IN THE
COMPANY
OF
GOOD AND EVIL

IN THE
COMPANY
OF
GOOD AND EVIL

A True Story of
Corporate Seduction and Betrayal

Ken Power & Craig Winn

CRICKETSONG
BOOKS

Published by

CRICKETSONG BOOKS

A division of Virginia Publishers,
a wholly owned subsidiary of The Winn Company, LLC
Charlottesville, Virginia 22901
CricketSongBooks.com

Cricketsong Books and its Cricket image are trademarks of
Virginia Publishers, a wholly owned subsidiary of The Winn Company, LLC.

Book and cover design by Ken Power
Photos by Doug Purvis

Winn, Craig.
    In the company of good and evil : a true story of seduction and betrayal
    / Craig Winn, Ken Power. — 1st ed.
        p. cm.
        LCCN 2001097724
        ISBN 0-9714481-0-8

        1. Value America.com. 2. Electronic commerce—United States.
    3. Internet marketing—United States.
    I. Power, Ken. II. Title.

HF5548.325.U6W56 2002   381'.1
                QBI33-169

To

Gayle and Katharine

without whose love, support, and patience
this story would never have been told.

CONTENTS

TO THE READER

Even though the events depicted in these pages actually occurred, we've written our story in the style of a novel, using dialog. The circumstances surrounding the meteoric rise and cataclysmic fall of Value America are too incredible to be relegated to dry, historical prose.

We were witnesses to, and participants in, these events until the early months of 2000; the story after that time is based on eyewitness accounts, correspondence, news articles, and court records. Over 20,000 pages of such documentation were examined in the process of researching this book. We have not knowingly changed any material fact. We have compressed some of the action for the sake of brevity and have shortened many of the quoted documents. While we recognize that our description of the company as it was being built may seem boastful and self serving, in reality the actual events and the reactions of others was far more favorable than we have presented.

Most of the dialog is reconstructed. Although much of what happened is a matter of public record, the conclusions, characterizations, thoughts, and motivations presented *In the Company of Good and Evil* are strictly the opinion of the authors.

We have endeavored to lay a solid business foundation so readers from all walks of life can appreciate the challenges faced by the firm's founders and the magnitude of what was ultimately at stake. As a result, you will be better informed than were most of the participants.

A word of warning: you are about to lose your naïveté. You will never again buy a product without reflecting upon the abuse someone endured to bring it to you. You will never again read a newspaper or magazine without wondering if you're being deceived. And you will never again look at business, politics, religion, or commerce in quite the same way.

Ken Power and Craig Winn

TO THE PARTICIPANTS

We owe a great deal to you, the characters in our story. Collectively, your deeds and interactions tell an important tale, one that reveals the qualities and organizational behaviors of builders and exposes the character and characteristics of those who destroy. Our story is principally a cautionary tale—designed to enlighten as it entertains.

For those of you who actually worked for, invested in, or were otherwise involved with Value America, our cast of characters may seem more important than our message. Since we wish no one any harm, a explanation of the methods we used to tell our story may be helpful.

We have distilled many years of business encounters into a few hours of reading, choosing only incidents we believed were the most relevant, the most edifying. Often we have coalesced several encounters into one, condensing the dialog to make the salient portions easier to understand. For example, the dialog in the final chapter actually occurred, but not in the abbreviated twenty-minute slice of time in which it is depicted.

We have also elected to group some topics rather than tell our story strictly as it unfolded. For instance, surviving our early days in an attic in Charlottesville, building the store's technology, selling consumer brands on our merits, and raising venture capital all occurred simultaneously. Yet we cover these subjects in successive chapters in an effort to make the story easier to follow.

This work was thoroughly researched. We collected, read, and evaluated tens of thousands of pages of documentation. Hundreds of hours of recorded interviews were conducted with eyewitnesses. Beyond that, we were participants in the events we describe. In fact, as the five founders, we are the central characters. No one knows more about these events than we do. We have done our utmost to accurately present this story. We have not conveyed anything of consequence we didn't believe, based on research and personal experience, to be true.

We have included excerpts from a number of contemporary documents—speeches, letters, and articles. Some have been edited slightly for readability. These documents are particularly important to our story. Without them, our tale might seem unbelievable, stranger than fiction. But you know better.

By necessity, most of the dialog is reconstructed. Obviously, we did not record these conversations as they occurred; we have had to rely—as all historians must—on our collective memories. Often we have found excellent source material that gives us great confidence that the dialog we have recounted was actually spoken. Other times, multiple participants had common recollections. On occasion we have simply written what we surmised was said, based upon what actually transpired.

Most importantly, we can only speculate as to your motivations, whether good or evil. Only you know your thoughts and rationale. Even today, many of you may not know why you acted as you did. Therefore, when we ascribe a motive or thought to a character, we have admittedly traveled into the world of opinion. Many of you, our characters, have gone out of your way to express yours publicly. Your opinions often differ radically from ours. When appropriate, we have included varying viewpoints, especially those you've made public. We've discovered that you have occasionally impaled yourselves on your own words. We have endeavored not to do so with ours.

Our narrator is a real person, one of the company's five founders, co-author Ken Power. Unlike fiction narrators, ours is neither omnipresent nor omniscient. He is at times opinionated and emotional. He is also witty, wise, and well grounded, an altogether human translator for Craig Winn's often lofty ideals and larger-than-life business persona. Ken's qualities serve as a handrail in what became a topsy-turvy world.

It was not our goal to embarrass anyone, especially private people. We are, in fact, uninterested in anyone's private life or personal values. This story is about organizational behavior, *corporate* values. As a result, we have often changed or omitted the names of the people, firms, and organizations that left their fingerprints on our company. You'll find a list of real and fictitious names in our Cast of Characters. Minor characters are presented using only their first names. But people who went out of their way to speak to the press about the company and those who built it have, in our opinion, become limited public figures in regard to Value America. In that they themselves showed no concern about expressing their views and giving their names, we are comfortable following their lead.

The destruction of Value America hurt many fine people. In writing this story, it is our hope that their sacrifices will not have been in vain. Dot-coms have collapsed, especially e-tailers, though they were once in a position to serve manufacturers and consumers in revolutionary ways. The solutions we invented and the grand strategies we envisioned are here for all to use. We only hope they will be used to "do well by doing good." We want others to learn from our mistakes—and yours. If the dark side of what we encountered is not understood, exposed, and thwarted, our country, and indeed the world, may be in greater peril than can possibly be imagined.

Value America's Five Founders

Bill Hunt
Joe Page
Ken Power
Rex Scatena
Craig Winn

A CAST OF CHARACTERS

ACKNOWLEDGMENTS

Although this book is based on our personal experiences, the timely and generous support of many people contributed greatly to its accuracy and insight. Most of these, not surprisingly, worked for or with Value America, some in leadership positions, and some in supporting roles.

Joe Page, Rex Scatena, and Bill Hunt, three of the company's founding fathers, spent countless hours in research and manuscript revision. Linda Harmon, Tracey Wingfield, Phil Intihar, Sean Flynn, Eric Cherna, Doug Schatz, and Aaron Schidler provided valuable eyewitness perspective on the company's decline—especially in the months following the departures of the authors. Ken Erickson, Andy Rod, John Motley, Mick Kicklighter, Jerry Falwell, Dean Johnson, and a host of others were important as sounding boards and memory joggers. The skills of Linda Harmon, Taylor Smack, and Celia Rocks proved invaluable in interview transcription and proofreading. We are also indebted to Jonathan Kirsch for his legal review of our manuscript. He is a credit to his profession. We wish to thank you all from the bottom of our hearts.

We would also like to thank the hundreds of great men and women who contributed to the growth of Value America. You were our constant inspiration for over a year as we worked crafting our story. We hope you will find the book worthy of your own selfless labors.

We would even like to thank those few whose self-serving ambition contributed to the downfall of our "Marketplace for a New Millennium." You provided us with a plot so twisted and sinister we could never have invented anything quite as compelling on our own.

Ken Power and Craig Winn

IPO FEVER

*J*ust because this was the big day, it didn't mean there wasn't work to be done. Linda Harmon picked up her note pad and walked to Rex Scatena's office, hesitating at the open door. The vice chairman finished his phone conversation and waved her in.

"Hi, Linda," he said, smiling. "Three more firms want to partner with us." As he rummaged through the papers on his desk, he grabbed his mouse and clicked the refresh button, as he'd done a dozen times this morning. Rex glanced at his screen. Linda's eyes followed.

This time, his Yahoo! Personal Finance page came alive. This was it— the very first public trade of Value America's stock. Linda had no idea what to expect as she squinted against the morning glare. Then, there it was. "Four and a half million." she said, genuinely pleased for her favorite boss. She smiled at Rex and then looked back at the monitor. "No, wait a minute. That's not right." Linda peered at the screen. "It's forty-five million!" she screamed. "Rex, you're worth forty-five million dollars!"

Rex, just north of fifty, was having a little trouble focusing on the screen without his glasses, which he'd misplaced again. But that *still* didn't look like it said $45 million. He squinted, and then remembered that they were pushed back into his hair. Linda leaned in for a closer look. There were an awful lot of zeros there. As they started counting them, the truth hit them both at the same instant.

Rex Scatena's shares were worth four hundred and fifty million dollars.

He sat back in his chair, his eyes glazed over, partially from utter fatigue and partially from the seductive mathematics of the morning. Rex was no stranger to money; in his former life he had been a prosperous environmental lawyer. But now, it appeared, he had attained wealth beyond the dreams of avarice. Rex was finding it surprisingly hard to comprehend.

❧❦❧

IT HAD ALL started three years before when Craig's improbable dream had been born in my little design studio on the other side of the country. As of 10:47 this morning, that dream was worth over *three billion dollars*. If I hadn't lived through it, I wouldn't believe it myself.

Today Value America had become a public company, the latest tech sensation making national headlines and creating instant millionaires. We had become the world's second largest online store by using a revolutionary blend of practical solutions and inspiring ideals. It had been Craig's brainchild, innovative from top to bottom.

His office was right down the hall from mine, and I wanted to thank him. But I caught myself smiling at the thought. Thank him for what? For doing exactly what he'd said he'd do? No, that wasn't it. It was more for giving me the most exciting three years of my life. I had given up my own California design company to join Craig Winn. Ken Power, CEO, had become Ken Power, Creative Director and Vice President of Marketing. I now created the ads that presented Value America to the world. Craig and I, along with Rex, Joe Page, and Bill Hunt, were its founding fathers.

As I stood up, I was confronted by a familiar face. Doug Schatz leaned on my doorframe, grinning. He had come to congratulate me. "So, Ken, how does it feel to be a bazillionaire?" He naturally assumed I had a boat-load of stock options. They came with the territory.

I didn't answer right away, but took a long breath and gazed out the window. Somebody was mowing the lawn across the street. It looked like any other bright Virginia spring morning. But today was different.

"Feels great," I said at last. "Strange, but great." *I wasn't making much sense.* "I mean, yesterday I was just a working stiff with a wife, kids, and a mortgage, doing okay but not gettin' rich. Today, I'm that same working stiff, but with stock worth millions. You've got shares, too, Doug. We can't sell 'em yet. So you tell me: are we rich, or not?"

Doug wasn't about to get sucked into a philosophical discussion. "Well, Ken, nobody deserves it more than you." I could never tell when he was being serious, because he always sounded earnest, always had a sincere mien, even if he were telling me that NASA had announced that the moon was made of mozzarella. "I mean that, Ken. I really do."

I was sure he did. Doug and I had been working together for what seemed like an eternity—about a year, which was tantamount to a decade in Internet time. Kind of like dog years, but you grow old even faster.

I was about to do the obligatory "You deserve this as much as anyone" speech (which in Doug's case was perfectly true) when Nikkii, my advertising traffic manager, popped her head in the door. "Have you seen it, KP?" she asked, as if I were the only one who had an interest in the price of Value America's stock. Nikkii was always looking out for me. "It's sixty-nine!" she gushed. "Congratulations!"

Congratulations, indeed! When I had joined Craig on this improbable journey, he had predicted that if all went according to plan, *someday* my shares would be worth as much as five million dollars. At $69, they were already worth three times that much. The stock was supposed to have opened at $23, but the start of trading had been delayed because there were no sellers, only buyers. Now that public trading had actually started, there was a feeding frenzy going on out there. It was dot-com fever, and we were the flavor of the week.

It was a glorious moment in time—a giant economic bubble, a euphoric aberration, and we were among the fortunate few in a position to capitalize. Dot-com was everywhere you looked, the lead story on the nightly news, on the front page of every newspaper, on the cover of magazines, the topic of discussion around every water cooler. The nation, the whole western world, was consumed by dot-com fever. The laws of economics had been suspended. What went up no longer had to come down. And we were where the whole world wanted to be.

One of my ad writers ambled by. "Seventy-one," was all he said, and poured himself a cup of coffee. I grinned and grabbed a mug. Might as well join him. Nobody was getting much work done this morning.

You couldn't blame us for pausing to do a little mutual backslapping. We were all in on it, all three hundred or so of us. We all owned stock, right down to the guy who shuttled our interoffice mail between eight buildings scattered all over Charlottesville. Some of us had a lot of shares and some comparatively few, but every single employee had a piece of Value America. Maybe that was why there was always electricity in the air. An indefatigable optimism seemed to permeate the place. Or maybe we were just excited about what we were doing; for once in our lives, we were doing something that actually seemed *worth* doing, something special, maybe even revolutionary.

ↂ

VALUE AMERICA HAD GROWN too fast for Charlottesville. In a mere three years we had grown from five people to the fifth largest employer in this quaint little university town, this cultural oasis in the middle of rural Virginia. At least half of us had moved here from somewhere else to be part of the excitement. For those of us who had actually read Craig's business plan, this wasn't just a job; it was something more, something deeper. We were *believers*. We sensed we were making a difference, making the world a better place.

The city itself was part of the draw. Charlottesville was invariably rated among America's top places to live. Though the town was small, it was big where it counted: in history, charm, and culture. But unlike Georgetown or Annapolis, C'Ville was immersed in the lush, green foothills of the Blue Ridge Mountains, not surrounded by big-city clutter. Seemingly endless hardwood forests stretched out into the hills to the west. Pristine farmland punctuated by thick stands of evergreens reached out toward Richmond on the east. A hundred miles north was the world's most powerful city, Washington, D.C.

Charlottesville is Jefferson country, and the third President's presence is still revered here. Monticello, Thomas Jefferson's magnificent home, sits on a hill just south of town. The University of Virginia, Jefferson's beloved "academical village," dominates the western third of the city. The place is steeped in history. Jefferson's two friends, Madison and Monroe, lived here, too. Meriwether Lewis called C'Ville home before joining Clark on their epic journey of discovery. The town was so old, it had been named in honor of an English queen, Charlotte, the wife of King George III.

None of this was lost on Craig. He saw Charlottesville's small-town values, its genteel southern charm, as a cocoon for our embryonic company, sheltering us from the distractions of big-city life as we endeavored to become the dazzling butterfly he had envisioned.

Ready-made office space for a company of three hundred people growing at the rate of ten souls a week was not to be found in this part of the world. So Value America was situated in a motley collection of buildings scattered all over town.

Our call center was getting ready to move downtown. Fifty employees strong, it was humming today, thanks to Candy Clifford, the queen of sales. A tall, heavy-set woman with jet-black hair and piercing eyes, she had a souvenir from another life hanging on her office wall that said it all. It was a vanity license plate that read "CLOZER." She lived to sell.

Just for a moment, Candy leaned back in her office chair, laced her fingers behind her head, and closed her eyes. A few months, that's all it had been since her move to Value America. She had been recruited by her old friend at IBM, Glenda Dorchak, who was now—*can you believe it*—president of the company; a far cry from her middle management roles at Big Blue. *How had she managed to pull that off?* Candy wondered.

Glenda had descended upon the place like a tornado. Yet on IPO day, the thin blond, along with most of the IBMers she had recruited, was keeping a low profile. "Team Blue" usually hung together, separate from the rest of us, but today it was more obvious than usual. Perhaps it was because none of them had been included in the IPO process. They may have felt under-appreciated. Or perhaps they were just biding their time. After all, the IPO marked our transition from entrepreneurs to "professionals."

ISSAC SALTZBERG was holding a supervisor's meeting in his cubicle on the third floor of the Yellow House. The tall, slender thirty-something was nothing if not production oriented. As his eyes wandered across his desk, he did a double take at the stock market ticker he, like Rex, had displayed on his monitor. "I don't believe it," he said, grinning.

"Sure you do," one of his writers said. "You've been preaching that our stock would go through the roof. Looks like you were right." He paused for effect. "There's a first time for everything."

Saltz was too elated to be annoyed by the good-natured poke. It was IPO day, and he'd been vindicated.

The Yellow House had been our only office for a few magical months back in early '98. Now it was home to but one of Value America's many departments, something called Presentation Marketing, a group that created the online demonstrations for the products we sold in our store. Nobody else had anything like them. They were the fulfillment of one of our most fundamental promises: enabling consumers to make better buying decisions.

Saltz had an infectious enthusiasm that ultimately played a large part in his choice as the leader of the forty-five person team when I left to write ads. He had, as the phrase went, "drunk the koolaid," our corporate metaphor for fanatical devotion to Value America and its mission. He didn't own a car, a TV, or even a real bed. He had sold them all to invest in the company back when the stock had been worth a small fraction of its present mind-numbing value. He had put his money—about $40,000 of it—where his mouth was. Today, his $40,000 was worth a cool four mil.

༄·ༀ

DOUG PURVIS had been at the FedEx building since 6:20 this morning, and right now he had no idea what time it was. Scattered on a table to his left were twelve pairs of diamond, sapphire, and opal earrings. On the table in front of him, a gorgeous heavy gold necklace rested on top of a piece of weathered wood from an old barn door, complete with rusty hinge.

The "FedEx" Building, of course, no longer housed the local office of the express delivery company. This modest industrial structure north of town was now home to our small but world-class photo studio and our equally small, equally impressive, sound studio. We were serious about the quality of our product presentations, and we'd found that to do things right, we had to do them ourselves.

Doug picked up the phone to hear Saltzberg's voice. "Jennifer is all over my case. She needs to get her new earring presentation online. Now."

"What earrings?" Doug asked innocently. He could hear Saltzberg's hair falling out.

"She hasn't gotten them over there yet? I'm gonna strangle her!"

Doug put him out of his misery. "Oh, put a sock in it, Isaac. The shots are done, although they shouldn't be. I just got the stuff yesterday."

Sometimes the only thing that held Doug together was his twisted sense of humor.

"You da man," gushed a relieved Saltz. "Are you watching the stock?"

"No, actually, I've been a little busy here. How we doin'?"

"We're in the seventies."

✌✿✌

INDIA HAMNER couldn't stop smiling. The excitement of the morning had bubbled over into hugs and handshakes, and she was right in the middle of it. India, our help-desk manager, embodied the ebullient spirit of Value America. She believed in the dream and came to work each day eager to serve.

On IPO day, there were seventy people in Operations and Customer Care. The prevailing mood in this sea of systems furniture wasn't, "Congratulate me, I'm a millionaire," although there were a few whose arithmetic worked out that way. Most were younger, more recently hired, with fewer options. What they felt, rather, was a sense of community pride, a sort of corporate patriotism.

"We did it," they smiled. "We went public." And when they said "we," they meant "all of us," including the nineteen-year-old girl right out of Albemarle High who checked with our vendors to make sure there were enough televisions or toasters to meet the demand. They meant "all of us," including the twenty-two-year-old college dropout who took care of customers on the phone, answering their questions with a smile.

They were right. Our firm wasn't all entrepreneurial fireworks and creative genius. It wasn't all brilliant merchandising *coups* and techno-wizards doing their thing. A very real reason for the success we were enjoying was the unceasing labor of a lot of regular people just doing their jobs.

✌✿✌

JENNIFER WAS ON the phone with Isaac. Again. She realized that, as our jewelry merchant, she was at a disadvantage because our customers saw her products through the low-resolution world of their computer screens. She even insisted on having her own dedicated graphics specialist, one on whom she could rely to get the most out of any photo.

I was pleased to learn that my daughter Chelsea, whom I had trained as a teenager, had been selected for this dubious honor. Chelsea needed a little aggravation in her life; it builds character. Nepotism, in the sense of hiring your idiot nephew as EVP was, of course, *verboten*, but family relationships abounded here. We had husbands and wives, parents and children, and several sets of siblings working at the company, usually in different departments. I think I held the record, with five of my kids or their spouses here at one time or another. For a while there, it looked as though I might even gain a son-in-law in the bargain.

"You've been here for years, Isaac," Jennifer said. "You're vested. You could sell your stock tomorrow!" It wasn't a complaint, just an observation. "It'll be a long time before this has any effect on my life."

She was right, of course, and had spoken for almost everyone. At the rate the company was growing, it was a given that most members of our team were rookies. Half had been here less than six months. A year ago, we had numbered less than fifty; two years ago, fewer than fifteen. Only we old-timers would be in a position to turn our options into cash anytime soon.

Saltz hadn't even considered selling his stock. For one thing, it would show a total lack of loyalty to bail out now. Bad form. And besides, who said it would stop here? This rocket was just taking off. Sell now? No way! On the other hand, he needed a car in the worst way.

❧

DOWN THE HALL from Jen's office, Bill Hunt's door was closed, his office dark. Bill was miles away, playing golf. It wasn't that he didn't care about the IPO. He had committed to be at this member-guest golf tournament at Hilton Head six months before. But as much as he loved the game, that wasn't where he wanted to be today. There were fires to put out, ruffled feathers to smooth, and congratulations to accept. And then there were all those black flies.

Bill was a VP, the firm's senior merchandiser. He had been employee number five, which was not surprising considering he and Craig had known each other for over twenty years. Graduating from the University of Virginia before heading off to executive positions with a string of respected manufacturing companies, Hunt had lived all over America, but his heart had never really left Charlottesville. Now in his fifties, he was part hillbilly, part MBA, tall, thin, bald, and thoroughly good natured.

Bill brushed away a swarm of flies as he approached the eighth hole. He glanced at his watch again. A little after eleven. Once again he grabbed his cell phone and hit redial. Every few shots he had checked in—9:00, 9:30, 10:00, and 10:30—but there had been no news. At last came the report he had been expecting: Value America was being traded—as well as the news he had *not* been expecting: it was trading in the seventies, not the twenties.

Today, all Bill's diplomatic skills would be put to the test. The day had brought some good news and some bad news—and it was all the same news. His contacts, vendors who were also close personal friends, had wanted in on the IPO. They were believers too. They had taken a chance when we were an upstart nobody in a new and unproven retail channel. And now, reasonably enough, they had wanted the opportunity to buy VUSA stock at bargain basement first-day prices.

A large block of shares had been set aside for "Friends of the Company," those who had supported us tangibly early on. But it had been clear for some time that there was not going to be enough to go around. Demand had outstripped supply twenty times over.

Bill didn't control the distribution of these shares. The investment bankers did, and they'd held their cards very close to the vest. Now, however, everyone on the list had been contacted. Everyone knew how much, or how little, stock they were going to be able to buy at the IPO price of just $23 a share. Craig had successfully fought for many more "Friends of the Company" shares than the underwriters had wanted to make available, but with demand so grossly exceeding supply, no one had been allotted as many as they felt they deserved.

❧∶❧

OUR HEADQUARTERS was in a modest office complex called Hollymead, just north of town. Although the interiors had been built especially for us, the space was gloriously cheap. Nobody had wasted any time naming the structures, either. They were simply labeled alphabetically counterclockwise A, B, and C going north, then D, E, and F heading back south. Someone had duct-taped their letters on the walls.

Building B housed our merchandisers: office supplies and equipment, books, home improvement, housewares, consumer electronics, sporting goods, toys, jewelry, health and beauty, computers, software, and specialty foods. It was all here, although some of the current occupants of B, our consumer merchandisers, were headed to Building D just as soon as Sales, which was overcrowding D, could move downtown, leaving all of B for the computer merchants. It was corporate musical chairs.

Building A housed the company's executives. Building F was home to

Operations and Customer Care. But that wouldn't last either. Soon they would move into larger quarters near the photo studio, making room for more technologists. Interoffice mail was getting to be a problem.

But on IPO day, Building E was where the magic happened. *Technology*—the one thing absolutely essential to an Internet store. If it didn't work, we were out of business.

It was no accident that Value America's first employee had been a technologist. Joe Page, our Webmaster, referred to himself as the Head Geek, never mind his official corporate designations, EVP and CTO. His genius as a programmer was readily apparent; his depth of character and engaging humility became obvious only after you had gotten to know him. Joe's Jeep bore a license plate that read "WEB GEEK." Page wore the term "geek" as a badge of honor, but he was anything but a nerd. Athletic and aggressive, a connoisseur of beer and pinball, Joe had guided the development of Value America's technology from the beginning.

Our site was dependent on the proprietary software he and his team wrote, and its conception was pure genius. When we had started, most content on the Internet was generated by static HTML, which meant that you had to be something of a techie to put your work online. Joe created an Authoring Tool, so our content could be developed and published by non-technical people—writers, artists, and merchants. The "Admin Tool" was another of Joe's masterpieces. It fueled the store's commerce engine. As these tools evolved, they gained some amazing functionality.

Talented Web technologists were in such demand that for much of our history we offered a handsome bounty to any employee who could entice, cajole, or shanghai a qualified computer professional to join us. The group had, not surprisingly, evolved into a combination brain repository and zoo. Yet the tech team knew that Joe was the one person who really understood how the whole thing worked. He was our medicine man.

Today, Joe became a folk hero of sorts, at least in Technology. One of his developers, a fellow with the curious name of Seshareddi Kamireddi—"Sesh" to you and me—wrote a program that calculated Joe's net worth based on the number of shares he owned and the current stock price. He made the result available via one of our intranet servers. The "Joe Ticker," as we called it, let you check his progress all day long.

Everybody in building E followed the rising fortunes of Joe Page with avid interest. Everybody saw his net worth climb to over *sixty million bucks*. And everybody in Building E, being in the same field, knew it could happen to them. Go, Joe.

IT DIDN'T have to happen. It wasn't inevitable. Going public wasn't listed in the Bill of Rights. But we had all worked for it. We had all counted on it. We had all watched it happen to other companies we knew didn't hold a candle to ours. We had come to the unshakable conclusion that we *deserved* this. Many of us conveniently forgot that the whole point of taking the company public was not to make *us* rich, but to raise the working capital we needed to grow and make our *shareholders* rich.

We had watched our founders depart, then return days later rumpled and bleary-eyed only to head out again a day or two later. The preparation for the IPO had taken a year, building to a grand climax with a two-week national road show for investors. But for all that, few of us had any first-hand experience with that mythical beast, the Initial Public Offering.

On this bright Virginia morning, though, it didn't seem to matter. Scores of us had instantly become millionaires. Euphoria was rampant. We were all walking around the halls shaking hands, sporting grins we couldn't have suppressed if we'd tried. Value America was now VUSA, one of the hottest Web stocks on the planet, and the world was scrambling to own a piece of us.

And well they should. We were an Internet store—*the* Internet store—with the vision to shape the future. We were going to give everybody, consumers and manufacturers alike, the things they had always wanted. We were going to be the first to make the concept of virtual inventory work. *Of course* people were buying up Value America stock like there was no tomorrow. We *were* tomorrow. We were, as my old advertising slogan had phrased it, *"The Marketplace for a New Millennium."*

Or so we thought.

☙❧

CRAIG WINN EMERGED from his office and shared a few quiet words in the corridor with Rex Scatena. Rex had been instrumental in helping get Value America off the ground. Had it not been for their enduring friendship and faith in one another, Value America would not have existed.

As Doug and I strolled toward the boss's office, Linda Harmon greeted us. Linda was the administrative assistant to our entire complement of senior executives: she served co-founders Winn and Scatena, plus President Dorchak and our new CEO Tom Morgan. "Congratulations, guys," she said. "This is so exciting!"

Linda's warmth and friendliness added something positive to the place. She was a hard-working single mom who had lived through the entire IPO process in the eye of the storm.

"Can you believe this?" I said. "Everybody's walking on air."

She smiled, but oddly, her demeanor changed. "Well...not everybody," she said softly as she nodded in the direction of Tom Morgan's closed office door. "What's up with him? What a grump. He's acting like he resents the whole thing. Okay, I know he's only been here a few weeks, but gee! At least he could pretend to be happy for the rest of us. We worked hard for this!"

"Aw, c'mon, Linda," I said. "It can't be all that bad. I mean, I can't say I really know Tom all that well, but he sure looks the part."

Linda lowered her voice and whispered, "I don't know. Something's wrong. It's weird. He's been here for almost a month, and I haven't seen anything come out of his office—no letters, no directives, not even complaints. *Nothing.*"

"Sounds like the perfect boss," I chuckled.

That brought a smile. Linda's tone brightened. "Hey, I'm sorry. I guess I worry too much. This means so much to my son and me. Anyway, it's been quite a morning, especially for our friends Rex and Craig."

WINN WAS a boyish-looking forty-four, but he had already built a resume you could easily divide among half a dozen hyperactive entrepreneurs. He'd had explosive careers in both sales and manufacturing, building several companies from inception to industry dominators. One of them had even gone public. Craig had had his triumphs and his tragedies, but it seemed to me that he was, all things considered, a good candidate for a poster boy for entrepreneurial over-achievement. Value America had not been an accident or a fluke. It was merely the newest pearl on the strand. Craig had invested twenty years of his life enjoying good times and surviving bad to become an instant star.

It wasn't that he didn't show any battle scars. They were there for all to see. But it was those scars, the failures in his past as well as the costly victories, that had given us confidence that he knew what he was doing. Despite his relatively tender years, Craig had been there and done that. We saw him as a visionary, a big thinker, disciplined and purposeful, and our industry seemed perfectly suited to his aggressive style. He used to tell us things things like, "E-commerce is the only business where we must sail our ship out to sea with all guns blazing while we're still laying the keel."

Oddly enough, on IPO day, Craig wasn't even in charge anymore. For reasons that didn't make much sense to me, he had stepped down as CEO weeks earlier. He had, in fact, worked on nothing but raising capital since the previous August. It had been some nine months since Craig had actually run the show. He was still our chairman, but boards don't run companies, management does. Value America's top-ranking execs were now CEO Morgan, President Dorchak, and CFO Dean Johnson. The baton had been passed from the entrepreneurs to the professionals, just as conventional wisdom dictates should happen.

Craig had been on the phone all morning, accepting his share of congratulations from major investors and fielding calls from a steady stream of reporters. Terry McAuliffe, President Clinton's close friend and future Democratic Party National Chairman, had called. So had conservative leader and Baptist minister Jerry Falwell. The callers were as politically diverse as they were uniformly congratulatory.

They had good reason to be. By all accounts, this was starting off to be one of the most successful initial public offerings in history. And the man responsible for its success, the success of the concept to which the market had reacted so positively, was Craig Winn. Value America had been his invention, his baby. When he had conceived the idea, its execution would have been science fiction, but here we were, a reality. In a very real sense, his whole life had been leading up to this day.

But the journalists calling this morning weren't interested in how he'd gotten here or where he was going next. They just wanted to know what it *felt like* to be in his shoes. They wanted to write, "Winn is jubilant, bouncing off the walls," and they were seeking his corroboration. After all, they thought, he had a right to be euphoric. With ownership of thirty-five percent of the outstanding shares, the arithmetic of the morning made Craig a billionaire. With a *b*.

He was not euphoric, though. He didn't even appear excited. He was having no trouble keeping his feet on the ground. He had told every reporter who would listen that he was worth no more today than he'd been worth yesterday. "You're never closer to tragedy than you are at the moment of your greatest triumph."

"Yeah, yeah," they all said, and rushed off to write their stories.

Craig was happy, of course, but it wasn't an "I won the lottery" kind of happiness. It was more an "I survived the plane crash" sort of thing. There was a downside to this.

This morning, he seemed to be the only one who remembered that a mere six months earlier, we had been written off for dead, the victim of a failed IPO. Eighteen months ago, our backs had been against the wall. We couldn't raise a dime at even one percent of the current valuation. Yet we had recovered, like a Phoenix rising from the ashes, and since those dark days, we had set records for raising private equity and for the scope and

quality of our IPO. But the offering was not the goal. It was only a quali-
fying heat, a necessary step toward getting us into the final race—a race
that Craig would not run with us, although his shadow, we were about to
learn, would keep pace quite nicely.

This morning, he was concerned. He had survived a year with investment bankers and analysts. Yet they still didn't appreciate our business,
what made it different, what made it valuable. The same bankers who
were gushing congratulations today had, just a few months earlier, been
embroiled in a bitter fight with our founder. Their conflict had left each
side wary of the other.

This morning, Craig was worried. He knew our stock wasn't worth $70
a share. It was worth $23, $25, maybe as much as $30. If it were actually
worth $70, we would have gone public at $70. What would happen
tomorrow, when reality dawned on thousands of investors who had
pushed the price so high? Sure, he knew that our first quarter's performance was much better than the analysts expected, but it would be five long
weeks before he could share that good news with anyone.

And this morning, Craig was annoyed. He had turned over the reins to
"professional managers" but had seen little professionalism, not much
management, and precious little reason to expect that anything would
change.

ঞ্জ:জ

SOMEBODY SHOUTED, "SEVENTY-FOUR! It's gone to seventy-four!"
from one of the little offices that lined the hallway as Doug Schatz and I
made our way toward the boss. Craig saw us coming and grinned.

"Dougie!" He extended his hand. Doug, whom no one *ever* called
Dougie, was one of his favorite merchandisers, one who understood and
appreciated our early achievements as few others could. But it was Craig
who was doing the honors. "Thank you!" he said. "You and the brands
you've brought to us are a big reason we're celebrating today. You have
endured 'the test of a thousand noes.' I'm grateful."

Doug wanted to thank the man who had conceived all of this, who
had recruited him, and truth be known, had lured most of the best brands
to the company. But before he could get a word out, Craig turned and
focused his attention on me.

He placed one hand on each of my shoulders. Craig and I are about
the same height, just shy of six feet, so I shouldn't have felt small, but I
did. I somehow knew he was about to single me out for praise, and I felt
uncomfortable. We had come to know each other well and had done
marvelous things together. Yet all this time we had never exchanged one

harsh word, though we had gone toe to toe hundreds of times over issues great and small. Craig knew my strengths, and he'd found ways to make me even stronger. He knew my weaknesses, and hadn't held them against me. The more comfortable I grew in challenging him, the closer our relationship became. For a man who knew my business as well as I knew it myself he was remarkably accessible, even vulnerable. He displayed his emotions openly. He wasn't just my employer; he was my friend.

This morning he spoke slowly, deliberately. "Ken, there is no one I'm happier for than I am for you. We began this journey together, in humble beginnings, not so very long ago. We've come a long way."

That we had.

"I have always said that you are our patron saint."

It was true. He had said that, although I hated it when he singled me out as if I were someone special. Maybe I was in his eyes. But just because I had adopted a few kids (okay, nine of 'em) and didn't make a secret of my faith, there was no particular reason to start envisioning a halo around my graying brow.

But Craig continued, "I knew God would never let anything bad happen to our company so long as you were here. Thank you, my friend!"

I mumbled something totally inadequate and shook his hand. Craig knew what I was thinking, even if I couldn't find the words to express myself. He smiled warmly. But his was not a smile of triumph, though he was uniquely entitled to one. Nor was it a smile of giddy greed-induced euphoria like the rest of us were wearing.

Craig wore the pensive, determined smile of a priest whose ministry it was to give encouragement to the parents of a dying child.

What did he know that had somehow escaped the rest of us?

THE PRICE OF SUCCESS

was dying to find out what he was thinking. You couldn't blame me. Craig should have been ecstatic. I know I would have been. He had *made* it: he had conceived and built one of the largest e-tailers on the planet, from scratch. Craig had finished building his grand home on a knoll overlooking the Blue Ridge. With his beautiful wife and two great boys, his life seemed perfect. What's more, the monkey was off his back: he had retired as CEO and had taken our company public. He had raised more money than any ten companies should be able to spend. Yet he wasn't celebrating.

Craig saw it in my eyes and motioned for me to sit down. As I walked into his office, the phone rang. His speakerphone was a modern octopus-looking contraption that sat in the middle of an antique table. The table itself wasn't very big, maybe four feet across. It had belonged to his children's one-hundred-year-old great grandfather. He walked over and pushed a button. "Hello, this is Craig."

"Howdy, pardner!" the voice boomed out of the conference phone.

"Hi, Bill." Craig brightened, recognizing his friend's voice. "How are ya and where are ya?"

"Just leaving the 18th green at Hilton Head," Hunt said sheepishly. "Although I'd rather be there with you." Even with the crackle of Bill's cell phone, we could detect a twinge of emotion in his voice.

"You're here in spirit, Bill," Craig grinned. "We're a team. This would never have happened without all five of us."

"You're right," Bill responded. "We built it together."

Craig leaned forward in his chair. "You and I go back a long way, Bill. We've done some pretty spectacular stuff together."

"That's for sure. As I played these last few holes, I kept thinking about that. Remember flying down to the Price Club? It all started there."

"We've got our roots in retail. We owe a lot to Sol Price. We copied the things that worked for him, and improved the things that didn't. Tell you what, if the folks driving our stock up today knew half of what you and I know about retail, we'd be in fine shape."

"So tell 'em, Craig," Bill said. "And don't give Sol all the credit. Most of what makes Value America great we brewed up ourselves. Remember that trip to San Diego with Scott Chrisman when you told him how you learned to sell? It was on that same trip that you explained how we were gonna change retail. You called it a *retail revolution*. Remember?"

"Yeah. Like it was yesterday," Craig said, drifting off....

"YES, I WORKED hard to get in, but I just couldn't bear the thought of spending the next three years in law school. I don't even *like* lawyers." Craig was telling Scott Chrisman and Bill Hunt the tale of how he'd gotten here.

"Here" was 5,500 feet above the California coast, headed southeast at 140 knots in Craig's Cessna. It was October 1985. Scott was in the pilot's seat, with the thirty-year old Winn acting as co-pilot. He had been working on his license for months now, mostly in his spare time, usually before sunrise.

It was a sparkling Tuesday morning, adorned with the kind of sky that makes the weather in this part of the world legendary. The three had just taken off from Torrance Airport, a small municipal airstrip nestled beneath the green, windblown hills of the Palos Verdes Peninsula, southwest of LA. The maroon and white Cessna Skylane 182 was loaded with samples of high-velocity ceiling fans made by Patton Electric. Bill was their VP of Sales. Their destination was San Diego's Montgomery Field, a forty-minute flight, and then on to a small but promising new customer, the Price Club. As a manufacturer's rep, it was Craig's job to create profitable partnerships between the people who made things and the people who sold them.

"You couldn't have picked a more unlikely candidate," he explained loudly over the plane's "David Clarks," the heavy green headsets worn by everyone on board. Communication over the engine's roar simply did not happen in airplanes like a 182 without electronic assistance. "My father was born for this, not me."

Bill Hunt nodded. He had known Craig's father, the gregarious Bill Winn, for fifteen years. Hunt was in his forties, tall, athletic, and recently returned from a stint at Harvard Business School. The story of Craig's rocky start was being told for Scott's benefit. Bill knew all about it. He had, after all, known the younger Winn since Craig was a teenager.

The elder Mr. Winn had taken the same shortcut from youth to manhood that so many of his generation had: combat in World War II. Twenty-five missions as a B-17 turret gunner over occupied Europe had made Bill Winn a hard man to shake. A post-war education at USC on the G.I. Bill had led to a career as a manufacturers' rep. It was started with bluff, bluster, and little else, but it had developed into a thriving little business, representing manufacturers like Patton to chain stores with buying offices in Southern California.

The operative word was "little." There were no actual employees, just Bill and two independent sales reps, one being his brother-in-law. Bill had none of the trappings even the smallest business would consider necessary. His "office" was a spare bedroom closet, equipped with a rotary-dial telephone, a hand-crank adding machine, and an old manual typewriter. His corporate stationery consisted of business cards and "from-the-desk-of" notepads. Bill's idea of good fortune was to find an uncancelled stamp he could soak off an envelope and reuse. A child of the Great Depression if ever there was one.

The William J Winn Company was successful for one reason—the outgoing personality of Bill Winn. A charter member of the old-boy network, he could charm paint off a wall. Born with the name "Billy J," a name that had too much personality even for him, he had had it legally changed to William J when he volunteered for the Army Air Corps.

By the late '70s, he had done well enough to consider retirement. It seemed like a good time to get out. The world was changing. It was getting harder to make a sale merely on the strength of one's friendships. Many of his old cronies had left, their places filled with younger buyers who didn't know him from Adam. And then they started hiring women as buyers. *Women!* Bill didn't know what they were thinking. Economic collapse was just over the horizon. *Women buyers!*

"So there I was, telling my father that I didn't want to be a lawyer after all." Craig continued his tale. "It was 1977. I had just graduated from SC and started law school," Craig said into his mike, "but I didn't make it through my first day. It dawned on me I'd never met a lawyer I liked. I wanted to spend my life *doing* things, not explaining them away.

"I told my father, and he said, 'I was about to sell my business. If you think you can sell, I'll give it to you. But...you don't have what it takes.'"

As cold as that sounded, Craig knew his dad was right. He had none of Bill Winn's easygoing personality, his gregarious relaxed manner, his seemingly effortless ability to charm people. Craig had seen his father at the top of his game—and it was a game to him—taking clients out to lunch, brilliantly holding up his end of a conversation, making his customers feel good. That's what being a salesman was all about, wasn't it?

Dad's shoes were going to be awfully hard to fill. Craig was smart enough, but he was introspective, analytical, and painfully shy. Not exactly a chip off the old block. If there was such a thing as a selling gene, he had failed to inherit it. On the other hand, he knew he didn't want to be a lawyer, so he decided he'd do what he'd always done—compensate. He would become a success through sheer force of will.

"The deal was," Craig continued, "I could call on any account not already being sold by my father or his helper, my Uncle Jim." That didn't leave much for the younger Winn. Craig was relegated to small specialty stores, newcomers, wannabes, and the chains that the other guys, with all their experience, had never been able to crack.

Craig systematically attacked the problem like a general going to war. He developed a hit list of potential customers using trade show directories, identifying anybody and everybody who had ever gone to a show. This was a logical move, since if you're attending a trade show, you're probably interested in what's being presented there. Cross-referencing the addresses of potential customers with his *Thomas Guide* map book, Craig worked out a schedule that allowed him to hit everybody in a small geographical area all at once. This way he could make an impressive ten to fifteen cold calls a day—all chosen because their map coordinates fell within block A-4 of page 27. That meant that Craig could get told *no* an impressive average of ten to fifteen times a day. He was Mr. Efficiency.

No one, it seemed, was much interested in the trash bags, plastic cups, or dishes that he had to sell. He got used to hearing, "No." Which is not to say he liked it. "It got to be so depressing," Craig confessed to his traveling companions, "I remember pulling my car off the road one day and saying, 'God, why me? This is hopeless. *I can't sell.*'"

Craig made just $12,000 that first year, about $2.75 an hour. During this same time, his father was bringing home $250,000 doing essentially the same job. That attorney thing was starting to look better.

"At the end of my first year, two buyers took pity on me. One was from Zody's, and the other was from Builder's Emporium." Bill and Scott knew both chains well. Zody's was a discount retailer with over fifty stores, and Builder's Emporium, a home improvement chain, was every bit as large. Both were destined to go the way of the dodo as the years passed, but they were very much alive in the late '70s.

"Each buyer," Craig said, "told me pretty much the same thing. 'Kid, you've come here every week on open buying days because you couldn't get an appointment. You've made your pitch and I've turned you down each time, yet you keep coming back. So I'm going to give you a break. You've earned it. Give me your best promotion, and I'll buy it.'"

At last! It was Craig's big opportunity. The buyer from Zody's, Dick Speas, bought lawn and trash bags from North American Plastics. Jerry Schwartz from Builder's Emporium bought Honeywell smoke detectors. If all went well, Craig might even make some money.

But all did not go well. Both promotions failed, so both buyers were in trouble. "I was devastated," Craig said. "My career as a salesman was over. I'd blown it."

Scott, still at the controls, was amused—and puzzled. "Excuse me. Didn't you just spend thirty-seven thousand dollars on this fine airplane with money you earned as a rep? Something tells me there's more to this story."

Bill Hunt just grinned.

"I took responsibility for the failures. One was my fault and the other wasn't, but either way, two good guys were in trouble. Since I'd been the one to get them in, I thought I should be the one to get them out. I covered their losses out of my own pocket—made their problems go away."

Scott just looked at him. "Nobody does that."

"So I found out. By acting honorably in the face of failure, I built a reputation."

Craig thought for a moment and glanced at Bill. "You know, those two guys gave me something far more valuable than purchase orders."

"Darn right!" Bill grinned. "Dick Speas gave you his wife."

"Your sales rep, Ginny Speas, is this guy's *wife?*"

"Yeah, Scott," Craig said, laughing. "Not long after this happened, she left FedEx and joined The Winn Company. Anyway, those two buyers helped me realize that I couldn't sell like my father did, scrawling orders on the backs of envelopes."

Scott adjusted the manifold pressure to 24 inches Hg and set the propeller speed to 2400 RPM. He still looked puzzled, so Craig explained. "It all started with Tim Snee, from Ralphs Supermarkets. I asked him a bunch of questions the first time we met, like what categories he liked to promote, margin goals, price points, cooperative advertising requirements, payment terms, and delivery criteria. I turned his answers into solutions.

"It was like somebody switched the light on. Buyers love talking about that stuff, since that's how they're judged."

"So what happened?" Scott asked as San Diego approach squawked on the radio, "Four seven November, there's traffic at ten o'clock, heading northwest, descending out of 4500 feet."

Looking out the left window, Craig pointed to the other airplane.

Bill chimed in, "Craig got *his* wife too."

"Naah. Say it ain't so," Scott moaned.

"'Fraid so," Craig answered sheepishly. "Ann Snee is Tim's wife."

"So these guys trusted you to the point they encouraged their wives to work with you. This must be some formula."

"Not really. It's pretty simple. I just stopped selling and started pre-senting. I got to know what the buyer wanted. Took a lot of notes. Then I'd go to our brands and say, 'This is what they need. We can restructure our standard program a little, give them what they want, and still meet our objectives.' A week later, I'd return and remind the buyer about what they said. Then I'd give them exactly what they asked for. Simple as that."

Bill chuckled. Scott laughed out loud. "That's your big secret? *Give 'em what they want?*"

"That's it. Works every time."

Craig didn't go into the rest of it—how difficult it is to actually give people what they want, even if you know what it is. The typical "born salesman," Craig had observed, preferred to wing it. But he'd developed the unusual *modus operandi* of reconciling the requirements of buyers with the realities of manufacturers. The process was tedious. Winn invested hours in preparation. There were always pages of written communication between Craig, his customers, and the brands, covering every miniscule detail. After all, he couldn't rely on his charming personality. His person-ality had no charm.

Even that wasn't the end of it. After he had an agreement with the merchant, Craig continued working, doing things that made life easy for buyers and their stores. He wrote their purchase orders. He handled the advertising and point-of-purchase displays. He arranged for delivery. He made sure their sales force had been trained. More importantly, if any-thing went wrong, he always made it right. Somehow, Winn never met a problem he couldn't solve. He learned to love problems, for solving them created value. His life's work became turning lemons into lemonade.

Scott pulled back on the throttle to begin his descent into Montgomery Field. Bill Hunt smiled. He knew all about Craig's penchant for prepara-tion. The two had spent an entire day getting ready. They *knew* they were going to get the order. They weren't even going to have to ask for it. Patton Electric made high-quality products, and the people they were going to see cared about their customers. Selling quality was part of the corporate mission. They had anticipated every possible question, knowing that a good answer today was worth more than a perfect one tomorrow.

༄

THE CESSNA ROLLED to a stop on the tarmac not far from the general aviation terminal. Their car was waiting. It was tired but cheap, a big old sedan that could be rented for the day by pilots who knew the system.

Craig smiled as he carefully extricated the samples from the plane's cramped interior. He inspected them one last time as he loaded them into the cavernous trunk of the ancient Cadillac.

It was usually the rep's business to convince the retail buyer of the merits of the brand's products. But in San Diego in the mid 1980s, the tables had turned. A fellow named Sol Price had started the Price Club, and top brands were staying away in droves.

Price Club wasn't a big deal; there were only a few locations. The "corporate headquarters" was still in the original warehouse. It wasn't fancy, just an old converted World War II aircraft assembly plant, a large metal Quonset hut affair, enclosing about 100,000 square feet. Warehouse-type steel racks were stacked to the rafters. Forklifts plied the aisles as customers scampered to safety with their oversized shopping carts. Neiman-Marcus it was not.

The Price Club was causing problems, making people nervous. Sol Price wasn't surprised. He'd made people nervous before. He had been the founder of FedMart, one of America's first discount stores. By the 1980s, FedMart had spawned many imitators.

When he had started FedMart, specialty and department stores had been furious. But Sol had figured out a better way to serve both consumers and brands. In the process, he had revolutionized the way America shopped. It was not to be the last time.

FedMart now had hundreds of stores. The revolution had settled down and become business as usual. Price had grown bored. As FedMart grew, Sol had hired professional managers from other retailers. They, quite naturally, had brought their prior understanding and experience with them, putting their own stamp on his vision. Changes in management philosophy ultimately quenched the flames of Sol Price's first retail revolution.

FedMart was no longer a challenge, and challenge was where the fun was. So Price sold the big discount chain to a German businessman. The deal included a non-compete covenant that prohibited him from reentering the retail business. But he was a tinkerer, an innovator, one who could think outside the box, even if it were a box that he had invented.

So Sol founded the Price Club, the first cash-and-carry *wholesaler* designed to serve the small business community. It wasn't a retailer, never mind the registers that lined the front of the warehouse (Sol wouldn't let anyone call it a store—it was always a warehouse or location). The key to the wholesale concept was that you had to be a member to shop there, and not just anybody could qualify for membership. You had to own your own business, be an executive in a business, or be part of a qualified organization. You couldn't just walk in off the street.

Beyond that, you had to pay for the privilege. Sol, in a stroke of inspiration, realized that people would be more likely to frequent his store, excuse me, *location,* if they had already paid for the right to do so.

And how could you get people to pony up $25 a year for the privilege of spending their money in one place rather than another? By offering significantly lower prices on higher quality merchandise, that's how. Works like a charm. If you know you're saving $50 on a $200 lateral file for your office, you're going to be impressed. Members always bragged about how much the Price Club saved them. The arithmetic was a no-brainer.

There was a rub, though. Selling things for significantly less than everybody else was a good way to go broke. But that's where the genius of charging a membership fee became apparent. Sol figured the *fees* were going to be his profit. His mark-up only had to cover his costs, and with his superior inventory management, those were as low as they got, hence the lack of amenities in the dingy old Quonset hut on Morena Blvd.

It was a numbers game. When he started, there were only a handful of members, but as time went on, the numbers became enormous. Eventually, over thirty million Americans would pay $35 a year for the opportunity to shop in the "stores" he inspired. Craig considered Sol America's greatest merchant. He was unquestionably the most inventive. Even WalMart's Sam Walton looked up to Sol.

Selling things at cost-plus meant that Price was operating on a razor-thin ten percent gross margin. Compare that to the thirty to sixty percent gross margins ubiquitous in the retail community, and you'll appreciate how happy his customers were and how angry he'd made his competition.

Actually, for the member, it was even better than these numbers might suggest, because retail gross margins are calculated on the selling price, not on cost. For Price Club to achieve a ten percent gross margin on an item that cost $90, they would charge $99.95. Another retailer, in order to achieve a fifty percent margin on the same product, would charge $179.99. A fifty percent gross margin doubles the price of the product. A sixty-five percent gross margin, common among catalog retailers, nearly *triples* the product's actual cost.

As strange as it sounds from this side of the cash register, Price Club's pricing strategy caused big problems for manufacturers like Patton. WalMart, for example, would tell Patton, "If you sell your Model XYZ fan to the Price Club, we won't sell it in our stores because we'll go broke trying to compete." This, of course, put Patton in a delicate situation. A big discounter with hundreds of stores could move a lot of Model XYZ fans. Sol had a revolutionary game plan but very few locations. Over a decade later, online retailers like Value America would be challenged with an even more extreme version of this same problem.

৩৯:৶৶

ARRIVING AT THE big, ugly, steel-walled building, Craig, Bill, and Scott wound their way through the aisles to a back corner. Flimsy temporary dividers hid a number of cheap desks. There fifteen or twenty mostly young men and women who shared Sol's vision ran the store accordingly. None of them wore expensive business suits. Every day was casual day. Most wouldn't even have thought of themselves as executives, though they were serving in those roles. Some had been senior merchants at FedMart, happily jumping ship soon after Price left. Others were new, just learning their craft, caught up in the excitement of corporate pioneering.

Adding to the excitement was stock-option euphoria. Sol Price was committed to sharing the wealth: every Price Club employee had stock options. They all owned a piece of the pie. They all believed that getting in on the ground floor gave them the potential to get rich.

Fortunately, the investment community understood that it took a retail chain at least five years to build the scale necessary to turn a profit. They knew that once scale was achieved, profits would follow. They recognized that new retailers needed time to attract customers, and that the surest way to attract them was with low prices, which initially meant lower margins. Emerging retailers also had to invest heavily in their infrastructure and systems. These costs represented a disproportionately high percentage of their early revenues, making their initial losses worse. Wall Street recognized that new retailers had to build a name for themselves too, reaching out through advertising. The cost of advertising further assured that profits would be delayed.

Yet most emerging retailers found the capital markets receptive—quite willing to give them the vast sums of money they needed to build their systems, advertise, and achieve scale, many years before they became profitable. Their value was calculated as a multiple of projected results. Long before unprofitable dot-coms were valued so highly by Wall Street, rapidly emerging retailers enjoyed the same good fortune.

Sadly, however, no dot-com analyst would ever grasp the correlation between the established mode of evaluating retailers and the new retail world of dot-com. From retail to railroads, from telephony to television, valuing companies based upon their potential was not some new gambit that had been pulled out of the hat to blow smoke in the eyes of tech investors. Although the media may scoff at the notion, valuing pre-profitable companies in emerging fields has been a valid, well-established, and productive strategy for well over a hundred years.

Price Club was a special place. Its founder's charisma, his noble corporate mission of serving brands and consumers alike, his willingness to share the wealth, all came together to give the firm a wonderful atmosphere, almost a religious fervor. It was as if the entire staff had become knights embarked on a noble crusade. Their members were their liege lord. The old retail world was the dragon they had set out to slay. And Sol's business plan was their sword. Every one of these corporate crusaders understood the company's mission and philosophy. They drank it in. They all valued its principles and followed its precepts. This wasn't just a job. It was a cause. Something about this powerful approach inevitably drew people in.

Hovering over it all was the great man himself, though Sol didn't even keep an office at the warehouse. To look at him, you would never guess that he was one of the most innovative business leaders of the twentieth century. He was about five feet, ten inches tall, in his early sixties, with thinning silver hair. The only remarkable thing about his appearance was his eyes. Sol had the strangest eyes. One bored holes right through you. The other was a free spirit. It had a tendency to wander about, quite independent of the other. It could be disconcerting to hold a conversation with Sol. There was no way you were going to make eye contact.

Trained as an attorney, Price was an active listener. His style was to ask a question twenty different ways. He wanted to discern if you really knew what you were talking about, if you believed in what you were saying.

჻

DURING THIS EXCITING TIME, Craig developed a close relationship with a FedMart merchandiser named Dick Gerhardt. A math major in college, he used a logical, calculated approach in negotiating with suppliers, many of whom were represented by The Winn Company. This endeared him to Craig, who could sell no other way.

It was in Craig's best interest for Gerhardt to stay where he was. After all, FedMart had hundreds of stores. Dick bought big. His orders were a huge part of Craig's income. But both could see the life slowly draining out of the once vibrant retail giant. Gerhardt found the new owner's process-oriented management style suffocating and paranoid; he came to hate his job. So Craig, seeing the writing on the wall, encouraged Dick to make the jump to the Price Club. It was a move neither would ever regret.

Craig, Bill, and Scott had come to make a presentation to the hardware merchant, Yale Conrad. Yale was in his thirties, short, with thinning blond hair combed straight back. He wasn't trained as a merchant, but he seemed sharp enough. Besides, how much damage could he do? It was supposed to be a tiny department. The Price Club, like so many successful retailers, was comprehensive. They sold some forty categories of merchandise, from office supplies for small businesses to bulk foodstuffs for convenience stores. Hard goods like appliances, housewares, and tools weren't critical. If he failed, no harm done.

It turned out to be a good thing they weren't *counting* on Conrad's failure. He didn't. He succeeded in spectacular fashion, in ways no one had anticipated. Yale was brilliant, tireless, and devoted. He and Craig shared a passion for the Price Club. Its mission was their mission.

Here, winning was all a matter of numbers, of performance. How many dollars could they generate per pallet, per location, per day? How could they maximize value for the member? Deals were negotiated on cold mathematics, as cold as the concrete floors in the big warehouse, not on what the traffic would bear.

Unfortunately, Yale Conrad was insecure, a problem that was given free reign when he came to recognize the power he had as a buyer. The power of economic life or death was his, one yes or no at a time.

Craig in time came to recognize the symptoms. Those suffering from insecurity have an overwhelming need for control, unquestioned and unchallenged. Insecure people are consumed with a suffocating craving for praise. And when they don't get enough, they personally proclaim their self-adoration. Yet their focus is seldom on their firm's accomplishments or its worthy mission; it's all about them. They must be the center of attention, and they won't hesitate to tear others down in order to elevate themselves. Their egos are out of control. They'll spend lavishly on the best clothes and the finest cars to create the illusion of competence.

They tend to be perfectionists. Their dress and personal hygiene can be fanatically fastidious. They won't tolerate an ounce of fat on themselves or their spouses. Their offices and homes are immaculate—any object out of place is immediately attacked; their souls are haunted until order is restored. The labels in their medicine cabinets all face outward. Their sock drawers tend to be a dead giveaway.

There is a dark side to insecurity. Rage can be triggered by the simplest things. Insecure people can't handle criticism, even when it's constructive and done in private. Many are abusive. Paranoia runs rampant. They become fixated on their foes and will stop at nothing to incapacitate them. Self ultimately triumphs over morality; yet they're invariably sanctimonious, piously justifying their unwarranted attacks on their rivals.

One of the more curious traits of insecure people is their tendency to undermine the credibility of those they fear. If their adversary has achieved something praiseworthy, they claim credit for themselves. Failing that, they mischaracterize the achievement, making a good deed look bad. The adversary is often accused of exaggeration or even lying. Evidence and logic never enter into the equation. It's all a matter of positioning and perceptions.

Craig was surprised to learn that insecurity did not manifest itself in overt shyness, as one might expect, but in compensation for their self-perceived inadequacies. Conrad was a classic case, and Craig studied him for years, observing and learning.

All the symptoms were there: a constant jockeying for position, a longing to be in control, the calculated undermining of those who failed to show blind devotion. There were rumors that he was abusive to his wife.

Relative stature was the key to Yale's insecurity. In order to elevate himself, those around him had to be torn down. He had a pathological need to have absolute perfection in his surroundings: the perfect wardrobe, precisely cleaned and pressed; the perfect office with everything in its place, every accessory precisely aligned; the perfect car, polished and spotless. If a speck of dust were to invade this perfect environment, the offending bit of soil would be dealt with immediately and ruthlessly. And ego? Conrad had a habit of telling sales reps, "To you, I am God."

Craig eventually learned how to work with Yale, finding that the more vile manifestations of insecurity are thwarted in the presence of altruistic corporate behavior. The more Conrad became dependent on The Winn Company, the better he behaved. Dependence, Craig found, was one of the most effective antidotes to the poison of insecurity.

Unfortunately, this would not be the last time Craig would do battle with this cancer. A decade or so later, he would discover just how much damage insecure people could do to him and his dreams.

෴

CRAIG CONCLUDED the ceiling fan presentation. He was confident. Conrad was pleased. Bill had reservations. "Here's the problem," he said to Yale. "Other retailers have told me they'll drop the Patton line if you buy it. Your prices make them look bad."

Conrad glanced at Craig. Yale was being placed on the defensive, and he didn't like it.

"So what am I supposed to do? Sign on with you and risk losing my biggest customers? You tell me. What would *you* do?"

There was a long pause. Yale was now glaring at Craig, silently screaming, *"Start earning your keep! Do something!"*

Craig had faced this concern before with other brands. He chose his words carefully. "The way I see it, you'd like to keep selling all your old customers and serve Yale and the Price Club too."

"Right," Bill replied. "That's why I'm here."

"Then don't compete. Patton has five styles of fan blades, and different brackets. You have four motor housings, eight light kits. Everything's available in three metal finishes. Right?"

"Yeah," Bill answered. "But we don't make or market even a tenth of those possible combinations."

"So let's create one just for Yale." As Craig spoke, he got up and placed several samples on the table. "The Price Club member deserves the best. These blades," he said, selecting the ones crafted out of real oak. "This solid brass motor housing, and remote control. We need you to combine these with this leaded-glass light kit." (He always used the term *we* to represent Price Club and *you* to represent the brand unless he was alone with the brand, and then they, too, were *we*.) "The Winn Company will design Yale's packaging and build his displays.

"Now, Bill," Craig continued melodramatically, "you know the rules. Anything special my friend Yale Conrad designs is his exclusively. Don't even *think* about selling this model to any of his competitors."

Bill smiled. "No. Of course not."

Yale got up and looked closely at his new fan. The others could see the wheels turning. *Yes. A Yale Conrad original. A Price Club exclusive.*

"This will work," Bill said. "Nobody else will have this model."

"Exactly. Everybody wins. Patton keeps its customers. Price Club gets to sell the best fan, and I still get to show my face around here."

That got a chuckle out of them. But Bill knew that what sounded simple, just combining parts in a new way, was actually quite complex. New bills of material had to be written, cost studies undertaken, and packaging procured. Winn had a knack for making the difficult sound easy and making the impossible merely appear to be an interesting challenge. He was so darn reasonable, how could you argue with him? He knew every nuance of Bill's and Yale's business as well as they knew them. Bill found himself loving and hating Craig at the same time. Solutions came too easily, and he was so confident they would prevail. Yet he always let others accept the credit, as he had for Conrad today.

Somehow, Bill thought, they would overcome the obstacles. They had done it before. Besides, now that Craig had made the offer and Conrad had accepted, they were committed. Handshakes were exchanged, and Yale excused himself.

"It's not going to last, you know," Craig said to Bill as they gathered their samples. "We've been planning as if our current customers are going to be around forever. They're not."

"What do you mean, 'they're not?'"

"What I'm talking about is the next retail revolution. Every ten years or so, somebody comes up with an idea that changes the way people buy and sell things. It's not that the old ways disappear; they just get eclipsed, left behind in the shadows. They become victims of commercial evolution, losers in the game of natural selection."

"Go on," Bill had to hear this.

"At the end of World War II, if you wanted to buy something, you'd go to the place that sold it. You'd go to Betty's Bake Shop, then to Harry's Hardware, Tom's Toys, and maybe the Curl Up and Dye Beauty Salon. There was plenty of personal service and good advice. In the fifties, as the suburbs took off, department stores did too. You could buy most anything from perfume to tires, from underwear to garden tools. They sold it all, so they were convenient. Of course, when you think about department stores today, you see high-priced apparel, cosmetics, and domestics, 'cause they've been run out of the categories that once made them strong."

"I'm with you so far," Bill said, following with interest.

"What hurt them was the retail revolution of the sixties: discounters. That phase was ushered in by none other than the white-haired gentleman standing over there." Craig nodded in the direction of Sol Price.

"FedMart."

"Right. Sol started FedMart about five miles from here, and the breed proliferated. Now, twenty years later, you've got WalMart, Kohls, Target, K-Mart, and Lord knows who else. Cutthroat competition is now a way of life. They're killing each other. Those that don't adapt will soon be extinct."

Bill stared at Craig. "Why don't you just take a gun and shoot me?"

"How do you think I feel? It's my living, too. Adapt or die, pal."

"So department stores owned the fifties, and discounters, the sixties."

"In the seventies, we saw the rise of shopping malls."

"Asphalt contractors loved 'em," Bill offered.

"You know, our malls have ten square feet of asphalt around them for every man, woman, and child in America." Craig smiled.

Bill sighed. *How does this guy come up with this stuff?*

"They function like department stores. Together in a mall, specialty stores are comprehensive. They save shoppers time. But today, department stores, regional discounters, and shopping malls are going south. Something new is evolving right under their noses."

"You don't mean...."

"Yep. Just watch. Before you know it, there'll be warehouse stores selling everything you can imagine."

Bill looked around him. The floors were concrete. The ceiling was the other side of the roof. There were no product displays, no sales staff, no air conditioning, no amenities of any kind. "Oh God, no," he muttered.

"This is the future," he said brightly. His attitude was an interesting contrast to the dimly lit warehouse. Craig always saw the possibilities.

"Come on. There's no way. Just *look* at this place."

"Look on the bright side, Bill. We'll sell tons of your new ceiling fans here at a hundred bucks apiece."

"Thank you, Doctor Winn. I feel so much better."

Craig's eyes scanned the warehouse. "Do you know how they do it, Bill? Do you know what makes Price Club better?" Bill hesitated, so Craig answered his own question. "Turn."

"Turn," Bill repeated. He knew what it meant, but he didn't know where Craig was going.

"Do you know how many inventory turns Sears averages?" Craig asked, not expecting Bill to respond. "One point two times a year."

"How do they stay in business?"

"Good question. It means that if they buy your product in January, they'll sell it in November. How many turns does Price average?"

"More than 1.2, I'm guessing." Bill was sharp today.

"Try eight. They buy your product in January, and it's gone by February. It's sold before they even pay us for it! Because their turn is so fast, they're never out of pocket. It makes them sort of like a bank—they're able to make a spread on other people's money."

Craig and Bill got up and strolled through the aisles of the Price Club. "Inventory management and distribution. That's what it's all about. Department stores and discounters have expensive warehouses *and* stores, but look at this place." As if on cue, the beep-beep of a forklift backing up punctuated their conversation. Craig and Bill moved out of the way and watched the operator take a pallet of pickles down from its perch. "Here, the warehouse is the store. It may not be pretty, but this is the most efficient solution yet."

ço:o

THE LATE AFTERNOON sun poured through the port side windows of Craig's Cessna. He had come to love this time of day, love the vague feeling of emotional fatigue that invariably followed a long but successful day of parry and thrust, give and take. He wasn't sleepy, but he closed his eyes against the glare, replaying it all in his mind.

Bill's mind was churning too, thinking it all over. As so often happens, answers had merely led to more questions, and now he had a head full of them. "Hey, Craig. Got your intercom on?"

"Yeah, Bill," he answered, adjusting his headphones.

"Remember what you said about retail revolutions? Where do you see us going *after* warehouse stores?"

Craig smiled and sat up. He had given this question a lot of thought. "Every new wrinkle comes in reaction to some need the previous revolution failed to meet. So ask yourself, as good as the Price Club is, where are they falling short?"

"First, there's no sales help or good point-of-purchase materials to explain why someone should buy our products."

"Bingo," Craig smiled. "You're one for one. It's up to the package to do the selling."

"They're inconvenient," Bill said. "It's a hassle to get to a Price Club and a bigger hassle to find what you want once you're there."

"Ka-ching! Give the man in the red sweater another point."

"The selection's not so hot, either," Bill added, hoping for a perfect score. "I'll bet they carry less than three thousand items."

"You're as sharp as a marble, my man. Three for three. All right, Bill, here's the future as I see it. All of the things Price Club does well will still resonate a decade from now. Better technology will mean more efficient inventory management, and that in turn will enable future retailers to sell stuff at better prices. Sol's commitment to quality is important, and so is his support of brands. I think the store of the future will emulate Sol's product breadth. You'll be able to buy everything. For my money, his idea of leading with office products is also genius."

"Okay. So much for adoration. What about invention?" Bill probed.

"The problem is that there's an information gap. It prevents consumers from learning what they need to know. And it's getting worse. Products are becoming more complex. They need *more* explanation, not *less*."

"Yeah. I agree."

"So we need a way to make consumers better buyers—to differentiate features, functions, and benefits, the same way you and I do for professional chain store buyers today."

"That's impossible," Bill said. "We can't sell every consumer."

Craig smiled. "Not today. But in the future, we'll be able to present things electronically, using multimedia: text, pictures, sound, even video. People will watch our product presentations right in their homes."

Bill smiled. When Craig got an idea into his head....

"Somebody will find a way to combine these new PCs we saw at the Price Club with phones and maybe even TVs."

"Is that why you bought that new computer today?" Scott interjected.

"No, I think this revolution is a ways off. But I'm told Dell is an up-and-comer. It's unbranded now, but the deal was too good to pass up. It's lightening fast, got an Intel *286* processor!"

"Wow." They were both impressed.

"Now imagine, guys, using this PC to view an electronic presentation of Patton fans. Buy them in your home and have them shipped from the factory to your doorstep. It'll happen. Someday."

"You've really thought about this, haven't you?" Bill asked.

"It's been, what, fifteen years since we put a man on the moon? Some of that technology has to trickle down to us common folks."

"So you're talking about bringing the store and the products to the customer?" Scott was having a hard time envisioning this.

"Exactly. Think about it—there's no store. No warehouse. No overhead. And non-existent inventory turns *very* fast. There's just the factory and the consumer. Supply and demand. The store is virtually transparent. It's the ultimate retail revolution. It gives everybody everything they want."

"Except manufacturer's reps," Bill pointed out.

"No more reptiles," Craig agreed. "So when this happens, we'd better be the ones making it happen."

Bill just grinned and shook his head.

Men listened to me expectantly, waiting in silence for my counsel—Job

THE SCHOOL OF HARD KNOCKS

*C*raig had seen the writing on the wall, and its message was too clear to ignore. The predictions he had made to Bill Hunt were coming true at an alarming rate. A whole new breed of "big-box retailers" had sprung up. They operated like the warehouse clubs but specialized in—and endeavored to dominate—a single category. The Home Depots, Circuit Cities, and Office Depots had arrived and conquered.

The bad news was that the overall buying base was shrinking, making the commissions Craig had become accustomed to earning, over $2 million a year by this time, harder to maintain. The number of buying offices in California had decreased from twenty-five or so to only a handful.

The discounters, so hot a decade before, were dropping like flies. FedMart was gone. Zody's, gone. Akron, Gemco, The Treasury, Two Guys, Builder's Emporium, Fedco, Ole's, all dead or dying. Darwin would have felt vindicated: commerce red in tooth and claw.

Against this backdrop of shrinking markets, Craig formed a new strategy. It had been a long time since he had earned lunch money beating his head against the wall, and he didn't particularly want to go back there. It had been a while since he had been a pivotal player in Price Club's rise. Years had passed since he had bought his father's business and started The Winn Company. His rep firm was now a giant with annual sales exceeding $100 million. The Winn Company, it could be safely said, was not his father's Oldsmobile. Nevertheless, Craig cringed at the thought of it turning back into an economy model, like Cinderella's pumpkin.

So it was that Craig, on a crisp October day in 1986, visited the palatial offices of the Price Club. They were no longer in the big Quonset hut on Morena Blvd. They had moved up the street into something that reminded him of an oversized self-storage unit. He met with a senior buyer, Alan Nellis, and his boss, Yale Conrad, now the Merchandise Manager.

Craig asked an intriguing question. "What's the dumbest industry?"

"The dumbest industry?" Alan tried out the words for size.

Craig clarified his question. "What industry has potential but is poorly managed—weak products, poor marketing, lousy values?"

Nellis didn't hesitate. It had been his own personal toothache for years. "Lighting."

"Lighting," Craig echoed. "What's wrong with lighting?"

"Everything," they answered in unison. "Poor quality, ugly designs, disastrous marketing...."

"We'd like to sell something better," Conrad said, "but we can't find it."

"That bad?"

"Come on, I'll show you," Alan responded as he stood up. The three drove to the warehouse. Craig was shown three lamps—a table, a floor, and a banker's lamp. Beneath them was a pallet of corrugated cartons. Each had a pitifully small photograph and such helpful sales copy as, "Table Lamp; Made in Taiwan; Model #12548."

Craig looked more closely. "How long have these been here?"

"About a month. Why?"

"Take a look at the brass plating. It's already starting to tarnish."

"See what I mean? It's pathetic! Think you can help us?"

Yale gave Craig a sideways look. "Going into the lamp business?"

"Why not? Any fool should be able to compete against this sorry lot."

Craig had sold thousands of things, but he had never sold a lamp. He didn't know the first thing about lighting. But life is for learning.

❧

THE CHINA AIRLINES Boeing 747 touched down with a jolt at Taiwan's International Airport outside Taipei. Katharine Winn felt the baby kick again. Sitting in her cramped economy seat, she looked over and smiled wearily at her husband. "I know you like to save money, Craig, but flying economy overseas is ridiculous."

Craig had to agree. It had been a month since he had formed his new lighting company. He called it Dynasty, figuring it would be better to grow into a name than worry about outgrowing one. This was his maiden voyage into brand dynamics.

The Winn Company was still very much alive, but Craig had now become a supplier as well, if not yet an actual manufacturer. The plan was simple. Find out what lighting products sold best. Find someone who could build these products. Design and manufacture them to a higher standard. Package and display them in a compelling way. Then price them so that their superior value would be readily apparent.

Craig had done his homework. The models he would produce first were considered commodities, models for which sales were certain. Conventional wisdom said that if you could sell these for a nickel less than your competition, you'd own the market. Dynasty's strategy was to buck the trend: make the lamps fifty percent better and charge twenty percent more. The reason he was here, 9,000 miles from home, was because Taiwan was the world's best source for decorative lamps.

As the jumbo jet rolled to a stop, Katharine had a bit of trouble getting onto her swollen feet, never mind how badly she wanted to. Craig stood, leaned over, and took his wife by the hand. When she got to her feet, he didn't let go but looked at her for a long moment. "Thanks for coming, Katie. Having you here is important."

"I know. Don't worry. It'll be fun." Little did she know the fun would include a dinner of bulgy-eyed fish heads, snake, and dog.

Taiwanese businessmen were pragmatists. They had learned long ago that when buyers came from America with their pockets full of money, they usually expected more than product demonstrations, plant tours, and contract negotiations. Most expected to be lavishly entertained. Five-star dining, free-flowing liquor, expensive cigars, and the occasional prostitute were all considered part of doing business. If a buyer wanted to spend his evenings in nightclubs populated with beautiful women in various states of undress, who were these practical businessmen to pass moral judgments? Fulfilling these wishes only increased the buyers' indebtedness, greasing the wheels of commerce. Where was the harm in that?

Craig wasn't about to negotiate with anyone on that basis. Having Katharine present at the initial meetings went a long way toward setting the tone. He made it clear that any such "favors" would quickly end their business relationship.

But what he did not do, the Taiwanese soon learned, was not nearly as unusual as what he *did*. As Craig visited factories, he asked them to "sell" him on their capabilities in the same way he routinely sold others on the merits of the products and companies he represented. They had never experienced anything quite like this.

Craig asked them how they could improve their products. They discussed materials and talked about manufacturing techniques. They analyzed features and benefits with an eye toward making a product that was significantly better. The Taiwanese, having become accustomed to hearing only one question—"What's your price?"—were thrilled.

Craig too got something unexpected out of the relationships he formed here (and it wasn't the same unexpected thing his competitors often got, for which penicillin usually did the trick). The Taiwanese had a reputation for being astute, resourceful, and hard working, but he also found them trustworthy. A handshake with a Taiwan businessperson was as good as a hundred-page contract.

Winn was not a trained designer, yet Dynasty's line would be marked by innovation, even though some of it was to be based on well-established forms. You don't have to reinvent the wheel to make a better tire. Craig adopted a technique that would serve him for years. He told the lamp makers what he wanted, often enhancing his explanations with photos from totally unrelated products to visually communicate what he was trying to achieve. The designer would then produce a loose sketch. Once done, Craig would pick the elements he thought held promise.

Looking at a sketch of a banker's lamp, he would say, "Let's make the post an inch longer. Change it from black to green marble. Ask your glassmaker to adjust the shade's color so when the light is *off,* it matches the dark veining. When it's *on,* try to match the color of the highlights. Now, while we're at it, marble is cheap, right? Let's make the column fatter."

The designer would make the corrections, and then they would go through the process again. React and rework. Craig kept making changes until he was happy with what he saw.

This process, of course, drove some designers nuts. Prima donnas didn't last, but talented professionals with balanced attitudes (i.e., thick skins) became the hands of Craig Winn, the designer. It wasn't that he wouldn't listen to advice. He would, and did, and sometimes changed his direction based upon it. But it was clear that the final call was his. By this process, he came to own over a hundred design patents.

Craig formed many long-standing relationships this way (including one with me, years later). It started with lighting designs but soon spread to packaging, advertising, corporate graphics, and a host of other disciplines. The common thread, it seemed to me, was that he had excellent taste, good judgment, and unerring design instincts. He *knew* what would sell.

The product designed, the next order of business was packaging, which in the lighting industry was universally excrementitious. Craig raised the bar so high, no competitor was able to compete.

Dynasty's cartons were magnificent. They attracted attention with sophisticated graphics, lavish environmental photographs, and well-crafted copy. There was always plenty of white space. Product information was well organized and motivating. Everything was graphically coordinated across the entire product line. The competition could only whine lamely, "Dynasty gives great box."

Under Winn, Dynasty broke every rule in the book, including the one that said, "Go slow." In the first few months following the "dumb industry" discussion with Alan Nellis, Dynasty sold $2 million worth of lamps. In their first full year, Dynasty did a stunning $16 million. The second year, $32 million. Third year, $64 million. Fourth year, $100 million. Pity about that fourth year. They had a nice pattern going.

❧

BETWEEN THE WINN COMPANY and Dynasty, Craig stayed busy. Although the markets had shifted, his dire prediction about his own commissions dropping had failed to materialize (hey, nobody's perfect). Now, in the summer of '89, he was still making a couple million dollars a year from his work at The Winn Company. He was also drawing a CEO's salary from his wildly successful lighting firm. His mother-in-law was starting to accept him.

During the third year of Dynasty's life, the company prepared to go public. It was a dance Craig would perform twice more before hanging up his shoes. He was almost relieved when his underwriters, Morgan Stanley and Salomon Brothers, said it would not be proper for the CEO of a public company to earn millions working for another company. The solution? The Winn Company would be gifted to Dynasty.

It made perfect sense. The two companies had a symbiotic, if not incestuous, relationship anyway. The Winn Company represented Dynasty in California, and was responsible for the majority of its sales. The merger of Dynasty and Winn was facilitated by Dwight Stewart, who had been Dynasty's financial backer from the beginning. An astute businessman and able manager, he had made his first fortune the *really* old-fashioned way. He inherited the Carnation Company from his father, later selling it to Nestlé, netting nearly a billion dollars.

Craig had met Stewart through a Kappa Sigma fraternity brother at USC. During lunch, he explained Dynasty's philosophy and its marketing strategy. Dwight, quick to recognize the potential, became an instant investor, writing Craig a check, right there and then, for one million dollars. The check, Craig noticed, had little sailboats on it. You've got to admire that kind of style.

What started as a handshake had grown into a major commitment for Stewart, and his investments were paying off handsomely. Within a year of that auspicious first meeting, Dwight had pledged $15 million, which had allowed Dynasty to buy inventory and build its manufacturing plants. He now owned forty percent of the firm, which, following the IPO, would be worth $400 million. So in order for Dynasty to go public, Dwight agreed to reimburse Craig for his proportionate share of The Winn Company gift.

To be fair, Winn asked the bankers at Morgan Stanley to set the price. They calculated that Dwight's forty percent share of The Winn Company, once public, would be worth $7 million. Then, to make absolutely sure Dwight was getting a fair shake, Craig cut their estimate in half. Dwight paid Craig $3.5 million over the next three years.

The Morgan Stanley-led IPO almost derailed, however. When it came time to set a value by comparing it to other public firms, Dynasty's nearest "comp" was a jewelry company named JanBell, but they were in trouble. Their largest customers, Price and Costco, both dropped them just prior to Dynasty's IPO. JanBell's stock price plummeted, dragging the estimated value of Dynasty's stock down with it. What JanBell's fortunes had to do with Dynasty's worth was never made quite clear. Nevertheless, Craig found himself with his back against the wall. He appealed directly to Sol Price, who saved the day by offering to buy shares in Dynasty's IPO. The road show started in San Diego, with a supportive Sol Price in attendance.

A month or so later, at the ritzy Pierre Hotel just off New York's Central Park, Craig gave his first investor's speech. Sandwiched between a credit card processor and a restaurant chain at a Morgan Stanley Emerging Growth Conference, he delivered what he felt was a conservative talk. About two-thirds of the way through his twenty-minute speech, two thirds of the nearly 500 institutional investors got up and left the room. Craig was dismayed, convinced that he had painted too pessimistic a picture of Dynasty's short-term outlook. Rattled, he finished his speech and left the ballroom.

As he began to apologize to Morgan's analyst for his poor performance, the small group surrounding him burst into laughter. It seems the investors had raced out of the meeting in order to buy his stock. Dynasty's share price had risen from $11 to $18 in less than an hour. Winn's net worth had jumped nearly $50 million.

Sadly, it wouldn't last. Saddam Hussein invaded Kuwait a few weeks later. The price of oil shot up, and the value of Nasdaq stocks, including Dynasty's, fell just as quickly. Craig never understood the correlation between desert megalomaniacs and solid brass table lamps.

ပ>:ၔ

THEY MET on a golf course, the first tee of the Mauna Lani on the Big Island of Hawaii. A good-looking stranger came up to Craig and Katharine and asked if he could join them. Rex Scatena proceeded to birdie two of the first three holes as they walked the green fairways that cut incongruously through the jagged black lava flows of the Kona Coast.

The tall Italian gentleman turned out to be an attorney with a personality, something Craig had never before encountered. Rex, as it transpired, was the founder of the largest environmental law firm in California, a position he was slowly growing to hate. He was getting rich but felt like he was losing his soul. Good news, bad news.

On Mauna Lani's back nine, the conversation revealed that the Winn and Scatena kids had become inseparable pals during the last few days at the resort's kids' club, Camp Mauna Lani. Craig and Katharine had heard nothing from Ryan and Blake but "Billy this" and "Billy that" for two solid days. Billy *Scatena*, it turned out.

Rex's firm had offices in San Francisco and in San Pedro, the port city serving Los Angeles, which was not far from Craig's home in Palos Verdes. So on his first trip south after their Hawaiian vacation, he called Craig and set up a lunch date.

In Hawaii, Craig had downplayed the size of his firm. But now, as Rex approached the nearly half-million square foot Dynasty factory, warehouse, and office complex, there was no hiding it; the place was gargantuan. Entering through massive bronze doors, Rex was greeted by a receptionist who introduced him to Jenny, Craig's administrative assistant.

As they entered Craig's office, he grinned, jumped up, and shook hands with his new friend. Craig offered Rex a seat, but Jenny interrupted. "Excuse me, Craig. I've just completed the written recap of our meeting with Sears. I've asked Rex—Rex Lundquist," she said for Mr. Scatena's benefit—"to do an artist's rendering of the department. Sears has given us their entire lighting department!"

"Wow!" Rex exclaimed. "This is some joint you're running. Got time to give me a tour before we go to lunch?"

"Sure." Craig beamed like a proud parent who's just been asked to show off pictures of his children. "Step right this way."

The two friends walked down a maze of intersecting corridors, all bustling with activity. The place was so big, the hallways were all named. They had street signs to help newcomers find their way around. Craig explained that while the offices looked grand, they were the deal of a lifetime. "It's hard to believe, Rex, but the landlord fixed up these offices for us on his nickel. He's only charging us thirty cents a square foot."

Rex stopped in his tracks. "We pay almost ten times that, and I thought we were getting a good deal. You want to negotiate my next lease?"

As they walked past other offices, people jumped out to give the boss an update. The excitement was infectious.

"Just got the directive to do the Sears' rendering," Rex Lundquist informed the boss. "We're on it!"

"Rex, meet Rex. Rex Lundquist is VP of marketing."

"This is a great job—like getting a paid education," Lundquist gushed. "We call this place Dynasty U."

A tornado with thinning red hair dashed down the hall with a triumphant smile. "We got it, Craig! We got the deal!" he almost shouted. "Home Depot said 'Yes,' a hundred lamps in most every store."

"Congratulations! Bentley, meet my friend Rex. I hired Bentley when I began The Winn Company. I think he 'bleeds orange'—that's Home

Depot's slang for vendors they really love—you know, orange logo, orange racks. It's their company color."

"Yep," he said proudly. "Craig and I go way back, grew up on the same street. I followed him to SC, but I joined a better fraternity."

Craig liked working with his friends, especially old friends, Rex observed. It was a defense mechanism. Craig knew that his ethics radar, his ability to detect personality disorders in others, was particularly weak. That made it possible for one of his greatest strengths to work against him. He had an uncanny ability to see the best in people, coupled with an inability to recognize their flaws until it was too late. He elevated and empowered those around him, taught them, led them by example, and put many on a pedestal. Unfortunately, his insistent praise attracted those most in need of praise, the insecure, that most dangerous of corporate viruses. Around old friends, Craig could let his guard down.

Rex and Craig made their way to Richard Gerhardt's office. He was another of Craig's old friends. Dick had been the buyer Craig respected most during the waning days of FedMart and the rise of Price Club. Gerhardt had been offered the most senior merchandising job at the now multi-billion-dollar firm. Rather than taking the promotion, he had asked Craig for a job at Dynasty.

The Price Club, in Dick's view, was no longer any fun. The entrepreneurs were now mostly gone, including their charismatic ringleader, Sol Price. Still chairman of the board, Sol no longer held a managerial position. He focused on building outside partnerships, much like Winn would do a decade later. So for Dick, what was once a crusade was now just another job—a big job to be sure, but definitely not an adventure. Richard yearned for excitement, and Craig delivered. Gerhardt's knowledge of the things that made the Price Club work—buying, inventory control, and systems—made him perfect for Dynasty.

Down the hall, the CFO was awash in a sea of paper. Although Mary looked as unkempt as her office, she was an amazing talent. She was a Fortune 500-caliber controller. Unfortunately, Mary was ahead of her time. Her gender had previously precluded her from rising to the level of her competence.

"How do we look, Mary?"

"Great!" she said. "The Street's going to love this quarter."

"Well, don't let us disturb you. I wanted Rex to meet our team."

"Make sure he meets Susan. She just finished the system upgrade."

The giant raised-floor computer complex was state of the art. Susan was immersed in a discussion with her team. So Craig explained, "This was our first IBM AS400, Rex. Susan and her team just installed this smaller version, which is actually bigger where it counts, giving us greater redundancy and scalability. The process of integrating bills-of-materials with sales, reporting, distribution, and finance is daunting. She and Mary have done a great job. Our system conversion was completed on time and under budget."

Craig led his friend past engineering, customer care, and the company's outlet store. He opened the steel door to the factory and warehouse. It seemed to go on forever. It was over five football fields long and a hundred yards wide—nearly half a million square feet. As they entered, Scott Chrisman greeted them with a wave. Scott was attired with his usual sartorial serendipity: shorts, Hawaiian shirt, and flip-flops.

"Hey Craig!" Scott shouted above the roar of pneumatic tools and the chatter of conveyer belts. "Come over here. You've gotta see this!"

It was all Rex could do to absorb the scene. He couldn't imagine how this chap he had met in Hawaii could be responsible for all of this. It was an unending sea of equipment, people, and products. There were conveyer belts and assembly lines running everywhere.

"Scott, meet Rex," Craig hollered over the din of the production lines. "Scott is the guy that makes this place go. If it makes noise or eats gas, he can make it purr."

"We bought all of this used, for pennies on the dollar. The forklifts, conveyer belts, warehouse racks, pretty much everything. This is what I wanted to show you," Scott shouted as he walked over to the new expandable foam packaging station he had built. "Got the guns and system in a barter deal. Let me show you how it works."

He asked the assembly worker to stand aside as he took the controls. In his element, Scott was already an expert. He picked up a DynaStone lamp that had been cast in Dynasty's Maquiladora factory in Mexico and carefully placed it into a beautiful blue and white South Coast carton.

Without any wasted motion, almost like an orchestra conductor, he fired the guns and filled the empty spaces with expansive foam. After placing the custom shade his team had produced on top, he sealed the carton. Then, without warning, he lifted the box three feet off the ground and dropped it flat on its bottom. Thud. Then he dropped it again, but this time on its side. Then a third time, on a corner.

Scott explained, still shouting above the noise, "Three drops from three feet on the bottom, side, and corner. It's the new UPS drop test. Sears' catalog operation will require it in a couple of weeks. I thought I'd jump the gun, so to speak, be ready for 'em."

As he opened the carton, Craig was sure all they'd see was dust. The firm's South Coast contemporary hydrostone lamps were stronger than the competitions', but passing this drop test was too much to ask.

Seeing the worried look on Craig's face, Scott intoned, "Oh, ye of little faith," and opened the carton with a dramatic flourish, extracting one DynaStone lamp, unscathed. *"Voila!"*

Scott beamed with the knowledge that he had once again exorcised his demons—the voices inside that whispered so convincingly that without a college education, he was not good enough to hang with the suits. Craig didn't care. He would rather have one Scott Chrisman than ten experienced managers. Scott was a builder; he got things done. "You're the greatest," Craig said in unfeigned admiration.

On the way out of the factory, Rex asked, "Is everybody here like Chrisman? He's a piece o' work." They started up the stairs.

"I wish. Scott is one in a million. He was unemployed when I found him, or more correctly, when he found me. He said he'd been discharged from the police department for busting the Chief's maid for cocaine possession. To hear him tell the story is a riot. Then Scott earned a living as a professional water-skier, but falling at over a hundred miles an hour smarts." Craig paused. "So Scott used his charm to enter a somewhat less painful career. He started working for beautiful rich women. To say he was a gigolo would be overstating it. He didn't get paid, but it did give him a pretty interesting lifestyle."

"Wow," Rex observed eloquently.

"Yeah. He's quite a guy. He taught me how to fly. He can mix with princes and paupers, priests and prostitutes. Everybody loves him. Well, everybody except the suits, our professional managers, but that's a long story."

Craig and Rex climbed the last flight of elegantly curved stairs and entered a series of giant showrooms, each displaying beautiful and innovative lamps and lighting fixtures. It was overwhelming.

"I don't know what to say." Rex, the master linguist, was out of words. It was a Kodak moment, the formation of a mutual admiration society. From now on, their destinies would be inextricably joined.

❦

THE FALCON 20 was a beautiful bird, a spacious powder-blue corporate jet that looked like a mini-Air Force One. But it wasn't there for looks—judging by the way the Dynasty team used it. Part freight truck, part taxicab, Pullman sleeping car, and time machine, it *wasn't* a luxury. Dynasty shared ownership of the half-million dollar jet with Williams-Sonoma, whose founder, Howard Lester, was a member of Dynasty's board and a friend of Dwight Stewart.

Most people would have assumed that it was glamorous flying around the country in a private jet. Craig knew it was just a tool. The Falcon was needed for quick access to Dynasty customers like Sears in Chicago, Home Depot in Atlanta, Kmart in Michigan, and WalMart and Sam's in Nowhere, Arkansas.

During Dynasty's rise, the company became the predominant supplier of lighting to Sears, winning their Vendor of the Year Award. Dynasty dominated the lighting departments of chains like Home Depot, Lowe's, Home Club, Sam's, and, of course, Price Club. By using the airplane like a carpenter uses a hammer, Craig personally generated the vast majority of Dynasty's revenue. The cost of owning the Falcon, compared to what it would have cost to generate those sales elsewhere, was insignificant.

၆၁-ၡ

WHILE SOME IDEAS are dogs, other ideas are cats. They have nine lives. For Craig, the idea of mastering seasonal product categories started way back at The Winn Company as a tabby cat. By the time it had grown up at Dynasty, the idea had become a Bengal tiger.

If a hot spell hits, the sales of fans can suddenly go through the roof. When this happens, the buyer calls the average supplier and arranges for a rush shipment, and more fans magically arrive—two weeks later. Craig recognized that the weatherman was not always that patient. A week after placing the order, the buyer might need umbrellas instead. So The Winn Company worked with Patton's Bill Hunt to engineer a system of warehouses and express freight companies (before they became popular). They did it again at Dynasty. When a buyer called, they got restocked the same day.

The secret ingredient of this system was trust, a commodity that could not be bought, only earned. The Price Club, for example, came to trust Winn to deliver when they needed him to. Winn in turn trusted Price to use the service they had made available at such great expense and risk. Amazingly, all of this—business worth tens of millions—was done over the phone and across the desk on handshakes. There were seldom any contracts, formal agreements, or even written purchase orders. It just happened.

Fast forward a few years. The Price Club's Yale Conrad spotted what he thought would be the hottest item for the upcoming holiday season: sequential Christmas lights. They produced an effect not unlike the moving lights of a theater marquee. Yale was sure they would sell, and he was seldom wrong.

He wanted someone he trusted to supply the new light sets. And who had time and again proved himself worthy? Why, Craig Winn, of course, especially now that Dynasty had so many manufacturing contacts here and abroad.

Dynasty jumped at the opportunity but didn't stop there. In typical Winn fashion, he saw not only the trees before him but the entire forest. Here was another industry, like lighting, that was under-performing. Dynasty got Conrad his sequential lights and then went on to build an entire division around lighted holiday décor, called Holiday Classics.

Soon, Holiday Classics became one of the nation's largest suppliers of seasonal goods. It wasn't hard to see why. Dynasty's new line did everything better. Over time, it grew into something wonderful.

Other people sold light sets. Holiday Classics offered (among other things) "Dancing Lights," featuring, as the catalog described them, "Innovative and ruggedly dependable super-bright lights. If any bulb burns out, or is even removed, all of the other bulbs will continue to light. Features a timed memory chip for automatic rotation of dozens of light show sequences, plus slow fade, wave, pulse, chasing, and random twinkle. Lifetime warranty...." And you didn't even need an advanced degree in astrophysics to plug them in.

Other people had Christmas wreaths. Holiday Classics offered (among other things) a "22-inch decorated Colorado spruce wreath, featuring 10 electric candles with flickering bulbs and 35 mini-lights, highlighted with natural pine cones, berries and holly."

Other people had...actually, *nobody* had anything like the Story-Telling Santa, a cuddly, hand-stitched version of the jolly old guy, designed to sit on a child's lap and "read" stories from the book he was holding. His mouth moved and his eyes blinked as he read the original "The Night Before Christmas" poem by Clement Moore. We're talkin' *cute* here.

The Price Club was the first to buy Holiday Classics designs. But it didn't take long for others to become interested, especially other warehouse clubs—especially Sam's, WalMart's Price Club clone.

꙳⁖꙰

ANOTHER SHORT NIGHT had passed as the Falcon 20 flew toward the Arkansas sunrise, robbing Winn of badly needed sleep. With him was Dynasty exec Mark Wong, President of the firm's overseas operations. Mark was a dashing Hong Kong businessman, impeccably attired in a custom suit. He was another of the insecure characters in Craig's life. He wondered where they all came from.

At breakfast, Craig sipped his coffee and wondered if all the hassle was worth it. No doubt it was just fatigue playing with his head. Sleep deprivation can make things seem worse than they really are. But it wasn't the travel that was starting to get to him. He could deal with that. It was the concessions Sam's Club was demanding.

First it had been exclusive products, so shoppers wouldn't find the same things in other stores. Dynasty had complied. They wanted point-of-purchase signs for their stores. Okay. Then, an end-of-season return program so they wouldn't be stuck with unsold goods. All these extras cost money, but jumping through hoops was what Dynasty did best. That's how they had earned the lion's share of Sam's business, starting with $2 million the first year, then climbing to $15 million. The third year, 1992, was to be the biggest yet—$25 million.

The meeting started promptly at eight o'clock. As Sam's senior buyer, Clay Steward, greeted them, Craig passed out copies of the revised program. It had grown to nearly one hundred pages of detailed documentation. He said, "Just so we're all on the same page, let's recap our progress. This lists the product mix you've agreed to buy, your revised quantities, and your updated delivery schedules. Your changes are underlined. The last three pages detail the shipping parameters you've asked us to follow." Craig wanted to say "demanded" rather than "asked," but since Sam's was now his biggest customer, it would have been bad form.

Craig had always thought it seemed a little odd that WalMart, with all of its "Buy-America" hype, ran the biggest buying offices in the Far East. But today, that was neither here nor there. "As you know, the factories in China can't wait any longer to buy raw materials and begin retooling their production lines. Manufacturing must start soon if we are to meet your delivery schedules."

"We understand all of that," Clay said.

"This program requires transferable international letters of credit because you want an end-of-season return program," Craig confirmed.

"That's right. We expect WalMart's import division to issue them any day now. But in the meantime, we need to make some changes...."

⚜

"CLAY, TALK TO me." Craig was in his office at the Dynasty plant, on the phone with Steward for the fourth time that week. "It's the third week in May, and I still don't have the letters of credit."

"I know, Craig," Clay replied. "I apologize. I know it'll happen. I just don't know when. I keep pushing WalMart for an answer."

"We're in trouble, Clay." There was a hint of desperation in Craig's voice. "If the factories didn't get started, you would've missed Christmas. We had to fund the raw materials and tooling ourselves."

"You did?"

"Yes, but that doesn't mean we should have. We've used our lighting division's credit lines to fund *your* program. It got us going, but it won't last. We've got to get your transferable international letters of credit, or we're as good as dead." Craig prayed he was exaggerating.

৵৽৻৶

"I'VE GOT SOME good news, Craig."

"What have you got for me, Clay?"

"I've got the letters of credit. Sorry it took 'til June."

"Transferable international letters of credit, right?"

"Well, ummm...no. They issued domestic LCs."

There was a long pause as Craig tried to regain his composure. It was a losing battle. "You're *killing* me, Clay. Domestic LCs aren't acceptable, and you know it! They can't be used to fund overseas production, and they're not part of international agreements. They don't automatically transfer payment when your products leave port. Are you starting to see the problem here, Clay?"

"Well, I...."

"Transferable international LCs," Craig continued with increasing frustration, "fund upon shipment. You take possession in Hong Kong, inspect the goods, choose the freight lines, pay the ocean freight, clear the goods when they arrive, pay the import duty, and truck the containers to your nearest distribution center. Read the program. That's what it says, and that's what you agreed to do in exchange for your end-of-season return privilege. We've confirmed it countless times in writing."

"Sorry, Winn. That's the best I can do." And then, remembering he was the buyer, he added, "Take it or leave it."

Craig took it. What else could he do? It was June already. Warehouses in China were filled with festive holiday village displays and lighted wreaths, high-tech sequential Christmas lights, and snow globes, all funded with the rob-Peter-to-pay-Paul method. Craig and company scrambled to make the best of a bad situation. After all, it couldn't get any worse.

But it did. Bank of America hated the deal even more than Craig did. In order to secure the necessary lines of credit, Winn had to put up his home as collateral. Then it got even *worse*. The domestic letters of credit enabled Sam's to continue changing the program to their benefit—and Dynasty's harm. Sam's required them to pay the ocean freight and import duty. They wanted all their products stored in American warehouses, palletized to their specifications, and the cartons side-marked with their labels, all at Dynasty's expense. This was a far cry from delivering shipping containers to an Asian port. Then Sam's delayed the arrivals. The list went on.

Every time Sam's added more restrictions, it delayed payment. These delays destroyed Dynasty's ability to fund its lighting inventory. Dynasty's asset-based line of credit with Bank of America was stretched beyond the breaking point. Soon the best-selling lamps were out of stock. No inventory, no shipments, no accounts receivable. No accounts receivable meant no advances on the asset-based line. No advances meant no inventory could be made or purchased. No inventory meant no sales. No sales meant no accounts receivables. It was an irreversible death spiral.

As lighting shipments became more erratic, bad things began happening. Dynasty's customers, notably Sears, Home Depot, Home Club, Lowes, Kmart, and even the Price Club, had to have something else to sell. So when Dynasty failed to deliver, they switched suppliers. Sensing Dynasty's troubles, they even started withholding payments from the firm, further starving it of cash.

Sam's and WalMart had dealt Dynasty a $25-million-dollar blow, a blow from which it could not recover. The giant retailer had strangled the golden goose. They hadn't meant to. It had been an accident. They had only meant to squeeze her for every last egg. Dynasty had been a good thing for Sam's. But their corporate creed had demanded that every advantage be taken, every opportunity be exploited, every ounce of clout be exercised. Never consider the consequences. And never, *ever* acknowledge the word "enough." Sears may have become famous for using their size to abuse their suppliers, but WalMart, it seemed to Craig, had perfected the art.

In the end, it didn't really matter if Dynasty's imminent fall was the result of Sam's and WalMart negotiating hard or being abusive, or whether it was caused by incompetence or outright greed. It was now clear that the huge and innovative lighting and seasonal goods manufacturer was descending inexorably toward bankruptcy. Five hundred jobs on this continent, and thousands more overseas, were in jeopardy. One hundred million dollars in business would go to other suppliers—or simply evaporate. It had taken a thousand transactions to build it, but only one to bring it down.

Dynasty Classics was five years old. It was too young to die.

෨෴෴

THE OUTCOME WAS virtually certain, but Craig refused to accept defeat. He worked directly with every Dynasty supplier, trying to create an acceptable payment strategy. He pursued merger options with other lighting manufacturers. Talk led to more talk. Then Catalina Lighting said they were interested. They sent in the troops, called customers, visited the manufacturing plants, and dissected the inventory. They agreed to buy the company and wrote a purchase agreement. The price was $2.00 a share, about $40 million. Craig breathed a sigh of relief.

Then it happened. Weeks after the deal was publicly announced, on the very evening it was to be consummated, a Catalina executive walked into Craig's office and said, "We have a problem."

At the last possible moment, they rejected the inventory numbers and cut their offer from two dollars a share to twenty cents. The words sliced through Winn's soul like a frozen dagger. He knew that the inventory had already been discounted to a fraction of its actual value. Why the eleventh-hour reversal?

The answer, it transpired, lay at the feet of Erwin Daffney, one of Dynasty's Sales Managers. He had turned Benedict Arnold. In the wake of his treachery, 500 people lost their jobs. But who cares? Daffney got himself a shiny new one: SVP of Sales for Catalina Lighting.

Winn tried to sell the Holiday Classics division for the benefit of the company's shareholders, finding a willing buyer in a wealthy housewares entrepreneur. It was the perfect addition to his holiday lines and a worthy complement to his imported brands.

In order to protect the company's employees, Craig praised the President of his overseas operations, Mark Wong, when presenting the division. But when Winn told Wong his plans, which included leaving Mark in the driver's seat, Wong smelled an opportunity. He flew from Hong Kong to Boston to cut his own deal, hanging Dynasty's shareholders and employees out to dry.

Not everyone involved in Dynasty's restructuring proved to be a scoundrel. Craig, working with Scott Chrisman, approached Najat and Quiel Nalic of Lights of America. These creative Pakistani-born brothers were leaders in energy-efficient lighting. They wanted to buy Dynasty, hoping to merge its marketing savvy with their awesome technology. Noble and exciting goals, everyone agreed, but no deal ever materialized.

During Dynasty's final horrific months, Craig concluded that his managerial skills were inadequate. His self-confidence was in ruins. Winn beat himself up over being blindsided by WalMart, and he vowed that if he ever built another company, he would replace himself as CEO just as soon as the firm grew large enough to attract a professional. It was a resolution he would live to regret.

Working to find potential investors, Craig found a turnaround guy and stepped aside to give him the CEO title. This fellow blamed the company's troubles on "lack of focus." He boasted that under his control, Dynasty would be a new, more professional company that would grow profitably. "It is time," he said, "to pass the baton from the entrepreneurs to the professionals." Winn prayed he was right.

The turnaround guy ran Dynasty with all the finesse of Blackbeard the Pirate, giving Winn an unwanted opportunity to see the underbelly of corporate behavior. One of his first official acts as the new, "more professional" manager was to alter his employment forms, increasing his salary by $100,000.

Meanwhile, Craig was taking the opposite approach. He made payroll out of his own pocket—for hundreds of employees. It was a valiant, heroic, yet futile effort to keep the company he had built and loved from going under. In the process, Craig became Dynasty's largest creditor. The new CEO filed Chapter 11 only two weeks later.

Craig was brokenhearted as he saw Dynasty being devoured by its new management team and the lawyers representing them. Before all was lost, he sold Dynasty to Seattle Lighting via their venture partner, Hancock Park. The new owners replaced the first turnaround guy with one of their own. He turned out to be little better than his predecessor. Dynasty slowly dissolved as they fought over the furniture.

As all this was going on, Craig and fellow board member Rex Scatena were preparing a lawsuit against WalMart on behalf of Dynasty's shareholders. They recruited Skadden, Arps, the nation's leading litigation firm, to assist them. So compelling and so well documented was the case against the giant retailer that the law firm agreed to take the matter principally on a contingency basis. They would profit only if they won.

Unfortunately, on the very day they were to have filed the suit in Federal Court, Hancock Park's principle reneged on his commitment to assign the rights to Dynasty's shareholders. He reasoned that the new task lighting department Craig had designed and sold to WalMart would be discontinued if the shareholders sought recompense. As a result, the case, all three billion dollars of it, died on the courthouse steps. WalMart discontinued the task lighting section anyway. Everyone lost.

At least there were no class-action lawsuits in the wake of all that had happened to Dynasty. Craig blamed himself for making enough mistakes to last a lifetime, for being unable to extricate the firm from the death spiral his sale to Sam's had set in motion.

Through it all, he witnessed a disturbing pattern. He had seen insecure parasites descend upon his firm, wait for an opening, and attack at the first sign of weakness. He would, unfortunately, experience this pattern again, but next time the corporate maggots would do their work in the glaring light of the national media.

So Winn found himself, in a way, right back where he had been after he graduated from USC—unemployed, alone, asking God, "Why?" But life is for learning. Dynasty had been Craig's school of hard knocks. It had taught him many valuable things. But the tuition had been a killer.

ৎৡৼৡৢ

ALTHOUGH SOME TIME had passed since they'd last played together, nothing much had changed. Rex's drive sailed straight down the fairway. Craig's had once again found the sand trap.

"God's teaching me patience," he muttered to no one in particular.

"He sure isn't teaching you golf," Rex replied breezily.

"I'll tell you something. Building Dynasty taught me stuff you can't learn anyplace else."

"Scars build character. It's all about what a guy does when he's in life's sand trap. That's what counts. That's when you learn what he's made of. I'd follow *you* into hell."

"Thanks, but there are enough lawyers there already."

Laughing, Rex ignored the affront to his noble profession. "I know the Dynasty story as well as anyone. You built a hundred-million-dollar business from nothing. You got the rug pulled out from under you, but you stood tall. You know what? I'd leave my law practice in a heartbeat to work with you. If you were to tell me that bat farming was going to be the next new thing in pest control, I'd be right there."

"Thanks," he said as he hovered above the ball and wiggled his feet to test the sand and improve his stance. "I hope we can work together."

"So what did you learn?" Rex asked. He was always interested in Craig's state of mind. He had come to consider Winn one of his favorite spectator sports. You never knew what the guy would think of next.

"I learned the ins and outs of how a brand functions." Craig grunted as he completed his swing, blasting his ball out of the sand trap. It landed softly on the green, above the hole, thirty feet from the cup. "I've learned how distribution works, how orders are processed, how inventory is managed."

Rex hit his 9-iron ten feet from the pin. "Okay."

"Did you know, counselor, that WalMart orders by store each week, based upon what people bought the previous week?"

"Huh?" Little did Rex suspect that what he was hearing would change his life. The two walked on, laying their bags down next to the green.

"The average retail order," Craig explained, "is *tiny*. But the brand has to receive it, enter it, pick the goods from their racks, and ship it. Each small order requires a separate freight bill. It's inefficient to the max."

"There's more, I presume," Rex led the witness.

"Abuse, Rex. I learned a lot about being abused."

"Wonderful."

"No, really, the system *encourages* retailers to abuse brands. It wasn't just Dynasty. Every brand suffers. Retailers have too much clout."

"That's what killed Dynasty," Rex added, eyeing his putt.

"Retail's dumb. It's broken. The more you know about it, the more you realize how foolish retailers are. They depend on brands, yet they abuse them. Remember the question I asked the Price Club before I started Dynasty?"

"Yeah. You asked 'em to name the dumbest industry."

"Well, they gave me the wrong answer. *Retail* is the dumbest industry!"

"So what can be done?"

"Not a damn thing. If brands sell to consumers directly, retailers will drop them. Besides, brands don't want to be in the retail business. But I'll tell you what they *do* want."

"What's that?" Rex asked as he sank his ten-footer for birdie and hoisted his putter into the air like it was a sword.

"Nice putt, even though you hit out of turn."

"You were on a roll, pal. I didn't want to interrupt," Rex shot back, encouraging his friend to sink his thirty-footer.

Undaunted, Craig continued to talk as he lined up his downhill putt. "Brands want to sell on the basis of value, not price. They want to present their products directly to the ultimate buyer."

"They can't do that."

"Not now, but someday. Imagine an electronic conveyer belt between factories and consumers."

"Okay," Rex prodded, "who's going to build it?"

"A new kind of retailer."

"A retailer!" Rex couldn't believe his ears.

"What if a store were run more like a rep agency—like The Winn Company, bringing people and products together?"

"Sounds great, but it's impossible," Rex countered in typical lawyer fashion. "The consumer can't place orders directly with brands, and brands can't afford to demonstrate their products to every customer. You can't serve the masses, one on one, one at a time."

"Actually, that's a myth. With computers, it ought to be just as easy to sell and ship to a *person* as it is to sell and ship to a *store*."

Rex thought about this for a moment. "How's this hypothetical retailer supposed to present products to the masses?" He watched as Craig stroked his putt.

"I think I've found an answer for that—an answer for a lot of things," Craig said as his putt hit the back of the cup and disappeared.

"What's that?"

"It was a bird, just like yours."

"I know it was a birdie. Great putt. I meant, what's the answer?"

"Ever heard of the Internet?"

"Yeah. Never seen it, though. What's it like?"

"It's like the early days of television. There isn't much there, and what's there is awful. But I'm telling you, it's got potential."

"You're actually thinking about doing this, aren't you?" Rex said as the two ambled up to the fourth tee.

Craig tried, but he couldn't suppress a grin. "Maybe."

"Well, it's not like you don't have any motivation." Rex was grinning now himself. Insanity was apparently catching. "The Internet, huh? Sounds like a long shot to me."

"Long shot? *This* is a long shot." The fourth hole was a downhill 220-yard par three. Craig grabbed his two-iron. He took a long slow swing. The ball jumped off the slightly open clubface. It hit a hill to the right of the green, bounced twice, and then rolled onto the short grass, following the break toward the pin. Closer. Closer. Craig held his breath.

Do not be surprised at the painful trial you are suffering, as though something strange were happening to you—Peter

LIGHTING THE WAY

"Welcome, my friend!" Najat Nalic greeted his new business partner expansively. His lilting near-eastern accent somehow made his words sound poetic. "These last few months must have been terrible for you."

"That and then some," Craig replied as he made his way across Najat's office, careful not to step on any of the engineering clutter scattered on the floor. "But you know, Najat, I wasn't alone. Dynasty's problems will come back to haunt America if something's not done."

"What do you mean?"

"Retail abuse, particularly the uneven playing field created by international letters of credit."

"I know all about retail abuse, my friend. We suffer through our share, but how are LCs hurting us?"

"International LCs are insurance policies against abuse. With American suppliers like you guys, retail chains can withhold and delay payment, make unauthorized deductions, and change the rules as they go along. They can't do that with foreign suppliers. International LCs prohibit it."

"So the foreign supplier," Najat realized, "is always paid on time, they're always paid the full amount they're owed and guaranteed their profit—while we get abused!"

"Did you ever look at packages in big retail stores like WalMart, Najat? Walk down the toy aisle sometime. Far more say, 'Made in Taiwan,' 'Japan,' and especially 'China,' than say 'Made in the USA.' Most people think it's because labor is cheaper, but the labor component of most products is less than twenty percent of the wholesale cost, right?"

Najat nodded. "The cost of overseas freight, the time value of money, and import duties offset the labor differential."

"Exactly. Without abuse, they've got the capital to invest. American suppliers don't." Craig was always pleased when a listener grasped an important concept. "The uneven playing field created by international LCs, *not* labor, is what's killing American manufacturing, especially in consumer products."

"It never occurred to me, but I suppose you're right."

The Nalic brothers had already made their mark. They were the embodiment of the American dream. These five brothers had settled in Southern California, worked hard, used their heads, and proceeded to build a manufacturing company they called Lights of America.

"Lights" and Dynasty, though both in the lighting business, had not been competitors. They'd made radically different products, and their market appeal came from opposite ends of the spectrum.

Dynasty, under Winn's direction, had made beautiful things. Quality and style were their holy grail. Lights of America, on the other hand, used advanced technology to build a better mousetrap. The Nalic brothers used their knowledge of electronics to squeeze more light out of less juice. But their products looked like they were designed by engineers. They weren't the wrong style, exactly. They just had no style.

Winn and the brothers Nalic came from two different planets. But sometimes, opposites attract. Winn was the possessor of a vast body of knowledge on lighting style, attested by his design patents. He had a track record no one could touch. No lighting company had ever grown so quickly or garnered so much attention. He had numerous manufacturing relationships on both sides of the Pacific.

The Nalics, for their part, had some of the best lighting technology in the world, with patents of their own, and a well-equipped factory. The plan was to have Craig design and build a line of stylish lamps and lighting fixtures using the Nalics' energy-efficient bulbs. Style *and* substance. A whole new brand was invented for the home décor line: *Lighting America.* Winn was to share ownership with the Nalics.

Unfortunately, it became evident that the new line would out-class the old one. Recognizing the problem, Craig volunteered to redesign and remarket Lights' current line. He would restyle what he could, create new items where he saw gaps, and delete others. This put the elegant decorative lamps and lighting fixtures he had designed on the back burner, their birth delayed by up to a year. But clearly his new line could not be allowed to upstage the stars that had brought Najat and his brother, Quiel, to the dance. So he agreed, but with a stipulation or two. Or three....

He asked that once the new concept was approved, he would have *carte blanche* over implementing the plan. "You will get to approve your new logo and the first package," he said. "Everything else will fall into place from there." He also wanted authority to select the design resources, conduct the budget negotiations, and make commitments on the firm's behalf.

Craig presented a long list of items he would produce, ranging from a two-story trade-show booth, to 5,000 copies of each of five catalogs, to 125 new product packages, designs for twenty new products, and a comprehensive sales plan, plus a new logo and corporate identity. "The cost," he said, "will be one million dollars, and the entire project will be finished in time for the August Hardware Show, just four months from now."

The Nalics' soaked it in like men taking a hot shower after spending a month in the desert. The monkey was going to be off their backs.

"The project," Craig told them, "must be coordinated and comprehensive. If you recarpeted your office, you'd immediately recognize the walls need repainting. Then the chairs, which look fine now, will look worn and dated. Replace the chairs and the desk will look out of place, out of character with the rest of the room. Repaint the walls, replace the carpeting, and buy new chairs, and suddenly the curtains will look bad. Gentlemen, as soon as we make one thing right, we're going to need to make everything right, or we'll do more harm than good."

Consistency was always important to Craig. It was central to developing and maintaining trust, whether in image or behavior.

"At the end of the project, if you are pleased with the results, if it remains on time and on budget, and if you guys elect *not* to go forward with our decorative lighting plans, I want a bonus of $350,000, equivalent to what I spent making payroll trying to keep Dynasty afloat. I don't want a job, gentlemen. I want a partnership."

Craig fell silent, waiting for their response.

It didn't take long. "The price you've quoted seems impossibly low," Quiel volunteered. "Our quote to build the trade-show booth alone is several hundred thousand. And the timeline seems incredibly short. If it were anybody else saying we could have this much, this fast, and this cheap, we'd say they were crazy."

Najat joined in. "We know you don't need this job, and you're only doing it to facilitate our partnership in decorative lighting. We understand—and accept!"

ويوۍ

CRAIG BEGAN THE PROCESS in his usual way. He commandeered the large upstairs conference room at Lights and proceeded to display, for his own edification, every scrap of graphic material he could find: packaging, brochures, and ads. He put it all on the big conference room table, a jumbled, inconsistent, discordant collection. It was not a pretty sight.

Frustrated, Craig went downstairs, asking himself why he'd volunteered for this mission. It looked impossible. Walking into Quiel's office, he asked, "What agency did you use to create your, shall we say, *colorful* array of images?"

Quiel grinned, unsuccessfully trying to hide his amusement. He was clearly enjoying this more than Craig. "It's an agency in Huntington Beach called Power Graphics," Quiel offered. "Ken Power runs it. He's a nice guy, but sometimes he just doesn't get what we're trying to do."

"I'd like to call him. I don't know if we'll be able to use them, but we should talk. It's only fair."

I GOT INTO the studio about nine thirty that Friday morning in April 1994, later than usual. I had gone to Costa Mesa to see a client about their noodle packaging.

I loved this business, the personal contact, the problem-solving aspects. Sure, some graphic designers were running larger outfits, and presumably making more money, but they'd paid a price. They didn't get to do the fun stuff any more, the actual design work. They had become salesmen. *Suits.* I felt sorry for them.

My assistant, Gloria, had taken the call just before I'd arrived. They wanted me up at Lights. They were by far my largest client, accounting for over a third of my billings. Whenever they called, I dropped whatever I was doing. It was a love-hate relationship: the money was good, but the quality of work I was allowed to do was marginal. Graphically, they were their own worst enemy.

"You're supposed be there at ten o'clock sharp to see some guy named Craig Winn," Gloria said. "Is he new?"

"Never heard of him. He *must* be new. He doesn't know it takes forty-five minutes to get there." I grabbed my briefcase and headed for the door.

Forty minutes later, I exchanged smiles with Lights' receptionist. "Hi, Ken. Mr. Winn is waiting for you in the upstairs conference room."

"Who is he?"

"You'll see," she said, grinning from ear to ear.

The psychological trauma of working with Lights of America was about to be taken to the next level. Opening the door, I saw my whole life flash before my eyes. There, on the massive rosewood table, lay everything I'd done for them, plus some things from before my time. Standing at the far end of the table was a fellow in an expensive suit, a decade younger than me, surveying it all.

"Craig Winn, I presume."

"Yes. You must be Ken Power."

He didn't waste any time. "I've been retained by Lights of America to completely revamp their product line and corporate image."

While I was still processing the implications of that remark, he continued. "I understand you're responsible for this rather interesting assortment of packaging and graphic styles. Now as I see it...." Winn embarked on a recitation of the major ills of their marketing materials.

"Yep," I replied when he'd had his say. "You're absolutely right. I've done some of my very worst work for Lights of America."

"You have?" Craig burst out laughing. "I mean, you *know* you have?"

My answer seemed to have taken him aback, something I've since learned doesn't happen very often.

"You've just cataloged the lion's share of my pet peeves. At the risk of sounding like I'm not willing to be held accountable for my work, I want you to know this is not my fault. I'm just the mechanic. I do what I'm told. They put up with me because my stuff is technically flawless. The film runs without a hitch, the boxes fit the cutting dies, that sort of thing."

"This isn't the way you'd do it, if given your head?"

I started picking up packages and picking them apart. "See this green series? They got on an ecology kick. So I came up with a deep forest green, very sexy, something deep enough to reverse copy out of successfully. But they overruled me, and changed the color to this bilious bright green. Sure, you can see the card from a hundred feet away, but you can't read the copy at two feet!"

"So I see."

"Please understand, I don't design crap like this if I have a choice."

"What kind of crap *do* you design?" he asked with a grin.

I opened up my briefcase and extracted a brochure I had done, a piece I always carried with me in case of emergencies, like the one this was turning out to be. "This," I said, "should give you an idea of what I can do. It's a brochure for one of the top prepress houses in L.A. I did the whole thing. Designed it, wrote the copy, art-directed the photos, updated their logo. Because this was to be a showpiece for a major film house, it had to be spectacular, the trickier the better, so it has lots of nice touches. Anyway, *this* is the kind of work I do."

Craig examined the piece, read the copy, ran his fingers over the subtle visual textures, and tipped it toward the light to see the high-gloss spot UV areas come to life. When he finally looked up, he glanced at the mess on the table and back at the brochure. "This is the most beautiful thing I've ever seen."

"It's nice, isn't it?" I said without a trace of modesty.

Refocused, Craig got to the point. "This project is too large, and the time too short, for one firm to tackle alone. I'm interviewing four others, and I'll use two. I'd like you to bid on the first phase. Are you interested?"

"It's what I do. When do we start?"

"I'll be at your office at eight o'clock Monday morning. Please do a little homework over the weekend so we're ready to roll first thing. I'm asking each of the finalists to provide three new logo variations and incorporate the new style into a sample package. I'll need you to supply a fixed bid on each. The new logo has to scream *America*. It should be red, blue, and gold, on a white background. Change the product name from

Compact Fluorescents to Electronic Lights."

I scribbled notes quickly as he barked out commands.

"Based upon what you've done for these folks, you're starting out behind the eight ball. But I like working with good people, hands-on folks who know how to get things done. You strike me as that kind of guy."

That I was, but I already knew that. The question was, who was he, and why had he mired himself in this predicament?

ᔕᐧᔓ

BILL HUNT LOVED challenges. Judy Hunt thought her husband loved them a little too much. His penchant for moving across the country to tilt at windmills was wearing thin. He had left one company for another, only to become the president of a third. When his last stint hadn't worked out, Craig had offered him a marketing job at Dynasty, SVP of something or other. At least they were getting to see the country.

Dynasty was already on a collision course with WalMart when Bill arrived in '92. In another year, it was all over but the shouting. Judy was not amused. She didn't know whether to laugh or cry when Craig called Bill again just months after Dynasty's fall. The new job: assisting him in pulling off a colossal redesign and marketing project for Lights of America. Bill needed the work and liked working with Craig. What's more, they wouldn't have to move again.

Bill was to be "stationed" at Lights. His primary contact was the head of marketing, Quiel Nalic, but in effect that meant he would be dealing most closely with Quiel's marketing assistant. Christi Reynolds was in her late twenties, a tall, enthusiastically self-confident woman.

She had known nothing about marketing when she had taken the job but was bright and willing to learn. Every chance Christi got, she talked to Bill and Craig about their experiences, becoming familiar with their history all the way back to the Price Club years. She listened with rapt attention as Craig outlined how retailing goes through revolutions, how the focus shifts, how new channels open in response to the changing needs of the market. Craig's experiences with Dynasty were fascinating to her, especially what it took to make it live—and why it died. She was interested in how it had shaped his perception of what the future would bring.

Craig told her that the next retail revolution would take place in people's homes. The store would come to us, and so would the products. She took it all in. As the project progressed, so did her marketing knowledge and ability. By the time the redesign was done, Christi had become in reality what her job designation had claimed.

CRAIG WAS WAITING in the parking lot when I got to my studio that first Monday morning. He was sitting behind the wheel of a gold Mercedes sports car, the only car in the lot at that early hour.

Power Graphics was a tempest in a teacup. Located in a corner suite of a small office building about half a mile from my home, it was 600 square feet of custom-made desks, light tables, and computers. Every square inch was used for something. It was like working in a sailboat. We had a little conference area, a table and four chairs. A darkroom housed my stat camera, once a gold mine but now seldom used.

I missed the old days, when you'd had to have some degree of skill just to get an image into print. Now, anyone with a Macintosh could do it. The computer was king now. Art boards, the medium that had borne information from idea to printed reality for the last eighty years, had been eclipsed by computer files. I had made the jump from art boards to computer media as soon as the better prepress houses were able to produce printing film more efficiently from data than from artwork. I'd watched as designers who were slow to adapt to the new methods withered and died.

I was principally a packaging designer. But restricting my business would have been restricting my income. So I took on any assignment I could get, in any print medium: litho, flexo, roto, serigraphy, designing brochures, composing ads, and creating point-of-sale displays. I did my best to master many design disciplines, becoming an illustrator, a typographer, a wordsmith, a production coordinator, and a salesman of sorts. I developed a wide range of skills on the theory that anything I didn't have to farm out was money in my pocket.

For the first time in my twenty-year career, I was about to need every shred of knowledge and experience I had accumulated. I was about to work with Craig Winn. He announced that we were going to be joined at the hip during the design process, a scary description that proved all too true. Craig pulled up a drafting stool beside my workstation and we proceeded to operate.

"The first order of business," he announced, "is the logo."

I opened a file with the five logos I'd developed over the weekend.

"Great start. They look good, especially that one!" Craig said, pointing to one of the five logo styles on my screen.

"It shouts America, just like you asked."

"You're on the right track, Ken. Give me a few polished versions of this design, and I'll pick one. We'll go from there."

That we did. The brothers Nalic loved it too, so we were off and running. We moved from logo to corporate stationery, packaging, brochures, displays, and ads.

We had hundreds of photographs in our files, but most didn't meet Craig's expectations, so he added hundreds more, photographed in his own elegant Palos Verdes home. Katharine didn't care for the mess, especially since the shooting took the better part of two weeks. But she was a good sport about it, although she did extract a promise from her husband that he would never do that to her house again. It would prove to be one of the few promises he broke.

A promise was kept, a contract was fulfilled, period. But Craig's more pessimistic predictions weren't quite so reliable. He had intended to use Power Graphics for half the project, and had told me as much. Early in the game, he turned over a small part to another agency, one he had used in the past. The job was simple, but they managed to screw it up. I bailed them out with some timely technical assistance, but he had been burned, and he wasn't about to be burned again. Power Graphics ended up doing the entire humongous job.

Being joined at the hip, as he put it, for four or five months, ten to twelve hours a day, we got to know each other very well. It turned out we were both Christians, so we shared a great deal in common. We spent many pleasant lunch hours (though never as long as that) discussing the finer points of theology in a local park under the warm Huntington Beach sun.

Craig fell in love with my odd family. You couldn't blame him. My wife, Gayle, was Mother of the Century as far as I was concerned. Of our eleven children, nine were adopted. Seven of them were from other countries, and most of them had serious problems ranging from early childhood abuse or neglect to profound mental retardation. Three of them were in wheelchairs. Two of them would die before another year had passed.

My new friend also saw something he liked in me. I liked getting my hands dirty, actually doing the job. He had seen many of his valued design sources reach, as the Peter Principle put it, their level of incompetence; gifted designers had become mere "front men," hiring lesser talents to do the labor.

It was late summer when we finished the project. When it was all over, I marveled that we had finished it all in so short a time—and for so little money. Craig was easily the best manager—and the best negotiator—I'd ever met.

He realized by then that there wasn't going to be a business partnership with the Nalic brothers. He loved and respected them but recognized they could never bring themselves to partner with anyone not named Nalic. It was a pity. Craig showed me the color renderings of products he had designed for them. Unlike anything I'd ever seen, they were stunning, radically innovative, yet quietly elegant.

Craig's two boys, Ryan and Blake, were growing up too fast, and he was missing it. So he decided to take some time off, coach Little League, do a little writing, some volunteer work, and maybe take his family on a long vacation—go back east, see historic America. Breathe.

Bill Hunt was asked to stay on at Lights, so we got to see a lot of him. A project of that magnitude is never really done.

Christi Reynolds left Lights shortly after the redesign project was completed. She went to work for Thermador, a manufacturer of ultra-high-end kitchen appliances.

At Power Graphics, life returned to normal. With the Lights project at an end, I never expected to see Craig Winn again. Pity. He was interesting, driven, and creative, even if working with him was a little like working in a hurricane with the windows open. After the pressure of the last half a year, a normal workload seemed like we were coasting.

But things were not back to normal, not really. This was only the calm before the storm.

PLANNING TO WIN

Strolling down the hall of his rambling oceanfront home, Craig covered the fifty-odd paces from his oak-paneled office to the kitchen. Mr. Coffee was down to the dregs, so he made a fresh pot. He leaned against the sink as the fragrant brown liquid filled the carafe, but his mind was elsewhere. His book was all but done. He was down to polishing prose. He had written a guidebook for entrepreneurs called *Winning: The Owner's Manual.*

The door from the back yard opened. Katharine had been working in her rose garden, doing battle with stray weeds and aphids. She sighed as she took in the scene: coffee can open, spoons, cups, the *LA Times* spread out in disarray, and her husband leaning against the sink with a dazed expression.

"Hi."

Craig was startled out of his reverie. "Oh! Hi, Katie!"

Katharine knew better than Craig himself how distant he could become when he didn't have a goal he was working toward. He had to be engaged, making progress. Craig didn't know the meaning of "pacing himself." She could see that this book was almost complete, and that meant trouble.

"You know, Craig, our marriage vows said for better or for worse, not for lunch. Don't you think it's time to start another company?"

Craig gave her a sheepish grin. "Yeah. You're right. But retirement's not so bad. I get to spend time with you and with the boys. You know I can't do something halfway. If I start another business, I'll play to win. It'll mean hiring people—becoming vulnerable again."

"You *are* a scum magnet. You've managed to attract some real losers over the years."

"That's not fair. After all, I attracted you, didn't I? Besides, for every insecure, self-serving low-life that managed to weasel their way in, my 'magnet,' as you call it, has attracted a whole lot more good people."

"Yes, but it only takes one bad apple to spoil the pie, remember?"

"Are you trying to talk me into this or out of it?"

"In, but I want some conditions this time," she warned. "Don't hire scum. Don't take it public. And don't build it here. Let's move to a small town, someplace where life is simpler."

Big-league hitters earn millions batting one for three. Craig would too.

FUNNY THING ABOUT phone calls. Even the ones that change your life start off sounding rather ordinary. "Hello?"

"Craig? I don't know if you'll remember me. This is Christi Reynolds. I used to work at Lights of America."

Craig smiled broadly. "Christi! Of course I remember. How are you?"

"I'm fine. Not working at Lights anymore. I went to work for Thermador. You know them?"

"Sure. A Masco company. Great outfit."

"Actually, I'm not *there* anymore, either. Moved on to something more interesting. Remember those conversations we had about the future of retail?"

"About how people were going to shop using their computers?"

"Yeah. Well, my job at Thermador was to implement a Masco directive—to create an Internet site."

"The Web's hot. Marc Andreesen of Netscape is on the front cover of everything." Craig was fascinated by the new medium. "Goldman Sachs took 'em public. Made our boy an instant bazillionaire."

"That's why I called. Masco's President, Ray Kennedy, got excited about the Web. He's convinced it'll be the next TV—thinks we'll all be using it."

"I don't know Kennedy, but people I respect think he's a visionary."

"It sure sounds like what you've been talking about." Christi went on, "Kennedy gave the Masco companies $25,000 to develop websites—that's $25,000 *each*, and there must be a hundred companies. Most Masco brands are still dragging their feet, but Thermador, thanks to their brilliant marketing director—that would be me—charged ahead."

"I thought you said you didn't work for them anymore?"

"I don't," she said. "You know me. Never could pass up an opportunity. I went to work for Internet Connect, the company Masco hired to put their companies online. We're content providers. Doing some radical stuff, developing websites out of databases, not just static HTML. You've gotta meet our CEO, Sid Golden. We can do everything you've been dreaming about."

✨

COMPELLED TO WORK even when he wasn't working, Craig returned to his keyboard. His manuscript for *Winning: The Owner's Manual* had a nice blend of philosophy, pragmatic advice, and personal experience. As he mulled over the conversation he had just had with Christi Reynolds, he went to work polishing prose.

PREPARATION—MANUFACTURING LUCK.

Too often we malign successful people by calling them lucky. We diminish their achievements by saying they were simply in the right place at the right time. It is as if circumstances swept them into prosperity. Some say they would rather be lucky than good, but in truth, luck is often the result of being good.

Luck occurs when inspiration, preparation, and determination coalesce. Winning entrepreneurs not only expect good fortune, they actually plan for it. Their lives and their companies' achievements become self-fulfilling prophecies. They not only earn their luck, they learn to be lucky.

He couldn't help but wonder if he were now in the right place at the right time. Was he about to be *lucky?* With that thought, he turned to the section of his manuscript that discussed hiring a management team. If he were to capitalize upon this opportunity, that would be his next move.

The selection of a management team profoundly impacts a business. Choose well, and your abilities are leveraged. Choose poorly, and the act of managing is akin to rowing up a waterfall. Successful companies are built by motivated individuals striving to accomplish a common goal. Builders routinely make sacrifices choosing the collective good over their individual self-interests.

The cost of hiring a dishonest or insecure person is astounding. Not only will they enrich themselves at the expense of others, their mere presence will destroy the firm like a cancer, eating it alive from within. When choosing between experience and character, select heart over head.

Craig had an inkling of the passage's truth from his experiences with The Winn Company and Dynasty. Yet he could not possibly have known how heavily his own words would weigh upon his soul not five years hence, or how eerily prophetic they were.

He agonized over the risks and rewards of being an entrepreneur. It's a lonely job. He had studied entrepreneurs for his book, of course, and had played the role twice before. His thoughts turned inward as he reflected upon what he had written:

THE ENTREPRENEURIAL 20-20 CLUB.

The fortunate few who endure as entrepreneurs have much in common. I have observed traits common to those who prevail. Entrepreneurs with the fortitude to survive the rigors of business and build mid-sized firms—those with annual sales over twenty million dollars—share twenty character traits. Unfortunately, the 20/20 Club is not an equal opportunity employer. Only the most inspired should apply. To this end, let's evaluate the current members:

1. Successful entrepreneurs strive to create value beyond all else. Making money is simply a by-product of a job well done....

2. Dynamic entrepreneurs appreciate the complex nature of our world, its history and culture. This bestows upon them a remarkable sense of perspective.... They recognize that the best predictor of future behavior is past behavior....

3. Most enduring business leaders are grounded in their faith. They embody the ethical values that once built our nation. They possess a clear understanding of right and wrong. They fight fairly and will not compromise to achieve a goal if this means divorcing their values. Corporately, they know, character counts....

4. Builders have what some call arrogance and others call confidence—a conviction so strong that their rivals often view them as conceited. A passion for their company, people, and products exudes from them. They thrive on challenges, believing every problem provides a new opportunity to prove their mettle....

5. Successful entrepreneurs conceive and implement a corporate philosophy. Their plan serves as a pragmatic guide from which harmonious execution occurs throughout the organization....

6. Leaders motivate and inspire every associate.... The corporate mantra creates an evangelical zeal. The company's mission becomes a crusade....

While reading through the list, Craig happened to glance down at a pad on his desk. He had written the words "Sid Golden" and "Internet Connect" during his earlier conversation. Suddenly, inexplicably, he knew destiny was calling.

✺

TIMES WERE HARD for ad agencies, especially this one. dGWB had laid off ten people in the last few months. For Sid Golden, that was good news. It meant cheap rent in a beautiful building in the most prestigious area of Newport Beach.

Sid and Christi were all there was of Internet Connect in California at the moment. The others were still in Michigan—making plans to move. California was the place to be, the land of new ideas, the land of techno-wizards, the land of doing business at a pace so fast it didn't matter if you were real or not. It was the land of Yahoos!

Internet Connect consisted of five developers, three graphic designers, and nine sales people. The fact that there were more people selling the service than providing it wasn't the only thing upside down. In reality, they were little more than a pyramid scheme, with Client B's fees paying for Client A's project while Client C was being courted.

It wasn't that Golden was evil. He was just over-optimistic—completely, almost criminally, over-optimistic. He couldn't help it. He could *see* it all being done. If he could just sell the next job or do the next deal, he could keep his company going long enough to...well, to sell the next job or do the next deal.

Internet Connect was almost as old as the Web itself. It was BN: Before Netscape. Designing for this new medium was something hardly anybody knew how to do. This was still the world of 9600 baud. 14.4K modems were just hitting the stores. 28.8K was a distant fantasy. 56K, the physical limit of a standard phone line, was a pipedream. Cable modems and satellite linkups? Not on this planet. They lived in the neolithic age of the World Wide Wait. Web pages were restricted to text, and precious little of that.

Business functions on the Web were in their infancy. Nobody had much experience with credit card transactions, much less inventory management, financial reporting, database integration, customer service, and logistics. The deepest Internet Connect had gone was to build dealer locators and email feedback forms.

Winn arrived at the advertising agency before eight. The offices were open but deserted. He used the time to check the place out. It was "Gen X" all the way, including a surfboard rack, just in case you wanted to catch a few waves on your way in to work. A ping-pong table took up much of the open area between offices. There was a basketball hoop and a cappuccino bar.

Examples of dGWB's work littered the halls. Each ad was the same: an offbeat headline, a picture of the product from an unusual angle, lots of open space, and precious little information. The brand's logo was buried at the bottom, insignificant. Craig dubbed the style "the urping snowboarder."

Standing alone in front of one of the agency's ads, a big smile came across his face. This was the competition, and they were awful. Not this agency so much; their work looked like everybody else's. His revolution was built around helping brands communicate the value of their products to the consuming public, and the competition was doing a terrible job. *His* new company would do this better than any ad agency. Using new tools, he could slash the cost of reaching consumers. He would charge brands less and accomplish more. Craig was excited; he couldn't wait to get started.

He had a secret. His vision—his retail revolution—wasn't really about retail at all. Deep down, the online store he imagined was simply a tool, a *conduit* brands could use to form informative and commerce-enabled connections with consumers. In his mind, it wasn't about retail; it was about *eliminating* retail—a concept that was way beyond most every audience he would ever encounter.

ഏൠ

CRAIG FOUND SID to be a bright, personable fellow in his late forties, a bit portly, with thinning hair and a quick smile. Words left his mouth like bullets from the barrel of an Uzi—in short, staccato bursts. Sid knew what he was talking about; at least he had the jargon down pat.

Winn began describing what he wanted to achieve. "I want a tool that helps brands and consumers. Each product, from cameras to computers, from barbeques to baseballs, must be presented using multimedia: photos, illustrations, animations, *obviously* text, but also audio and video. Let's make consumers better buyers.

"Everyone should be able to shop in the way that's most comfortable for them, so the store has to be dynamically generated out of a database. It must be able to rearrange itself so each customer can shop by product, category, brand, by what's on sale, what's new, or even by related products. If they buy a vacuum cleaner, I want to take them directly to the bags for the model they've bought. No hunting around—a variety of menus, all feeding from the same database."

He went on as Sid listened. "The store must greet each customer by name, thank them for their last purchase, and ask them to rate the products they've purchased, so we can provide the first ever *real* consumer reports. I want the store to retain credit card and shipping data for customers, so they can check out with a single click. I want it to be graphically attractive and uncluttered." Sid nodded and smiled.

"The back-end will be the hard part. We need to validate the customer's credit card, process the payment, send the order to each factory using EDI, calculate freight, communicate shipping data, and then audit the financial transactions between consumers, factories, carriers, and ourselves, all electronically."

Sid didn't see any insurmountable problems with any of this. He never did. Never mind that there were only a handful of stores on the Web at this time. Never mind that he had no clue what Craig was talking about. The scope of the project was unlimited, and the guy was rich. That's all Sid really wanted to know.

Golden explained that applets could make incredible things happen on the client side. Databases could be used to dynamically generate online presentations. He seemed particularly knowledgeable in the area of multimedia. Sid's mind, like Craig's, lived in the realm of what could and would be, not what actually was.

"Products are going to be shipped directly from the factory, so EDI has to be an integral part of the system."

"Okay," Sid said. "I gather you've had some retail experience."

Craig gave him the short version of his experiences over the last twenty years. As he did, Golden came to recognize that sitting before him was a man uniquely qualified to pull this off. Winn knew retail, he knew manufacturing, he knew marketing and sales—all from first-hand "insider" experience. This was no ordinary project, and this was no ordinary businessman.

"What you're proposing is going to change everything!" Sid enthused.

"The thought had occurred to me. I've been planning this for ten years."

Sid's mind was racing. He wanted to be a part of this, and not just as the hired help. "I want to be your partner. I've got the team; they're still in Michigan, but we're moving out here. With your experience and vision and my company's technology, we can turn the world upside down. We'll end up on the cover of *Time: The Men Who Revolutionized Retail!*"

Winn just smiled. That was the last thing he wanted. "The way I see it, we need three things to get started: a partnership agreement, a business plan, and a budget. You write the partnership agreement, outlining each party's responsibilities and benefits. I'll write a comprehensive business plan. We can use it as a roadmap to build a budget for the project."

"Fantastic. If I have a plan to follow, I'll be able to budget my part down to the last nickel."

They shook hands and thanked Christi for her introduction. They scheduled another meeting a week later, when the business plan would be completed. Sid had no idea how Craig expected to get it done by then, but Craig knew. He was already halfway home.

As he neared the Palos Verdes Peninsula, Craig stopped at a little magazine shop on Pacific Coast Highway. The Web was too new for books, too esoteric for mainstream, general-interest publications. He was looking for anything he could find on, or near, the subject of Web technologies: bandwidth, multimedia, applets, audio and video technology, software developments, and what would come to be known as convergence. Geeky stuff. He bought a dozen thinly distributed tech magazines and headed home to study.

Sid Golden got on the phone and called his wonder-boy in Michigan. "Joe, it's Sid."

"What's up? You sound like you're out of breath," Joe Page answered.

"Get your butt out here!"

JOE PAGE TURNED left off of PCH and stepped on the gas. The rear tires of the bright red '72 Mustang chattered, then grabbed the pavement, pushing him back into the seat as the car flew up the hill. Two gorgeous blond heads turned as their owners jogged down the sidewalk. Yes, this was definitely going to be the car for Joe's new lifestyle. No more snow. No more four-wheel-drive Jeep Grand Cherokee. He'd left that behind in Michigan with the rest of his life.

He reached the top of the hill and stopped for the light. A teenage couple strolling on the sidewalk caught his attention. The girl, maybe sixteen, wore the boy's letterman's jacket loosely over her shoulders. Joe smiled. He was instantly transported back to his high school days in Grosse Pointe, where he had earned a varsity letter or two for himself, and to his time at the University of Michigan, where he had been captain of the school's Lacrosse team. His best sport, though, was not Lacrosse, but computers. He thought he should have worn the Captain's "C" for leading the school's computer team.

There is a proverb widely held among baby boomers: if you want to get your computer to work, ask a kid. The personification of the "kid" was Joe Page, still in his mid-twenties.

Joe still smiled at the thought of high school computer meets with scores of homely computer geeks vying for team honors and prize money. He'd won several thousand dollars, a hundred bucks at a time, by acing them. He was a natural. Joe had an uncanny ability to home in on the essentials, cut through the clutter, and produce an elegant solution using a minimum amount of code in a minimum amount of time. It was a gift.

Page had graduated from the University of Michigan with a degree in computer engineering, combining electrical engineering with computer science. His education covered not only the programming side, computer languages, but also thermodynamics, logic, and circuit design. He had learned things like how to dope silicon to get electrons to behave properly, a skill he admittedly didn't use on a daily basis.

His introduction to the dichotomy between the computer world and the "real" world involved writing software for Chrysler Motors. Chrysler had spent a couple million dollars on a software package that would let them dovetail their inventory control and production scheduling requirements. It sounds simple enough until you realize there were about seven hundred variables to juggle in this sophisticated linear algebra program.

The problem was that the program had to be used by ordinary people—"curmudgeons" in Joe's parlance—at Chrysler's engine assembly plant. They were used to working things out with pencil and paper. Joe wrote the documentation to see how the curmudgeons were going to handle the new approach. "Use it for a while; call me if you need help."

They called the next day.

"Where's the problem?" he asked.

"Well, we need to know what to do next."

"Okay, show me where you're stuck."

"Right here," they said, a bit more frustrated.

They didn't know how to turn their computers on. Their PCs had been there for months and had never been used. "I think I see the problem," Joe said. "I'll be back."

About a week later, he returned with new documentation, starting with a picture of a computer and a big arrow pointing to the power switch. From that point on, Joe Page never lost sight of the fact that computers were for people, not the other way around.

Joe worked in the auto industry and at the University of Michigan Computer Center throughout his six-, almost seven-, year plan. He tried his hand at a few things after graduation, mostly to broaden his experience. His first job was to develop software systems to control laser drilling and electrical-discharge machines. He wrote screen-saver programs for a few months, a job he parlayed into a position with Microsoft—almost. Their Seattle facility was too much like a college campus for his taste. He'd been there and done that for what seemed like an eternity.

Then he saw it. *The ad.* "Programmers Wanted: $5 a Web Page." How could he resist? The rub was, he didn't know the first thing about the Web. It was all too new. Before he took the job with Internet Connect, Joe had never even seen a Web browser. He figured getting $5 a Web page was going to be a paid education, nothing more.

On his first day, Joe found Andy, his supervisor, frantically trying to get a project done for the boss, Sid Golden. He wasn't happy about having to train a new guy, but he hastily showed Joe the ropes. One rope trick in particular, though, caught Joe's eye. Selecting "View Source" on the browser revealed the HTML code that made up a Web page.

That was more than enough. Joe spent the next hour or so becoming an HTML developer. By lunch, he was ready and offered to help. The project involved a lot of repetitive work, so Joe asked, "Isn't there a way to automate this? I was just reading about a scripting language called PERL...."

"Don't mess with that stuff!" Andy interrupted. "We have to get this done by the end of the day."

Joe could see that it was victory enough that he had convinced his new boss to let him help. He went back to his desk and manually updated a dozen pages before the "Joe Factor" got the best of him. He downloaded

PERL, along with some documentation. In a couple of hours, he had written a program that automated the process.

The next morning, Sid asked for another change. Andy came over and apologetically handed Joe the whole six-hour task. He wasn't in his seat for five minutes before he returned to his boss's desk.

"Stuck on something, Joe?" Andy asked in a mentoring way.

"Nope. I'm done."

In time, by surfing the Web and reverse-engineering the sites he visited, Joe became indispensable. By the time he was called to California, Joe was, in all but title, the CTO of the company.

When Sid's biggest opportunity yet came along, he naturally turned to Page. Sid was trying to convince Masco to use his company to create websites for over a hundred brands. At the upcoming meeting, there were going to be plenty of corporate types: marketing, advertising, and of course, technical people.

Sid asked Joe to wear something as close to a suit as possible. He was reassured to hear that he owned one "big boy" outfit for just such an occasion. Joe didn't have any real sense as to what the impact of getting a contract like Masco meant for the firm; he had only been an employee a short time. But he knew that if the boss was not merely asking him to wear long pants and something that didn't say "Wolverines" on it but rather a full-blown suit, it must be important.

The next morning, they drove to Masco's offices in Taylor, Michigan. Golden made an impressive two-hour presentation and then pointed to Joe saying, "I've brought my chief technology officer with me today to answer your questions." Hearing the CEO refer to him as CTO was a pleasant surprise.

Masco started asking easy questions about operating systems and hardware. Then came a tough one. "What kind of interface do you have to the backbone?" asked one of the techies.

Joe had no idea what he was talking about. He had just recently seen his first Web page. He didn't even own a modem. He quickly tried to size up his tormenter to determine if this were a real geek or merely a suit pretending to be technically savvy.

"Exactly what do you mean by interface?" Joe asked calmly.

"Do you have a ISDN line or a T-1?"

Joe knew that a real geek would never have given him a multiple choice. He would have fished for a more detailed response. This guy was just parroting some key words he had overheard. Unfortunately, Joe had no idea what an ISDN line or a T-1 was. He wanted to flippantly respond, "T-1, T-2, whatever it takes." Little did he know how funny that would have been, since only T-1s and T-3s are used. But instead he said, "We use a mix of both to accommodate the different levels of service for our many clients."

The inquisitor nodded his head slightly and scribbled a couple of lines on his pad. The meeting proceeded a few minutes longer before it broke out into the smiles, handshakes, and card swapping. When Sid and Joe were alone, Sid said, "Where did you learn this stuff?"

"Just picked it up along the way."

"It was great the way you handled the one about the T-something. I'm really glad you were there for that. I wouldn't have had a clue."

"Don't feel bad, Sid. I have no idea what a T-1 is either!"

"You're *shittin'* me!"

"Nope."

"You and I are going places, kid," Sid said with a glimmer in his eye. He had found himself a techie who could wing it—his own personal gold mine.

"Say, Joe, I understand we're paying you five bucks a Web page. How many have you done so far?"

"*None.* I've been reconfiguring your systems. I've replaced those two-hundred-dollar-an-hour buffoons you hired. I've optimized processes and wasted my time in meetings with a bunch of 'suits.'"

"Let me write you a check for the work you've done. It's only right."

"That's okay, I'm cool with five bucks a page. Just be prepared to give it to me when I hook some scripts to our client databases. I'll instantly create thousands of Web pages."

"You can *do* that?"

"Sure."

"Is anyone else doing this stuff?"

"Not that I know of, but someone must have done it, or at least will do it. Any geek worth his pocket protector should see the potential."

Months passed like days for Joe and Sid. They were in early, and they had staked their claim. It was a gold rush, and like the big one in 1849, the gold was in the rolling hills of California. Sid started bugging Joe to set up an office with him in the Golden State. Joe liked the idea but knew money was tight. Making payroll had become a bi-weekly challenge.

But then it happened. Sid handed Joe some guy's business plan for a pioneering shift in retail. Joe instantly realized everything else at Internet Connect was Web fodder. *This* was what the Internet was about. No one else was doing anything remotely like it.

KATHARINE SMILED. Her ol' business hound had gotten the scent back. He was on the trail of something; she didn't know quite what, but it was consuming his thoughts, not to mention most of his time. Strange acronyms were starting to creep into his vocabulary: WWW, HTTP, HTML, EDI, TCP/IP....

It had all started the day he had returned from a meeting in Newport with an armload of magazines about the Internet. He said he was working on a new business plan. That was a good sign. Now if he would just get himself an office somewhere else so she could have her kitchen back....

Craig was spending six hours a day reading about the Web. He was determined to learn how it worked, where it was going, the equipment that ran it, the people who were shaping it, *everything*. He bought a faster modem and got a Netscape browser.

Another eight hours were spent working on the business plan. He came up with a list of fifty or so possible names for the new enterprise, but one emerged as his favorite: "Value America." It became his working title, then his strong preference, then his obsession. No other name would do. These two words said it all.

Over the next week, Craig poured his experiences with The Winn Company, The Price Club, and Dynasty into a business plan for Value America. He punctuated his thoughts with analysis, philosophy, and future predictions. He pulled heavily from his book, *Winning*. Originally a hundred pages, it soon grew into a nearly two-hundred-page blueprint for the construction of the next retail revolution. It began:

EXECUTIVE SUMMARY

Value America is destined to be the world's best store. We will create multimedia presentations that properly demonstrate the best products from the world's leading brands. Customers will shop in the comfort of their homes and offices....

Brands need a more direct distribution channel—one that brings them closer to the consumer, diminishes their cost of sales, and effectively communicates the value of their products. Many traditional retailers have simply become inefficient parking spaces for inventory and contribute little to the actual sale. Value America will solve these challenges by integrating the synergistic power of advanced technology and pragmatic electronic distribution. We will change retail forever.

Craig outlined his philosophy. Part attitude, part game plan, this section was to provide the moral roadmap. The company would prove unstoppable as long as it lived by these twelve tenets.

CORPORATE PHILOSOPHY

1. CREATE VALUE: Value America shall only present the highest quality affordable products, and sell them at the best value....

2. LEAD THROUGH INNOVATION: We shall create and innovate by developing exciting interactive technology and efficient acquisition and delivery systems....

3. CREATE WORLD-CLASS PRESENTATIONS: Marketing is the voice of the company.... Great marketing is the outward symbol of inward inspiration....

4. IMPLEMENT EFFICIENT TECHNOLOGIES: Greater efficiency, service, and productivity are all derivatives of intelligently embracing technology....

5. FOCUS ON OUR STRENGTHS: We shall strive to do what we do best, only what we do best, and will do it better than anyone. Value America will focus on its core business—bringing people and products together....

6. CREATE INNOVATIVE SOLUTIONS: Revolutionize retail by inventing and executing effective solutions to common problems. Value America will implement pragmatic solutions that eliminate inventory and reduce burdensome overhead....

7. SELL THE MERITS, NOT THE PRODUCTS: We shall communicate the merits of our company, and the suppliers we serve, rather than simply selling individual products....

8. EMPOWER THE TEAM: Hire the best, reward them with ownership, empower them with knowledge, and lead the team with a clear vision....

9. AGGRESSIVELY PURSUE EXCELLENCE: Greatness is achieved when excellence is executed aggressively. Excellence is that middle ground between mediocrity and perfection. Mediocrity meanders and perfection is slow to start....

10. BE PEOPLE OF PRINCIPLE: Say what you mean and do what you say. Tell the truth. Make a habit of under-promising and over-delivering. The best deal is one in which everyone wins....

11. ACHIEVE VALUE THROUGH FRUGALITY: We shall spend money prudently and hire people cautiously. It is easier to generate revenue than profit. Acquire only those things that can be clearly demonstrated to reduce costs or make the company more valuable....

12. CREATE A BETTER WORLD: We have a duty to help others.

The next section detailed the marketing concept, explaining what was wrong with the retail world as it existed and what Value America would do to correct the situation.

MARKETING CONCEPT

Productive innovations solve common problems. In such cases, marketing is simplified because the problems are widely known and the solutions are greatly appreciated. We have all experienced the frustration of searching for a particular product. We must fight traffic, find the right store, locate the desired item among the clutter, and endure long checkout lines, only to find needlessly inflated prices. Retailers burdened by excessive inventory, exorbitant leases, extravagant advertising, and expensive personnel are forced to sell goods well beyond their worth. Barring a few advertised specials, most retailers *double* a product's already burdened cost. Sadly, retail products are seldom presented appropriately, rarely demonstrated, or intelligently compared. The world awaits a better way to shop.

Now, imagine shopping in the comfort of your home. Envision a wealth of products properly presented and demonstrated by informed people. Consider a world where thousands of interactive multimedia and video presentations are accessible on demand, each answering important questions, actually demonstrating the salient features, and revealing unique benefits. Simply press a button to purchase the best the world has to offer. No hunting for stores, no long lines, no wasted time. This remarkable vision is emerging to serve the world's consumers.

Value America will be the first interactive, multimedia, product education and discount acquisition service. Factory-direct shipments eliminate the need for inventory, driving value pricing. Video demonstrations replace anemic store displays and untrained salespeople. Interactive menus function as aisles and store directories. Technology replaces costly personnel and expensive offices.

With specific examples, the business plan demonstrated that the challenges faced by traditional retailers could be solved. This was a whole new ball game on a whole new playing field.

RETAIL LIABILITIES EMPOWER VALUE AMERICA

Businesses thrive when they solve problems encountered by their competitors. We will prosper by avoiding the challenges endured by traditional retailers.

INVENTORY: No burdensome inventory to control or finance. No inventory shrink, pilfered products, markdowns, imbalances, or obsolescence.

BUILDINGS: No leases, store ownership costs, or displays. No warehouses or distribution facilities.

FINANCE: No expensive and restrictive asset-based lines of credit, bank loans, or inventory audits. No negative cash flow, bad debt, or bounced checks.

CONVENIENCE: No searching for products or pushy, uninformed salespeople. No driving from one specialty store to another, or waiting for stores to open.

PRESENTATION: No struggling to learn an item's features, function, or performance from its package alone. No wondering why one is better than another.

QUALITY & VALUE: No excessive returns to burden costs, because goods are handled and shipped only once. Efficient operation means no high mark-ups.

The benefits of shopping at Value America were delineated next. The plan described the Internet the way Craig knew it would be, not the way it actually was at the time. A final short paragraph summed up his groundbreaking concept. It read, "Value America's superior business model will enable lower prices, broader product offerings, interactive product presentations, and responsive customer support. It will generate tremendous growth by satisfying consumers and supporting brands."

In the detailed two-hundred-page plan, Craig explained what customers would see when they visited the store, how they would navigate the site, view the product presentations, and check out. He described how transactions would take place between the store and its suppliers. He reviewed the markets in great detail. He projected revenues, margins, expenses, and earnings five years out, dovetailing his knowledge of traditional retailers' growth rates with what he had read about the expected growth of the Web.

Issues of future connectivity were covered, as were comparative gross margins in competing markets. The plan detailed the store's merchandising strategies and provided a product category "hit-list" and timetable. The business plan ended with a five-page listing of technical, financial, reporting, and logistics requirements and their interrelationships for the benefit of the systems designers.

The resulting document was thorough to the point of being overwhelming. It took a totally focused mind to take it in. Those in business were likely to find its premise, strategy, and detail fascinating, unless, of course, they were going to have to compete against it—for those, it would be terrifying. It was designed to hold the company together, moving everyone in the same direction.

လွှာ

SO THERE HE WAS. Joe Page in Newport Beach. He had arrived with one bag, moved into Sid's place, bought a classic Mustang, and gone to work. Unfortunately, Sid, for some unexplained reason, had run into a little money trouble and wasn't paying him. But he wasn't charging him for rent or food, either. Joe could do this for a while. Sid, of course, promised to give Joe a big slice of the company just as soon as they made it. Joe was nothing if not loyal.

Sid Golden, not surprisingly, found Value America's business model eminently doable. "No problem," was invariably his response to anyone with money. He told Craig, "With this plan as a roadmap, I can build your solution." The cost? If Craig would put up $100,000 in cash, plus give him a sizable stake in the new company, Sid would provide the operating system that would make all of these wonderful things happen. "The job can be done in six months," Sid promised.

When something sounds too good to be true....

Joe Page skimmed the business plan once more the day he arrived in California. He pondered the geeky parts. Then he read them again, slowly. Frustrated, he went to see Golden.

"Sid," he said. "We've got to talk. Value America's business plan...."

"Amazing, isn't it?" he responded brightly. "This is going to change the way people shop! And *we're* going to own thirty percent of it!"

"We?" Joe wasn't sure how much equity his "free" services had earned him thus far. "What do you mean, *'We?'*"

Sid was light on his feet, as always. "Joe, my boy," he stalled for time. "You got me. That just slipped out. It was supposed to be a surprise."

Joe didn't say a thing.

"It's predicated on the Value America deal going through, but when it does, you and I will be partners."

Yeah, right. "How much of a partner?" In the current state of things, *complete* ownership wouldn't buy him a cold beer and a game of pinball.

Sid had hoped the question of percentages wouldn't come up, but then again, Joe hadn't been hired for his good looks. "Fifty percent," he blurted out, figuring that his remaining stake in Value America was still going to be worth millions. Sid was really good at counting unhatched chickens.

"There's only one problem, Sid," Joe said. "Value America is impossible. I understand what he wants to do on the front end. Sure, it would be great, but it can't be done. Not this much, not this fast! And the back end, well, that's way beyond me."

The smile never left Sid's face. "Not to worry, Joe. I have faith in you. Just get started. You know, get some pages up. We'll get the money, and we'll figure the rest out later. Oh, and by the way, Winn will be here Monday morning. Try to come up with something positive to say."

"Okay," Joe muttered under his breath, "I'm *positive* this can't be done."

∽∘∼

"LET ME GET this straight," Rex said. "You want me to give up my job as a lawyer and give my partners my share of the firm *I* founded. You want me to ante up fifty thousand dollars now and a lot more later. You're asking me to work for free for a couple of years helping you start a new retail business that's dependent on cutting-edge technology, even though I know nothing about technology *or* retail. Did I get that right?"

"Yep, that's pretty much it," Craig said happily.

"Hell, yes, count me in! How could I turn down an offer like that?"

"Great. I already FedExed you a copy of the business plan. You should get it in an hour or so. Give it a read."

"Okay. How about golf at PV tomorrow?"

"I'll pick you up," he offered.

As he hung up, Rex began to wonder about what he had just done.

CRAIG LOOKED OVER at Rex and started to laugh. "Hey, pal, is this any way to start a partnership?"

"Some things never change," Rex grinned. Craig was even par but already one down to his new partner. Rex was still laughing as he started his back swing. He stopped when the trap swallowed his ball.

Winn chuckled, stifling his grin. He flattened his swing to take the right side out of play. His ball, working from right to left, flew past the trap to the left side of the fairway, landing fifty yards from the pin.

"So we're going to be partners," Rex said, "and build your 'retail revolution.' Your magical communication machine turned out to be the Internet after all. You've written the business plan and found somebody who can do the computer stuff."

"Maybe."

"Why maybe?"

"The guy was far too eager to say yes. I think he knows his stuff, systems and programming, but I don't think he knows *our* stuff—retail and brands."

"I'm not sure *I* do, either. But you haven't asked me what I thought of your plan." He grinned. "Best damn thing I've ever read, at least the parts I understood." Rex would eventually read it twenty times, start to finish. Even with a lawyer's disciplined mind, he had a hard time comprehending the full dynamics of the buy-sell relationships and the complexity of their interdependence. Yet he was inspired by what he could assimilate.

"I'm glad you liked it, but you can still change your mind, you know. Sure you want to chuck it all on a flyer?"

"Heck, yes. We've been talking about this for years. I want out of the law business; I want to be your partner. I'm *in*. When do we start?"

Craig watched as Rex, in true Scatena form, blasted his ball to within a few yards of the hole. "Man, you're good!" he proclaimed.

"Darn right, I'm good. Not so much at this game, although I'm better than you. I know how to be a good partner. You can trust me. I don't know retail like you know it, but I *know* how to make a partnership work."

"That's why I called you," he said as he stroked his putt in for a second consecutive birdie and temporarily pulled even with his friend. "You already know my greatest weakness. Sometimes I trust the wrong people. You're going to need to protect me—us."

"Can do, pal," Rex said as they hiked up to the elevated fourth tee.

"Before we start, there are a couple more things," Craig warned. "I promised Katie I would never take another company public. We won't be able to honor that pledge, I'm afraid. Value America won't be competitive without access to the public markets."

"I understand." They stood looking out over the lush rolling hills with the sea shimmering in the distance. "What do you need me to do?"

"I need you to be the spokesman for the company. The press can be very mean spirited. With Dynasty having filed Chapter, they're going to be merciless. I'll be opening old wounds. I don't want to be in the press again, to be a public figure. This is very important to me and my family."

"Okay, I'll do it, but I think you're wrong. Those wounds are the very reason I want to be your partner. The way a man handles himself when he's down tells you what he's made of. I saw what happened at Dynasty. You were there for them. I'll be there for you. When do we start?"

Craig looked up into the cloudless sky as if to see if God was listening. Then he answered, "Right now. We'll both need to write $50,000 checks, and we're off."

"Okay. Here's mine—partner." Rex pulled out a check he had written before he left home and handed it to Craig. They shook hands. That was the full extent of their partnership agreement. Ever. A handshake: good enough.

"Thanks, partner. Now for the fun part. Let's turn this fifty thousand into fifty million!"

SOMEBODY HAD BEEN fired at the ad agency, leaving an empty office. They hadn't finished moving their things out; files and personal effects littered the floor. Craig settled in at the empty desk, his cavernous black briefcase resting on the floor at his feet like a faithful dog. It was ten before eight, Monday morning.

At a quarter past, Joe Page breezed in. The place looked awfully quiet. Sid wasn't there, and most of the ad agency folks didn't arrive until after nine. The receptionist smiled at Joe and pointed in the direction of the office where Craig had camped out.

The door was open, so he walked in. Craig looked up from his paperwork and smiled. "Hi, I'm Craig Winn," he said. "You must be Joe."

Joe held out his hand. "Joe Page. I guess I'm here to write your application."

Craig rose and shook Joe's hand, then motioned toward an empty chair. "I presume you've read the Value America business plan."

"I have."

"What did you think?"

"Well, the *concept* is spectacular. There's nothing like it. It's why I'm here." Joe paused, tried to find the right words, "positive" words. He gave up. "It can't be done, you know. I don't know what Sid told you, but what you've described is impossible." Joe launched into an explanation, dumbed down for Craig's benefit, of why the things he wanted were beyond the scope of the existing technology.

"The bandwidth, or data flow rate, that's currently available is too limiting to allow the pictures, text, audio, and video you want. There's no way to control the geometry of the screen the way it's described in your plan either. It can't be done. Sorry."

"Other than that, Mrs. Lincoln, how'd you like the play?" Craig quipped, undeterred. "I know the front end is a little demanding, considering the current state of affairs, but where's your sense of adventure?"

"I'm as daring as the next guy," Joe shot back.

"Good, 'cause I don't want this designed for today. I want it optimized for the way things are going to be two years from now. The Web's going to get faster and gain functionality."

"Okay, say you're right. I think the front-end stuff is probably doable in time, but the back end is way beyond me, beyond any team of Web designers."

"Not to worry. I know the back end like the back of my hand. If you can write the customer interface, create dynamic page generation out of a database, and create the menu structure, I'll teach you everything you need to know about order pipelines, EDI, logistics, and financial reporting. Deal?"

Joe was at a loss for words. The silence was about to kill him. It was obvious that he shouldn't have dumbed down his "It-can't-be-done" speech. He thought about the business plan again. His programming life began to flash before his eyes—the countless times he had written elegant code for the curmudgeons. Suits were hopeless; yet sitting three feet from him was a suit who could talk to a geek and make sense. Maybe this was a battle *worth* losing, if for no other reason than to find out where it all would lead. "Deal."

Thus began an extraordinary relationship.

✺

THE NEW PARTNERS were back in Winn's oceanfront office, sitting around his oak and green marble desk. They had agreed that Craig would start full time, but would not take a paycheck for the first year or so. Rex would stay with his law practice for a while, helping out whenever he could. Both understood that they would have to raise additional money, which would dramatically dilute their holdings—that is, presuming they would be lucky enough to attract outside capital.

"Every time I read your business plan, I learn something new," Rex said. "But right now, the most I can do is handle the legal work. What do you want done?"

"Sid Golden, the Web developer, was supposed to come up with a contract," Craig said. "I want you to do it instead. Matter of trust. We'll also need to incorporate. Can you do that?"

"Consider it done. I presume you want to use 'Value America?'"

Rex made sure the agreement was airtight. It turned out to be a good thing. Even before the ink was dry, they were expressing doubts about Golden's ability to tell the truth. They discovered as time passed that Golden had a bad case of selective memory. He never took notes and often had trouble remembering the commitments he had made the day before. Craig, on the other hand, could remember almost verbatim conversations that had taken place years earlier—it was one of his most annoying traits.

The first crack in the dam appeared as soon as Craig started working with Joe on a daily basis. Sid hadn't counted on that, even though it was clearly spelled out in the contract that Value America was to have Page full time. Joe, however, had other earlier projects going. Christi Reynolds' Masco projects, for instance.

Sid was used to dealing with people who signed the contract, delivered the money, and then conveniently disappeared, leaving Internet Connect alone in a vacuum for a while. He had sold Joe's time as a dedicated asset to several companies, figuring no one would ever be the wiser.

But Craig didn't work like that. When you were employed on his project, he was your Siamese twin, your constant companion, your hyperactive shadow. For Internet Connect, this led toward confrontation.

The crack in the dam widened when Sid, as part of his contribution to the partnership, volunteered to officially register and protect the name "Value America." After weeks of insisting he had taken care of it, he couldn't come up with the papers from the trademark office. It became apparent that he had neither researched nor registered the name. Sid Golden's credibility was failing fast.

The final irreparable rip came when Craig discovered that Joe Page was, in effect, working for room and board. Sid wasn't paying him, even though their sizeable check to Golden had been cashed some time back. They had grown protective of Joe, and didn't have any use for the twisted Stockholm-syndrome loyalty their talented new friend was showing his boss. They knew the ownership carrot Golden had dangled at the end of Joe's stick was nothing but a plastic phony.

For his part, Joe knew Internet Connect would fold if he left. There were a score of people back in Ann Arbor who needed their jobs, many of whom were living from paycheck to paycheck. So Page gritted his teeth and hung in there.

That was it. It was obvious that Golden had an allergy to the truth. He hadn't delivered what he'd promised. Internet Connect was *history*. Craig asked Rex to draw up a separation agreement.

As a result, Value America was nearly stillborn. Surviving the dismemberment of a partnership this early in a new corporation's life is almost always fatal. The young company could not afford the time, or cost, of the legal battles that routinely follow a break-up. On a more basic level, who was going to write the code that would empower the grand vision? The partners were faced with their first twenty-foot sudden-death putt. It was do or die, sink it or kiss their investment—and their dreams—goodbye.

Woe to him who uses his neighbor's service without wages and gives him nothing for his work—Jeremiah

A CAST OF CHARACTERS

*M*y studio was only a half mile from home. If I had blinked, I would have missed the majesty of the morning. It was so clear that day, it seemed as if I could have reached out and touched the snow-capped mountains. Now, three hours later, I had other things on my mind.

"Power Graphics," my assistant Gloria said cheerfully as she answered the fourth call of the morning. I looked up from the computer where I was working on a syrup label. She had a funny look on her face. "Hi. How are you? Sure, he's here. Hang on." She covered the mouthpiece. "It's Craig Winn!"

Gloria seemed surprised to hear from Craig. I know I was. After the Lights of America project, he had disappeared off our radar screen. But there he was on the phone.

"Hi, Craig," I said. "What's going on?"

"I'm starting a new business called Value America. I'd like you to design the logo and some sales materials. Are you interested?"

"Of course. When do we start?"

I thought I heard Gloria groan.

Craig descended on Power Graphics like a cloud of locusts, poised to devour every available minute. He brought the large, black open-topped briefcase we had come to refer to as "the black hole," because anything in the vicinity—sketches, printouts, documentation—was likely to get sucked into it. The first thing Craig pulled out was a humongous business plan. He asked me to take it home and read it.

Then he pulled out a manila folder filled with clippings. "The first thing we need to work on," he said, "is the logo. The logo sets the tone for the entire company. It establishes the identity, style, and character. It tells the world what the firm is all about...."

I couldn't help but smile. "I'm the designer. I'm supposed to be telling you these things." It was strange working with someone who took such a personal, hands-on interest in my business.

He opened the folder and laid the clippings on the table. "Here are some things I like. Just for inspiration." The images were all contemporary and all looked good against a white background. "This isn't a store you can drive to. It's just electrons on a screen," he said. "So first and foremost, we need to look credible, reliable...real!"

"But it's also the Web," I countered. "Fluid, dynamic—*new.*"

"That's right. Part of the logo needs to reflect the dynamic, ever-changing nature of the Web. So write 'Value' in a free-flowing script. It needs to look shiny and fresh, so new the ink has yet to dry. And 'America'—make America solid and dependable."

I grabbed a sketchpad and started fooling around.

Sitting down at my Macintosh, I typed "AMERICA" in large, red, Palatino caps. Then, with tracing paper, I wrote "Value." I superimposed the two words on a light table, moving the sketch around until I liked the relative position. Then I traced "Value" again electronically using my computerized drawing tablet, so the image appeared on my screen. With America in red, Value just had to be blue.

"Great, so far," Craig said, looking over my shoulder. "But it still needs a graphic element to help symbolize our business—bringing people and products together. How about earth?"

"Perfect." I showed him a shot from one of my stock photo books. "What you're doing is environmentally sound. It will make the world seem a little smaller by bringing us all together. This NASA image from outer space can also symbolize cyber-space." I did a quick scan. The whole thing had taken no more than fifteen minutes. I was starting to appreciate the speed of Internet development. Too bad I was billing by the hour.

We looked at the "finished" sketch. "That's it!" Craig said, wearing the proud smile of a new parent. He studied his logo on my screen. "We could work for weeks and not come up with anything better."

I had to agree. So much for the sketch stage. Of course, it took hours of computer illustration, and days of tinkering, adjusting, and tweaking, before we were satisfied. We added a tag line, "The Living Store" beneath the logo in gold. That's how we were coming to think of Value America— as a store where products were taken out of their boxes; they came alive.

That night I read the business plan. The first thing that went through my mind was, "This can't miss. He's thought of everything." The plan eliminated all of the things consumers hate about shopping and at the same time had given manufacturers the things *they* wanted.

The second thing that occurred to me was, "This could put me out of business." I was a packaging designer. My work was designed to be seen at the point of purchase, attracting, educating, and motivating people to exchange their money for my clients' products. With Value America, the point of purchase would no longer be where the package was. It would be where the *computer* was—in people's homes and offices.

Value America's presentations would be able to explain a product's merits in far greater detail that any package I could design. And they could be instrumental in differentiating between products—helping consumers make better choices, something a package could never do.

Taken to its logical conclusion, there would be no need for packaging graphics at all. A shipping carton would be all you'd need. As I finished the business plan, the seeds of an "If-you-can't-beat-'em-join-'em" mentality began to grow in my mind.

❧

CRAIG WAS TIRED of the little steak place, but Quiel apparently still loved it. For what had seemed like a hundred lunches, they had always sat in the same booth. They had always had the same thing to eat, although they didn't actually order any more—the steak sandwiches just *appeared.*

Today Craig had a very specific agenda. Between bites, he laid out his concept for Value America. Then he explained how Lights of America fit into the picture. "We need a way to show brands the awesome potential of our Product Presentations," he said. "And what better products than yours? Your Electronic Lights are incredible, but they're also incredibly difficult to sell."

"You're right. Once you know how good they are, you can't live without them," Quiel offered. "But getting the idea across...."

"Exactly. So we'd like to use Lights of America for our first series of Product Presentations. You're perfect—high-quality products with a story that needs to be told."

"So what do you want from me, my friend?" Quiel asked.

You now own an awesome collection of design resources—photos, charts, computer illustrations, research, and the like—and they're all at Power Graphics."

"So you want to use *our* products and *our* materials to demonstrate how *your* store will work," Quiel asked rhetorically.

"Yes. I want you to be our first brand. I'm willing to give you an exclusive in energy-efficient lighting in exchange for letting us use you as the poster child for our new concept."

Craig searched Quiel's poker face for a reaction. "We'll be offering our multimedia presentations for five thousand dollars per product category, and we'll add a video demonstration for another five thousand. I'd like to create five comprehensive presentations for you, including multimedia and video, at just ten thousand dollars apiece.

"You know from experience, Quiel, that it costs many times that just to get a professional video done. The ad agency I'm working out of is charging their clients over a hundred grand for websites that do a lot less than ours will," Craig pressed. "Best of all, Value America will become one of your customers."

"I've got to tell you," Quiel said, "I really like the idea, especially the video demonstrations. But it sounds too cheap. Can you really do all of this for so little? What's it going to cost *you?*"

Craig reassured Quiel he had done a thorough analysis. "Five presentations at ten thousand each," he said. Half down, twenty five thousand, will get us started. The other half is due when they're Web-enabled."

Quiel was astounded. Craig's proposal looked like a giveaway.

"My friend, you have a deal. I'll have a check cut immediately." The money wasn't a big deal for a company grossing $100 million a year, but it was huge for the infant Web retailer, a godsend.

Grateful, Winn sweetened the deal, "The Internet isn't ready yet for the caliber of presentations I've envisioned, so we'll be cutting a CD-ROM version of our store. It will feature your product presentations. As a way of saying thanks, I'll give you a hundred copies."

I was the first person Craig sought out when he got back from lunch with Quiel. He was positively euphoric. Try as I might, I couldn't muster as much enthusiasm as he obviously had. My reaction was rather one of profound relief that the work I'd done so far wasn't going to end up on the cutting-room floor.

I needn't have worried. As it turned out, the week I had put onto the product presentation project was merely the smallest tip of the iceberg. Value America was destined to become Power Graphics' ball and chain for the next five months.

For the founders, it had been their second twenty-foot sudden-death putt. Had he not convinced Lights of America to partner with their new enterprise, there might not have been a Value America. I now recognize what Craig knew then—without the immense collection of spectacular graphics, beautiful photography, and intellectually compelling products that we had at our fingertips, there would have been no earthly way to compose the caliber of product presentations needed to persuade the world's leading brands to pay to partner with a store that didn't exist.

"The first one is the hardest," Craig observed as he placed his hand on my shoulder. That made sense. If you could point to one big, successful company that had invested in your idea, and could show others what wonderful things you had done for them, it stood to reason other brands would be less skeptical and more receptive.

❧

NOW THAT WE had our first brand and products to sell, all we needed was a store. And all that stood between us and a store was the way it looked and the way it worked. I was prepared to tackle the design, but we were a little short on technologists.

Hiring Joe was the answer. We could look at the $15,000 advance the partners had wasted on Internet Connect as a finder's fee. We had been impressed with Joe's programming skill and business acumen, but there was more to him than that. There was evidence that Joe Page was a man of character. Loyalty, even to a deadbeat, was more important to Joe than money. Had not the business plan plainly stated that virtue was to be desired over all else?

Day after day, Craig pleaded with Joe for hours on end. Desperation helps you focus. Finally Joe cracked. He became the first employee of Value America. It was April Fools' Day, 1996.

"This is going to be your desk," Craig said to Joe. "I know it's tight, but it's only temporary." Considering what day it was, Joe could be forgiven for thinking it was all a joke. But it wasn't.

"Tight" was putting it mildly. The company had now moved into the palatial 600-square-foot office of Power Graphics. Except for the lack of room, it made perfect sense. Craig was spending all his time here anyway, working on the marketing and sales tools for his new enterprise. So we had taken the logical, if somewhat painful, next step. We had another couple phone lines put in, cleared off some space next to the coffee pot for Craig's stuff, and had Value America business cards printed up with our Beach Boulevard address. The company picked up half our modest rent and part of Gloria's salary as well.

Just because Joe was now receiving a paycheck instead of peanut butter and jelly sandwiches, his opinions hadn't changed. He had serious concerns about making the programming magic happen. Despite his reservations, we plowed ahead, using a print-graphics software program just to get our ideas into viewable form. We knew that for Joe to "see" the store Craig envisioned we'd first have to picture it on paper.

Joe Page, the Web geek, set about teaching Ken Power, the print guru, just what it was that made Craig's front-end ideas so improbable. Craig and I were used to a world where people saw pretty much what you wanted them to see. If you placed a headline at such and such a size in such and such a place, it stayed there, right next to the photograph that had also been carefully sized and positioned for the proper graphic effect. Print was predictable. There was even a computer graphics term, an acronym, for seeing your exact page layout on the computer screen. WYSIWYG (pronounced wizzy-wig), meant What-You-See-Is-What-You-Get, a capability that had revolutionized my industry.

With Web pages, things were not so simple, especially back then. The page layout was controlled by the viewer's browser. This caused several problems. First, the *user* could set some graphic parameters like the size of the text. Second, there was more than one browser. Some people still used the feature-poor Mosaic, though most were using Netscape, and there was a new one from Microsoft. Because it was from Microsoft, Internet Explorer might eventually dominate the market, so we had to pay attention to its quirks and idiosyncrasies. Third, each viewer's monitor size and the resolution they chose played a part in altering the final image. Someone with a 24-bit, 20-inch Sony Multiscan monitor running at a 1,024x768 pixel resolution could see something quite different than someone using an 8-bit, 14-inch NEC with 640x480 resolution.

There were many parts to the Value America graphics project. First was the store itself, its story, how it worked, why it was better, what it would do for you as a shopper. At its heart was the design of the product presentations and purchasing panels. Both were eloquently described in the business plan, but Craig knew that most people were incapable of really "seeing" what he'd envisioned. They needed more than words and more than a plan—they needed visual imagery. That's where I came in. Craig and I took every part of the store and brought it to life.

Our second big project was the printed materials. We set about designing two brochures. *The Retail Revolution* explained the problem, the existing retail environment, which relied on expensive advertising, poorly informed sales people, and inadequate point-of-sale materials to educate consumers. Value America's Living Store with its interactive presentations was the solution. *The Retail Revolution* was designed to encourage brands to partner with us.

It's About Time presented our corporate mission. It revealed how we were going to enable consumers to become better buyers. Suppliers, or brands, as we called them, would triumph by realizing their dreams of increasing sales through closer customer intimacy. And the company's factory-direct efficiency was sure to save everyone money. The brochure described tomorrow's communication network, where consumers, manufacturers, and freight companies all came together through electronic financial transactions and data management.

Of course, none of what it presented actually existed. Not in our store, not in *any* store. Nobody was doing any business to speak of on the Web. Even Amazon, the innovative online bookseller, was but a fledgling reality. Our new sales tools, both electronic and print, presented things as we were sure they would soon be. It was our job to present, build, and sell the future.

The best example of this became project number three. We created a fully functioning version of our store on a CD-ROM. It was the only way to demonstrate how our store was going to work and how our customers would interact with it. Craig could paint an exciting word picture, but comprehending this concept without an audio-visual aid was beyond impossible.

People could view the CD-ROM on their PCs, and it would work just like the real—i.e., virtual—store we intended to build. It proved to be an extremely valuable tool for the next year, until there was an actual store, doing actual business, with actual customers. Unfortunately, it was expensive, a real budget buster. If Quiel had not been willing to sponsor its production, I wouldn't be telling this story today.

Technical experts scoffed at the interactive multimedia store we created on the CD-ROM. They said it was impossible to execute online. So we must have done the impossible: Value America's first actual online store looked and worked exactly like what we'd said it would. It was but one of a thousand bold predictions we willed into reality.

Sometimes we felt like we were working within an Escher print. Everything was upside down, mirror imaged, and backwards. The current technology would not allow us to operate in the present, and the tools of the future didn't exist yet. So we had to rely on our past to present our future. Solomon was right: there's nothing new under the sun.

Working with concepts in lieu of reality, it was only natural that symbols and metaphors would become our *lingua franca*. Very early in the game, one image emerged as our symbol for the whole idea: a butterfly. It probably wasn't the first time a butterfly had been used to exemplify a new commercial venture, and it certainly wouldn't be the last. Even mighty Microsoft has come to use these small, colorful creatures.

The idea was metamorphosis. Value America had emerged from the cocoon of a greedy and voracious caterpillar, the existing retail world. Our caterpillar, named MalMart, was a member of the species *buggus retailus*. It represented everything we thought was wrong with retail. High prices, grumpy and uninformed salespeople, long register lines, and sticky price tags were attributed to this ugly little critter.

MalMart had had his day. Now *buggus* was being transformed into the beautiful Value America butterfly, of the species *wholesaleus educatus*. More than merely beautiful, our butterfly was a symbol for freedom, moving effortlessly and gracefully throughout our store, visiting and investigating whatever struck its fancy. Okay, maybe we were taking our metaphors a little too seriously. But we were having fun.

The butterfly played a starring role in an animation we called *"The Good Buy Machine,"* a fanciful illustration of how factory-direct shopping worked. *The Good Buy Machine* started with a shopper sitting at his PC, clicking his mouse to buy a product. Our butterfly fluttered from his computer to a teeter-totter springboard, which launched a young lady in a graceful dive into a pool of water, which splashed, startling a sleeping cat, who jumped into the air with a terrific yowl. This got the attention of a dog sitting on a conveyor belt. As the dog ran toward the cat, the conveyor belt started to turn, tripping a lever attached to the dog's leash that caused a pair of mechanical hands to place the shopper's order on a ramp. It sent an electronic message to an airplane, which came swooping out of the sky, grabbed the box with a dangling hook, and flew it to the shopper, where it was dropped gently into his waiting arms with a fluffy parachute. It was all set to music with sound effects punctuating the action.

I was skeptical, but Craig assured me that this was how it was done.

৩৯৹৵৶

We had a "Catch 22." A store is not a store without brands and the products they make. Yet there are no brands or products to sell until there is a store. So to produce our first product video demonstrations, Craig found a small production company willing to do the job on a shoestring. They assembled a team of actors and technicians—makeup artists, Teleprompter operators, and sound techs—and we proceeded to make a liar out of Craig to the one person who really counted—his wife.

We had no choice, really. There was simply no other way to do it. Craig had made a solemn promise to Katharine when he had used their home as a glorified photo studio during the Lights of America packaging project that he would never ask her to go through that again. But here he was, doing exactly that. Well, not exactly. This time it was broadcast-quality video production. There were five times as many people and ten times as much equipment as before. She was not amused. The whole idea had been to get her husband *out* of her kitchen.

The battle plan, though, was brilliant. As we shot the video clips, we used a still photographer to shoot the people who were shooting the video. After all, we need to show future brand partners what they would be getting.

The place was a zoo. For three incredible days, we had movie sets in every corner of the house, even spilling out to the poolside patio and the rose garden overlooking the ocean. Actors were holding forth in the living room, the dining room, the office, and out by the cabaña. Lights of America fixtures were installed and photographed in bedroom ceilings and in front-yard security applications.

Craig and I were all over it like a swarm of mosquitoes, suggesting scene locations, helping the crew get set up, making minor changes in the scripts as they were loaded into the Teleprompters, and telling the photographer what we wanted him to shoot. There were cables running across the floors in profusion, light stands everywhere, make-up cases, wardrobe racks, 'prompter computers, sound booms, power packs, and portable editing equipment.

Frugality being the watchword, we used whatever and whomever was at hand. Rex Scatena modeled for us, as did Craig's kids, Ryan and Blake. Jane Scatena, Rex's stunning wife and professional thespian, played roles in several of the videos. Even Craig's photogenic and cooperative yellow Labrador, Crystal, got into the act. A shameless scene stealer.

The final result was a graphic presence that made Value America look as if we had been in business for years. The materials gave us the appearance of professionals who knew what we were doing. The catalogs and the multimedia CD-ROM store clearly showed that we had the skills to perform for our brand partners. Our virtual version of the virtual store looked great. We were virtually ready.

ɛ৯:৫ɔ

"WELCOME TO BRAVO Burger. May I take your order?" Oh, yeah. Craig and I knew fine dining. Whenever we felt like we needed a break from the grind, we'd get out of my claustrophobic studio, grab a bite at one of the local drive-thrus, and head for the park. Perry Park was just around the corner. It was two acres of grass, trees, benches, and playground equipment snuggled amongst the nice but aging tract houses in my Huntington Beach neighborhood. There was a grammar school adjacent to the park, and we both enjoyed listening to the kids' chatter as they played outdoors.

"When we're all through with this," Craig announced one fine day in March, "I'm going to move to Charlottesville, Virginia, to build the company." He took a sip of his iced tea. "It's the perfect place. Lots of history and charm. It's home to the University of Virginia and Monticello."

"Like on the nickel, right?"

"Right. You don't have to be in a big city to run an Internet store. You could do it from a cornfield in Iowa, or in Sam Walton's back yard next to a chicken coop in Arkansas. You just have to have the basic services. Charlottesville is beautiful, full of writers. And it's close to the Internet hub in Pentagon City. Did you know that Charlottesville has more published authors per capita than any other town in America?" Craig asked, munching an onion ring. "It should be easy to attract and hire good people.

It's such a wholesome place."

"They got trees?" My wife and I had always dreamed of moving out of Southern California to settle in some place that was greener.

"Oh, yeah. Lots of trees. Charlottesville is in the foothills of the Blue Ridge Mountains. There are oaks, poplars, maples, black walnuts—dogwoods and redbuds too. And some of the prettiest farmland you've ever seen. Jefferson called it Eden."

"Sounds beautiful," I said. "So how did you find Charlottesville?"

"That's a long story," Craig said.

"I love a good story." I took a bite of my burger.

"Okay. A couple of years ago, when we were doing the Lights project, my oldest son, Ryan, was having trouble in school. Couldn't concentrate."

"Ryan?" I asked rhetorically. That didn't sound like the Ryan I knew. Sharp kid. A lot like his dad. They looked the same too, almost like twins, just thirty years apart.

"Yeah. The school called us in and said they thought he had ADD...."

"Attention Deficit Disorder," I said. As the parent of several "special-needs" kids, I was familiar with it.

"That's right. So we took him to a psychologist, and she put him through a battery of tests. She said that things weren't checking out for ADD, and asked if she could test his IQ."

"So what happened?"

"She called us frantically after the test, all excited, but worried at the same time, very emotional. She had tested thousands of people, adults and children, over the last twenty years. She told me that Ryan's IQ was off the chart. That explained why he was doing poorly in school. He was bored stiff—a nine-year-old boy whose mind was working like he was in college."

I thought of my sweet little Molly, whom Gayle and I had adopted at about one year old. She had made it to three before she died. Molly had a *minus* IQ—pre-newborn. The most advanced thing she ever learned how to do was smile, during the last few months of her short life. "Well, at least it was good news," I said.

"No, that's not what the psychologist told us," Craig mused. "She said, 'This is the worst news I could give you. Studies on profoundly gifted children aren't real encouraging.' A lot of bad stuff can happen, especially in adolescence. Then she gave me some advice: 'Get your son out of California, out of public schools. Find a more wholesome environment. You may have to educate him yourself,' she said."

"You've got two boys, right?"

"Yeah. Katie suggested testing Blake."

Blake was fifteen months younger than his brother. He favored his mom, right down to the twinkle in his eye.

"She called again, shell-shocked. Apparently Blake had turned the IQ test into a game, like Jeopardy. He'd fire off answers before she could finish the questions, no working it out, just boom, here it is, with a big grin. She told me he may be smarter than his brother."

"Really?" I shook my head. "So how does that lead you to Virginia?"

"I was trying to figure out how I was going to handle the challenge— being both dad and teacher. I boned up on my math, science, and history, and tutored the kids where I could. I'd bring in computer tutors and others to teach them in areas where I couldn't."

"So, Professor Winn?" I laughed.

"Yeah. Katie and I took the boys on an educational trip to show them how America was born and how we had to struggle for our freedom. We took them out of school and flew to Boston, and then we worked our way down the East Coast, stopping at every important historical site, Philadelphia, Gettysburg, Washington, Mount Vernon, Williamsburg, Yorktown...and one of our stops was Charlottesville."

"Home of Thomas Jefferson," I recited.

"Jefferson, Madison, Monroe, Meriwether Lewis, among others. It was early spring, and they were celebrating the 'Dogwood Festival,' complete with parade. The whole thing was so charming, we couldn't believe it. We found ourselves asking around about schools and real estate. Turns out there was a private school equipped to deal with the special needs of my kids. And of course, there's the university—it dominates the city."

"Sounds like you found the perfect place," I said, a little jealous.

"Yep, I think so," Craig replied happily. "We've been looking for a farm close to town. Katie has loved the idea of moving to the south ever since she met the Governor of South Carolina. Some time ago he tried to entice us to build our company in his state. So Katie thinks we should build Tara, you know, as in *Gone with the Wind*."

I could feel myself turning green, and it wasn't the greasy burger. But there was no time for envy. We had work to do.

⋐⋑

"I'M GOING. I don't care."

"Bill, please, listen to me," Craig pleaded. "As much as I believe in this, Value America is a long shot. I don't want you to leave Lights to take a chance on something that could easily fail. Besides, you're needed there. We've brought them from a bow-and-arrow marketing to cruise missiles.

In the wrong hands, that arsenal is dangerous."

"They're driving me crazy, Craig," Hunt admitted. These guys won't rest until they've taken your cruise missiles and changed them back into Sopwith Camels. The brothers are great guys, but...."

Craig sighed. "Still, we've sold one brand so far. *One*...somebody who already knew and trusted us. Your employer, I might add. It's going to take a lot more than that to give us the right to hire people away from good jobs."

Hunt relented. "Okay, but don't say 'no.' Say 'maybe later,' all right?"

"Sure, Bill," Craig knew how much Bill loved Charlottesville.

"Listen. There's someone I want you to meet. He was my roommate at Harvard when I did my post-graduate studies. We're still close friends. Now he's the president of a hardware conglomerate. I think he may like what you're doing."

"I'd love an intro. Who is he?"

"Ray Kennedy. He runs...."

"Masco: Baldwin, Thermador, Hot Springs, Delta, and Peerless? *That* Ray Kennedy, right?"

"Yeah. Why? What?" Bill could see that Craig was genuinely amused.

Through a big grin, Craig explained the coincidence of the century to his old friend. "You remember Christi Reynolds?..."

෨෧෨

A WEEK LATER, Craig, Bill, and Rex walked through the front doors of Masco's corporate headquarters. They had FedExed their new brochures ahead. The demo CD-ROM was hot off the presses. This was to be its maiden flight.

It was a little intimidating walking into Masco. They were the most successful home-improvement corporation in the world, and the building had been designed to display that success. "Opulent" was hardly a big enough word to describe it. The artwork alone was worth a fortune, but it was the selection of art that told the real story. Classic American paintings lined the walls. A magnificent collection of Remington bronzes graced the public areas. America had been good to Masco, and the company seemed determined to return the favor.

Among such luxurious surroundings, it was easy to imagine that arrogance and greed could have been instrumental in amassing so much wealth. Knowing Ray Kennedy, Bill knew better already. Craig and Rex were about to learn that nice guys often finish first.

Kennedy had moved fast to gather an appropriate audience. The head of each business group was there, as was the VP of Marketing. Good thing. The boys from California had a remarkable tale to tell.

Craig began by telling his audience what he was going to share. He told them why partnering with his new company was in their interest—including just enough detail to legitimize his rationale. He provided insights into their business to show he'd taken the time to appreciate their challenges. Then he concluded by summarizing what he had presented.

The smarter the audience, the more impressive the presentation. Winn studies them as he speaks, analyzing their body language. Are they leaning forward or back, are their arms crossed or open, are they fidgeting or motionless? He dissects their expressions: are they comfortable enough with the presentation to make eye contact, are their brows raised or lowered, are their lips lifted in a smile, lowered in a grimace, or flat-lined with bewilderment? He studies their hands: are they placed over their mouth trying to restrain a question, on their cheeks as they listen intently, or are they engaged in taking notes? Everything is tailored to the audience: pace, length, breadth, humor, detail, and depth of insight.

With some audiences, he will begin by teaching the basics of retail or the Web, making them more receptive to his story. Other times, he moves directly to his innovative solutions, recognizing that those listening share a common understanding of the challenges.

With the most enlightened audiences, he leaves his strongest points unspoken, knowing someone will ask the right question. That's when he's in his element. He seems as comfortable on his feet as a politician at a press conference—funny when appropriate, serious when necessary, always articulate, and never without an answer.

There was magic in the air that day. Winn had found a compatriot in Ray Kennedy. The man was brilliant and wise, compassionate and tough, idealistic and realistic. Like Craig, Ray had been in the trenches. He had led by example. He knew his business. When Craig talked about replacing warehouses with technology and inventory with systems, Kennedy stayed right there with him every step of the way. The presentation became a discussion.

"So you're going to do one better than WalMart," Kennedy observed. "They send us small orders each week by store based upon what their customers bought the prior week. You're just compressing the process—transmitting orders by customer, in real time."

"Precisely."

"I assume you intend to use EDI?"

"Indeed."

"So when you send the order to us electronically," Ray asked, "you're planning to attach a file that includes the customer's name and address so we can automate the label printing process and eliminate the need for a stencil, right?"

"Correct."

"How large do you think the average order might be?"

"My plan calls for two hundred dollars," Winn answered, knowing that number was ten times larger than what the experts were predicting for online sales and identical to that of most traditional retail orders. "We've made a commitment to sell only the best products from the best brands. By doing that, I believe we'll earn our customers' trust. And our product presentations should enable us to sell better goods than our competitors."

Ray Kennedy's body language did all the talking. His hand covered his mouth. His brows were raised, his eyes danced, he leaned forward. "Our existing customers already require us to have the kind of infrastructure needed to accommodate your 'inventory-less model,'" he said.

Craig smiled. "Karl Marx once said, 'Capitalists will sell us the rope we'll use to hang them.'"

"Gentlemen," Ray told his team, "they're right. What they're asking us to do is ship their customers directly, bypassing the retail store. We've invested millions setting ourselves up to do this very thing. In fact, what they want us to do is even easier than what we're required to do now. I like getting closer to the real customer, too—the consumer."

The assembled suits were all nodding. They, like their leader, had earned the right to be there. They knew the score. They knew retail was broken, inefficient, and abusive. As they drilled down layer after layer into the esoteric and arcane world of business structure, the Masco executives became more and more convinced that this was the right idea at the right time, and that these were the guys who could make it happen.

"I love your product presentations," Kennedy concluded.

Thank God Lights said yes! Craig thought. "Ray, your companies have prospered by making great products. Yet you have no way to tell the customer why Delta's single-handle faucets and washerless systems are superior. No package, and certainly no retailer, is able to explain the merits of your 'Brilliance' lifetime tarnish protection. Imagine empowering the president of each company to make an individual presentation directly to every consumer with a full range of multimedia tools."

"These guys are prepared to give us what we want. The way they've anticipated our needs, the way they've designed their solution to mesh with our systems, gives me every confidence they'll succeed in building this thing," Kennedy said. "They have unified our interests with theirs—and with the consumer's." With that, he slapped his open hand on the conference table and stood up. "We would be proud to be your partner."

A list of brands was drawn up, along with a preliminary estimate of the number of presentations each would require. Masco corporate would partially fund the effort, the various divisions making up the balance. The hook was set, but reeling in this huge fish—getting each of the divisions to sign their listing agreements and provide the money to get started— would take months. Building something new is never easy.

Yet the three Californians believed that success was within their grasp. They left with a commitment from some of the country's most reputable firms. That, and a store that actually worked, was going to be all they needed to turn their dreams into reality.

Bill looked at Craig, grinning. "Guess I'm movin' to Charlottesville."

"Yes," Craig laughed. "I guess you are."

Rex was quiet, thinking about all the things he didn't know yet. He was ecstatic but worried at the same time, like a skinny little tight end on a high school football team who's just caught his first pass, only to discover four burly defenders between himself and the goal line. He'd have to move fast or get creamed.

꙳

THE INITIAL GRAPHIC PROJECT was all wrapped up, and I found myself examining my life for the first time in ages. I had been in business for nine years, good years for the most part. I had always earned more than my previous job, even in that first harrowing year, but the stress of owning my own business was a killer. I could never plan too far ahead, because I never knew when I would hit a dry spell. It happened often enough to keep me off balance. Sometimes I longed for a regular job with a regular paycheck, just like other people.

My family demographics had changed in those nine years. When you have eleven kids, it sometimes feels like you're running a small country. But by '96, most of my kids were gone, one way or another. Six of them were grown and living on their own. Molly and Jill, our two profoundly handicapped children, had passed away—two weeks apart—the previous summer. That left our three youngest—and a wife who felt like she had lost the best job in the world when her girls had died. Both my parents and Gayle's mother were gone as well, and her father had remarried.

It occurred to me that for the first time in decades, there was nothing in particular tying us to Southern California. It was a strange revelation. I started thinking about trees.

Craig had mentioned his future staffing needs, but I didn't know if he was fishing. He had dangled some bait, but he'd been pretty coy. "Under the right set of circumstances," I said, "I might be persuaded to come and work for you in Virginia."

"Really?" He sounded pleased. "You'd be perfect for the job. I'd love to have you join our team. But could you really leave Power Graphics?"

"I'm having my second mediocre year in a row," I said, truthfully. "My kids are mostly gone, my parents are gone, my wife has been wandering around like a lost lamb ever since we lost Jill and Molly. The only thing I'd miss about California is my church. So yes, I might."

He asked me what my net earnings had been last year. I told him. He said that would be fine.

I told Gayle what I'd done. "Are there trees?" she asked.

"Lots of 'em."

"Sounds good to me. Let's go."

Gayle and I, as usual, were on the same wavelength. You don't adopt nine kids without an overly developed sense of adventure. "Maybe we should see if he was sincere about his offer first. All he said was, 'Fine.'"

The next morning Craig confirmed our conversation—in writing. He listed my title as VP of Marketing and threw in some pluses, including stock grants representing one percent of the company's total shares, vesting over three years. It was exactly the same deal Joe Page had. Gayle had already called information for the number of a realtor in Charlottesville.

❧

LESS THAN A WEEK passed before Craig asked Joe and me to fly with him up to San Jose to attend a trade show displaying the latest Web technologies. Rex, still living in San Francisco, was going to meet us there. I got to LAX in plenty of time, went to the gate, and found Joe. We waited for Craig to arrive, but he didn't show. They called our flight. Still no Craig. Last call, but no boss in sight. Finally, at the last possible moment, Craig came strolling up to the gate and got on board.

"Cutting it a little close, aren't you?" I asked.

He smiled. "I've flown all over the world, traveled in over 120 countries, been in scores of airports, and caught thousands of flights. In all that time, I've only missed one."

There was a pregnant pause before he spoke again. "That one crashed."

"Crashed! You've gotta be kidding."

As we flew on to San Jose, he told me the story. "I went to Africa one summer during college. One night at Victoria Falls, in what was then

Rhodesia, I was watching the moon create swirling rainbows at the base of the falls with a girl I'd met. I was bitten by a Malaria-carrying Tste-tste fly. Two weeks later, I found myself wracked with fever, doubled over in pain.

"Unfortunately, I was now in one of the most primitive and remote places on earth, Ghondor, Ethiopia, chasing down rumors about the twelfth tribe of Israel. They claimed to have the Ark of the Covenant there. Anyway, the place was so inaccessible, the only way in or out was aboard a flying relic, a DC-3. One would occasionally land in a mountain pasture if the weather was good. It was raining. So there I lay—dying."

I hadn't heard any of this before. I was riveted.

"They finally got me out. I'd lost thirty pounds. I looked so emaciated that when I reached Cairo, a ticketing agent took one look at me and changed my flight. She booked me directly back home."

"So what happened?"

"My original flight had me returning on TWA from Tel Aviv via Rome. That flight...." Craig paused to regain his composure, "That plane was the first victim of aviation terrorists. It exploded over the Aegean Sea. All seventy-seven aboard perished. Don't know why my life was spared, but I decided to make it count. I was—am—living on borrowed time."

Tste-tste flies and terrorists. The stuff of destiny. Most people, most Americans at least, would have brushed it off as a remarkable coincidence, a lucky break. Craig Winn saw the Romans 8:28 implications, "All things work together for good...." and let it shape his perspective from that day forward.

I didn't really mind flying, but suddenly I felt better having Craig Winn in the same airplane.

৩৯০৫

A FEW WEEKS later, Joe Page and I again found ourselves together in an airplane, this time headed for Washington, D.C. We were on our way to Charlottesville, a two-hour drive south from Dulles. Craig was already there. He wanted us to get a feel for the place.

Page was on the payroll. I had agreed to start in August; it would take me that long to tidy up my affairs.

Joe and I bummed around all day Saturday in our rental car. At one point, a real estate sign led us to a vacant lot on a road called "21-Curves." I was stunned with the beauty of the place. Looking up at heaven from this clearing in the midst of a forest of tall hardwoods was like being in a cathedral.

We met Craig for lunch at Glenmore Country Club, where he was buying an interim house while his dream home was being built on his new farm on the other side of town. He gave us his take on navigation in C'Ville: "All roads have four names and go in a circle." I suppose that would apply to any town with a layout based on eighteenth-century wagon ruts that had been strung together and paved over.

We did a little off-roading in our rented Dodge out at Craig's new spread. It was a huge parcel of rolling hills overgrown with waist-high tangles and hedges gone wild. There was barbed wire everywhere. Much of this had been productive farmland a hundred years ago. But now, the neglect was palpable. You *had* to be a visionary to see the possibilities in the place. All I saw was work, and lots of it.

The agent my wife had called found us a perfect home. It was like *déjà vu.* It had the same cathedral-like feel as the lot Joe and I had visited. I called Gayle. "Get yourself a plane ticket. I've found the perfect house...."

Her answer blew me away. "I trust you. If you like it, buy it." Buying a house for a woman without her seeing it is not an exercise for the faint of heart. But that's exactly what I did. I would not know until August whether I had chosen well or not.

I sold my business to Gloria, put my house on the market, and took my first vacation in years—driving across the country in my wife's Continental with my three remaining kids in the back seat. It was something I had always wanted to do. I'll never do it again—at least not with three kids in the back.

As we pulled up the drive, I could see the expression on my wife's face changing from relief to delight to excitement. Yes! She loved the house, loved the neighborhood (she couldn't see our neighbors), loved the sound of late-summer cicadas in the trees—and loved me.

Of course, there wasn't enough cupboard space.

If God is for us, who can be against us?—Paul

LIFE IN THE ATTIC

Nothing seemed to rattle or shake, so they must have done a pretty good job putting the Jeep back together, Joe mused as he cruised south on US 29. It was the last leg of his ten-hour drive from Michigan to Virginia.

The Grand Cherokee had not betrayed any evidence of having been thrashed and rebuilt. Joe smiled as he mentally replayed taking the Jeep off-roading the first day he owned it, driving it so aggressively he had broken both axles—then having it rebuilt, only to roll it the following week. He laughed out loud when he pictured the poor service manager trying to find a gentle way to inform him that the damage would not be covered under the warranty.

Joe had spent the Fourth of July holiday with his family, having flown home to Michigan from California. But now, with all of his worldly possessions in the car, he was arriving in Charlottesville in the middle of the night. He asked himself the logical question, "Now what?" Having no place to go, he caught a few hours sleep in the car.

The next day, Joe picked Craig up at a local hotel. He had arrived earlier the same evening. The hotel, strangely enough, was hosting a *Star Trek* convention that day. Funny—we too were off to boldly go where no one had gone before. Joe wanted to have a couple of Klingons "arrest" Craig, just for giggles, but he didn't know the boss well enough yet to risk yanking his chain.

Being Joe, he was about to pull the trigger anyway when he was distracted by the spitting image of Scotty, Chief Engineer of the Starship Enterprise. But the illusion was broken when the portly fellow turned to his family and said, "Cm'own ya'll—we gonna miss all da fun." Must have been from southern Scotland. Welcome to Virginia, Joe.

Unlike Joe, Craig *did* have a place to hang. Craig closed escrow on his new home at Glenmore. Then he and Joe paid a visit to the local WalMart *(No hard feelings, right?)*. They acquired a couple of sleeping bags, pillows, and some towels, and moved into their temporary bachelor quarters. No furniture, no family, no food yet, but hey, it was home. The two camped out on the floor.

Katharine loved the idea of becoming a country girl, so long as Craig built her a white-columned classic southern manor house, surrounded by acres of picturesque rolling countryside. He had already sketched the layout. He combined the footprint of Mt. Vernon, Washington's home, with the architectural style of Monticello, Jefferson's Palladian manor. Craig called his final design a "George Jefferson."

While it may sound opulent, the math worked out quite nicely. Craig and Katharine were able to sell their California homes at prices well above what it would take to build Tara. Things were cheaper in paradise.

Building his home, however, would take time. Craig was looking at a year of backbreaking weekend labor just clearing the brambles, barbed wire, and poison ivy. He would soon become very familiar with his John Deere tractor and Husquavarna chain saw. Doing the work himself was his way of fitting in, of becoming one with the land and community.

He had found a home for the company, too. The building, which actually *looked* like a home, was on the east side of town, in an area known as Pantops (Jeffersonized latin meaning "panoramic views").

None of us knew a soul in C'ville prior to our modest invasion, so Craig wanted to have a few contacts established before we—all five of us—descended upon the place. On earlier trips to Charlottesville, he had visited everybody who had anything to do with the Internet.

One of the companies he'd visited, Commonwealth Clinical Systems, operated its own ISP and had some vacant space above their offices. They quoted us a buck a square foot, gross, with additional benefits like free furniture, free janitorial service, the services of their receptionist, free Internet access, and free consultation with their network administrator. They even let us put our sign, small as it was, on the building.

At about a thousand square feet, the two rooms were palatial compared to the setup Joe, Craig, and I had endured in California. Yet being on the top floor didn't mean it rated the title "penthouse." It was more like the attic.

Lad McCaile, our new database specialist, looked up at the company's Webmaster. Joe was standing on his cheap pressed-board desk trying to gain access to the crawlspace above the attic. Lad said, "I'll go look for a ladder." His gentle Irish brogue sounded a bit out of place in rural Virginia.

He and Joe were on a quest, which was degenerating quickly into a vendetta. The building had been used by more than a few former tenants, each of whom had installed their own network wiring. The collection of cables now resembled fettuccini alfredo. Some of the wiring ran down the walls to the servers in the basement; some just lay there adding to the ambience. Some was appropriate for a local area network, and some was actually television cable.

Our internal network was going to be our circulatory system, our veins and arteries. But it was suffering from abnormally high packet losses. Joe knew the wiring was one of the reasons. The boys had come to the grim realization that they were going to have to clean out the crawl space and rewire the whole thing from scratch.

The bad news was the direct result of the good news. The reason all of those wires were there in the first place was that Commonwealth was one of Charlottesville's few Internet service providers. The arrangement gave us a LAN connected directly to the Internet, a nice, cost-effective bonus that most start-ups have to do without. Besides, the rent was cheap. And cheap, in those days, was a very good thing.

August in Virginia is hot and muggy. Ninety degrees outside meant that the crawl space was running a hundred and ten. Between the heat, the humidity, and the dust, Joe's wire-pulling technique deteriorated as the project progressed. He realized with chagrin that this was what entrepreneurs meant by "getting your hands dirty." As he pulled on one particularly stubborn wire, it snagged. When it finally let go, Joe was completely off balance; his foot landed between the rafters and sank deep into the insulation, which lay directly atop the drywall ceiling. Joe quickly shifted his weight to keep from falling, and, hearing no comment from Lad in the room below, congratulated himself on a narrow escape. It was only after Joe descended the ladder that he saw the result.

"Quite a hole you put in the ceiling," Lad said.

"Why didn't you say something?"

"No point. Your foot had already come and gone," McCaile answered with exasperating logic.

"Great. We've hired Mr. Spock."

That had been the idea. Early on, Craig and Joe had concluded they were going to need a database expert to work on the store's back end— the business aspects—while Joe developed the front end—the customer interface.

The solution to that search had come as the result of another, less successful one—the search for commercial software that could be used to run Value America's online store. Even before we arrived in Charlottesville, we recognized that our virtual store was going to be as dependent upon its database as regular stores were on their shelves. We knew the best databases were made by Oracle. So that seemed like a pretty good place to look for a database administrator.

Craig called them and asked for the name of their Mid-Atlantic sales rep. The man responsible for the east was named South—Kyle South. Kyle took a liking to Craig and an even bigger liking to our plan for the store of the future. He claimed that the best DBA in Virginia was a fellow working at General Electric's automation division located just north of Charlottesville, an Irish immigrant named Lad McCaile.

Craig interviewed Lad and sent him our business plan. He was hooked. They agreed on a compensation and equity package identical to the one Joe Page, Bill Hunt, and I had been offered. Craig and Rex were on the books for a lot more of the company's still-worthless stock, but while responsible for meeting the young company's burgeoning payroll, they were drawing no salary of their own. Ah, the joys of capitalism.

Lad McCaile turned out to be a good fit for Joe Page. Joe was something of a cyber-cowboy—enthusiastically charging ahead into the unknown, acting spontaneously on his blinding flashes of intuition, even when it meant chasing his train of thought into the wee hours of the night. Keyboard on lap and shoeless feet on desk, Joe was something to behold. Lad had a more "professional" demeanor. He was quieter, more businesslike and organized, more CPA than circus performer. His feet never left the floor. He was tall and thin, with curly hair and a ready grin. When I was introduced to him and to what he did, the image of a vaude-villian horse costume, with Joe Page occupying the front end and Lad McCaile taking care of business in the back end, involuntarily popped into my mind. It was a terrifying picture; they were Dean Martin and Jerry Lewis, Mr. Spock and Scotty.

ᴄᴏ:ᴏᴄ

THERE WAS A RUMOR that Netscape was building a merchant software solution, so Craig, Joe, and Rex made their way to the Silicon Valley. The whole idea of selling things on the Web was so new, it seemed logical that the company making the most successful browser might also have the best enabling software.

Their initial discussions with Netscape's engineers quickly dissipated any hopes they had of a quick, painless solution. As they set about trying to explain how their product worked, our team got the distinct impression they were clueless. They knew nothing about logistics, distribution, credit card processing, the integration of financial applications, or EDI. They knew even less about the product return process, what would moti-vate a consumer to buy, or what consumer brands needed or wanted.

In preparation for the meeting, Craig had analyzed Netscape's appli-cation. For his own edification, he had drawn up a diagram, a flow chart, based on his observations. In engineering parlance, it showed how each of the components, servers, databases, and applications would have to inter-act to support the requirements of an online store. Simply said, it ex-plained how the darn thing should have worked. But now, since Netscape's engineers were having so much trouble explaining how their application supported online commerce, Craig found himself rummaging around in the Black Hole until he found his flow chart. He placed it before them.

"This is *our* perception of what your software needs to do," he said. "Did we get all of the components and applications in the right place? Are their interrelationships correct?"

They looked. They studied. They conferred. They smiled. "Well, ahh, yes! As a matter of fact, this is...." You've never seen a room full of engineers move so fast. "Could we make a copy?" they questioned as they stampeded out to the Xerox machine.

Craig and Joe just looked at each other. Netscape wasn't the answer. Yet ironically, as the leader of this brave new world, Netscape had the *chutzpah* to charge nearly $300,000 for their software. This was well beyond our meager means. But we figured that since there were so few players in e-commerce, the price might be negotiable. Sadly, it appeared that even if Netscape *gave* us their software, it would have no value. Then, sure enough, even as we said, "Thanks, but no thanks," Netscape sent our fledgling company two complete sets—free. Both cases sat in a closet, unopened.

While still in the Silicon Valley, they tried another company offering online commerce software, called BroadVision. It was pretty much the same story. They had produced a great one-to-one marketing tool, but their commerce systems were inadequate and inflexible.

Next, with their sons in tow, Rex and Craig flew off to Boston to visit a company called Open Market, yet another firm attempting to play in this new field. Their software was slightly better than Netscape's, but it too was flawed. They wanted a million bucks for it, even though the transactional engine was not all that well developed.

Open Market had built a solution for existing retailers and large brands. It was designed to work with their existing legacy systems. Thus there were no financial applications, inventory management tools, EDI links, or credit processing modules. They assumed that their target audience, those already selling products in the real world, would not need to replicate these tools in order to venture into the virtual world. Value America, of course, had no legacy systems, no distribution capability, no financial applications, no *nothing*. We needed everything from soup to nuts.

Ironically, three years later, the founder of Open Market would come to us when he needed a robust e-commerce engine. His new company, I-Belong, in partnership with a leading financial institution, would trust the solution we eventually built even more than their own. But not today.

On this day, Craig was coming to the conclusion that this was going to be a long, hard road. He had visited the big three of e-commerce and had yet to meet a single person who had any retail experience. If there were no tools we could buy, we would have to build our own. Craig recognized that everything he knew about sales, marketing, retail, manufacturing, inventory, and distribution was going to be needed to get our little team into the market with our own software solution. But even with his natural entrepreneurial optimism fully engaged, this was going to be the biggest challenge of his life.

It's one thing to build a company from birth to prosperity. It's altogether something else to do so as a pioneer, in a new industry, without any tools. Craig knew the odds. Less than one firm in ten survives to celebrate its fifth birthday. Fewer than one in a thousand ever manages to achieve $20 million in annual revenues—the level most consider mid-sized. Only one in a million ever grows to become what is considered large by corporate standards (though still insignificant by retail standards), with revenues of $100 million and 500 or more employees.

He also knew that the rare and fortunate firm that grew that large took twenty years or more to reach the Promised Land. More importantly, he knew Value America would have to reach this plateau within a year of our advertised launch, and be ten times larger a few years later, if we hoped to survive as a retailer. And now he knew we would have to do it without any help. We would literally have to build the tools before we could build the store. The realization was sobering, but we were too far along to turn back now.

◈

RETURNING FROM BOSTON empty handed was devastating. But Craig hid this grim reality from us. He simply set about the task of working with Joe and Lad to choose an operating system. Should it be NT or Unix? That would determine the platform. A database had to be engaged. What EDI package should we integrate? Who would process the credit cards? What financial tools would be the easiest to adapt to the virtual world? And those were the easy decisions; at least we had choices. The hard part would be creating the incredibly robust and dynamic consumer front end from scratch. But even that, we knew, would be easier than building a proprietary back end for the inventory-less retail revolution.

As we pondered these questions we asked, "What about Oracle?" They held promise. Rumor had it that the world's second largest software company was working on their own application engine. Oracle, we all agreed, was king of databases, and our interactive structure was going to necessitate a healthy database integration. This could be a perfect fit.

The three intrepid Value Americans returned to Silicon Valley. As they approached Oracle headquarters, they got an eyeful of the kind of opulence that unrestrained success could bring. Glittering round "crystal towers" were punctuated by fountains and water works. The software business had been good to these guys.

Our team met senior Oracle executives in their central tower. Craig delivered the pitch, delineating what we were planning to accomplish. Oracle came back with a proposal that would have been a very good deal —for them.

They said, in effect, "Teach us what you know about the retail business, brands, marketing, sales, inventory management, and distribution. Explain how they interrelate, and we'll *give* you an operating system."

It was the devil's own bargain. The price was right, to be sure. But the cost was far too high. What they were saying was that Winn's unique qualifications were a gold mine whose riches they might tap. He understood how brands think, because he had been there. He understood how retailers acted, because he had done that. More importantly, he knew how they worked together, because he had been a manufacturer's rep, an expert in uniting the two disparate worlds. No one had entered the virtual world with those credentials. No one ever would.

If Oracle had built an operating system based on Craig's business endeavors, he would have lost much of the advantage his life's experiences had gained him. With tools ready made, any bozo with the price of admission would be able to follow in our footsteps. Thanks, but no thanks.

ക്കൈ

MURRY SILVERSTEIN THOUGHT he'd struck it rich. His little Atlanta-based coupon and direct-mail advertising company had never done all that much business, but now there was this lawyer from California on the phone who wanted to pay him thousands of dollars, not for his services, but for his name. Not Murry Silverstein. Value America.

Rex Scatena was still stewing over Sid Golden's shortcomings. Internet Connect's inept CEO had dropped the ball in securing the Value America trademark. And then, to add insult to injury, Rex had discovered that the company couldn't even incorporate under that name in California because there was a wrecker service, a tow-truck company, already registered with the same name. So Value America—the Internet store—was incorporated under the laws of the great state of Nevada instead.

Rex's trademark search looked pretty clean. There were no retail businesses using our name or anything like it. Nor were there any Internet, technology, or media companies using Value America. Rex breathed a sigh of relief. We were way down the line with this and didn't want to think about having to start over with a new name.

Rex submitted the necessary applications for Internet and retail store usage. But sure enough, a guy working out of his apartment who made coupons for pizza parlors, hair salons, and health clubs was using our name, and he objected. Rex tried to reason with the trademark office that we were not remotely in the same business. "Look. There are Ritz Crackers and Ritz hotels, and nobody is likely to confuse the two...." His wit fell on deaf ears. They wanted a sign-off from Mr. Coupon before they would give us a green light.

Rex called Mr. Silverstein and said, "We would like to purchase your permission to allow us to use Value America for a non-conflicting online business, sir. What do you think?"

Murry jumped at the bait. "Of course, as long as the money is right."

They negotiated a deal for $5,000. And then Rex asked him, "Mr. Silverstein, how much would it be if we just bought the name from you outright and then licensed *you* to use it?"

"Oh, boy," he stammered. "That would be a lot more." *Reach for the stars,* Murry told himself. "How about another $10,000? A total of $15,000." Murry held his breath and crossed his fingers.

"Fine," Rex said. "We'll send you the $5,000 now with some paperwork to sign. We're too strapped for cash to complete the transaction now, but if things turn out good for us, I'll call you back."

There's something comforting about knowing who you are. But Value America had to wait until our first private investment funds came in to say we actually owned our own name.

◈

AUGUST 15, 1996. The first day of the rest of my life, as the saying goes. Here I was, officially employed as Value America's VP of Marketing and Creative Director. For the first time in years I was no longer an outside consultant. I was now part of a team, small though it was—just Craig, Rex, Joe, Bill, Lad, and me.

My first job was to create the presentations that would communicate the merits of our brands' products. It was an entirely new kind of stress. I felt a little like a field-goal kicker. I was only a small part of the team, but everybody from the head coach to the water boy was relying on me to do my job. As I saw it on that first day, there were three problems. Or rather, challenges.

First, there was no website yet. There was no way to put my work into circulation on the Internet, at least not in a format we were willing to show the world. Joe was working on it, but he wasn't ready yet.

Second, the pressure to produce was enormous. The only income generated so far had come from selling Product Presentations. The second half of the fee wasn't paid until they were done.

Third, nobody had ever done one of these. Forget the Lights of America demos; there would be no made-to-order marketing materials, no filing cabinet full of outstanding photos, no Craig Winn looking over my shoulder co-authoring them. I was going to have to dig for every scrap of information, for every graphic resource. Nothing was going to be handed to me on a silver platter. I would have to invent the methods, procedures, and style.

To my mind, this kind of design work was about fifty percent psychology, knowing the audience; forty-five percent craftsmanship, knowing how to use graphic and communication tools; and five percent inspiration. The psychological part had to be figured out first. In order to get into our shoppers' heads, we would have to know who they were.

Our audience, at least in the beginning, was expected to be very affluent, college educated, two-thirds male, and, of course, computer literate. That was the demographic profile of the typical Web user at the time. But it wouldn't stay that way, and we all knew it.

Over time, relative affluence would be less characteristic of our typical shopper. Computers with Web access would become more affordable, eventually becoming as ubiquitous as the telephone or television. I likened modems to VCRs a few years before. At first, they had been mysterious, complicated, and expensive. Now everybody had one and used it, even though half of 'em constantly flashed 12:00, 12:00, 12:00....

Women, I knew, would overtake men as users of Web services, particularly online shopping. This would happen, I surmised, when the computer became less self-important and became a mere tool, important for where it could take you. It was like photography. Men wanted the latest 35mm Nikon autofocus SLR camera with 6-segment 3D matrix metering, five-zone AF detection, a 35 to 70mm f/2.8 aspherical Nikkor zoom lens, and all the bells and whistles. Women just wanted the pictures.

Oddly enough, as the technology became more sophisticated, computers would actually become simpler to operate. That too would affect demographics. The bottom line was that our typical shopper was going to be, in the long run, a pretty ordinary person—with one important distinction. I believed that we would always be dealing with intelligent people. After all, they were going to be smart enough to shop at Value America.

Most writing for general consumer audiences is "dumbed down," with vocabulary and concepts geared to the average sixth grader. But we decided that our shoppers deserved better. We would give them credit for having the intelligence, and the desire, to make good choices when provided with reliable and pertinent information. We would, in short, treat them with respect. How's that for a revolutionary idea?

✎❦✎

THE MASCO CONTRACTS had started to come in before I got to Charlottesville. I was going to need help if we were to crank out their presentations in a timely fashion—writers, graphic designers, and data-entry specialists. I could do each thing, but not nearly fast enough to keep up with the demand.

Many of the early hires proved to be wonderful, as staff and as people. Rick Major was a young African American looking for his first job. He was right out of art school and knew Photoshop, the principal software tool for our graphic artists, backward and forward. Stocky of build and quiet of demeanor, Rick was a true gentleman, but, we found initially, a little distrustful of us white folks. That was pretty funny to me: I had *children* of every conceivable color.

Craig liked hiring minorities too. Gender made no difference, nor did faith, color, or orientation. If a qualified black Jewish lesbian had applied, she'd have been on the team. Craig even forged Rick's name on his stock option grants just to make sure he'd get his fair share, as Rick was reluctant to sign the paperwork. Rick was worth the risk.

Isaac Saltzberg started early in '97. A writer with incredible talent, he was a journalist, a novelist, a sometime tennis pro, and a full-time hustler. Isaac was Jewish, from a well-educated family of academics and doctors. He was a doctoral candidate himself when we found him, a Jefferson Fellow, just a chapter or two shy of completing his dissertation on the Civil Rights movement in the American South.

Mary Carlson had a silky-smooth writing style that was often under-utilized on our nuts-and-bolts work—seven product presentations for Masco's Peerless Faucets, for example. With flaming red hair and a personality to match, Mary had a Ph.D. in southern literature; turned out she was one of the foremost authorities on author William Faulkner. Laudy!

Pete Gudaitis was the curmudgeon of the group. He was hired as a graphics specialist but turned out to be a great utility infielder. Trained as a biochemist, Pete had a good handle on technology. We found out almost by accident that he could write. *Boy*, could he write. Pete could take an arcane technical subject and make it crystal clear.

In retrospect, it's amazing how many of the core group that started in the Attic stayed with the company for the duration. But the line separating those who prevailed from those who failed was neither education nor experience. It was simply a matter of attitude, of corporate character. Those who built Value America read the business plan. They understood our mission and were committed to our collective cause. They routinely made sacrifices for the greater good.

During these magical days, sales reps came hoping to sell us their wares, only to change their minds and sell us *themselves* instead. The Attic was literally buzzing with energy. The first of these was Kyle South, the sales rep from Oracle who had introduced us to Lad McCaile when we were still in California. Kyle was so impressed with the company, he left Oracle to become our first technology merchandiser.

Ken Erickson stumbled across Value America's site—actually just an early prototype—while surfing the Web and thought it looked promising. It reminded him a lot of Costco, a Price Club clone, where he had been one of the original employees. Ken now worked for Fabricant, the world's largest jewelry manufacturer. He called, set an appointment, and was on the next flight to Virginia.

Ken arrived, delivered his pitch, and was on his way back to the airport when it hit him. These guys were sitting on a gold mine. They had figured it out. He stopped his car, pulled over, and called Craig. "You know?" he said, "I think I sold you the wrong thing. I should have been selling myself. Let me build your jewelry department. I'll get every brand to participate. I'll even get my wife to build your sporting goods area...."

"Okay, Ken. Sounds good to me. We can't pay you much, but we can give you stock options."

৩৯৫৫

IBM WAS BIG, but they had an awfully small vocabulary. The only word they seemed to have mastered was "No." We had called everybody at Big Blue and had run into more brick walls than Evel Knievel. "No," they weren't interested. "No" to the Internet. "No," we don't pay for presentations. "No, No, No." But finally they condescended to send out a sales rep. Monica Link took one look and decided we had potential.

We regarded that as a compliment, because Monica was bright, well educated, and articulate (you worried when idiots liked your ideas). She was an African-American woman in her twenties. I wouldn't presume to make value judgments about a woman's appearance, but suffice it to say that half the guys in the office risked neck injuries the first time she walked into the place. Joe even gave her a personal tour.

Her first reaction was, "I'll find a way to get IBM to support Value America." But, like Ken Erickson, her tune had changed even before she left Charlottesville. "I'd rather be a part of this—hire me as your technology merchandiser, and *then* I'll find a way to lure IBM." The only problem was, we already had a technology merchandiser, Kyle South. The fact that Kyle wasn't having much success didn't change the fact that he was already here. Winn thought that a division of labor might help focus Kyle, so he hired Monica Link to handle business technology while Kyle concentrated on the consumer side of things. There was plenty to go around.

 споэ

CRAIG WAS ABOUT ready to call it a day. It was nearly eight o'clock. Time flies when you're wearing six hats. As he reached for his briefcase, he noticed that his wastebasket had reached critical mass. As he started for the dumpster, the phone rang.

"Value America," he answered.

"Bill Hunt, please," the voice said.

"I'm sorry, he's gone for the day. Can I help?"

"Oh, shoot!" the caller said. "I forgot about the time difference. It must be eight o'clock there. You're working late, aren't you?"

"Yeah, I guess," Craig laughed. "Just doing a little janitorial work."

"Well, anyway, this is Brad Reeves, from Amana. Bill and I have been talking. I had some questions about the company's presentations."

"Hi, Brad. My name's Craig. I know a little about them."

"Well, okay," Brad said, still thinking he was talking to the janitor. "Here's what I don't understand...."

Craig sat back down and opened the Amana file on his computer. It included a copy of the company's standard marketing literature, plus a customized Product Presentation Agreement for Amana.

"What do you mean by 'recommend company' in your presentations?"

"It means Value America will endorse Amana, Brad. We'll inform our customers that we've done our research and have found that Amana makes superior appliances."

"Okay. I understand. Now can you tell me why Bill recommended doing an important category like Microwaves with a Basic presentation?"

"I'm sure Bill didn't mean to slight your Microwaves. He was just trying to save both of us some money. We'd like to present everything using Multimedia, but it's expensive. We're too small to ask big companies like yours to comply with *our* wishes."

"Your presentations are great. There's nothing else like 'em."

"We agree. For us, serving great brands like Amana is what it's all about. No one goes to a store to buy the store. They go to buy top brands."

"The stuff Bill sent me does a fine job of explaining that. It helped me show my management what you guys are all about. I especially liked your CD-ROM. The 'Good Buy Machine' is a hoot. And your catalogs are first rate, better than ours."

"Did you get our *Frequently Asked Questions?*"

"Yep," Brad said. "They answered my management's concerns. Made me look great, well prepared. I even found your *Vendor Requirements* helpful. It's reassuring to see a retailer so *into* the details, so committed to getting it right, leaving nothing to chance." He looked at the information package Bill had sent him once again. "Amana is coming to Charlottesville next week. We're taking the company jet."

"Great, Brad. I look forward to meeting you."

Smart janitor, he thought. If he's that smart, what are the rest of these folks like? I'd better read through this stuff one more time....

THE FUTURE OF RETAILING

The fastest-growing retail channels are Home Shopping, Factory Outlets, and the Big-Box retailers. Value America's Living Store synergistically combines their many advantages and adds a whole new dimension of consumer education, convenience, support, and value.

Factory Outlets are prevailing because consumers like buying quality, branded products at factory-direct prices. Manufacturers like them because they can control their distribution and avoid abusive retailers. However, the success of outlet malls has come at a price. Brands are forced to be as good at retailing as they are at manufacturing. Selling under their own name, brands must compete with their customers. And sadly, most of the inefficiencies that plague the existing retail environment still exist in outlet stores. Value is more illusion than reality.

Home Shopping has eclipsed all other forms of retail, with sales exceeding $500 billion. Product information is more prevalent, and direct shopping is more convenient. Unfortunately, production and mailing costs are high. As a result, many sell memorabilia, cosmetics, jewelry, and apparel, where they can charge higher margins and offset their inflated costs. Home Shopping is not interactive. Consumers can only buy what is being presented when they tune into their channels or open their catalogs.

Big-Box Retailers, or Category Killers, are derivatives of the original warehouse club concept. Their single-category focus makes them less convenient, and they seldom provide any effective sales support. Their concentrated volume on a specific industry has increased their tendency to abuse suppliers.

Value America synergistically blends the advantages that have caused each of these distribution channels to flourish. And we provide pragmatic solutions to the problems that make each less than ideal. It is little wonder leading suppliers are joining Value America to capitalize on the future of retailing.

INCREASING SALES WHILE DIMINISHING COSTS

Value America is more than just a new customer in the world's most explosive distribution channel. We create incremental sales. We effectively present the merits, features, and value of your products to the consumer.... Just imagine how much more you will sell when everyone appreciates why your products are better, and can buy them affordably, without ever leaving their homes or offices.

Remarkably, Value America's powerful operating systems and efficient distribution mean you will earn more on these incremental sales. Our store does not require expensive color packaging, retail point-of-purchase displays, showroom samples, slotting allowances, or in-store service. Retail markdowns to clear slow-moving inventory are a thing of the past. We never ask for guaranteed sales, and never return shopworn cartons or discontinued products. Value America creates consumer sales presentations, so advertising expenses can be reduced.

Suppliers never see freight bills when they sell through Value America, because we pay these bills ourselves. Complicated routing guides are eliminated. Automatic labeling machines replace shipping stencils and side-marked cartons. Our informative sales presentations and consumer support systems will even reduce non-defective returns.

The entire ordering process is automated, so our suppliers net more on each sale. Imagine, incremental sales at higher net margins. No wonder leading suppliers trust Value America to increase their sales and profits.

୨୬∘୧ଓ

WHEN BILL PICKED UP the Amana delegation at Charlottesville's airport a few days later, Brad had already put two and two together, and they all had a good laugh at the janitor's expense. Bill and Brad's team hammered out the final details; then they introduced Brad to me.

"Welcome to Value America," I said. "I'm Ken, and I'll be your writer today. May I take your order?"

Brad and I hit it off immediately. I started by explaining the finer points of Value America's presentation philosophy.

"So how do you write a presentation?" he asked.

"We use our Authoring Tool. It's like an electronic production line. Even though the content of each presentation is custom, we follow a framework that's the same for all of 'em. We just fill in the blanks. The system Web-enables the content."

"Fill in the blanks." Brad, having seen what we had done with other brands, was incredulous.

"Yeah," I grinned. "The trick is knowing what to put in the blanks. If you were a consumer and wanted this information, the best place to get it would be directly from the company, right?"

"Right. But before you guys came along, consumers couldn't do that."

"Correct. So when I write these presentations, I conduct in-depth interviews with the brand's most knowledgeable people."

"At Amana, I would be one of them."

"So I've heard. I want to ask you twenty questions about each product group, but I might let our conversation wander if it's taking us to interesting places. I'm almost always surprised; invariably I learn something that, properly explained, gives a product greater appeal. So...you ready?"

Brad was a terrific source of insight and information. We talked for hours about washers and dryers, dishwashers, microwaves, freezers—and their pride and joy, refrigerators. And just as I suspected, their brochure hadn't even *mentioned* Amana's exclusive double-dimpled egg trays.

◈

LOOKING BACK AT LIFE in the Attic, two things immediately come to mind. One, those were great times, exciting, heady, inventive, live-life-to-the-fullest times. Two, let's not do that again.

There's something to be said for living your life with your back against the wall, as long as you believe what you're doing is right. That's how we lived during those first months. The adrenaline flowed. The tension was palpable. It seemed like every person we met was either a skunk or a saint. Everything was black or white, do or die, feast or famine, now or never. It was the best of times. It was terrifying.

Craig and Rex, bless their hearts, concealed a lot of the nasty stuff that went on from those of us who had simpler jobs—no sense in all of us having ulcers. Craig conferred with Rex, worked out the problems, and shielded us from the blood-curdling details, figuring that if the problem brought the company down, we would find out about it soon enough, and if it didn't, we didn't need the distraction. Imminent corporate death was placed on a need-to-know basis.

On the other hand, if they were dancing on the ceiling, it was pretty hard to hide, and the reasons were explained with grins and congratulations. The atmosphere in the Attic was "casual hysteria." The dress code was loose—no, non-existent; anything that covered the crucial body parts was acceptable. Craig's dog, Crystal, roamed freely, always on the lookout for a pat on the head, a kind word, or a surreptitious French fry, not necessarily in that order. Crowded into two big rooms, dialog flowed freely. It was impossible not to be creative in an atmosphere like that.

The building itself lent us its personality. When it rained, water poured in through massive cracks around the double-hung windows, causing havoc and threatening to short out the power. At the first sign of showers, those of us along the outside walls would cover our computers with plastic trash bags—and go back to work. The power went out at the drop of a hat, so often that Commonwealth, our host, had installed a huge generator in a garage out back that sounded like a 747 taking off. The carpeting was blood red, giving the place a sense of passion or making it hideously ugly, depending upon your point of view. The furniture added to the ambience. It was worth every penny we had paid for it—nothing. We jammed our desks so close together, one held the other up. It was like living in an anthill.

Our technology was as cheap as possible, with predictable results. We were all daisy-chained together with a temperamental 10-base-t Ethernet network. If Rick Major happened to roll back his chair too far, he'd dislodge a cable and the whole network would come crashing down.

In the tech room, our only server was protected with an uninterruptible power supply, or UPS—one we had managed to obtain for free from a vendor. It protected the server from voltage spikes and kept it going during power outages, but it had a downside. An alarm sounded whenever the voltage spiked. It was a shrill, screeching, *pay-attention-to-me* sound. And it stayed on until the unit was reset.

Unfortunately, the reset button was also the power switch. So you either put up with the racket or shut down the computer, which defeated the whole point of having a UPS. Joe shoved the offending device into a small filing cabinet and stuffed an old sweatshirt around it to muffle the sound, reducing it to a faint but persistent buzz. Whenever visitors asked about the annoying sound, he'd open the drawer, pull out the sweatshirt, and give them an earful. I think Joe missed the Attic when we finally moved out.

As we staffed up, we were in constant danger of outrunning our resources. It was as if we were in a big, wooden roller coaster, and our train was struggling to reach the top of the first hill. We knew we were dangerously overloaded, but we felt sure that if we could just reach that first peak, we'd be in for one hell of a ride.

A little one shall become a thousand, and a small one a strong nation—Isaiah

A BRAVE NEW WORLD

*F*ace chapped and body bruised, Dan Lucier had just returned from a trek through the Himalayas. If it was dangerous, he loved it. If Dan wasn't kayaking on a Class 5 rapid in the Andes or scaling the granite face of El Capitan in Yosemite, you'd find him in a dark corner of Commonwealth's server room. He'd be the one in the well-worn hiking boots, old blue jeans, and long-sleeve shirt rolled up past his elbows, poring over a white paper on some esoteric network design. Paid by Commonwealth, Dan actually worked for one of their tenants, the guys in the Attic.

"It's now or never," Joe said as he searched Dan's mind. "I've always been a UNIX guy, but I'm being pulled by the dark side of the force. Tell me again why we should build this thing on NT."

Dan was a genius when it came to networks, servers, firewalls, and hosting facilities. Most techs fixate on a single operating system or platform; they're either carnivores or herbivores. But Dan was omnivorous. "Faster and cheaper," was all he said.

Joe let out a sigh. "Thanks, but I was looking for a bit more substance."

Dan leaned back in his chair and plunked his well-traveled hiking boots onto his desk. "See all those servers over there?" he said, pointing to a fifty-foot row of sleek, black rack systems. "There's enough horsepower there to run ten Commonwealths. Do you know how much that speed and capacity would *cost* if we were running RISC machines?"

"Yeah," Joe countered, "but we could run UNIX on Intel boxes. I know there aren't a lot of applications on those platforms, but heck, I helped write some of the code for early versions of Intel/UNIX."

"It's inefficient, Joe. It takes constant optimization and tweaking. NT does most of that for you; it makes it a heck of a lot easier to monitor and analyze stuff, especially at lower volumes." He thought for a moment. "I know you don't have any usage data yet, but what about projections? Did Winn tell you what to expect?"

Joe smiled. "Oh, yeah. I've got it all: store traffic, length of visit, media demands, number of products, orders, even average order size. Craig's got it all broken down by quarter, five years out. I brought a copy of our business plan so you'd see what Lad and I are up against. Look at his multimedia requirements," Joe said as he opened to the section for Dan.

MERCHANDISING TIMELINE

A chart projecting our five-year merchandising plan follows. We will begin modestly, encouraging three suppliers in each of three divisions within three industries to sponsor an average of four category presentations. This will require the production of 100 multimedia demonstrations in 1997. By year five, we will be selling products in fifteen industries, with twelve divisions each. We anticipate 100 suppliers per industry, each sponsoring ten category presentations and offering 100 products.

Yr	Industry	Divisions	Categories	Demos	Total	Products	Total	Factories
97	3	3	3	4	100	15	1,500	25
98	6	4	3	7	525	80	5,250	75
99	7	5	4	8	1,200	175	12,000	150
00	8	6	5	9	2,250	300	22,500	250
01	9	7	6	10	3,500	425	35,000	350

Dan took a little time to absorb the ramifications of the chart. "That doesn't sound too ambitious to me," he said at last. "If I'm reading this right, he's only figuring on bringing in 250 factories between now and the end of '99. He thinks you're going to sell about 1,800 of your multimedia demos in that time frame. That seems manageable, even if they *are* memory and bandwidth hogs. Let's see, 12,000 products in '99. Entering and maintaining that should be easy for any platform. Actually, the plan looks pretty sound." Dan looked up at Joe. "I thought Winn was a salesman."

Joe laughed. "Craig? He's scary. Plans everything. You can't tell him anything he doesn't remember. If I tell him we can't do something, he asks why. By the time I finish explaining the technical limitations, he's found a way to turn my answer into a solution. Pushes the limits on everything. These presentations he's talking about here are big-time important. You want to see the scars on my back from the last time I suggested we scale them back? Here, see for yourself..." Joe said, pulling up his shirt.

"Please, no, that's alright," Dan choked out. He read on instead. "Category Presentations play an important role initially. They represent the store: without them we have nothing to sell; with them we are the world's most exciting retailer. The margins from these presentations will fund our initial development. If we can automate their production, margins should exceed eighty percent...."

Lad McCaile poked his head around the server room door. "I heard you guys were hiding down here."

"I was about to get Dan's opinion on our system requirements. He was going to tell us why we don't need UNIX."

Lad grinned at Dan, pointing to the business plan in his lap. "Just so you know, everyone who reads that thing ends up working for him. It's like a curse. Don't say you weren't warned."

"One step at a time," Dan said. He cleared his throat and read on.

"Visits and transactions...." Lad looked over Joe's shoulder as the three shared two copies of the plan. Dan scanned the document, summarizing. "Okay, he's using the Nielsen numbers—fifty million people using the Internet as of the end of '96. 'An additional two million get connected each month.'"

Lad theorized, "He's figuring that if we actually do everything he's asked for, we could be one of the Web's hottest sites."

"Yeah," Joe interjected, "but that's one humongous *if.*"

"First things first. NT or UNIX?" McCaile was focused.

"Hang on a minute, Lad. It says here, 'If one percent of those using the Web visit each month in '98, the sales estimates in the forecast would need to be increased by 700 percent.' Apparently he's hanging the big number out there so guys who build networks and hosting facilities, like me, know what's possible—so the systems are ready to handle the load, just in case."

"Look at this bit," Joe said, pointing to the headline. "'Percentage Purchasing Product.' I didn't know any of this stuff before I read this. What he's saying is online selling is really just retail. So even though we don't have any history, we can still forecast using the historical numbers of other retailers. Check this out...."

The home shopping industry is the most similar to online retail. It is comprised of Shopping Networks, Infomercials, and Direct Mail Catalogs. On average, cable home-shopping firms receive orders from 20% of those that view their programs. Well-managed catalog firms with quality mailing lists generate revenue from 10% of their catalog recipients. Considering that visits to Value America will be planned, we should perform better.

With infomercials and home-shopping networks, customers have to endure twenty hours of memorabilia, miracle health-care products, and cheap jewelry presentations before they see something they want to buy. Our demonstrations are better than any catalog or home-shopping presentation, further increasing the likelihood we will exceed industry norms.

Our lower margins will allow us to sell better-quality goods for less than half of the prices charged in catalogs or home-shopping networks, encouraging greater response and revenue. Infomercial margins average 65 to 80%, catalog margins average 50 to 65%, and home-shopping networks average over 50%. Value America's margins will average 15 to 20%. Considering these factors, the forecast underestimates the percentage of visitors who will buy by a substantial degree.

"Interesting," Dan said. "Does he have a chart in there projecting visitation? It would be nice to see how he correlates visits to sales."

"Yeah. Right here."

PROJECTED ACCESS & REVENUE:

Yr	Web Users	% Visit ValAm	#Visit ValAm	% Buy	#Buy ValAm	Aver Buy $	X's Return	Projected Revenue
98	50 M	1.0%	0.5 M	10.0%	50,000	$100	4	$25M
99	75 M	2%	1.5 M	10.0%	150,000	$200	3	$120M
00	100 M	3%	3.0M	10.0%	300,000	$200	3	$240M
01	125 M	4%	5.0 M	10.0%	500,000	$200	4	$500M

Dan stared at the chart and its supporting documentation in disbelief. "Where did you find this guy? He not only gives you the charts five years out, he gives you all of his assumptions. He even tells you where his assumptions are weak and what impact they'll have on his numbers if he's wrong."

"Yeah, yeah," Joe said with a smile. "So, can we do this on NT?"

Dan studied the chart for a minute. "Well, these visitation numbers are fairly high, but nothing the new dual-processor Intel servers running NT can't handle. As for the revenue projections, NT can accommodate a lot more transactional volume than what's projected here. That's certainly true for '98, and probably true for the hundred-plus number he's hanging out there in '99. So yes, I'd say Intel and NT can do the job. Of course," he said raising his eyes, "if you actually do *more* business in '99, you'll be able to afford beefier UNIX/RISC systems, won't you?"

"Not so fast," Lad said. "It's not quite as simple as that. Before you swear NT will work, listen to what he says about the assumptions that underlie these numbers." Lad picked up a copy of the business plan and read aloud. "'We believe annual revenue per product will exceed $5,000. Our projections increase to $10,000 in the second year and to $15,000 per item in year 2000. With product retails averaging $175, we are forecasting sales of just twenty-nine units an item in 1998. This represents only two sales a month, increasing to four units per month in '99. It is possible that initial product sales will exceed $25,000 and escalate to over $50,000 within a few years. This favorable variance would serve to triple our estimates.' Still with me, or is the math getting a little tough for you?" Lad asked, as he lowered the page again.

"Enough background," Joe said.

Dan took a minute to absorb what Lad had read. He looked at another chart or two. He scanned the accompanying assumptions. What he read predicted retail sales commencing in '98 at up to $40 million and growing to as much as $175 million in '99. "I think your guy's a closet math major," he mumbled. "He obviously didn't get his fill of algebra in school. You know what he's doing here? He's taking away any excuse for failure. You're never going to be able to whine, *you didn't warn us.* But I'll tell you what—this is some plan. Can I keep this?"

"Sure," Joe responded. "But just so you know, it gets worse. If you really want to know what we're in for, take a look at the systems requirements." Joe flipped back to the last few pages. "The Transactional Requirements." They reviewed the plan together until they saw the line, "Reconcile All Ordering, Shipment, Invoice, and Payment Records."

"All of this front-end, database-driven stuff is nothing compared to the network of logistics, reporting, and financial systems we'll need to support this plan. However, that's all back-end stuff, so *I* don't have to worry about it." Joe chuckled, glancing at Lad.

"The number of variables we're talking about is significant," Lad added, ignoring Joe's attempt at humor. It was the understatement *du jour.* "I've gone through this stuff with Craig a dozen times. Each time he rattles off a list of the processes we need to track, and explains how they're interrelated. There's a lot more to this than meets the eye."

"As if that weren't enough," Joe interjected, "we have to make the system handle exceptions like backorders, partial shipments, and credits."

Dan was getting it from both sides. Now Lad jumped back in. "Everything has to be attached to an order file, compared, differences reconciled, and then entered into an accounting system. And get this—we have to make the data, most of it anyway, available to the *customer.*"

Joe's turn. "And that's not the end of it. We've got to build an integrated customer-service system too." Dan was starting to get dizzy.

"As you can see," Lad said, sounding undaunted by the challenge, "the list goes on forever." He flipped open the plan again. "Look at this...."

SHIPPING AND COMPLIANCE
    Electronic Order Transmission and Acknowledgment
    Create Electronic Shipment Labels for Printer in Distribution Center
    Create an Electronic Bill of Lading for Shipper
    Fill Rate Calculations, Scheduled and Average Lead Time Reports
    Compliance Standards and Evaluation of Vendor Performance
    Forecasting Tools for Merchants and Inventory Level Notifications

FREIGHT AND DELIVERY
    Member Freight Options, Freight Rate, and Delivery Time Calculation
    Electronic Freight Designator to Vendor & Electronic Notification for Pick-up
    E-Mail Shipment Confirmation and Notification to Member

ACQUISITION SEQUENCE
    Present Testimonial Consumer Reports Ratings and Data
    Confirm Desire to Acquire and Create PO Number

Select Quantity, Color, Size, and Options (Attributes)
Select Freight Carrier and Present Freight Cost Calculations and Alternatives
Enter Special Instructions for Delivery and Present Estimated Delivery Date
Present Home, Office, and Other Address; Confirm Ship-to Address
Automatically Insure Selected Shipments and Waive Signature Requirements
Calculate State Sales Tax and Accumulate Sales Tax by State
Retrieve Member's Credit Card Data from Behind Firewall and Decrypt
Tabulate Appropriate Cost, Freight, and Sales Tax Total
Require Mother's Maiden Name for Selected Orders (>x $ or unique ship-to)
Secure Credit Card Authorization and Attach Number; Notify if Denied
Encrypt Credit Card Data *en route* and Unscramble Data Encrypted by Sender
Electronically Receive Credit Card Reimbursement
Acknowledge Receipt of Funds and Attach Data to Order File
Present Charity Options and Acknowledge Contributions in Member's Name
Thank Member for Purchase

RETURNS
Communicate Procedures and Provide Address and Authorization
Notify Vendor and Get an RGA from Vendor
Arrange Return Pick Up with Carrier, E-Mail Instructions, and Mailing Label
Confirm Delivery with Shipper and Factory
Debit Factory's Accounts Payable and Document Debit
Charge Factory for Return and Outbound Freight
Credit Customer's Card; E-Mail Acknowledgment of Credit to Member

REPORTING
Sales and Profits by Unit, Dollars, Source, Category, Division, and Industry
Sales and Profit by Day, Week, Month, Quarter, Year to Date, Rolling 12 Months
Forecast and Reconciliation with Inventory Management Plan for Vendors
Member by State, Region, Interests, and Demographics
Contact Frequency, Average Transaction, Computer Capability, Connectivity

GENERAL LEDGER
Accounts Payable and Receivable Aging
Financial Modeling and Budgeting, Actual Performance *versus* Budget
Financial Reporting, Balance Sheet, Income Statement....

Dan looked stunned. "This is worse than trying to climb El Capitan in flip-flops. You realize, of course, there's no off-the-shelf application that can do this stuff. Any one of these items could be deadly. This plan could keep an army of developers writing code for years. Now I see why Craig isn't forecasting any revenue from product sales until '98. It's going to take at least that long to build a store that can do half this stuff."

Joe and Lad nodded knowingly. They'd come to the same conclusion.

"Listen guys, if it's just a decision between NT and UNIX you're after, that part's easy. Go with NT. It'll take you twice as long to build this thing using UNIX. That's the good news. The bad news is that if you can't find some existing application to hang your code on, you're as good as dead."

"We know," Joe agreed. "Dan, you love a good challenge, don't you? It doesn't look to me like there's much difference between doing this and climbing straight up El Capitan."

"Yes, there is. El Cap has been climbed before."

৩০৵৩

"HI, JOE. Burning the midnight oil?" Driving home from dinner, Craig had noticed Joe's light was on.

"I think I've found it."

"It? What's *it?*"

"I was surfing the Web, checking out some geekie sites, and I found this. It's called IDCHTX. It's from Microsoft—designed to dynamically generate HTML pages from a database."

"Catchy name. Pages from a database, huh? Think we can use it to automate production?" Craig asked his chief engineer.

"It's a little early to tell, but yeah, maybe. I'm working on it. There's been a rumor going around that Microsoft is trying to write an online retail program, and I think this might be part of it. Hey, go home. It's after ten. I'll let you know tomorrow how this works out."

"Alright, Joe. Don't hang too long."

Right. Joe was known to come in at noon and work until four in the morning if he was on the trail of something. Craig reached the door and turned around. "With this Microsoft thing, does that mean you guys are thinking about building the store on NT?"

"Yeah, that's what we're thinking." Joe explained, "Lucky for us we have an NT network guy downstairs. He's pretty excited about what we're doing. He loves anything on the ragged edge. This afternoon, he helped Lad and me set up an NT server. It took us two hours. I've done the same thing a hundred times with UNIX servers but never in less than two days. NT's fast, and Dan's good."

"So you think we'll be able to snag him?"

"Pretty sure, but not while we're hanging in the Attic. Besides, his guys aren't giving him enough work to keep him awake. We already get most of his time, and we don't even have to pay for it."

"Just so I understand, could you explain why you're giving up on

UNIX? There are some serious budget implications."

"We're not giving up. It's just that NT's better for a start-up. NT's got a GUI interface, point-and-click stuff, and lots of the routine coding steps are automated. Sure, we'll have to reboot our systems more often than we would if we ran UNIX on RISC machines, but at least we'll have a store to reboot. It's like Microsoft's SQL Server; it's not quite as good as Oracle, but it's faster to set up, and it costs next to nothin'."

"Why do they call it 'Sequel Server?' A database isn't a server, and it doesn't sound like it's the sequel to anything."

Joe laughed. Craig didn't often embarrass himself, but this time he had. "It's not 'Sequel,' its 'S-Q-L.' It's an acronym—stands for Standardized Query Language. It's got more than enough horsepower to get our demo store online. Like I said, it's quicker and cheaper. We can always upgrade later."

"Quicker and cheaper are good," Craig smiled. "'Night, Joe."

NOBLESTAR'S OFFICES WERE hidden among the forest of glass and steel office buildings along the western edge of the Washington Beltway. One of their geeks had written a book on the ins and outs of SQL Server. Lad, our Oracle DBA, had called the book's author one day in desperation. During their discussion, Lad had discovered that Joe had been right. Microsoft's IDCHTX had led to a beta product called Merchant Server. NobleStar had been given a beta copy to help evaluate the code. And since we wanted to get our hands on it, we were off to NobleStar.

Joe, Lad, and Craig arrived early. As the sixth-floor elevator door opened, they were greeted by a receptionist. She removed her headset, offered them coffee and soft drinks, and escorted them to a nearby conference room. The receptionist was pretty. The office was *gorgeous*.

Five expensive suits entered the room, each occupied by a NobleStar team member, complete with notepad and coffee. They looked more like investment bankers, Craig reflected, than developers. They began by peppering him with questions. This was natural enough—online selling was so new, there wasn't even a name for it. The term "e-tail" hadn't yet been coined. The boys soon discovered that these folks had no retail experience. The fact that they had been chosen to evaluate retail software was hilarious. The blind were leading the vision-impaired.

Craig explained the challenges of selling online and asked Joe and Lad to elaborate on the progress they'd made. By the time they were through, the NobleStar suits recognized it would be in their best interest to provide us with a beta copy of Merchant. They were green, but they weren't dumb. The whole application fit on a single CD-ROM.

A second meeting followed two weeks later. NobleStar's certified experts were to tutor us on Merchant Server. However, Lad and Joe had learned so much about the application in the intervening weeks, the teachers became the students. Lad had become expert in integrating the back end of Merchant with the SQL Server database. He discovered how the application partially enabled credit-card processing, especially when linked to outside applications. Joe worked with the SQL "calls" and learned to push the envelope on the front end.

Merchant Server provided the tools we needed to build our version of e-tail. It didn't do anything on its own, so there was nothing we had to disable or work around. Other e-commerce applications provided forms for entry of data into *their* model. But our model was different. Joe knew it would be more work undoing what they had done than to design what we wanted to do. Merchant was a toolbox that allowed us to build a solution our way.

Merchant also provided a skeletal structure that could be used to support the elements of the order pipeline. It tied things together, enabling us to build our code on something that was both flexible and connected.

Another ingredient sweetened the recipe: Microsoft had clout. They unlocked doors we could not otherwise hope to open. Every off-the-shelf application, from finance to firewalls, credit-card processing to tax collecting, servers to audio streaming was designed to work within Microsoft's framework.

Merchant Server was a good start. Joe and Lad may have been clinging to the sheer rock face of El Capitan, but now at least they had ropes.

✥

"I DON'T MEAN to be nosey, but I couldn't help noticing the UPS logos. Do you work for them?" Craig asked the man across the aisle.

"Yes. I work out of Atlanta. I'm flying home. What do you do?"

"I'm with Value America; we're an online store based in Charlottesville."

"Internet commerce! We've got a whole team dedicated to it. We think it's going to be *huge.*"

"You mean you're ready to support guys like us?"

"You bet. Give me your card, and I'll have our team leader call you."

"Great," Craig said, pulling out two business cards. Another unbelievable coincidence was unfolding. "We've been getting the runaround from

FedEx. I'm having trouble getting anybody to call us back."

The UPS exec smiled. "I assume the reason you handed me two cards is that you want our account manager to give you a call too, right?"

"Absolutely," Craig said. "For us to give our customers the right deal, we have to negotiate the right deal on freight. It's a big part of our cost."

"Oh, I know. That's why we're committed to online retail. Both guys will call you. When will you be back in the office?"

"Day after tomorrow, Friday."

"Consider it done. Now, can I ask you a favor? I couldn't help but notice your Value America brochures. Could I have a copy to pass around?"

"Sure, I've got extras." Craig reached into the Black Hole, smiling.

༺·༻

"WHO'S BUYING TODAY?" Lad asked as we headed out for lunch. We all knew where we were going, even without asking. A local Chinese buffet restaurant a few blocks away had become our company cafeteria.

"It's my turn, but I forgot my wallet," Joe quipped. "I guess that means it's your turn again," he said, pointing to Craig.

"Alright, I'll buy, but it's going to be a working lunch. UPS is here tomorrow." Craig poked his head into my cubicle. "Ken, you going?"

"Sure," I said. I never missed lunch when Craig was buying.

The Shanghai was a family affair, a minute from the office. The buffet was good and, more to the point, fast.

We piled our plates high with General Tsao's Chicken, Beef Broccoli, Sweet and Sour Pork, and a Crab Rangoon or two. Following the customary feeding frenzy, Craig called the meeting to order.

"Where do we stand with our freight calculator, guys?"

Lad looked at Joe to see who was going to flinch, i.e., relinquish the chicken wing and answer the question. Joe never lost a game of chicken. "We've got all we're going to get out of UPS," Lad answered. "Their Internet-based freight calculator works okay on their site, but I'm afraid it's not designed to accept an outside query."

"That's true," Joe said, waving a chicken wing in the air, "but I learned enough looking at the source code behind their site to build our own calculator. As long as we make sure to download the UPS freight table updates, we'll be just as accurate, and a heck of a lot faster, since we won't have to connect to their site."

"He's automated data entry too," I added. "We now have tools in Presentation Marketing to feed the calculator. He's linked the Authoring Tool to the Admin Tool, so now we've got a Web-based application with a great graphical interface. It supplies the purchasing panel and the trans-action engine. Saves us a ton of time, not to mention cutting down on data-entry errors."

Joe summed it up. "I just borrowed UPS's logic, freight tables, and zone information. I linked it with the data Ken's gang has entered on products and suppliers. It calculates the actual freight. I've written code for UPS Ground, Second Day, and Overnight. Set the default to Ground, of course." Joe paused. "But we're going to need to negotiate a discount from these boys tomorrow. Using their published rates, the numbers are *ugly*."

"That's the idea," Craig said as he asked for the bill. "Sounds like you guys have made great progress. Can you demonstrate it tomorrow?"

"Yeah, it's ready now," Joe said. "I've even managed to incorporate the functionality of Microsoft's Wallet into the calculator. Pretty slick."

"Lucky Microsoft's *got* a Wallet, Joe; otherwise I doubt you'd know what one looks like." Craig handed the waitress his credit card.

"Oh, hurt me, in front of my friends. I represent that statement."

"Speaking of representing," I chimed in, "think it's about time to change the imagery we're using to represent our freight carrier? It's purple and orange on a white truck and airplane, remember? It still says, 'ExPres.' Looks like we need to make it UPS brown and gold. Pity, though. The 'ExPres' FedEx knock-off was pretty clever."

"Yeah. FedEx is classier, a better fit for the image we're trying to create. Who'd ya rather see pullin' up to your front door, a FedEx van with their fancy electronics or UPS's Teamsters?"

"Hey, careful there, big boy," Joe laughed, "or I'll send my dad after you. You know where he works, don't you?"

"Chief Counsel for the UAW. You gonna unionize us, Joe?"

"You never know...."

❧❧

"I'VE HEARD YOU present our store a hundred times," Joe said. "I've watched you go point by point through the whole process. Something good always happens. But not this time."

Craig was shaking his head. He had just hung up with Wells Fargo's credit-card manager. "The way they treated me, you'd think I'd tried to hold up their damn stagecoach. What is it with these people? We're trying to give them business. It's not like we want to borrow money!"

"So what are your revenue projections for calendar '98, Mr. Winn?" Joe said in falsetto, impersonating the lady's voice he had heard over the speakerphone. Then, mimicking Winn's deeper voice, Joe carried on, "Our forecast is rather modest; we're projecting $40 million, with more than eighty-five percent of that coming in the second half." Then falsetto: "And you say you haven't sold *anything* yet, nothing we can use to base your merchant account application upon?" Then back to Craig's voice, "Of course not. We're an Internet store. Until we can accept credit cards, we can't sell anything! That's why we're calling you...*you moron,*" Joe added for emphasis. Laughing hysterically, he concluded his charade, "Then, Mr. Winn, we will require you to deposit one million dollars to cover our exposure."

They might as well have asked for a billion. Craig tried to hide his concern. He knew that VeriFone was the dominant credit card processor. Their "swipe" machines were in virtually every retail store. Yet for Internet sales, VeriFone had authorized only two banks. Both of them had asked for more than we could possibly give. *We've come so far,* Craig agonized, *slain so many dragons, and now we're going to fail because we can't open a credit-card account? Every mom-and-pop nickel-and-dime operation in the country has a merchant account—even if they're charging pocket change for a pack of gum or a carton of cigarettes.*

"You know why we're having this problem don't you, Joe?" Craig asked. "Online stores have been skewered by the press."

"Yeah." Joe had put the pieces together. "You've got Netscape working with Visa and Microsoft working with MasterCard. They have different security standards. Each lobbed a grenade into the other's camp, trying to point out their weaknesses. The press had a field day with it. They blew the whole security thing all out of proportion, creating the false impression that buying something online is somehow riskier. In reality it's just like swiping your card through one of those machines at the store. They both encrypt data and send it over regular phone lines."

"What do you think is safer—giving your card to a waiter who disappears with it into a back room of a restaurant, or an encrypted transaction that takes less than a second?"

"Why do you think the media never bothered to ask an expert what was really happening?"

"It's a better story this way, Joe. From what I can tell, there aren't many reporters left, only storytellers. Why let facts get in the way?" But he brightened. "Anyway, not to worry, Joe. There's another game in town, not as big and well established as VeriFone, but at least their application is designed to work online. We'll shift gears and give CyberCash a try. I'll find a bank that's willing to work with them."

Joe found both the business and technical contacts. On the business side, they were most accommodating—unfortunately, they were less so on the tech side. In his discussions, Craig discovered the process CyberCash used to bring new banks into their world of electronic cash for the electronic age. He talked to our hometown bank (named Jefferson National, naturally) and persuaded them to apply. They came through, following a month or two of negotiations.

The business side of e-commerce was now enabled. Although Craig had projected sales of $40 million in '98, he told the folks at Jefferson National that, being a new business in a new industry, he could only provide forecasts for the first half of the year—about a million dollars in Q1 and four or five million in Q2. This lowered the bank's perceived risk enough to provide a merchant account without a monetary pledge. Good thing; we didn't have any monetary to pledge.

With Craig's battle won, Joe and Lad were faced with their own nightmare. CyberCash didn't work—at least not very well. For example, if a customer double clicked the purchase button, as people are apt to do, CyberCash charged their card twice. That tended to make customers cranky. They made the auditors cranky too. At the time, CyberCash was unable to provide any payment information. They would process the customer's credit card and acquire authorization, but that's where it ended. Cybercash was unable to tell us how much money was actually paid, or when.

Our quest for a solution ultimately led us to a new California company named Segue. Working with Joe, they were able to transfer "flat" files on the final cash transfers in a way that enabled us to attach them to the customer's order file. This was essential for the financial audit trail, not to mention any semblance of customer service. Segue went on to become PaymentNet, and Value America went on to become an Internet store that actually worked.

Soon after our high-tech store went "live," we discovered that we were an easy target for old-fashioned chicanery. We learned the hard way that the authorization number we got from the credit-card processors meant very little. It wasn't a guarantee of payment, we found to our dismay. In the virtual world, the card is not physically present, so there's no way to verify the customer's signature. The fact that signature checking is seldom done in regular retail stores didn't seem to matter to those setting up the rules. If the card was stolen or its number purloined, we would not get paid, authorization or not.

To make matters worse, solving the problem fell squarely on the shoulders of Value America. Our average checkout was thirty times greater than that of our online competitors. Amazon was averaging less than $20 a register ring; we averaged over $750. If you were a crook, would you steal a $20 book or a $750 diamond ring? Right. The thieves came to the same conclusion; they shopped Value America like Imelda Marcos at a shoe sale. Early on, nearly ten percent of our orders were from crooks.

Eventually, we were able to hire a guy away from Federated Department Stores who had faced, and slain, this dragon before. He wrote a fraud-detection strategy that automatically checked for things that were likely to occur if there was fraudulent intent. For example, did the delivery address match the credit card billing address? Was the customer buying a product, like jewelry or a notebook PC, that was easy to fence? If we called to verify the order, had they given us their real phone number? It even checked an online database of stolen credit cards. The new program cut fraudulent orders to a fraction of one percent. Another dragon was dead, or at least very depressed.

Just when we thought we were making progress, yet another dragon raised its ugly head. No accepted financial system worked without inventory, under the reasonable theory that you couldn't sell what you didn't own. Forget that Craig had spent years as a rep doing precisely that. Yet his rep business had been all cash positive. It didn't require investors in order to grow and prosper. Value America would.

Investors would mean audits, and accounting firms required financials—general ledgers, income statements, balance sheets. So we had a problem. Without inventory, no accounting program would work. Without a working financial application, there could be no financials. No financials, no investors. And without investors, there would be no Value America.

Joe came to the rescue, God love his devious mind. He decided to "give" the financial programs, like Platinum and Sterling, what they wanted—inventory. Joe created a virtual warehouse that received and shipped our virtual inventory. It worked beautifully. Turn was terrific, and the financial programs loved it. The accountants, however…well, that's another story.

৩◌৶

WINN FOUND HIMSELF in an airport again. Chicago. His pocket began to ring as he jogged down the interminable corridors of the United complex at O'Hare. He flipped open his cell phone. "This is Craig," he said, panting.

"Hi, this is Doug, with Premenos. Can you talk?"

"Hi Doug. Actually, I'm trying to catch my flight to Dulles so I can make another connection and go home. Can you give me an update while I'm hightailing it to the gate?"

"Sure. I've given all of your questions to our technical staff, our developers and engineers, and they've come back with some answers. You realize," he chuckled, "we've never had anybody ask these questions before. Anyway, first off, we're writing a version of our EDI application to run on NT. It's going to be a whole lot cheaper, they tell me. As you may know, most of our current customers use...."

"Yeah, I know. They use IBM AS400s. I used to be one of them."

"AS400s. That's right," Doug said. "We found that our app can port information to your database. Most of our clients are using IBM databases; some have gone to Oracle. Our guys can make it work with, it says here, 'S-Q-L.'"

"That's pronounced sequel. It's Microsoft's database, SQL Server. Did you find out if it's ODBC compliant?"

"No, it's not, just flat files."

"Too bad. That's a significant roadblock. When will you have the NT version ready? How much will it cost? How much of the functionality will it retain? Oh, and what level of transactional volume is it calibrated for?"

"I don't know. I'll ask our engineers and I'll get back to you."

The EDI conversations with Harbinger and Sterling didn't go much better. The only differences were that one had a tie-in with IBM, and the other offered an integrated financial package. The one promising survivor appeared to be GEIS, GE Information Systems. They were the biggest player and offered the additional advantage of operating the most commonly used VAN, Value Added Network. There was only one problem: they were *expensive*.

Joe had hated EDI ever since he had first heard the acronym. Lad had eventually come to the same conclusion. Electronic Data Interchange was arcane, little more than a complex version of e-mail transmitting on a slightly more secure network. There were differing versions, ridged rules, ANSI standards, and seldom-used protocols that had to be understood, accommodated, and integrated. Even when you did all this as well as it could be done, you still had to "map" your EDI to the vendor's for the darn thing to work.

Lad recommended purchasing the GEIS starter version. It was ancient, so old it actually ran on DOS, and was therefore cheap. It would suffice, though, until the store's transactional volume surpassed its meager capabilities. Craig approved the purchase begrudgingly, hating the idea of running the store of the future on the EDI of the past. He promised Lad he would try to climb up through the GEIS management chain until he found someone willing to partner with us. Working together, he reasoned, we could develop a more cutting-edge solution without having to pay for it.

It wasn't long before the CEO of GE Information Systems invited Craig to a Washington Redskins game in his private box. They knew many of the same people, and they talked the same language. They even shared their private impressions about the work being done out in California by Netscape.

GEIS agreed to partner with us, virtually *giving* Value America the latest version of their EDI software. In return, Value America worked with GE to make EDI more effective online and integrating it more seamlessly with databases. We promoted the partnership as an essential element of the new world order. Dragons, it seemed, were becoming an endangered species.

ভঃৎ

"I CAN'T BELIEVE anything this simple could be so difficult," Craig said. "C'mon, Joe, is it really that complicated? I'm *just* trying to reduce the number of SKU's we have to manage." Winn knew what he wanted, knew why he wanted it, and wasn't about to give up. "My head is killing me," he announced abruptly. "I'm going to the drugstore for some Advil."

I could use some myself, Joe thought. Craig was doing it again, using his favorite four-letter word, "just." Every time he used that dreaded word, Joe's life disappeared for a month, dissipating into mind-numbing solutions to simply stated goals. Interminable hours, late-night pizza deliveries, and aspirin were all part of the formula. *Just* build something that can fly to the moon on gossamer wings.

This time it was accommodating "attributes." It was tantamount to trying to achieve two mutually exclusive goals: selling individual products *versus* selling product "types" that had common variables.

"OK, Joe, this can't be that hard. We need 'attributes' to handle products that have options, like…this shirt I am wearing. It comes in, say, five sizes and ten colors, both short and long sleeve. So there are three attributes, size, color, and sleeve type, giving us a hundred possible combinations. All one hundred variations come from the same factory, and all have the same price. I want to list it in our system as a single shirt, a single Stock Keeping Unit—but with color, sleeve, and size *options*. If we burden our members with all of the variations, they'll give up, and we'll lose the sale. If Ken's team has to enter and manage every variation, we'll go broke. We have to simplify this."

Joe sighed. "I know it sounds simple, but our store is built on products—individual products. How can you sell something that's not entered as a SKU? What happens if we want to sell the long-sleeve version for more than the short-sleeve? What if the manufacturer wants to charge us more for the Extra Large than for the Extra Small? And here's another wrinkle: what happens if someone decides to eliminate one of the ten colors, or worse yet, eliminates the color in some sizes but not every size. We'd have to keep the data for historical sales even when the store no longer sells the option. And we'd have to prevent customers from ordering the discontinued item. This is not as easy as it sounds...."

⁖

SOLVING THE ATTRIBUTES puzzle was tough, but it was child's play next to Craig's grand scheme of giving our members multiple ways to shop. He had envisioned fifteen of them. We never got around to implementing them all, but Joe made a good start.

The first of these was similar to what drove our competitors' sites—shopping "by product." It was simple enough. A window was provided to let the customer "search" by typing in a product's name. If you were shopping for books at Amazon.com, and you knew the title or author, you'd just type in *The Firm* or "John Grisham," and Amazon would take you right to it. But who knew the name of a toaster or television. You could enter "TV," or "Panasonic," or even "Panasonic+TV+25-inch," but they make a bunch of them, all with different features.

Sometimes the brand names themselves were elusive. Do you know the names of any pants other than Dockers and 501 Jeans? What's the name of Amana's innovative line of bottom-freezer refrigerators? "Easy Reach" is the answer, but who, other than Amana and the Creative Director of an Internet store, knows that? Craig had a point. Using a search engine for products like we were selling was less than ideal. There had to be a better way.

Joe was asked to enable shopping "by category." Virtually every retailer since the dawn of time has been organized this way. Even down at Crazy Abdul's in Ur of the Chaldees, I imagine, they sold the rugs in one place and the frankincense in another. Within every industry, there are divisions and categories. Housewares, for example, is an industry. Appliances are a division of that industry. Toasters are a category within that division. Within the Toasters category, there are dozens of brands and hundreds of products.

We may have been the first online store to create a graphical menu structure that allowed our customers to search for products by industry, division, category, and type. Winn had dedicated twenty pages of his original business plan to this concept for the benefit of our merchants and developers. The reason it worked was that Joe made sure our store was dynamically generated out of our database. Things could be called up and grouped for presentation virtually any way we wanted.

The third way to shop was our favorite. Shopping "by brand" was a natural for us since our whole philosophy was brand-centric. Each brand had their own exclusive department. Their logos were pictured on the landing page of their particular industry. By clicking on the logo, the customer went directly to the brand's "store within a store." We gave them their own URL, or Web address: VA.com/HP went directly to a department devoted exclusively to the world of Hewlett-Packard products. With the exception of some designer shops in upscale department stores, the idea of creating a department around a brand, rather than around a category, was unheard of.

The fourth way to shop was by "related products." If you bought a vacuum cleaner in our store, a coffee maker, or an ink jet printer, we could take you directly to the bags, filters, and cartridges for the specific model you owned. It was convenient because it was personalized.

Fifth, we highlighted products that were "on sale." If you wanted to shop by category or brand for the products that were discounted, we brought them all together for you. It was like a giant virtual sale table.

The sixth method was a nod to the "gatekeepers" among online shoppers. The "What's New," section highlighted newly added brands.

The seventh way to shop at Value America was called "Featured Products." It was equivalent to what retailers call an end cap. In traditional brick-and-mortar stores, this is the highly visible section at the end of a gondola, along the main aisle. Our Featured Products were pictured to the right of every menu page, along with a sale price. As in regular retail, they consumed about five percent of our "floor space" but generated more than twenty-five percent of our revenues.

There were more ways to shop, which never made it off the drawing board, that would have made the store even more interesting. But it was enough, I suppose, to have built a virtual store that actually worked. These unrealized dreams included Comparison Shopping, Highest-Rated Product, and Most-Popular Product. We also wanted an Express Checkout, in which items you purchased regularly would be kept in your customized Express Checkout area, ready for one-click ordering. Automated Delivery was a derivation of this idea: products your family or your business consumed on a predictable schedule (e.g. toothpaste, diapers, copier paper) could be scheduled to arrive automatically at some predetermined interval.

The original business plan talked about a Personal Shopper. Craig suggested a butler, which later became Ask.com's imagery. The Personal Shopper was actually enabled in early versions of our store, manifesting itself as a genie. Our genie, thanks to the creative folks at Microsoft, actually listened to what our members said and talked back to them—nicely. When you entered the store, our animated genie, a cute little blue guy with a turban and a smoky tail, moved about the screen pointing out things of interest. He greeted each member by name. The genie made an appropriate remark in a computer-generated voice: "It's only been five minutes since your last visit. Did you forget something?" Our engaging blue mascot thanked our members for the last product they purchased. He also reminded members about important upcoming dates in their lives.

One idea that never quite made it into production was an automated floral service. The idea was genie genius: tell us the dates that are important to you, your anniversary, your spouse's birthday, Valentines Day, and Mother's Day for example, and we will automatically send flowers. That would have been very, very cool. When's the last time a store improved *your* love life?

ভ়ৎ

LOOKING BACK, it seems impossible. In only eighteen months, we built a store that actually worked, from scratch. It was ours. We wrote the code. Value America was a proprietary solution from front to back. We slew dragons and invented innovative features, many of which have still never been replicated. We created thousands of multimedia product presentations. The software we used to build them and the incredible functionality that enabled them existed only at Value America.

We built the Internet's most comprehensive store—at a time when no other online store offered more than one category. It let each customer shop in the way he or she found most comfortable. In an era of static HTML Web pages, our site was dynamically generated. We were the first online store to communicate with our suppliers using EDI and the first to build an automated freight calculator. We were the first to have electronic fraud detection and to run autonomously, independent of ISPs.

In an age of biplanes and barnstormers, we had created a space shuttle. Was it perfect? No. Would it fly? Yes, indeed! All we needed now was something to put in the cargo bay.

Who are you to say, "We will carry on business...." You do not even know what will happen tomorrow—James

GETTING TO YES

Broke. Craig sat staring at our checkbook. It was late. Everyone else had gone home. He felt completely alone. Calling this a problem would have been wildly optimistic. We were a week from being out of business. Sure, plenty of vendors had agreed to sponsor presentations, but that was not the same as saying, "Here's a check to get you started."

The first bold Masco visionaries had signed Presentation and Listing Agreements totalling $340,000. Other companies, like West Bend, Amana, Zenith, Braun, Canon, Sanyo, Hoover, Iomega, Toshiba, Singer, and Philips Magnavox, had signed up for $360,000 more. Their fifty percent deposits had kept the machine running—so far. But we were now a team of fifteen souls, all but two drawing salaries, all using expensive (by our parsimonious standards) computer equipment. When Craig and Rex had ponied up another $150,000, the looks on their wives' faces told them that was about it for the ol' out-of-pocket.

So Craig sat there on a cold February evening, just staring at the checkbook—which for all intents and purposes comprised the company's accounting system. He looked at the balance. He looked at the vendor projections from the merchandisers. He agonized over the upcoming payroll. And he started talking to himself. *We're not going to make it. We moved across the country and put four hundred grand into this thing, invested our heart and soul, and it's about to go poof.*

It did not go "poof," at least not yet. The first break came when AT&T agreed to lease back all of the equipment we had bought. At first blush, it seemed to be an unbelievably good deal, considering that any computer bought today can be expected to be worth nothing moments after you've installed it. But the lease wasn't really based on the market value of the equipment. Craig and Rex had agreed to guarantee it, making it tantamount to a personal loan. Still, it was a timely influx of capital.

That was the essence of capitalism, was it not? Intrepid entrepreneurs putting their resources at risk in hopes of reaping a commensurate reward. Craig and Rex knew our concept was sound. We'd be in fine shape if only we could get enough vendors signed up. That would make the finances work like a charm, never mind filling the store's cyber-shelves with products, which was the whole idea.

As Craig looked at the numbers, he knew we were going to have to secure more brand participation, faster, or die in the attempt.

✥

"WHAT WE NEED here is a new strategy, Bill." Craig was sitting on the corner of Bill Hunt's desk the next morning, chewing thoughtfully on a bagel. Crystal eyed him expectantly. Her tail twitched, but nothing else moved. "These Hewlett-Packard guys sound like IBM. Their favorite word is 'No.'"

Bill gritted his teeth. "What I keep hearing is, 'We have no established policy for selling on the Internet, and therefore we have no way to evaluate you as a business partner.' It's maddening. Trying to crack Hewlett-Packard is like driving a car into a brick wall."

"Maybe we're using the wrong vehicle."

"A tank, perhaps?" Bill asked with a twinkle in his eye.

"I was thinking of an airplane. Let's go *over* the wall."

"Find somebody higher up."

"Exactly. We need to find the person *above* the people saying 'No.' HP is too smart to opt out of the future."

Crystal's persistence was rewarded with the last little bite of Craig's bagel. Maybe the same technique would work on HP.

֎

THE BUNGALOWS looked like they ought to be rented by the hour. Craig suspected the last time this Las Vegas dump had been redecorated had been under the personal supervision of Bugsy Siegel. The rooms were small, smelly, and cheap. This was where the *low* rollers stayed.

Bill had at long last gotten through to the people above the people saying "No" at HP. One of these had magnanimously agreed to grant Value America an audience at the Consumer Electronics Show being held here in the gambling capital of the West. How appropriate.

HP's retail account manager, his boss, and *his* boss, the potentate of all North American operations, were assembled in a conference room. If these guys couldn't make a decision, nobody could. Pleasantries were exchanged, and Craig proceeded to demonstrate our store. He began and ended his presentation from a position of strategic weakness; call it *enthusiastic humility*. "Value America's store," he said, "was specifically designed to partner with great companies like HP—those that make better quality goods and strive to sell them on their merits. I believe HP is the world's best brand."

As he finished, he studied their expressions. The HP team seemed impressed, though he had the feeling these folks didn't impress easily.

The senior suit declared, "You've built a new solution to a very old problem. You're doing things we want done, keeping our line together, presenting us as a brand rather than a collection of unrelated products."

The second-in-command added, "Forming a closer relationship with the consumer is one of our top goals."

The third continued, "We're committed to making better products. We want to sell our products based upon their actual value. Your tool enables us to do that. This is an outstanding value proposition!"

"I agree," the senior exec stated. "We realize the Internet is going to lower the cost of going to market. Tell you what," he said, "HP has never done business with an online company, but we'd like you to be the first. We'll sponsor a test on our consumer printer line. We'll call it TAP, for Target Account Program. If it works, we'll add other products."

In one breath, he had filled our sails and then run our boat aground. The concept didn't work that way. The idea was to present the whole company, not just one division, even if HP *was* the biggest manufacturer of consumer printers in the world.

Craig paused for a moment, looking down at the table and forcing himself to smile. "Thank you for your kind offer. It is an honor to have HP be willing to partner with such a young company as ours. But for our store to be of value to you, we need to present *you*—all of you—not just one product line."

The HP team glanced at each other, letting out a collective sigh. "We're not prepared to do everything. Not yet."

"That's a pity. We'd be good for each another."

The three Valuable Americans didn't say much as they left the meeting. Even the blistering Nevada sun couldn't dissipate the gloom.

"Listen," Craig finally said, "we're no worse off than we were before the meeting. We told our story to the right audience. Give it time to sink in. They're smart people. They'll come around. After all," Craig rationalized as the other two looked at him incredulously, "they didn't say 'No.' What I heard was, 'Not yet.' It's not over 'til it's over."

"Want to go over to the MGM Grand tonight, Craig?" Rex asked. "I hear the Fat Lady's singing...."

Meanwhile, back in HP's little conference room, the weight of Value America's concept still lingered. They flipped purposely through one of the brochures we had left behind, the one called *It's About Time*.

"It's about time," one said to the others. "It *is* about time!"

༼·༽

HEWLETT-PACKARD WAS replete with geniuses, and these three were as bright as they came. The next meeting took place in our tiny Attic conference room. It didn't get started until nine o'clock in the evening. After an hour of discussion, the leader of the delegation cleared off our whiteboard and proceeded to graph HP's complex business model. On the left, he listed their manufacturing divisions, their "silos." Down the right side, he listed their customers—businesses of various sizes, consumers, educational entities, and government agencies. And right in the middle were the intermediaries, a convoluted mass of boxes and arrows depicting the middlemen: distributors, retailers, and value-added resellers. It was the *corpus callosum* of their new world order. "This," he announced, "is what we're trying to achieve."

Craig got up and studied the board for a moment. "This may be what you want," he said, "but I don't believe it's what you *need*." The HP team traded glances. Craig walked around the table, which was two sizes too large for the room. He picked up an eraser and rubbed out the entire middle section of the diagram, leaving only HP on the left, and their customers on the right. Then Craig drew a line joining the two sides with an arrowhead on each end.

"This line is an electronic conduit between you and your customers," he said. "It's a direct link between your products and the minds, offices, and wallets of the people who buy and use what you make."

As the concept sunk in, heads began to nod. Their faces brightened with receptive smiles. They began taking copious notes.

"This line," Craig concluded dramatically, "is Value America. *We* are what you need."

❧

"IT APPEARS WE'VE got even more good news from HP," Bill said.

"What happened?" Craig was all ears.

"Well, you remember how many times we were told no because HP had no policy for online sales? Well, they've decided they need one."

"Do tell."

"More people are coming next week to assess the opportunity."

They arrived like a mighty army. HP sent their Wholesale Business Products Manager, their new TAP Manager, and the managers for Marketing Development, Product Marketing, and Imaging Products.

Winn loved to play to a smart audience, and these folks all fit that description. Now a relative expert in HP corporate parlance, he was able to punctuate our story with humorous insider anecdotes. They ate it up.

One manager said, "What you've built here is compelling and forward-looking. We've come in here and overwhelmed your team with our people—heck, you've met more HP execs than I have. I promise, your patience will be rewarded. But," he said, "there's still one more thing we're going to ask you to do. As you know, we have no policy for selling online. We'd like *you* to help us write one."

The fox was being invited into the hen house. Not to eat the chickens, but to keep the weasels out. "I think we can accommodate your request," Craig almost choked as he struggled to regain his composure.

What Craig and Bill would recommend looked suspiciously like our business plan. "You want companies that present your products so customers can learn what differentiates them from the competition; you want menu-driven shopping convenience; you want every division together. An online customer should be EDI-enabled; they should be willing to honor your MAP strategy, serve small and medium business as well as consumers...."

MAP, or "Minimum Advertised Price," policy was a big issue for HP. (They operated under a variant called UMAP—Unilateral Minimum Advertised Price. The "U" meant that U couldn't even discuss it.) It was kind of like a strong leash for a stupid dog. Retailers chafed at it, but it kept them from hurting themselves.

MAP had come about as the result of a series of events that had started decades back. Well into the fifties, fair trade laws in America were a fact of life. Brands routinely told retailers what they could charge consumers for their goods. If they didn't agree, they simply weren't allowed to sell their products. In the '60s, the pendulum swung back. Legal action involving FedMart and others precipitated laws that made price-fixing illegal.

As a result, retail stores began structuring their promotional pricing around the most recognizable products and advertised them *at cost*, or even below, in hopes of attracting more shoppers. The idea was to charge a lot more on everything else to make up the difference. The theory was that once lured into the store, consumers would assume that every price was as low as the advertised item. This is why the milk and eggs are always in the back of the store.

Since retailers have no way to differentiate between items on any basis other than price, Store A felt they had to lower the price of Product X to below their cost because Store B had done that a week before. Then Store A, realizing that they were losing money hand over fist, went to Brand X and said, "We're going to have to drop you unless you lower your price; we can't make any money with your products." Meanwhile, Store B was telling them the same thing because Store A had matched their price. Eventually, Brand X went under. And Stores A and B went under as well. Everybody lost but the lawyers.

The brands came up with an answer. It wasn't price-fixing, exactly, but it was its kissin' cousin. The feds allowed brands to impose "Minimum Advertised Pricing." It said, in effect, a retailer could sell products for whatever price they wanted to in their stores, because price-fixing was illegal, but they could not *advertise* them below the price the brands had set. If they did, brands had the right to refuse further shipments. (Ever wonder why every retailer seems to sell branded products at the same price? Now you know.)

In this way, the retailers were prevented from doing grievous bodily harm to themselves and the brands they carried. Retailers no longer duked it out in the Sunday circulars. Brands no longer looked like cheap floozies. Consumers paid fair, realistic prices. Everybody was happy, more or less.

But then somebody invented e-commerce, and it was a whole new ball game. As far as MAP policy was concerned, the new issue was *what constituted an ad?* Some held that an online store was just that, a store; hence, listing a price was not an ad *per se*. Others felt that because the price was viewable outside of the confines of a "store," the website *must* be a form of advertising. That's why we addressed the issue, recommending that HP's online policy include a commitment to adhere to MAP. After all, *not* adhering to MAP would mean no "factory authorization," and without authorization, there would be no legitimate sales.

But we had an ace up our sleeve. We had several ways to give our customers a better deal without violating MAP. Our customers earned a one percent credit they could deduct from the cost of future purchases. We donated another one percent to a charity of their choosing. We provided free shipping on MAP items, which saved the customer more. The real *coup*, though, was Bonus ValueDollars.

This is how they worked. Say our member bought a big-screen TV for $1,500, and the margin was twenty percent, or $300. If we needed $150 to make our business model work, we could cover the $50 freight and give another $100 in discounts and still profit. But if we deducted the $100 from the price, we'd be in violation of the MAP policy. So instead, we put the money into the member's "ValueDollar" account, which they could spend on their next purchase.

This arrangement encouraged membership; we couldn't track your ValueDollars if we didn't know who you were. It encouraged repeat business. And we hadn't violated MAP with our gift because it wasn't deducted from the price of the item, but rather from the *next* purchase.

About a week after we'd given HP our recommendations, they got back to Bill and announced that they had formulated their policy. It's amazing how fast you can work when you've got the right tools.

"That's great," Bill said. "When can we get started?"

"Started? Oh, no. We have to evaluate our applicants first."

"Applicants?"

"Of course. You'll have to apply, and then we'll decide who qualifies."

"Oh." Bill suddenly felt as if he had somehow fallen through Alice's looking glass and was carrying on a conversation with the March Hare. "Okay. How does one do that?"

"Well," the exec said, "if you'd like to apply, I'll send you the forms." *Would we like to apply?* "Yes, please."

The next day, Bill felt like a naughty schoolboy with stolen answers to the big test. HP's application looked like it had been lifted from our business plan. So it was no surprise when, a few days later, the HP exec called and gave him the good news. Craig listened in on his speakerphone.

"Congratulations," she said. "Value America is one of our finalists."

"*Finalist? One of?* Are you saying somebody *else* fits the profile?..."

"Yes. Well, not exactly," she said, "but you *are* one of two finalists."

"That's great," Bill lied. "Who's the other one?"

"Coincidentally, they're also located in Virginia."

"Virginia?" *Oh, God, No!*

"Yes. The other finalist is AOL."

America Online was only the biggest Internet company in the world. Ostensibly an ISP, they had their tentacles into every online endeavor—including e-commerce. This wasn't David *versus* Goliath. This was David's pet hamster *versus* Goliath's rogue elephant.

"*Please,*" Craig tried to reason with the HP exec. "Long-term, we can do more for you than anyone. We're a pure-bred, value-oriented online retailer. We've got the systems and the desire to present everything HP does. But let's face it. AOL is a whole lot bigger than we are. This is hardly a fair contest. Why don't you choose both of us?"

"No," she replied firmly. "We've decided to choose only one. We're sending out an evaluation team on Monday, next week."

Craig and Bill looked around the Attic. The place was held together with duct tape. The cumulative value of every piece of second-hand furniture, underpowered PC, and antiquated network component wouldn't buy lunch for the executive team at AOL. We needed a miracle.

We were up first. Bill collected the Hewlett-Packard delegation at the airport. We were already one stroke behind, he figured. Maybe it was a little thing, but one annoying fact of life in C'ville was that most people couldn't fly here without changing planes. The biggest things that flew into town were cramped, noisy turbo-props, like the De Havilland Dash 8 on which the HP team would come—and leave.

We had reserved Commonwealth's big conference room downstairs, ostensibly because it was larger, but also because Ken Erickson was now using the upstairs conference room as his office during the day. The Attic was hummin'.

It was a milestone of sorts. For the first time, we delivered our pitch using the *real* store. We talked about how our product presentations brought brands like HP closer to their customers and how they elevated the perceived value of their products. We described how a customer could get anywhere they wanted with only a few clicks. We talked philosophy and concept, because HP loved that stuff as much as we did. We outlined our thoughts on the benefits of membership, charity donations, and special personal touches the likes of which no brick-and-mortar store had provided in half a century—if ever.

We explained that we weren't after individual sales so much as we were trying to build relationships—between HP and their customers. We shared our belief that Value America was destined to become the one place consumers and businesses could "go" to find most everything they needed for home or office. We talked about Electronic Data Interchange, the grease that kept the wheels of the inventory-less revolution moving.

The HP team was engaged and receptive, but we weren't over the hump yet. They still had to visit AOL, who had a huge building, the finest equipment, thousands of people, and a long-standing position of leadership—they had everything. Well, almost everything.

An HP exec, a few days later, told us what they lacked. "You know, Bill," she explained, "when we came to Charlottesville, you guys treated us like we were important, respected, *wanted*. AOL didn't. It's as simple as that. To them, we were just another company."

"Really?..." Bill's eyebrows were raised in amazement. Forget good manners. HP was, well, *HP*.

"Yep," she replied. "I'm pleased to tell you, the deal is yours. Hewlett-Packard has selected Value America. Congratulations!"

And so it came about that the most significant vendor we had ever signed—the one we had worked so hard to impress with our unique business model, our elegant technological solutions, and our unparalleled grasp of the complex relationships between manufacturers and consumers—had in the end made us their exclusive online partner because we were nice to them.

EVERY DAY IT BECAME clearer that the office products industry was ready for Value America. They were right in our power-alley. Product acquisition was not discretionary. If a business needed it, they bought it. No one let the wheels of commerce grind to a halt for lack of a ballpoint pen or a printer cartridge. The things every office needed were considered (as in the clever name of one of the big chains) *staples*. Every office used these things and never ran out of them.

Those that bought office supplies tended to be early adopters. This is where the first personal computers showed up. It's where the most active Web connections were. Consequently, this is where we could expect to find the greatest comfort level with online shopping.

Convenience was important. There was work to be done, and sending an employee to the office supply store was expensive. Our product presentations were particularly valuable in this space. Companies made more than one product for a reason: people's needs varied. Businesses needed to be able to make smart buying decisions in order to stay competitive. Information was the key to better buying.

Selection was also important. Whereas all one company may have needed was a good pair of 9" editor's scissors, another couldn't get along without a 36" flat-bed paper cutter with a carbon steel blade and a full complement of Federally mandated safety features. The typical brick-and-mortar office store only stocked about 5,000 items. There wasn't room for any more. But with our virtual store and inventory-less model, "shelf space" was unlimited. In the end, we would offer over *30,000* business products to the professional community.

And then there was the question of product appropriateness. It was a little-recognized fact that the big office superstores like Staples were not authorized to sell business computers. If you wanted a room full of IBM business machines with full networking and remote administration capabilities, you'd have to go elsewhere. The closest thing to a business box that Office Depot carried was likely to come with *Reader Rabbit* software—it was a consumer PC in sheep's clothing. Value America understood the distinction, and we worked hard to gain factory-authorized status in both business and consumer computer lines. We were the first online company to accomplish this feat.

Sol Price had figured this one out years before: small businesses owners have homes, families, and money. By definition, they have jobs and thus paychecks. And they buy things that have absolutely nothing to do with business. If Value America could attract these people, we would have a ready-made audience for the other couple hundred thousand things we wanted to sell, *including* home computers with *Reader Rabbit*.

HP was the first major computer, and one of the first office-equipment brands, to recognize the efficacy of our model. But they weren't prepared to jettison their entire distribution system to accommodate it. Implementation of the factory-direct model would have to wait. In the meantime, we were instructed to choose one of their existing distribution partners. Bill Hunt turned this challenge into an opportunity.

HP authorized five distributors to work with us. Choosing among them was our prerogative. So we decided to select our distributor based upon which of them was most cooperative in introducing us to the other quality brands. The "winner," we decided, would be the distributor that helped arrange the most brand partnerships—the best "matchmaker."

United Stationers sent their senior team to Charlottesville. But they were an industry giant, and like most giants, they moved rather slowly. Azerty was the new kid on the block. A specialist in the technology side of the business, they were a young, energetic company, the most nimble of the lot. They were on us like a duck on a June bug, quickly arranging to hold our first business-products vendor day.

Azerty wasn't the only one who had to move quickly. We were not about to approach the major office-products brands without showing off our new—and exclusive—relationship with HP. That meant my crew and I had to drop everything else and concentrate on their presentations.

Our website was up, but downloading a page could take a while. The lack of online infrastructure was a problem. It was hardly a way to make a good impression on a room full of busy executives. The solution was a "store-in-a-box." Joe transferred our entire store onto the hard drive of a notebook computer. The only thing "fake" about it was the connectivity.

Azerty persuaded thirty vendors to meet with our team at their facilities in Buffalo, New York. There were about a hundred industry pros in attendance, from industry leaders like 3M, Sony, Polaroid, Avery, Belkin, Imation, Texas Instruments, Brother, Sanford, and Canon. Each brand came equipped with their sales materials and a healthy dose of curiosity.

Their training room served as an auditorium. Using our newly created store-in-a-box, Value America was projected onto a large screen, replicating the experience of shopping online. The presentation was smashing, and it was universally well received.

Upon its conclusion, the audience was divided into four groups, one for each member of our merchandising team, and the real work began— the categorization of their product lines. There were so many companies, each was allotted only thirty minutes. Within that time, an interview was conducted, the sales materials were examined, and the product line was dissected to determine the best way to present the brand's wares in our store. For the most part, the company's brochures told the tale: they had six of this, eight of that, and seven of the other thing; they were already separated into distinct categories.

The ability to publish category presentations that were neither anachronistic nor fleeting in their ability to communicate was something brands had never had before. If their product's specs changed, we could update our presentation in minutes. Best of all, the presentation was made at the point of sale. Once impressed, the customer could actually buy something. This was a better mousetrap if ever there was one.

About twenty brands said, "Yes," at the Azerty vendor's day. Twenty brands, each signing up for an average of three $5,000 Multimedia Presentations, made it a $300,000 day. The experience also taught us something about group dynamics. Value America was, by anybody's standards, a tiny company. We had about the same mass as navel lint. Normally, we could not possibly hope to command the attention of industry giants. But big brands are fiercely competitive. What one had, the others wanted. It was a law of nature; when a brand saw their competition sign on, they were suddenly put in the awkward position of "make dust or eat dust." Peer pressure was a wonderful thing, we decided.

JOHN MOTLEY knew everybody in his industry. The office-products business was good to him, and he was good to it. John was not only the industry's leading manufacturer's rep, he was its biggest fan.

It was surprising, then, that a question like this one could catch him flat-footed. The president of one of the companies John represented had just heard something that seemed too good to be true, so he called Motley.

"Azerty introduced some brands to a new Internet store called Value America. They're leading with office products. I just wondered if you'd heard anything. I think they're in your territory, down in Charlottesville."

John thought for a moment. "You've got me. First I've heard of 'em. Value America, you say?"

"Yeah. The guy's name is Winn. Greg Winn, something like that."

"Give me twenty-four hours." John promised, "I'll tell you all there is to know about Value America."

"Great. If what I heard is true, it could be good for us."

Motley's offices were near Washington. Charlottesville was in his back yard. He dialed directory information and got the number.

"Value America." Commonwealth's receptionist answered our phones as part of the lease arrangement. Nice voice.

"Greg Winn, please."

"Yes sir. One moment." A short pause.

"This is Craig."

"Mr. Winn, my name is John Motley. We haven't met. I'm a manu-facturer's rep in the office-products industry."

Craig's ears perked up at the mention of "rep" and "office products." "Yes, sir," he responded brightly. "I like reps—I was once a reptile myself. And your industry is important to us. In fact, just last week we met with a group of brands at Azerty. What can I do for you, John?"

"Actually, I'd like to invite you to the U.S. Open this weekend at Congressional here in Washington. I'm a member, and I thought you might welcome the opportunity to get away from the office. Of course," he laughed, "I have an ulterior motive. I want to hear about your Internet store—apparently you've been causing some commotion."

Get away from the office? Craig sighed. "I wish I could. It sounds great, and, yes, I'd love to tell you about Value America. But I'm afraid there just aren't enough hours in the day for a diversion like that." Craig had become the proverbial "blind dog in a meat market." He didn't know where to turn next. He felt like he had to make every minute count.

"I understand, Craig, but if you want, you can keep working. The top executives of the largest office products companies are going to be there. Oh, and the largest distributors too. They'll all be attending a dinner I'm hosting, and then they'll be spending the next two days at the tournament as my guests. I'd be pleased to introduce you."

These were the very people he had been trying so hard to meet. "In that case," a grateful Craig replied, "I accept."

৽৽৽

I'VE SEEN CRAIG WINN behind a podium. He is a dynamic, forceful, and entertaining speaker. But he's lying to you. He's not actually like that at all. The real Craig can be painfully shy, especially in social situations or unfamiliar surroundings—*especially* at cocktail parties.

So as he pulled his Chevy Suburban into the parking lot at Morton's Steakhouse, he wished he were somewhere else. Anywhere else. Inside were people who knew each other well, colleagues and friends. They had become comfortable with each other. Craig felt like a fish out of water.

He opened the door and looked around. The place was expensive, filled with beautiful people. Rich oak paneling and the faint, tantalizing odor of a perfectly cooked New York strip filled his senses. He didn't know a soul, not even his host. Craig stood there for a minute as his eyes adjusted to the dim light, then caught the *maitre d's* attention. He said he was looking for John Motley.

"Of course. Follow me, sir." He led Craig to a large private room in the back of the restaurant.

There was a party going on. Craig's shy nature begged him to run away. He stifled it, swallowed hard, and looked around the room. A short, dapper gentleman in an expensive custom suit and Hermes tie glanced in his direction. Donning a broad smile, he stepped forward.

"Craig Winn, I presume."

"Yes. And you must be...."

"John Motley," he said as he shook Craig's hand. "I am so glad you could make it. Your company is the hot topic of conversation tonight." Before Craig could comment, John turned toward his guests and announced in a loud voice, "Ladies and gentlemen, may I have your attention? I would like to introduce our very special guest, Mr. Craig Winn, founder and CEO of the new Internet store you've all been talking about, Value America!"

ॐॐ

UNITED STATIONERS may not have landed HP's core business, but that didn't stop them from seeing our potential. They wanted in. Sure, the vendors who had signed listing agreements at Azerty would remain theirs, but there were other office-products brands we needed.

Recognizing the scope of the opportunity, United's EVP of marketing and their VP of sales came to Charlottesville a second time. On a beautiful spring morning, the 30th of April, they played golf with Bill and Craig. After the round the four men gathered at the "19th Hole," an intimate bar and grill at Glenmore, for a bite.

"Gentlemen," Bill said, "little Azerty is eating your lunch. If you want to have any vendors in our program, you'll need to act."

"It takes time to arrange a vendor day with so many brands."

Knowing that cash for a new company was like blood to a vampire, United volunteered something rather tasty. "What if we were to pay some presentation fees up front for the brands we want?"

"Which brands did you have in mind?" Craig asked.

"Well, I was thinking of Avery, Fellows, ACCO, GBC Quartet, 3M, Apollo, US Robotics, and APC," he answered.

"Just how much support were you thinking about?"

"How much would it take?"

Craig thought out loud, "Eight brands times a minimum of three

Multimedia plus three Basic Presentations each. They cost five thousand and twenty-five hundred respectively, so let's see, that's a hundred and twenty thousand plus sixty for a total of a hundred and eighty grand.

"Knowing these brands, they'll most likely commit to twice that. I'm guessing three hundred and sixty thousand dollars—but to be fair, why don't you guarantee a hundred grand toward whatever their actual commitments turn out to be." They shook hands on it and confirmed the arrangement in writing that afternoon. It was a very profitable round of golf. (Craig missed guessing the actual combined commitments of these brands by only $8,000: they would sign up for $352,000.)

With United's commitment, our team set about making preparations for our biggest vendor day. The process began with a letter in which we said, "Our management team has owned manufacturing companies. As a result, we have created a store that works as well for you as it does for the consumer. Just imagine how much more you will sell when every customer has access to a world-class presentation on your products and can buy them in their homes and offices."

About 400 office-products execs responded to the invitation. Collectively, they represented over a hundred brands. For the occasion, United rented the grand ballroom of a Westin hotel near Chicago. Our team arrived early, set up the store-in-box computer, and hooked up our new 3M data projector. The hotel had a huge screen that came down from the ceiling. However, true to Murphy's Law, their sound system failed. Fortunately, Craig, knowing Murphy, had lugged his own speakers along.

"The room looks great," Craig said as the United team walked in. "How many people are we expecting?"

"At least four hundred."

"That's great." Craig turned to the hotel's representative. "Sir, can you get someone to remove about fifty of these chairs?"

"Yes sir," he said, scratching his head, "but I was told to set up chairs for four hundred guests."

"Yes, I know. So if we need them back, I assume you'll have someone here to accommodate our guests?"

"Yes sir, we can do that."

"The spirit of a meeting is dampened when the audience comes into a room that's set up for a bigger crowd. But if the room has too few places to sit, it looks like the event is exceeding expectations."

As predicted, the Grand Ballroom filled to overflowing. Craig gave the office products industry a guided tour of our virtual store. "You'll notice," he began, "that when you enter Value America, you're greeted by name." he turned toward the giant twelve by eighteen foot screen just behind his left shoulder, where in an attractive gold script the audience saw *Welcome Member—Craig Winn.* "That's pretty sociable, wouldn't you say? How many stores greet their customers by name?

"We show a picture of the last product you purchased." The screen showed a Tiffany lamp. "We say thanks, and ask a question: 'Did this product exceed your expectations, merely meet them, or fail in some way?' If it failed to meet my expectations, I would be taken directly to customer service.

"By asking our customers' opinions, we have created the first real 'consumer reports.' Consumers who have bought a product can report on its performance. If a product is consistently rated poorly, we will remove it from the store. We attach our customers' ratings to the purchasing panel so our members can view the ratings prior to deciding which item to buy."

A new screen appeared. "Our store is telling me that my son's birthday is coming up and reminds me of my wedding anniversary too. We plan to add an automatic floral delivery service to send flowers to your wife the day before your anniversary, her birthday, Valentine's Day, and Mother's Day. Gentlemen, you'll never have to spend another day in the doghouse."

The crowd broke into laughter, sat up a little taller, and collectively seemed to wonder where this store had been all of their lives. Craig launched the main menu. "There are six ways to shop at Value America, and because this is a database-driven store, not a collection of static pages, our customers can shop any way they want. The technology that makes this happen is proprietary. We designed it."

He explained. "Some folks like to shop by brand. Some like to shop by category, like office products. Some, like my wife, like to shop by what's on sale. One of these days, she's going to save us right into prosperity. Some like to shop by what's new, and some by related product—they bought a printer from us, and now they need the right cartridge. We take them directly to the one that's right for them.

"Can you imagine a retailer willing to rearrange their entire store for each customer, however they want to shop, whenever they want to shop, every time they enter the store? That's exactly what we do." The skeptics were starting to soften. This was not what they had expected.

"Say you want to shop by category. Click on the office icon, and our Office Products department instantly appears. It includes printers, copiers, faxes, phones, writing instruments, calculators, furnishings, and supplies, just as you'd expect." Most everyone leaned forward, focused on their category, and then, almost in unison, sat back, recognizing they *belonged.*

"If I were to select 'Phones,' as you can see, I'm given a choice of types." Craig reversed gears and with a single mouse click went back to the main menu. "But what if you wanted to shop by brand? Let's return to the office products menu. Here you see some of our favorite brands, represented by their logos. We could choose 3M, Canon, Avery, Brother, or HP. Let's click on HP." Of course, Craig chose HP. They were well respected, and more to the point, their presentations had actually been completed. "Here we see eight Multimedia Presentations on Hewlett-Packard products. Let's say we're interested in their inkjet printers."

Craig clicked his mouse and let the HP DeskJet presentation run. Now the store was doing the talking. The audience heard our voice-over talent explain what the products were all about. A man's voice and a woman's switched pages between them, using different words than the written copy, somehow chattier, more conversational. But it didn't sound like a sales pitch. It was friendly advice. When the voice stopped, the page automatically advanced.

With the powerful projector, the store's pages were huge. Craig was justifiably proud, enjoying himself. As the audience watched the presentation, he studied their faces. After five pages, he clicked on the "World-in-a-Box" icon at the bottom of the page, going directly to the purchasing panel.

"What you just experienced is a Multimedia presentation. The audio you heard is blind launched—you don't have to do anything to start it. This feature exists only at Value America. It's streamed in real time from one of our servers. Did you notice that the pages changed automatically? Again, only at Value America. We even delay the audio stream by three seconds so that our visuals don't compete for bandwidth with the audio."

Turning back to the screen, he said, "We are now in the product purchasing area. Here we can buy any HP DeskJet. Let's say we've decided to buy this one." He clicked on the product's image.

He walked them through the buying process. "The store remembers who I am and it knows my favorite addresses. So now it's giving me a choice of where I want my new DeskJet printer shipped. Do I want it shipped to my home, to my office, or maybe to my mother-in-law's house in Bakersfield? All I have to do is choose and click." By this time, Craig had transformed the audience from vendors whom we were trying to sell into consumers who were thinking, *I can't wait to go shopping.*

"You'll notice the store didn't calculate a final delivered price. That's because it needs to know where the product is going. We've built a freight calculator that instantly calculates the cost of shipping. I'll click the 'buy' button and... sure enough, there's the freight cost.

"It's been said that there are only two things certain in this life, death and taxes. In our world, taxes are only a sure thing if you live in Virginia. You'll notice that I've been charged 4.5 percent sales tax because I'm a Virginia resident. If I lived elsewhere, we wouldn't have charged any tax.

"Okay. How do I want to pay? See my MasterCard, here? Watch. I'll click here...." A swooshing sound was heard as the image of another credit card appeared. "I can choose my VISA card instead." Winn clicked the "Purchase" button, and our animated "Good Buy Machine" filled the screen. It took about ten seconds to run, entertaining the audience while his credit card was being verified. "My order has now been processed, and my printer is winging its way to my home."

There was spontaneous applause, not something you ordinarily experience after your average retail transaction. He smiled broadly. He couldn't help but love this stuff. "Now, a moment ago, I shared that we offered some other ways to shop. More than half the people that grace the doors of Office Depot or Staples go there for one of two reasons: to buy an HP print cartridge...or to return the one they bought by mistake. How many of you have a printer at home or in your office?" Craig asked as he raised his hand. Most everyone raised theirs too. "Now, how many of you know the model number of your cartridge?"

Out of 450 in the audience, about four hands were still raised. They all belonged to the HP delegation, Craig noted, getting a laugh. "Okay. If you walked into a Staples or Office Depot and said, 'I bought my printer here a year ago, but I don't know the model number or what cartridge it takes,' what do you think they'd say?" More laughter.

"We've all bought things like printers not knowing what supplies or accessories go with them. We look up and down the aisles, pick the wrong thing, take it home, and then return it to the store. Well, at Value America, we'll find it for you. A moment ago, I bought an HP printer. So now it's stored under my receipts and in the related products area." Craig was navigating through his account-info page as he spoke. "If I click here," he said as the cursor hovered above the HP printer, "we'll go to its related products. Here are the results: a black cartridge, a color cartridge, and a printer cable. If I click my mouse on any of these, it'll show up on my doorstep tomorrow."

Excited murmurings exploded as they processed the implications.

"A lot of people have a drawer somewhere, or an old shoebox, where they keep their receipts and product warranties. We have a place like that too, and you can visit it any time you like. You'll find information on everything you've ever bought in our store. We call it our 'Shoebox.' Here we attach an electronic version of the product's warranty to your receipt.

"Anybody here like a good sale?" Twenty or thirty hands went up, mostly women, laughing. We've got you covered," Craig said. He clicked again, and a dancing animated mouse appeared, wearing a sweatshirt that said "VA" on it. "Meet 'Crazy Joe'—named after our Webmaster. He's the mascot of our bargain basement. If we get special buys, closeouts, promotions, or the like, we pass the savings on to you.

"There's another way to shop at Value America; you can check out 'What's New.'" Craig clicked his mouse. "As we add new brands, you'll see their logos here, along with a funny line inviting you to take a closer look. For instance, beside Hoover's logo, it says, 'Now that Value America has Hoover, our store really sucks.'"

He continued through the laughter, "The lawyers at Hoover had a field day with our presentations. Early on, we encouraged our brand partners to review them for accuracy. So Hoover had their lawyers affirm our claims. They edited down our ten-minute presentations on the benefits of owning a Hoover to a minute of 'some Hoover products may clean your floor under ideal, but not all, circumstances.'" The crowd continued to roar. "So we came to two conclusions. First, Hoover's *lawyers* sucked— that is, they sucked all the vitality out of the presentations. And second," he went on, hardly controlling his own laughter, "for the good of the cause, we'd never let another lawyer near our copy. These aren't ads; they're *our* opinions. That's the whole idea of providing an endorsement."

As they settled down, it was obvious that there wasn't anybody in the room who wasn't imagining what his or her company's products might look like in our store. This was not turning out to be the boring pitch they had been expecting. It was looking like something that could fundamentally change the way they did business. That didn't happen every day.

But he wasn't done. "We believe that we should leave the world a little better than we found it. We donate one percent of every dollar a consumer spends in our store—that's gross revenue, not profit—to charity. And here's the good part. The customer gets to choose where our money goes, from a long list of worthy causes. If you're having a bad day, just click here, and we'll tell you how much we've donated to the charity of your choice." Craig scrolled through the list. Everyone spotted something they had supported. Their expressions and their murmurings clearly revealed their thoughts: *these guys had thought of everything.*

"Of course, some of you may be saying, 'My favorite charity is my hip pocket.' Well, okay. Value America also gives one percent of everything you buy back to *you*. We call 'em 'ValueDollars,' and they work like frequent-flyer miles. One day we'll even have our own credit card," he said as a picture of a Value America Visa card flashed on the screen. "An additional one percent of anything you buy anywhere in the world will be electronically transferred to your ValueDollar account. But we're not limited to one percent. When selling MAP'd items, we offer 'Bonus' ValueDollars—larger awards so our customers get the right deal while we comply with your policies."

Craig left the store presentation and articulated the reasons Value America had been created. He continued to speak extemporaneously but had a well-orchestrated complement of computer-generated visuals. He knew that visual imagery combined with his spoken words would enable his audience to grasp, and retain, our revolutionary message.

"Value America was created to do good things for two groups of people: the people who buy things and the people who make them," Craig explained. "The existing retail environment serves itself quite nicely, but it does a poor job of serving these two groups, even though it relies on both for its very existence. We start by giving consumers the seven things they want most. First, quality products, things that actually *do* what they're supposed to do—that meet, or better yet exceed, our expectations. That's why we partner with reputable brands like you." The audience's reaction told him he was on target.

"The second thing you and I want as consumers is value. We want to get our money's worth.

"Third, we want convenience. That's why we embraced shopping malls. That's why we spend billions each year on things we can buy at home with catalogs. Online shopping is the most convenient retail channel ever. No matter where you are, we're down the hall, not down the street. Even the slowest modem is faster than the shortest drive.

"Those who write about such things tell us that convenience is the primary motivation for online shopping. Sure, a store that's in your home and office is convenient. So is one that delivers products to your doorstep rather than requiring you and me, as consumers, to be our own delivery vehicle. But what could be more convenient than a store that brings it all together?

"The fourth thing consumers want is information. Access to good, reliable information is the number-two motivation for Web shopping. We produce thoroughly researched presentations about what we sell, because customers want their questions answered.

"Fifth, we want selection. One of the cornerstones of Value America is our desire to present and sell a brand's *whole* line, not just a couple of hot products. If you make twenty-seven kinds of staplers, we see no reason why consumers should only be able to buy three of them.

"Sixth, we want great customer service. We're frustrated when we can't find someone to process a return or help us find a product. This is why we've integrated a customer-care call center.

"And seventh, as consumers, we have a conscience. That's why Value America gives back one percent of every purchase to charity."

Craig scanned the room. "If you think about it, the best way we can serve consumers is to serve brands like you, the folks who make and market the products that make the world work.

"The sad and painful truth is that your biggest customers have become your adversaries. Privately, hundreds of you have shared your horror stories with us.

"Everyone here makes his or her living in the office products business. That means that seventy-five percent of your retail sales are made to only two customers—Office Depot and Staples. You can't afford to alienate either of them. You know it, and they know it. If you made products in a different category, the story would be the same. In the home improvement industry, seventy-five percent of your retail sales would be to Home Depot and Lowe's. Can you imagine being a home electronics brand and losing Circuit City, or a sporting goods manufacturer without access to Sports Authority?

"Retailers routinely use their accounts payable, your accounts receivable, to exercise their clout. They justify their deductions by issuing hundred-page routing and compliance guides. I can tell from the looks on your faces that I'm hitting pretty close to home. The good news is, we're different. We're here to *serve* brands, giving you the things you need most.

"Everyone wants to expand sales in the newest and fastest growing distribution channel. What could be better than harnessing the momentum of the Internet and partnering with us here today? You know what they say: 'If you're not the lead dog in the pack, the view never changes.'"

The audience was getting the picture, and they liked what they saw. "The second thing you want is to sell your products based upon their merits, rather than on price alone. So who ya gonna call...Office Depot? Your *advertising agency?*" Craig asked as the crowd chuckled.

"A few minutes ago, we saw an HP DeskJet presentation. All of you are in the office products biz, but I'll bet there's not one of you," Craig said as he raised his hand, "that didn't learn something new about HP."

A few hands went up, amidst laughter. "Oh, great. The folks from HP didn't learn a thing." He gestured toward the Hewlett-Packard team in the front. "Anybody else?" His point was made.

"The third thing brands want is the ability to bring your whole line together—to be able to sell everything you make—in one place. You want the consumer to think of you every time they're in the market for something you make. Existing retailers have no interest in putting your scissors near your paper clips just because you make both. Value America has changed that. We want you, all of you, everything that makes you great. We give each brand its own exclusive department.

"There's another thing brands want—to get closer to your customers. You want to know who they are, what they're thinking, why they bought this instead of that. You want to communicate directly with them and do business with them without all the inefficiencies of the existing channels. Value America provides a virtual link between you and your customers.

Wouldn't you like to know what percentage of customers come to you because of the power of your brand? Or was it just your category that brought them into our store? Are you interested in their demographics— male *versus* female, how much they earn, where they live? Wouldn't you like to know how the demographics of those people who bought your products differed from those who saw your presentation but elected not to buy? All of that data is kept by our company, and once a quarter, we'll share it with you in aggregate terms.

"We'll break down the physical barriers, too. Previously, inventory was managed like Sears manages it. Let's say you made red pencils. Sears would have you ship a truckload to their distribution center. From there they'd be shipped to the stores in hopes consumers would love them as much as the buyer did. Sam Walton came along and decided to put a handful of red pencils in each store, along with intelligent registers to keep track of them. His systems reported how many he had sold in each store, and an order would go out to you, via EDI, to replace them. Walton made the consumer, in effect, the buyer. Now, we've taken the next logical step. Rather than sending you orders by-store-by-week, we send them to you by customer, in real time.

"WalMart transfers all of the costs associated with distribution and inventory to you. In case you've grown used to jumping through hoops, let me recount the tale of your average order. It averages less than two hundred dollars. You receive them under some EDI variant that doesn't sync with yours, so you have to manually enter it into your system. You send it to your distribution center, stage it on your shipping dock, and side mark each individual carton. Then you're required to put a bill of lading on one particular carton. You have to follow a convoluted routing guide that designates shipping times and carriers. Then *you* get to pay the freight to get it to *their* store. You have to invoice each store individually. And because the routing guide and the compliance agreement are purposely designed to be impossible, you can expect deductions."

As he reminded the brands of the abuse they routinely suffered, he was making them uncomfortable with the intolerable state of affairs they had been forced to endure. He was also demonstrating that he knew what made their industry tick, down to the smallest detail.

"Once you've done all this, you have to prove there were no concealed shortages or damage. If you don't, retailers will delay payment and make deductions. Ever wonder why they don't let you invoice them by EDI? Some of you know. EDI is too fast and accurate. If there are no mistakes, they can't make deductions. If there are no deductions, what excuse do they have to delay payment? By the time you get your money, you're beaten down. That, my friends, is abuse, pure and simple.

"We don't do business that way. We *pay* our invoices; we *want* to be invoiced electronically. We want to be billed accurately, of course, but we make this promise: even if there's a discrepancy, we'll pay the undisputed portion when it's due." For this, they gave him another ovation.

Craig wrapped up his remarks with one of his favorite comparisons. "Ladies and gentlemen, we believe what you have experienced here today is as innovative as the idea Fred Smith, founder of Federal Express, conceived in order to compress time and deliver value."

About forty vendors signed up on the spot, and soon thereafter virtually all of them elected to partner with us. Other meetings would follow, with other companies, but for sheer volume, there was never another gathering the likes of the United Stationers vendor day in Chicago.

Were it not for the office-products industry, Value America may not have survived its turbulent childhood. The confidence shown by so many brands in that industry became a critical factor in convincing top brands from other fields to partner with us.

The record books say Ernie Els won the '97 U.S. Open, taking home $500,000 in prize money. But we believe the real winner was a company named Value America. The relationships formed that weekend brought in over $1.4 million in listing agreements over the next six weeks, all because of one gentleman, short of stature but long on vision, Mr. John Motley.

If only they were wise and would understand this—Moses

A CAPITAL VENTURE

*R*ichmond wasn't like Charlottesville. C'Ville had no real aristocracy, no old-money upper crust. Newcomers were welcomed here. But in Richmond, being a fourth-generation blue blood still counted for something, even if the money, old as it was, had dwindled in generations past.

Kyle South's blood was blue enough. His family went back generations, and with that genealogy came status, and with that, connections. Being a graduate of the prestigious Darden School of Business at the University of Virginia didn't hurt, either. The old-boy network still thrived, even if the boys were not all that old.

He didn't comport himself as your average over-privileged rich kid. Kyle worked hard in his role as technology merchandiser. He was enthusiastic, organized, and systematic. He contacted vendors and was able to explain our concept as well as Bill Hunt, and that was saying something. But Kyle South couldn't seem to get to "Yes."

Craig, of course, was batting a very high average. He struck most people as the most persuasive fellow they had ever encountered. It was no surprise that Bill was generating a reasonable number of yeses, too. He was a pro with decades of experience and a lifetime of great contacts.

Rex Scatena, still living in California, was spending more and more of his time selling Value America and less of it practicing law. Even though he had never sold a thing in his life outside a courtroom, he had a remarkable rate of success, even better than Bill's. Rex had a ton of money invested in the venture, and we sometimes wondered whether his success was due to his ability or his motivation.

But Kyle wasn't making it happen. He seemed to be making all the right noises, but a disproportionately large percentage of his consumer technology brands had declined to participate. He knew only too well that his compensation was predicated on his performance, and that his contribution to the company's coffers was falling far short of what he was getting paid. Clearly, it was time to look for other ways to make himself valuable. It was time to tap the old-boy network.

To Kyle South, the obvious place to start was the law offices of Caise, Perkins, in Richmond. Justin Caise was an attorney specializing in solving the problems encountered by emerging businesses, including the biggest problem: raising money. This was invariably the Achilles heel of entrepreneurial enterprises like Value America.

The law firm of Caise, Perkins came highly recommended. The partners included one Jim Gilmore, soon to be Governor of Virginia. George

Allen, the current Governor and future U.S. Senator, was a close personal friend. The list of high-rolling notables on a first-name basis with Justin Caise, in both politics and business, was impressive. And Justin knew Kyle South. How fortuitous.

Justin's appearance wasn't exactly what Craig had expected. It wasn't his face or build, which were pretty ordinary, but his hairstyle—swooped straight back and fixed into place. Justin's style sense was either way behind or way ahead. Craig prayed it was the former.

Hairstyle aside, Caise was a professional, and we had pressing issues. Re-incorporation in Virginia was high on Justin's list. He told Craig that takeover issues and board protections were superior to those in California or Nevada. But the "staggered" board structure Caise recommended would later prove to be less than ideal.

Craig had drafted stock agreements for the original employees that suggested grants. He told Justin that he wanted to make these legally binding. Justin's counsel was to use options instead, and he outlined good legal and tax reasons for doing so. Winn understood, but knew that it would take some time before the company could afford to pay the $15,000 in legal fees required to implement the plan. He had a choice between taking care of the stock program—which he needed to do sometime soon— or making payroll that week. He chose the latter.

Justin helped Rex out on some trademark issues and generally made himself useful as the company's new legal counsel. Yet his most significant role would be guiding us through the tricky and dangerous shoals of private investment funding.

✑

"I KNOW THEY'RE small. So are we."

Kyle had a point. But the bigger issue was that the Madison Company had never raised funds for a technology firm. Yet we needed money. Kyle's friend at Madison, Lyle Timmon, a fellow Darden alumnus, said he could help.

We were trying to raise a million dollars on a valuation of ten million. One million, we thought, would be enough to get us over the hump. The problem was the valuation. Rex had tried it out on his friends, and Craig had done the same. The only reaction they were getting was polite amusement. Ten million dollars? This was an Internet store with about fifteen employees, hanging out in an Attic in Nowhere, Virginia. A helluva business plan, but *ten mil?* No, I don't think so.

Madison didn't see it that way, though comps were hard to come by.

About the only comparable company was Amazon.com. They were just then in the process of going public, so their numbers were readily available. The interesting thing was that Amazon's pre-IPO worth, calculated for their private investment rounds, had been based not on profitability, but on forecasted revenue. As a private company, Amazon had been valued at sixty percent of projected future sales—sixty percent of the revenue they expected to generate in the upcoming year.

By that math, Value America was worth a whole lot more than anybody thought. Craig's revenue projection for 1998 was $40 million; sixty percent of that put the company's value at $24 million. Even rounded down to an even twenty, it doubled our valuation. Using this math, the prospects looked good for raising $2 million in working capital.

Pessimists do not start businesses. Entrepreneurs, who do, are optimists by nature. It is therefore common for their growth projections to be sinfully inflated. It bears mention here that such was not to be the case with Value America's unabashedly entrepreneurial top management. As far back as late 1996, Craig and Rex had predicted revenues of $40 million in '98 and $175 million in '99. Both numbers proved correct—on the conservative side. So much for starry-eyed optimism.

Raising venture capital begins with writing a description of the company and its business prospects. When preparing for a public offering, this document is known progressively as the "S1," the "Red Herring" (the pre-IPO version, characterized by the red text on the cover), and the post-IPO "Prospectus." In the world of private investments, it is simply known as "The Book." It begins with an executive summary, followed by an analysis of risk factors, a description of the company, and its financial projections, for which an independent audit must be performed.

The requisite audit was to be our company's first. Half a dozen large accounting firms were interviewed, but we chose a small local company, to save money and to expedite the process. They confirmed that while as an entrepreneurial company it was necessary to know where every dollar was at any given time, presumably because there were so few of them, there was another method of accounting with which the financial community was more comfortable. Thus began the discussion of cost *versus* accrual accounting.

When you're strapped for cash, as we were, the only thing that counts is how much of it you actually have. Thus, you'd use cost-based accounting, which told you, "This amount came in, and that amount went out, leaving you this much." It's accounting based upon one's present reality—not unlike a checkbook.

Accrual-based accounting is more Dickensian in nature. Its reality takes into account the Ghosts of Christmas Past, Present, and Yet-to-Come, which is a poetic way of stating that it allocates costs and profits over the entire period in which they should be properly recognized. This method is expected of companies engaged in raising or borrowing money. So every publicly traded firm, and those planning to go public, find themselves using this somewhat less straightforward form of arithmetic.

In practical terms, all of this meant we had an accounting issue with the money generated by our product presentations. Mind you, it was the only revenue we were earning. Technically, our fees just covered the labor it took to build them, including a substantial margin. But since we agreed to host them online for three years, that made their *useful life* three years for accounting purposes.

For bookkeeping, then, should the presentations be sold like cattle—cash on the barrelhead—or amortized over their useful life? If the commonly accepted valuation basis for companies like ours was shifting from "past profits" to "forward revenues," then shifting to accrual-based accounting was a no-brainer. It was the best of all possible worlds: we already had the cash, but it wasn't counted as "revenue" until next year or the year after that, making the company look all the more valuable on paper.

In due time, "The Book" was completed. The documentation was in order, and the "due diligence," the formal investigation of the company's financial soundness, had been given, well, *due diligence*. Madison was poised to introduce Value America to the local venture community. It wouldn't come a moment too soon.

As time went on, a remarkable pattern began to emerge: the Darden connection. It seemed that almost everywhere we went, there was someone in a position of influence who had graduated from UVA's Darden School of Business, often in the same class as Value America's merchandiser, Kyle South. Getting a foot in the door of the east coast investment community appeared to be quite a bit easier if the foot happened to be wearing Kyle South's size-ten Gucci loafer. How could one guy know so many of the right people?

Private investment rounds like this are precursors to public offerings. Investors aren't putting their money at risk just because they think the company's concept is sound. They're doing it because they've calculated that the odds are good the company will go public in the near term, so they can cash out. Venture capitalists are gamblers at heart, but gamblers who won't place a bet until they know how the deck has been stacked.

Craig and Rex got good at presenting our company to the venture capitalists. Practice makes perfect, and they got a lot of practice during the spring and summer of '97. It was basically the same presentation that they gave to the brands, but geared to an audience with a different agenda. The presentation never varied much, and invariably it had a positive impact.

A Richmond investor representing Jefferson Capital made the short trip from the state capital to meet with Craig and her friend, Darden classmate Kyle South. "Kyle, so good to see you again," the diminutive blond said as he greeted her in the lobby. "Nice little building." The Attic was in a charming white brick house with black shutters, just east of town. One could see Monticello peeking through the trees on a hill less than a mile away. Our hosts didn't even have a sign outside, but we did. Our two-foot-square, hand-painted rendition of the Value America logo made it look like we owned the joint, humble as it was.

"Our offices are upstairs," Kyle said, "but let me show you around."

They toured the server room in the basement, which looked impressive with its banks of humming glass-enclosed computers on a raised floor for cable management. In reality, it was overkill for Commonwealth and, for the moment, extreme overkill for us. But it sure looked good.

Once in the Attic, he introduced Jefferson to Craig, who until now had been a disembodied voice on the phone. After a quick tour of Presentation Marketing and Web Development, Craig and Kyle escorted her to the big conference room on the main level, where she and another potential investor, Smithers, were given the pitch.

After making several such trips, both venture capitalists said "Yes." Jefferson Capital's Darden grad asked to be our lead investor.

The search for capital went beyond Virginia. We traveled to New York to visit the prestigious investment firm of Wasserstein Perella. We wondered if the northern halls of power and wealth would respond as positively as had genteel southern money. Sure enough, they joined a rapidly growing chorus of venture capitalists who saw our potential.

We visited two firms in Washington D.C. The first was Allied Capital, who joined the others chanting "Yes." The Carlyle Group said "No." Carlyle, a successful and politically connected venture firm, made it clear, however, that their negative answer had nothing to do with Value America *per se*. They said the Internet was not a sector in which they were making investments. They had no one who could properly analyze the merits of an online retailer, or any Internet-related company for that matter. Several of their principals would later become individual investors in our star-studded "Series C" round. Their "no" really meant "not yet."

As Madison's Lyle Timmon witnessed the uniformly positive reaction of venture capitalists on the east coast, he offered to take Value America west, to California. The heavy hitters in the Silicon Valley were Kleiner

Perkins and Softbank. Both had sterling reputations investing in Internet start-ups. They had backed all the right players.

But a bit of research revealed something disturbing about them. In Japanese business culture, it's called *keiretsu*, mutually beneficial corporate back scratching. If they invested in Yahoo, for example (which they did), and also in Amazon (which they had), they would be in a position to influence both companies, though they would surely characterize it as "suggestion." Amazon, for example, might be "encouraged" to buy an anchor position on Yahoo's portal—at, say, $5 million a year. At the same time, Yahoo might be "motivated" to give Amazon preferential treatment, like giving them exclusives. It was all geared to make both Amazon and Yahoo! look more valuable, thus increasing the value of the investors' holdings.

It was all perfectly legal, as long as they didn't go too far, but there was a dark side. It was rumored that if these 800-pound gorillas in the venture world decided your goals were no longer consistent with theirs, they had not only the power, but also the will, to shut your business down. The founders decided that we could do without another challenge and asked Lyle to politely unschedule us. There were plenty of willing, even eager, fish in our pond. And old money was just as green.

⚜

"JOHN," CRAIG SAID into his speakerphone, "your lawyers are about to do you in. I *told* you I'd take care of you."

Motley replied in their defense, "They're considered one of the best firms in Washington. They've never steered me wrong before."

"Listen, John, I like you and your family. I appreciate everything you've done for us, so I'm going to go over all of this again." Craig gave John chapter and verse on stock options, vesting, strike prices, and exercise periods. "If you're willing to trust me, I'll give you everything I've promised. If the market holds out, and if we're able to deliver on our corporate promises, you'll do just fine. But, I'm only going to do this if you tell your lawyers to back off and stop hounding me."

"Okay. I'll call them," John said with some trepidation.

"Good. Katie, the boys, and I are going to Wintergreen this weekend. Do you know where it is?" Craig asked.

"Sure."

"Meet us there. We'll work out the details." They did, and in time, just as Craig had predicted, John Motley became a rich man. No one deserved it more.

ৎৡৢঌ

TO JOHNNY-MOT AND BITS (i.e., John Motley Jr. and his little sister, Elizabeth), it was just school. But to their parents, it was something more. The Potomac prep school was one of the finest in Washington.

Rich Fairbank's kids also attended Potomac. John, the master of personal networking, had gotten to know the Chairman and CEO of CapitalOne, as he had many of the Potomac parents. Motley had become convinced that Value America was poised for greatness, so we were on his mind as he was greeted by his friend following a school function.

"Hello, John. Bits did a great job in the program—cute as a bug."

"She's definitely got her mother's talent," John said proudly. After exchanging pleasantries, Motley brought the conversation around to business, as men are wont to do. "How's the credit card business these days?"

"Just keeps getting better." CapitalOne had made its mark by exploiting a niche market that others, not recognizing its potential, had avoided. They provided credit cards to people with less than perfect credit. Ordinarily, this could be a formula for disaster, but CapOne had done its homework. They had hired dozens of MBAs to do financial modeling. Together, they had invented ways to identify deadbeats while finding those, despite their questionable credit profiles, who were acceptable risks.

Rich Fairbank and his team had discovered an often overlooked truth—a truth as old as the Bible: there is no correlation between a person's wealth and their propensity to pay their bills. The honoring of one's debts is a matter of character, not of income. The tip-off for CapOne's analysts turned out to be absurdly simple. No matter what else the applicants put on their forms, if they listed an accurate telephone number, they were likely to pay their bills; phony phone number, they'd try to stiff you. They may be a little over their limit, and they may pay a few days late, but they'd pay.

Credit card companies like CapOne depend on direct mail advertising to grow. But it's an expensive hit-or-miss proposition when the solicitation is addressed to "Occupant," or even to the more warm and sincere "Resident." Any direct mail marketer will tell you that your mailing's success rate will only be as good as the quality, accuracy, and appropriateness of your list. Paying to print and mail a catalog full of frilly lingerie to a fifty-two-year-old bachelor auto mechanic without a credit card is, entertainment value aside, a guaranteed waste of money.

But in a coordinated effort, credit card issuers and direct response retailers could form an incredibly profitable symbiosis. If you knew that your solicitations were going exclusively to people who had credit cards, and who had purchased the kind of things you were selling, then you had a recipe for success beyond your wildest expectations.

"Rich," John said, "I recently met a guy whose company is poised to make some breakthroughs in Internet commerce. His name is Winn. The company is Value America. They're doing some remarkable stuff."

"E-commerce?" E-tail was the electronic incarnation of direct response. Rich was immediately interested. The attention the new field was getting on Wall Street and in the media was hard to miss.

"Yes, and you know, at some point they're going to want their own credit card. Maybe you two should put your heads together."

"That's a good idea, John." Rich pulled out his business card and scribbled a name on the back. "Why don't you get him in touch with this gentleman. If he likes what he hears, we'll go from there."

Craig had a word for them, *homo-chromos*—short for homogenous chromosomes. All of these MBA types, it seemed, had been stamped out with the same cookie cutter: same age, same haircut, same suit, same advanced degrees from the same prestigious colleges, same high class standing, same lack of experience, and the same arrogant superiority toward lesser life forms—especially entrepreneurs. This one was no different. He was certainly bright enough, polite and business-like, but Craig got the distinct impression that he had gone to kindergarten wearing a suit and tie. Enthusiasm and passion were apparently signs of weakness.

Yet this fellow was responsible for business development at Capital-One, so Craig, who indeed foresaw the need for a store credit card, was happy to give him a tour of Value America. The nameless, faceless MBA must have thought the concept held promise, because he immediately set up a meeting with his boss, Rich Fairbank.

The rendezvous took place at Fairbank's retreat on Gibson Island, a private enclave in the middle of the Chesapeake Bay, situated between the historic ports of Annapolis and Baltimore. Craig and John had brought the store-in-a-box, the big 3M projector, and a large screen. But it was a beautiful day. A deep cerulean sky was punctuated with puffy white clouds. The porch provided a perfect view of sailboats gliding along the Maryland coastline, so they decided to give the pitch outside on the patio.

Craig proposed a rather unusual alliance, uniting "the key and the door," as he saw it. The key to e-tail was the credit card. Without electronic money, there was no "e"-commerce. And Value America was the ultimate online doorway between consumers and brands.

Forming an alliance with CapOne presupposed that Value America would have been given the opportunity to serve their customers. That would give us several advantages. Everyone on their customer list, by definition, had a credit card, and let's face it, it's really hard to shop online without one.

Second, the list was accurate. It had to be, because it was comprised of the cardholders' billing addresses. You could spend years, and a whole lot of money, trying to compile such a perfect customer list.

Third, those on the list trusted its keeper. After all, CapOne was their bank. Endorsed by CapitalOne, Value America would gain instant legitimacy. Fourth, CapOne knew where their cardholders shopped and what they liked to buy.

Craig was also desirous of partnering with CapOne's call center, which used the best technology for routing and managing tens of thousands of phone calls a day. Unlike most Internet prognosticators, he firmly believed that the telephone would play a critical role in the implementation of any successful Web retail establishment.

Rich, after absorbing the presentation, came to the conclusion that their two companies could indeed be very good for each other, but the partnership need not stop there. He asked if CapitalOne could become the sole investor in our private funding round.

After a moment's reflection, Winn realized that we were too far down the road with the other investors to let one company have the whole deal. But there was no reason CapOne couldn't be a lead investor. In the final analysis, with their credit card, customer data, direct mail solicitations, and call-center capabilities to sweeten the pot, CapitalOne's money was greener than anyone else's.

❧

"WE'VE GOT A problem, Rex," Craig said with a grin. "We've got more investors than we've got company to invest in."

"There's not enough stock to go around."

"Jefferson wants two million. Allied Capital thinks that anything less than a million isn't worth bothering with. Wasserstein Perella wants at least two million. Smithers wants in too. Now with CapOne wanting more than two million, plus an alliance that could blow the doors off e-commerce, we've got too much demand." Craig paused. "For a company two paydays away from being broke, we sure are popular."

"Maybe the round's valued too low. After all, it's been a few months since we started beating the bushes. We've made a lot of progress since then, especially in signing up brands. You saw the reaction at United Stationers—it was like a stampede! We're performing much better than we said we would. What if we raised the price?"

"It would tend to weed out those who aren't serious. As soon as some-body backs off, we'll know we've zeroed in on the right number. Our worth, apparently, is no longer a matter of arithmetic, it's a matter of per-ceptions—craziest thing I ever saw."

"So long as we don't slow down the process," Rex cautioned, "I say we raise the valuation. Thirty million has a nice ring to it."

❧

HE SURE DIDN'T look like the typical CapitalOne "suit." He arrived in a van reminiscent of the hippy era. He wore his hair in a ponytail, and he didn't talk at all like a financial guru. But, like everyone else we had encountered at CapitalOne, he was definitely smart.

He was a techno-wizard, CapOne's CIO, and he had come to evaluate our systems. He knew, as we had discovered, that there was no off-the-shelf software available—at any price—that could do any of the mar-velous things we claimed to be doing. Were we for real, or were we just a house of cards?

Joe and Lad spent hours with him. He wanted to know how we drove our site dynamically out of a database. How did our authoring tool empow-er artists and writers? How did we make our EDI solution work with everybody else's? How had we solved the problems of blind-launching audio and automatic pagination? He asked a plethora of intelligent ques-tions.

Joe and Lad demonstrated how it all worked. They showed him thou-sands of lines of code. They opened his eyes. The CapOne techno-guru went back to Richmond armed with the knowledge that Value America had actually accomplished things no one else had even *attempted*. Should they invest? *Hell, yes!*

❧

REX SCATENA had finally moved to Charlottesville. His law practice was history, yet few of Value America's employees had any idea what Rex meant to the company. He had just shown up one day with the title of President. He was an executive, a merchandiser, and an ex-lawyer who had a lot of meetings with Craig, now managed the company's check-book, and traveled to most every trade show. That's about all anybody, except for Joe Page, Bill Hunt, and me, knew about him. Craig was more relaxed now that Rex was here; that much was obvious, at least to me.

Our one-year anniversary had come and gone without anybody noticing. We were too busy just trying to survive. But enough time had passed for us to have developed some concept of our place—our value to the firm.

I tried to be scrupulous in treating my Marketing team members with respect, praising them when they'd earned it. I knew how far a little encouragement could go in a stressful situation, especially among creative types. Unfortunately, that didn't mean that I was in a position to give them raises, no matter how much they deserved them.

Rick Major, my senior graphics guy, finally wearied of getting put off whenever he'd ask me about a raise. He decided to go over my head, straight to Craig. The withering look he got told him the whole story. It wasn't going to happen. Rick wisely retreated.

It was a little thing, but it made everybody more aware of just how precarious our situation was. As for me, it made me realize that I needed reassurance too. What did Craig think of the job I was doing? In the early days, he and I had challenged each other regularly; mutual constructive criticism was part of our daily regimen. But now his attention was focused elsewhere. Sure, he was complimentary from time to time and never uttered a harsh word, but I needed more.

I mentioned my concern to Rex one day, almost in passing. Frankly, I was a bit reluctant to bring it up with Craig. What if he *hated* my stuff? The next day, he called me into his office. Rex had spoken with him. I remember only one word of that conversation: *"spectacular."* I needn't have worried. I was still the same guy he had hired. Felt good, though.

The problem was that Craig could be intimidating. He didn't mean to be, but he clearly wasn't your average guy. His door was always open; anyone could go in and rap with him about anything. But if you wanted to challenge something he believed in, you'd better have your act together—be able to support your position.

Craig is an active listener and that, I suppose, was part of the problem. You couldn't rattle on for half an hour without interruption. He always wanted to dissect your first point, understand it clearly, and evaluate its implications before you moved on to the next.

Countless times, Joe was asked by others less sure of themselves to confront Craig about something that was troubling them. They'd invariably say, "*You* go talk to him. He listens to you."

Joe always responded the same way: "His door is open for a reason. Go on in. He'll listen to *you* too. Just don't babble. Make sure you can support whatever's on your mind. He's going to ask questions, and he'll remember what you say."

If there was one person questioning his status in the company, it was Kyle South. Craig had made it all too clear that Kyle's performance was not up to par. He had a lot of irons in the fire, to be sure, but he was having a terrible time getting his brands to say, "Yes."

Our merchandisers all had a sales quota. It was by no means an impossible goal to reach, for Craig was routinely exceeding it tenfold, and Rex, with no sales experience, was doing almost as well. Bill Hunt and Monica Link met theirs, as did Ken Erickson. Kyle South did not.

In our early days, it was not uncommon for several people to have a hand in the signing of a single vendor. But we were becoming increasingly impatient with Kyle's arithmetic, in which merely having been in the same room with a vendor who'd signed on counted as an "assist."

The partners had no illusions about the value of Kyle's introductions to Lyle Timmon at Madison or to Justin Caise at Caise, Perkins. While they were appreciated, the fact remained that both firms were charging for their services—they were hardly doing us any favors.

South knew in his heart that his days were numbered. But if they had taught him anything in business school, it was how to leverage contacts. If his leaving the firm empty handed wasn't a problem for us, then maybe he could find something—or someone—to exploit that would be. After all, he had put four whole months of his life into this thing.

❧

THE CICADAS WERE starting to sing, and the darkening sky revealed the first of the million or so stars that would soon dust the Virginia sky on this perfect late-summer evening. Joe, Lad, Kyle, and Ken were all relaxing on Lad's deck. But Kyle hadn't come for relaxation. He had come for *agriculture:* he was about to plant some seeds.

"Boy, Lad," Kyle said. "Must feel good to have that first third of your stock vested already. You and Joe really deserve it, you know? Without you guys, this company would be nowhere."

Joe glanced at him sideways. It had taken total commitment by half a dozen people, and months of hard work from a dozen more, to get the company to where it was now. Sure, tech was important, but....

"Must kind of frost you, though," Kyle said under his breath. "I mean, Winn's buddy Scatena just waltzes in and gets handed thirty percent of the company's stock. You've been here since day one, working your butt off, and you've only got, what, four or five percent?"

"Two." Lad looked up from his beer.

"What?" Kyle asked.

"I have two percent of the company. You're telling me Rex has thirty? What has he done that's worth anything close to thirty percent?"

Joe piped up. "He put up a lot of money really early in the game. Don't you guys know anything about capitalism?"

"It's a question of overall contribution," Kyle snapped back. "From what I can see, Scatena hasn't earned it."

Ken Erickson sipped his beer and didn't say anything. Yet.

༄·ༀ

"I'M TELLING YOU, Craig, you've got a problem." Ken had cornered Craig downstairs in Commonwealth's little kitchen. He had finished the pot and was about to brew some more. "This has been going on for weeks now. Kyle shows up after work at Lad's house, and they sit around grousing about how the stock distribution is unfair. Kyle's got Lad believing he's under-appreciated. He's building his own Irish green-eyed monster. I have no idea why."

"I do," Winn said, frowning. "What about Joe? Is he in on this?"

"Joe has been there on several occasions. He's Lad's bud. Doesn't say much. I've heard him defend your position once or twice, but Lad is more susceptible."

"Thanks, Ken," Craig said softly as he picked up his coffee cup. "Keep me posted, would you? Make it seem like you're with 'em."

"Sure. I didn't want to see you get blind-sided."

Winn was furious, but he did his best to hide it. When he got back upstairs and sat down at his desk, his hand was trembling, spilling coffee. *Get hold of yourself, man.* He asked Rex to join him in his office and closed the door.

"I don't know exactly what's coming," Craig said, "But it *is* coming. Kyle is planning some kind of mutiny. Erickson's been hanging out at Lad's, watching this thing build for a couple of weeks, playing along. It appears that Kyle has come to the conclusion he's on his way out, and he wants to either leave with his pockets full or somehow force us to keep him on. Damn! I just hate these games!"

"So what's he got for a bargaining chip?"

"Not what. Whom. He's got our brilliant but naïve Lad McCaile all worked up about his ownership percentage. He has him convinced that he's due more stock. And the bone of contention…"

"Don't tell me," Rex said. "It's me and my thirty percent."

"You got it, pal." Craig almost spat out the words. "They have no conception of how capital works. They have no grasp of what it's like to plunk down your savings on an idea—to leave your own business and work fourteen-hour days for no salary at all, trying to get something going. Think *they'd* sign a personal guarantee for a quarter million dollar equipment lease? I've explained stock ownership and options to them 'til I'm blue in the face. They just don't get it."

"Okay, calm down. Knowing it's coming is half the battle. Let's look at the likely scenarios. What's Kyle going to ask for? What's Lad going to want? How does Joe figure into this? Can Kyle hurt us?"

Craig blanched at that last question. "He's close to three of the five investors in our venture round. They're all Darden grads."

"What if one or more of them decides to bail?" Rex asked. "Will the round survive?"

Winn knew the answer but elected to change the subject. "Kyle's not pulling his weight. His departure wouldn't even be a mosquito bite. Lad's leaving would be more like getting run over by a buffalo—we'd survive, but it would really hurt. But if Joe leaves, we're dead."

"We need to find out what he's thinking," Rex said. "Right now."

Joe was whisked into Craig's office, pumped for information by our worried founders, and offered a raise and more option shares if he'd stay. "Look, thanks for the offer, but this really isn't necessary. I know you're worried about Lad leaving, and you're right to, 'cause he *is* thinking about it. He doesn't want to. He really likes it here. He's just concerned that he's not getting a fair shake. Lad knows Kyle is gonna get fired if he doesn't quit. But you don't have to worry about me. I'm not going anywhere. I believe in what we're doing. Besides, you can't afford it."

"You got that right." Craig and Rex breathed a collective sigh of relief. "You don't know how pleased we are to hear you're not bailing on us."

"Oh, I probably have some idea," Joe smiled. "Look, Lad is my best friend in Charlottesville. Outside of work, we play soccer and hockey together, go dirt biking, that sort of thing. That doesn't mean I agree with him. He's got this idea that in an Internet business, the geeks are the most important thing. Kyle is in there fanning the flames. Lad has a point, I suppose, but our company is a lot more than its technology."

"That it is," Rex agreed.

"I wouldn't characterize Lad as being evil here," Joe continued. "He just thinks the stock allocation isn't fair. He doesn't know much about the value of capital, and he's conveniently forgotten that he's been drawing a salary all along. I've tried to talk to him, but..."

"Okay, Joe," he said. "Worst cast scenario. Can we make it if Lad leaves? Do you know the back end well enough to continue building it?"

Joe thought for a moment. "Yeah, I think so. I've spent an awful lot of time on the back end. I know how it works. We'll make it."

As Joe got up to leave, they stopped him. "We want to thank you for not holding us hostage. You're a class act. As our way of saying thanks, Rex and I have decided to give you another one percent of the company."

ERICKSON GLANCED BEHIND him as he walked into Craig's office, making sure no one else was within earshot. "Tomorrow morning," he said. "Lad and Kyle are planning to hit you with their ultimatum tomorrow, first thing."

"Okay. Thanks for the heads up."

Craig and Rex met early the next morning.

"Here's how it lines up. The due diligence is done, with a valuation of thirty-five million. The round is due to close tomorrow." The founders were sitting at the round antique drop-leaf maple table in Craig's office. Papers were everywhere, in semi-neat stacks on the table and the floor nearby. "The lead investors are in for two million apiece. So is CapOne. Allied Capital is in for one. Smithers is investing five hundred thousand. That comes to seven and a half million on a thirty-five million valuation.

"That's the good news," Craig continued. "The bad news is that any minute now, Kyle and Lad are going to walk through that door and make their demands. This isn't going to be pretty."

As if on cue, Kyle South popped his head in the door. Lad McCaile was standing beside him.

"Come on in, guys," Rex waved them in. When Lad saw that Rex was there, he hesitated, but it was too late. He followed Kyle into the room. "Have a seat. What can we do for you?"

Kyle and Lad glanced at each other. Lad spoke first. "We feel that there are some inequities in the way the stock has been distributed. It doesn't accurately reflect the contribution of every employee."

"Meaning you two," Craig offered.

"Ahh, well, yes," Lad's speech had been rehearsed, and Craig had thrown his timing off. "Among others, I mean." His prepared text was out the window; he'd have to ad lib. The bottom line was simple. He wanted more stock—a lot more—and he wanted all of it vested immediately.

He felt that since we were a tech firm, the techies should get a bigger slice of the pie. With that picture in mind, he produced a sheet of paper and drew a circle on it. "This circle represents the company," Lad said. "Draw a pie chart that shows the value of each person's contribution."

Craig wouldn't bite. "I'm not going to do that, Lad. It's clear that you have a fundamental lack of understanding about the value of capital, of sales, of marketing, of partnerships. You're a great guy and a darn good DBA, but you're inexperienced in business matters. You've had no exposure to the entrepreneurial environment, to capitalism, to incentive stock options. I trust you will someday. Kyle here's a Darden grad. I'm surprised that he hasn't enlightened you."

South said nothing.

"As far as vesting all your shares immediately, asking us to do that belies a fundamental misunderstanding of the nature of incentive stock ownership. Forget the fact that our agreement clearly delineates a vesting schedule spread out over three years. The whole point of an incentive stock option plan is *incentive*. It's a reward for hanging in there, finishing the job, doing your part to make the company successful. As far as day-to-day contribution, that's why you're paid a salary. Salaries, by the way, are something that neither Rex nor I have enjoyed. In fact, it's our money that's paying yours."

They talked for some time, the founders trying to convince Lad that he was being given a fair, even generous deal in light of the circumstances. Lad tried to get them to see things his way. It was clear that, even though he wouldn't name a figure, he thought his two percent was off by an order of magnitude. Also, the concept of his percentage being diluted by raising capital through private equity funding was impossible for him to grasp. Lad dug in his heels and refused to budge.

Craig looked at Kyle, who as yet had contributed nothing to the discussion. "And what about you, Kyle. What do you want?"

South sat up a little straighter. "I feel pretty much like Lad, that my talents and contributions are being shortchanged. I've worked hard for this company, and I've introduced you to some very important people. That has value, whether you realize it or not. Bottom line, I want my shares to vest immediately, based upon my overall contribution."

"We can't do that, Kyle. Not for you, not for Lad, not for anybody."

Kyle put both hands on the table, pushed his chair back, and rose. "I thought you might say that. I've stated my position in a letter. I'll email it to you. As you consider my conditions, I suggest that you keep in mind that several of the key players in this investment round are looking to me for guidance. After all, what can I tell my fellow Darden alumni if I no longer have faith in the soundness of their proposed investment?"

Craig's voice remained calm. "Are you blackmailing me, Kyle?"

South smiled slightly. "No, of course not. Just negotiating."

"Negotiation," Craig said coldly, "is where I offer you something good in exchange for something good in return. *Tough* negotiation is offering something that's sort of good in exchange for something very good. But when you say 'Give me a good thing, or I'll do something bad to you,' that's *blackmail*. Think about that before you send your email."

Kyle and Lad left Craig and Rex to absorb the implications of what had just transpired. Rex lamented, "I thought this might get ugly, but...."

After an hour or so, Craig checked his email. "Message from Kyle South. Here it is." He opened it up with Rex looking over his shoulder.

"Blah, blah, blah, vendors that I played a key role in securing... Eighty-seven thousand dollars! I'll buy his role in signing Samsung, Hitachi, and UUNET. These would total, let's see, twenty grand. The rest of these, GBC, Sanford, Targus, he played a minor role, if any."

"I signed most of these myself," observed Rex. "Bill signed these two. Where does this guy get his numbers?"

Craig read on. "Stuff that might close within sixty days...more accounts that he thinks he should get credit for...okay, here are his demands—excuse me, his 'proposals.' One, we pre-vest his shares. Fat chance on that. Two, 'If we can put together a mutually agreeable severance package...blah, blah, he promises to be a good boy.... Oh, *shit!* Look at his third point, Rex. 'I will assist in keeping the financing process on track and attribute my leaving the company to a combination of personality issues (differences in management style) and family issues.'"

"In other words," Rex analyzed, "If we don't give him a severance package for his four-month tenure here, he'll do everything he can to derail the venture capital round. He'll go to all his Darden contacts and tell them that the company isn't viable without Lad McCaile."

Craig slumped in his chair. *This can't be happening.*

"So what do we do next?" Rex queried.

"First we accept Kyle South's resignation. Then, damage control. Who's from Darden? Let's see, there's Lyle Timmon, from Madison...."

"The lady from Jefferson Capital, Chip from Allied Capital...."

"Right, and if you can believe it, the Treasurer and CFO of CapOne is from Darden. The deal doesn't go through without his sign off."

♋᠁ℛ

"THEY SURE DIDN'T waste any time." Rex was sprawled in one of the chairs near the antique table. His eyes were glazed over.

Craig read the score. "One terse note. One phone call from an underling who doesn't know anything about us. Of the lot, only Smithers is even willing to talk about it. Rich Fairbank isn't returning our calls. The Jefferson lady isn't available—*like hell she isn't.* It's like we've got leprosy or something. Rex, my friend, I'm afraid we're screwed."

"Yeah. "How could people who were so positive one minute turn so negative the next? How could one slick Richmond blue blood and a naïve Irish immigrant do so much damage in, what, twenty-four hours? They never moved that fast when they worked here."

Despite himself, Craig had to smile at that. You almost had to admire the efficiency of their treachery. What had taken months to build had been torn apart in a matter of hours. He sighed. "When you have too little information, bad information can be very seductive."

The founders had no idea how fraught with portent those words were. They had more pressing things on their mind. Craig got back to business. "I've been keeping Timmon and Caise appraised of the situation ever since Ken gave us the heads up. Right now, I don't even know where they stand. I only know three things. One, we're almost broke. Two, Caise and Timmon are the only two people on God's green earth who might be able to breathe some life back into our funding round. And three, both of those guys are in tight with Kyle South."

"Well," Rex said. "Looks like you were right about one thing."

"What's that?"

"We're screwed."

ANGELS AND DEVILS

"I was afraid of that." Lyle Timmon was on the phone, rubbing his forehead and talking over the day's disaster with Winn and Scatena. "Kyle South called me and told me what he'd done. The inference was that I should warn investors off. I want you to know I did no such thing."

Craig responded with incredulity. "I appreciate that, Lyle. But frankly, I'm a little surprised, considering your Darden connection."

"The old-boy network brought us together, but it's not going to tear us apart. I think the boys made a huge mistake, not that I could do much to prevent it. You guys have done everything right. But be straight with me. With Kyle and Lad McCaile gone, can you still pull this off? If you had enough money, I mean."

"Yes," Rex answered without hesitation. "After spending some time going over the back end with Joe Page, we're convinced he knows it every bit as much as Lad did."

"Don't get us wrong. Lad made a valuable contribution, but...well, let me put it this way. If Joe and Rex had bailed out instead of Kyle and Lad, I'd be folding up my tent and going home. Lad wasn't as essential as he thought he was. Kyle won't even be missed. So yes, Rex is right. We'll do just fine, if you can get us some dough."

There was a lull in the conversation. After a few moments, Rex broke the silence with the question *du jour*. "What do you think are the chances of putting something together? We really don't need seven and a half million. We could stay afloat with...well, with a whole lot less."

After another interminable pause, maybe five seconds, Lyle spoke. "You're aware investment bankers don't normally invest money ourselves."

"Of course."

"I'll tell you what I'm thinking. Why don't you guys come down to our offices tomorrow. Give your investor presentation to my partners. We could do a limited funding round between us, you know, pass the hat. The documentation is in place, the due diligence is done, the book's written. If you can convince my partners you're still viable, I'll bet we can raise a few hundred thousand."

Craig and Rex had seen some gutsy moves, but this was downright heroic. Lyle's proposal was as risky as it was essential to our survival.

The partners shared a moment of restrained enthusiasm before dialing Caise's private line. "Lad and Kyle actually went through with their blackmail scheme, Justin," Rex said.

"Yeah, I know. Looks like the investors bought it too. What a shame."

"It doesn't take much to kill a venture deal. A little noise and every-body gets spooked."

"But you may not be dead yet. Timmon just called me. He said you're headed to Richmond to present the company to his partners tomorrow. Madison is only a few blocks from our offices. When you're through, why don't you do the same thing for us? I'll get some of my partners together. I want in."

CRAIG AND REX walked into Madison's offices knowing their chances of survival lay somewhere between slim and none.

At five minutes before nine, they were ensconced in a conference room. Timmon introduced several partners, and Craig gave the presenta-tion. It was the same investors' pitch he had given dozens of times before.

He found himself sharing how the company had been able to achieve big things on a small budget. This was no hopeful entrepreneur with another wild-eyed idea. Nor was Value America a black hole, where investment dollars got sucked in with no prospects of ever emerging.

We had proved we could solve problems no one else had tackled, not even the industry giants. The company had shown it could form partner-ships with quality brands. But we were still a couple of months away from having a fully operational online store. We needed the breathing room that only adequate funding could provide.

Two hours later, the founders arrived at the more opulent offices of Caise, Perkins, Attorneys at Law. Here they covered much of the same territory. Six or seven of the firm's partners squeezed into one of their conference rooms and were given a personal tour of the store.

The consensus, from both meetings, was that the venture capitalists who had withdrawn their support had done so too hastily. The company had lost one key employee, a good and valuable man, but we had not suf-fered a fatal blow. Money invested here (and now) at a $30 million valua-tion would likely be worth substantially more later.

We had dodged a bullet. Both the bankers and the lawyers invested. Rather than taking *our* money, they gave us some of theirs. Together with Smithers and Motley, they contributed $1.2 million. They were our angels. They gave us wings.

JOHN MOTLEY didn't feel quite right about this, but he couldn't pin-point why. He only knew he couldn't turn Debbie down. His wife seldom asked him for favors, especially ones that involved his business. But she felt sorry for her old friend. Seth Rossi, she said, had gotten into a "situation" with his boss and had lost his job. Couldn't John find something for him to do? Perhaps he could introduce Seth to Value America. They were growing. Surely they could help. John, the last of the true gentlemen, did as his wife requested. *It's an introduction, that's all. What could it hurt?*

And yet there was this little voice in John's head telling him, *"Don't do this. Seth's too slick—too self-centered—not enough substance there."* But Seth claimed to be connected. He said he knew a lot of people with money. Maybe he could help Value America. So John called Craig. Of course, he told him nothing about his reservations. That wouldn't be proper. *If you haven't got anything nice to say....*

A few days later, five people arrived at Value America's palatial offices in the Attic. John Motley led the delegation, having told Craig only that Seth Rossi was his friend and that Seth's companions were supposedly well connected. That was good enough, Craig decided, for an hour or two of his time.

Rossi was introduced as an out-of-work call center executive. Casual, with thinning hair, he was the picture of country club living, if you could judge a book by its cover.

Rossi was accompanied by a tall, craggy, white-haired gentleman in his sixties. He looked like he should be a senator or perhaps the pastor of a Southern Baptist congregation. He had an indefinable air of dignity about him, a resonant voice, and commanding presence. He was introduced as Derk Quinton, a career businessman who now owned the United News Service.

That got Craig's attention. We couldn't afford to advertise yet. But if we were allied with a news agency, our future corporate milestones could be announced as *news*. That was intriguing, to say the least.

By the time the presentation was finished, both Derk and Seth wore broad smiles. Their heads were dancing with ideas. Derk said, "I'd like to introduce you to my writers at United News Service. What you're doing is newsworthy, and that's our business. I also have some friends that are connected with the credit card bank MBNA. I'll make that introduction too, if you'd like. I'll even call my friend Tom Volpe with the investment bank Volpe Brown Whalen. He'll go crazy when he sees what you've built here."

"Okay, okay, and *okay,*" Craig replied. "Just tell me when and where!"

Seth waited impatiently for his turn. "I have friends too," he said, not about to be outdone, "who could be interested in this. One in particular manages pension plan investments for the largest unions."

As Rossi spoke, Craig's mind went into high gear. Organized labor? Unions? This seemed to be the antithesis of the Internet's present upscale demographics. If they could be served as a group, a whole new and previously untapped customer base could be developed overnight. And what better people to benefit from our concept than the men and women who actually made the things we sold in our store?

"I'd like to introduce you to Rafe Durn. He manages the pension funds for the AFL/CIO, SEIU, the Teamsters, and Plumbers. You might be able to do something together."

"I agree. Let's meet Mr. Durn."

IF YOU STAND on the steps of the Capitol in Washington and look around, all you see are Smithsonian facilities and union headquarters. Most of these are built in the Greek revival style of architecture. But Union Labor Investment Company's building is a starkly modern, knife-edged black affair, looking for all the world like Darth Vader standing between Aristotle and Plato.

The unions know where the real power in Washington lies. Their edifices are situated at the end of the Mall, near Capitol Hill. Congress holds the purse strings.

So Craig Winn and Rex Scatena, on a cool October morning in 1997, left Charlottesville headed for D.C. in Craig's Chevy Suburban. It was a two-hour drive. Rex smiled as his mind went back to his first experiences with organized labor. "I've dealt with unions before. Did you know that?"

"No, really?"

"Yeah. It was back in the early '80s. Right out of law school, I got this job at a San Francisco shipyard, a family business. The owner's name was Sal. He was a big, tough, John Wayne type of guy, no formal education or anything, but very bright—a self-made man. I just loved him. He'd started out in the ship-repair business as a union welder.

"Anyway, at one point, the Feds put Sal's company under indictment for bribing Navy officials. This in itself was kind of peculiar, since back then not offering perks was considered bad form, tantamount to 'biting the hand that feeds you.' But I never saw any evidence that Sal was really guilty of anything.

"To be in the shipyard business, you've got to have a license—one issued by the Feds. When they indicted Sal, they revoked his license—in effect declaring him guilty until he was proven innocent. No license, no livelihood. So here he was, with multiplied millions of dollars worth of shipyard equipment just sitting idle and over a thousand workers with nothing to do. Naturally, Sal was totally stressed out. Then one day—we were both in the men's room takin' a pee—Sal hollers over to me and says, 'The only thing I can think of is to transfer ownership of this thing to somebody outside my family. If I don't own it, there's no reason for the government not to reinstate the license.' So...."

"You're kidding," Craig laughed. "You mean he...."

"Yep. Sal signed the whole shootin' match over to me. Sal trusted me, so tens of millions were transferred on a handshake."

"So what happened?"

"We got our license back, put the crews back to work, put together a defense team, and eventually won our case. After it was all over, we were sitting in his office after work, and he poured a couple of shots of his cheap rotgut scotch into styrofoam cups. Cracked me up. The guy was worth about a zillion dollars, but he was just as down-home as an old shoe. He raised his glass and toasted me. Then he said, 'I want my stock back.'

"It was such a great moment. I told him I'd think about it. If he'd get a better brand of booze than this swill, *maybe* I'd reconsider."

Craig was laughing so hard he almost drove off the road.

"Of course, I gave Sal his stock back. But for a couple of months there, I owned my own shipyard. Anyway, that's where I got my first taste of dealing with organized labor."

"What's it like?"

"Awful. We had eleven trades represented under a collective bargaining agreement. Sal was what made it all work. He was a dues-paying member of the welders' union until the day he died. He could weld better than any of 'em, and they knew it. They all respected him, and the feeling was mutual. But there was a growing rift between the union leadership and the rank and file. These were good, decent, hard-working men and women with families and mortgages—dreams. There had been a time when the unions had provided a necessary service, but some had outlived their usefulness. The leadership forgot why they were there. Funny thing," Rex added, "for a while, I was a union leader myself."

"No way."

"Yeah. We were leasing the shipyard property from the Navy, but the equipment was ours. Our deal specified that we had to maintain the facility. But then we had a strike. The maintenance workers wouldn't cross the picket line. The longer the strike, the more the shipyard deteriorated. So Sal came up with a brilliant solution. He started his own union and gave his new union all of the equipment. We hired the maintenance guys from our old company. As long as they paid their dues, the old union couldn't complain. They weren't technically crossing the picket line any longer, 'cause the 'union' owned the equipment!"

"An elegant solution," Craig concluded, smiling.

Craig and Rex rode in silence for a while, their minds mulling over similar thoughts, like a couple of old married people. Rex spoke first. "What if these union guys offer to buy us?"

"Funny you should say that," Craig said. "The thought crossed my mind. But I don't see it happening. We're going to talk about partnerships. Nobody's said anything about money, much less buying us out."

"I know these guys. The type, anyway. It's just the kind of thing they'd do. We ought to be prepared, that's all. How much should we ask for?"

Craig chuckled to himself. Early on, he and Rex had teased one another about the idea of Bill Gates buying Value America. *Someday, five years from now, he's going to offer us a hundred million dollars!* Their failed funding round, at a $35 million valuation, should have tempered their enthusiasm. It had died so recently the body wasn't even cold yet.

"You want to say a hundred million?" Craig asked.

"I like threes. Good things happen in threes."

"*Three* hundred million dollars?" Craig choked.

"Yeah."

〜❦〜

"PRETTY OPULENT DIGS for the people who are supposed to be serving the working man," Craig observed as they entered the gleaming black tower a few hundred yards from Capitol Hill. "We're Craig Winn and Rex Scatena. We're here to meet Seth Rossi and Rafe Durn," Rex said.

"One moment," the guard warned as he picked up the phone, talked, then put it down. "Mr. Rossi has already arrived, and Mr. Durn has been informed you're here."

They glanced at each other, as if to say, "Why all the security?"

Seth obviously knew his way around the place. He led Craig and Rex to a giant conference room and asked them to wait for Durn. The room was as big as a barn, nearly a hundred feet long, maybe thirty feet wide, with an enormous table running down the middle, flanked with a couple dozen expensive chairs. A fine breakfast had been prepared and sat waiting against one wall.

Slick union brochures had been laid out for their edification. Craig flipped through a copy. Coal miners, steel workers, and other noble tradesmen immersed in the sweat and grime of their respective professions graced their covers. Superimposed on their images was a photo of

Union Labor Investment Company's President. He was in his opulent private conference room, dressed in an expensive Italian suit. The nation's Capitol could be seen through the windows behind him. It was an artful dichotomy—emphasis through contrast. The Union leadership apparently didn't see the irony. The image that sprang to Craig's mind was 1789, the France of Louis XVI, a day before the Revolution.

A little after nine thirty, Rafe Durn and five other executives entered the cavernous conference room. Durn was about six feet tall, white haired though only in his late forties, bright, and articulate. He appeared to be every inch the powerful Washington lawyer he was.

Rafe hadn't come up through the union ranks. There was no coal dust in his lungs. It turned out he was a political operative, a bigwig in the Democratic Party; Durn had once been Vice Chairman of the DNC, or some such thing. As introductions were made, coffee was poured, and the group settled in.

Rex emphasized the communication capability of the store. He talked about our proprietary Authoring Tool—the means we used to build multimedia content. "Our presentations need not be limited to providing information about products. They can just as easily be used to present ideas. Organized Labor could use them to promote union benefits. Working together, we could make the speeches of the AFL/CIO's John Sweeney available at the click of a mouse. We could use text, graphics, audio, and video to present the history of the American Labor Movement, telling all the good things you've done—get the word out, on the members' schedule, even if they're on the swing shift."

Changing gears, Craig described how Value America could help to put a PC into the home of every worker and by so doing make exceptional prices available on thousands of other products. "Access to the store could be a privilege of union membership. We could even provide union locals with their office equipment and supplies, reducing their overhead. At the same time, we could contribute one percent of each sale to the unions' pension funds, using our charity contribution feature."

The Union delegation sat quietly, taking it all in. About halfway through Craig's presentation, Rafe Durn put up his hand, stopping him in mid-sentence. "Gentlemen," he said. "Would you excuse us for a moment?" Durn rose, as did the other union executives, including Seth Rossi. Just as abruptly, they all walked out, leaving a bewildered Winn and Scatena staring at the door.

"What happened?" Rex asked.

"Maybe they found out we're Republicans," Craig quipped. "I guess we'll have to wait 'til Seth gets back to find out what offended them."

"Don't know about you, but I'm amazed that we got to talk to these guys at all. I wouldn't have missed this for anything."

"Me neither, but I guess we just don't speak 'union.' It looked like a great opportunity, though. For them and for us."

After fifteen minutes, the group came back into the conference room. They were smiling. Everyone sat back down at the far end of the long table. Durn folded his hands and looked over at Rex and Craig. "Gentlemen, we're impressed with what you've shown us here today."

They expected the next word to be "But," but it wasn't.

"We've been actively trying to acquire radio and television stations on behalf of our member unions," Rafe said. "We've known that we needed a more effective way to get the union message out. The Internet is clearly the medium of the future, but we need to do something better than just build a website. We want to give our members a good reason for 'tuning in.' You've provided that reason: a pro-union marketplace."

"Several things struck a chord with us," Rafe continued. "Your Authoring Tool, as you call it, provides the ability to communicate using audio and video. This could be very effective for us, just the tool we need to fulfill our mandate."

Scatena and Winn looked blankly at each other, then back at Rafe, as he went on. "We're interested in partnering with companies that have a symbiotic relationship with unions. You're planning to ship everything UPS. That's a Teamster company."

They didn't tell them that we would have preferred to use Federal Express, but they wouldn't return our phone calls.

"Another objective," Durn went on, "is rewarding union workers. I like your idea of a dedicated union-members-only marketplace. With them being such loyal customers, I can envision one of our unions going to a big factory and saying, 'We'll sell your products in our union store, but only if you agree to collective bargaining.' We'd have something positive to offer, instead of being confrontational."

After recounting reason after reason for developing a working relationship, Rafe Durn finally dropped the bomb. "Craig, Rex, we want to buy Value America." "Buy" wasn't at all the same thing as "invest in," and it wasn't even on the same planet as "partner with." His conversation with Rex notwithstanding, this caught Craig by surprise.

"Rafe, we're flattered by your vote of confidence." Craig, for once, was uncomfortable. "But we came here looking for a strategic partnership, not an acquisition. We're open to an investment, especially from someone who wants to partner with us. However, the company's not for sale."

Rafe smiled and shook his head slowly. "Everything's for sale. How much?"

Craig glanced at Rex, who gave him an encouraging nod and a smile of his own, as if to say, "Just say the words—you can do it."

"Okay," Winn said, although he felt like an idiot. "Three hundred million." Surely that would quiet them down.

"Done," Durn said to the accompanying smiles of his team. "We'll have our attorneys call you in the morning." With that, the management team of Union Labor Investment Company started gathering up their notes, along with the propaganda the guys had brought them. It was the same package we sent to our prospective brands—a portfolio containing our two brochures, several position pieces, and our CD-ROM. Craig reflected that, based on all this stuff, we probably *looked* like we were worth $300 million. Just don't show up at the Attic—you could still write everybody's names on the back of a business card.

"Wait!" Craig blurted out. "Wait just a minute. Please. We really don't want to sell the company. I'm sure we can find an investment strategy that meets your objectives, but selling the whole company is more than we had in mind. Why don't we talk this through over dinner and *then* have your lawyers call us?"

"Sure," Rafe said. "That'd be fine."

ᘛᘚ

THE DAZED PARTNERS found a park bench facing one of the many museums that comprised the Smithsonian Institution. They sat down, emotionally exhausted from the morning's excursion into the twilight zone.

"Don't you just hate it when I'm right all the time?" Rex asked. "This is scary. These guys clearly don't have any conception of what they'd be buying. I mean, we may have the recipe for the best cake in the world, but at the moment, we're just ingredients in the bowl. There are still a thousand ways to screw this up."

"You've got that right, pardner," Craig said thoughtfully. "You know what picture keeps popping into my head? Don't laugh. I keep seeing the smiling face of Jimmy Hoffa." Rex looked quizzically at Craig.

"Say they buy us outright for three hundred large. I don't care how much money they've got, that's a considerable chunk of change. So now it's their company, and they'll try to manage it professionally, right?"

"Right so far," Rex said.

"So what would you do if you were in their shoes? You'd hire the best managers money could buy, wouldn't you?"

"Umm, yeah."

"Okay. Now picture yourself as one of these managers. You're in control. You're going to manage things your way, 'cause that's all you know. It's worked before, or at least it's what you were taught in some MBA class. Only this time it doesn't work, because what we do isn't like anything that's been done before. You aren't going to have a clue about what brands want or what retail's all about. All you'll be able to do is look at the numbers and move people around—confuse process with progress."

Rex cleared his throat. His mouth suddenly felt dry.

"And then what do you think happens?" Craig went on. "Their managers will fail. They'll look for an alibi. That'll be us, the loose cannons, the entrepreneurs. So they'll get rid of us, which ought to be okay, because we'd be rich. But they'll fail even faster with us gone. So what do you think they'll do then—accept responsibility? Not a chance in hell. They'll tell our union friends that we stiffed them, sold them smoke and mirrors, a house of cards. Our friends won't be pleased, not happy at all."

"No, not happy at all," Rex repeated glumly.

"Yeah, but they won't be angry at *their* managers. These types don't accept responsibility. Oh no. They'll blame us. *Us,* my friend. So what do these guys do when they're really unhappy?"

"I suppose three hundred million takes the situation a little beyond broken windows and slashed tires."

"Cement shoes?" he joked.

"Oh, man, I hope not."

⚜

THE CAPITOL GRILL was one of those places in D.C. that you don't take the kids. Dinner is about $40 a plate, before you start drinking. Craig met Rafe and Seth in the bar, and the three were escorted to a table near the back of the restaurant—Rafe's regular table, it appeared. The place was elegant, with dark wood paneling, polished granite floors, and miles of leaded glass. Rafe was greeted by several people on their way. He was apparently on a first-name basis with many of the town's notables.

As dinner began, the conversation naturally returned to Value America. Craig delicately explained that the proposed $300 million outright buyout was ill-advised, for a couple reasons. First, all the key employees were owners—and were motivated as such. Pay them off now, and you'd turn them back into mere employees.

Second, the venture capitalists we'd talked to recognized we'd be better off taking the company public than trying to run it privately. Going public was the only way to gain the credibility and notoriety we'd need to prevail in cyberspace.

"I have a counter proposal for you, Rafe," Craig said. "I think it'll give you what you're looking for. It's predicated on four things, none of which should be objectionable. I suggest you buy ten percent of the company, not all of it. To make that percentage more attractive, we'll reduce the valuation from three hundred million to one hundred million. At the same time, we'll give you a ninety-day option to purchase up to eighty percent of the company at the three hundred million valuation."

Rafe stabbed a piece of prime rib with his fork. "And your four requirements?" he asked.

"Okay. First, we're interested in developing an automotive division. The Internet is destined to become a significant sales channel for vehicles of all types. So we want you to help us. The United Auto Workers holds seats on the boards of the big three, right?"

"Yep," Rafe said.

"We'd like to talk to them."

Rafe swallowed and smiled. "Shouldn't be a problem."

"Second, we want Value America to be the Marketplace for American Labor. We've already talked about this. We'll create a custom store for union members. As a reward for shopping in the union store, we'll make a two percent donation to the member's pension fund, plus give two percent of each sale back to the member in the form of Value Dollars. For your part, we want you to bear the cost of promoting the store to the rank and file."

"Rafe, how many union members are there in this country," Seth asked.

"About twenty million," Rafe said.

"You understand the math here?" Craig asked. "Every time a union member buys something in the Union Marketplace, you get more money to invest, and the value of your investment increases. The more they spend, the more you make—and the more you're worth."

"What's not to like?" Rafe observed between bites.

"Third, we want each union local—how many are there, Rafe?"

"More than ten thousand...."

"Okay, we want all ten thousand locals to purchase their office supplies and business equipment from Value America. That'll give us a revenue boost and will increase the value of your shares. And remember, two percent goes right into the local's pension fund. Win-win."

"Uh huh."

"Lastly, this must close before the end of the year."

Rafe looked over at Seth and back to Craig. "That's cutting it pretty tight. It's October already...."

"I realize these things normally take six months to hammer out, but we don't have time to putz around. We need to finish our infrastructure, get the website launched, start advertising, and take the company public. Going slow serves no one in this space."

Rafe Durn thought for a moment, then simply said, "Done."

Things are never quite that simple, however. Rafe smiled, took a sip of his fine California Cabernet, and added, "We'll meet all four of your requirements. As you said, they do as much for us as they do for you. But you must meet one requirement of mine."

Craig nodded.

"We won't proceed with this negotiation until you have taken care of my man, Seth, here. He is going to manage this on our behalf. So before we talk again, make sure he's covered."

Winn had a sinking feeling in his stomach, and it wasn't the steak. He had hardly eaten a bite. It was the implications of Rafe's request. So far, all Seth had done was provide an introduction. During the initial meeting, he hadn't said thirty words. He had introduced himself as an out-of-work call center executive. But Rafe wasn't asking for anything unreasonable, Craig thought. Seth had provided a valuable introduction.

"I don't know what finders get these days, Rafe, but we'll do the right thing," Craig said. "You have a deal."

The next morning, Seth Rossi was ready when Craig phoned to discuss his fee. "Yes, I thought you'd be calling," he said.

I'll bet you did. "I suppose we're talking about a finder's fee in the ten to twenty thousand dollar range, is that correct?"

"Oh, no, my friend. I'm not a finder. I'm an investment banker."

He had to smile. Seth Rossi had gone from unemployed to investment banker over dinner. "Really!" Craig played along. "My mistake. I didn't catch the name of your investment bank."

Seth was undeterred. "I was thinking of calling it 'Capital Advisors.' What do you think?"

"Clever. I like the play on words. Capital and Capitol. Are you going to spell it with an 'O' or an 'A?'"

"Haven't decided."

"So—what does an investment banker of your standing want for this introduction?"

"An investment banker's fee, not a finder's fee."

This wasn't going anywhere. "Tell you what. I'll ask around and find out what investment bankers earn these days for this kind of thing. I'll get back to you."

ॐ

"5-4-3-2-1. IT'S CALLED the Lehman Rule." Justin Caise was explaining the most common formula for compensating bankers for their services. "It works like this: the banker gets five percent on the first million, four percent on the second million, three on the third, two on the fourth, and one percent thereafter. Depending on the size of the deal, the percentage often goes down to a fraction of one percent."

"Anything else?" Craig asked.

"Only the obvious stuff. It should go without saying that this is a fee for services rendered. It presupposes that the investment banker is the real deal. The banker's expected to manage the book, coordinate the due diligence, and manage the legal negotiations." Justin chuckled. "Even investment bankers are supposed to earn their fees."

Equipped with this new information, Craig called Rossi back. It didn't go any better the second time. Frustrated, Craig hung up the phone. "I don't get it," he said to his partner, seated across the desk. I don't know what Seth wants. He turned the Lehman Rule down flat, but he won't say how much he thinks he deserves."

"The Lehman Rule sounded a whole lot more generous than he's worth," Rex said. "Let's call Durn and get his take on all this." Craig dialed the number and got Rafe on the speakerphone.

"Morning, gentlemen. What can I do for you?"

"Well, Rafe, it's our discussions with Seth Rossi. We're trying to work out a deal with him, but frankly, we're confused. He wants more than one would expect, especially since we both know he won't be providing the normal investment banking services."

"Gentlemen, perhaps I didn't make myself clear. We're not to talk until you take care of my man. When he tells me you've consummated your deal with him, to his satisfaction, we'll talk again. Not before."

"Uh, okay, Rafe. That's pretty clear."

"Good. Goodbye."

Once again, Craig and Rex found themselves sharing "that look."

"This is smelling awfully fishy," Craig said.

"Then don't breathe."

"Huh?"

"Look," Rex suggested quietly, "The less we know about this, the better off we are. Just give Rossi what he wants. Don't ask any questions. Is *that* clear?" The look he gave Craig was a lesson in jurisprudence.

"Maybe there's a logical explanation," Craig thought out loud, trying as usual to see the positive side. "Durn is a busy guy. He's not used to reviewing stuff like this without a banker involved. Since there isn't one, he's using his pal."

Wisely, Rex summed up the situation. "Look. It doesn't matter. We need money to finish the store, hire people, and advertise. Ten million, give or take, will get it done."

"So pretty much whatever Seth wants, Seth gets."

ৡৄৢ

"FIVE PERCENT? You want *five percent?* Of the whole transaction?" Craig couldn't believe his ears. Perhaps the phone was playing tricks on him. *"Half a million dollars?"*

"Yes," Seth said. "You sound upset, Craig. I don't understand. My introduction puts nine and a half million dollars at your disposal. Look, if it makes you feel any better, I'll be willing to settle for one percent on the three hundred million dollar option."

That came out to three and a half million for dinner. Great work if you can get it. "I'm not upset, Seth," Craig lied. "Just a little surprised, that's all." He swallowed hard. "Five percent it is. No problem. Let's just sign the deal so we can get to work."

As they hung up, Craig turned to Rex. "I feel like I need a shower."

A greedy man brings trouble—Solomon

FUZZY MATH

"Well, that was fun." Rex had just finished arguing with a California lawyer representing the union investors. "Looks like we're off to the races. But I've gotta tell you, I don't think I've ever met a more difficult, dare I say, *unpleasant* individual as this lawyer they're using."

"Well, you know lawyers," Craig grinned, and then got to the point. "Do they have the deal points right?"

"Yes, finally. In principle at least. But speaking of principles, you know what bugging me? It's not so much Seth Rossi and his finder's fee. It's this Quinton guy he introduced us to. I just don't know. We haven't really done anything with him yet, but I'm concerned."

"Rex, Quinton's news wire could be perfect." Craig saw the bright side, as usual.

"Right. It'd give us more credibility than issuing press releases, that's for sure. Anyway, maybe he'll come through, maybe he won't. I worry when guys get too clever. Do you recall him saying something about tax avoidance on stock in closely held companies after they go public?"

"Vaguely."

"He said you could put a collar on your stock by placing puts and calls on the same shares. Then you put the money in a trust and borrow it back from the fund. You pay interest on the money you borrow. But since the money isn't taken as income, you avoid paying taxes on it, and since you're paying interest on borrowed money, the interest is a write-off. So you spend the money, postpone your taxes, and leave it to your heirs to duke it out with the IRS."

Craig shook his head. "Sounds more like tax evasion than tax avoidance. This smells like the kind of thing that could land you in jail."

"I don't know if he was seriously proposing this, or was just trying to sound clever, but...."

"But...let's be careful around this guy."

"Remember what you said the day we started Value America?"

"Yeah. I told you it was supposed to be your job to keep the bad guys away."

"Well, my radar tells me you're three for three here. Quinton, Rossi, and Durn are all going to be trouble."

❧⋅❧

ONE OF THE things that really rankled us was that when the venture capital round had cratered, the relationship with CapitalOne had disappeared along with the cash. So we were particularly eager to meet Derk Quinton's friend at Kessler Financial Services, a valued partner of financial giant MBNA. To this gentleman's credit, he had managed MBNA's co-branded credit card for Gateway Computers—the "Moola Card" (it's a cow thing).

As the discussions began, Craig explained that we were going to need a co-branded credit card. *No problem.* An installment plan for major purchases? *Yes, we can handle that for you too.* How about access to their customer data to help jump-start our custom marketplaces? *Of course.* Things got off to a promising start.

And then the rumors began floating through the grapevine. Craig and Rex were told some disturbing things about the head of KFS, Howard Kessler, from an investor. Should they pay heed to these stories? It was tough trying to figure out whom to believe. The guys hated making important decisions based on hearsay.

Then as the discussions progressed, Derk's contact made an unusual request. He asked that all communications about this transaction go to his home, not his office. The deal was to going to be directly with him, he announced. And the payment for his services, including Value America stock, would be going not to KFS but directly to his personal accounts.

Craig and Rex balked. This fellow was being paid by his employer to perform these very same functions. For him to moonlight the project was, they felt, unethical. Uncomfortable, they bailed.

Some time later, it should be noted, we found out that the rumors we had heard concerning Howard Kessler had been quite untrue. In reality, the man was a class act, completely worthy of the trust MBNA had placed in him. That revelation made one other fact all too clear: it was getting harder and harder to distinguish the good guys from the bad guys.

৯৽৽৽৶

I GUESS OL' DERK does have some contacts, Craig thought as he escorted the two executives up the stairway to the Attic. They were from Volpe Brown Whelan, one of the largest independent investment banks focusing on dot-coms. Quinton said he had placed a call to his friend Tom Volpe. We would learn later that it had actually been John Motley who had started the wheels turning, but today Derk was happy to accept the credit.

Mark McNay, the firm's senior investment banker, was one of the classiest Craig had encountered. It wasn't just "the uniform." They all wore expensive Italian suits and silk Hermes ties. It wasn't just his polished manners or the picture of confidence he projected. What impressed Craig was that the substance matched the image.

There are two sides to an investment banking house. On one side are the investment bankers. They put the deal together and manage the relationship. They work with the company, its accountants, and the lawyers preparing the S1 for SEC scrutiny as well. Mark McNay was such an investment banker.

On the other side are the analysts, who, as the name would imply, analyze the company to determine its viability and value. The analysts communicate with investors, write research on the firm, and explain the company's model to the investment community.

Naturally, nothing much happens unless both sides of the investment banking equation are in sync. That's why McNay brought his analyst along. Her name was Andrea Williams. A tall, slender African-American woman with a dazzling intellect, she was every bit as polished and apparently just as knowledgeable as her partner.

Craig ushered them into his office at the top of the cramped, poorly lit stairs. He gave them the grand tour of the store, outlined the company's five core concepts, explained the seven things that consumers want most, and discussed the four things brands need. He showed them just how close we were to being open for business.

He brought them up to speed on where we stood financially, including the union's commitment to fund a mezzanine round at a $100 million valuation. He explained how we intended to invest the money we raised— solving our remaining technical challenges, hiring more merchandisers, and getting our initial advertising campaign off the ground.

Mark peppered Craig with questions. Good questions, Craig observed—questions that told him the guy knew his stuff. "Amazon's the biggest player in the space," Mark said. "You have to pay attention to what they're doing. They're moving away from their dependence on book distributors like Ingram Media and Baker & Taylor. They're talking about building their own warehouses. Bezos thinks you've got to own inventory in order to satisfy the customer. Are you going to sit here and tell me he's wrong?"

"If that's where he's heading, yes. He's wrong," Craig said. "But look, Mark. Amazon's not being run by a retailer, or even by a manufacturer. It was founded by an investment banker. I know Bezos has built a hell of a site, but he apparently doesn't understand inventory. If he buys it, you watch, it'll be his downfall. His overhead will increase by fifteen percent managing inventory—oh, not initially, because of the GAAP rules on burdening inventory. With GAAP, Amazon will look more profitable while they're building inventory. But the rules will hammer them the first time they find themselves overstocked."

Mark nodded, as if he agreed.

"When you add the five to ten percent they'll need to manage the company to the five to ten percent they'll spend in advertising, and then add the fifteen percent they'll waste managing inventory, they've exceeded the twenty percent margin they're going to make selling books. I'll be amazed if they ever turn a profit, no matter how much volume they do. No, the way to achieve customer satisfaction, and ultimately profit," Craig concluded, "is to fine-tune the inventory-less model. That means using technology to enable distribution partners to ship orders quickly."

"Your ideas," Mark said dourly, "are counter to Wall Street's view."

"Yes, I know. Hopefully, they'll discover the truth before somebody gets hurt."

Mark changed the subject. "What about the fact that Value America has no agreements with the big Internet portals, Yahoo!, Lycos, Excite, or AOL? Nobody in your space has gone public without having their anchor and tenant positions locked up."

"Ask yourself, 'Whose brand do you want to build, anyway?' The way we see it, Mark, we could pay America Online five million bucks a year— well, we could if we had it—but that wouldn't build our brand; it would build theirs. No, we've got a better idea. We're going to use *offline* advertising, direct mail catalogs, newspaper, radio, and TV—not the Internet— to drive online sales."

"Nobody's ever gone public without a portal agreement."

"As you may have noticed, we aren't particularly interested in what's never been done."

"Uh huh," Mark said.

Andrea Williams watched the conversation as she would a tennis match. Back and forth. She was analyzing. That's what analysts do.

"All right, then," Mark continued. "Let's talk about your product presentations. They make you look like a content provider, not a retailer. Nobody does this. You're just going to confuse investors, you know."

Oh, that's not hard, Craig thought, but he said, "It doesn't have to be either-or. We have many reasons for creating these presentations, one of which you just touched on. Nobody else does them. We believe it's important to provide the kind of information consumers need to make better buying decisions. If we're the only place they can go and get the straight scoop, they'll come to us, and they'll buy from us.

"Beyond that, we want the best brands to be our partners. We call it 'having skin in the game.' We want brands to be invested in the solution we're providing on their behalf. We're forming symbiotic, mutually beneficial relationships, hundreds of them, ultimately thousands of them. That strategy is fundamentally sound. It's at the very heart of what online commerce should be all about—forming factory-authorized relationships to sell the best for less, not this convoluted notion that you're valuable because you give stuff away."

"Well, okay, let's say I buy that. What about this convergence idea of yours? You want to give people a choice of buying online or over the telephone. C'mon. Are you a dot-com or a 'ma bell'? This is never going to fly on Wall Street."

"It should. Think about it, Mark. Say you bought a refrigerator online, and you get it into your kitchen, and the door opens on the wrong side. What are you going to do? Peck away at your email, hoping somebody will respond? No. You're going to pick up the telephone! You'll want to talk to a real person who can solve your problem. Unless we move toward solutions that work in a converged world, we'll be old before we're even born."

"Well, I'm not sure...."

Andrea couldn't take it anymore. She slammed her palm down on the table. "Mark! Would you please just...*shush up!* This is the only model in this space that makes any sense. This guy understands what e-commerce ought to be. It's genius! Every one of his five core concepts is right on the money, including the one you haven't trashed yet, the one about being comprehensive. His idea about building the infrastructure to bring brands and consumers together is exactly how online retailing should work. I don't know what *your* problem is, but *he's* right."

Mark McNay rocked back in his chair. He had a big grin on his face. "I know that. I was just trying to see if our friend Craig here could stand the heat. Apparently he can. The Street's got a lot invested in the Amazon model, and his plan is radical—a whole new paradigm.

"You know as well as I do, Andrea, when other analysts hear this stuff, they're gonna come down hard on Mr. Winn. He's going to gore every one of their sacred cows, and they aren't going to take it lying down. People have made too much money to let somebody waltz in and prick this dot-com balloon. I just wanted to make sure Craig here could handle the pressure, that's all."

Andrea tried her best to give Mark a dirty look.

"Yes," Mark said, "I don't think we have to worry about your communication ability. You did a right fine job. Sorry about hammering you like that, but the Street's got a vested interest in their view. Normally my advice would be to keep low, not rock the boat—you know, don't point out the flaws in their reasoning. But I can't see that you have much choice. Everything you stand for flies in the face of what they believe."

Craig analyzed what Mark had said. "So if I run the company in accordance with their metrics, I'm dead because they're wrong. If I stand up and present the merits of our model, I'm dead because it's in their interest to say I'm wrong. Do I have this right?"

"Yep, that's pretty much it in a nutshell."

"Sounds like a classic Greek tragedy. So where do we go from here?"

"We want to lead your IPO, that's where," Mark replied. "Damn the torpedoes." Andrea agreed, nodding her head. "We'll get a proposal to you. What are your revenue projections again?"

"Forty million for '98, a hundred seventy-five million in '99."

"So if we take you public in June of next year, which is probably the best timing, your forward-looking revenues will be a hundred seventy-five million. That means you'll earn a valuation close to that amount. Your comps are trading on forward revenues, you know. If things continue the way they're going, it could be twice that amount."

Twice $175 million was several times higher than the value of the current union round. It was even higher than their blue-sky buyout option of $300 million. Things were looking good.

"Before we get carried away," Craig said, "I have a problem. You need to know something about me before you sign up for what could be a suicide mission."

"What's that?" Mark asked.

"My last business, Dynasty, was a public company—a deal co-managed by Morgan Stanley and Salomon Brothers. Dynasty filed for Chapter 11 at the end of its fifth year."

"We know," Mark said. "We did our homework before we came. It's not a problem. Listen. OnSale's founder, for example, has a past far more checkered than yours, and his company is now public and doing well. The investment community wants to back people with battle scars, especially in the new frontier. This is no place for rookies or for people who don't know what it's like to lead, struggle, build something, make payroll. Besides, the way you handled yourself during Dynasty's fall should be worn as a badge of honor."

"Thank you, Mark, but if we're going to go out and do battle, I want you to know the whole story—no secrets, the unvarnished truth."

"We don't need to know anything more, Craig," Andrea said. "The very fact you thought it was important to volunteer this information speaks volumes."

It didn't normally work like that, of course. Investment bankers didn't often say such nice things. And they didn't usually make house calls on companies with fifteen employees either—especially ones hanging out in somebody else's Attic. On the other hand, impressing one investment bank did not an IPO make. If we were going to take Value America public, we were going to have to hit the road.

Companies getting ready to go public naturally endure more intense scrutiny than closely held "private" corporations. Value America was quickly getting to the point where we were going to have to have a real board of directors, something more substantial and broad based than Craig and Rex talking things over during lunch at the local Chinese restaurant.

Justin Caise was a natural choice to join Rex and Craig on the board. He was a respected attorney who had been a valuable ally for some time now. John Motley, too, had earned his place on our board with his timely introductions and tireless support.

ULIC's Rafe Durn would soon be in a position to command a seat on the board by virtue of his organization's timely and sizable proposed investment. Rounding out our brand new board of directors was Derk Quinton. His place on the board was based more on promise than performance. The United News Service connection was too tempting to ignore, and besides, Derk had asked—vigorously—to be included. After having taken credit for the Volpe Brown meeting, Quinton seemed to be a natural. He certainly looked the part.

⚜

SO IT WAS that between John Motley's friends and one of Derk Quinton's contacts, an introductory road trip was planned. Winn, Scatena, Motley, and Quinton would make the rounds of all the big players. That would mean a trip to New York City's financial center, Wall Street. But it wasn't to start there. The journey would begin at Alex Brown, in Baltimore.

Dynasty, otherwise known as the University of Hard Knocks, was now history, gone but by no means forgotten. Craig could only hope that Mark McNay's intuition about the Street's attitude toward costly battles was right. Alex Brown's emerging growth analyst had covered Dynasty.

When they arrived, they found that the same analyst was still with the firm. Now, to their consternation, they discovered that he had become Alex Brown's analyst for dot-coms. The trial by fire had begun.

It quickly became obvious that the analyst remembered Craig, and unfortunately, remembered Dynasty all too well. But that wasn't the biggest problem. The analyst wasn't actually there. He was on the telephone. Couldn't make the meeting in person, something about the market acting up. That complicated matters. Value America, after all, was a visual sort of thing. How could one adequately describe the Mona Lisa over the phone?

They talked about old times, of course. To Craig's surprise, the analyst had no inclination to hold Dynasty against him. On the contrary, the way he had handled himself under pressure—making payroll out of his own pocket and working to the bitter end to salvage value for the shareholders, to the point that there were no lawsuits—was what he remembered most. Dynasty, strange as it seemed, had been miraculously transformed from a liability into an asset. The analyst understood that Dynasty provided the motivation to solve the problems that had brought it down.

But that in itself didn't mean the Value America team was able to make a dent in Alex Brown's armor. They left with the distinct impression that without the visual aspect of the presentation, they had failed to pique the analyst's interest. The fact that Alex Brown was in the process of taking another Internet retailer public didn't help much either. Nor did the day's record 500-point drop in the Dow Jones Industrial Average.

No go, apparently. But tomorrow was another day.

ço:ę

STANDING THERE ON the sidewalk in the heart of New York's financial district, team Value America looked up at the tall buildings. The twin towers of the World Trade Center dominated the skyline, like sentinels proclaiming this place to be the very center of America's economic soul.

"Looks like you're earning your stock options today, John," Rex said to Motley. "Four meetings in a row, with the best of the best. Ready, Craig?"

"I'm ready for them," he answered, still looking up. "The question is, are they ready for us?" Craig didn't want to worry his traveling companions, so he changed the subject. "Can you believe our luck? What happened to the market yesterday? It crashed, down five hundred points! These guys will probably be too distracted to pay attention."

"Biggest one-day point drop in the history of the Dow," Rex shook his head. "Boy, we sure know how to time these things."

"It remains to be seen if anybody is even going to show up for these meetings," Winn said apprehensively. "You couldn't blame them if they all said they've got more important things to do today."

With that, he looked at his watch. Six thirty. "We start in half an hour." Craig mulled over what was really worrying him. Goldman Sachs' lead analyst was one of the most respected, most credible presenters of dot-com gobblety-gook—the notion that popularity was more important than performance. With their colleagues at Morgan Stanley and Robertson Stephens, Goldman was responsible for the metrics, the corporate measurement criteria, upon which dot-coms were valued. Craig knew he was about to tell them that they were wrong. *This,* he thought, *isn't going to be pretty.*

Goldman Sachs wasn't the largest investment bank on Wall Street, but they were arguably the most prestigious. If Goldman Sachs elected to take a company public, especially as the lead firm, the company stood to gain instant legitimacy. And it was a given that the after-market support would be spectacular.

But there was a downside. Goldman Sachs had a reputation for under-pricing their deals—and they had good reasons for doing so. First, setting the IPO stock price conservatively assured that all of their deals would actually get done. But beyond that, these under-priced stocks invariably ramped up, making huge profits for their investors. The problem for the company going public was that less working capital was raised in the process. And raising working capital, for the company at least, was the whole idea. That's not to say we would have turned up our noses at Goldman Sachs. Oh, no. All they had to do was whistle.

The conference room was spectacularly situated on an upper floor in a corner suite overlooking the harbor. Lady Liberty stood out there, centered in the conference room window, with her torch lighting the way toward national prosperity, or so it was believed within these walls.

By seven o'clock, ten of the most influential people in New York were assembled. The Goldman Sachs team was led by Roth Latour, a brilliant investment banker, and by Rusty Kincade, one of the most famous Internet analysts on Wall Street. Kincade had written volumes on Internet commerce, and the guys had been hoping that he would attend the meeting. Craig had read everything he could find of Kincade's work, and he had weighed his presentation against what he knew of the analyst's thoughts.

As the financial experts filed in, the conference room took on the atmosphere of a sports stadium, although a gladiatorial contest is probably a more apt metaphor. Entrepreneurs *versus* Analysts—a fight to the death. Would the bankers give us a thumbs up or a thumbs down? A projector was brought in, and a large screen was unfurled from its recess in the ceiling. Goosebump time. If you're in business, presenting your company to Goldman Sachs is a good as it gets. So let the games begin.

As he began to talk about our five core concepts, Winn was all too aware that the first words that left his lips would probably manufacture a room full of enemies. As Mark McNay and Andrea Williams had discovered, our company followed no one's preconceived notions. Value America was more merchants and manufacturers than Internet geeks and investment gurus. We toed no man's line.

The truth was that there was very little "line" to toe, even if we had been of such a mind. Amazon.com was the poster child for e-commerce, and in the minds of the investment community in the fall of 1997, no one else was big enough to matter. There were portals, of course, and auction sites like OnSale were starting to appear, but in the pure world of "e-tail" at this time, Amazon was about the only game in town.

More to the point, Amazon had made these people rich. Their word was gospel. They were Wall Street's sacred cow, and we were about to fire up the barbecue.

"Ladies and gentlemen," Craig waded in, "Value America is driven by five core concepts—five principles that define who we are and how we operate. Each is based upon years of experience in the areas central to the success of online commerce—retail, brands, and the marketing and sale of consumer products.

"The first of our core concepts is comprehensiveness. We will sell products in over twenty categories, not just one, from computers and office supplies to appliances and home electronics, from sporting goods and toys to specialty foods. Value America will be the one place online where you'll find most everything you need for home and office.

"I realize that comprehensiveness is inconsistent with the model most analysts are touting. Clearly the most well-established company in our space is Amazon. They're a single-category store—just books. If success is to be measured by being like Amazon, then becoming King of the Niche would seem to be the right road to follow. I don't think so. I predict that even Amazon, whom I admire, will soon see the wisdom of *our* approach and expand beyond the sale of books into other fields. They'll be related at first—music perhaps. But soon they'll be adding categories farther and farther from their core business."

"I talked to Bezos just last week," Rusty interjected, "and he's committed to books. Jeff didn't say anything about being 'comprehensive,' as you call it. And as you acknowledge, his model is playing just fine here on Wall Street."

"Rusty, I believe that will change. But for now, let me give you three reasons for being comprehensive: scale, convenience, and comfort. It's going to cost a lot of money to build effective online systems, and even more to build a recognizable brand name in the virtual world. There's not enough revenue in one category to cover the costs. Profitability will occur sooner for a comprehensive store than it will for a niche player.

"Second, convenience. We can save people a lot of time by providing one convenient place for them to buy most everything they need.

"The third is comfort. Even though we know buying things online is safe, the general public is still worried about using their credit card. So there is something to be said for a store that has more of what shoppers want to buy. People don't want to give their addresses and credit card numbers to twenty different sites for twenty different kinds of products, especially when one store will have everything they're looking for.

"Convenience is a big factor in the success of traditional retailers. The world's biggest retailer is comprehensive. WalMart sells everything from tires to t-shirts. Every shopping environment has a learning curve. A comprehensive store will have a decided advantage in the consumer's mind over a collection of unrelated niche sites."

As his audience endeavored to absorb the ramifications of his first point, Craig turned on the firehose again—giving them more information than they could swallow. "Our second core concept focuses on the communication of valuable information. In a moment you're going to see our store. As we take our virtual tour, you'll see that we provide far more product information than other sites. We're committed to helping consumers become better buyers. The more they know, the more they'll buy, the happier they'll be with their purchases—and the less likely they'll be to return them, saving everybody money.

"Most retailers stand as a wall between brands and consumers. We, on the other hand, act as bridge. Our mission is to be transparent—a conduit through which brands and customers can communicate and interact.

"Before Value America came along, brands were restricted to inefficient and ineffective ways of communicating the features and benefits of their products to consumers. A product's package has limited space and capability. Quality sales help is a thing of the past. Have you ever asked the clerk at your local WalMart...come to think of it, you don't have a local WalMart or anything like it here in Manhattan, do you? Have any of you ever shopped in a WalMart?" Craig asked. No one raised their hand or said a thing.

It suddenly became clear to him. How could these people purport to understand retail, much less position themselves as experts, if they had never even been inside the world's largest retailer?

"Well, next time you're out on the road, conduct a little due diligence. Go into a WalMart, veer left, and walk back to the electronics department.

Ask the clerk what the megapixel rating of a digital camera means, or anything else for that matter. Try it sometime. You'll find the experience entertaining. Like it or not, that's what all of us online types are competing against—and it's always a good idea to check out the competition."

The crowd chuckled. The very thought of WalMart's blue-collar image being competition for their dot-com superstars was, well, funny.

"The upshot of all of this," Craig continued, "is that brands have no effective way to communicate to the customer why their products are better. The solution is our multimedia product presentations, like the ones you're about to see. We research the products we sell, use them, and interview the brand's most knowledgeable people, then share what we've learned. Brands love this, and they pay us to properly present their products in our store. In so doing they become our partners.

"But we're not just a content provider. These presentations appear at the point of purchase, the best possible place. Wouldn't you prefer to shop in a store where you could get the real story about a product—without pressure, without hype, on your schedule, and without leaving home? We're using the Internet for what it was designed to do—share quality information."

Craig looked around at his audience. This was starting to sink in. He saw a lot of head nodding, note taking, and spontaneous, involuntary smiles. "Some of you may be thinking to yourself, 'All this information is going to take forever to download.' And I'll admit, if today's 14.4 modems are as fast as the Internet is ever going to run, we may have overdone it. But compression techniques are improving, bandwidth is increasing, and modems are getting faster.

"All of which brings me to our third core concept: convergence. We are building Value America to work today and triumph tomorrow. When hockey legend Wayne Gretsky was asked why he was so good, he said, 'I never skate to where the puck is. I skate to where the puck is going.' That's why we're skating toward convergence. We believe that the productivity of the personal computer, the impact of television, and the communication prowess of the telephone will all come together—they'll *converge*.

"That is why we record sound tracks for our multimedia product presentations, and why we produce video demonstrations that will be streamed in real time. Will it work at today's 14.4 world? Not very well. Will it work tomorrow? You bet. And Value America will be ready when the technology arrives with the best multimedia content on the Web.

"For online retailers, however, the most important part of convergence is how you integrate the telephone into sales and customer service." As he spoke these words, the smiles turned to grimaces. The thought of people helping people on the telephone was as blue-collar as shopping at a WalMart to those in this circle.

It was an Amazon thing again. Books are easy to ship, and they don't break, so you don't need customer service. You don't *sell* them either, at least in the sense of explaining features. So Amazon had convinced everybody (on Wall Street, that is) that customer service call centers were passé—a victim of their superior technology.

"What if you live in a home without a Web-enabled PC? Today, that's seventy percent of America. How are you going to buy something online in the first place? Folks, the telephone is essential to serving customers in the virtual world. And this will all become seamless in the converged world."

Craig knew he was making an impact, but he also knew he was about to take a cattle prod to another of their sacred cows. "Now, the Web is getting to be a pretty crowded place. Every day, it seems, there are more places you can visit, get information, or shop. So how should we get the word out about Value America? He waited to see if anyone would rise to the bait.

Rusty Kincade knew the answer. This was a no-brainer. "Follow the lead of Amazon," he said. "Get your anchor and tenant positions locked up on the big portal sites, Yahoo!, Excite, Lycos, and AOL."

Oh God, Craig thought. How could such smart people be so out of touch with reality? It was as if their virtual world had no contact with the real one. "Ladies and gentlemen, let me introduce our fourth core concept. We are going to drive online revenues with *offline* advertising."

Instant murmuring. It wasn't done that way. You could see it in their eyes—*this guy's trouble.* "I know that sounds radical to many of you, but please hear me out. You've been thinking of online stores the same way you think of portals. But they're not the same. AOL and Yahoo! are media companies. Amazon is not. You *should* judge media companies by how long people hang with them; but the proper yardstick for retailers is how much people buy. Their key metrics are sales growth, advertising productivity, and operations cost as a percentage of revenue. It's popularity *versus* performance.

"I think you all view Amazon as an Internet company that just happens to sell stuff. That's true, of course, as far as it goes. But this business of e-tailing, as your compatriots at Robertson Stephens are now calling it, will make a lot more sense if you look at us as retailers who just happen to conduct our business online."

The room grew icy cold and silent. These were fighting words, threatening words. Goldman Sachs was a stakeholder—*the* stakeholder—in the ultimate gold rush. They were getting rich and their clients were getting rich, mining the glittering gold of the virtual realm. Now this guy Winn hikes in here with a pick and shovel and says that the glitter really isn't gold after all....

"Ladies and gentlemen, I have been in and around the retail business all of my adult life. It is something I know from the inside out. Half the battle in retail is about building your brand and changing people's buying behavior. The other half is diminishing the cost of inventory, but we'll get to that in a moment."

The crowd sat back and sized up their adversary. They placed their hands in front of their mouths and bit their lips. Craig knew he was playing to a hostile audience, but he could see reason for hope—especially with Roth Latour, the group's lead investment banker. He went on, "I have seen no evidence that convincingly correlates money spent on portal relationships with revenue. Have you?"

There were no volunteers this time, so Craig carried on. "It seems to me that giving a portal five or ten million dollars for a button that links their viewers to our site is something less than a bargain. I believe we can accomplish more, and sell more, using offline media like newspapers, direct mail, radio, and television. Why? Because there, the money we invest will build our brand, not the portal's brand. Plus, we can connect our brand to the brands whose products we sell.

"What's more, we can reach more people offline because more people read newspapers, have mailboxes, and watch TV than surf the Web. Offline advertising for an online store is a win-win proposition. If you think about it, it seems terribly provincial to assume that the only people who can benefit from online shopping are the people who are already shopping online. We'll be expanding the customer base for the entire sector—especially when we sell consumers Internet-enabled PCs. We want to be inclusive, not exclusive. We want to empower people, not limit them. The only thing we wish to limit is the cost of building our brand name and achieving scale."

He continued to give them far more than they could assimilate. "Ultimately, we intend to build our customer base by forming alliances, partnerships if you will, with great organizations like unions, faith groups, charities, and banks—especially credit card banks. We've created a custom store capability that allows us to do some pretty incredible things, but that's more than we have time to discuss today."

The analysts were beginning to squirm. Winn had poked big holes in the theories they had preached as gospel, theories that had made them rich. What was worse, there was no logical way to refute what he had said. But he wasn't quite done with them yet.

"Our fifth and last core concept is that we're going to do all of these things without owning inventory. Ultimately, in retail, the battle is won or lost over the issue of distribution and inventory management. Sam Walton is a logistics and inventory expert. He has automated reordering. In essence, he has made his customers buyers.

"I know you probably have a picture in your minds of huge tractor-trailer rigs pulling up to the WalMart loading docks. Sorry, folks, apart from ads, it doesn't work that way. The average WalMart reorder is by store, by week, by brand. It's less than two hundred dollars. It's based upon what consumers bought in that store the prior week. We found that since the brands were willing to ship to individual WalMart stores in these small amounts, many were willing, and more importantly, able to ship to individual consumers—our customers—directly and swiftly."

Craig saw their eyes starting to glaze over, so he retreated to more familiar territory. "Interestingly enough, Amazon started out with an inventory-less model, just like ours, only simpler, since they were dealing with a single great distributor, Ingram. And yes, I know they've begun talking about building warehouses. From what I hear, they say they're doing this in the name of customer satisfaction. Am I right?"

"Yes, that's true," Rusty said. "Bezos believes that owning inventory is necessary to satisfy the consumer. You know he's fanatical about satisfying the customer, don't you?"

"Yes, I am sure he is. So are we. But I respectfully submit that owning inventory is not the answer. It's the problem. I don't wish to be the bearer of bad news, but owning inventory will be Amazon's undoing. Jeff Bezos is a banker, is he not?"

"That's right," Roth replied. "He's one of us."

Winn took a deep breath and studied the room. "Folks, I've probably *forgotten* more about inventory, its costs and its problems, than anyone in the dot-com world knows. There isn't time to explain the consequences of owning inventory. For now, all I ask is that you envision the possibilities of a new paradigm. We can replace inventory with systems, and distribution centers with technology. We can build, in fact we *have* built, an electronic conveyor belt between factories and consumers. This is the real promise of the virtual world: linking supply and demand."

The analysts were awake again. Their sacred cow was once again bellowing. Craig didn't care. "Do the math," he told them. "It's my considered opinion that the numbers will never add up. Amazon will *never* turn a profit."

The analysts in the room were not happy with Winn's pronouncements.

Strangely enough, their partners, the investment bankers, were pleased. They appreciated his business logic. Our team had managed to divide the room into warring camps, based solely on whose reputation would be trashed if we were right.

But few of them, whether investment banker or analyst, had ever gotten their hands dirty working in a business. They were naïve, having earned the right to be Goldman's golden boys merely by getting good grades in school. It was becoming obvious that dot-com euphoria was being built on a truly flimsy foundation.

Undeterred, Winn took them on a tour of the store. It was the same basic presentation he had given a hundred times. He knew beyond a doubt that his logic was flawless and his message was compelling. As he proceeded, the investment bankers became more convinced that he was on the right track, and the analysts grew more uncomfortable and antagonistic. It was starting to look like Verdun.

Craig had presented the store so many times, he could now do it on autopilot. It was during one of these hypnotic moments that Roth Latour's comment, "Yes, he's one of us," finally sunk in. It all dawned on him: *Bezos is a banker, not a retailer. When he took Amazon public, he needed comps. There were no online retail companies with which to make a comparison, and offline retailers had less dazzling valuations—so portals, he must have thought, were perfect. They're valued more highly than gold; I'll use them for my comps.* While simple and benign in itself, this idea started a catastrophic series of events that no one could have imagined on this day.

The partners patiently explained that with the economies and advantages of Value America's business model, taking us public would be good for Goldman Sachs. If our view of the virtual world was right, Goldman would have hedged their bet. Besides, an early IPO would put Value America on the fast track to becoming the first Internet retailer to turn a profit. And wasn't that—profitability—what it was all about? Craig assumed it was a rhetorical question. Turns out it wasn't.

"Mr. Winn," interjected Rusty Kincade, "Profitability isn't the issue."

"It isn't?"

"No," Kincade explained. "There's a whole new market dynamic in play, and profitability doesn't count for much. What counts today is market share, revenue growth, and first-mover advantage."

Team Value America tried hard to follow his logic.

"In this space, you're either number one or you're nothing. Investors aren't interested in number two."

"With your brand partnerships, you could become profitable sooner than others, a couple of years perhaps," Latour added. "But by that time, the market is going to be saturated with e-tailers like you—well, maybe not *just* like you, with your 'electronic conveyer belt,' slick presentations and such. But they'll be there all the same. They'll kick your butt in the revenue department and scoop up all the investment capital."

"In the new economy, it's grow fast or die," Kincaid concluded.

We had planned on growing like an oak tree, strong of root and thick of limb, able to weather any storm. And here were these guys, the acknowledged experts in the field, saying we had to be kudzu instead: grow like a weed.

Roth Latour spoke up. "Assuming you had enough cash to advertise, how much revenue could you generate next year?"

Craig quickly ran the numbers in his head. Strangely, he was not thinking about how much he could sell with an unlimited ad budget. He was calculating how fast the store could grow without hopelessly bogging down customer service. He knew that the bigger the number he gave Roth, the more interest there would be in taking us public, and the more we would be worth. He also knew this crowd devoured those that over-promised and under-delivered. And he knew they would write down whatever he said.

We had previously projected $40 million for 1998, easy from an advertising and revenue perspective. But more importantly, systems and customer care could handle the load. But there was a problem. The number was too small and too big. Forty million was tiny compared to the nearly two hundred million Amazon was projecting. And it was unbelievably large. How does a company grow from nothing to forty mil in its first year out of the chute? Craig said it anyway. "Forty million."

Roth showed no reaction. "And your revenues for the year after that, 1999?"

Rex, who had been quietly watching the drama, now spoke up. "A hundred seventy-five million is our projection."

"Gentlemen," Roth said, "the reality is that companies like yours are being valued on multiples of forward-looking revenue."

"Multiples," Craig tried out the word for size.

"As in more than one," Rex clarified. This was definitely a new and welcome concept.

"Yes," Roth replied. "Two, three times, who knows how high it will go. The point is, if you go public sometime in summer of '98, we'll use your hundred seventy-five million number...."

"Whoa, wait a minute," Craig said. "It's our philosophy to under-promise and over-deliver. Let's ramp up to, say, a hundred fifty million. That's twenty-five million less than we actually think we can sell."

"Okay. That would put your valuation at three hundred million dollars," Roth said. "If we take off the standard twenty percent pre-IPO discount, and another twenty percent to give our investors the bump they need, that puts the number around two hundred million. The IPO, with you on the road show, could be done at two hundred fifty mil, maybe two seventy five. You're a good speaker, and the store presents well. After you're public, that valuation should jump to somewhere between three and four hundred million dollars. That's the math *du jour*."

"I'll have a cup of that," Rex chuckled.

Rusty ignored the levity. "It's not about operating efficiencies, advertising productivity, or even profit. Right now the Internet is hot. It's all about growing fast and gaining market share. This is the way the game is being played."

"You've got a great model," Roth shared. "It makes a lot of sense, but you've got no chance of attracting any serious venture capital, or public equity, unless you start playing by the rules. Frankly, I can't believe you've made it this far without a venture capital round."

Winn and Scatena shared a look. *Oh, let's not go there.*

"Anyway, two hundred million, ramping to four, is about it."

We were practically broke, had twenty under-paid employees jammed into an Attic in a building we didn't own. The store wasn't even fully functioning yet. Two hundred million? Is that all? It was another surrealistic Alice-in-Wonderland moment. We were getting our reality directly from the lips of Tweedle Dee and Tweedle Dum.

✥

LATER THAT DAY, Value America's team visited Morgan Stanley. It was a *déjà vu* experience. Craig had been all through Morgan's world before. He had great memories of Dynasty's IPO, memories of his first investor speech, when the stock had jumped in one hour from $12 to $18 a share. The pain was there, too. Morgan's analyst had since moved on, but Winn remembered him like it was yesterday. He had been awesome during Dynasty's Road Show, Craig's tour guide on a ride few get to experience—the incredible roller-coaster world of Wall Street's magical journey called an IPO. In the end, the analyst had bailed. *Couldn't blame him*, he thought. *It wasn't his fault.*

Our team was escorted into Morgan's large glass-lined conference room. Rex fired up the laptop and demonstrated the store. The reaction was pretty much the same—enthusiasm on the part of the investment bankers, wariness on the part of the analysts, and a new kind of math that said two plus two equals somewhere between seven and thirteen, depending on how fast you can add it up.

The really amazing thing was that they too came up with a valuation of $200 to $300 million if we went public in the summer of 1998. The new math was certainly friendly, Craig thought, even if it was a mass hallucination.

༄༅

ROBERTSON STEPHENS was a San Francisco-based investment banking firm, but they maintained an office on Wall Street. Our gang was looking forward to meeting their lead analyst, Dale Dandridge, the man who had coined the term "e-tail." But the previous day's record stock-market decline had Dandridge distracted, harried, and more to the point, absent. Once more, we were faced with communicating the virtues of the store over the telephone.

The Mona Lisa? Well, she was an Italian girl. From Florence. In her late twenties when Da Vinci painted her in 1505. Brunette, having a really bad hair day when she sat for Leonardo. No sense of humor at all. She just sat there with her hands crossed, but Leo told her dirty jokes until he got one tiny smile out of her, and that's what he painted. Now that little smirk is the only thing anybody remembers about her. Explaining Value America over the phone was something like that. Inadequate.

Although no earth-shaking impression was made upon Robertson Stephens during that first encounter, they would later become our lead investment banker when we finally did go public. Never say die.

༄༅

OUR VISIT TO Union Bank of Switzerland had come about through a friend of a friend. It seems one Stan Garmin, a friend of John Motley in the office products industry, was a keen supporter of a European industry publication called *OPI—Office Products International*—whose publisher was Mike Jefferies, who in turn had ties with this European investment bank with an office in New York. They were supposed to have enormous worldwide cash reserves. It certainly couldn't hurt to talk to them.

Their Sam Abrams wasn't your typical investment banker. He was part analyst, part hustler, and part-time TV commentator. He introduced himself as a "shameless self-promoter," and their initial conversation seemed to bear out his assessment.

As introductions were made, he said to Quinton, "You look familiar."

Derk explained that he probably knew him from a student loan venture he had been involved in, a deal that had gained him some notoriety.

"Yes," Abrams said with a smile, "of course! I must tell you, Mr. Quinton, you're one of my heroes. I followed that whole thing when I was in school. What a performance!"

Well, he certainly seems impressed with our Mr. Quinton. I presume that's a good thing.

UBS's reaction to our store was unbelievably positive. They not only wanted to do a deal, they wanted to do it *immediately*. They had apparently never heard of terms like "coy" or "playing hard to get." They committed to an IPO right then and there. Sam said he and his firm would "crawl over five miles of broken glass to lead Value America's IPO."

Craig brought the discussion back into perspective. Enthusiasm was one thing, due diligence was another. "Gentlemen," he said, "why don't you send a team to Charlottesville? See what we're doing. If you're still impressed, write a letter of intent, explaining how you would handle the IPO. Tell us why we should choose UBS."

They did exactly that. They came, they saw, and for a moment it looked like they were going to conquer. They wrote a letter that said Value America was worth two hundred and fifty million casabas. Suddenly we were within shouting distance of the incredibly optimistic $300 million pipe dream we had used to cool off the union's ardor such a short time ago. The $100 million valuation for the current round was looking positively cheap.

The letter did not sit idly gathering dust. It proceeded with great haste to the nearest fax machine, where it was sent to Mr. Durn of the Union Labor Investment Company. *Hey, Rafe, we thought you might be interested in this....*

⊱⊰

THE TOUR MADE one more stop before returning home. It had begun one Saturday at a car wash. John Motley had overheard a friend talking about his business with an upstart investment house called Freedman, Billings, Ramsey. In typical Motley fashion, John asked his friend for an introduction. Now, in an office overlooking the Lincoln Memorial, the boys encountered a different type of investment banker.

It was obvious they weren't on Wall Street anymore. FBR had a different style. It wasn't that they couldn't afford the thousand-dollar Italian suits; they just preferred blue jeans. They were hot, and they knew it.

FBR was on a roll, having just completed the IPO for a remarkable businessman, John Ledeky. The IPO for his United States Office Products had created a company poised to sell four billion dollars of pens, pencils, and paperclips annually. John hadn't built the firm; he'd bought it—sort of. More correctly, the companies that comprised USOP had bought into John's idea. Hundreds of regional office products distributors and related office supply and services companies sold their business for stock in USOP. If all went well, they stood to make millions.

The lesson to be learned, if only one had a crystal ball, was that the corporate life of an entrepreneur is a mere vapor, here one moment and blown away by the capricious winds of fortune the next. John Ledeky would be gone within a few short months of his company's multi-billion dollar coming-out party, replaced by a man named Tom Morgan, who would in turn...ah, but I'm getting ahead of myself.

The bankers and analysts at FBR listened to our pitch. They too asked to take us public.

The Motley crew had now seen seven investment bankers. The score was one no, three solid maybes (one of which would later change to a leading-role yes), and three yeses (one of which was punctuated by a melodramatic pledge to crawl over miles of broken glass). Not too shabby for a store that had yet to open its doors.

❧❦

JOHN MOTLEY SEEMED NERVOUS, uncomfortable. John was a man of impeccable manners and unquestionable good will. He would never stoop to demeaning anyone, never say anything bad about a mutual acquaintance. But this was different. Seth Rossi had just finished belly-aching to John about how Derk had stiffed him. Seth evidently thought he was somehow entitled to a piece of whatever Quinton was going to get out of his relationship with Value America. While a provocative and tasty *hors d'oeuvre,* this admission was bland compared to the dish Seth served up next....

"Craig," John said shakily into the receiver, "I just don't know how to put this. I—I'm really uncomfortable saying anything about what I just heard, and it's nothing but a rumor. It might not even be true."

"What's wrong, John?" he asked.

Motley continued beating around the bush. "It's just that I could never forgive myself if you found out, I mean, if it turned out to be true. But...." There was a pause that lasted for what seemed like eternity. John was really struggling with whatever it was. "But...I, I mean, there's a rumor in town that says...Derk Quinton, well, Derk has spent some time in jail."

"In jail," Winn repeated.

"Yes, well actually," John said, "in *prison*. But it's just a rumor. You know how people love to conjure up vicious rumors about successful people. But you may want to check this one out, you know, just to be safe, especially with him being on the board now."

He did check it out, calling Quinton himself, and asking him point blank. "Derk, there's this terrible rumor going around. I'm sure it's not true, but I'd be remiss if I didn't ask." Craig was more direct than John. "Have you ever been convicted of a crime? Have you ever spent time in jail?"

Derk was miffed. "Gimme a break. That's ridiculous. Don't you think I would have disclosed something as important as that? I don't know who makes this stuff up...."

Craig was relieved and tried to smooth Derk's ruffled feathers. "Okay, thanks. I knew it couldn't be true."

"LISTEN, CL," I said, "Take a couple of guys and go over to the new building. There's a furniture truck there. Give 'em whatever help you can, and call me if you need more bodies."

"Sure, Pop." My son took off with the only two guys he could find who would admit to having a minute to spare. Half an hour later, he called me. "There's a huge tractor-trailer rig here. It's loaded to the roof with boxes. The drivers told me they weren't going to unload anything. They've gone to breakfast!"

"How many guys are we going to need?" I asked.

"All of 'em!"

At least we were finally going to move out of the Attic, I reflected. Having twenty-plus bodies packed into a space that could reasonably hold six had gotten a little old.

Once we had received the checks from the angel investors Craig had signed a lease putting us into a 9,000 square foot building across town. He worked out a deal with some of the nation's biggest suppliers of office furnishings to swap our Multimedia Presentations for chairs, desks, filing cabinets, and systems furniture. So here we were, entering the new economy by borrowing an idea as old as time, barter. We had been in business for almost two years. Now, for the first time, we were actually going to *look* like it.

The Yellow House, as we came to know it, would be our home during our most exciting period. But on that cool November morning it was a blank canvas—miles of empty space, the smell of fresh paint, new color-coordinated carpeting, and network wiring all over the place.

The truck out in the parking lot gave us our first hint of just how large our infrastructure needs had grown. Everybody dropped whatever they were doing in the Attic and pitched in. Technologists, writers, designers, and merchandisers all became stevedores for a day, unloading the big trailer, hefting boxes up the stairs, uncrating furniture, assembling chairs, and sorting hundreds and hundreds of module pieces for the cubicles.

With a bit of technical help from the furnishing manufacturers, we assembled the cubes and put the desks together ourselves. Craig had measured the place and drawn the schematic we used to lay out the furniture.

Working together, manual laborers all, we knocked it out, got it done. In a couple of days, it was home sweet home, not opulent by any means, but certainly businesslike and professional—a stunning contrast to the claustrophobic rummage-sale atmosphere of the Attic.

We would have enough elbow room for at least the next three months.

৩৯৽৵৻

JUSTIN CAISE WAS on the phone, talking faster than usual. Rex sensed that the change in Justin's demeanor meant something. "As I understand it, Derk Quinton was supposed to receive stock options if United News Service helped us get the word out on Value America," Justin started in.

"Uh huh," Rex said. "'Course, he hasn't done anything yet."

"Well, his attorney's pushing real hard. I've had some experience with guys like this. Whenever one of these tough-talking types tries to negotiate a one-sided deal, I get nervous."

Rex tried to envision where Justin was going with this.

"Anyway, on my own initiative, I decided to run a Nexis Lexis check on your buddy Derk. Are you near a fax machine, Rex?"

"No," he said, "but I can be. Why?"

"Give me the number."

Rex did.

"Go stand by the machine. You're not going to believe what I found."

Justin hung up, leaving Rex both puzzled and worried. He walked down a narrow hallway and stationed himself by the second-floor fax, right outside Craig's new office in the Yellow House. As Rex took up his post, he could see Craig through an internal window, talking on the phone. On cue, the fax machine started buzzing. Out came the first of thirty-five pages—the record of the Federal indictment and trial transcript of one Derk Quinton.

Rex turned white. Out spewed page after page of legal documents stating that Quinton had been arrested, tried, found guilty, and had spent time behind bars in a Federal penitentiary. The worst part was the nature of his offense.

About seven pages into the fax transmittal, Rex staggered into Craig's office. One look at his ashen face told Craig something was desperately wrong. "He's an ex-con!" Rex said through his teeth as he waved the fax pages in the air. "Derk Quinton is a felon. He's done time. And not for something simple like armed robbery or mass murder."

Craig's eyes grew large. "Oh, no...."

"Oh, yes," Rex said. "SEC violations. Securities fraud. Non-disclosure!"

"Oh, my God!" Craig gasped. "We just put a convicted felon on our board! We're dead, Rex. Dead."

WHEELING AND DEALING

"You've got two choices." This was lawyer humor. In reality, Caise was telling Rex that he had *no* choices. "You can promptly kick Quinton off the board and revoke any potential stock options...."

"Or?" Rex asked.

"Or you can try to convince the SEC that securities fraud is not such a bad thing—that he's really just a nice old guy who was unfairly railroaded by some eager-beaver Federal Prosecutor. Just because the Feds sent him up the river for a couple of years for non-disclosure—which is, by the way, what he did to you—it isn't the worst thing he could have done. He could have, well...okay, I can't think of *anything* worse for a company trying to go public."

Rex listened in stunned silence as our legal counsel and newest board member, Justin Caise, painted a dire picture. "He failed to disclose his checkered past, knowing full well that if he had, you wouldn't have had anything to do with him, right? There's a pattern here."

Rex let out a sigh audible enough to let Justin know he understood.

"The bottom line is that if you don't rid yourselves of Quinton, you may not be able to go public. The SEC will make it nigh on impossible. Keep him and you can kiss your dreams goodbye—including, by the way, the investment my partners and I just made in your fine firm."

"Alright. You've made your point," Rex finally replied. "He hasn't delivered on his promises anyway. A simple goodbye letter should suffice. Besides, can you imagine a guy with an SEC conviction having the *cojones* to sue us?"

Justin had an answer for that one. "He can sue all he likes, but he can't win. He deceived you. Motley was the one who arranged most all of the meetings with the investment bankers, not Quinton. You can forget about his United News Service too. Word's out it's up for sale. You've got no exposure, Rex."

"You're right. Draft the letter."

"Consider it done," Justin said. "Now, have you found a CFO?"

"No luck so far." We were under no illusions. The financials required to close the $100 million valuation ULIC funding round would easily overburden our QuickBooks accounting system. We were going to need a Chief Financial Officer, and more professional books, in a hurry.

"I've come up with several candidates," Justin said. "One looks particularly promising. He lives in Charlottesville, and he's built and sold a couple of businesses. He's currently unemployed, too."

꧁❖꧂

IT WAS A GIVEN that a CFO with the skills, stature, and experience we needed would command a six-figure salary. Even with the partners working free, we'd be cash starved until we got the union funding. But we couldn't close the union round without the services of a qualified CFO. So since we were as good as dead without such a person, Craig dialed Dean Johnson' number, not even knowing where he'd find the money to pay his salary.

Dean picked up the phone on the second ring. Craig introduced himself and gave him a five-minute overview of Value America. "Please come by for an interview."

"Sure," Dean said. "Sounds interesting. When would you like to meet? Sometime early next week, perhaps?"

Winn laughed. "We're an Internet firm. How about in fifteen minutes?"

"Please," Dean protested, "I'm wearing jeans. I haven't even shaved. I'm not dressed for an interview...."

"I don't care. I've seen suits before."

It was Dean's turn to laugh. "Okay then. I'm on my way."

An intrigued Dean Johnson arrived at the Yellow House on time, looking preppy in blue jeans and a sweater over a long-sleeved oxford shirt. He was in his late thirties but had braces on his teeth. Better late than never.

He told Craig and Rex how he had graduated from the Darden School of Business, and how he had started, built, and sold two tech-based companies. He had done his time under the big tent too. He had been one of the senior managers in Lehman Brothers' London office. Maybe that explained his polished and proper air. Dean seemed to possess a perfect balance between an entrepreneurial, roll-up-your-sleeves builder and an experienced professional manager.

The three immersed themselves in the subtleties of the arcane world of Generally Accepted Accounting Practices, audits and auditors, lawyers and venture capitalists, investment bankers and public offerings. It was like plunging into a bowl of alphabet soup. Our CEO and future EVP/CFO discussed IPOs, S1s, 10Qs, GAAP, and CTOs. They were like two peas in a pod.

Rex gave Dean a copy of Value America's business plan along with a couple of hours to read it. He outlined our plans for growth and explained our pending investment round. He described our recent meetings with investment bankers and was pleased with Dean's reactions. Johnson could certainly talk the talk, and there was every indication he could walk the walk. That didn't necessarily mean we could afford him.

"Dean," Craig finally said, "I think Justin Caise was right. You sound like the perfect CFO for a young, growing technology firm. I may not even hold your Darden MBA against you...."

Dean was about to protest that Darden was a first-rate institution, a top-tier business school, when Rex's laughter stopped him. "Don't worry about it," he said. "Just a bit of Value America lore. Ancient history. We'll tell you about it sometime. Anyway, we're prepared to offer you this job under one condition."

"What's that?" Dean figured it would have something to do with long hours or horrendous travel.

"We have a rule around here," Craig said. "Our management team all has skin in the game. I believe our CFO should be on the board and should be an investor. So we'll need you to invest the equivalent of your first year's salary, $100,000, into the company. It aligns our interests."

The investment request was as ridiculously high as the salary was low, but a considerable quantity of stock options sweetened the pot. After an in-depth tour of the online store and a long discussion about the business plan, Dean was ready to invest, job or no job. "Yes," he said. "Count me in." With that, Dean Johnson stroked a check to the tune of $100,000, becoming Value America's CFO. But it was the man, not his money, who helped pave our way.

ᘐᑛᘎᕉ

CRAIG AWOKE, STARTLED. He looked at the bedside clock—a little past two. Moonlight poured through the window like warm honey. Reflecting off his lake, it danced on the bedroom walls. His head was filled with numbers. What did they mean? Had he been dreaming? He couldn't remember.

Slowly, it all started coming back into focus. Volpe Brown had sent their letter valuing the company at $175 million. UBS had said we were worth $250 million. If the multiple of forward-looking revenues used by these investment banks went up to three or four, as they were predicting, the company could soon be worth billions. Yet as of tonight, the company was nearly broke. Building the next retail revolution wasn't cheap. It was all becoming surreal, incomprehensible. Were we rich, or poor?

Dreaming or not, he knew the answer. We were living on a veritable shoestring. The proceeds from the pass-the-hat funding round were dwindling. Requiring new hires to invest in the company was a clever strategy, but it had its limitations. Brand presentation fees were coming in, but not fast enough to impress an investment community fixated on revenues rather than profits.

We wouldn't be able to generate enough revenue to go public until we raised enough money to advertise. Our virtual reality was that we couldn't generate sales until we had funding, and we couldn't get funding until we generated sales. It made the chicken and egg thing look like a no-brainer.

His mind drifted to the odd world of Rafe Durn and Organized Labor. *If we could just close the ten million dollar union round,* he thought, *we could launch the store, stock the "shelves," prove the model, shake down the systems, drive revenues, and go public. But, every time we claw our way forward, the union buries us under another giant pile of reality.*

Katharine rolled over beside him, making that little humming noise she did. *God, she was so beautiful.* Craig's thoughts drifted away from numbers, investment bankers, and organized labor to his wife. In the midst of such turmoil, it's good to be loved. He drifted back to sleep, troubled no more.

ၑၖၞၟ

"SURE," RAFE DURN was saying. "As soon as you convince Union Privilege to partner with Value America, we'll close the funding round."

Craig felt his blood pressure rising. This was supposed to have been Durn's responsibility, not his. Once more, the union was adding a burden onto this already overloaded camel, changing the terms of the deal with no apparent motive other than to flex their prodigious muscles.

This new requirement put us in a rather ticklish position. The managers of Union Privilege had crafted a piecemeal solution for providing services to union members, some of which would become redundant if our far more comprehensive program were adopted. If they supported us, they might be putting themselves out of business—something politicos and union leaders are seldom willing to do. This was just swell.

But he had to try. Without the union investment, it didn't look like we would live to see the store's grand opening.

Craig presented the merits of Value America to the leaders of Union Privilege. He explained the ways we could serve Organized Labor, especially the rank and file. We could recount the great union accomplishments of decades past. We could prioritize union-made products in the Union Privilege store. Craig proposed using the marketplace to help build union membership and enhance the lives of union members.

He shared a strategy that would enable us to give a computer with Internet access to every union member out of the proceeds from the store. "Imagine," he said, "the notoriety you'll receive when you help union families fulfill the aspirations they have for their children's education."

Winn laid it on thick.

Using the most non-threatening language he could find, consciously placing himself in a subservient role, he stressed how we could enable the mission of Union Privilege. Craig portrayed this as a symbiotic relationship. It wasn't an act; he believed it. Forget that we were as good as dead if he couldn't convince them.

In the end, Union Privilege said they would work with Value America. Another of Rafe Durn's hurdles had been crossed.

Sadly however, they never followed through with their commitment, and union families never got their Internet-enabled PCs. Despite the promises and good intentions, self-interest won out over the common good. Pity.

❧

"REX, IT'S JUSTIN." Rex Scatena was in his office reviewing a thick stack of vendor listing agreements.

"Yes, counselor," he said cheerfully. "What can I do for you?"

"It's about Derk. You remember he wanted an opportunity to prove that his being on our board wasn't going to be a problem for us?"

"Sure," Rex replied. "It was one of the highlights of my day. A little levity to break the routine...."

Justin chuckled. That had been his reaction as well. "I have before me that 'proof.' Actually, it's just an opinion letter from his attorney."

"I guess that proves that you get what you pay for."

"Provided you pay enough," Justin finished his sentence. The two attorneys shared a laugh. "The letter contains a thinly veiled threat of a lawsuit if we don't agree."

"Naturally."

❧

"OKAY, DEAN," CRAIG SAID. "Here's how I'd like to handle this. I'll work with Rafe Durn, handle the negotiations, and the legal documentation. Meanwhile, you work with the union's accountants. Rex will handle their obnoxious California lawyer. In time, you'll learn to love this guy as much as we do. Their in-house counsel is a fellow named Chip, and he's actually pretty reasonable, for a union lawyer."

Dean smiled. *A union lawyer named "Chip." Alright.*

"Now as far as accounting firms are concerned, the union is using Coopers & Lybrand. We've been using a local firm. They've been doing a respectable job, but with the union, and hopefully an IPO, we're going to need one of the big six accounting firms. Somebody other than Coopers, of course."

"Of course."

Craig explained that there was another reason he didn't want to use Coopers & Lybrand. A year or so before Dynasty's IPO, Coopers had won a bid to handle their audits and tax filings. But his idea of an accounting firm's proper role was not merely to be an auditor or historian, recording past transactions for the benefit of posterity and the taxman. He wanted a firm that could spot and report potential weaknesses, points of vulnerability in his business, while they were still on the horizon, still small enough to fix. In short, Winn wanted auditors who could *help.*

The Coopers team had not been willing to provide much help beyond recording history. So in its third year, Dynasty put its accounting needs, including the work that would be needed for its upcoming IPO, out to bid again. The winner, in both price and promise of managerial support, was Ernst and Young. Craig wanted to make the switch well before Dynasty went public, realizing that it is next to impossible to switch horses later.

But Coopers had other ideas. They announced that they had underbid the initial Dynasty contract in order to get their foot in the door. The implication was that this gave them the perpetual right to charge whatever they wanted. While Craig wondered what might be contributing to their hallucinations, Coopers played their trump card. They decided not to release their work papers, documents Dynasty had already paid Coopers to prepare. These files were needed by Ernst and Young to complete the S1. No papers, no S1. No S1, no IPO. It would take another payment to loosen the papers from their grasp—a "transfer fee" of $100,000.

It sounded a lot like blackmail, at least by Winn's definition. But it couldn't be, could it? A big reputable accounting firm, guardians of the public trust, would never stoop so low, would they? Call it what you like, he paid the ransom, but as the money left his hands, he swore he would never deal with Coopers & Lybrand again.

Ordinarily, major accounting firms wouldn't have much interest in working with a little fish like Value America. But our founder had learned some interesting things about dealing with big fish. The largest accounting firms, investment bankers, and lawyers are competitive by nature. Even though they might swim right past a little fish, they'll part the seas to compete against each other. So he told Dean to solicit bids from Price Waterhouse, Ernst and Young, Arthur Anderson, anybody but Coopers.

The bids Dean received were astonishingly low and all reasonably close to each other. He wanted to use Price Waterhouse, the theory being that their tech team was more expert in the Internet/technology space. Craig wanted Ernst and Young because they were retail experts. But in the end, he deferred to his new CFO, knowing that to do otherwise would hurt Dean's ability to manage. It would turn out to be a costly mistake.

DURN SENT A TEAM down from Washington, D.C. to collect due diligence information on Value America. Rafe never actually visited the company himself. His associates were accompanied by his man Rossi. With his customary slicked-back hair and loafers with no socks, Seth regaled the team with tales of feminine conquests and a litany of colorful union stories.

Craig, still confused about Seth's relationship with Rafe Durn and ULIC, asked him to elucidate. Rossi informed him that it wasn't actually Rafe he was closest to—it was Durn's boss, ULIC's president. "You have to understand," he said, "I'm a made man, of sorts."

"Oh, you're self-made, you mean?" Ever the optimist.

"No. I mean I'm a *made man*," Rossi said. He explained precisely what that meant in this context as Winn stared in wide-eyed disbelief.

While Seth was educating Craig, Dean entertained the due-diligence doers. He recognized that the process could be approached in two ways. One was to fight it, nit-pick and analyze every request, asking, "Do you really need that?" Dean Johnson took the opposite approach. No matter how absurd the request, Dean was happy to comply. Even if it were going to take three thousand pages to copy all of the documentation on an issue, his response was, "Fine, no problem."

That's because he knew we had nothing to hide. There were no skeletons in our closet. And even if we had had something to hide, full—really full—disclosure would be the best way to conceal it. If your dirty little secret was on page 15,673 of 24,586 pages, what was the likelihood that anyone would spot it? No, Dean knew you never fought due diligence. If somebody wanted to look for a needle in a haystack, we'd provide not only the needle but a very nice stack of hay as well.

Craig and Dean were joined at the hip. They now checked with each other several times each day. "Watch your step," Johnson said, grinning. His office floor was covered with three-ring binders, each filled with compliance documents. There was a narrow pathway between them leading to Dean's chair. "Due diligence, for the union deal," he explained unnecessarily. "We've already sent some of it up. I'm going to need more of these binders."

TO THE UNINITIATED, it would have sounded like a tempest in a teapot, much ado over the most insignificant sort of minutia. But to Value America, it was a matter of life and death. The issue was revenue recognition, or more precisely, the accounting method used to determine it. This was important because the value of the company was now based on a multiple of forward-looking revenues.

We, like every retailer, counted our revenue as the full price our customer paid us for a product. But Coopers & Lybrand, the accounting firm representing the union, said, in effect, because you are operating on a virtual inventory model, your revenue is not the price of the product you've sold but rather the profit you made selling it.

Obviously, if profit (or more precisely, margin) were the measure of revenue, we were worth a whole lot less than we'd thought. On this basis, we wouldn't be able to raise enough money for our own funeral.

The founders were livid. It wasn't hard to see where this harebrained idea had come from. They suspected that the union wanted to acquire us cheap, not recognizing that while the Golden Goose might make a tasty supper indeed, it would make infinitely more sense to keep her alive, happy, and laying eggs.

We defended our position using sound accounting principles, not blue-sky wishful thinking. The crux of his argument, ironically, was something we considered a modest liability, a necessary evil. The fact was that we incurred risk of loss while the product was in transit, from the time it left the manufacturer's warehouse until the customer accepted it. Technically, we owned the product while it was *en route*.

The key was risk. If the product were lost or damaged *en route*, we were responsible, although there was a remedy with the freight carrier. If the customer was not satisfied for some reason, we were responsible for crediting back the purchase price. We had the remedy of sending the product back to the manufacturer; but there was still the risk that the manufacturer would not honor the credit, even though we still owed them for the original sale. So technically, there was risk of loss at several points, though Value America had systems in place to minimize it.

Our newly appointed accounting firm, Price Waterhouse, explained this to Coopers. They determined that we had indeed been using the proper accounting method for revenue recognition. But neither Coopers nor ULIC accepted their assessment.

They decided the final arbiter should be the Securities and Exchange Commission. Typically, the SEC first reviews accounting policies in a pre-IPO document called an "S1." They pass judgment on this document before it is printed and distributed in the form known as the "red herring."

By the time it becomes a prospectus, the SEC has sprinkled enough holy water on it to float a battleship. If the prospectus reflects a particular accounting method, it's a fair bet the SEC thinks it's gospel.

Newly christened as a public company, OnSale used precisely the same method of revenue recognition we did. The details were conveyed right there in OnSale's prospectus, just as Craig had explained it to Durn and his accountants. This was our "get out of jail free" card. Surely this would convince them.

Coopers wavered, becoming aware of how incredibly foolish they were beginning to look, but Rafe Durn held his ground. Logic had no effect on him. Indisputable proof wasn't good enough. This whole fiasco, it appeared, was nothing but a ploy to drive the price down.

So it came down to a battle of wills. "What's it going to take to convince you that we're doing this right, Rafe?"

Durn wasn't ready to give up. "The SEC is the final authority. I want an opinion letter from them confirming your policy."

"We already have that," Craig said, hoping his frustration wasn't too apparent. "The OnSale prospectus describes exactly the same method we use. The SEC's opinion is right here in black and white."

"Not good enough. I want a letter from them."

There was a long pause while Craig processed the ramifications. In order to ratchet down the company's valuation, Durn was willing to open Pandora's Box. The SEC, the supreme authority in this arena, was already struggling with astronomical dot-com valuations. But Rafe wanted us to ask them, in effect, "Are you really sure about all this?" Our request for clarification would imply we were questioning the rules upon which we would be valued.

"Rafe," Craig said at last, "this is in no one's interest. We're six months from going public. What part of this sounds smart to you?"

"Get the letter from the SEC supporting your accounting method, or we lower the valuation. Clear?"

It was clear we couldn't make it without investment capital, and we were out of time. We no longer had the option of going through the six to nine month process of raising venture capital. So here we were, at the business end of Rafe's gun. Our Price Waterhouse accountants thought it was the dumbest thing they'd ever heard of. Caise thought the same. I don't have to tell you what Craig thought.

It was a pointless, frustrating, and humiliating exercise, but we had no other options. Craig capitulated. He had our accountants send the letter, and in due time, the SEC responded. Yes indeed, rules are rules. GAAP was still GAAP. "Risk of loss" was still alive and kicking, in more ways than one. In their initial telephone response, the SEC said in essence, "Value America's method for revenue recognition is consistent with our prior rulings. Frankly, we're surprised that you couldn't figure this out for yourselves...."

৵৽৹৵

THE IDEA OF a co-branded Value America Visa card was never far from the top of our wish list. So when one of CapOne's brilliant young "homochromos," Erik Taylor, made himself available, Craig hired him without hesitation. Erik's job? Make the card happen.

Erik, Craig, and Rex soon found themselves sitting with Terry Flynn, Vice Chairman of financial giant MBNA. They discussed a symbiotic relationship where MBNA's cardholders would receive an extra one percent bonus, rather like frequent-flyer miles, that would automatically be credited toward their ValueDollar accounts in our store, no matter where they shopped. MBNA would cover sixty percent of the cost of the program, and Value America would absorb the rest. Good for them, good for us, and good for their cardholders.

We discussed creating marketplaces for the largest of MBNA's 5,000 affinity groups. Our store would be their store. By working together, we would quadruple the amount each organization earned on their members' credit cards. MBNA's clients would be the foundation of a direct mail marketing campaign. With such an accurate, affluent, and focused customer list, our "success rate" would instantly exceed any catalog retailer. In turn, our success would translate into more business for MBNA and greater contributions to each of their affinity groups. Win-win.

During a break, the founders called Sam Abram from UBS to bring him up to speed. Since he had been the one offering to "crawl over five miles of broken glass" to lead our IPO, he'd no doubt want to know that we had finally cleared the last hurdle in closing the union funding round. With Rafe Durn's reluctant surrender on the revenue recognition issue, the deal was going to close. Value America was ready to start its push toward the IPO. We also needed to tell Abram we had parted ways with his hero, Derk Quinton.

Abram's reaction was not at all what they had expected. It wasn't, "Congratulations! This is the highest valuation any Internet company has ever achieved pre-IPO," which it was at the time. It wasn't, "It's amazing you bypassed the usual venture vultures and formed a symbiotic affiliation, with all the promise that implies." His reaction was, "This is getting too big. I just don't know if I feel comfortable...."

If our guys thought the conversation was strange, the letter they received the following morning was downright bizarre. In it, Abram announced that UBS was backing out of the deal. This presented Craig with a dilemma. UBS's high valuation had done its share in encouraging Durn to invest union pension-plan cash. With UBS no longer in the picture, did that mean that their valuation had gone poof as well? When Rafe found out—and he would find out, because we never hid things like this— there was a very good chance that the deal would be dead again.

The savior turned out to be none other than Seth "the investment banker" Rossi. He did some research into Abram's past and announced that he had done this very thing on at least two previous occasions. Chronic cold feet, apparently. We never found out where Seth got this information. We never even discovered if it was actually true. But it didn't matter. Seth's timely tidbit and his relationship with Rafe Durn made the UBS bailout a non-issue. Maybe Seth *was* an investment banker.

Naaaah.

෧෴෴

IT WAS QUICKLY getting to where you couldn't tell the players without a scorecard. The movers and shakers were beginning to, well, move and shake. Stan Garmin, the investment banker with Union Bank of Switzerland, was mortified by the ignominious retreat of Sam Abram, his analyst. So Garmin jumped ship, moving to Robertson Stephens to head up their Business Supply sector.

While it might not sound terribly exciting when compared with the sizzling technology sector, the business supply industry was comprised of some of the largest corporations around—supply companies like Office Depot, Staples, Corporate Express, Boise Cascade, United Stationers, and US Office Products. It also included what was known as "the channel," huge distributors of business technology, companies like Ingram Micro, Tech Data, and Merisel.

Garmin quickly arranged an appointment. Unfortunately, he missed the last connection into town. So the Robertson Stephens' team consisted of their top analyst for the office products industry along with an investment banker—both women, it turned out.

They seemed to appreciate our grasp of the challenges that permeated the office products industry, the retail world, technology, brands, distribution, and VARs (Value Added Resellers). They were amazed at our understanding of the esoteric thing they called the channel. Few outside this convoluted domain even know it exists. Fewer still know it well enough to philosophize about its problems and opportunities.

The analyst and the banker went back to San Francisco recommending that Robbie Stephens take us public—in the business-products sector. But Dale Dandridge, the technology analyst who had been too busy to see us, got wind of this and alerted Gordon Conover, a Managing Director, their investment banker for tech stocks. They quickly mobilized to prevent their teammates from running away with their prize. After all, they had not gotten where they were by letting the Business Supply sector upstage them. Heated competition, once again, had turned into a beautiful thing. It was nice having people fight over us, even if they were on the same team.

Gordon Conover's boss, firm co-founder Sandy Robertson, had been instrumental in persuading many of the nation's leading technology executives to help fund the presidential campaigns of one William Jefferson Clinton. And the man who had arranged the meetings between Sandy Robertson and these influential and moneyed tech magnates was a gentleman named Miles Julian, who subsequently spent the first three years of Bill Clinton's presidency in the White House managing technology initiatives and granting presidential access to the favored few, especially dot-com founders. After leaving the Clinton administration, it was only natural that Miles would join Robertson Stephens.

That was how the experienced and financially savvy Gordon Conover and the extremely well-connected Miles Julian found themselves sitting in the modest office of Craig Winn, CEO of an up-and-coming (well, not quite up yet) Internet store in Charlottesville, Virginia. Rex once again explained the plan, showed off the store, and expounded on how Value America would be good for brands and customers alike. Then Craig outlined the union deal, which was within days of closing. He also explained the merits of the strategic alliance.

"This partnership with Union Privilege could be the prototype for strategic partnerships with a whole broad range of groups, from commercial affiliations like credit card issuers to organizations of like-minded people—university alumni, for instance, charities, and faith groups."

Miles liked the sound of that.

"The beautiful thing about it," Craig continued, "is that these strategic partnerships do something good for everyone in the loop. They're the classic win-win scenario. We spend a whole lot less on advertising and help great organizations raise money."

Miles Julian's political background brought a fresh insight. "I don't know much about being an investment banker, and I have no conception of what it takes to win in the retail business. But I know a great deal about politics, about building relationships, and about perceptions, and I can tell you this. You folks hold the high ground here. This concept is the most worthy idea to come along in a long time."

"That's been the idea since day one, Miles," Rex replied.

"The real question is how to present your store to the world. The way I see it, there's really very little difference between your store and a political candidate. Both have a story to tell, a message to get across. Now, it's my experience that the message will be best received if there is a personality the audience can identify with.

"In politics, this would be the candidate. They're carefully positioned as champions of the greater good. But it works in the commercial world too—Virgin Atlantic had Branson; Chrysler had Iacocca. I'm not talking about a spokesman here, mind you, a mere talking head. I'm talking about a symbol, the founder, someone who can honestly say, 'This is a good thing; I built it and I'm proud of it.' For Value America, Craig, that's you."

Winn wasn't comfortable with this. He didn't want to be in the spotlight. For a multitude of reasons, he had come to mistrust the media. Julian went on anyway. "Here, reality and perception are the same. Heck, with politicos, the perception itself is usually all it takes. Reality is just a bonus. But you? You're the real deal—you're doing well by doing *good*. This is the stuff of heroes."

Miles had nailed it. "Doing well by doing good" was really what Value America was all about.

Gordon Conover grinned. "See, guys? That's why you want Robertson Stephens in your corner. We know how to position you, how to market you. Choose us to lead your IPO."

"Getting the message out is a big reason we're going public," Rex explained. "There's not enough money on earth to advertise our way into the national psyche. Public dot-coms have gained prestige by virtue of the free media coverage they've received." Scatena had learned his craft.

"That's quite right," Gordon said.

"But the press hardly ever reports on privately held companies," Craig said, "no matter how successful or innovative they are. Know why?"

Gordon and Miles looked at each other.

"It's because they're unwilling to do the research to tell a credible story about a private company. Private firms are allowed to have secrets. They don't have to make a public announcement every time the CEO takes a pee. It takes real investigative journalism to find out what makes a private company tick. I can assure you, their stories are no less compelling.

"Ah, but with a public company, the research is easy. Just look at the public reports or call the analyst. It's all there in black and white, mandated by the SEC. That's why we have to go public," Rex completed the thought.

"We're the right guys to get you there," Gordon stated again. "Our analyst, Dale Dandridge, is the biggest promoter of Internet stocks. You can trust us to do the job right."

REX WAS ALL SMILES. "So Robertson Stephens and Volpe Brown Whelan are going to co-manage our IPO."

"Right," Craig replied, "and FBR will assist. I'm pretty sure we'll get H&Q on board too."

"Robbie Stephens; Volpe Brown; Hambrick and Quist; Freedman, Billings, Ramsey—the number one, two, and three pure tech investment bankers in the country along with the hottest and fastest growing regional firm. This is a dream team. No doubt about it."

"Rex, old buddy, it looks like this is actually going to happen. Now if we can just get the ULIC round closed, get the store turned on, and generate some sales...."

OKAY, HERE'S THE PLAN. We take over Times Square. Set up a computer that's hooked up to the mega-screen TV, so everyone can see what's happening. Then we get La-Z-Boy recliners set up all over the place, and people sitting in 'em with laptops, shopping online at Value America. And all this happens on the Friday after Thanksgiving—it's the biggest shopping day of the year, so all of the networks will have to come up with some kind of news on the shopping scene. We can have all the big reporters there because this year, you're what's happening. Everything is dot-com this and online that. Value America will gain national notoriety overnight!

Pennington was one of the biggest PR firms around, and when they had proposed this grandiose scheme two months before, it had all seemed doable. Even the price, $250,000, including pre-event publicity, hadn't seemed out of range.

But Craig, ever the pragmatist, knew there was a vast difference between conception and execution, between saying and doing. He suspected that once the contract was signed, we would be turned over to the underlings, the $15-an-hour worker bees, who wouldn't have a clue how to pull it off. So he had put a caveat into the contract that made our relationship with the PR firm dependent on the success of this event. It had to be delivered as promised and as priced.

It's no fun being right when right is wrong. The grand event became a comedy of errors. We had given them every scrap of material we had on the store, its operation, and its philosophy. Pennington's worker bees had proceeded to butcher it. Their presentation came out incomprehensible, or worse—repellent. They couldn't even get the publicity right. Neither could they get the technological wrinkles ironed out in Times Square. They couldn't figure out how to get proper connectivity to the site, couldn't get access to the giant TV, and couldn't seem to understand that Times Square was an outdoor venue—what happened if it rained? They had no contingency plan. And the budget? *Well, ah, we're running a little over....*

Disappointed, we invoked the escape clause Craig had wisely put into the contract and said goodbye. But we wondered how we were ever going to publicize this thing if someone as prestigious as this firm couldn't pull it off.

Now, in November, it seemed the Julian approach might be the ticket. Reluctantly, and now out of options, Craig began to think in terms of publicizing the store as one might build a political campaign—structure it around a press conference. That would give us a sense of being real, which was always an uphill battle when talking about a virtual business, and give us a focal point (though Craig characterized it as being a lightning rod) with which people could identify.

We hadn't solved all the technical problems with the store, but we had gotten it to the point where it would at least work. One could visit us online, choose from among a couple hundred thousand products, and buy them. We were ready to launch the store, to announce our presence to the world, to spread our wings and fly.

Capstone was a public relations firm specializing in promoting political candidates. Their specialty seemed to dovetail nicely with the Miles Julian-inspired marketing strategy. We decided to hold a political-style press conference. The venue would be, as they say, fraught with portent: the National Press Club in Washington, D.C., where many a high-ranking notable had made monumental pronouncements.

Capstone set it up for the first week in December and promised to have a hundred or more journalists in attendance, who would, it was expected, generate dozens of articles on the future of retail. For our part, we would have banks of computers set up so the audience could try the Value America shopping experience for themselves. Every shopper would have a "coach," someone on our staff who could guide them through the store, answer their questions, and keep reporters from floundering. The store was pretty deep, after all, and if you weren't used to surfing the Web, you could get lost.

Craig chose for a theme, "Let's go shopping now, everybody's learning how, come along and shop with me," a shameless appropriation of a great old Beach Boys surfin' song. It made great sense to tie shopping to surfing, the universal metaphor for exploring the World Wide Web.

The only problem was that the media event was a bust. Only a few actual reporters showed up, mostly for the free lunch. The room would have been virtually empty were it not for thirty or so Value America staffers (virtually all of us), a large group of vendors who had been invited, and a motley collection of fringe players who had crashed the party hoping to sell us one thing or another.

The post-game analysis revealed that not a single story ever appeared in the press as a result of our big coming-out party at the National Press Club. Value America's virtual doors were open at last, but we were still a secret.

That's not to say nothing exciting happened that day. Chip, the union's in-house attorney, called on behalf of Rafe Durn. "Craig," he said, "Mr. Durn has decided how he wants you to handle your dismissal of Derk Quinton."

"What are you talking about, Chip?"

"We found the dismissal letter in the books of documents you sent us."

"So you're saying that because we were good guys and gave you a copy of his veiled threat, you're going to hold it against us?"

"Not hold it against you. Rafe just wants it resolved."

This wasn't going to be pretty. "Resolved? Derk Quinton is an ex-con whose very presence has the potential to sink any chances we have of going public. Quinton is history."

"Not quite," Chip said. "Our lawyer is drafting a clause that says you will guarantee to resolve the Derk Quinton issue to Mr. Quinton's satisfaction within sixty days."

There was a long silence. The words "Mr. Quinton's satisfaction" hung in the air like the smell of rotting fish. Craig thought perhaps he had misinterpreted what he had just heard, so he asked Chip to repeat it. No, he had heard correctly. Stifling the urge to scream, he tried to calm himself enough to enumerate the reasons why this was the dumbest demand yet in a long series of dumb demands.

"Chip, listen to me. This is insane. First, there is absolutely no risk here. None. Even if Quinton had performed on our behalf, which he didn't, even if he had spent a single hour sitting in on a board meeting, which he hasn't, there would still be the little matter of non-disclosure. He committed securities fraud, got caught, got sent to prison, and then tried his best to hide his background from us. Sure, he can sue us, because anybody can sue anybody for anything. But he can't win. There's not a judge or jury in creation gullible enough to find in his favor, and you know it."

Chip sounded apologetic. "It doesn't matter. Rafe's decided."

Craig tried again. "Look. Rex and I will personally indemnify him, the company, ULIC, and God knows whomever else you want, for both the legal costs associated with a potential case and whatever hypothetical settlement might be awarded. We'll put it in writing that if Quinton, by some unbelievable twist of fate, gets a judgment, we'll give him any stock he's awarded out of our own holdings. If you don't want to get stung, don't kick the beehive."

"That's not going to be good enough," Chip countered. "You either sign the clause or there'll be no investment."

Winn grit his teeth and tried one last time. "Chip. This is suicide. You've got to make him understand that if we sign off on that clause, it becomes part of our public record! The SEC will spot it when we prepare the S1, and they'll have a field day. If we don't go public, what happens to your investment? Nothing, that's what. Quinton will see it too—you're *inviting* a suit. What part of 'crazy' don't you guys see here?"

"I'm sorry. I can't help you...."

As he hung up the phone, Craig felt as if he'd been kicked by a mule, and not just figuratively. He was still sitting quietly, rubbing his temples, when Rex walked in. He told him what had just transpired.

Rex sat down and tried to think like a lawyer. "I've got a theory, but it sounds...." He scratched his head. "Well, anyway, let me tell you what may be going on. You've told me, and my experience bears this out, that Rafe Durn won't make a move without his lawyers, right?"

"Right."

"So his lawyers know it, and they're feathering their nests. All the while, they're on the clock. That means billable hours."

The revelation didn't make him feel any better. "First they spend time creating the problem, and then they spend more time rectifying it."

"And don't forget, Durn won't be paying the bill. We will. Their fees come out of the investment funding. Pretty slick, eh?"

During the next twenty-four hours, Scatena and Winn called everybody they could find to get their take on the issue. Dean Johnson, John Motley, Justin Caise, and yes, even Seth Rossi. They all just rolled their eyes heavenward. How could you reason with the unreasonable?

They called Rafe, but he predictably said he wasn't doing anything contrary to the advice of counsel. Finally, they traded words and faxes with the lawyers—proposals and counterproposals. But nothing worked. ULIC's lawyers wouldn't budge. You could almost see them smiling in their plush California law offices. They probably enjoyed this.

Finally, Rex said, "Let's call their bluff. No one's this stupid."

"Weren't you the one who taught me that you couldn't play chicken with unions? Weren't you the one who told me that expecting reason to prevail with these guys is a fool's errand?"

"Call his bluff," Rex repeated. "He'll blink."

Craig wanted desperately to believe his friend was right. He took a deep breath and dialed Durn's home, for it was now late. Craig told the union executive that they couldn't in good conscience sign the "Quinton clause." He told Durn that it was not only bad for Value America, but it was bad for him as well. He listened for a moment and then hung up the phone.

"What did he say?" Rex asked.

Craig appeared calm. "What did he say? He said, 'Thank you very much. We will not be investing in your company.' That's what he said."

Rex looked stunned. "I was *sure* he'd blink. *Nobody's* that dumb."

"Well, one guy is," he said as he picked up the phone and hit re-dial. "Rafe, Craig. Please accept my apology. We would be pleased to sign the clause. Yes, we'll fax it to your lawyer immediately and UPS-overnight the original tomorrow. Yes. Thank you. Good night." Crow *à l'Orange*.

The founders signed the document with scrawls no handwriting expert would have recognized as theirs—angry, steaming scribbles, but on the proper lines. They both felt as if they had just sacrificed their second-born child in the hope of saving their first. Rex turned to his ashen-faced partner and said, "This will cost them. I don't know how, and I don't know when, but if there is any justice in the world, they will live to regret this."

۞

ON DECEMBER 20, 1997, Value America was the recipient of a wire in the amount of $10,000,000 from the Union Labor Investment Corporation. After half a million had been deducted to cover the cost of Seth Rossi's "investment banker's fee," $350,000 had been paid for the masochistic pleasure of the union's lawyering, and Caise's legal fees had been paid, a little over $9 million remained.

For the first time in our young life, the gas tank was full and the open road beckoned. Only Craig and Rex knew that the vehicle we were driving had a time bomb in the trunk.

IT'S COOL TO BE BLUE

*O*nce again, the ball got rolling with a kick from John Motley. He knew virtually everyone in the office products industry, but he also knew folks in other fields: finance, law, politics, even advertising. In John's tireless enthusiasm for Value America, he had sent some of our printed materials to a west coast ad agency with whom he was acquainted.

Weller-O'Sullivan was at the top of their game. They had engineered many successful and memorable ad campaigns for both commercial and political interests. One look at our materials, and they asked John to provide an introduction.

Craig was spending the night at John's home, as he often did when working in Washington, so Motley had a captive audience. "I have a video tape and a brochure from an advertising agency I want to show you," he said as he popped the tape into a player. It contained a series of first-rate commercials for everything from Maxwell House coffee to Burger King.

The timing was fortuitous. With the store now open for business and the union investment a reality, it was past time to start getting the word out. Craig reviewed the Weller-O'Sullivan pitch, grinned, and asked John to arrange the meeting.

They came armed to the teeth. Television ads. Print ads. Radio. Even Internet banners. I knew nothing about these new developments until I got a call from Craig one Thursday afternoon asking me to attend a meeting in his office. As I shook hands with two guys in suits named Weller and O'Sullivan, he introduced me as the company's Vice President of Marketing and Creative Director, the "voice" of Value America. I had no clue who these guys were or why they were there. Craig explained that we were about to start advertising and that these gentlemen had come to present their ideas.

A twinge of jealousy crept up my spine. The look and feel of Value America had always been my responsibility, my baby, and I was reluctant to see it—any part of it—fall into the hands of strangers.

I don't know if Jim Weller sensed any of this, but he quickly transformed himself from a stranger into a trusted colleague. With charm and disarming humility, he explained how he had researched our company by reading my stuff online and had come to the conclusion that the reasoned, informal, almost folksy writing style I had developed was as powerful a communication medium as he had ever encountered.

The newspaper ads they had brought with them were pretty clever. *The*

ATM machine changed the way you bank. Value America will change the way you shop. It was easy to see why Weller's creative mind had won his firm so many awards, so many prestigious clients.

There were a hundred examples he could have used of recent developments that changed our lives, but the ATM was probably the strongest. To most people, the ATM represented freedom, the successful application of computer technology to an old and annoying problem.

Weller-O'Sullivan also brought a rough-cut TV ad, and this was what got everyone's blood pumping. It was inspired by the classic science fiction film *2001, A Space Odyssey*, complete with Strauss' *"Also Sprach Zarathustra"* theme music. The visuals were primarily NASA file footage of shuttle liftoffs and space walks. It wasn't the execution, however, but the idea that grabbed us all. The ad declared that the future—Value America— had arrived three years early, not in 2001, but today, in January 1998.

I don't know how many copyright violations we would have committed had we proceeded with that TV ad. We never found out. The agency, in attempting to fine-tune it, was never able to duplicate the spontaneity and power of that first rough cut. But seeing the ad was enough to make us all stop what we were doing and reflect on just how close we were to glory. Seeing ourselves on the TV screen crystallized it. We had been focusing so closely on the potholes in the path at our feet, some of us had lost sight of the horizon, and the horizon was now almost close enough to reach out and touch.

Sadly, Weller's newspaper ads didn't make it either. Jim's brilliant beginning was turned over to his agency staff, who promptly sucked all of the finesse out of them. I suppose it would have been asking too much to expect Weller to personally execute our ads. Big-agency principals don't *do* production work. But the same frustration we had experienced during our initial foray into the world of public relations had come back to haunt us. Craig showed their first finished jewelry ad to me, hoping I would say he was overreacting, hoping it could somehow be fixed. But all I could do was shake my head and ask, "What happened?"

We were beginning to feel like the early rocket pioneers. We were pretty sure we knew what we were doing, but we were having a terrible time getting anything to fly.

❧

"BDS. DON'T ASK me what it stands for," Joe said. "But their developers are the best we've interviewed. They just finished building the commerce engines for CarMax and Barnes & Noble.com." Page appreciated talent.

"I think these are our guys." A lesser man would have been jealously guarding his territory. Joe just wanted the job done.

"Okay," Craig agreed. "Let's hire 'em. Just make sure their marching orders are clearly spelled out. Their fees must be project based, as we discussed. Investment money or not, we can't afford to be wasteful. Fact is, we never will."

Although the store worked beautifully from the customers' viewpoint, there were several secondary issues lurking just beneath the surface. The big problems had been solved. But it was like the old Chinese proverb: It wasn't the mountain that would wear us down—it was the pebble in our shoe. Only the details remained, but those could become major annoyances if left unattended. Now that we had money, solving them became our top priority. BDS was given their marching orders.

First, we asked them to finish integrating our customer-service tool. Joe and team had developed a proprietary system that was pretty spectacular. It was intuitive and practical, automatically providing our customer-care reps with the information they needed to help folks with their orders.

The second challenge was to streamline the order pipeline. Straightforward transactions were no problem. But while it was one thing to simply charge the customer's credit card and process a new order, it was something else again, something a hundred times more difficult, to deal with exceptions.

What if a product were returned? What was the best way to verify the return and credit the customer's account without becoming vulnerable to thievery? What if only part of the order were shipped? How should we deal with backorders? These unruly side issues in the order pipeline would require man-years of very sophisticated coding.

A far more fundamental issue still had to be resolved: how to account for virtual inventory. There was no way the accounting community would accept financial data generated with software you wrote for your own company. *Don't touch those numbers. You don't know where they've been.*

Commercially available financial software packages—providing such essential functionality as general ledger, accounts payable, accounts receivable, income statements, and balance sheets—assume the presence of inventory and accounts receivable. We had neither.

Diminishing the cost of inventory by maximizing "turn" was what separated successful retailers from dead ones. The Price Club had prevailed by combining the distribution center with the actual store. But they still owned their inventory, albeit for a comparatively short period of time. our plan was to make inventory exposure virtually non-existent. You could call it "hot-potato" inventory. The customer bought the item, the factory shipped it, and the customer received it; *we* never actually touched it. Short of "Beam me up, Scotty," it was the most efficient distribution model on the planet.

Problem was, financial software packages assumed that you had to own something before you could sell it. It was a logical position, I suppose. Typically, if you sold something you didn't own, a felony was in progress.

Complicating the problem, we had no accounts receivable. Our customers paid us up front, before we ever asked anybody to send anything anywhere. It was great for business but terrible for bookkeeping. BDS had their work cut out. Thankfully, they had more patience with the auditors than did Joe.

⁌⁍

WE NEVER REALLY planned on inventing a whole new advertising genre. As a matter of fact, the idea of producing ads ourselves—in-house—had never even been a part of the original master plan. But you can't calculate everything. Sometimes you just have to follow your nose.

Conventional retail advertising said, "We have this product for sale, and it costs this much." The implication was invariably that the price was lower than the competition's. That concept was out of sync with our environment, where better quality products were offered on the basis of their merit. It dawned on us that there wasn't an ad agency anywhere who knew how to sell like this.

Craig agonized about it for all of five minutes before he called me. "I really don't want to pull you off what you're doing, Ken, but this is important. I want to run a test ad, and I think the only way we're going to get it the way we want it is if you and I work together."

That brought a smile; images of the good ol' days working joined at the hip, of thoughtful lunches at sunlit parks. Craig wanted to create an ad style the same way we had worked out so many things in the past: one on one, thrust and parry, me pounding away at my workstation and him merrily barking out suggestions as fast as I could field them. But it took fast reflexes and a thick skin for a designer to work *mano a mano* with the strong-willed Winn, and I was out of practice.

Together we finished the jewelry ad Weller-O'Sullivan had started, and we ran it in one or two newspapers. We quickly discovered that our jewelry department was going to be a lightning rod for every con artist in the country. Our fraud-prevention procedures were going to need a little fine-tuning. I suppose you could call the ad a qualified success; so many computer thieves responded to it, we were sure a lot of nice people had seen it too. It was a start, at least. Our toe was in the water. And for the first time in a year, I found myself back in the world of print.

❧

"OH, THAT'S IMPRESSIVE." I was down in the basement getting a cup of coffee when I ran into Joe in the hallway. "What are these things?"

Joe grinned like a kid at Christmas. Gleaming black boxes with small blinking lights and understated blue lettering lined two walls in what had been an office the last time I'd paid any attention. Now, there was barely enough room to turn around. "Netfinities," he said. "They're IBM servers. Just came in."

"A bit more horsepower than that old refurbished HP we used in the Attic," I observed.

"Just wait until our T1s are in," said a disembodied voice. Dan Lucier was curled up on the floor behind one of the systems, hooking something up. I hadn't noticed his hiking boots sticking out amid the clutter.

"Does that explain all the mess out in the street?" I asked. "I couldn't help but notice all the trucks and backhoes this morning."

"Yeah," Joe said. "Real connectivity. And that's not all. We're getting Cisco routers and switches too."

"We're upgrading, now that we have some money," observed the network guru. "And no offense, word-guy, but it's nice to see us spending it here first."

"Yeah," Joe said. "Can you imagine what would happen if we got an ad campaign going and we were hit by thousands of customers? Without this new infrastructure, our site would be as slow as Michigan molasses."

"Believe it or not," I said, "I agree with you. Technology has to come first. We're going to run very few ads initially, so you guys have all the time you need to shake down your new systems."

"We're about ready. So when are you pullin' the trigger?" Joe asked.

"Soon. Ready or not, world, here we come."

❧

CRAIG SAT AT his desk all alone, chuckling. This was the most inventive solicitation letter he had ever read, and the samples the guy had sent along were first rate.

Phil Ramsey was just what we needed, a real, honest-to-goodness advertising manager. He was both creative and knowledgeable about the ins and outs of all phases of the business—print, radio, and television. He was an expert in direct-response advertising to boot. Craig figured Ramsey would be a good bookend paired with me, since I didn't pretend to know the first thing about the *business* of advertising—I was a fair designer and passable writer, but the advertising business required cutting deals and managing money. Craig knew I couldn't negotiate my way out of a paper bag.

Phil brought with him more than talent, experience, and an infectious personality. He brought contacts. And among the most valuable of them were the energetic and resourceful people at an advertising agency in Washington called Stevens, Reid, Curcio. SRC was a specialist in political campaigns, having worked for the likes of Ronald Reagan and the elder George Bush.

The fact that SRC had few if any non-political clients deterred neither Phil nor Craig. There was a little-known silver lining to this cloud. They explained that Federal law mandated that the media must disclose and offer their lowest rates to political candidates. Knowledge, as they say, is power. In this case, it was *buying power*, for SRC knew exactly how low every newspaper, magazine, radio station, and TV and cable network would sell advertising, if pushed hard enough.

So we signed a deal with Stevens, Reid, Curcio that said we would run all of our advertising through them, like a media-buying service. For this exclusive arrangement, they slashed their commissions (we never paid top dollar for anything), and they booked space for us at the rock-bottom direct-response rates. Yes, we were cheap. No apologies.

This wasn't the only way to save money on newspaper ads, we discovered. Papers sold "remnant space" at a healthy discount. The ad may run Wednesday instead of Tuesday, but it would still run in whatever section we wanted. As a result, we paid as little as $20 thousand dollars for full-page national newspaper ads, a fraction of the published rates.

❧❦❧

NOTHING HAD HAPPENED to dim our admiration for HP. As far as we were concerned, the technology giant was our most important brand. So it made perfect sense to kick off our advertising campaign with Hewlett-Packard. The jewelry ad had just been a dress rehearsal. Now we were ready to rumble. Craig and I mapped out the territory, but we didn't get far before I realized I'd never even *seen* an ad that did what we wanted done, much less designed one.

"This first HP ad," Craig said, "is going to be the prototype for everything we do. It's going to establish our format, philosophy, and style from now on."

Nothing like a little pressure to start the day off.

"The ad has to enhance the HP brand."

Serve the brands. I read that somewhere.

"At the same time, the ad has to 'brand' Value America and connect us in the reader's mind to HP. We want to be perceived as a conduit, the very best way to buy HP products."

One ad, two brands. Got it.

"We want the ad to mirror our store, you know, provide the same kind of information with the same informal flavor. Let's help folks make better choices. Doug Schatz is our merchant for HP, if you've got any questions. He's got a good-better-best scenario: PCs, monitors, and printers."

We're going to need a bigger newspaper.

"Oh, and make it funny," he said as he turned to leave. "And I almost forgot. Somewhere in the ad I'd like to see a collection of brand logos, to show the kind of direct relationships we've developed."

Oh, that'll make for a nice clean presentation.

"This should be easy for you, Ken. It's *print.* Things don't move around."

Wonderful. "Full-page ad?" I said, trying not to look rattled.

"Sure."

"What papers?"

"Does it matter?"

"Yes. Some of 'em have oddball sizes. I'm going to have to research this and verify the dimensions."

"Okay, then design the ad for *USA Today.* These are Pavilions, HP's home line. They wouldn't make sense in *The Wall Street Journal.*"

"Fair enough. Are they live?" Being "live" meant that our customers could visit our website, view the presentation, and buy whatever we were selling. But we also had something called the "Staging Store" where we assembled the Product Presentations. The public never saw this phase. Obviously, there was no point in advertising something the consumer couldn't actually buy.

"Most of this is in staging now. It'll go live tomorrow."

This isn't impossible, I thought to myself. *Just highly improbable.* There was so much to say in so little space. Conventional wisdom in ad design insists that people don't want to read, so one should keep the text to a minimum. But it's always been my contention that most ads simply aren't worth reading. They preach. They cajole. They schmooze. Few impart any useful information with wit and style. If we had learned anything from doing the in-store presentations, we had learned to be sympathetic with our audience, not adversarial—to have a conversation, not deliver a speech.

Text-heavy, clean, and balanced, my first important Value America ad took shape. Although we would change some of the details, the basic structure would stand firm, in time becoming an instantly recognizable entity. *Oh! Here's the Value America ad. What are they featuring today?*

৩৯⋮৶৶

MONICA LINK HAD begun to feel like Sisyphus. The ancient Corinthian king had been condemned by an offended Zeus to roll a boulder eternally up a hillside in Tartarus, only to have it slip from his fingers every time he neared the crest.

Monica was, after months of uphill effort, beginning to doubt her chances of landing the one brand she had been counting on—IBM, her *alma mater*. Sisyphus may have had it coming, but Monica had never shown any disrespect to the all-powerful geek god.

Eventually, though, her perseverance paid off. On January 27, 1998, IBM signed a $27,500 Product Presentation and Listing Agreement. That touched off a frenzy of activity in the Yellow House. We gave the prestigious new brand the full-court press. Every available staffer was enlisted. Within five days, we'd created eight Multimedia Product Presentations and had built an entire IBM store with hundreds of individual products.

The reason for the big push was simple: IBM was the biggest fish in the business-computer pond. And we needed business PCs to complement our office products offerings. An excited Monica Link informed me we were going to launch the new department with an ad—a full-page *Wall Street Journal* look-out-world-here-we-come sort of thing.

The only problem was, we were going to feature an end-of-life business machine. It was ancient—all of three months old—thus relatively slow, with an outdated chip and, by today's standards, a mere teaspoon of RAM. What it had going for it was the price, $699. At the time, a new Dell business box cost thousands. In a world in which speeds and feeds were everything—the latest this, the fastest that—this poor old guy didn't have it. This was the kind of product that, as ad fodder, would separate the men from the boys. I swallowed hard and dug into the all-but-incomprehensible vendor specs.

I wouldn't have fully appreciated the value proposition without Craig's perspective. (For his part, he liked nothing better than coming up to my office and working on ads. It got him away from the auditors, lawyers, and investment bankers who had descended on us like a plague.) He explained, though not in these terms, that if a home PC is like a thoroughbred horse, a business computer is more like an ox. One is made for speed—for video games and other RAM-hungry applications. The other is made for work; it needs to be reliable, easy to maintain, and productive. Blazing processor speed is not a terribly high priority, because battling space aliens from the planet Zorg is not usually a big part of an office worker's job.

Craig came up with the headline. He recognized that IBM had an identity problem. They were generally viewed as being a bit dated and stuffy. They were "Your father's computer company," to borrow a phrase. Nobody really seemed to appreciate that IBM's technology was every bit as advanced as it was esoteric. He wanted to make IBM appear as chic as Dell, so he titled the ad: "It's Cool to Be Blue....No one ever got fired for choosing IBM."

It was, admittedly, not the kind of thing one usually said about stodgy old business institutions. I followed up with this explanatory subhead: "IBM is the company that invented the PC. And everyone knows they're big, advanced...and expensive? Well, two out of three ain't bad. Big? Oh, yeah. Advanced? Definitely. Expensive? Think again. Value America and Big Blue can save you lots of green on a business machine."

Next to the photo were a few bullet points stating the specs. And right up there almost as large as the headline was the price: $699, with a mouse-type disclaimer beneath it, "This is not a misprint." By now we had pretty well established that while this was an IBM PC, it was *not* an IBM ad.

We figured they'd stopped burning heretics a long time ago, so we proceeded to tell our audience the unspeakable truth about business computers: "How much computer do you really need? The trick to buying a business computer is getting precisely what you need, no more, no less. IBM's GL is designed to be the perfect fit for most businesses."

The ad continued. "It's business as usual today, but no one knows what tomorrow will bring. That's why IBM is the perfect choice. Industry experts acknowledge that it's memory, more than anything else, that governs the power and capacity of a PC. This PC's memory is readily and affordably expandable to 128MB. Instant obsolescence is for newspapers, not your IBM."

We took a paragraph to discuss fax/modems, Ethernet cards, expansion slots and bays, soundboards, CD-ROMs, and IBM's impressive three-year on-site warranty. Then we explained what made this a *real* business PC: "IBM's taken the sting out of managing a network. Your IBM PC comes equipped with TME 10 NetFinity, Wake on LAN, Flash on LAN, LANClient Control Manager, CoSession, QAPlus, and it's DMI v1.1 compliant. Loosely translated, this means that IBM virtually eliminates the need for a technician to visit the PC to keep it running perfectly. It's all designed to lower the cost of owning a computer in a commercial network environment."

IBM's Product Presentations were live by the time I finished the ad, so we sent it out to *The Wall Street Journal* and held our breath. We were not prepared for what happened next.

❧

ANDY SIPPED HIS coffee as he flipped through *The Journal*, just like thousands of other businessmen were doing the morning of February 5th. When he got to page nine, he paused and smiled. He couldn't help it. He loved unexpectedly spotting his company's logo. And there it was, the Pentium mark with "Intel Inside" nestled in the body copy of this full-page ad. "IBM must have a new agency," he observed. "This doesn't look like their usual stuff."

As the co-founder of Intel, Andy Grove was familiar with the "stuff" his customers—like IBM—put out for public consumption. His processors drove their machines. His fate was inextricably linked to the likes of IBM, Compaq, Dell, and HP, companies whose logos....*Wait a minute! This isn't an IBM ad. Half my customers are listed here in the left column. What's the deal?*

As he read the body copy, he couldn't believe his eyes. Nobody talked like this. Value America...they must be something new. Grove picked up his phone. "Lou, it's Andy. Did you see *The Wall Street Journal* this morning? Yeah. Front section, page nine."

Lou Gerstner had indeed seen it. The CEO of IBM had been just as intrigued as his longtime friend and supplier. "I've never seen anything like it," Gerstner said.

"Nor have I. Who are these guys?"

"I don't know, but I will soon enough."

❧

BILL HUNT COULDN'T stop grinning. His triumph had been made sweeter by month upon month of "No—go away—leave us alone." This wasn't just any yes. This was arguably the best yes in the home improvement industry, the backyard equivalent to HP: Weber barbecues. We were cookin' now.

With their agreement in hand and their check in the bank, the presentation team had completed Weber's online product demonstrations. Now it was time to take the relationship, as they say, to the next level: advertising. Weber and Value America were about to find out what it was like to grab the tiger by the tail.

Once again, the campaign had its challenges. Weber's products were "MAP'd," so we were restricted from advertising them for less than our principal rivals, Home Depot and Lowe's, even though we were more efficient. But the big boys rarely advertised the grills we'd be featuring. They'd be more likely to promote Weber's bottom-of-the-line Kettle, a good product but one that only hinted at the line's grandeur. Selling worse for less was the order of the day, but not at Value America. Our unlimited "shelf space" and inventory-less model enabled us to "carry" every barbecue, smoker, accessory, and option in the entire Weber line—over a hundred SKUs. You'd never catch Home Depot doing that.

"The Greatest Advance in Outdoor Cooking Since Fire" was the headline. "Og discovered fire," I wrote, "but then for the next couple of million years, nothing much happened. Now, fire is making a comeback."

"Delicious Decisions. With over a hundred Weber grills and smokers to choose from at Value America, you'll need to think with your head, not just your stomach. Do you want to cook with gas or charcoal? Are you cooking for a small army or just the two of you? Do you want it portable, or built-in? Do you want your Weber to last the rest of your life, or do you want to give your grandchildren a shot at it? Some models come with twenty-five-year warranties!

"If you think you can't afford a Weber, consider those T-bones you burned beyond recognition last Saturday on your cheap imitation barbecue. Years from now, when your neighbor is throwing away his third rusted-out grill, you'll still be the top dog of the backyard barbecue with your trusty Weber from Value America."

We ran the ad several times. We used Weber grills as the backbone of our fledgling direct response program—a program we knew would eventually have to play a leading role in our advertising efforts. We started selling Weber grills. Dozens of them, then hundreds of them. It got ridiculous. For the first time ever, Weber had to run their factory year-round and put on a second shift just to keep up with the demand.

Bill Hunt couldn't stop grinning.

❧❀❧

EMPHASIZING PCs WAS an unhealthy trend, I thought. The good news was we were selling tons of them. The bad news was we were in danger of becoming type-cast. That, of course, wasn't a problem for IBM.

Lou Gerstner arranged for Value America to meet some of his senior managers in Raleigh-Durham. The PC company's headquarters was in Research Triangle Park. For Monica Link, it was like going home after winning the big game. Congratulations were the order of the day.

IBM, like HP before them, had no plan for selling online. They had what they called their "seven channels," a comprehensive description of their marketing strategy. So Craig prepared a document called *The Eighth Channel*, fitting our concept into their corporate parlance. In it, he explained our role as a conduit, an electronic conveyor, between them and their customers. As a result, our relationship with Big Blue blossomed.

While at IBM, Monica introduced Craig to their Mid-Atlantic Sales Manager, a tall, energetic blond woman named Kim DeJong, who had been Monica's boss's boss's boss, or something like that. Kim had talent written all over her. It was only a matter of time before she came to work for us.

During the meeting, our ad, "It's Cool to Be Blue," was praised for what it had accomplished. Enthusiasm was nearly universal. But one exec, an advertising manager, had a problem with it. Glenda Dorchak, a corporate type with short blond hair, took one glance at the ad and told Craig, "You can't do that. You can't use IBM's 8-bar logo."

Winn's least favorite word is "can't." He explained that since we'd paid for the ad, we could do most anything we wanted. "If you want to pay for the next ad," he said, "I'm all ears."

"Sorry," Dorchak said. "Its use is restricted...."

Craig was incredulous. "You mean to tell me that IBM has spent thirty years and billions of dollars promoting their famous logo, only to develop a policy that says the logo can't be used?"

"Yes," Glenda said glibly. "That's our policy." Managers love policies.

For a man who wanted to scream, he handled himself quite nicely. He just turned and walked away. If only he'd never looked back....

❧

THE WASHINGTON POST wasn't playing ball. As we expanded our coverage to include a selected group of power cities like Los Angeles, Chicago, San Francisco, Washington, and New York, the only newspaper that refused to run our ads at the ridiculously low direct response/remnant rates was SRC's hometown paper, the *Post*. The publication that had brought the Nixon White House to its knees was no pushover. So Phil Ramsey and his friends at Stevens, Reid, Curcio decided they needed a little persuading.

Radio advertising was complementary to newspaper. When we were running print ads in Philadelphia, for instance, we would run a few radio ads there as well. The idea was to build "top-of-mind awareness." They'd see our ad in their morning paper, hear a radio spot on their way to work, and then another one on their way home. They'd have to be either dull or dead to miss us. That was the theory, anyway.

So Phil took every dollar we planned to spend on print ads with the *Post* and spent them with radio stations in the Washington-Baltimore market. Radio ads may be fleeting in impact and short in duration, but they're cheap. You can buy an awful lot of airtime for the cost of a full-page newspaper ad. And that's what we did.

Newspapers can't afford to ignore local newscasts from radio stations. Electronic media has an immediacy about it that papers can only envy. Newspapers monitor news programs for their self-preservation. Thus, every time somebody at the *Post* turned on a radio newscast, there we were, sponsoring it. When they got into their cars to go home, they'd catch our ads again.

And it wasn't like the ads were easy to forget. Phil wrote things that got under your skin. He had observed that the kind of information and insights we were providing in our Product Presentations hadn't been available since Mom-and-Pop neighborhood stores lined Main Street. The irony was that this technological marvel, Value America, was actually just like your next-door neighbor, sharing experiences over the back fence. Phil wrote ads like this:

"Every life's a story. A collection of life's stories is a community, a place for the comings and goings of a people, once strangers, now neighbors and friends. No one is unimportant.

"A place called Value America has its story. We've been lingering in the minds of consumers for more than a hundred years. We've seen small-town merchants close their doors...people on their way to shopping malls...and all the music lessons and soccer games in between.

"The old towns have mostly gone away, and so have the mom-and-pop merchants. We've come to miss their old-fashioned sense of service, integrity, and product knowledge. Strange as it may sound, all these years, you've been waiting for Value America.

"We would be proud to have you shop our store on the Internet. You'll be struck with the quality, service, and integrity of it all. Come see for yourself why ValueAmerica.com has become America's premier Internet retailer."

Phil hired a voice talent that sounded like your favorite uncle, the one you went to for advice when you didn't trust what your dad was telling you. A deep, resonant, mature sort of voice, thoughtful, genuine, and honest. You could *believe* this voice.

Every few days, SRC would call their friends at the *Post* and gently remind them that Value America was investing money in the Washington metro area. Too bad they weren't getting any of it.

Eventually, they caved. Everyone was happy. More or less.

⚜

I OCCASIONALLY CAUGHT myself having just a little too much fun. I was doing what I loved to do and was actually getting paid for it.

Although we wanted to strengthen our reputation in the office products industry, most products falling under that general description just didn't make advertising sense. Ball point pens? Reams of copier paper? *Staples?* You'd have to sell carloads of these things to justify doing an ad.

Once again, it was John Motley to the rescue. He called a colleague at GBC Quartet and suggested co-oping an ad. Frustratingly few people saw the need for some of their products. If I could just plant the seed....

And what did GBC make? Shredders—from little guys that sat on top of a waste basket and would cut bank mailings and other potentially damaging "trash" into little strips, to high-horsepower mince-monsters suitable for erasing the paper trail of the Pentagon itself.

Despite the efforts of the TV news magazines, people didn't heed the dangers lurking within their wastebaskets until they'd had their identities stolen or had seen their company's secrets revealed. The title of the ad emerged as Craig's all-time favorite: "A Little Paranoia Isn't All That Crazy."

We weren't surprised that a lot of people were coming to know who and what Value America was. Our reputation had taken wings. The gratifying part was that we had caught the eye of not only the man on the street, but also the movers and shakers of American business.

Our first IBM ad, "It's Cool to Be Blue," resonated with corporate America. A senior business executive at Citibank clipped out the ad and later wrote a partnership proposal based upon it. Fred Smith, founder of Federal Express, read it. Intrigued, he took pains to learn more about us. Both of these contacts would eventually lead to significant developments in our history. CEOs of retail giants like JC Penney and marketing mavens of cutting-edge firms like Apple Computer cut out our ads, hung them on their walls, and used them for inspiration.

One interesting story came about as a result of an executive round table in which Craig was asked to participate. It was a meeting of some of the brightest lights in the corporate world, sponsored by *Chief Executive* magazine. Among the participants was the president of one of the nation's largest and most influential advertising agencies, J. Walter Thomson. He told Craig that he had not only noticed our ads, but that they had even been discussed at his agency. Their view was that we had created an entirely new genre—ads that were neither "brand" nor "retail" but both at the same time. They called it "the Value America style."

It had never been our intention to reinvent the wheel. We just wanted to create ads that told our story. They were unique because *we* were. But that didn't mean they would stay that way. Every week, somebody on my staff would clip out an ad that was so obviously an imitation of ours, I had to smile. Our merchandisers started telling me anecdotes about CEOs cornering their VPs of Sales and asking, "Why aren't our products in these ads?" Stories were told of corporate execs demanding that their agencies produce ads for them that looked, and worked, like ours.

ৎঔৄৎ

EVERY ONCE IN a while, an ad worked too well. Consider Amana.

The challenge with most of Amana's products was that they were too big to ship via UPS, and they often required some kind of hook-up—an icemaker, a water supply, a drain—simple but necessary tasks that many homeowners were not equipped to handle. So Bill Hunt spent months negotiating an agreement to deliver items as big as refrigerators. He found a firm that could do it all—everything our customers needed.

Amana was in the same league as HP and Weber. In their industry, they were as good as they came. Their products, like HP's and Weber's, were sold under a Minimum Advertised Price policy. Yet they had no problem with us popping for the freight and installation. At the MAP price, we could afford to pay the freight, even on a refrigerator, and still make money. So we ran an Amana ad featuring refrigerators, microwaves, washers, and dryers.

"How Can a Mouse Lift a Refrigerator?" The intriguing title was supported with a photo of a big Amana side-by-side refrigerator, doors wide open, plus a list of features and the price: $999. The subhead read, "Your appliances should simplify your life. So we've made it simple to buy the best. Great prices. Free delivery. Free hook-up. Just visit us online at ValueAmerica.com. Your mouse will do the rest."

Our deal with the delivery firm was for the continental U.S. and only for "standard" deliveries and installations. So in the first paragraph, we covered ourselves: "Now that's convenient!" I began. "Thanks to Value

America, the convenience begins before you dispense your first ice cube or spin your first load of laundry. Visit ValueAmerica.com or call us toll free, and we'll do the rest. Standard delivery is free. (If you live up six flights of stairs, or in Alaska, we need to talk.) Installation and hook-up are free too, assuming the appropriate plumbing and electrical services are in place. And we'll even haul away your old clunker if you like. Value America convenience and Amana quality...now that's the way to buy an appliance."

We ran the ad in *USA Today*, a national publication—national, as in "including Alaska." If the guy from Anchorage had called our toll-free number, we would have told him we couldn't deliver to Alaska. But he didn't. He went online and bought the big refrigerator. We had a problem.

It was trial by fire—or should I say, ice—for Neal, our new logistics specialist. He was faced with getting a refrigerator delivered to Alaska. Undaunted, he found that the Amana distribution center nearest to Anchorage was in Seattle. There was a regularly scheduled ferry between the two points, so he arranged to have the cooler sent north and installed.

It took a week to get the big side-by-side from Seattle to Anchorage, delivered to the man's home, and hooked up with a water line for the ice-maker. We even hauled his old refrigerator away, as promised. We hadn't delivered ice to Eskimos, but it was the next best thing.

You'd think our Alaskan customer would have been happy, but he was not. He was mad as a cornered grizzly. Why? Because he was the local Amana dealer! He'd only bought the thing to prove Value America was a fraud. He called Amana headquarters in a rage, demanding to know how we could get a refrigerator shipped from Seattle to Anchorage in a week when it took him—the authorized Amana dealer—thirty days. Good question.

OFF TO SEE THE WIZARD

"We tried it three times. Couldn't make it work," Dorchak said, explaining what Winn already knew. It was nearly impossible for a company—even one as large as IBM— to sell their products through both traditional channels and via their own direct operation.

"Your 'Eighth Channel' idea has come at a perfect time." Glenda continued, "We shut down IBM PC Direct just before Value America showed up on our radar screens." The veteran IBMer bragged that she herself had managed two of IBM's last three attempts to compete directly against Dell and Gateway. Even the best generals, she implied, sometimes fought losing battles.

Our proposal to empower "IBM Direct" had begun to bear fruit. Kim Dejong negotiated a daunting maze of red tape for Value America to secure the privilege of selling IBM products to the federal government.

One does not sell things to the government of the United States of America by ringing the doorbell of 1600 Pennsylvania Avenue and presenting one's wares like a Fuller Brush man. The procedure is a bit more complicated. The key is GSA, the General Services Administration, which is the central clearinghouse for the myriad of things the government wants to buy. And in order to get on the GSA Schedules, you must be authorized.

As you might imagine, it is not particularly easy to achieve this coveted status. But once achieved, GSA authorization can lead to sales volumes that make ordinary business-to-business business pale in comparison. We were eager to expand our sales into federal agencies. You could do worse things than becoming authorized to sell IBM products to the U.S. government.

The pursuit brought Craig to an IBM office building just outside Washington. He was between meetings, the first with IBM's Vice President for Government Sales, the second with the Director of the General Services Administration. IBM had assigned a woman to manage our account, and she graciously offered Craig the use of her office. When he called in to check his messages, he found that Rafe Durn had called.

What now? Craig had just had dinner with Rafe and Seth two days earlier. ULIC had confirmed that they were going to exercise their option to buy eighty percent of our firm. That meant that Winn and Scatena would *personally* receive *$240 million*.

"Rafe, it's Craig. I understand you called."

"Yes," he said. "Thanks for getting back to me so quickly." There was a conciliatory tone in his voice that Craig didn't think he'd heard before.

Durn was never far from his thoughts. There was a thorn that kept Rafe's smiling face high on his awareness meter: the written *carte blanche* guarantee that Derk Quinton's demands would be met—whatever they might be. "No problem, Rafe," Craig said. "I called as soon I got your message. What can I do for you?"

"Well, ah, I have a little problem, and I'm hoping you could help me."

"I'll do what I can, Rafe," he said evenly. *I'd be glad to hold your coat for you just as soon as you remove the gun from my head.* "What's the problem? You sound troubled."

"Yes, we, I mean my lawyer, ah, made a mistake. When we invested the first ten million in Value America…"

Oh, no. Here it comes.

"…we took the funds from the wrong account. We have something called Special Account P, which pools funds from a variety of different pension plans. He shouldn't have used that account."

Craig found himself grinning in spite of himself. After all the abuse Rafe's lawyers had inflicted upon him, after all the "I can't make a move without the advice of counsel" crap that Durn had fed him, after all the money we had paid their firm—their lawyers had muffed it.

"Uh, gee, Rafe," he commiserated, "I'm sorry to hear that, but what, precisely, does that have to do with me?"

"Well, you see, the Feds say we can't make follow-up on investments in a company if we've used funds from a pooled account. That means we can't exercise our option to buy Value America."

"I see," said Craig. *Goodbye, two hundred and forty million dollars!*

"Good, I'm glad you understand," Rafe answered. "But I think I've found a way to save the deal." *Hello again!*

Craig wasn't so sure this was good news, in light of all that had transpired in bringing the first union investment round to a close. Besides, the firm's recent gains with IBM and GSA could easily lead to valuations even higher than $300 million. But he let Durn have his say. Two hundred and forty million birds in the hand were better than three hundred million in the bush.

"I need two things. First, I need an extension of our deadline. No matter what happens, we can't consummate this deal by the end of March."

"Go on."

"The second thing is that we want your permission to assign our buy-out option to another qualified investor."

This request was clearly in a different league than merely adding two months to the deadline. At the heart of the issue was the fundamental difference between investing and buying. If you buy a company, you're buying it from its shareholders.

The union option was to buy eighty percent of the company for $240 million, not invest in it at a $300 million valuation. With a purchase, the money would have been paid directly to Craig and Rex, as the primary shareholders. (Craig had arranged for everyone owning stock options to have been paid off, even if they were not yet fully vested, but that was chickenfeed by comparison.)

From then on, the buyer—in this case, the unions—would have owned most of our company. They would have been responsible for funding and managing it as they saw fit.

If you invest in a company, however, a different dynamic is in play. Using the first ULIC transaction as an example, Value America sold ten percent of its shares for $10 million, agreeing in effect that the company was worth $100 million at that time. That meant the founders now owned roughly ninety percent of a $100 million company that had $10 million in cash. That, in theory, was equivalent to owning one hundred percent of a $100 million company that had no cash. The owners' shares had been diluted by ten percent in exchange for getting the cash to grow.

The rub was that the option Durn wished to reassign was an option to *buy* Value America. It was clear that although investors were welcome, selling the company outright to someone out of the blue was like stepping out of a perfectly good airplane with a parachute packed by a complete stranger. A lot would depend on who was doing what to whom.

"Who is this investor, Rafe?" was the obvious question. The underlying thought was, *How many guys do you meet in a typical day that have $240 million lying around?*

"Paul Allen. You may know the name," Rafe replied.

"Paul Allen, as in Microsoft co-founder Paul Allen? Smartest technologist and second richest man on the planet Paul Allen?" Craig's eyes got big and round. The proposed parachute packer was practically perfect.

"That's the one. What do you think?"

Winn smelled opportunity. Allen was one of only two or three people on earth who not only had the money to consider a venture like this, but who might also be interested for reasons beyond the mere prospect of profit. Besides, who wouldn't have been just a little curious about meeting a living legend?

"Rafe, tell you what. I'm willing to do both things, plus one more, something you'll need. I'll change the option from a purchase to an investment, with eighty percent going to the company." Craig knew that an infusion of cash prior to the IPO would enable us to enhance our systems, hire merchandisers, and increase advertising—all of which would make for a stronger offering. Plus, it would keep the nature of the transaction in the realm of investment, as opposed to buyout, keeping the management of the company in the hands of the people who'd built it.

Winn also knew that smart men like Paul Allen seldom buy companies. They invest, because they want their money to stay in the company, not walk out the door. He is no fool who gives up that which he cannot hope to keep, to gain that which he could not otherwise acquire.

"But I want you to do something for me in return."

"What's that?" Craig could have asked for a lot, and Rafe knew it. He braced himself.

"Discard the Derk Quinton agreement. It has no legitimacy. It never should have been written." He didn't belabor the fact that the offending document had the potential to adversely affect the IPO, putting the unions', or should I say, Special Account P's, shares in as much peril as his own.

"Done," Rafe said simply. *You're on your own, Derk.*

It was turning out to be a roller-coaster day. Sure, the partners were a couple hundred million poorer, but it was never about the money anyway. Well, not completely.

෨෴෴

IN JANUARY 1975, a young computer programmer working for Hewlett-Packard in Boston came upon an ad for a microcomputer kit in an issue of *Popular Electronics*. Frustrated by his own limited access to mainframes, he saw the ad as a harbinger of the future, of widely available personal computers. So Paul Allen persuaded his friend, Bill Gates, to team up with him to create software that would make these new machines useful. Microsoft was born.

Paul held the fledgling software company's senior technology post, spearheading development of some of their most successful products, not only the revolutionary MS-DOS operating system but also Windows, Word, and the Microsoft Mouse (all tools I find myself using at this very moment). But a serious illness in 1983, Hodgkin's Disease, led him to re-evaluate his personal priorities. He left the company he had helped launch.

But Paul Allen didn't leave his dreams behind, or his money, for that matter. His Microsoft stock became the launching pad from which he ascended to the status of one of the world's wealthiest men. For almost twenty years, he had used his money to further the dream he shared with his friend Bill so many years ago, the dream of a Wired World.

In '85, Allen began investing in companies he felt could further digital communications, at first concentrating in enabling technologies, and later shifting his focus to innovative content. Through his wholly owned investment vehicle, Vulcan Ventures, (named after the emotionless and logical race in *Star Trek*) he invested in e-commerce, networking, security, hardware, and electronic entertainment companies.

Then, in early 1995, Vulcan Ventures purchased an eighteen percent interest in DreamWorks SKG, the multifaceted entertainment studio led by three of Hollywood's most brilliant and creative minds, Steven Spielberg, Jeffrey Katzenberg, and David Geffen. Allen, now a member of the board, was the studio's largest private investor—his interest in the company was said to be valued at somewhere north of $500 million.

DreamWorks is aptly named. Not only is it owned by a dream team of the most creative minds in Hollywood (the state of mind, not the place), but it is also in the business of making the impossible look real on the big screen. These days, you don't do that by dreaming small. You must dream big, spend big.

DreamWorks wanted to build a big studio—the finest you ever saw, with state-of-the-art equipment. It would be the most opulent such place in a town constantly inventing new meanings for the word. They wanted to build their new Taj Mahal in Playa Vista, a swamp strategically situated near Beverly Hills, LAX, Malibu, and other points of interest in the land of La. Needless to say, it wasn't going to be cheap, even for these high rollers.

Bankers, of course, are in the business of loaning money. But they like assurances they're going to get paid back. This project was working out to something like $800 per square foot, a bit hard to swallow considering the industry's unpredictable nature and their penchant for creative accounting. Disaster was never more than a big budget flop away.

So how were Spielberg, Katzenberg, Geffen, Allen, and company going to raise the necessary capital to build their new DreamWorks studio? Enter Rafe Durn, investment manager extraordinaire. *Sure, we'll loan you the money. All we ask is that you build every stick of your new studio with union labor. You scratch my back, I'll scratch yours.*

It was through this connection that Rafe Durn became familiar with the way Allen invested, his interests and strategies. He recognized that Winn and Allen would be a perfect fit. So when his little tactical error with Special Account P was exposed, Rafe saw an opportunity to pass the baton. Keeping the company well funded was in his interest, after all.

JUST BECAUSE THE option to buy Value America had been assigned to Paul Allen, it didn't necessarily follow that it would be exercised. Five hundred companies are introduced to the Wizard's team each year, scores are examined by his elite advisors, but Paul Allen personally reviews, and invests in, a mere handful. In a good year, the odds are one in a hundred.

Within his theme of "The Wired World," the companies he chooses invariably have proven management talent, a solid business plan, traction, and innovative products or services. He has an uncanny instinct for knowing where technology is headed.

Rafe Durn gave Seth Rossi the job of getting the ball rolling. Seth set up a series of telephone interviews between Craig and Vulcan Ventures' advance team. The initial contacts knew almost as much about retail as Craig did intergalactic space travel, but somehow they communicated well enough to take the next step.

That step was taken by Thurston Stark, who had been the CIO for one of Paul Allen's Internet holdings. The soft-spoken Stark contacted us, saying he was representing Paul Allen and wanted to do some due diligence.

The tall, thin, dark-haired technologist must have liked what he saw. He seemed particularly impressed with the company's proprietary software. "JoeWare" had become a pragmatic solution for a series of complex problems. What Thurston loved most was Joe's Authoring Tool, the software that dynamically generated our Product Presentations. This, Stark knew, would be well received by Allen, who was always trying to demystify the computer.

We naturally assumed that Thurston had come out from Seattle. But he was now working as a freelancer. He had left his fast-paced west coast lifestyle in search of a more wholesome place to raise his family. He had moved back to his hometown—Charlottesville. Craig smiled at yet another coincidence and offered Thurston a job.

❧❦❧

THE PRE-MEETING BRIEFING was a bit disconcerting. Rumors were one thing, but to hear these things directly from Allen's own staff was a little strange. Craig had flown to Seattle with our CFO, Dean Johnson, and Rafe's representative, Seth Rossi. Sitting in a small public cafeteria in the basement of Vulcan Ventures' offices, he was told, "Please don't be put off by Mr. Allen's appearance or behavior. A man of his intellect and influence might be expected to display a few, shall we say, eccentricities."

"Fair enough," Craig and Dean agreed.

"Mr. Allen will probably not be present when the meeting begins. Go ahead with your presentation anyway. Our staff will fill him in on the parts he missed. Expect him to walk into the room halfway through your presentation. He won't greet you, won't make eye contact, won't ask you any questions, won't seem to engage or be interested. Mr. Allen may not even look at what you're showing. He may seem bored.

"Don't let this bother you, gentlemen. I can assure you, he will grasp every word. At some point, he may abruptly get up and leave the meeting. Strange as that seems, you shouldn't view it as a negative sign. Continue your presentation. The staff will brief him later," the young exec said.

After a moment's reflection, Craig concluded that this was not arrogance but rather an unusual form of mercy. Only a very small percentage of the companies reviewed by Vulcan ever sees any investment capital. If Allen were to appear interested, he would be sending a false message to the vast majority of people he saw. By remaining aloof, he not only protected himself but also kept the presenters from jumping to the wrong conclusion.

As they prepared to leave, a diminutive blond man walked into the tiny cafeteria. He passed his colleague without so much as a wave. He proceeded to pick up a cookie and gave it a slap shot across the counter toward the register as if it were a hockey puck. Then just as coolly as he had arrived, he departed. "Oh," the young exec explained, "that's Frank Flowers. He's the boss. He manages all of Paul's holdings. He'll be in the meeting too."

"Friendly," Dean said under his breath.

With the ground rules established, they found their way to Allen's conference room. Every possible convenience was made available: backlit projector screens, Internet connectivity, surround-sound, even beverage service. The conference table itself was a full-blown command center. There were all sorts of buttons and switches that were supposed to make wonderful things happen.

The system did everything but actually work. They had to scramble to find someone who could turn it on. The first group of technologists brought in others. For a while, it looked like a high school civics class with a substitute teacher. They finally got the systems working, and not a moment too soon.

The execs arrived. Among them was the president of Vulcan Ventures, Frank Flowers, head of Paul Allen's entire investment machine. Trained both in computer science and in finance, Flowers had been an investment banker, a CFO, and a corporate president before joining Paul. Also among them was Paul Allen, on time and looking more like a college professor than one of the primary movers and shakers in American business.

He may have been a billionaire, but he didn't look the part. No one would have mistaken him for Donald Trump.

No time for pleasantries. Warned that the meeting couldn't run over, Craig began the pitch he had given so many times, this time geared specifically for what he knew about the gentleman sitting next to him. Allen's vision of the future dovetailed nicely with his own, especially in the area of convergence technology, a cornerstone of both companies' strategies. It had been part of Craig's plan since day one, and he had been delighted, if not surprised, to see this paragraph in Vulcan Ventures' brochure:

"Television, telephone, and personal computer technologies are converging. As video and audio information takes digital form, the distinctions are blurring among television sets, PCs, [and] telephones.... Information devices have merged into intelligent consumer electronic products that perform entirely new functions."

Winn wanted to say *I told you so* but settled on a thorough explanation of how convergence would impact online retail, Value America style. He knew Allen's thoughts, for Paul was often quoted, saying things like, "Periodically you see ways to marry technologies. Then you try to push the envelope and ask what wholly new applications, products, or services you can do. I'm trying to come up with those. It's high risk, but you can't schedule revolutionary ideas." If any quote ever supported our concept, this was it.

Frank Flowers sat stone-faced as Craig proceeded. Paul started out cold as well but became increasingly interested, attuned, and thoroughly engrossed as the story unfolded. Craig smiled inwardly. *Who are you, and what have you done with Paul Allen?* You could almost see the wheels turning. His eyes danced. He made eye contact. He smiled. He nodded. He remained animated and attentive all the way through the presentation. Truth be known, he was a hell of a nice guy.

As Craig finished, Paul leaned back and exclaimed, "Yes!" with a big smile. "This is exactly what Bill and I envisioned." Even before they'd started Microsoft, they had foreseen a world in which everyone would have a PC, all connected, sharing information and providing services, just like Value America. "This is what e-commerce was meant to be!"

Through a remarkable series of unlikely events, the company had gained a powerful and resourceful ally, one whose involvement had the potential to make us the dominant force in the world of Internet retailing. It wasn't money. It was synergy—the process through which Paul Allen's holdings became greater than the sum of their individual parts. His strategy was to go beyond investment, adding value to the companies with whom he was involved by contributing his insights and by exploiting points of contact between his mutually beneficial synergistic endeavors. Allen was the catalyst, and dozens of cutting-edge companies were his chemistry set.

During the remainder of this and other meetings in Seattle, spirits ran high. Paul expressed a desire to invest, recognizing our potential. The magical words "the Microsoft of e-commerce" were spoken. These were not times for the faint of heart.

Craig requested three things from Paul. First, he asked to partner with his cable TV holdings. The possibilities of an Internet retailer joining forces with a cable-shopping network were too exciting not to explore. Allen agreed. Second, Craig asked to partner with Allen's PetSmart stores in facilitating our sales of pet supplies online. Allen agreed. Third, he asked Paul to lend us his technological expertise so we could develop our systems more expeditiously. "Pay us a visit in Charlottesville." Allen agreed to this as well.

For someone who had the reputation of rejecting a hundred deals for every one he accepted, Paul Allen was turning out to be one of the most agreeable fellows Craig had ever met. But there was something else brewing; something he couldn't quite put his finger on. He could see it in Allen's eyes.

After handshakes and cards were exchanged, Allen boarded one of his personal jets, perhaps his private Boeing 757, and flew off to watch his personal basketball team lose to the Lakers in Portland. Our team flew the red-eye back from Washington State to Washington, D.C., and then drove to Charlottesville, arriving around eight thirty the following morning.

It wasn't long before Frank Flowers called expressing his boss's wishes. Like the union before him, Allen wanted to *buy* a controlling interest in Value America, not just invest in it. As problems go, this was a pretty good one.

ക്ക

"FOR YOUR EYES ONLY," the document said. *"Do not copy or distribute. Please return after reading."*

Oooo! Spy stuff. Craig had been right. There *was* something brewing. Paul Allen wanted more of Value America, much more. Flowers asked Craig to compose a document explaining how different Value America would look if it were the *centerpiece* of Allen's Wired World, "the Microsoft of e-commerce."

Craig cloaked everything in secrecy, not even having his response typed. He didn't share the contents of his handwritten memo with others on our team. There were things in it Craig didn't want made part of the public record, something that easily happened to documents from companies preparing to go public.

Goal: Swiftly execute a strategy that combines Value America's superior vendor relationships, pragmatic e-commerce capabilities, and direct response expertise with Vulcan's core Internet connectivity, bandwidth, and advanced technology to become the dominant business and consumer marketplace.

No point in being shy, Craig figured. The question was: what could Value America accomplish if we had unlimited capital and unlimited access to all things Allen?

Incremental Investment: The equity capital required to accelerate our execution from our current very aggressive mode to that needed to become the 'Microsoft of e-commerce' is outlined below. We would have to execute at near perfection to implement a plan that consumes an additional $50 million over the next year.

We were tightwads back then.

Allen had asked Winn to consider a large infusion of private capital rather than a public offering, suggesting that he would fund Value America himself. Craig was open to the idea, even supportive, but he wanted Paul to appreciate the pros and cons of this unusual path.

IPO: E-commerce is perhaps the only enterprise in which the company is easier to run public than it is private.

• A public company's credibility is enhanced in an environment where credibility is essential.

• It becomes easier for a public company to attract vendors and persuade them to fund product presentations. Both factors are essential to growth.

• The editorial coverage required to make us the dominant brand and to add credibility to our advertising is dramatically increased post-IPO....

• The market is currently very hot for e-commerce, and we have already done eighty percent of the work required for the IPO.

• Alliances are more readily initiated following an IPO. Cybershop and Shopping.com are vastly inferior solutions that have been able to gain mindshare as a result of being public. They were unknown when private.

If Vulcan's concern with an IPO in sixty days is 'cheap stock,' as Frank indicated, we should structure a deal that minimizes this risk.

The "cheap stock" issue loomed large for Vulcan. If a big investor bought stock in a rapidly developing company, the IRS could decide that the stock had really been worth more than they had paid for it, creating an immediate taxable gain.

Our current plan is to file the IPO at a $450 million valuation and use the road *show to increase the value to between $500 and $575 million. We plan to issue only ten percent new shares for the IPO and thus raise about $50 million. We believe investors will recognize that our 1999 forecast is understated…at $140 million in revenue. In addition, our post-IPO multiple of forecasted revenue is five times— thus we would have a valuation of from $700 million to $1.25 billion by late summer to early fall. We currently plan a secondary stock offering at another ten percent to raise an additional $125 million. I cannot measure the increase in valuation Vulcan's participation adds….*

No wonder Craig had wanted to keep these numbers under wraps. The company had been flat broke less than three months before. To be projecting a billion-plus dollar valuation now would have raised a few eyebrows. Yet his estimates would prove to be amazingly close. He knew his numbers. He knew what we were selling and how fast we were growing. In the context of the moment, these projections may have seemed ludicrously optimistic, but in the light of historical hindsight, they were perfectly rational, precisely accurate.

I would like to focus our discussion on what Vulcan specifically plans to bring to Value America [besides money, was the inference]. *Your suggestion that it would be the centerpiece of Vulcan's Wired World sounds great, but to sell a controlling interest in the company forty percent below its IPO value—and at less than half of its late summer valuation—deserves some detail….*

No kidding. The benefits of Paul Allen's vaunted synergy would have to be clearly spelled out. Craig followed this caveat with nine pages of charts, facts, and figures outlining, as promised, what would be required if we wanted to swiftly become the Microsoft of e-commerce—to give it the full-court press. It delineated how much more we would need to spend in technology, merchandising, marketing, direct response advertising, public relations, business development, customer care, sales, management, and finance.

The projected bottom line, the equity capital that could be required in the next twelve months to achieve market dominance, was $69 million— as a worst-case scenario. But the document was peppered with phrases like "If market conditions remain reasonably consistent," and "if we optimize this opportunity…." Nobody was suggesting this would be easy.

Winn ended the fourteen-page document with fourteen issues he felt needed to be addressed. I have included some of them:

IPO Timing: Value America must continue to move ahead between now and the time we reach a definitive agreement. We would prefer to postpone the IPO for only the minimum time required to resolve the 'cheap stock' and alliance issues.

Valuation: Valuation for an early May deal for common stock with a split of twenty percent for primary shares is $300 million…. The union option was one hundred percent primary shares at a March valuation of $300 million. While this option has expired…we approached Vulcan under its terms. My partner and I would prefer one hundred percent primary shares and a July IPO, but we are willing to compromise.

Whereas "secondary shares" are bought directly from the company's founders, personally enriching them, "primary shares" are newly created shares that are bought from the company itself, providing working capital but diluting the founders.

Ownership:…We began our discussions with Vulcan in the five to ten percent range. Subsequently, at your request, we have increased this to 30% if Vulcan is prepared to bring very substantial long-term value to Value America. During our recent visit…I increased this to thirty-five percent. I recognize you want forty to fifty percent, but this means I would own less than Vulcan of a company into which I have invested twenty years in preparation and two and a half years in execution.
Board: Three board members out of nine is okay with us….
Mechanism: Common stock and simple agreement. I would like our ownership status to be the same, so our long-term goals are the same.
Employment Agreement: My partner and I are both willing to sign long-term employment agreements. The only thing we would like more than managing Value America is doing so with Vulcan as our partner.
Stock Options: Every employee has stock options, and we wish to continue this practice. Employees currently have options totaling twelve percent of the company.
Evaluation: We believe the more you know about us, the more you will value the company, its strategy, people, systems, and vendor relationships….
Vulcan Contribution: We would like to know specifically what Vulcan intends to bring to Value America, how you would like to work with us, and how your other companies would complement us. I would be pleased to create a plan for maximizing the value of Marcus Cable. I can create a Microsoft 'wish list' that you could favorably influence. I can list the benefits of aligning Value America with an ISP. You alone, however, are in a position to specify and commit.
Desire: We are very impressed with Vulcan and would love to build the 'Microsoft of e-commerce' together with you.

The confidential document outlined a program that had the potential to take Value America to the pinnacle of the dot-com world. It would take somewhere between $50 million and $70 million to pull it off, depending on whether you were talking aggregate numbers or net of incoming cash, and best case or worst case scenario. It was predicated on completing the transaction in early May '98. It was also dependent on the development of synergistic relationships with other Vulcan companies.

Sadly, after making such a bold offer, and after asking Winn for his thoughts, Flowers and Allen faded into the woodwork. Craig would not talk to either of them again for many months. Their only response to the proposal they had asked him to prepare was silence. They got distracted, purchasing one of the nation's largest cable companies. Pity. We would have made beautiful music together.

ॐॐ

"I'VE GOT TO tell you, Rafe, I'm worried." It was a little past seven o'clock on a Wednesday evening in late May. Craig was in his car, talking on his cell phone with Durn, hoping to persuade him to use his influence to move things along with Vulcan Ventures.

The timing, after all, was critical. The due diligence for the initial public offering was complete, and the company was poised to file its S1 with the SEC. But we couldn't do that until the Allen investment was consummated. The reasons were technical in nature, but the implications were indisputable. The SEC would require several weeks to review the S1, and then our legal team would have to respond to their comments before our IPO could even be scheduled.

Looming on the horizon was the *piña colada* factor. Investment bankers didn't stagger their summer vacations. The industry virtually shut down every year, starting in late July. They returned to their offices when their children returned to school in September. No investment bankers meant no IPOs. If you weren't ready to roll in late June, you were out of luck until fall. Who knew if dot-com fever would last, if this euphoric bubble would survive the summer break?

"You wouldn't think an investment of this size could get lost in the shuffle, would you?" Rafe commiserated.

"No," Craig agreed. "But evidently one cable company wasn't enough. They've diverted their energies to other things. These are billion-dollar deals. Their lawyers can't seem to do three things at once."

"These things take time," Rafe said, trying to cool Craig down.

Craig pulled the big tan Suburban into his garage, threw it into park, and turned off the engine. He was not cooling down. "Rafe, just call 'em and see what you can do, okay? I've tried to reach Frank Flowers, but it seems he's always out. If we don't close this thing in the next couple of weeks, we're going to miss the summer IPO window. If we don't move right now, we're assuming a huge market risk. Waiting until September is incredibly dangerous. We're accepting far more risk than we should. And it's not necessary!"

"Just be patient," Rafe said evenly.

"Rafe, this is important. Make the call. *Please!*"

Craig didn't know it as he sat there in his car, fuming. But he had just had the single most important telephone conversation in the history of Value America. It had not gone well.

So I gave them over to their own stubborn heart—Asaph

DRINKING THE KOOLAID

*L*ater it would be reported that as he finished his inspirational speech, the sun broke through the clouds, a rainbow appeared in the sky, a white dove fluttered in from nowhere and landed upon his shoulder like a blessed omen from on high, and we all said, "Wow."

It didn't happen at all like that, except maybe for the part where we all said, "Wow." It was remarkable enough, frankly, that most everybody in the company had gotten out of their warm beds on this chilly Saturday morning to come down to the office to hear Craig tell us what was going on.

The rumor mill worked fine, of course. What it lacked in accuracy, it made up for in speed—and none of us knew quite what to believe about the amazing things we'd heard.

We were somewhat compartmentalized—by design. People in one department didn't really need to know much about the challenges being faced by folks in other areas. That meant that the issues that affected all of us were harder to explore. We could have published a company newsletter, I suppose, but there were only fifty of us. Why not get together for breakfast and get the word straight from the horse's mouth? Q&A and all that.

So here we were at eight thirty on a Saturday morning, woofing down scrambled eggs and sausages, bagels and bacon, fruit and flapjacks. We had no room big enough to hold all of us, but the weatherman smiled, so we all met in the parking lot behind 2340 (a building we had spilled over into, a few doors down from the Yellow House, aka 2300. Everything was on Commonwealth Drive, so we just referred to our locations by their numbers).

I milled around with my paper plate, catching up with old friends I seldom got to see anymore and introducing myself to some of the new kids on the block, who were proliferating like rabbits. I ran into Bill Hunt, who re-introduced me to our friend from Weber Barbeques. Sporting a big grin, he complained that Weber had had to put on another shift to support my ads. It felt good to know my stuff was valuable for something other than lining the bottoms of bird cages.

Rex Scatena stood on a retaining wall and welcomed the group, giving a short rundown on our recent successes and introducing several new folks who would be filling key positions. Everyone was politely enthusiastic, but we hadn't really come to hear Rex talk about the recent past. We had come to hear Craig talk about the near future.

We wanted to know more about ISOs—incentive stock options. All of us had them in one amount or another, and they were having their intended effect: we didn't think of ourselves as employees of Value America, but as its owners. Most of us had taken pay cuts to come here. The incentive part was the key for everyone. If we all worked hard and made the company a success, the value of our shares would increase, and we could all make a lot of money. But very few of the newer employees/owners really understood what stock options were or how they worked. Craig was going to explain it all this morning.

He was careful with his words, explaining what could happen, what might happen, what he thought should happen, and what it would take to screw it all up. He shared insights into his meetings with Paul Allen. He explained what an IPO was and what we were doing to try to bring ours about. He took the time to present how investment bankers and analysts worked together. He told us who the managers of our IPO would be and what they were saying about how companies in the dot-com world were being valued—which had everything to do with how much our shares would be worth.

Winn made the complex world of stock options approachable, telling us how vesting periods worked, what it meant to exercise an option, and how strike prices affected the outcome. He blanketed his explanations with caveats. "There are two enormous conditions," he said, "that color everything I've said here this morning. The first is that market conditions must remain relatively constant. They can improve, of course, but there's no guarantee that will happen. If the market for dot-coms erodes, it will negatively affect us all—no matter what we do."

None of us said it, but we all thought it: *that won't happen.*

"Second, we must, as a company, under-promise and over-deliver. We must build a store that performs well and serves our customers. We must form partnerships with more great brands and keep creating ads that generate revenue. We must do all of these things better than we have promised we would do them."

And every one of us vowed, "Yes, we can do that. We *will* do that."

Then he at long last answered the question on everyone's mind: what are my options worth? "First," he said, "a company must have 'comps'—companies comparable to ours that are already public, so investors have something to compare us to. Our closest comp is Amazon. They currently trade at three times next year's projected revenue. We're expecting to sell forty million this year and a hundred seventy-five million next year, in 1999. If you multiply a hundred seventy-five million dollars by three, you get five hundred twenty-five million. That would be our market capitalization, or value. We have ten million shares outstanding. Divide five hundred twenty-five million by ten million shares, and you get a price of fifty-two dollars a share.

"IPOs are usually priced at twelve to fifteen bucks a share, so we'll need to split our shares three to one. That means if you have ten thousand option shares at a strike price of three bucks a share, after the split you'll own thirty thousand shares at a dollar a share. A strike price, by the way, is the price each of your shares was worth on the day they were issued to you.

"If we continue to do better than Wall Street expects, sell more than forty million this year and start off strong against next year's forecast, a year from now we'll be valued on our projected year-2000 revenue. At current multiples, that could mean as much as fifty dollars a share after the split—a billion-five market cap.

"Now, all of this is very hypothetical. The market and our company both need to perform well for any of this to happen. But if it does, and you own ten thousand shares today at three dollars a share, you would multiply the potential fifty dollars a share future stock price less your one dollar a share net strike price by the thirty thousand post split shares you'll own. Using this example, the number comes to just under one-point-five million dollars."

Even though he reiterated his caveats, the warnings went in one ear and out the other. We were naïve, but we weren't stupid. We all could do the math, and we all *did* the math. We all figured that we were going to be millionaires. Craig Winn said so.

But he had said no such thing.

ço:ول

IT'S EASY ENOUGH to see in hindsight, but we didn't know it then: this was the golden age of Value America. We could do no wrong—everything clicked. We had gotten over the hump of anonymity. Investors were starting to see the possibilities; vendors were lining up in droves and customers were responding to our ads and buying things at a dizzying rate. Value America was working just like we'd planned.

We knew that people were the key. In order to make our dream a reality, we had to understand the dream. So Craig preached the gospel, and we soaked it in. His mission became our mission. Many of us had read the entire business plan; those who hadn't were told about it, about all the things in it that set us apart. We held informal meetings every month in the parking lot or on the front lawn of the Yellow House just to make sure. Food? Oh, yeah. Burgers and dogs on the grill, pizza, sandwiches, ice cream, maybe a spread from Big Jim's Barbecue.

On one such occasion, Craig said something that struck us all a little differently. After sharing the status of our investment rounds, reinforcing the four things we did to serve brands, and reminding us of the seven things we did for our customers, he added, "I know I speak for all of us when I say Value America is far more than just a job. For many it is a noble crusade. Together, God willing, we'll make our world a little better. There is nothing virtual about our calling, nothing 'pretend' about what we've accomplished. But I want you all to know," he said, looking at each of us individually, "we are called to serve more than ourselves. We must serve two masters." He didn't elaborate.

Some thought he meant that by serving our company, we served ourselves. Others recognized that we now had investors—shareholders—and that it was our job to serve them. Some, weaned on Craig's business plan, heard something different: our two masters were our brand partners and our customers. He was speaking of all of this and more. It was all about service.

For a few magical months, Value America was the greatest company in the world. The plan was coming together; we could see it happening before our eyes. We were all together in one place, crowded and noisy and alive with a buzz so palpable you could scoop it with a spoon. The moment began to feed on itself like a nuclear reaction, and we were all swept up in it. We had followed our pied piper and had given our all to make the dream live. We were on a mission, devoted and passionate. Value America was *our* company—we were going to change the world. We had all "drunk the koolaid."

During this wonderful time, we had an unofficial company policy that people could rise to whatever level they were capable of handling. And this sometimes led folks in odd directions. Dawn Robinson, our office manager, was an energetic and vivacious ex-army intelligence officer, a single mom who had been with the company since our days in the Attic.

After we moved to the Yellow House, it became clear that we would need to hire a janitorial service, and she researched it. When Dawn found out how much they wanted for the job, she said, "For that much, I'll do it myself!" So for months, she could be found after hours pushing a vacuum cleaner or a toilet brush, often with her cheerful pre-schooler in tow. She later became the head of our customer care department, and later still she developed our training program for new recruits. We all figured you could run a multinational conglomerate with ten people like Dawn.

My own number-two son, Chris (known around here simply as CL) hired on in the Attic as a data-entry person, a $15,000 entry-level job any reasonably bright person could handle. But as time went on, he emerged as our resident expert in the care and feeding of Joe Page's Authoring Tool. CL became its official drill instructor, training all the new data-entry personnel, artists, and writers in its proper use. As its features advanced, so did CL's relationship with it; he developed an uncanny ability to root out the bugs in the code. He was eventually asked to start and run our QC department to test the company's voluminous output of proprietary software, learning his craft in the saddle. The department was by all accounts an unqualified success. Makes a papa proud.

Isaac Saltzberg moved into my old job as head of Presentation Marketing and promptly changed the job description. I had functioned as a mentor of sorts, a guide, showing my team by example how best to communicate the features of the products they were presenting—without resorting to "snappy ad patter." We had a style, a voice (which sounded a lot like mine), and we were all singing in the same choir.

Isaac was more like a general on a battlefield. He split the department into platoons, each team led by a senior writer supervising three or four less-experienced wordsmiths and one graphics guy. The ever-increasing workload was assigned and attacked in methodical fashion. Quotas were set. Deadlines were pronounced. Meetings were held. Quality suffered. But Isaac got a lot of meals out of the kitchen.

Bill Hunt and Rex Scatena had shifted roles too, but in more subtle ways. It had always been their job to bring new vendors into the fold, to convince them that Value America was a better mousetrap, so to speak. In the beginning, this had been an uphill struggle, sort of like a century before when Ransom Olds had tried to sell automobiles in a country where there were few good roads and no gas stations.

Even though Internet use was doubling every quarter, Value America was growing even faster. We were tripling our revenues one quarter to the next. During the last year and a half, the typical reaction to the our proposition had gone from "Huh?" to "Not me—pioneering is too risky," to "I'm impressed with what you've done, but it won't work in my industry," to "Where do I sign?"

Bill and Rex had a new problem: how to deal with the stampede. By mid-summer Value America had twenty computer brands and fifty-five peripherals brands. We had two hundred and fifty brands of office products. In consumer electronics, we carried thirty-four of the biggest and best brands in the world. There were a dozen toy brands and no less than eighty-seven separate brands in our health and beauty department.

We made a distinction between brands and manufacturers, because our customers made those same distinctions. For example, Procter &

Gamble was a big, well-known company, but no one ever bought "Procter & Gamble" shampoo. They bought Head & Shoulders. No one bought Procter & Gamble baby diapers. They bought Pampers. No one bought P&G fragrance, but they bought Giorgio, Hugo Boss, Wings, Red, and (right here in the same sentence) Old Spice—by the bucketful.

With household products, foods, apparel, home furnishings, giftware, housewares, jewelry, home improvement, software, and sporting goods, we carried 500 brands. Some of them were merely well known in their own industries. But many of them were household names: Panasonic, Compaq, Tide, Toshiba, GE, Mattel, Epson, Brother, IBM, Kodak, Microsoft, Pepto-Bismol, Rubbermaid, Waterman, Comet, Sony, Hewlett-Packard, Vidal Sassoon, Canon, Pulsar, Tampax, Casio, Elgin, Norelco, Calvin Klein, Sanyo, RCA, Olympus, Max Factor, Avery, Zenith, Polaroid, West Bend, Sharp, Amana, 3M, Weber, Delta Faucet, Kitchenaid, Ram Golf, Hoover, Seiko, Rolodex...see any names you recognize? 500 brands and counting, but we were a mere shadow of our future self.

જ઼ૐ

THESE DAYS CRAIG was spending less time bringing brands into the store and more time developing alliances with influential people and innovative companies. These included investment bankers, of course, and individual investors like Paul Allen. But often he found himself just taking advantage of opportunities he hoped would lead to other opportunities. You never knew where a good introduction might take you.

To Craig, the business world was comprised of gazelles and elephants. Some companies were small, fast, and nimble. Others were big and strong, but slow and hogtied in bureaucracy. We needed each other—we were *good* for each other. Big firms needed access to our ideas, spirit, and swift execution; we needed their clout, and access to their customers.

John Ledeky wanted to meet Craig Winn. The founder of United States Office Products had heard the buzz about Value America, as had the heads of virtually every Fortune 500 company by this time. So he asked John Motley to arrange an introduction.

USOP was a huge office products firm, now doing about $4 billion a year in sales. It was a "roll-up," formed by buying up many smaller, independent businesses and "rolling" them into one large conglomerate—the antithesis of the way we had built our business. Not that it mattered.

John Motley, of course, was happy to comply. Bringing people together is what he did best. A round of golf was arranged with Ledeky and his recently hired Chief Operating Officer, a guy named Tom Morgan. He had come from S.P. Richards (an office products distributor along the lines of United Stationers but now much smaller). So Winn, Scatena, Ledeky, Morgan, and Motley met at the Congressional Country Club.

First impressions can often tell you a lot about a person. But Craig's radar was attuned to John Ledeky, not Tom Morgan. Although he had noticed that the dapper COO's outfit was as beautifully coordinated as anything he had seen on a golf course, Craig didn't jump to any conclusions about Tom, even when the first thing out of Morgan's mouth was a slam at his boss.

"You've got to be careful with Ledeky," Tom said quietly when he and Rex were a discreet distance from the others. "He means well, but you need to watch yourself around him. He can go off at any time."

Normally, that kind of thing would have screamed *this guy's insecure, political, and power hungry—stay away!* But unfortunately, as they proceeded through their eighteen holes, Ledeky kept saying things that made Morgan's observations seem plausible. Gregarious and charming one minute, he could instantly change demeanor, chewing out someone for making a noise during his practice swing. He told great stories, but some of them were whoppers, like the one about trying to outbid Rupert Murdoch for ownership of the Los Angeles Dodgers. Unbelievable, even if true.

With every hole they played, Tom's sad pronouncements, "He's a loose cannon," and "I've got things under control now because he's moving off to the sidelines," seemed less like political maneuvering than a realistic assessment of the actual situation. But, as Craig reminded himself constantly, there was more to a company than one person's impression of its founder.

Winn tried to turn the fledgling USOP connection into something good for everyone. They owned Mailboxes Etc., the nationwide chain of mailing convenience centers. It occurred to him that people living in cities would often have a real problem ordering online because there is usually no one home at their apartment to receive deliveries. *Have UPS just leave the parcel in the hall outside the door? No, the thieves should have to work for it.*

But Mailboxes Etc. could receive these packages, he thought, and provide a safe place for the shopper to pick them up. The shipping rates would be lower because the destination was a business, and MBE could keep the difference as their profit. For that matter, we could work out deals with big computer makers like IBM and Compaq where folks without computers could even shop online at MBE locations. They could also facilitate returns. This could open up a whole new world for people who were residence-challenged.

Value America was assigned to a fellow named Tom Starnes whom Tom Morgan had hired to manage business development for USOP. Starnes was tall, good looking, pleasant, and professional, but incapable of getting anything done. The deal never materialized.

ᆼᆼᆢᆼᆢ

TO SAY WE were out of space was putting it mildly. It was bad enough upstairs in Presentation Marketing where we now had two writers to a cubicle in a room through which you could have safely fired a cannon a few months before. But the basement of the Yellow House was where we had reached critical mass.

The basement was home to both Technology and Merchandising. The little offices down there had been intended to house the merchants since they needed little but a quiet place to work, a telephone, and a pizza now and then.

Did I say quiet place? Fat chance. This was also home to Tech, who had consumed every square inch with bodies and hardware. Programmers were stationed two to a desk, four or five to an office. Several rooms were now filled wall to wall with big IBM Netfinity servers in gleaming black cabinets, putting out so much heat the air conditioners couldn't keep up.

The congestion got to be almost proverbial. When all of the offices had been occupied to their maximum capacity (which is to say, about triple what the fire marshal wanted to see) we started to notice things, like a storage closet on the main hallway being turned into an office for some poor, presumably thin, soul. There was a telephone equipment room beneath the stairs that people had been storing stuff in. One day a sign appeared on the door, saying, "This is not a closet." The first thing that went through my mind was, "Oh, no. They've turned it into an office." When someone stored an unused desk in the men's room, well, you know what we thought.

We had, of course, bought a new phone system when we'd moved into the Yellow House, but our volume had increased so rapidly the switch melted down. So we replaced it with one that would last "forever." Three months later, that one was hopelessly overwhelmed. Finally, we bit the bullet and installed a big AT&T/Lucent G3 system with a switch the size of a refrigerator—and prayed it would hold up under the strain.

Joe Page finally got some high-powered help too. The company policy offering a $1,000 bounty for any employee bringing in a Web technologist was starting to pay off (merchants were only worth $500; writers like me would get you a handshake and our hearty congratulations). We needed brains in the place. We got DBAs, EDI specialists, developers, project managers, testers, and encryption gurus. Joe, who still wore the title "Head Geek" with pride, now had a dream team—and an office he shared with three other guys.

❧❦

IT WASN'T THAT he was nervous—excited, maybe. It was an unusual feeling for Craig Winn, but the men he was going to meet on this trip were his heroes in a way, like sports figures or rock stars might be to us as kids. Craig was no kid, though. These guys were heroes of the business world.

The old guard in American business was represented by the likes of Fred Smith, founder of Federal Express, Price Club's Sol Price, and Intel's leader, Andy Grove. As innovative as their companies were, they had been built on solid, old-fashioned business principles into some of the most respected firms in the world. The transition from old- to new-economy companies was represented in Craig's mind by Microsoft, one of whose founders, Paul Allen, he had already met. And then there were the new-economy innovators, led by Yahoo!'s Jerry Yang. These were the stars in Craig's sky, and on this one trip, he was going to meet *two* of them, Jerry Yang and Andy Grove.

Both meetings took place in California's Silicon Valley. The meeting with Andy Grove was arranged by *Chief Executive* magazine's CEO, Arnold Pollard. Craig arrived early. He didn't know if he would be allowed the time to present Value America to Grove or even if he would be able to discuss his vision for an Intel-Value America partnership. As his driver approached the enormous Intel complex, the vista had its desired effect. Intel's corporate headquarters is overwhelming—a monument to the success of the computer and to Andy Grove's role in transforming our modern world.

Craig walked to the reception area. "Hello, my name is Craig Winn. I'm here to...."

"Yes, Mr. Winn. Mr. Grove is expecting you. I'll call his assistant to let her know you're here."

Shy of being told, "The President is waiting for you in the lobby," these words were about as good as it gets. He was excited as Mr. Grove entered his conference room. Andy Grove is an unassuming man, about five feet nine inches tall, lean, with thinning hair. He wore a ready and ample smile and reminded Craig a lot of his old mentor, Sol Price. He had the same caring demeanor, the same compassion, the same intellect, and the same way of driving right to the heart of an issue. Andy seemed interested in exploring what made Value America special, so Craig opened his lap-top and attempted to deliver a presentation that was worthy of his audi-ence. As they discussed Value America's mission, its performance and prospects, Andy seemed intrigued.

"This is powerful," he said. "You're really going to shake up the indus-try with this. Your competitors will either have to copy what you've built or face obsolescence."

"Thank you, Andy," Craig said, feeling pleased. It's not every day you get to impress a legend. "We've worked hard to build this. We're still small, but I believe we have something to offer great brands like Intel."

Andy smiled as Craig proposed, "We'd like to partner with you, exclu-sively, just as Dell has chosen to sell only Intel-based PCs."

"Craig, while I appreciate your kind words, neither Intel nor I can ask you to partner with us exclusively."

"You didn't ask. I volunteered. There's nothing improper about our company coming to the conclusion that your firm makes the best proces-sors. Partnering with the best is central to our mission."

"Tell me, Craig," Andy questioned, "why are you partnering with the big computer makers at all? From what I've seen, they need you—what you're doing—a lot more than you need them. Why don't you just make your own machines, under your own name?"

"Andy, I think we can do more, better and faster, if we partner with IBM, HP, and Compaq than we can if we compete against them." He wondered whether Grove was testing his loyalty to Intel's biggest cus-tomers or if he was looking at Value America as the Internet's incarnation of Dell, his biggest customer. Craig sensed it was the latter, but he refused to take the bait. More to the point, he knew he was not ready to take the bait.

"If we don't serve these brands, Dell and Gateway could end up being your only customers. That's not good for you, or anybody. If nothing is done to help IBM, Compaq, and HP compete, especially in the consumer and small business arenas, they're gonna die. As it is, IBM's consumer line is hanging by a thread. Value America was designed to give these brands the ability to compete directly against the likes of Dell and Gateway. Our systems and product presentations are better, and we can provide a customer-direct interface for less money than they can build and manage themselves."

"I agree," Andy said, analyzing every word, "but there's nothing stop-ping you from competing against them, especially after you become frus-trated by their inability to react at the pace your world requires."

"I think elephants know they need to partner with gazelles if they're going to survive," Craig challenged. "We'll all be better off if we focus on building our solution. The distraction of designing and assembling our own PC is more than I think we can manage, Andy."

To have our business model complimented was nothing new. To be praised by the likes of Andy Grove, however, was not your everyday occurrence. "You've demonstrated a very powerful solution here. From where I sit, your two biggest challenges are going to be infrastructure and customer care."

Craig outlined our infrastructure advances, explained our systems architecture, and reviewed our network design. He was having fun.

Andy smiled and shook his head in amazement. "What about customer service? At the rate you're growing, keeping the customer satisfied is going to be your biggest challenge."

Winn explained that our customer-care team was still small but that it was growing exponentially. Two heavy hitters were now managing it. One had built call centers for Federated Department Stores and Bloomingdales. He was an authority on fraud prevention. The other had won the Malcolm Baldridge Award for Excellence for his work with the credit card division of AT&T. "Your concerns are valid, Andy. I believe our people are strong, but we've still got a long way to go."

As he spoke, Craig's thoughts drifted to the soldiers in the trenches. His heart was with the troops. We had hired as many people as we could from Charlottesville's "inner city," such as it was. For many, this had been their first decent job. Having been trained and given a position of responsibility, they'd responded with enthusiasm, appreciation, and fierce dedication. They had a talent for empathizing with the people on the other end of the line. Seeing all that happen was one of the most rewarding parts of the job for all of us. Heartwarming success stories abounded here.

Winn left the meeting at Intel with a sense of destiny. One of the most powerful and innovative men on the planet had recognized that Value America was indeed something special.

৯৽৵

PRESIDENT CLINTON'S technology-guru-turned-investment-banker, Miles Julian, was good friends with Yahoo!'s Jerry Yang, the first of the new economy's Internet billionaires. Miles arranged an introduction.

Yahoo.com was the ultimate portal, a doorway to the wonders of the World Wide Web, designed to be a user's first stop in the day's cyberjourney. At its heart was a powerful search engine where users could find virtually anything they desired. It offered intelligently organized links to multitudes of different subjects, as well as a plethora of services like email, news, and discussion boards. With all its depth, Yahoo! was free to the people who used it. The company made its money by selling advertising to other dot-coms, complete with links taking you directly to the advertiser's website. The concept appeared brilliant. It quickly became the model all Web portals would emulate.

As Miles introduced his friend Jerry, Craig found him, like Paul Allen, to be a very unlikely billionaire. Jerry Yang was unassuming and down to earth. It was obvious he was not only well educated but also intelligent (concepts that are by no means coterminous). His business card bore the title "Chief Yahoo!" He certainly had a sense of humor.

Yahoo!'s offices shouted that this was a different kind of company than Intel. The computer-chip maker's headquarters were grand and clinical; Yahoo!'s were scattered throughout a series of leased buildings, and were decorated in yellow and purple, the company's colors. They looked more like a college dorm. Instead of a water cooler, you'd find an espresso bar or juice dispenser. This was designed to be a fun, creative place to work. Conformity didn't count for much here.

Craig Winn and Jerry Yang were at opposite ends of the Web. Jerry had been on the front cover of *Time*, shown surfing into celebrity status following his wildly successful IPO. Value America was still small, just beginning to make a name for itself. Still, they had much to discuss.

They began in the world of finance. Jerry talked about venture capitalist John Doerr and his firm, Kleiner Perkins. He spoke of his rich friends at Softbank. He explained how the VCs had used a heavy hand in the name of *keiretsu*, the Japanese version of symbiotic partnerships between businesses. "Amazon and Yahoo" he said, "initially benefited from this arrangement. Amazon used money the venture companies invested in them to buy anchor positions here at Yahoo. That helped us establish the value of these things and garnered Amazon a lot of attention."

Craig didn't know if Jerry Yang was implying that Value America needed to do the same thing to be successful or if he was just complaining. He soon found out that it was a little of both.

"It helped us initially, especially with Wall Street. But now I think it's time they left us alone," Jerry said candidly before switching gears. "It's interesting that with all of the advertising you folks are doing, you don't have any portal agreements. The idea of advertising offline to drive online sales is pretty radical, especially if you're planning to go public."

Our goal was to build our brand and the product's brand simultaneously—a devilishly hard thing to do in a tiny online banner ad. "We want to bring new customers to e-commerce, not merely lure people away from other sites."

"Doesn't do a thing for me," Jerry quipped.

"No, I don't suppose it does," Craig smiled. "But this bubble's only going to stay inflated so long. It's like balloons—as long as the VCs keep providing fuel to keep 'em all hot, they'll keep rising. Dot-coms will spend the money they've raised here at Yahoo! to increase their sales and increase their valuations. Then they'll raise even more money, at even higher valuations, to pay you even more, to increase their sales. But what happens when they figure out this is all hot air? Their balloons, and yours, will all come crashing down. There's no such thing as perpetual motion."

That was not what he wanted to hear, but he was smart enough to know where Craig was going. Jerry was conflicted. Part of him wanted to go along, but he, more than anyone, was enjoying the ride the present reality was providing. No matter how misguided the euphoria, no matter how absurd, Jerry was flying the biggest, most spectacular balloon of all. "Before you bring us all back down to earth," he said, "you might want to check out the view for yourself."

Winn laughed. "Well, maybe, Jerry. But before I abandon reason, I'd like to propose something a bit more, ah, grounded. Retail! Have you ever considered a co-branded e-commerce solution for Yahoo!? We could help make that happen."

"I'm afraid that just as you surmised, we're victims of our own success. The Amazons are paying our way with advertising that directs our users to their stores. If I open up a competing e-tail operation, they'd drop me, and who could blame them? But I realize that e-commerce is ultimately the engine that'll keep us flying. We'll eventually need to be a portal for commerce as well as for information."

"It *is* possible, Jerry, to test e-tail and not compete with any of your current advertisers. Take jewelry, for example. With the exception of watches, there aren't any brands. It's a painless way of getting started. What do you think of 'Jewelry for Yahoos'?"

"I like the sound of that. Yeah, 'Jewelry for Yahoos!' Can you build a prototype?" Jerry asked brightly.

They talked about future possibilities. They discussed Yahoo!'s dream of partnering in an online office products superstore, about the PC configurator that was in the works, about a search engine that would land you in the information-rich pages of Value America's consumer electronics department. Some plans were implemented; others were not. Good ideas are like eggs. They won't hatch unless you keep 'em warm.

"HI, CRAIG," I said. "What brings you up here?"

"Got a project for you, Ken. The store's stable now, so I think it's time we offer an online tutorial. Explain the benefits of shopping at Value America, how to get the most out of the experience. We need to answer their questions about security and privacy. Give it the Power touch, folksy and funny. Use our picture, headline, copy format. I'd like to expand on the 'everybody's shopping now, everybody's learning how' idea."

"Cool, dude." I flashed the "hang loose" sign. "When do you want it?"

"This afternoon?"

"Piece of cake," I lied. "I'm on it."

A week and a half and 13,000 words later, I had covered the subject and had run it past Joe for accuracy and anachronisms. The exercise had given me a new appreciation of just how big Value America had grown, how much we had to offer, and how far ahead of the rest of the online world we were.

I took a draft of the whole thing downstairs to get Craig's blessing, only to find he had gone to Washington to speak at Price Waterhouse's "Technology Conference." Amazing, I thought, what a little online success could do for your popularity as a public speaker. My boss had been the one chosen to lecture some of the country's foremost tech-savvy executives on the future of e-commerce. He had come a long way from a plan and a prayer in my little graphics studio in Huntington Beach. His speech, *E-Commerce 101*, spoke of partnerships, symbiotic relationships where every company could focus on what it did best and rely on others to expand their horizons. It was way ahead of its time.

Of course, what I called "a little online success" was a bald-faced understatement. We had opened the store for business right before the end of the year and had taken our first baby steps into advertising in February. It was one thing to plan on growth, but this was ridiculous. In the second half of the first quarter of '98, we did $1.2 million sales—an annualized pace of $5 million. Respectable. In Q2, that jumped to $5.2 million, or $21 million annualized. Then we started attracting attention. Q3 was spectacular. We soared to $15 million, a $60 million annualized pace.

Winn had done the studies. He knew that less than one company in a thousand ever grew to be "mid-sized," that is, achieving over $20 million in sales and employing over a hundred people. Those that did usually took decades to get there. We had become a mid-sized company in a single fiscal quarter. Businesses, even those that are run well, can be expected to grow about as fast as people do. But our "toddler" was now six foot one, 190 pounds, studying differential calculus, and playing varsity football. What would this thing look like when it hit puberty?

⚜

ROTH LATOUR WAS back in Charlottesville, just as he'd promised. The Goldman Sachs investment banker felt vindicated as he shook Craig's hand. He had taken a risk when he had defended Winn's crazy scheme, especially when the analysts at his prestigious firm had been confrontational. He knew Value America's unique model had merit, and he had been proven right.

We had once again under-promised and over-delivered. The Q3 numbers showed clearly that his $40 million 1998 revenue projection was well within our grasp. As Roth caught up on the latest advances coming out of the Yellow House, he shook his head and smiled. "Some said you could drag this horse to water, but you'd never get him to drink. Well, from what I can tell, the horse has jumped in the water, has drunk his fill, and now he's doing the backstroke. Congratulations, my friend! If I have anything to say about it, I'd like to see Goldman Sachs lead your IPO."

Craig appreciated that, but the fact remained that Rusty Kincade still had his reputation to defend. If he backed Value America, he would be admitting that he had made a horrendous miscalculation with his Amazon-based media metrics. You couldn't have it both ways. What's more, Rusty had signed on with a baby version of Amazon, e-Toys. They were ideal: cute name, niche player, portal-dependent, warehouse-bound, and media metrics friendly. They were perfect.

At the end of a great day, Craig personally flew Roth back to Washington to catch his connecting flight. He quickly discovered that he had never flown in a small plane. Latour may be African American, but he turned white in the copilot's seat of Winn's Cessna 206. As they said their goodbyes at Reagan National, he somehow knew it would be the last time he would see Roth Latour. It wasn't the flight; it was his analyst.

⚜

ACCORDING TO *ADVERTISING AGE*, IBM's ad budget was expected to exceed $100 million. And that was just for the PC division in North America, a mere ten percent of their global ad allowance. Chickenfeed.

Ogilvy & Mather was running the campaign. Advertising Age called it, "…the most unified effort to tie product ads into corporate brand building. The goal of aligning product ads with corporate branding is the Holy Grail of tech advertising," they said. *Oh yeah,* Craig thought. *That means they've taken the radical step of actually putting a picture of a computer in their ads, a couple of bullet points, but still no price. And why should anyone buy this thing? Because it's an IBM!* It was arrogance personified, but what the heck, it was only a hundred mil. This year.

Craig had a better idea, and he told them so. The General Manager for Marketing and Integrated Offerings (advertising, to you and me) for IBM's PC division, and his lieutenant, were in Charlottesville. They were trying to figure out how an upstart Internet store had sold so many PCs.

He said, "Give us ten percent of your ad budget, and we'll match it, dollar for dollar. With your ten mil and ours, we'd be investing a total of twenty million. Now, my guess is, being poor, we buy advertising cheaper than you do through your agency. We know that our print ads in *The Wall Street Journal* cost us half of what they cost you. Therefore, your ten million, in our hands, will buy advertising you'd pay forty million for."

"How can this be?" the GM exclaimed. He looked more concerned than pleased. His lieutenant, Glenda Dorchak, knew that the numbers Craig referenced were true although she chose not to react.

"If we're doing the advertising, there is a purchase mechanism attached to the ads, just like with Dell and Gateway. Short of selling direct—which you've tried three times unsuccessfully—Value America is the closest you'll get to a direct link between you and the customers you're ultimately trying to reach."

All the red-hot agency guys thought IBM's ads were great, very stylish. But beauty is in the eye of the beholder. "Sure, they're artsy, but they don't do much of a job communicating the value of your products. There are no prices or commerce links."

That hit home. IBM had suffered at the hands of its more progressive competitors. True, they had made a bit of a comeback from the billion-dollar operating loss they had recently endured, but their sales were still lagging behind. Compaq's growth was double theirs, and Dell had experienced a massive sixty percent surge. Catching them wouldn't be easy.

"Do you want to turn ten million in advertising into forty million and then into hundreds of millions in incremental direct response sales? We've proven that our ads work. If you'll co-op our advertising and make certain we have a steady supply of machines, we'll deliver the sales to turn your division around," Craig proclaimed. *No point in being shy.*

The GM was struggling with the idea of sharing his ad budget. Yet he understood the concept of outsourcing. The modest inroads IBM had made in reducing manufacturing costs had been achieved that way. He understood targeting Dell too. IBM openly envied Dell's success.

Dorchak, quiet up to now, told her boss to think of Value America as an effective "Eighth Channel"—a customer-direct channel. IBM would be outsourcing its direct sales objectives. She explained in detail how this model would allow them to sell direct but without competing against their existing customers. She called it "direct in drag." Value America's systems were so efficient, she explained, that we could do more for IBM than IBM could do for itself—without the risk of alienating current resellers.

She had done a fine job of explaining our vision. "That was good," Craig said. "You've captured the essence of this opportunity."

"The 'Eighth Channel' white paper you presented made quite an impact," Dorchak explained.

As they left the meeting and stepped through our conference room door, the GM said under his breath, "Glenda, don't you go to work for them." There was no humor in his voice.

Glenda brushed it off. "Don't worry. Nobody's offered me a job."

"They will," he said. "They will."

ᘒᘒ

A WEEK LATER, Craig was still thinking about Glenda's performance. She had done such a masterful job of making our message clear to someone who clearly wasn't getting it. There was leadership ability there, and we needed someone to manage Sales and Marketing. Dorchak had been at IBM over twenty years. She had been involved in two of their direct-sales initiatives. She understood advertising and call-center sales.

Winn had studied growing businesses. He knew that pioneers with the ability and passion to build value from ideas were often the wrong people to manage mid-sized firms. And mid-level managers—so essential to the success of mid-sized firms—were all too often overwhelmed by the demands placed upon them by large corporate entities. In other words, one needed three different, successive teams, with three different attitudes and skill sets, in order to grow from small to large.

Still, Craig thought, his character radar was notoriously weak. What did he really know about Dorchak? No less than he knew about Dean Johnson, Ken Erickson, or Doug Schatz, and they had worked out fine. But IBM had a distinctly different corporate culture than we had. Would she be able to make the transition? Would she drag IBMers along with her? He relied on Rex to steer him around conundrums like this, but Rex hadn't met her. On the other hand, it was only a Vice President position. It wasn't like we were considering her for President or CEO or something like that.

Craig picked up the phone.

Glenda said she was interested. She said she had turned down similar offers from both Dell and Micron, much to the relief of her supervisors. But Dorchak was beginning to feel like she'd hit the glass ceiling at IBM, never having risen above lowly Director positions. Who knew how far she could go in a less established company? Weren't these the people who had just hired Kim Dejong, also from IBM—as a division president, no less? What did Kim have that Glenda didn't? Nothing she could see. This could be her chance to show the world what she was made of.

But risk was a problem for Glenda. She was making about $100,000 at Big Blue, including bonus. Since she had assumed the role of primary breadwinner in her family, she didn't want to leave the security of the big firm if Value America wasn't solid.

Glenda's references checked out, so Craig continued to court her off and on over the summer. He knew our risks were diminishing, especially the risk of testing the company's revolutionary business model and proprietary e-commerce engine. It was all working even better than we had planned. Value America had gained traction. Our revenues were tripling every ninety days. He told Glenda that we were expecting to go public in the very near future. This, he said, would be her last chance to get stock options at pre-IPO strike prices. That was all it took. She signed our standard employment contract and bid IBM *adieu*.

Glenda's job description read:

"As the Senior Vice President of Sales and Marketing you are to manage direct response advertising, the call center, and the marketing department. Hire, manage, train, and motivate a team of telephone sales associates to serve consumers, GSA, state and local government agencies, higher education, trade unions, charities, and corporations. Evaluate performance and tune the direct response model. Improve the value proposition and diversity of ads to maximize sales, margins, and service. Work with our merchandisers to negotiate more cooperative advertising. Expand the Intel relationship. Manage the direct response initiative on technology and office products. Expand the sales effort to include catalogs, direct mail, co-branded stores, and telephone sales. Develop promotional partnerships with leading vendors to increase their involvement and support of our sales while increasing soft dollars and market-development funds. Coordinate advertising and marketing presentations in the store. Manage the Product Presentation team. Enhance the quality and appropriateness of product presentations and increase the quantity of presentations per writer. Develop, manage, and evaluate traditional and direct response advertising campaigns."

"Sure, I can do that," she said. If only she had.

৩৽৵৹

ROCOCO'S WAS AN Italian restaurant just down the street from the Yellow House. Three days after Glenda Dorchak began as SVP of Sales and Marketing, Craig, Rex, Joe, and almost every member of the management team met there for an informal welcoming dinner.

Joe Page picked up on it: Glenda was all business, dressed impeccably in an expensive designer suit and wearing a triumphant smile. She exuded success as she rose to jocular shouts of "Speech! Speech!" Joe listened to her corporate patter for a while and thought, *She's been here all of three days, and she's already decided she can dispense with our business plan. She may have jumped onto the band wagon, but she has no earthly idea what it took to build it or what we went through to get it this far.*

Perhaps it was because Joe had an allergy to corporate bureaucracy, but as he sat there, he wondered if he were the only one in the room who somehow knew that this was the beginning of the end.

The lips of an immoral woman drip honey, but in the end she is bitter as wormwood—Solomon

ROWING UP A WATERFALL

*H*e was supposed to be on vacation, but it wasn't working out that way. Katharine and the boys had insisted he join them on the Outer Banks, knowing he needed a break. Finally Craig acquiesced, only to find himself parked in a deck chair, his toes buried in the warm Carolina sand. Relaxing? Not exactly. There were problems. His cell phone was glued to his ear.

"Rafe, you know the arrangement with Rossi—five percent on the first ten million and one thereafter. But now that we've paid him half a million dollars, he's hired a lawyer and wants to change the deal. Your friend's killin' us. Did you know about this?" Craig knew the answer. He just wanted to see if Rafe was as interested in his investment as he was in his friend. "We should have closed this round. We can't schedule the IPO until it's done, and like I said, if we miss the summer IPO window…."

Durn, characteristically, wouldn't budge. "I can't help you. You need to work out your differences with Seth, so I'd suggest you give him what he wants and move on."

Winn wanted to scream *the company you're hurting is partly yours, you know*, but he didn't. He merely gritted his teeth and related the rest of the tale. "He's also demanding that we sell him Value America stock at one third the current price. The company can't sell under-priced shares without sending up flares at the SEC. This kind of thing makes 'em real testy."

"That's your problem," Rafe observed helpfully.

He hung up and called our attorney's private line.

"Justin Caise."

"Hi Justin, it's Craig. I know you've told me that the company can't sell Rossi under-priced shares, but I have an idea. Can *I* do it?"

"Yes, but you'd be cheating yourself. Why would you do that?"

"Because the choice is either cheat myself or cheat everybody else. If we don't figure out a way to give our boy what he wants, we'll never get this round closed. That means no IPO. And I don't think I need to tell you what *that* would mean."

"No, I understand." *It'd mean I might not get paid.*

"Draft the paperwork, okay, Justin? Take the shares from me."

"Alright, if you say so."

❧✦☙

REX FINISHED SENDING his fax, and Craig waved him into his office. "If one more thing goes wrong…."

"What now?"

"Know how Caise couldn't handle the drudgery of writing the S1, so he turned it over to an underling? Well, *he* got out-gunned by under-writer's counsel. Our S1 looks like the prospectus for the Prince of Darkness."

"Yeah. I've never seen so many silly risk factors."

"McNay and Volpe Brown are doing their part, but not Conover. He promised to be here for us—but instead we get Miles Julian, who by his own admission is a politician, not a banker. Gordon's never around."

Rex shook his head. "Yeah. Miles is a nice guy, connected and all, but he doesn't know when, or even how, to stand up to the lawyers or the auditors. Gordon *knows*, but he's not here, so they're walking all over us."

"Well, wanna hear the latest? Conover just called. Said they're no longer willing to co-manage the deal with Volpe. He said his firm is 'too big and prestigious' to accept equal billing on our prospectus. It would be 'damaging to their corporate psyche!'"

Rex couldn't help himself. He burst out laughing. "They're afraid they're going to damage their *corporate psyche?* We're risking our corporate *life*, and they're worried about the humiliation they'll suffer if they co-manage our IPO with a smaller outfit? And I thought lawyers had egos!"

"I'll bet it has less to do with corporate psyche than with corporate profits. As the lead manager, they'll get the lion's share of the deal. They'll control the book, and with it the allocation of stock. And guess whose clients will get to feast on us?"

"Right-o," Rex said. "On the other hand, their corporate paranoia may have had an upside."

"How's that?"

"Remember how Dandridge, their analyst, thought Flowers, Vulcan's honcho, was 'unprofessional'? That all shook out as a risk factor in the S1, but to me it looks more like a big sign saying, 'Buy this stock!'"

Anticipating the closing of the funding round, the new risk factor said in effect, "Don't pay any attention to the fact that Paul Allen, the world's second richest man and one of the most technologically savvy people on the planet, has examined and analyzed this firm and chosen to invest in it at a $300 million valuation. You shouldn't take him seriously."

"With enemies like this, who needs friends?"

"We do." Craig brought Rex back to earth. "We've lost as many friends as we've made. Sure, Volpe Brown has been with us all along. They were the first to visit, the first to commit to managing our IPO, and they're still our most reliable friend. But Goldman Sachs has been sitting on the fence so long, I'm sure their collective butts are numb. It's a shame. Latour's great. And remember UBS and the 'shameless self promoter?'

They bailed at the first sign of success."

"Then there was FBR," Rex said through his laughter. "They looked terrific. But they got into a spat with Dale and got deep-sixed."

"Then Dandridge introduces us to Suzzi Maupin of Hambrecht & Quist. She loves us, but we haven't seen hide nor hair of their bankers. I presume they have them."

"How'd we end up with Robinson-Humphrey?" Rex queried.

"They're the leaders in the office products and computer channels— our two most important categories."

"Oh, right. So with them on our team, the cover of our prospectus is going to read: Robertson Stephens, Volpe Brown Whelan, Hambrecht & Quist, and Robinson-Humphrey." Rex smiled. "Quite a lineup. We must be doing *something* right."

෧෴෬

"THE SITUATION IS completely intolerable," Glenda said. "How do you expect me to develop sales for this company if the whole B2B division is outside my control?"

Winn breathed a heavy sigh. A catfight was the last thing he needed right now. Glenda Dorchak had been our SVP of Sales and Marketing for one week, and already she was getting territorial. "Seems to me you've got your hands full managing marketing, advertising, the call center, and online sales," he said. "Read your job description lately? Developing our direct response capability is a full-time job in itself. You don't need to be in control of everything to be important, Glenda."

Craig didn't say what was he was really thinking, that he was once more witnessing the classic symptoms of insecurity that had hurt him so badly in the past. He wasn't about to let it happen again.

"You're missing the point, Craig," Glenda said flatly. "If this is going to work, there has to be horizontal communication. Kim DeJong is running her own little kingdom over there, independent of me. There's no process. It's helter skelter."

Oh, I see the problem. You can't stand to see another person, especially another woman, especially another IBMer, in a role in any way competitive to your own. So you're going to claw Kim's eyes out. But what he said was, "Kim DeJong, like it or not, is doing a marvelous job leading our Business-to-Business sales initiative. Everything about that division *should* be handled independently, with different methods than online and inbound consumer sales. She's set an aggressive budget for her division, and she's managing to exceed her objectives. B-to-B is important. B-to-C is important. You do your thing, and let Kim do hers." His phone rang. As he picked up the receiver he wrapped up the conversation abruptly: "Just do your job."

◊

RISK FACTORS WERE nothing new for Internet companies. As a group, dot-coms were risk personified. Their prospectuses were filled with red flags. After all, none had made money. The whole industry was being invented on the fly. The bankers had told us not to worry.

But our team was worried—or, at the very least, annoyed. Risk factors, even though they were listed in the S1, were routinely ignored. They were usually so obvious as to be laughable: "The Company expects to experience significant fluctuations in future operating results due to a variety of factors" (like every other firm in existence). "The Company is entirely dependent upon manufacturers and distributors to provide merchandise for sale" (as is every other retailer on the planet). "The Company's performance is substantially dependent on the continued services and performance of its current senior management" (Yeah, they might all of a sudden decide to play golf instead of going to work). Virtually every risk factor talked about perils faced by every company every day. They were supposed to be there to protect naïve investors, but in reality they were crafted to cover the "professionals" writing them.

"Reportable conditions," however, were a horse of a different color. These were specific and serious problems that the auditors performing their due diligence had discovered (or at least that was what they were supposed to be). Investors took them seriously, as well they should. What annoyed Craig about this one was that it concerned a condition that no longer existed, one that had never really been a problem in the first place.

The brouhaha was all about how to account for sales that took place at the very end of each quarter. The Price Waterhouse team Dean Johnson had brought in knew all about Internet companies but considerably less about retail. Their lack of experience had become a problem.

The invoice is considered the definitive document for confirming a shipment or sale. This document was particularly significant for us because we did not actually take physical possession of the thing being sold. Our sales were counted as revenue only after shipment, and the evidence for *that* was the invoice. It didn't matter that we had already received the customer's money.

At issue was the speed at which our suppliers' invoices could be received and matched. Value America had been designed to communicate with our suppliers via EDI, but when we first opened the store, most brands were accustomed to mailing invoices. This meant it could take a few days, rather than a few minutes, to transmit these documents. Even then, it was not a problem except for the last few days of a quarter.

No one was suggesting that we were misstating revenue; there was never a question of how much we had actually sold. The only question was how fast we could determine the quarter in which the sale occurred. And even then, it was only a problem in the thirteenth week of a given period.

When the problem had first been noticed, it was theoretical—we weren't advertising yet and were selling very little online. Craig's solution to the theoretical conundrum had been pragmatic, not to mention common: understate revenues, the same percentage each quarter. What didn't get picked up in Q1 would get reported in Q2, and what got missed in Q2 would show up in Q3. As long as you weren't overstating revenue, what did it matter? The potential error was only some fraction of one thirteenth of a quarter's sales. Even if it were understated and reallocated, it would be a positive adjustment, something that brings smiles, not suits. So who cared?

As it turned out, Price Waterhouse cared. They wanted the whole thing calculated down to the penny. After all, they were auditors. But that wasn't the reason Craig was upset. As soon as we had collected the first union investment funds—$9 million after fees—we had hired BDS to solve this and other technical challenges. After sitting through a four-hour technical review, even PW acknowledged that they had done their job. For some time now, Value America had been able to give the auditors timely revenue numbers for the oh-so-critical thirteenth week.

So what was the problem? Price Waterhouse told us, in effect, "We're historians. We are reporting a condition that existed in the period we're auditing, i.e., 1997. Now, in the middle of '98, you've fixed the problem, but that's not germane. We're not auditing '98, only reviewing it. So the reportable condition stands." It was another straw on the camel's back. How much more weight could the IPO stand before it collapsed?

It got worse. Craig's least favorite S1 insertion wasn't required either. The lawyers decided they wanted to tell everybody about Dynasty's Chapter 11 in Value America's prospectus. Never mind the SEC regulations, which only required that a prior Chapter filing be listed if it had occurred within the past five years. Anything before that was considered irrelevant, ancient history to everyone except the lawyers we were paying to draft our disclosure documents. Not only did they insist on its inclusion, they put it where it would cause Craig the most grief—in his bio. A founder's bio is the first place every journalist looks before they write.

Preparing for the initial public offering was monumentally stressful. It was bad enough behind the scenes working with lawyers and accountants who were running amok. But the primary public document upon which the company would be judged—the prospectus—was shaping up to be a poor reflection of the company, this retail revolution of ours. Craig felt like a mother whose child was about to enter a beauty contest only to be given a bad haircut and a black eye.

❦

THE FOUNDERS were chatting in Rex's office at the end of another long day. "About $25 million, Rex, less Rossi's fee and another hit from the lawyers. Not bad," Craig smiled. "Five million of it came our way, too."

"Yeah, but because this round was based on the union option, it was *all* supposed to come our way. I'm not complaining, mind you."

"The bad news is that the Series B round should have closed in May. It's what, June 26th? We sent the S1 off to the SEC, but we're not going to receive their comments for at least four weeks. By the time our team responds and we're cleared for takeoff, it's going to be August. We've missed the summer IPO window, Rex." Craig forced himself to look at the bright side. "At least we've got fuel in the tank."

Rex did the tally. "Fifteen million from Allen's Vulcan Ventures and half a million from President Clinton's friend, Terry McAuliffe. You think we'll get an invite to the White House?"

"I already got one. Dinner with Terry and the President. Katie was sick the day he called, so I decided to stay home."

Rex raised his eyebrows.

"Funny thing. Terry and Rafe told me that one day when they were both at the White House, they began discussing Value America with the President. They even went online and checked out the store."

"They buy anything? Cigars, perhaps?"

"I have no idea. But I do know that a lot of Rafe's friends invested. You've got to give Durn credit. Almost half of the dough in this round came from his political pals."

"Yeah. I noticed."

"The most interesting names, though, were Frank Flowers and Allen's investment banker, Michael Yagemann. Did you hear how that happened?" Craig asked.

Rex shook his head.

"Mike called me on my cell phone about a week ago. He introduced himself as the managing director of a big investment bank and said he'd managed most every Allen deal. After chiding me for not using him, not using *any* banker, he went on to say that Allen had told him we were one of his best companies. Mike asked if he could personally invest. I said no, that we needed to close the round. Then Flowers calls, tells me he's investing too, and asks me to take care of his friend. First time I'd talked to Frank since he asked about buying us out."

"So they're both in for a half million. I wonder if they've ever personally invested in an Allen deal before."

"Don't know, but the fact that they invested is a good sign."

"Sure makes Seth's self-serving claim that Flowers had a problem with you look ridiculous," Rex said. "Come to think of it, most everything Seth says makes him look ridiculous. Just for the entertainment value, ask Dean what he thinks of him."

"Oh, I know. Dean thinks he's dangerous, a loose cannon who's going to blow up in our faces."

Rex shook his head. "I warned you. But in spite of it all, we've done pretty well so far. We closed the 'pass the hat' round in October at a thirty million valuation, the union round in December at a hundred million, and today we closed Series B at a three hundred million dollar valuation. Not bad for a couple of duffers."

"Our valuation is growing almost as fast as our business. But I've got a bad feeling, Rex. I called Robbie Stephens ten minutes ago just to confirm our schedule. Conover said we were looking at the middle of September, when the investors return from their vacations and start looking at IPOs again. That means we'll finish our road show in early October. You know about October and the stock market, don't you?"

Rex knew. The two biggest crashes had taken place in October. "So the real question is will the market be ripe or rotten when investors get back?"

"Maybe I'm just being paranoid, but I have a funny feeling the dot-com honeymoon's over. I don't mind selling our company on its merits, but a little market momentum never hurts."

"One thing's for sure. All this extra time we spent screwing around with Flowers, Durn, and Rossi trying to get the round closed has given the lawyers and accountants plenty of time to monkey around with our S1."

"They've left us with no wiggle room. One little glitch, one untimely hiccup, and we're history: pack up our tent and go home. And *nobody* gets a second chance at an IPO."

Rex peered at Craig over the top of his reading glasses, flashing a wry smile. "How *do* we get ourselves into these situations, anyway?"

જ઼ઃૡ

CRAIG STOOD IN my office door. He wasn't smiling.

"Hi," I said. "What's up? You look...down." This was a different look for Mr. "Always-See-the-Good-in-Everything."

He wasn't angry, at least not with me. He was embarrassed. I don't think I'd ever seen him like this. He was almost shuffling his feet.

"Um, Ken, as you know, Glenda's been in one of the offices in the old Protein Solutions area since she got here a few weeks ago." Protein Solutions was a nutrition company that had occupied a small portion of the main floor of the Yellow House when we'd arrived. Our cancer-like growth had been too much for them, so they'd moved out, leaving their few precious square feet of office space for us to infest.

"Yes." I knew she had an office down there. She was my boss.

"Well, she wants a bigger office, one more in keeping with her stature...."

A blind man could see where this was going, so I put Craig out of his misery. "She wants my office. Give it to her. Look, don't worry about it. It's okay. We're all on the same side in this war, aren't we? I'll just find a new foxhole—I'll shift some bodies and move into one of the cubicles. It'll be okay as long as I'm still close to my ad team."

Craig looked relieved. "You're not upset?"

"I didn't say I wasn't upset. About moving, no. We all make our little sacrifices. But I *am* upset, yeah. Look at this!" In the jumble of paperwork on my desk, I found the printout of a newspaper ad format Glenda just had asked me to design. I handed it to Craig and said, "What's wrong with this picture?"

He was at a loss for words. What he held in his hand was a handsome five-column ad. It was divided into nine boxes. Each contained a separate product. "This does nothing to promote us or our brands. Hell, there are five, no, six brands in this one ad. No text, just bullets—precious little reason to buy any of this stuff."

"Bingo. Like you've told me a thousand times, any idiot can sell on price, and most idiots do." The relationship we were building with our customers and brands set us apart; we had something special going, a voice, a personality. We were creating a reason for shopping here. But with this new format, Glenda was throwing all that away.

"Worse than that. In a newspaper, it's a fool's folly. The picture-bullets-price format works in catalogs, in color inserts, but...."

"But there's a reason no one does this in newspapers."

I could see the turmoil behind Craig's wrinkled brow. He stared at the ad, though I don't think he was looking at it but rather through it. He breathed a heavy sigh. Finally, he spoke. "What you and I designed put

Madison Avenue on its ear. The big agencies are calling our style a 'whole new genre.'" It was doing everything we wanted, helping to set us apart, build our brand. More importantly, it was *working*. We were growing at three hundred percent *quarterly*.

More than just propelling our growth, our conversational, brand-centric style was clearly doing what we wanted. It enabled us to sell goods based on their value, it endeared us to our brand partners, attracted new brands, and even helped us generate co-op advertising money.

"So what do you want me to do?"

"Nothing," he said thoughtfully, almost sadly. "Let me see what I can do. She's wrong, dead wrong, but it's never a good idea to cut your people off at the knees—to give them a job and then override their decisions. It kills morale, makes them impotent. We've just given Glenda the Sales and Marketing job, Ken, and advertising is one of the tools she has to get the job done. I want her to succeed at her job, so I have to *let* her do her job. I'll try to explain the merits of what we've been doing, so she understands. Maybe she'll change her mind."

Having been in his shoes, only on a much smaller scale, I knew what he meant. Somehow, I should have known he would say something like that. "Okay. Glenda's my boss. I'll do what she wants. Hopefully, you'll get her to understand. I'd hate to see her destroy what we've built." Unfortunately, I had a feeling he would fail. Glenda would dig her heels, get defensive, and assert her professional status.

Craig nodded and turned to leave. Two steps later, as he reached the door, he stopped and looked toward me. He felt impotent, unable to help his friend. The pain was written all over him. He too somehow knew he was going to fail, and that his failure would be costly. He opened his mouth to speak, but said nothing. He just bowed his head, turned, and walked slowly toward the stairs.

♋∶♋

THE TIME HAD finally come. It was now the second week in September. The boys had edited, tweaked, fine-tuned, and polished the Value America investor presentation, and now they were ready. Craig, Rex, and Dean had a tight, crisp twenty-minute talk prepared—five minutes for an interactive demo of the store and another fifteen to explain the store's core concepts, capabilities, and financial picture. It was all supported with PowerPoint slides and the store-in-a-box. Dean explained the financials, Rex talked about our people. Their lines were so smooth they appeared to be speaking extemporaneously, but the speeches were in fact memorized.

The three arrived at the Robertson Stephens offices in Bank of America's Giannini Building, overlooking the San Francisco Bay. Rex announced offhandedly as he gestured toward a plaque on the wall, "We're related. Did you know that?"

"Who?" Dean asked.

"The Scatenas and the Gianninis. The man who built Bank of America into the biggest bank in the country was my grandad's cousin. As a matter of fact, Amadeo Giannini, known to everybody as 'A.P.,' actually asked my grandfather to join him back in '28. Grandpa turned him down."

Dean let out a low whistle. "Can you imagine how rich you might be if he hadn't?"

Rex just smiled. "Actually, what happened *before* B of A is why folks remember Giannini here in San Francisco. He started the Bank of Italy in 1904 to serve the city's working class. Two years later, on the morning of the great earthquake, he borrowed a produce wagon from my grandpa and drove down to what was left of the bank. A.P. sifted through the rubble and surreptitiously loaded the wagon with two million dollars worth of gold, coins, and securities, hid the loot under a pile of vegetables, and drove home. Then, while all the other bankers took a 'wait and see' approach toward reopening, A.P. set up shop down there," Rex pointed in the direction of the waterfront, "on the docks, loaning San Franciscans the money they'd need to rebuild the city. No matter how much money he made, Giannini's heart was always with the common folks. Remember what Miles Julian said about how Value America was 'doing well by doing good?' Ninety years ago, that was A.P. Giannini."

Upstairs, team Value America was ushered to a small conference room and gave the presentation a dry run. They had an audience of one: analyst Dale Dandridge. He gave the presentation "an eight and a half on a scale of ten." He said, "I've never given anyone a better rating than that."

As much as he liked the presentation though, Dandridge wanted to make some changes. They were not insignificant. Craig's speech talked about why we thought our model was different from—even superior to—Amazon's. Touting Amazon was how dot-com analysts had made a name for themselves. Any comparison belittling the industry's poster child for dot-com wonderfulness was *verboten*. So the sections dealing with the "relative strength" of our model had to come out.

The fact that Paul Allen's Vulcan Ventures had invested in Value America seemed to Craig to be a significant indicator of our company's merit. He hadn't factored in the low esteem in which Dale Dandridge held Frank Flowers. Dandridge demanded that Allen's investment not be mentioned: "His name is not well respected in this space," he claimed.

Moments later, they met with the firm's syndicate manager in another conference room. Bentley Hollis managed the "book," ultimately deciding how the IPO would be priced, who'd get allocated shares, and how many they'd get. He walked into the room like a doctor with bad news.

"There is something you should know," he said at last. "We've just pulled all of the IPOs we're leading. This is the worst IPO market we've ever seen!"

Rex and Dean looked at each other blankly and then turned to Craig, who was as stunned as they were. *Now what?*

Hollis continued. "The only IPO out there right now is eBay, and they've been struggling. They still have an outside chance because Goldman Sachs is lead, and the deal's under-priced. Goldman may have enough clout to get it done, but it's going to be tough. We're a co-manager." He paused and took a sip of his coffee.

"We like your model, so that's why we're proceeding with you...."

"Wait a minute!" exclaimed Craig. "You're *not* cancelling our IPO?"

"No. Didn't I explain that?"

There was a collective sigh that sounded like air leaving a slashed tire. "Uh, no, you didn't."

"Oh, sorry," Hollis said with a little smile as he took another sip. "You have a great model, exponential growth. You're bigger than eBay. So we think we can get you out there and get the deal done, even in this market."

Dale revived team Value America from their near-death experience and escorted Rex, Dean, and Craig to the firm's large auditorium. Along the way he said, "Our sales force was not very happy this morning during my 'teach in.' They've been burned recently—bad market and all—and they're overly sensitive. They don't like your risk factors. Don't be surprised if they hammer you with some really tough questions."

That in itself was a recipe for disaster, but it got worse. The audio-visual equipment in the conference room didn't work—the audio tracks accompanying the product presentations couldn't be heard. Although the conference room was filled, our team was faced with giving a presentation to people who weren't there. The sales force was scattered all over the country, and they had been "brought" into the room with a sophisticated video-conferencing setup. It was a less than ideal way to demonstrate an Internet store designed to be experienced intimately on your desktop.

Craig felt all the life and excitement drain out of his speech as he read it from his butchered notes. Dale had made so many changes, he was afraid he'd revert back into the familiar word patterns he'd memorized before leaving Charlottesville. Dean and Rex delivered their short segments.

It wasn't their best effort either. Then the questions began. This was normally Craig's favorite part. He knew retail, brands, marketing, and technology better than anyone in his audience.

But the questions were not about Value America's business, retail, brands, marketing, or technology. The sales force, especially the group in Chicago, grilled him on the reportable condition listed in the S1. Craig had seen that one coming and patiently brought the sales force up to speed on what had been done to correct "the problem" and why it had never really mattered in the first place. They hammered Craig and Rex on Dynasty's demise. Their coherent, concise response turned this into an advantage. Dynasty's experiences and lessons had provided the motivation for Value America. The pitfalls that had hurt them six years earlier were now pylons in the course we were running—clearly visible and easy to avoid.

But like a group of teenagers whose party has been shut down by their parents, this audience was in no mood for reason. Why should they be nice to Value America? The bloom had fallen off of the dot-com rose, and their clients had been hammering them about the risks of investing in Internet IPOs. Turnabout was fair play. Their frustration was palpable, and their resentment lurked just beneath the surface. They characterized every well-prepared answer as "glib," every thoughtfully considered response, "facile." The Value America team was dismissed as being "too slick." Any *less* "slick," of course, and they would have been written off as bumbling amateurs. There was no way to win.

The curse continued when they took the demonstration to Volpe Brown Whelan. It was bad enough that they were still smarting from being asked to step down from being co-lead. It was challenge enough that their conference room was long and narrow, not at all suited for the visual communication the Value America presentation required. Worse, their offices were under construction. Craig, Rex, and Dean tried to deliver the pitch, shouting over the din of hammering, sawing, and colorful construction jargon.

Things went no better at Hambrecht and Quist. Now playing third fiddle, their egos were damaged beyond recognition. They were clearly a better firm than Robertson Stephens, they thought. Who needs this humiliation? *Oh, yes,* Craig mused. *There's nothing like placing your future in the hands of an excited, motivated sales force.*

The Robinson-Humphrey presentation was delivered over the telephone. They were back to describing the Mona Lisa.

৩৽৻ৎ

THERE WAS NO time to lick their wounds. When Craig, Rex, and Dean got back to C'Ville, they only had a couple days to tweak the presentation to Dandridge's specifications, make new PowerPoint slides, and polish it all. The appointments had been set. The road show was about to begin.

The itinerary looked fatal, or at least impossible: Monday, 9/14/98: three meetings in Los Angeles; Tuesday, 9/15: four in San Diego, two in Los Angeles; Wednesday, 9/16: seven in San Francisco; Thursday, 9/17: two in Minneapolis, three in Chicago, one in Baltimore; Friday, 9/18: four in Baltimore; Saturday, 9/19: home for a shower, shave, and a good, stiff drink; Sunday, 9/20: travel; Monday, 9/21: six meetings in London; Tuesday 9/22: two in Frankfurt; Wednesday, 9/23: seven in Boston; Thursday, 9/24: seven in New York; Friday, 9/25: seven more in New York; take the weekend off, back in C'Ville; Monday, 9/28: two in Milwaukee, two in Kansas City; Tuesday, 9/29: eight in Denver. What fun.

Before all that fun though, Justin Caise asked that the team start the road show in Richmond. How could they refuse? Justin had helped save the company from early extinction, not to mention being instrumental in bringing Dean Johnson on board. Craig smiled at the parallels between this and Dynasty's IPO years before. Sol Price had been the savior, and his hometown, San Diego, had been the site of that road show's kick-off.

The Richmond meeting was to be held at the Commonwealth Club, and Justin promised to invite 200 or so of his contacts. The list read like the Who's Who of Virginia. Craig welcomed the opportunity to present to a friendly audience before entering the lion's den.

Glenda Dorchak had had nothing to do with the IPO. She had only been with the company for a few weeks when she asked Craig if she could ride along to witness the kick-off presentation. *Why not: It would be a good opportunity for Glenda to absorb some of the vision, the excitement of the whole idea.* From every indication, she had neither read the business plan nor understood our mission of doing well by doing good. This might help.

It takes about an hour to drive from Charlottesville to Richmond. As they began the trip, Glenda made it clear that she was a little put out at not being asked to be part of the road show. Craig gritted his teeth and tried to make the situation clear.

"Glenda, you've got a big job to do," he reasoned. "Managing Sales and Marketing should be your focus. Rex and I founded the company; we orchestrated its growth. Dean Johnson is CFO. He has to be there. You have no history with the firm. You've made no investment in the company. The investment community wouldn't take you seriously."

"I'm not sure *you* are taking me seriously, Craig."

"What's that supposed to mean? I've placed more people under your supervision than anyone else in the company. If I didn't have faith in your abilities, would I have done that?" Actually, it was Craig's usual *modus operandi* to give people more responsibility than they had ever handled, or thought they could handle. He pushed people to excel, even if it was uncomfortable for them—*especially* if it was uncomfortable for them. If they thought they could go a mile, he asked for three, and when they came up short at two and a half, they were still amazed at how far they had come. Some balked, dug in their heels, and hated him for it; some surprised themselves, discovered new talents, and loved him for it; and some were never satisfied no matter what happened.

Glenda was one of those. "The way the company is structured, I can't do my job. You've got all these independent silos, Presentation Marketing, the Call Center, Advertising, Technology—and they're not connected. How's a company supposed to move forward if each leg is moving independently, doing its own thing?"

"We've been over this ground before, Glenda. Each leg is working together and moving in the same direction because our managers have read the business plan. They know where we're going and how we're going to get there. Besides, at this stage, there is no advantage in Presentation Marketing knowing how Finance is managing our books, or in Advertising knowing what Technology is planning to develop. It's a waste of time, a distraction. It prevents people from doing their jobs."

"IBM," she countered, "couldn't run for a week without the kind of horizontal process I'm talking about."

"We're not IBM," Craig shot back, "and with any kind of luck, we never will be. If we wanted to pattern ourselves after a big company, it wouldn't be IBM anyway. It would be HP, who *does* run their business with independent silos. We're still relatively small and all in one place. If Advertising needs to know what Merchandising is doing, they can walk downstairs and ask. And they do. There are plenty of points of contact."

They had reached the suburbs west of Richmond. Eastbound Interstate 64 widened to three lanes, then four. We were within ten minutes of beginning our road show. That's when Glenda dropped her bomb.

"I'm sorry, Craig, but I can't continue to work under these circumstances. You have a choice. Either you name me President and Chief Operating Officer so I can do my job the way I think it needs to be done, or I'm going to resign."

To his credit, Craig didn't swerve off the road and hit a tree. But he was clearly no longer in control. Glenda Dorchak had him right where she wanted him. True, she had done nothing to build the company, and she had had nothing to do with the IPO. But she was smart enough, or more correctly, crafty enough, to know the IPO couldn't survive another hiccup. With market conditions this bad and with our risk factors so overdone—especially with a reportable condition—the slightest glitch would cook our goose. For an officer of a company—whose name and bio were listed in the red herring—to leave for *any* reason on the eve of the IPO was one glitch too many. Furthermore, she *had* to know that a failure of the IPO would likely spell the demise of the company. Second chances at going public were about as rare as any other resurrection from the dead.

It grew very quiet in the car.

Craig reviewed his options as he gripped the wheel tightly with both hands and stared straight ahead. Option One: let her quit. Consequences: the IPO is put off, we run out of operating capital in three months, and the company goes under. Option Two: give her what she wants. Consequences: the IPO proceeds, and we give Ms. Dorchak a couple choices of our own when the deal is done. What goes around, comes around. It wouldn't be pretty, but at least we'd survive. Option Three: cross your fingers and hope she lets it drop. Consequences: a state of limbo ensues, increasing tension and stress, but there would be no "disclosable event." This was easily the preferred choice. If Craig said anything to her either way, he would have to make his decision public.

Glenda broke the silence. She had been thinking about her options too, as in how many she could get. "As President and COO, I'll be needing a substantial raise, of course. My guaranteed bonus must increase, commensurate with my new title. There must also be a substantial increase in my stock options."

So much for Option Three. *Damn.*

'Course, there was still Option Four: open the door and kick her out.

"I want a seat on the board and my own employment contract," Glenda squealed. Option Four was starting to look pretty good.

Craig knew he couldn't give her a definite answer without jeopardizing the IPO, so he did the only thing he could. He stalled. "Listen, Glenda. I'm going to have to talk this over with Rex—between us we own seventy percent of the company. We'll think about it." He hoped that sounded non-committal enough.

But his head was swimming. A dozen conflicting thoughts vied for attention, not the least of which was that Ms. Dorchak had instantly transformed herself into the object of his most sincere loathing. *How could I have been so wrong about her character? My wife's right: I'm a scum magnet. Could her timing have been any worse? Will the IPO really crash if she walks, or am I being paranoid about this? Alright. Don't panic. Maybe having everything under one manager isn't such a bad idea. Surely this can't be as bad it seems. After all, she put in twenty-three years at IBM. I've really only known her for a few weeks. But what would she do with our company if she had more power? Maybe I'm just overreacting. Whoa!—Look out for that trash truck! I can't deal with this right now, going into an IPO with this terrible market and a prospectus to match. Will the company survive if the offering is postponed? What are the odds against getting a second chance? How can I continue to work with someone who's black-mailed us like this? I hate these games. We called Kyle South's bluff, and it almost killed us. Now, there's a lot more at stake—so many people are depending on us, so many investors are counting on us to come through on the IPO. If we cave in to her demands and succeed in going public, can we fire her when we get back? Oh, man! Was that my off ramp I just passed?*

ೋ⋛⋌⋚ೋ

"DID YOU SEE the paper this morning?" Rex asked Craig and Dean over coffee. They were standing on the sidewalk outside Starbucks in La Jolla. "The news is grim. All our comps are cratering, even Amazon."

"Perfect timing. It's our second day on the road, and the dot-com world is a disaster area," Dean added.

Craig smiled grimly. "On the other hand, we were well received in L.A. yesterday. It's not over yet. But it is six thirty, gentlemen. Time to get started."

The San Diego area held a lot of memories for Craig. The Price Club had begun here, and a very young Craig Winn had helped make that happen. His first IPO had started here as well. And now on this bright Tuesday morning, they were to kick off the day with a seven o'clock visit to a firm who had been heavily invested in Dynasty. The offices of Wall Street Associates were just a five-minute stroll from their hotel in this deceptively quiet seaside village.

After listening to the pitch, the response was, "Very impressive, gentlemen, but I have a question. Why are you trying to raise money in this market? You couldn't have picked a worse time."

Craig answered, "We have no choice. Nobody can afford to advertise their way into the national consciousness. Web firms are saturating the media. Public companies are soaking up all the free ink.

"That said," Craig continued, "we *do* have to advertise, and heavily, at least in the beginning, to make people aware of our brand and what makes us special. That takes money, the kind of money you can't come by any other way. The infrastructure enhancements we'll need to manage our growth aren't cheap either. The bottom line—we *have* to go public to be competitive."

The investor rubbed his chin. "Okay, so that leads me to my second question. What price are you willing to accept?"

That was out of bounds. He shouldn't have asked, and Craig wasn't about to answer. Pricing and projections remained the purview of the investment bankers, not the investor or the investee.

The IPO had been structured to sell five million of the company's thirty million shares at $14-$16 per share. We had split three to one, just as Craig had predicted. With our new shares, our filing valuation was $450 million, half again as high as the Series B round we had closed just two months before at a $300 million valuation. It was, to the dollar, the valuation Craig had predicted in his "For Your Eyes Only" letter to Paul Allen. So any way you looked at it, the next question was like a bucket of cold water in the face.

"Would you accept $7 a share? In this market, that may be the most you'll be able to get."

Seven dollars would put us below our last private valuation. That would be a very bad thing. A lot of covenants would be violated. The lawyers would have a field day.

"You know I can't answer that," Craig said. "We've just started our road show, and markets go up as well as down. Granted, conditions are horrible. We're realists. We'll do the right thing. But I must say, I'm glad you're interested in buying our stock." Craig always found a reason to smile.

৩৽৻৻

THE NEXT STOP was in Rancho Santa Fe, another suburb of San Diego. The investor had been with a prestigious New York firm but now ran his own fund out of a room above his garage. Glenn met our boys in shorts and sandals. His workspace was strewn with baseball memorabilia. It was haunted by the ghosts of summers long past. Manhattan this was not.

Craig knew enough not to let this relaxed atmosphere cloud his judgment. Glenn had been around for years and was highly respected. He had, in fact, bought a big stake in Dynasty's initial public offering. It was certain they would spend some time reminiscing.

Craig braced himself with Rex's admonition, "Don't apologize. You stood tall while the world was crashing around you. Without having learned those hard lessons, you could not have built this company. You learned about brand abuse, about distribution, about the real cost of owning inventory. You learned not to borrow money from banks to build a new company. It taught you not to concentrate too much business with anyone. You might say Price Club taught you what to do, and Dynasty taught you what *not* to do."

Glenn may have learned to hate neckties, but he had earned respect. So Craig delivered his pitch as if he were addressing the world's biggest institutional investor: "Value America is an e-commerce marketplace for business and consumer products—an Internet store for over eight hundred leading brands. We have built exclusive technology to produce multimedia product demonstrations, integrate a call center, and deliver the convenience of a comprehensive store in an inventory-less model. We have built an engaging front end for the consumer and linked it to our own back-end transactional solution.

"Value America uses the Internet to bring the best products and people together. As a result, our average checkout is nearly fifteen hundred dollars. This is ten times greater than our nearest competitor, and a hundred times that of our largest competitor. We have motivated national brands to pay us ten million dollars to present their products in an environment where most thought we would have to compete strictly on price. Manufacturing giants like GE and Amana have agreed to be our warehouse, shipping our customers directly, one at a time.

"We have created an authoring system to efficiently produce interactive product presentations that blend visual imagery, audio, and video. They empower consumers with the information they need to make better buying decisions. Our demonstrations are equally powerful on the supply side because they represent the first chance brands have had to correctly present their products directly to consumers. As a result, hundreds of brands have chosen Value America as their only online partner.

"We cast a broader net by using traditional advertising to drive revenues and brand share. We enjoy the benefits of co-op advertising, where the brands pay us to sell their products.

"Twenty years ago, while working with the original Price Club team, we launched the last retail revolution—the last time buying behavior and selling strategy were fundamentally changed. It is important to appreciate the things that drove Price Club because we have integrated these into our solution. They had a commitment to quality. Like before, our job is to encourage the best brands to sell through our new channel. Price Club was efficient, which was why they could sell the best for less. Value America uses an even more efficient version of the same strategy. Ultimately at less than five percent overhead as a percentage of revenue, we will sell the best products at lower prices and still profit. Price Club chose to lead with business products, recognizing that business people are early adopters. So have we.

"We believe the Internet is where the next retail revolution will occur. Value America was created to lead this revolution by providing online shoppers with the seven things they want most:

"First, quality products from trusted brands like Panasonic and Weber, PCs from IBM, HP, and Compaq. We are the only online store factory-authorized to sell consumer *and* business PCs from the big three.

"Second, value. We're more efficient, so we can sell the best for less. Third, information. We produce multimedia product demonstrations so consumers can make better buying decisions. Fourth is convenience. Consumers want a store that's always open, a store that instantly arranges itself for the way they want to shop, a store so big most everything they need for home or business can be found in one convenient place.

"Fifth, consumers want service. That's why we've built a store that greets them by name, thanks them for their last purchase, and takes them directly to customer service, should they have a problem. Sixth, consumers want selection. Someday we'll serve thousands of brands and feature millions of products. And seventh, trust is essential, particularly online. This is why we give members instant access to the information they need, their receipts, warranties, and customer service."

All of this was supported by PowerPoint slides. After demonstrating the store, they told Glenn, "Our customer solution is only half the equation. Value America is about constructing productive partnerships with leading brands.

"We have built an electronic link between consumers and factories. Ultimately, what we do costs less and works better. Manufacturers get to keep a higher percentage of the ultimate sale, and the consumer gets a better deal. This is a whole new way of doing business—a comprehensive solution designed to capitalize on the Internet's power to drive revenues up and costs down."

Glenn listened attentively, leaning forward in his chair. Maybe these guys *had* learned something from Dynasty. Nobody else, it seemed, had even pondered these problems, much less crafted a solution to solve them.

"Today, we present and sell products in a dozen categories, from office products and computers to jewelry, from housewares and home improvement to electronics, from sports and fitness to health and beauty. Soon we'll be adding books, music, pharmaceuticals, and apparel.

"Now, you may be wondering why we did this the hard way, why Value America is comprehensive, not just another niche player. We don't think consumers will learn to navigate and purchase products from hundreds of sites. Nor will they share personal and financial information on a wide scale. We believe they will gravitate to the handful of comprehensive sites that provide everything they need. Amazon, whom we respect, has recognized this reality. We are an 'Amazon' with brand relationships, an 'Amazon' without the burden of inventory, an 'Amazon' with informative product presentations, and an 'Amazon' with a model that supports product sales in a dozen industries, not just one."

So much for Dandridge's admonition to drop the Amazon comparisons. Dale wasn't here—he never made a single road show appearance.

"What works in consumer products applies to business products as well. We have brought two hundred fifty office products, business technology, and peripheral brands together for the first time. Our direct business partnerships include PC manufacturers, peripherals, and office supplies. In the office products world, we see ourselves as a Dell with two hundred and fifty brands, not just one."

Craig went on to discuss our technological achievements, particularly our proprietary authoring and administration tools, the order pipeline and audit capabilities, and our EDI-driven back end. He highlighted our in-house advertising capability, our brand relationships, and growth.

Rex talked about our people and their areas of responsibility. Dale had wanted all references to our team taken out of the presentation, but Craig knew better. We were the reason they were here. So our people were brought along through a series of clever themed photographs. Each employee/owner was pictured with his or her team wearing Value America golf shirts, color coordinated by department.

After presenting our people, Rex handed the baton to Dean, who explained our financial model. A few minutes later, Craig resumed explaining how we expected to grow. He spoke of expanded relationships with existing brands; new brands in existing categories; expansion into new product categories; custom stores for businesses, unions, faith groups, and the like; and even Value America credit cards.

"We think we're in the right place at the right time with the right solution," he said. "Our business model is strong, and so is our team. We have the best brand partners. Our solution is scalable, proprietary, and has mass appeal. We are building market share and have tremendous momentum. Value America is all about bringing people and products together. This is why Tim Forbes called Value America 'the best business model,' and why Andy Grove said that to compete, others will have to copy Value America. Paul Allen believes we have created what he and Bill Gates envisioned years ago, and that we have the potential to become the *Microsoft of E-Commerce*."

Glenn was impressed, or at least said he was. But the schedule was tight, and there was no time to chat. Thirty minutes after they had rung his doorbell, team Value America was gone and headed back to downtown San Diego for their third and fourth meetings of the day, with Duncan Hurst Capital and Nicholas Applegate. They flew back to Los Angeles for afternoon meetings before departing for San Francisco.

As the road show progressed, a pattern began to emerge. Almost no one had taken the time to read the red herring. Few had visited the store. More often than not, the presentation wasn't finished before the Q&A impatiently began. The team fielded each question like tennis players returning a serve.

There are no words to adequately describe the trauma of these thirty-minute encounters. In this short time, our team had to earn the investors' trust and respect, describe our industry, explain what we did, and share how and why we did it. The questions were often designed to skewer presenters. This was the world's most jaded audience; they had seen and heard it all. Most every day, a team of aspiring entrepreneurial gladiators charged into their arena and attempted to pry millions from their tightly clinched fists. Like Roman gladiators, few survived a failed encounter.

The third meeting on day three was a bit of a surprise. For everyone. Jake Gambini of Gambini Associates had apparently forgotten about it. He arrived late. Moments into the meeting, as Craig gave Sol Price credit for Value America's attitudes and strategies, Gambini's eyes lit up.

"Sol Price!" he said. "I was the largest investor in Price Club. Still own most of my stock. I was the first to invest in Home Depot, too."

"Then you must know that Sol and Bernie are good friends."

"Yes indeed, as am I with them."

"I know Sol better than Bernie," Craig shared. "I admire them both, the way they use their corporate philosophy to motivate. Working with either of them is like being on a crusade. They ooze charisma."

"They're great," Jake agreed.

"So you speak retail."

"Like a native."

Craig grinned. "Listen, Jake," he said. "Let's put the presentation aside for the moment and just talk. I haven't been able to do that."

"I'm not surprised. You know, in addition to Bernie and Sol, it wasn't that long ago Jeff Bezos of Amazon sat at this very table. I was one of the largest investors in his IPO." Craig was now conflicted, but knowledge in common can be like glue, bonding men together. Rex and Dean became bemused spectators as Craig and Jake shared their experiences. Craig wanted to regale Jake with horror stories of ignorance on the part of financiers as they tried desperately to distance e-tail from retail, but he knew better. There was a dichotomy brewing. Jake, he learned, was the godfather of Dale Dandridge's newborn son. Dale served on his board. Jake had just shared how heavily he was invested in the portal-inspired Amazon model. He had made a fortune buying Amazon stock.

They had known each other less than twenty minutes, and yet Craig found himself asking Gambini if he would consider a seat on our board. It would have been a *coup* to partner with an investment maven who understood retail. As they parted, Jake promised to visit us in Virginia.

As the elevator doors closed, Rex was the first to speak. "Listening to the two of you talk about Home Depot and Price Club was mind boggling. Who would have thought?..."

"That's just it, Rex; *nobody* thought, not even Jake. That's why I kept the discussion focused on Price Club, not Value America."

"Say what?" Dean questioned. "I thought you were bonding. Now you say no one's thinking? You just asked that guy to serve on our board."

The elevator door reopened, and the three Valuable Americans headed down a flight of stairs and on to their waiting limousine. "Don't get me wrong. I'm as pleased with our meeting as you guys are. He's going to buy our stock. It's what he said about Amazon that has me worried. We may be rowing up a waterfall."

"Maybe you could translate that," Rex requested as Dean unfolded his itinerary and told the driver where to go next.

"Alright guys. Bezos was an investment banker, not a retailer. He needed comps during his IPO, just like we do today."

"Yeah, like we need them to stop falling so we can get our IPO done," Dean interjected, putting away his itinerary.

"At least we *have* comps. Bezos had none. So he and his investment banking pals used portals, with their media metrics. Thus began the popularity contest—page views, stickiness, and customer acquisition. All rubbish, but nobody cares."

"So what does that have to do with your buddy, Jake?" Rex questioned, riding backward in the limousine.

"The problem is so pervasive that even a guy like Jake, who should know better, doesn't. He's in denial, because the delusion is in his interest." Craig painted a troubling picture for his compatriots. "You see, despite this recent hiccup, Amazon stock has soared. So in the minds of investors and the media, it must be a good company—doing things right. They've defined 'right' using popularity metrics and justified it being right with the fact that Amazon's stock has increased in value. It's circular reasoning, logical suicide. Amazon is popular, Amazon was the first e-tailer, Amazon is growing, and their stock price has climbed. Therefore, it stands to reason they must be a winner. If *they* say owning inventory is right, it must be. Everyone's invested in Amazon, one way or another. Investors, analysts, and the media have become cheerleaders. No one wants their bubble popped."

"So why consider giving Jake a board seat?" Rex probed.

"Because if we can awaken *him*, we have a chance. He's one of them. He's in the epicenter, Dandridge's pal. He'd be the perfect messenger."

❧❦❧

IT WAS ALL downhill from there. In Minneapolis, they had apparently never heard of the Internet. Or good manners. Craig and company found the people at American Express Financial so rude, they cut the meeting short and folded up their laptop.

In Chicago they were nice, at least. But in the early fall of '98, they were light-years behind, it seemed. The meetings were pleasantly unproductive.

On to Baltimore. The venerable T. Rowe Price had arranged to have their senior investment manager, Ron Dunler, meet with the Value America team. Another Dynasty alumnus, Dunler naturally wanted to hear Rex's and Craig's take on what had happened. He could hardly wait for Art Costello, Robbie Stephens' banking representative, to complete the introductions and recount the analyst's financial projections. As the team delivered the pitch, Ron remarked with a wry smile that the boys had learned their lessons well, even though they had been at his expense.

Dale Dandridge caught up with our team as they were heading out of Baltimore. Not in person, mind you—on the telephone. Costello's cell phone rang as the four raced toward the airport and their flight to Philadelphia. Meetings with Turner, PNC Equity, and Delaware were less than an hour away. Even though he had been scheduled to accompany the troupe on some of the road show stops, the analyst had remained in San Francisco the whole time, trying to hold his clientele together. The market was in a state of siege. Amazon (who *had* to do well because the investment bankers had staked their reputations on it) was looking about as perky as a hound dog's ears. Dale's heart, it seemed, wasn't in our IPO.

"I think we should pull the plug," he said. "eBay's deal isn't happening either. Even though Goldman's still bullish, our G2 says otherwise. Most everyone is interested in you, but *at what price* is the question."

Bentley Hollis jumped in, "At this point, we'd expect the book to be a little weak. It doesn't start to build until after Boston and New York. You haven't been to either place yet. But our indications of interest are softer than we'd like. This is a buyers' market, and our investors want a deal.

You might have to accept a price below your filing range."

"Alright. We'll accept whatever it takes to get it done. But we want to continue," Craig said with unmistakable resolve.

Listening to Craig's end of the conversation and seeing the look on his face left little doubt in the minds of Rex and Dean as to what the phone call was about. Dean's panicky whisper, "No, no, no!" and his frantic palms-out gesturing reminded Craig, as if he needed reminding, that we needed the working capital.

"Mitch, Dale, please," Craig pleaded. "Just get us the best price you can. We need to complete the IPO. How much demand do you have?"

"We've got enough to get the deal done, maybe, but like I said, at what price? You're going to take a haircut," Bentley answered. It was a rather odd prediction, considering his earlier revelation regarding the dominance of New York and Boston firms.

Craig swallowed hard. "Just don't pull the plug. We'd rather raise less money and come back in six months with a secondary than walk away empty handed." The thought of a failed IPO was horrifying.

The team went on to finish their meetings in Philly. But a giant cloud now loomed over their heads.

෨඄෯

ONE DAY OF R&R was all they were going to get. Craig, Rex, and Dean were scheduled to fly the Concorde to Europe, first to London on Sunday morning, then on to Frankfurt. When they returned to the States, the crucible awaited, the heart of any IPO: Boston and New York.

The Winns had moved into their beautiful new home just west of Charlottesville months before. Craig was now thankful that it was big enough for a man to get lost in. Saturday afternoon arrived too soon. As the hour of departure approached, he went to the basement and made like a mushroom. An hour of veg time. Whatever he could get.

Somewhere in the distance, he could hear a phone ringing. Three rings, then it stopped. A minute later, he could hear Katharine calling from the top of the stairs, "Craig, are you down there?" She sounded far away. Maybe it was he who was far away. He couldn't tell. He walked across the large open game rooms that comprised his basement, and picked up the phone. The voices were familiar, yet somehow strange. "Craig, it's Dale Dandridge, Bentley Hollis, Gordon Conover, and Miles Julian. We're glad we caught you before you left for the airport."

Craig made a game of predicting the outcome of phone conversations in the first few seconds by the tone of the caller's voice, their choice of words. The words, "caught you before you left," were not encouraging. It appeared that the dragons might win this round. Up to this point, the score had been Winn and Scatena-10, Dragons-0. There had been a few ties, not that it mattered now. In the world of entrepreneurial conflict, you only get to lose once.

"Look, we won't beat around the bush," Gordon said. "We've got some bad news. We're pulling your IPO."

Craig was not surprised, just numb. It felt like he was dreaming. Any minute now he would wake up and....

"There's a reason we're doing it now," Dale claimed. "If you go on to Boston and New York and we pull it then, you're dead; your credibility's shot—you'll never go public."

Craig was certain that given the opportunity to present our firm and its mission to the financial elite in New York and Boston, we would have prevailed. But logic and reason no longer carried any weight. We were being sacrificed on the altar of expediency.

"It's not your fault," Bentley added. "This is the worst market any of us can remember. It went from bad to worse. Everyone you met was impressed, but the strength of their commitment is a product of the market. I can't guarantee we can get it done, even at ten dollars a share."

Earlier in the day, Mark McNay had called Craig. He'd predicted Robbie Stevens' about face and asked Craig to let his firm finish the IPO as lead. It was noble, yet improbable. Such a maneuver had never been done, even in a good market.

It was Miles' turn. "Conditions haven't been this bad in half a century. By all accounts, you were doing fine out there."

Craig responded somberly, "I assume this is no longer up for debate. Our desire to continue no longer matters? Your decision is final?"

"Yes," they said collectively.

"Then I want three things. First, write a letter that says what you just told me: This was not our fault, we were well received, and you wouldn't hesitate to take us out again when the market improves. We'll need this letter for the media, our investors, and employees."

"It's all true. I'll write it," Miles said.

"Second, I believe Stan Garmin, the office products guy that brought us together, is managing private equity for you now. We need you to raise ten to fifteen million in private capital *post haste*. You got us into this mess. The least you can do is get us out."

"I'll take the lead on that one," Gordon answered. "I'll put a call into Stan this afternoon. He'll call you first thing Monday."

"Third, I want to be back on the road and finish the IPO just as soon as the market recovers—whether that's two weeks or two months."

It was Dale's turn. "I can't make any promises, but I think we can have you back out there just as soon as you have your Q3 numbers reviewed. We can reprint Reds and use the updated numbers as a justification for returning. Your numbers are going to be good, aren't they?"

"Your model has us growing from five million in Q2 to ten in Q3, right?" Craig already knew the answer.

"I think that's right," Dale responded, a little unsure of himself. "It's a huge jump quarter to quarter, even for an Internet company."

"We're going to do fifteen million dollars. *Triple* Q2."

"Impressive," "Strong," "Incredible," and "Great," were the reactions.

"Alright, gentlemen, that's the plan. Get it done," Craig said resolutely. Then he heard himself thanking Dandridge and the team for the call. Even condemned royalty tipped the executioner, did they not?

Craig called Rex and Dean and told them the bad news. First thing the following morning, they'd assess the damage.

৩৺৶

CRAIG SUSPECTED IT was a death sentence. How long would we last without an influx of capital? In keeping with our need to exceed expectations, we had been burning through our technology and advertising budgets at a prodigious pace. We couldn't keep that up for long, and we hadn't reached "critical mass" yet, not by a long shot. When we ran out of advertising funds, people would simply forget about us, and our revenues would evaporate. There would be no second chance.

Sunday morning's brilliant fall sun did little to brighten the mood. Dean, Rex, and Craig met at the Yellow House. They gathered around the antique table. "I didn't want to say anything yesterday because I wasn't sure, and there wasn't anything we could do about it anyway," Dean began. "But I've talked with Caise. I have some bad news, and some *really* bad news."

Craig shared a glance with Rex.

"As of this morning," Dean announced, "we have less than four million dollars in cash available to us. We've got ten million in the bank, but the rest is tied up supporting our merchant account and lines of credit. In other words, we won't be able to meet payroll and keep advertising."

Craig took a deep breath. "We're going to have to go out and raise some private capital between now and the time the market recovers. It's gonna be hard, but not impossible."

"Not hard. Not impossible," Dean said. "Illegal. That's the *really* bad news. The SEC says you can't raise private equity for six months after you've filed a registration statement. I'm sorry, Craig. Unless we can figure out a way to raise money without giving people shares, we're dead."

"Do you know the names of any good loan sharks?" Rex asked.

"They call them 'swing loans,' but the rates and terms would make a mobster blush," Dean answered.

Saddened, Craig volunteered, "I'll call the board, give 'em a heads up."

"I'd like to be there and listen in on your call to Durn," Rex joked bitterly. "That ought to be fun."

"Bet you a buck Rafe's supportive," Craig shot back. "Despite his colorful ways, Durn has always been there when we needed him."

"Hey, if you've got a buck to spare, give it to me. We're going to need it to make payroll," Dean lamented, leaving Craig and Rex sitting alone in stunned silence.

Rex broke the spell. "It's over, isn't it?" He wasn't asking. Slowly, he placed both palms on the old table, pushed back his chair, and stood.

"Looks that way, pal," Craig agreed as he rose to his feet. "We gave it our best shot. I'm sorry I dragged you into this. I...I really thought we were going to make a go of it."

Rex had been staring vaguely at the floor, but he suddenly lifted his head and looked Craig in the eyes. "I have only one thing to say." He didn't say anything for a moment. Then, looking back down, he murmured, "Thank you." Forcing himself to establish eye contact, Rex displayed the depth of character that had endeared him to Craig so long ago. "It may be over, but I don't regret a minute of it. This has been the greatest time of my life. I'm proud to have been a part of it." He couldn't take the eye contact any longer but instead gave Craig a manly hug. "You know what? Given the chance, I'd do it all again."

Rex started to leave but turned around before reaching the door. "You remember watching cartoons when you were a kid?"

"Sure," Craig smiled.

"Ol' Wile E. Coyote got hammered every time he tried to catch the Roadrunner, didn't he?"

"Yeah, he sure did."

"Well think about this. No matter how deep he cratered into the canyon floor, he was always back the next Saturday morning."

Be strong and of good courage, for you must go with your people to the promised land—Moses

CORPORATE POVERTY

"Listen Craig," Dean said, "I'm not suggesting we're going to get a loan from somebody that's got 'Bank of...' in their name. The guys that provide loans like these go by a different name...."

"Yeah," Rex reminded him, "they're called loan sharks."

"Okay, guys, have your fun. But I want you to apologize when ol' Dean comes through with the dough-re-me."

"Rex, Dean's right. There're four or five outfits that can provide a two-million-dollar, ninety-day swing loan for us. 'Course, they'll take their pound of flesh, high rates plus warrants."

"Are you sure this is our only option?" Rex asked. "I don't think much of borrowing money, and I know you don't either."

"While I don't like debt," Craig said," the idea of telling Paul Allen and our union buddies that we're toes up...well, I like *that* a whole lot less."

"Actually, raising capital *could* be just a matter of semantics, guys." Johnson loved words; they were his hobby. "We could raise some dough by *borrowing* it from investors. Our 'lenders' could have the option of being paid back in stock after the SEC restrictions are lifted."

"Gordon Conover pledged to raise $10 million when Robbie Stephens pulled the plug, did he not?" Rex thought out loud.

"But now," Dean concluded, "he can jolly well follow through on his promise with private loans, convertible into equity."

"That would certainly be a good place to start."

"Actually," Rex said softly, "we need to start closer to home." He looked at Craig and swallowed. "Count me in for a quarter million."

Craig was suddenly overcome with half a dozen emotions—gratitude, thankfulness, pride that he had chosen a friend and partner who would stay the course. "Rex," he said, "I don't know what to say."

"Say you'll top it, stupid."

"Yes," Craig laughed. "Count me in for three hundred thousand."

"I'm in for another hundred grand," Dean shot back.

"Now, if we can just get people to follow our lead," Craig mused, "and if we cut expenses to the bone, we might just survive our own funeral."

Rex smiled. "We'll get that Roadrunner yet, Wile E."

❧

FAIR'S FAIR. These company-wide parking lot meetings had always been used to deliver good news, rally the troops, and bring the team up to speed on our progress. Now that there was bad news to deliver, Craig chose the same forum. Mass email was just too cold, too impersonal, too *chicken hearted*. So here we were, not twenty-four hours after our intrepid trio had been cut off at the knees, standing in the parking lot behind 2340, listening to Craig explain what had happened.

He didn't sugarcoat it. He made it clear we were in deep trouble. Not one company in a bazillion recovered from a failed IPO, but we were going to do it or die trying. He explained the impossible market conditions and the fact that there had been no new IPOs for a record-setting twenty-seven straight days. He told us we'd have to tighten our belts, and that we would all have to accomplish more with less than ever before if we wished to survive. Craig went on to share that our lead investment banker, Robertson Stephens, had unilaterally made the call to pull the offering but had also been sufficiently encouraged by our performance on the aborted road show to state their willingness, publicly, to take us back out when the market recovered.

The SEC precluded companies in our pickle from accepting conventional investments, he explained. We were looking to borrow money from whomever would be willing to loan it to us. It was risky business, he said. He wanted to make that very clear. On the other hand, we had the business plan, the people, and the motivation to make it, if anybody did. Then Craig announced that he and Rex Scatena had loaned the company money. Their loans were unsecured and repayable as cash or stock at the lender's option, just as others would be. If any of us, he concluded, would like to follow their example, his door would be open.

♋❧

IT WASN'T THAT Craig was omniscient. But he had had a bad feeling about the NEC deal from the beginning, and now he wished he had stopped it when he'd had the chance. The NEC notebook computers we had committed to sell were by anyone's standards expensive, and Craig had smelled trouble. But Glenda had brushed off his trepidations, assuring him that we hadn't made any guarantees, and if the NECs didn't sell, the distributor, Tech Data, would sell them elsewhere. "Get it in writing," Craig had warned. Glenda hadn't. Tech Data wouldn't.

The NEC deal had brought another top tech distributor into the fold, which was a good thing. But the letter of credit we'd had to issue guarantying the transaction was tying up $1.5 million, money that was now a life-or-death matter to us. It didn't help when Glenda tried to shift the blame to Kim DeJong. Craig was finding Ms. Dorchak's excuses increasingly hard to swallow.

Not everything was Glenda's fault, of course. Much of the collateral we'd had to post as a private company was scheduled to be released the moment we were public. It couldn't come a moment too soon. Our neighborhood bank, Jefferson National, with whom we had negotiated a merchant account, had been gobbled up by a larger institution, Wachovia Bank. Johnson pointed out to Craig that our historic product return rate had been far below the originally estimated level, minimizing the bank's exposure. To free up badly needed capital, Craig tried to renegotiate a reduction of the nearly $3 million we'd been forced to put up in collateral, but without success. His requests were met with intransigence at every level, all the way up to the bank's president.

Since they obviously didn't care if our company sank, Craig thought, why should they continue to enjoy our business in the unlikely event we managed to stay afloat. He heatedly told the bank's top executive, "I can assure you that if we save this company—and we *will* save it—we will do everything we can to part company with you." Revenge: one more motivation for staying alive.

Justin Caise jumped into the fray as well. He begged the SEC for mercy. Amazingly enough, his pleas fell on sympathetic ears. Since it had been market conditions that had derailed our IPO at the last minute, the SEC gave us a break. They said we need wait only sixty days before raising private equity capital—they knocked four months off the normal requirement. Pretty nice, we thought.

We didn't have enough unrestricted cash to last sixty days, of course, but certain death had been transformed into mere probable death. Familiar territory.

"PERFECT TIME TO fire her," Rex told Craig. "The IPO is history. Let's dump her before she can do any more damage."

Craig sighed deeply. He wanted desperately to see Dorchak gone, but....

"We can't do it, Rex. Not now, anyway. It's going to take everything we've got to pull this off. Dean with the lenders, you with the friends of the company, and me with the union and Paul Allen. I can't even imagine a worse situation. If you think it was hard managing the last two rounds, fasten your seat belt. This ride's really gonna get rough."

"Guess you're right."

"Look, right now, we have one job to do: find money. If we don't do that, it's all over, no matter what. If we fire Glenda now, we'll have to beat the bushes trying to find someone to replace her—and who'd take the job now that we're running on fumes? We don't have time for it. Besides, I'm not entirely convinced that what she wanted—centralized control—is a bad thing, although I hate what she did to get it."

Rex reflected on the ramifications, shaking his head. "We aren't in the Attic anymore, are we?"

"No, friend, we're not." Craig was thinking of the two hundred families who now depended on Value America for their livelihood, for their mortgages and bills. And then there were many hundreds of brands that had believed in the mission we shared, paying to partner with us. We owed it to them to stay the course, to focus on the task at hand. "It's not that I don't want to axe her, Rex, but if we fail, she's gone anyway, just like the rest of us."

❧⋅❦

ONE BY ONE they came, poked their heads through Craig's office door, and said silly things like, "Are you busy?"

Phil Ramsey plunked himself down in a chair opposite Craig's desk and launched into a folksy, long-winded explanation of why he had come to work for Value America. It wasn't that he needed the paycheck, he said. He craved the action, to be doing something *worth* doing, something he was really good at. But he wasn't there to tell a story. He was the first stone in an avalanche.

Phil wanted to loan the company $80,000. Karen Wiles and Erik Taylor from finance came in and offered substantial amounts. Joe Page and Bill Poletti from tech, Andy Rod in business development, Kim DeJong and Steve Sabatini from the business to business division, Derick Roberts, who did the heavy lifting for Glenda in the ad purchasing world. They stepped forward like an army to show their support and, more to the point, loan the company the funds we'd need to survive.

Craig had mixed feelings. He had invested more of his own money, as had Rex, over a half a million between them; that would not have surprised anyone. But we were standing about three inches from the edge of the abyss. He knew that panic was contagious, and that having to share your office with the grim reaper tended to be bad for morale. It was hard for people to do their jobs when all they could think about was polishing their resumes. Yet he was amazed at how quickly and unhesitatingly the good people of Value America rose to the occasion. And as they did, we moved back from the precipice, step by step, until our survival seemed more likely than not.

Only when they had reached that "confidential divide," that mental Rubicon of confidence that separated desperation from determination, did Craig, Rex, and Dean feel they could approach the friends of the company.

These friends, who in the past had been supportive of Value America, were now in a position to save her. They began making the calls.

Raising money was part of the solution; conserving it was even more critical. Rex suggested a hiring freeze.

"Yes," Craig agreed. "But there are two areas where a freeze doesn't make any sense."

"Technology, of course," Rex offered.

"Right. Every technologist we hire replaces a far more expensive consultant. That's simple math. We should continue hiring merchandisers too. They pay their own way with presentation revenues. The more good merchandisers we get, the more money we bring in, the better store we build and the more brand partners we have in our corner."

"Nobody's going to give us money if we're not squeezing every dollar 'til the Presidents wince," Rex recognized.

"True. Value Land is about to become fat free."

ഏ:ര

CRAIG CAUGHT UP with Rafe Durn in his Washington, D.C. office. He took the news remarkably well. Maybe he didn't realize just how poor the odds were against getting a second chance at an IPO.

"Craig," he said, "if *you* couldn't get it done, nobody could have. The papers are calling this the worst IPO market in three decades. Just rotten timing, that's all."

"I appreciate your support, Rafe."

"I have faith in you," the unions' pension fund manager assured him. "I have no doubt that you'll get Value America public as soon as conditions allow, hopefully as early as November."

"I hope so. The trick's staying afloat until we do. We were counting on the IPO, so without it we're running on fumes. If we want to go public we're going to have to drive revenues, and that means advertising. With the holiday season upon us and precious little money available, we're going to have to make every penny count."

"I assume you've put together a new budget?"

"Of course. First thing we did."

"Good."

"No, not really, the picture's pretty bleak. We need dough, Rafe."

"I'm not surprised." Rafe responded in a way that indicated he might help.

"As I'm sure you've heard, SEC rules say we can't raise any private equity for two months—actually, the rules say six, but they've given us a special dispensation. Dean is trying to arrange a loan. Our covenants with you on Series A require your approval. I assume we have it. In fact, I was hoping you'd want to participate."

"Maybe."

Craig told him of the heroic actions of the employees and friends of the company. He explained some of the new fiscal restraints he had imposed. He shared his plan for a selective hiring freeze. He wanted to assure Rafe he wouldn't be throwing good money after bad.

"Tell you what, Craig. I'm in. I'll raise another five million."

Durn was as good as his word. Before the day was out, he had called Craig back with a proposition. As usual, it was good news, bad news. ULIC would come up with some; the rest would come from Rafe's friends. But all of it would come with some serious strings attached.

"Okay, Craig," Rafe said. "We'll commit to raising five million to get Value America over the hump: two million will come from our own coffers, and we'll also raise another three from other sources. This'll have to be a convertible deal. It needs to be done at a level above the last round's valuation, which was three hundred million. There's no going backwards. So we're going to need some warrants to sweeten the pot."

Craig found himself back in Wonderland, having a pleasant chat with the March Hare. The average company, upon failing an IPO, would be expected to dissolve, close the doors, and fade into oblivion. We, on the other hand, had to find a way to plausibly say we were worth even more than before.

"I think we can get that done, Rafe," Craig said. "We're going to need more stock if the loans convert to equity. If we use the same ten-dollar-a-share price we used in the Series B Paul Allen round, then we're there. Say we go from thirty-five to forty million shares; even at the same price per share, the elevated number of shares creates a four hundred million dollar valuation."

"Perfect," said Rafe. "We can't look like we're losing ground."

"No, of course not."

"Now," Rafe cautioned, "I have to impose a few conditions. I'm sure you'll understand."

"I'd expect nothing less." Craig was willing to endure the inevitable.

Durn proceeded to codify the efforts we had already made, building them into his proposal as conditions to be met. He turned good-faith commitments into contractual obligations. It saddened Craig to witness the process, but he reminded himself that as difficult as Rafe Durn could be, he'd always kept his word, always come through when the chips were down. All things considered, he was an ally worth having.

"We have no intention of going down this road by ourselves," Rafe said. "So we're going to stipulate that Rex's and your five hundred fifty grand stays in until we're over the hump—having 'skin in the game,' I think you call it."

"That was our intent, Rafe."

"We'll expect you to raise another half a million from Value America's employees."

"That's not our commitment, it's *their* commitment, and it's an incredibly noble endorsement from the very people who've built the company. But they've already *made* it, as in past tense."

"Good. And you'll raise another million from friends of the company."

"Rex is handling that, but I think he's *already* received commitments for more than that."

"We just want to make sure that there are a lot of people besides ourselves committed to your success."

"Of course, Rafe. We may be about out of money, but we're not out of friends. What else?"

"The hiring freeze. You've been hiring people like there's no tomorrow, and if you continue, there won't be."

A total hiring freeze would compromise our ability to diminish development costs. "If we can exempt the Tech department and Merchandising from the freeze, it would make better financial sense."

"Forget it. The hiring freeze is total, or there's no deal."

Craig sighed. If only the man would listen.

CRAIG AGONIZED OVER the severity of our belt-tightening. He would have to make it painfully clear to everyone that we were going to have to choose our battles. He went over his budget with a fine-toothed comb, cutting here, snipping there, holding the line in this other place. We had reverted to survival mode. He went back to simple cost-based accounting, using a pad of paper, pencil, and a calculator. He agonized over his new, lean budget, for it was to be our map out of corporate purgatory.

Our biggest single budget item, not surprisingly, was advertising. Most was spent on newspaper ads, in over twenty major metropolitan areas. Phil Ramsey was also doing award-winning ads for radio and television.

Craig called Glenda into his office. Rex and Dean were already there, poring over the details of the skinny new plan. As she sat with the others at the old maple table, Craig slipped her a hand-written rundown of her new spending parameters.

"Read it and weep," he said. "Poverty sucks. Until we can raise some serious capital and take this company public, we have to cut expenditures. All of 'em."

Glenda peered at the sheet. Her jaw dropped.

"I know this represents a serious reduction to your ad budget," Craig proclaimed, "but it can't be helped. With our new reality, we can only spend a million dollars a month." If all went well and we succeeded in raising capital, Craig projected investing another $4 million in December to boost Christmas sales, for a total of $6 million for the quarter. Corporate poverty was no more fun than any other kind.

The newly anointed "President" was incredulous. "There's no way I can stretch it this thin," she said. "If we expect to come anywhere near our revenue projections...."

Craig cut her short. "The revenue projections are out the window. We just finished a fifteen-million-dollar quarter; I'd be ecstatic with ten in Q4. That's what I've told the analysts to expect. But even that is going to take a miracle. Point is, that's all we've got to spend. Invest it wisely. Drive as much revenue as you can. But whatever you do, don't go over budget!"

Glenda frowned at the pitiful numbers. "I understand," was all she said. *I understand I'm getting the shaft from this two-bit dreamer with his handwritten joke of a budget. He can't treat me like this.*

ക്കരു

PHIL RAMSEY KNEW the business side of advertising better than anyone in the company, having run his own agency, and this didn't look right to him. Glenda had personally scheduled a series of two-page ads in *Business Week*, and Phil had half a dozen serious issues with that decision.

First, our experience with magazine ads had been disastrous. Their production lead times were so far out, any price-driven product offerings were likely to have disappeared by the time the magazine hit the stands, causing confusion, bad feelings, and accusations of bait-and-switch tactics. Our magazine ads were a colossal waste of money.

Second, *Business Week* was all wrong. Not only did its demographics mesh poorly with ours, it was far from the best choice among its genre. *Fortune,* perhaps, thought Phil, maybe even *Forbes*. Not *Business Week*. They had all the credibility of a supermarket tabloid.

Another thing that rankled Phil was that Glenda had gone outside approved channels to buy the space. She had a friend at *Business Week* from her days at IBM and had done the deal directly with her. Phil had developed a unique and profitable relationship with Stevens, Reid, Curcio, through whom all our ads, according to our contract, were supposed to be placed. SRC was furious. They had concluded we were cheating on our agreements. Fact is, we were.

Phil asked SRC to determine how much the space would cost if they were running the ads in accordance with our contract. When they ran the numbers, it turned out that Glenda was paying double what our agency could have bought them for. We had a problem.

Since his own money was now on the line, Phil was incensed. (Actually, he would have been anyway.) He stormed into Glenda's office, without an appointment (horrors!), and demanded to know what the hell she was up to, or words to that effect.

Glenda merely smiled condescendingly and told Phil not to worry about her *Business Week* indulgence. It was none of his business, she said. She had her own reasons, and he needn't bother himself trying to understand.

For some reason, Phil Ramsey never really trusted Ms. D after that.

ജ്യൂ

TROUBLES OR NO TROUBLES, Craig couldn't say no to this one. It was a black-tie dinner on the floor of the New York Stock Exchange. The event's host, *Chief Executive* magazine, had invited him. Intel's Andy Grove would be there. So would the CEOs of many of America's most powerful and innovative companies.

Craig found himself chatting with Jack Welch, the CEO of GE, about our collaborative efforts to e-commerce-enable GE Information Systems' EDI software. Jack was well versed on our progress. He told Craig that the Value America model had made quite an impression on his team. The door was open for a future alliance, assuming, of course, there would be a future.

Craig greeted his new friend Andy Grove as if they'd known each other for years. Andy spoke first, "I read about your IPO in *The Journal*. Sorry, rough timing."

"Yeah. They're calling it the worst IPO market since, well..." Craig looked around, "since this place crashed back in '29."

"Right," Andy agreed. "How are you doing, my friend? Are you okay?"

"I'm doing fine, Andy. We'll figure something out." His stiff upper lip didn't fool anybody. Craig was hurting, and it showed, but he realized that depression is seldom endearing, especially to successful men. Besides, Craig wasn't interested in pity.

"Well, hang in there. Keep your chin up. You'll come through this."

As they sat down to dinner, Craig was dying inside. Not only had he lied to Andy, he had lied to himself. He wasn't fine, not even remotely. A great man had made himself accessible. He'd reached out expecting, deserving, a straight answer, and Craig had come back with a flippant platitude. He felt awful.

Eventually, Andy got up to stretch his legs, and Craig caught up with him. "I lied to you, Andy," he blurted out. "You asked me how I was doing, and I didn't tell you the truth."

"I know," Grove answered softly. "I knew it at the time. You wear your emotions openly. But I admire you for being able to say it now."

"Truth is, I'm worried and scared. I don't know if we're going to make it."

"Let's take a little walk, shall we?" As they slowly strolled, Andy related a little of his personal history. "I met Michael Dell when he had less going for him than you do now. His idea wasn't as strong as yours, and yet look how far he's come. I also met the guys at Compaq way back when they were smaller than Value America is today. Good company, but their potential wasn't half of what yours is. I believe in you and in your company, Craig. You're going to survive and be stronger for it. I'm convinced of that. If you need anything, anything at all, you call me. I'll be there for you." When a man of Grove's character and substance talks to you like that, it's hard to know what to say.

৶৽৶

SKIP DIDN'T WANT to cater this particular lunch. He'd do it, because Craig and Rex had befriended him, supporting his restaurant, but he hated the idea. After all, Skip was openly gay, something that didn't seem to bother Craig, but Craig's guest today was going to be Jerry Falwell.

Our introduction to the famous television evangelist had been arranged through InService, a Lynchburg-based company that had been instrumental in helping us build Demand Alliances—mutually beneficial arrangements with organizations like charities, educational institutions, and faith groups like Falwell's. Supporters of Falwell's Liberty University, for example, could make an automatic donation to the school simply by shopping at a special Value America custom store we'd create for them.

Craig had offered to meet Jerry on his turf in Lynchburg, an hour or so south of Charlottesville, but Falwell insisted on making the trek himself. He arrived in his Chevy Suburban, just like Craig's, and found his way to the CEO's office. As the two visionaries sat and talked around

Winn's little hundred-year-old table, Crystal, Craig's yellow Labrador, who still came to work with her master every day, got up from her customary spot by his desk, ambled to the table, and plunked herself down on Jerry's feet. He smiled, reached down, and gave her a pat.

"She likes you," Craig said. "She's a good judge of character."

"I like her too," Jerry laughed, "and you, your company, everything you've built here, your whole demand-alliance concept. Remarkable, especially your ability to create custom marketplaces. Your corporate heart really impresses me. The fact that you've made it a priority to help charities, universities, and faith groups like ours is amazing…especially for a businessman."

Craig explained that the idea of giving something back with every sale wasn't an "add-on" to the plan. It had been part of Value America's fabric from the very beginning. As they talked, Falwell became convinced that his ministries and university should be working with us. But Craig cautioned him to move slowly. He wanted Falwell to understand the ins and outs of how it all worked before he committed.

"You couldn't cheat me if your life depended on it, Craig," Falwell said. "I'm a pretty good judge of character myself. I believe you've been called to achieve something remarkable. I believe God has something very special planned for your life."

Jerry Falwell, this larger-than-life man of God, had achieved so much, Craig reflected. Yet the media had unfairly tarred him with the same brush as his failed televangelist colleagues. Through it all, Jerry had remained faithful to his God and his mission. To hear such prognostications from this man's lips was humbling. Craig did not feel worthy.

As mid-day approached, Craig said, "I realize that it's probably hard for you to eat out at restaurants without being bothered all the time, the curse of celebrity and all, so if it's alright, I've arranged to have lunch catered at my home."

"Wonderful," Jerry said.

Everyone "knows" that Jerry Falwell is anti-gay. It's all the media seems to be able to say about him. But he's not, really. He's not particularly anti-anything. He isn't any more preoccupied with homosexuality than he is with anything else the Bible describes as sin (like envy, pride, greed, adultery, or gossip, for instance), but truth doesn't sell newspapers, scandals do. "Homo-phobia," is juicy stuff. No wonder the poor caterer was uncomfortable.

As Craig learned that morning, Falwell seems to love everybody, making it his goal to hate sin while loving sinners, judging no one because we all fall short. As Skip served the small party an excellent lunch in the

Winns' elegant dining room, Jerry engaged him in conversation, listened to what he had to say, learned all about his life, his beliefs, his attitudes. As they ended the meal, Jerry went to the kitchen, shook Skip's hand, and congratulated him on a fine meal. He gave him a hug and said he'd like to visit Skip's restaurant the next time he came to town.

By the time they were getting ready to return to the office, Skip was almost in tears. "I can't believe it. I completely misjudged him," he said.

Craig smiled. *There's a lesson worth learning,* he thought. *You can't necessarily believe what you read about a guy.*

☙❧

"WELCOME BACK. How was Atlanta?"

"Hot," Craig answered.

"I'll bet it wasn't as hot as the steam under your collar when you read *The Post* article," Rex guessed, gesturing at the paper in Craig's hand.

"Well, at least we're getting some ink," Craig said bitterly as he tossed his *Washington Post* on the desk. "The article trashes us, gets the facts wrong, and generally misses the whole point. But at least they spelled our name right."

"Nobody in the media seems to get it, do they?" Rex commiserated. "They love trashing companies, even if they have to make up the facts. Like the *Journal* article that came out announcing we'd postponed the IPO. The first part was accurate, but that one paragraph...."

Craig remembered it well. Lifted right out of the risk factors, it had said "Value America, in its filing, acknowledged that it faces development hurdles. The company cited constraints in its customer service capacity and...said that its electronic order systems aren't yet fully in place."

"Can you believe it?" Rex questioned. "They report that our electronic order systems, that would be EDI of course, 'aren't yet in place.' Yet they don't mention that the same document said, 'Value America's systems were 97% EDI enabled.' That's better than most retailers that have been in business for decades. It's so misleading. Why do they do that?"

"Fun with statistics," Craig said. "They regurgitated our red herring's risk factors like there was something unique about them, 'cause they fit the story they wanted to write. The facts were readily apparent, but *they* didn't fit their story, so they ignored them. Investigative journalism died a long time ago."

"Sure did," Rex agreed. "The one thing in the risk factors that's worth reporting—the Paul Allen 'warning'—they missed. And the reportable condition was fixed six months ago, but they didn't report that either.

Doesn't do us any good to bellyache, though. How did your visit go with the IBM team in Atlanta?"

"Great, but nothing like I'd planned. The guy I was supposed to meet called in sick just as we landed. Boy, that's a long flight in a 206. I like flying, but sitting in a tin can for four hours gets old."

"You were supposed to meet with their top education guy, right?" Rex asked. "To help us with our custom store for American School Supply...."

"Right, but we hit the jackpot instead. I met a guy named Dave Boucher. We talked about IBM shipping our customers directly, you know, using Value America to help IBM compete against Dell. The Dynasty lessons really paid off, Rex."

"Told ya."

"We talked about distribution, inventory management, bills of material, component constraints, build-to-order *versus* build-to-ship. I earned his confidence because I was able to speak the same language. It's amazing how a common appreciation of the details can help people frame an issue, form bonds of trust, even help resolve nagging problems. It was great. The guy's a 'ten.' You'd love him, Rex. We finally found an IBMer we can work with."

Some time later, Dave Boucher, one of IBM's most lauded senior executives, would tell the press: "I recall Winn flew down to our Atlanta offices to meet with someone that had, unfortunately, called in sick. I went in to say hello as a courtesy. But he was armed with a laptop presentation and a hell of a sales pitch. What I thought would be a five-minute in-and-out turned into four hours. We sat in one of our conference rooms talking about all manner of things. Based upon Winn's presentation, we signed an agreement with him to ship IBM PCs directly to Value America's customers, the only such agreement in IBM history. I see the partnership as a wedge for IBM to gain market share against online competitors like Dell. [The Value America team] were pioneers. I think they've helped us blaze a new trail."

∽◦∾

DEAN SAT BACK in his chair, his feet propped up on the only unoccupied corner of his paper-strewn desk. Craig knocked on his door and entered, not waiting for a response. Johnson appeared to be talking to himself, but closer examination revealed that he was having a phone conversation using a lightweight headset, ostensibly so he could shuffle through the stuff on his desk and take notes while he talked. Craig figured he used it so he could talk with his hands when he got excited.

As he hung up, Dean grinned at Craig and shook his head. "I wouldn't have believed this a week ago. So many people have come forward saying they want to invest, it's just amazing. You've got to give the Vice Chairman credit. Ol' Rexy-boy really came through for us. If Robertson Stephens is true to their word and the IPO gets back on track in a month or two, we're going to make it. I've got that two-million-dollar swing loan nailed, by the way. And you guys were laughing at me."

"Dean, you're the best," Craig replied. "You and Rex have given us some breathing room."

"My pleasure."

"Tell me about the loan."

"Short fuse. We have to pay them back in December, and the interest rate's high, but less than I thought. Like you said, it's like going to Guido. Not a lot of fun."

"The things we do when our backs are up against the wall. Thankfully, we're not without friends, though."

"No, we're not. Ray Kennedy from Masco is coming in with three hundred grand, and his three sons are putting in ten thousand apiece. John Motley is helping out to the tune of a hundred and fifty thousand, Justin Caise says he's in for two hundred and, if you can believe it, even Seth Rossi has said he's going to invest three hundred thousand."

Craig picked up on the theme. "There are a ton of suppliers who want to be part of this too—not the companies, their founders and senior managers, the guys we've been working with. HP, Fellows, Avery, IBM, Targus.... Ram Golf's CEO is in for a quarter of a million. Even Mike Jefferies, the founder of *Office Products International*, the magazine, is in for a quarter mil."

"The response from the company's management has been almost universal," Dean said. "It's got to make you feel good when your *employees* invest over a million dollars in your company. Especially after a failed IPO. Their support speaks louder than words."

"It's humbling, Dean. Heck, even my dentist wants to be included." Craig paused and took a deep breath. "Of all our senior executives, there's only one who didn't step up."

"Glenda Dorchak," guessed Dean.

"Right you are," Craig said. "Big surprise."

A bit later, the *real* surprise would be announced: "Fifty million dollars this time." Frank Flowers' news took Craig's breath away. Another investment from Paul Allen's Vulcan Ventures, especially one of this magnitude, would save the company—again—and make it possible to operate for whatever time was needed to resurrect the IPO. Craig immersed himself in the irony of the thing: fifty million was more money than we'd hoped to raise in the failed IPO.

"You'll need to come up to Seattle again and give Paul an update, show him the progress you've made. I don't anticipate any problems though. You've done what you said you were going to do. Paul and I respect that," Flowers concluded.

∞:∞

GLENDA, STILL FUMING over being told to cut the advertising budget, decided to solidify her position by writing a letter to each Value America board member outlining her early "achievements." They were, in her eyes, quite remarkable, considering the short time she'd been with the company.

So Caise, Motley, and Durn, along with Craig, Rex, and Dean, were regaled with a rundown of Dorchak's accomplishments. She had shortened shipping lead times significantly, she reported. She had molded the company into a cohesive whole by introducing horizontal process into its operation. She had introduced a new advertising style, designed to increase revenue by presenting more products per ad, a far more efficient plan than the brand-centered foolishness in which we had indulged to this point. Now, because of her brilliant leadership, the company was moving forward into a bright future, free of the chaotic atmosphere that had held us back. The company was at last in good hands. Hers.

Craig thought he was going to puke. Much of what she said she'd done was fabricated; the rest was worthless. Her "process" concept was being achieved at the expense of progress—tying up scores of people in useless three-hour meetings each and every day. Her "brilliant new ad concept" came at the expense of a format and philosophy that had endeared us to hundreds of major brands, had sold millions of dollars of merchandise, and had been acclaimed in the top echelons of the ad world. In two short months, we had "progressed" from raising the bar, from being the envy and inspiration of other retailers, to being a laughingstock.

Winn was livid as he stormed into her office past her wide-eyed secretary, shutting the door behind him. He told her in no uncertain terms to can the political positioning games, to stop undermining everything that had been achieved by others, and to just *do her damn job*. "...And don't you *ever* go to the board again," he seethed. "If you do—you're toast!"

What Glenda hadn't said in the letter was that she had decided to completely disregard the new ad budget. Now that she was in charge, she was determined to top that $15 million Q3 revenue number the entrepreneurs had achieved. The easiest way to do that was to place ads, lots of them.

Her first quarter managing the company would show *progress*. She was going to show the world what she could do, whatever the cost.

৯ৄৣ৶

THE ORIGINAL IDEA was simple enough. Merge an Internet portal with an e-commerce company, so people could shop online in the obvious place—the site they first visited when going online. This one, though, had a fascinating wrinkle. The portal was owned by the one of the biggest computer companies on earth.

Nate Gould was an investment banker and a friend of Mr. Eckhart Pfeiffer, CEO of Compaq. Gould called Craig, introduced himself, and related the story of how Pfeiffer was trying to merge his Web portal, AltaVista, with Shopping.com, an e-commerce solution that, in theory, competed with Value America. They were having a bit of trouble, however, with the due diligence. Craig was not surprised: Shopping.com was a hastily thrown together "picture-bullets-price" sort of website with no brand relationships, no product information, and no sales to speak of. Shopping.com was to Value America as paper plates were to fine china— same basic function, but worlds apart in execution, style, and scale.

Would Craig be interested in talking, Nate wanted to know. *Sure.* Craig is always interested in talking, even if he has no idea where the discussion will lead. But as Gould would soon discover, Winn is not what most people would call a "good listener." He'll keep hammering away until he either knows exactly what the speaker is trying to say or becomes convinced they don't know what they're talking about. A conversation with Craig Winn can be quite an experience.

Glenda correctly assumed that if Compaq acquired Value America and merged it with AltaVista, she'd be out of a job. Day after day she came into Craig's office in tears over the prospect. She had done so much, in her mind, to better herself—I mean the company—during her three-month career. "It just wasn't fair," she cried. Craig counseled Glenda. They spoke often and openly about her insecurities. He shared his experiences with other insecure people, trying to help Glenda better understand her problem. It did no good. She did everything she could to thwart the deal, surreptitiously casting aspersions on our firm.

Yet Compaq must have been more impressed with the opportunity than they were unimpressed with Dorchak. They dispatched Gould and some Compaq executives to Charlottesville to see our operation, meet Craig and Rex, and explain what it was they were trying to achieve.

After letting them fumble around for a while, Craig suggested, "What you want to create is a comprehensive closed-loop Internet solution, a union of all the disciplines that could benefit from an online alliance. You start by making a computer that has a special button taking you directly to AltaVista, your portal. The portal has a built-in shopping engine— Value America—and you make a percentage of every sale because you own the shopping vehicle. You highlight presentations that show the business and consumer solutions made by Compaq, so you've got a head start there too. At the same time, you have your own ISP, and you get a percentage of that. So it's a closed-loop environment with all the basic Internet services provided—simple, comprehensive, profitable."

"Well," they said, "we hadn't really thought about it in those terms, but yes, that's exactly what we want! Would you mind repeating what you just said, a little slower this time so we can write it down?"

Somehow it had happened again. Compaq's simple merger idea had become, in Winn's fertile mind, the basis of a whole new paradigm. Craig took the floor and proceeded to improvise. "Gentlemen, you're all familiar with the Internet's hot programming language, JAVA. I would like to propose "CAVA," Compaq, AltaVista, and Value America, the world's first comprehensive Internet solution. In it, the best companies are brought together to serve their customers. It would start with the computer hardware, from Compaq. Dedicated buttons on the keyboard would take people directly to AltaVista and Value America. But it doesn't stop there."

Craig now had them on the edges of their chairs. "Convergence technologies from the likes of AT&T should be built in. I recently spent some time with Michael Armstrong, the CEO of AT&T, at 'Camelot,' the Kennedy compound in Palm Beach. His plan to converge telephone, cable, cellular, and Internet technologies is perfect for this.

"An alliance with a top freight company would help too; UPS perhaps, or better yet, Federal Express. The company that delivers the product you buy, from the store we own, operating on the machines you build are all part of the same team—a giant electronic *keiretsu*.

"Each company spends hundreds of millions attracting new customers and even more retaining the ones they've got. Working together we'd reduce each company's advertising expense, diminish churn, and pass some of the savings on to the customer. Everybody wins. Best of all, nobody has to do anything differently than they're doing now. We just work together. Serving customers and improving their lives—that's CAVA."

Wow. You could see it on their faces. "A financial partner would also be valuable. CAVA should provide its own credit card and financing options. We could capitalize on our relationship with MBNA. Serving their customers would be a virtual gold mine. We'd know where to find them, know what they like, and know they have money—electronic money."

As Craig wove the CAVA tapestry, a pattern began to emerge. His audience began to grasp the beauty of it all: a symbiotic alliance of companies, all doing what they did best, all working together to provide the ultimate Internet solution. The Compaq execs moved from interest to excitement, unable to scribble their notes fast enough to keep up. They asked Craig to write a proposal for CAVA.

Nate Gould, as enthusiastic as the others, spoke of Pfeiffer's desire to take the newly merged company public at the end of the first quarter of '99. AltaVista would be, according to Wall Street metrics, worth $1.2 billion by that time. Craig, knowing there was little substance backing the valuation of this or any other Internet portal, told Nate that Value America would be worth the same amount. "I won't quibble with you whether or not AltaVista is overpriced at $1.2 billion, and you won't quibble with me over a similar valuation for Value America. We're worth the same," Craig asserted. "Makes life easy. If Compaq wants to own us, the price is $1.2 billion. I'll write the business plan, manage the IPO, and do the road show, but that's the price."

"Sounds good," Gould and the Compaq team responded. "We'll set up a meeting between you and Pfeiffer early next week. But we've got to get the due diligence done *now*, over the weekend." So for forty-eight blistering hours, they investigated everything one could imagine. Unlike Shopping.com, however, Value America was given a clean bill of health. So far, so good.

Gould arranged to pick up Craig and company at Charlottesville's little airport in his own Citation 10 corporate jet—the only such machine capable of traveling near the speed of sound. With Nate at the controls and Craig in the co-pilot's seat, the group flew to White Plains, New York, where they changed planes. This time it was an amphibious Cessna 208 Caravan on floats, which Nate landed flawlessly in the Hudson River. A limo picked them up at the dock and took them to Gould's office for a planning session.

Gould and team Value America soon found themselves headed for Texas, again in the Citation 10. The response to CAVA had been universally positive, but in the end, only Eckhart Pfeiffer's opinions carried any weight.

Craig found the Compaq CEO to be cold and overly structured, the worst sort of Germanic stereotype. He came to the conclusion that there was no way Pfeiffer's ego would allow a partnership. Pfeiffer was a dictator. Craig knew that as a dot-com company, CAVA could prevail only if it were free to move at the speed of the Internet. We would fail if we were tied to the directives of a huge, bureaucratic manufacturing entity like Compaq. Pfeiffer didn't buy it. CAVA was stillborn.

This wasn't Pfeiffer's first failed merger. Compaq exec's believed that the proposed Gateway-Compaq merger had been stymied for the same reason—Pfeiffer's suffocating style. The irony, however, was just beginning. Pfeiffer ended up spending $200 million for Shopping.com, which was promptly disgraced for all sorts of SEC irregularities. Pfeiffer was fired as Compaq's CEO—the same week he was featured on the cover of a national business magazine as one of the best CEOs in America.

✥

THE EBAY IPO succeeded, though its "failure" had been the primary justification for pulling our public offering off the playing field. But like the little engine that could, eBay persevered. The offering had been so grossly undervalued by its investment bankers, the price of their stock had skyrocketed in the first few days to four or five times the IPO price. This didn't do a thing for eBay's corporate finances, but it did wonders for the market. Dot-com frenzy was back.

"Let's go out now, Gordon," Craig pleaded. "The market's hot. We had a great third quarter, triple Q2. Let's do it on the strength of Q3!" He stopped short of whining *besides, you promised*.

Gordon said, "I'll see what I can arrange. Let's get Dale's input."

The phone grew heavy against Craig's ear. He must have been on hold for five minutes. This did not bode well. Finally a sheepish Gordon returned, this time with Dale. "No, I don't think we should go out now," chided a reluctant Dandridge. "You need to have another strong quarter or two. Then we'll see about taking you back out."

And how are we going to do that without money and with the stigma of a failed IPO hanging around our necks? Craig wanted to scream, but he somehow found a polite way to ask the question instead.

"I can't help you with that," Dale answered. "I need for you to get a couple more quarters under your belt. Then you'll have a proven track record. Nobody will be able to say it's too early. End of March, Craig." So much for his earlier promises. *How did we get hooked up with this guy anyway?*

"There's a problem with your theory, Dale," Craig countered. "Since the IPO cratered, we're on a shoestring budget. Sure, we've got promises of big money from Paul Allen, but it's almost certain that our fourth quarter numbers are going to decrease, rather than increase—we just don't have the ad dollars to invest. I'm not an alchemist."

As before, nothing he said mattered. We were on our own. Our allies had become our adversaries. It occurred to Craig for the fiftieth time that trying to get an IPO done with Robertson Stephens was like trying to get a hyperactive four-year-old to go to bed. It was more work than it should have been.

If we were going to survive without a timely IPO, the second Paul Allen round would have to be consummated. There was no way around it. And between Frank Flowers, Rafe Durn, Seth Rossi, and an army of lawyers, Vulcan Ventures couldn't exactly be counted on to operate like an automatic teller machine. Nor could Robbie Stevens be counted on to keep their word and raise private equity for us. Not in this millennium. Once again it looked like "do or die," or at least "do or get severely pummeled."

Fortunately, Paul Allen still wanted to follow through with his huge investment proposal—$50 million, which would bring his total stake to $65 million, not exactly pocket change, even for him. Frank Flowers passed Paul's sentiments along, stating their intention to fund the round quickly this time. We gathered a team to visit the Wizard again and bring him up to speed on our progress.

So it was that Joe Page and several of our top technologists accompanied Craig to Vulcan's headquarters. Allen appeared, as usual, slightly disheveled, the very picture of the stereotypical computer genius. As Joe reported on the current capabilities of the store, Allen found himself in the surrealistic position of not recognizing his own child. He had, after all, invented the Windows NT operating system we used. But Joe Page and friends had stretched it so far beyond its normal capacity, Paul found himself shaking his head and thinking *NT can't do that*.

The same was true for Microsoft's SQL Server, which Joe had also trained to perform unheard-of feats of daring-do. Value America, just six months after our first meeting with Paul, was processing over fifteen times more revenue through its proprietary commerce engine than we'd achieved during the first visit.

As incredulous as he was that our technologists had accomplished so much with so little, Paul came to the inescapable conclusion that we wouldn't be able to expand much further using the Windows-based system. We would have to make the expensive jump from NT to Unix, from Intel to RISC, from SQL to the dreaded Oracle. And Paul Allen's money would enable us to do that. Stranger things have happened, but not many.

As he had during the first investment round with Allen, Craig asked him to visit us in Charlottesville, advise us on our systems, and provide symbiotic access to some of his other holdings. Paul wanted to do all of these things but never got around to doing any of them.

But it was appropriate to ask Frank Flowers to serve on our board at this point, taking an active role in the guidance of the company. He agreed, but the "active role" part failed to materialize. Some things never change.

And the $50 million investment? *Patience!*

The poor you will always have with you—Jesus

THE WHITE KNIGHT

reat news sometimes comes when you least expect it. Craig had been out of the office the better part of the day. By the time he returned, it was well past business hours. He slumped into his chair and punched up his phone messages. The fourth message started, "Ah, hello, Mr. Winn. This is Fred Smith of FDX Corporation in Memphis, Tennessee. I've been studying your business, and I'd like to meet you." He left a phone number.

Fred Smith, as in the founder and CEO of Federal Express? He didn't recognize the FDX moniker, but it sounded like an abbreviation. *Oh, I get it,* Craig thought, *since I've been hanging with the likes of Andy Grove, Jack Welsh, and Paul Allen, why not Fred Smith? How many times have I compared Value America to the concepts that drove FedEx? It's just a practical joke. Still...*Craig dialed the number. A woman's voice answered. "Executive offices, FDX Corporation."

"Uh, hello," Craig stammered. "I, ah, I got this phone message from Fred Smith, and this is the number he left. Is this Federal Express?"

"Yes," answered the polite but slightly amused voice. "You've called on Mr. Smith's direct line. He's not in now. May I take a message?"

"Oh, yes, please," said the slightly rattled CEO. "My name is Craig Winn, that's C-R-A-I-G W-I-N-N, from Value America. Please tell Mr. Smith that I returned his call and that I'd be pleased to meet with him."

༄•ঌ

CRAIG MISSED FRED SMITH'S return call and found himself playing telephone tag with one of the legendary figures in American business. "Hello, Craig," the second message began. "This is Fred Smith, from FDX Corporation. I've read everything I can find on your company, and I'm impressed with your business model. The way you're using technology to manage logistics and inventory is great. I've been reading about your failed IPO and thought you might need a friend about now."

"Hey Rex," Craig said. "C'mere. You've got to hear this!" Craig played the message for Rex, then for Dean.

"Uh, maybe you ought to call the man back," Rex suggested.

Craig grinned sheepishly. This time Smith was actually in his office, and the two founders had a long chat. They hit it off immediately. Fred said he viewed his "freight" company as a technology firm. Even though we were in different "businesses," both companies were engaged in using technology to compress space and shorten time—both were about bringing people and products together, he shared.

Pretty profound, Craig thought. As the conversation progressed, the brilliant mind of Fred Smith manifested itself in his ability to grasp complex details and difficult concepts quickly. Craig found that he wasn't able to finish explaining a thought without Fred comprehending it well enough to finish his sentences for him. *I've met some bright people along the way, but this fellow is flat-out amazing.*

"Let's meet," Fred proposed.

"Sure." Craig explained that he owned a Cessna 206, hoping that a common appreciation for things that fly might help cement the relationship. "I'd be pleased to fly to Memphis as soon as your schedule permits."

"Oh, there's no need for you to fly here, Craig. A 206 is a fine little plane, a real workhorse, but I've got a better ride," Fred laughed. "Actually I'm often in Charlottesville. I have a son and a daughter enrolled at UVA. I love the town. As a matter of fact, we even thought about moving our headquarters to Charlottesville."

"You're kidding."

"No. Much of what drives our business happens in Washington. It would have been convenient. Anyway, my next trip to D.C. is in four days, and I'll be coming to C'ville afterward to pick up my kids. Why don't we meet then?"

Fred asked for background material and explained that he was a voracious reader. So an information packet was prepared: our two brochures, *The Retail Revolution* and, appropriately, *It's About Time.* The executive summary was included; a list of our brand partners, almost a thousand of them by this time; a document that explained how we lowered costs while increasing revenue; frequently asked questions; and a streamlined version of the business plan, shortened for public consumption to about fifty pages. The red herring from the failed IPO completed the package. Not quite enough to make a good novel, but there was plenty to read.

Fred didn't disappoint. By the time they met, he had read—and understood—most everything. Smith had obviously earned his success. But unfortunately, Fred's hearings in Washington were running late, so he wasn't going to be able to visit our offices as planned. "Let's say hello anyway," Fred told Craig over the phone. "I'm still going to pick up my kids and fly them back to Memphis. Why don't you meet me at the FBO around nine o'clock. We'll schedule another business session."

Smith finally arrived at the General Aviation terminal in Charlottesville about five or six hours later than he'd planned. Since it was now past dinnertime, Craig brought Katharine and their two sons, now twelve and thirteen, to meet the legend. Rex and Jane came too. It turned out that the man stepping off the Challenger 604 corporate jet was a dad first, business mogul second. Fred told Craig, as he got down on one knee to greet Blake and Ryan, that the last of his ten children was about Craig's boys' age. "I named him Cannon," he noted with a twinkle in his eye, "because he was my last shot."

Craig greeted Fred's daughter and his son, Richard. Conversation then turned to the Value America materials Craig had FedExed to Smith. Fred looked Craig squarely in the eye and said, "Yours is the best damn business plan I've ever read." Since Fred's plan is considered by most to be the best ever written, the statement was shocking. So there would be no confusion, Fred added, "...even better than my own."

Craig managed to blurt out something self-deprecating, talking about the undeniably earth-shaking changes the man before him had wrought. "I don't care," Fred said with disarming simplicity. "This has more potential than anything I ever did at Federal Express."

Wanting his kids to stay engaged in the conversation, Craig responded, "Boys, do you know that Federal Express grew out of a paper Mr. Smith wrote for one of his classes at Yale?"

They didn't, of course, but Fred played along. "Yeah, my professor didn't like it very much. Gave me a 'C.'"

"So the legend is true?"

"Well, not really. I don't remember what grade I actually earned, but it wasn't a 'C.' Some reporter got it wrong, and others picked up on it, so everybody now thinks it's true. It's good for laughs."

"When can we meet again?" Craig asked as he shook Fred's hand.

"Soon. I'll call you tomorrow. My guess is that you probably need a friend, and some money, right now."

As Fred gathered his children and left the FBO, Rex turned to his partner and said, "Now there's a man we can trust."

❦

THREE FOXTROT ECHO taxied up to the terminal again. It was a little before nine o'clock on a brilliant fall morning. Craig hadn't noticed the tail designation or the purple and orange FedEx stripes on the white Challenger during the last visit.

No Chevy Suburban today. Craig picked up his jet-set friend in his Jaguar XK8 roadster. They took the back way into town, down Earlysville Road, winding through the rolling hills of Albemarle with the top down, enjoying the brisk air, the falling leaves, and the company. In less than ten minutes, they had arrived at the Yellow House. All too soon.

Craig could have shown Fred the store and its operation himself. But he didn't. He was proud of his team and as anxious for us to meet the legend as he was for the legend to meet Team Value America. So he asked the leaders of each department to prepare a presentation for Mr. Smith. This would give Fred the opportunity to ask questions of the people who were actually working out the answers. All day long, small groups trudged through Craig's office, explaining our presentations, technology, merchandising, finances, customer care, advertising, and operations.

We immediately fell behind schedule. That was because Smith, like Winn, was an active listener. Understanding, remembering, and acting upon good ideas are the three hallmarks of the active listener (as opposed to the "good," listener, who just sits there open-eared). Smith probed and questioned. He was liberal with his praise. By the end of the day, he had developed a deep understanding of what Value America was all about, from the point of view of the people who were building it. He weighed the progress we were making against the materials Craig had sent him. As the day wore on, he formulated a plan of action in his mind.

Sitting with Craig at the old drop-leaf table, Fred grew wistful. "You know something? Value America reminds me a lot of Federal Express in the early days. We were once like you are now, exciting, driven, nimble, able to implement cutting-edge ideas. We could attract the best and brightest because we were inventing a new world. Like you, we were disintermediating space and time."

Disintermediating space and time, Craig thought. *Great phrase. I'll have to use that.*

"Unfortunately, we're a victim of our own success. We've grown too big and bureaucratic to move as fast as you folks do. These days, the best we can do is partner with companies like yours. It gives our people access to those blazing new trails, those fighting tomorrow's battles. That's the reason I want Federal Express to invest in your company. By rubbing shoulders, our people will get exposed to the kind of out-of-the-box thinking that makes your company great."

Craig explained that we were putting together a "friends of the company" investment round at a valuation of $400 million, $10 a share. If the FedEx investment happened quickly, it would have to come in the form of a loan, he said, but they both knew that FDX was far too big and ponderous to get a deal done within the SEC's sixty-day moratorium. "We've also had some positive feedback from Paul Allen," Craig said. "He's expressed his desire to invest another $50 million."

"That's the number I had in mind," Fred said. "Tell you what. You aren't going to need that much from both of us before your next IPO. To his credit, Allen got here first. You should give his people the first shot at anteing up. If they want to invest $50 million, we'll come in with five. But if they want less, we'll invest fifty. How's that sound?"

Sounds like all we need now is a recipe for roadrunner fricassee.

We had come a long, long way from not being able to get the regional FedEx rep to return our phone calls. We obviously wouldn't have any problem getting Federal Express to ship our stuff now. That thought gave Craig pause. Rafe Durn, Mr. "Anything-for-the-working-guy," would doubtless have something to say about who shipped Value America's products. Teamster Union members drove UPS trucks. Non-union personnel made Federal Express deliveries, although their pilots were unionized. There was trouble brewing.

❧

THE NEXT MORNING, nothing had changed but the outlook. We were still short of money, long on friends, and uncertain how, or even if, it would all work out. Craig sat at his desk, dealing with little things like keeping the company alive. At about ten o'clock, his phone rang.

"Hello, Craig," the voice said. "My name is John Tigrett, and we're having lunch today."

Craig pulled out his calendar and saw that he was penciled in for lunch with someone, but he wasn't named Tigrett. He had never heard of John Tigrett. "Uh, my calendar begs to differ, sir," Craig replied, not knowing quite what else to say.

The voice chuckled. "Well, I'm a friend of Fred Smith, and my calendar says we're having lunch today."

"It does, does it?" Craig laughed. "Well, I see. Yes indeed. I must have been looking at the wrong date. Yes, there it is, Tigrett, lunch today—twelve o'clock."

They both laughed.

"I'm looking forward to meeting you," said the voice. "I'm at the Omni. I'll meet you there at noon? I'll be the distinguished-looking gentleman."

Intrigued, Craig dashed upstairs to Dean Johnson' office. "Ever heard of a guy named John Tigrett?"

"No. Why?"

"I'm having lunch with him today," Craig said. "He's somebody special. I could hear it in his voice. Look, could you see what you can find out about him? I'd like to know who I'm dealing with. All I know is he's a friend of Fred Smith."

"Sure," said Dean. "There's this thing I heard about called the Internet that's great for looking things up...."

About five minutes later, Dean strolled into Craig's office with a print-out in his hand. "You're not going to believe what I've found."

"Money?" Craig asked, still focused on his overwhelming priority.

"No, sorry, but I found out that Fred's friend Tigrett is one of the 20th century's most intriguing characters. Ran things at Occidental Petroleum, started a couple of successful toy ventures, ran a large bus company, was considered one of the world's foremost financiers, and he's the world's *best* negotiator. As in second to none. Oh, and he's on FedEx's board."

Craig arrived at the Omni Hotel, and Tigrett immediately walked up and introduced himself. He was indeed dashing, another larger-than-life character. John was in his mid-eighties, but the years had not blunted his mental acuity or his wit. Indeed, his stunning intellect had now been tempered with the wisdom life's experiences leave in their wake.

The two walked the short distance to the elegant Downtown Grill. Dean's quick research had revealed that Tigrett was sort of a Forrest Gump with brains—he had interacted with dozens of the century's most influential people, from Winston Churchill, Dwight Eisenhower, and Douglas MacArthur to Howard Hughes, Jimmy Hoffa, Armand Hammer, and J. Paul Getty, to the Shah of Iran, and Libya's Mu'ammar Gadhafi. He was on a first name basis with both Ronald Reagan and Leonid Brezhnev. Not many people can say that. But Tigrett didn't really want to talk about himself.

"In all the years I've known Fred Smith," he began, "I've never seen him so excited about a person or a company. You have impressed him, as has your company. I just wanted to see for myself what all the excitement is about. You know," he said with a grin, "it's not healthy to get all worked up, not at *his* advanced age." (John had to have a good quarter of a century on Fred, but no one knew for sure because John was known to lie about his age.)

"I'd be honored to share the Value America story with you, John," Craig said as they sat down to lunch, "but could you indulge my curiosity? I did a little homework, and you seem to have led a rather remarkable life. You've engaged the most fascinating people of the 20th century."

With a little goading, Craig induced John into telling the story of how he had saved Winston Churchill's life. "I was a corporal during World War II," John said. "I would get orders to go here or there, and it occurred to me that there wasn't much thought to the process. I asked around and found out that somebody in Washington was just pulling names at random out of a central file.

So the first time I got a few days leave, I bought a case of scotch and went up there. I found out who the fellow was and gave him my case of scotch. I asked him what the really good assignments were, and how a guy like me might go about getting one of them. He asked me, 'What do you like?' and I said I liked people, airplanes, seeing the world, and I think I'd make a pretty good manager. Then the guy said that a C-47 couldn't make it all the way from the States to London, so they stop for fuel in Iceland. 'If you were there,' he said, 'you'd get to meet all kinds of interesting people.' I said I'd take it. Next thing I knew, I was stationed in Reykjavik.

"I heard one day that a planeload of bigwigs was coming through, so I decided to meet it personally. And there he was, Winston Churchill himself. He asked me if there was any place a man could get a glass of scotch, a good cigar, and perhaps a shower. I told him, 'There's only one shower, and it's in my quarters. It's not very big, but you're welcome to it. I've got some scotch too, sir—my scotch is your scotch. The cigars I'll have to work on."

Tigrett was quite a storyteller. Craig was hooked. Lunch took four hours, but Craig didn't care. John Tigrett was the most inspirational and charming character he had ever met. He wanted to soak it all in, somehow hopeful that John's indomitable spirit might be contagious.

"Churchill wanted to continue his journey, but there was a big storm brewing in the North Atlantic, too big to fly around, too dangerous to fly through. I told him I wasn't going to let his plane take off that evening."

"You were a corporal, right?" Craig asked the obvious question.

"Yes. The place was crawling with four-star generals, not to mention the Prime Minister of Great Britain, who wasn't known for taking no as an answer. I told him, 'I understand our relative stature, sir, but my job is to decide which airplanes leave and which don't. Now, you can relieve me of duty, you can have me thrown in the brig, you can do pretty much whatever you like, but unless I've been relieved of duty, your plane's not taking off. Not tonight. Sir.' Churchill looked me straight in the eye, and said, 'Let's have another scotch.' I lit a fire, and we sat and talked all night. And I kept pouring the scotch—I watched Churchill drink thirteen doubles. Never phased him. Amazing. The next day, the weather cleared, and he and his entourage went on their way."

"So how did you save his life?" Craig asked.

"Another C-47 did take off that night. Somebody let it slip that the Prime Minister was flying out, and the Germans got wind of it. They shot that airplane down. The next day, it was reported in the German press that they had killed Winston Churchill—the war was as good as won.

Loose lips sink ships, the wartime phrase went. Only this time, the treachery was deflected."

John treated Craig to several other stories, including a memorable anecdote describing how he found himself in the midst of the most significant oil negotiation of the century with Mu'ammar Gadahfi's pistol pointed at his forehead. The Libyan dictator possessed, he said, a unique negotiation style. John talked about famous "rascals" he had known, like J. Paul Getty and Armand Hammer. It was clear that John loved rascals. He then said something that gave Craig pause. "Fred is a rascal, you know. Can't be trusted."

He explained the remark: "When we met, he asked me to serve on his board, and I said no. He pressed, asking me what it would take. I finally told him I'd take a pair of first class, round trip tickets to any destination in the world I'd choose. My wife and I wanted a vacation. Did I ever see those tickets? No," he said with a grin. "The man's a rascal. Be careful."

છ•ન

HAVING THE FOUNDER and CEO of a company like FedEx verbally commit to investing in a company like ours is not exactly the same thing as having the money in your pocket. The process of due diligence must be endured, baring the recipient's inner workings to the scrutiny of the investor's army of experts. No one wants to buy a pig in a poke.

Like so many others before them, FDX's team descended upon Value America in search of problems. They were led by their CIO, a man responsible for as large a technical team as any in America. Their CFO was scheduled too, but there was a labor dispute brewing, and he had to stay home to tend to more pressing matters.

As our employees acted like the owners they were, and as our friends stepped forward, precise shareholder data became a moving target. There were new influxes of capital every day or two in the form of loans, most of which would eventually be converted to equity at the lenders' option. When and if this happened, it meant new shares would be created. This process would dilute, in effect, the percentage of ownership of other shareholders, even though the value of the shares would remain constant.

What this meant to FDX was that the more successful we were in raising funds from other sources, the smaller their percentage of ownership their five million would buy. They couldn't just say, "We want to own 1.25% of Value America," for instance. The same investment that represented 1.25% today might work out to 1.23% tomorrow, depending upon how aggressively our employees and friends stepped up.

Their CFO had apparently never worked with a company of this nature before. Big companies like FedEx raise money, of course, but not with a process like ours. They use more esoteric vehicles that circumvent the dilution issue.

When Dean Johnson provided FedEx with an updated chart reflecting Durn's $2 million loan/investment from ULIC, the CFO realized that FDX would ultimately own a microscopically smaller percentage of Value America than their original expectation. He cried foul, telling Smith we were, "changing the deal." Most investors understood that, in theory, the process of dilution gives them a slightly smaller slice of a slightly larger pie. Net loss: zero. But explaining dilution to the CFO of a Fortune 500 company was sort of like lecturing the Pope on Catholicism. It's not supposed to be necessary.

As this drama was taking shape, Craig and company were calling on FedEx in Memphis, first in Fred's spacious but homey office and later in one of his large conference rooms. Craig pitched what he envisioned as Value America's future, something we came to call "Demand Alliances."

Our concept was to create a custom online store exclusively for FedEx employees, another for FedEx's business clients, and a third for consumers, the recipients of FedEx deliveries. They would all offer their own individualized value proposition. And they would all feature free delivery. "The best products, from the best brands, delivered by the best...free!"

In return, we would receive the endorsement of Federal Express, along with mutually beneficial access to their customers. "This," Craig shared, "would diminish our cost of sales and end our industry's costly dependence on advertising. It would also strengthen FedEx's position in e-commerce. Demand Alliances give Value America a ready-made customer base, motivated and trusting, acquired and served at a fraction of the cost of any other means," Craig proposed.

This also explained the emphasis Craig had placed on direct marketing in Glenda Dorchak's job description, in which he had listed the subject no less than five times in a single paragraph. FedEx, he hoped, would be but one among many such Demand Alliances, each with its own custom marketplace. Each would have its own methods of motivating customers, whether it was free delivery, discounted prices, patriotic loyalty, or just a painless way to make charitable contributions.

As these discussions progressed, Craig discovered an ominous political undercurrent running through the FedEx organization. Some of FedEx's earliest employees were devoted beyond reason to the cause of Federal Express and its fearless leader. Others, more recently hired, informed Craig discreetly that they viewed Fred and the company differently, as if their interests were mutually exclusive.

There was a feeling among some of the FDX suits that they had to watch Smith, to keep him from going off and doing something crazy with *their* company. The fact that it was more his company than theirs, having founded, nurtured, and led it since its inception, was apparently lost on them. Fred was an entrepreneur, an innovator, and therefore dangerous. There was no obvious movement to force Fred onto the sidelines, of course. He remained CEO and thus held *the* position of power. What was happening, rather, was a chipping away at the edges, a subtle undermining of the founder's credibility. The problem wasn't with Fred. He was the real deal. It was with his antagonists.

It wasn't as simple as all that, however. Access to Fred Smith, CEO, holder of supreme power at FDX, was the thing most highly prized among these same managers. Being close to power was power itself, and power was like catnip to these corporately insecure bureau-cats.

It followed that somebody new, somebody who was able to get close to Fred, was a potential threat. Those who had his ear could exert undue influence. John Tigrett was such a man, but he clearly had no personal agenda. He was simply Fred's moral compass, his mentor, his unshakable friend. He was old. His bite had been dulled by the passage of time.

Craig Winn, however, was another story. He would have to be watched. The suits were appalled at how quickly Smith had taken a liking to the e-commerce pioneer.

⤜⦂⦂⤛

FEDEX'S CFO WASN'T the only one who had an interest in stopping FDX's investment in Value America. Rafe Durn's pro-union position naturally made him antagonistic to any FedEx alliance. Durn believed, and had said, "That company is anti-Union."

Craig was beside himself. Until and unless the Paul Allen deal closed, Value America would need every friend we could get. He, unlike Durn, didn't care about what piece of the pie the Teamsters got. Craig's loyalty was to Value America, to our employees, brands, and shareholders. An alliance with the technologically superior FedEx for an e-commerce company dependent upon reliable delivery was as good as good ever gets.

But Craig had anticipated this eventuality a year earlier. In his negotiations with ULIC's lawyer, he had negotiated a clause allowing Value America to use any freight company it desired so long as at least "some or all of its employees were operating under one or more collective bargaining agreements." Rafe was evidently under the impression that this precluded us from using Federal Express. Craig knew better. He had negotiated this specific language just in case such a possibility arose. As abusive as ULIC's lawyers had become over minutia, Craig relished trumping them on a material issue. He was enjoying the moment.

And then, as if on cue, on the eve of the Christmas shipping season, the FedEx pilot's union threatened to strike, seeking a seventeen percent pay increase over five years. Although the union caved in by late November, the incident served to remind Rafe Durn that there was indeed a union at Federal Express. If he had been thinking like an investor and not like a union pension fund manager, Durn would also have been aware that UPS's Teamsters had staged a crippling fifteen-day strike only one year before. It was a strike that would have brought Value America to its knees had we been doing business at the time.

These facts didn't stop Durn from acting belligerently. Covenants in his Series A investment gave Rafe the power to block any new capital, including FedEx's. As an investor, that wasn't in his interest. But Durn, now aware of the language Craig had negotiated, knew he couldn't legally block the company from using Federal Express.

He was conflicted, to be sure. Smith, in Rafe's eyes, was anti-Union. But Value America needed cash and friends, or his union investment would turn to dust. In a tense and nerve-rattling confrontation at the Union Labor Investment Company's offices, a frustrated Winn dug into his pocket and placed the keys to Value America on the table. "If you think you can do a better job running this company, they're yours."

They laid there for what seemed like an eternity. Neither man spoke. The keys on the table spoke for them. Finally, Durn backed down and approved the transaction. But it would come at a terrible price.

Rafe hissed, "If you ever do a deal with that anti-union company, I'll bring you down."

The threat was personal, and Craig knew it. Sure, putting himself at risk was nothing new. That's what builders do; they place the common good over self-enrichment or self-preservation. It's written somewhere in the job description. But this personal threat from a union big-shot was a bit much. "Thanks, Rafe," Craig said as he got up to leave. "I've got a company to save."

IN 1973, JOHN TIGRETT, then in his sixties, had wooed and wed a multi-talented southern beauty named Pat Kerr—then in her twenties. An unlikely love match, perhaps, but John and Pat were anything but average. Their son, Kerr, was the same age as Fred Smith's son, Richard. As close as their fathers were, it was not surprising that the two young men became close friends as well. They were, in fact, both students at the University of Virginia, both members of the same fraternity.

Education is relatively easy to come by, albeit expensive. What's hard to get is your first meaningful job. So Craig hired Kerr Tigrett and Richard Smith to work at Value America as their college schedules would allow. He hoped to see something of their illustrious fathers emerge, and he was not disappointed. Kerr and Richard worked hard and acquitted themselves admirably. Their value exceeded their salaries many times over.

One day, life's road took a funny twist. Kerr and Richard unwittingly brought Value America to the brink of disaster. Drinking is a common pursuit at UVA, and Kerr had had a few, though Richard hadn't. As they tell the story, they, along with two other Delta Kappa Epsilon brothers, decided to visit the local 7-Eleven for some snacks at about two o'clock one morning. On the way back, they encountered Alexander Kory walking on Rugby Road, apparently drunk, shouting obscenities at them. Smith, Tigrett, and Brad Kintz, seeing no good reason to sit idly by and be verbally abused, got out of their car and confronted the inebriated freshman. Words were exchanged. The gregarious Kerr enjoyed trading gibes with Kory, who was not having quite as much fun. As the belligerent freshman grew more vociferous, Richard stepped between them, as a peacemaker, to calm things down.

And then it happened. Kory went too far.

Richard Smith had gained a few pounds since his days on the UVA football squad, and Kory took the cheap shot: "What are ya gonna do about it, fat boy?" So the 265-pound Smith took a shot of his own. He popped Kory in the mouth. One punch was all it took. The foul-mouthed frosh landed on his butt, got up, and ran off. Smith, Tigrett, and Kintz shook their heads in disbelief, got back in the car, went home, and thought nothing more about their brief encounter.

The next day, the buzz on campus was that some guy had been attacked and beaten up by a vicious street gang. As Richard and Kerr joined their peers bemoaning the rise of violent crime in small-town America, details began to emerge as to the time and place of the incident. Then it dawned on them. "Oh, my God," Kerr said. "That was no street gang. That was us!"

They went to the Dean of Students to explain what happened. No big deal, they were told. Later, the police came by the fraternity house and asked them to come downtown and make a statement. When they arrived, however, they were arrested and put in jail. Fred Smith flew back from business in Alaska to bail his boy out of the slammer.

Richard pled no contest to misdemeanor assault and battery—$2300 worth of dental work—and was sentenced to a two-month jail term and 400 hours of community service. If that seems a bit stiff for one punch on the jaw, factor in the scuttlebutt overheard shortly thereafter at the Glenmore Country Club: the local District Attorney was heard boasting that he had "nailed Fred Smith's son." Nobody was going to accuse *him* of showing favoritism. He was a real crime-buster.

But what happened next was the UVA version of a public lynching. The student-run Judiciary Review Board scheduled a hearing on the matter but told the accused they'd cancelled it. Then, after Richard and Kerr had left town for a trip home to Memphis, the Board held their hearing anyway, in their absence. Not surprisingly they were found guilty. The punishment: expulsion from UVA. Jefferson could be heard turning over in his nearby grave. Kerr's only crime was talking, yet he was expelled from the university founded by the man who had written the world's foremost treatise on freedom. The press had a field day with the whole incident, stopping just short of running banner headlines: *Rich Kids Get Their Comeuppance.* The Tigretts and the Smiths were quickly losing their taste for Charlottesville.

৩৩৹৵৬

BOTH CRAIG and, curiously, Rafe Durn, were touting the FedEx investment commitment. This enhanced our company's credibility with other investors. Smith had even encouraged Craig to do so. And one didn't keep a thing like this a secret. As a result, Fred Smith's call put our company right back on the edge of the abyss.

The gist of the message was, "I've decided not to invest in Value America. I am told by my CFO that our deal has changed. More importantly there are pressing personal matters I need to attend to." A complicated dynamic was suddenly in play. It was easy enough to figure out what the "pressing personal matter" was, but it hardly seemed like a plausible reason for bailing out of the investment. On the other hand, the CFO of FDX had made it clear he didn't like the deal.

Craig could instantly envision the reaction of other investors, from Paul Allen on down: *Fred Smith found some horrendous problem with Value America, and they got out while the getting was good. We should too.*

The message was repeated in a letter Fred faxed to the company. Craig, Rex, and Dean sat in stunned silence at the antique table, staring blankly at it. Dean finally spoke. "Once again, gentlemen, we're dead. I know we've said that before, and somehow we've managed to drag ourselves out of the funeral pyre. But not this time...."

Rex knew. "The minute word gets out, we're toast. And it *will* get out, because we're obligated to keep our investors informed. As soon as we tell them what's happened, our credibility's shot." It's one of life's great ironies. When you tell people something they don't want to hear—even if it's the truth—the *messenger* loses credibility. "No one will trust us after this," Rex concluded. We're *finito*.

"It's a long shot," Craig said, gazing out the window. "But it's the only thing I can think of."

Rex and Dean turned and stared at him with incredulity. "What?" they said in unison.

"Fred Smith is a good and decent man. He's been misled. He's made a bad decision based upon incomplete and inaccurate information from his own people. Give me a couple of hours. I've got a letter to write."

Three hours later, Craig had composed a 6,000-word tome. He sent it to the CFO and cc'd Fred Smith. It was conciliatory in tone, edifying, calm, reasonable. It recounted the entire history of the Value America/FDX business relationship, how we had done everything possible to keep them informed, how the misunderstanding concerning dilution came about, and how the relationship could mutually benefit both companies if allowed to proceed. Written between the lines, Craig informed them that we had justifiably relied on their commitment and made public comments about it. For them to pull out now, claiming it was due to a personal matter, would cause us grave and irreparable harm.

The letter specified three possible courses of action FDX could take, any one of which would be acceptable to us. The first would allow them to own a big piece of the company for $50 million. With it we offered an anti-dilution provision. The second option was a bit more complicated, but at its core, it prescribed a smaller investment than option one.

The third was the obvious choice, a sort of "get-out-of-jail-cheap" card. "We have relied on Fred's commitments," it said, "and per his instructions, announced our relationship. A failure to invest now would be devastating and could destroy the company and all that so many of us have worked so hard to build. Thus, a symbolic investment of as little as $5 million on the same terms as the $50 million option would allow us to save face and to continue to make progress in implementing the mutually beneficial alliances we reviewed earlier...."

Upon reviewing the letter with Rex, Dean, and Caise, Craig faxed it to FDX, and they held their collective breath, though not for long. We received a response within the hour, not from the CFO, not from Fred Smith, but from FDX's legal department. The salient paragraph of the faxed response read, "FDX disagrees sharply with many of the factual assertions in your letter, and the Company is deeply disappointed by its threatening overtones. Nevertheless, subject to the conditions set forth in this letter, FDX Corporation is prepared to negotiate a $5 million investment in Value America...."

Rex and Dean couldn't believe Craig's letter had worked. The odds against a reconciliation leading to an investment were one in a million. Yet all he had done was convey who had said what to whom. Nonetheless, the cadaver was breathing again. Value America was starting to make Lazarus look like a warm-up act.

❧❦❧

PRESSING PERSONAL MATTERS my ass, thought Craig. This near-disaster had been precipitated by an incident that had been blown all out of proportion by people with an axe to grind. These were good boys. They didn't deserve this. Something needed to be done.

The Chairman of the Board of Education for the Commonwealth of Virginia happened to work for Caise, Perkins. So when He told Justin about their latest hair-raising saga, Caise said, "I can help. There's a fellow on our staff...."

Craig turned the Smiths and the Tigretts on to him. In the process of trying to get Richard and Kerr reinstated into the University, the three families grew close. Although there wasn't any direct connection, Fred in time grew bullish on Value America again. The reason was John Tigrett.

"You know, Craig," Smith said during one of their now frequent visits, "We committed to invest $5 million, but if Paul Allen doesn't come through, I'd still like FedEx to do the $50 million deal with Value America."

"I appreciate your confidence, Fred," Craig said. "It means a lot. But I've gotta tell you, what I value most is your introduction to John Tigrett. He's the most remarkable man I've ever known."

Fred concurred. "He's my best friend, the wisest man I know. You ought to hear what he says about you." Craig had an idea. John had written and called often. His words of encouragement were dear to Craig.

"Anyway," Fred went on, "here's what I'm thinking. There are a lot of people who will look at the FedEx investment and say, 'They're a big company. Five million is nothing to FDX.' But from me, it's different. So what I propose is to invest $5 million of my *own* money in addition to FDX's five."

An immensely grateful Winn thanked Smith profusely and said, "You know what I'd really like, Fred? I'd like you to serve on our board."

"I don't do boards, Craig. I'm on some charity boards, but I haven't served on a corporate board for many years now."

Craig gave him that look.

"I'll think about it, okay?" Fred said with a smile he couldn't repress. "I'll think about it."

The next evening, Craig received a call from an attorney he didn't know. He introduced himself and said he was calling on his cell phone from a duck blind. "My friend and client, Fred Smith, tells me I'm supposed to wire five million dollars from his personal account to your company. He says the paperwork isn't done yet, but he trusts you." The attorney laughed. "I'm doing my official due diligence here. Actually, I'm calling to find out what kind of guy could induce my friend Fred to send five million dollars to somebody without documentation! I've known Fred for years, even served on his board. This takes the cake."

After all the brouhaha over minutia, Fred was telling Craig to treat his money as if it were his own. He told him to send the paperwork and stock certificates to him whenever it was convenient. With those instructions, Craig and Fred's attorney talked for the better part of an hour about Value America, Fred Smith, John Tigrett, and the value of friendship. No ducks were harmed during the making of this conversation.

୧୨·ୡୠ

A WEARY WINN taxied up to the Charlottesville FBO at the controls of his Cessna. It had been a long day. He brightened when he saw the Challenger, 3FE, parked on the tarmac; its door was open. He climbed the stairs and peeked inside. To his delight, he found his two friends, Fred and John, sipping merlot and waiting for their families.

"Craig! Come in. Join us." The three sat in the jet's spacious cabin and talked of recent events, for it was now May, and a great deal had come to pass. But this wasn't a time to talk business. Chance meetings are the glue that holds our most cherished memories together, and so they talked of friendships and families, of love and life. As Craig bid them farewell, he didn't know that it would be the last time he would see John Tigrett. John was swallowed up in history that night. His heart, in the end, had proved to be no match for his indomitable spirit, a spirit that lives on in the best of us, in our best moments.

A man who has friends must himself be friendly—Solomon

PLAYING CHICKEN

*O*nce again, Craig, Rex, and Dean found themselves seated around the old maple table. It had moved. Our new offices were just north of town in a group of five office buildings collectively called Hollymead.

What the three had before them was unbelievable. The final tally from the private funding round showed that not only had we moved back a safe distance from the edge of the abyss, we had actually brought in more cash than we had hoped to raise during the failed IPO. Putting the achievement in perspective, Dean pointed out that we had raised more private equity capital than any dot-com ever—this was one for the record books.

As the three men formally closed the funding round, setting the stage for a new run at an IPO, they reviewed the last few months like a tailback reviewing the instant replay of his ninety-five-yard touchdown run. They felt proud, exhausted, exhilarated, and motivated, all at the same time. They were victorious, for the moment, but the game was far from over.

It had not been easy. As far back as Christmas Eve, the Paul Allen investment, a gargantuan $50 million influx of capital, had looked imminent. Then Rafe Durn and Frank Flowers had squabbled over who would have what preemptive rights, and they had demanded warrants to sweeten the deal in the event Value America failed to attain a public market valuation of at least $600 million during 1999. What had happened to the good old days, just a short time back, when a $300 million valuation had seemed wildly optimistic?

The problems had been ironed out, finally, and the money had at last begun to flow into Value America's coffers, and not just from Paul Allen. Fred Smith and Federal Express had each contributed $5 million. Global Crossing's founders, Rafe Durn's friends Don Tarpin and Gary Winnick, invested $10 million. And the employees and friends of the company had given millions more. It was immensely gratifying because all of the "loans" made in the first sixty days after the failed IPO had been voluntarily converted to equity. The folks who knew us best *believed* in us.

The world was finally starting to take notice. *Retail Week* had proclaimed that Value America was one of the world's most innovative retailers....

Tucked in a lush pocket of country where east coast bustle fades into quiet green hills, Craig Winn has assembled an Internet company whose chief strategists profess no special love for the Web. Hundreds of miles north, in New York, or a continent away in California, entrepreneurs run themselves ragged trying to wring money from the ether-world. Though it's a simpler pace of life in

Charlottesville, executives at Value America, too, burn their days in double time. Others talk of customer acquisition costs and focus-group findings, but the architects of Value America use a different vocabulary. They aspire to nothing less than building the world's next retail revolution....

It is Winn's enthusiasm that fuels his team's 12-hour shifts. "He appeals to my intellect," said Phil Ramsey, VP of Direct Response Marketing. A year ago, Ramsey was capping a successful consulting career. "Now I'm hooked," Ramsey said. Others followed Winn from California where he worked closely with the original Price Club team that pioneered the warehouse-store concept.

Ken Power, SVP and Creative Director, met Winn four years ago. He produces the folksy newspaper ads that make Value America the one Internet company able to make traditional marketing tactics work online. Power's copy and style extends into the company's Web store. Its logical layout, plain-English descriptions, and copious illustrations lend an approachable air.

"People never really buy anything until they trust someone," Ramsey said. "We want to make our mark doing what other retailers can't. We're a one-stop shop." An analyst at the *IPO Monitor* said, "You've got to take WalMart and put it on the Web." Or Price Club, as the case may be....

Richard Gerhardt, Value America's President of Consumer Products, and Price Club staffer at the time, said, "Winn convinced manufacturers they could eliminate costs by supplying Price Club with great products that could be sold to consumers at a low overhead. This same model persists at Value America today." The firm takes possession of inventory only while it's *en route* to customers. Manufacturers coordinate the deliveries. In return, brands pay fees for online listings and multimedia product presentations. "This was a unique opportunity for us," said Chuck Gangi, Sales Manager for Targus. "They're unlike any other Internet retailer. With Value America, we're all part of the same team."

"Retail is in need of repair," Winn said earlier this year. "Almost every manufacturer of consequence views their retail customers as their enemy." Value America is Winn's bid to flip-flop the retail channel, selling the best quality merchandise in the store with the lowest overhead.

AS WE CONTINUED our quest for dot-com's holy grail, the initial public offering, our due diligence efforts proceeded apace. The investment bankers, lawyers, and auditors had been busy collecting risk factors. Generally, we didn't mind, because they were like cheap insurance—"You can't say you weren't warned." But this was getting silly. They seemed to be writing risk factors on everything they could think of, real or imagined. It got to the point where some of the risk factors were simply untrue.

Bill Hunt had found himself at the epicenter of one risk factor controversy that irked Craig no end. Bill had addressed a group of footwear and stocking manufacturers, and during the course of his speech he had made what appeared to be a "forward-looking statement"—a bad thing, the lawyers had declared, according to their view of SEC regulations.

In reality, all Bill had done was say we were filing a registration statement (correct), and that we had grown faster than the Web itself (correct again). He referenced a recent *USA Today* article that said Internet use was doubling every ninety days. Our first IPO's red herring had proclaimed that we were *tripling* every ninety days. Unfortunately, his speech was picked up and reported in the *Dow Jones News*. So the lawyers accused him of hyping the stock.

He had done no such thing. The SEC ruled that it was perfectly proper to share positive new developments with business partners like Bill's hosiery brands. In fact, to refrain from doing so would have constituted a breach of fiduciary duty to our investors: one was *expected* to "sell" one's company to potential allies. They even had a term for the acceptable behavior: "puffery." Being of a business mind, the SEC knows nothing happens until somebody sells something. Our lawyers didn't care. They crafted a risk factor that maligned the truth and embarrassed Bill.

Companies are strongly discouraged from hyping their public offerings in the media, especially in the days leading up to an IPO. An overly favorable or inaccurate newspaper or magazine article can derail a stock offering before it gets started. The technical term for the offense is "gun jumping." The SEC wants the company's merits to be judged strictly upon what was published in the S1, red herring, and prospectus—a devilishly hard thing for us to achieve, considering we were up to our ears in the information age. This was why the February issue of *Chief Executive* magazine caused such a stir.

Chief Executive didn't have a very large circulation, only 30,000 or so. You couldn't even walk up to a newsstand and buy a copy. You had to be a mover or shaker in the business world, a top executive of a large corporation, to get it. Naturally, when Craig told the lawyers about the impending article, their here-comes-trouble meters pegged.

Craig insisted that the article had not been written to support the upcoming IPO. In fact, he had been having discussions with Arnold Pollard, the Chief Executive of *Chief Executive*, since the previous April. Arnie was intrigued with Craig and the company he had founded. They had become good friends by this time. But it wasn't until Pollard's staff asked if they could come and take a few photographs that Craig knew that they were planning an important story. At Pollard's suggestion, the photographs were taken in Craig's elegant home, with his wife and his dog.

He figured he dare not wait until the issue was actually published to find out if it were accurate and devoid of hype. He asked Arnie to let him preview the text. "I won't ask you to change anything editorially," he said, "but a misstatement could sink our IPO."

"The piece is going to press in twenty-four hours, Craig," Arnie said. "It's going to be our February cover story, the first time we've ever devoted our cover to such a young firm. So, if we've gotten the facts wrong, we'll make corrections. Otherwise...."

The story was spectacular. Its tone was so positive, Craig's pulse raced as he devoured every word. Based upon his experience with the media, he just *knew* there had to be a time bomb ticking away in there somewhere, but he couldn't find it. The story was provocative and entertaining, yet truthful.

The magazine went to press as written, and all hell broke loose. The story at first blush made Value America look too good to be true— inspired leadership, revolutionary business plan, bright prospects, friends in high places. Underwriters' counsel demanded that the IPO be pulled. This *had* to be hype, they charged. But closer examination revealed what Craig already knew—the story was precisely accurate, verifiable, and totally consistent with the statements contained in the S1. There was no hype, no forward-looking statements, nothing at which to point an accusing finger. The lawyers didn't care. They wanted blood. The story at the heart of the controversy said, in part:

At first glance, the story sounds familiar: a young, energetic, tech-savvy entrepreneur starts up a company on a wing and a prayer, with a fascinating premise and a dream of becoming the next Gates. The company chugs along, announcing strategic alliances and releasing new products until it either secures a place as leader of a niche—or fades off quietly into cyber-oblivion. But if you think you've heard Value America's story before, you may want to think again; this online retailing company isn't just another Internet.com. After all, it isn't every day the CEO of an e-commerce start-up secures some $120 million in private placement from some of the world's most noteworthy investors.

Some of those who now own pieces of Value America (which has also just filed with the SEC to go public with 5 million shares of common stock): FDX's Fred Smith (he and his company are in for $5 million each), Microsoft co-founder Paul Allen (he has a total of $65 million invested through his company, Vulcan Ventures), Gary Winnick, CEO of Pacific Capital Partners and co-chairman of Global Crossing, Don Tarpin, co-chairman of Global Crossing, and the respective principles of both the Carlyle Group and CIBC/Oppenheimer. Organized labor, oddly enough, has invested a total exceeding $20 million. And all of this was accomplished without help from investment bankers. That means no fees to pay out—which, in turn, means a whole lot of cash to play with.

Not that Winn will have trouble finding ways to spend it; competing for share of the online wallet requires constant reinventing, developing, and evolving. The virtual retail world is a space in which all is new—or at least most things are. In fact, Winn's company is built on a business plan he wrote some 20 years ago. Back then, Winn was working as a representative helping retailing legend Sol Price. Winn's job was to convince brands to partner with Price, but it wasn't an easy sell.

To increase the vendors' comfort level, Winn explained that retailing had historically undergone periodic revolutions, that the Price Club represented the latest of such shifts, and that they shouldn't miss out on being part of it. It was a reasonably effective pitch, but some brands wanted to know more. "They said, 'If you're so smart, tell us about the next retail revolution,'" recalls Winn. He painted a futuristic picture of multimedia product presentations and direct shipments from manufacturers that eliminated the need for inventory sitting on retailers' shelves. And he liked what he heard himself saying. "I decided that while this idea was fresh, I might as well write the business plan."

The missing ingredient was the technology that would make it possible. So Winn worked as a manufacturers rep, and then founded Dynasty, a lighting manufacturer that he eventually sold. In the meantime, PCs proliferated and the Web arrived, making Winn's old business plan feasible. In 1996, he and partner Rex Scatena incorporated Value America, and since have been working to revolutionize retail.

But so, too, have thousands of other companies that have taken to the Web. Entrepreneurs are trying out new business models to see what will make money in the new and rapidly evolving medium. Winn's vision, then, is just one of many vying for the attention of customers and investors. But his approach is one of relentless logic, methodically ticking off point after point, while tempering his arguments with considerable personal charm and enthusiasm. In short, he makes a powerful pitch—one that has convinced a large number of high-profile backers of his model's merits. So impressed was Fred Smith, in fact, that he will serve on Value America's board—his only other board besides that of his own company.

Winn says that the Value America business model stands out from the Internet crowd because of a handful of key factors starting with scale. Rather than one or two types of products, the company offers goods from more than 1,000 brands in 20 industries—everything from computers and jewelry to coffee and Post-it notes.

Another critical element of the model is an emphasis on well-known brands, such as Panasonic, HP, Amana, and GE. Winn says that the trust engendered by such brands is important in a medium where people can't touch the merchandise, and where a lingering suspicion of Internet security and legitimacy keeps many from buying on-line. To support the sale of branded, higher-end goods, Value America gives customers a wealth of product information in the form of multimedia presentations that describe features and strengths in detail.

Value America has also bucked Net tradition in its approach to advertising. The company has focused heavily on traditional vehicles, such as newspapers. The company's ads, which are often humorous, are created by an in-house advertising staff. "It's our biggest expense area, so it better be a core competency, right?" says Winn. "That's especially true if you want to have a unique voice."

Value America is based on an "inventory-less" model. The company is essentially a conduit between consumer and manufacturer; it has no warehouses, and owns products only while they are on their way to consumers. The company has created sophisticated systems that will seamlessly take orders online and pass them electronically to the brands. The result, he says, is "what we believe to be the first totally electronic and automated link between supply and demand.

"We are in the business of creating friction-free capitalism," he adds. While the most efficient retailers operate at 18-to-22 percent total overhead as a percentage of revenue, he says, "We have designed Value America to run ultimately at 5 percent." The approach, he adds, is "very much like being a bank. A bank typically makes a 3 percent spread on your assets. We are margining other people's assets."

Such efficiencies, as well as the relationships Value America has with manufacturers, were key to attracting Paul Allen's Vulcan Ventures firm, says Vulcan president Frank Flowers. "It's clear to me that the challenge in on-line retailing is to keep your infrastructure costs as low as possible. Any time you can deliver customers directly to manufacturers and allow the manufacturers to ship products to customers directly; you have eliminated a significant amount of risk from the business model. So the appeal of the Value America story is its finely tuned back end, as much as anything else."

In the following interview, Winn talks with *CE* about the merits of Value America's business model, and the travails of creating a business on the Internet.

Q. Why is having a broad range of products so important to your business model?

A. We're convinced the consumer isn't going to learn to navigate and bookmark hundreds of sites or share personal and financial information on a wide scale. So we're comprehensive. Most everything you need for home or work can be found in one place. The other reason is the stunning amount of capital that is necessary to build a brand in e-commerce. If you're applying those promotional dollars to a single category, it would be difficult to ever be profitable.

Q. That approach means you've had to establish relationships with a great many manufacturers. Has that been difficult?

A. It's the hardest thing we do. Every brand relationship started with a "no."

Some told us no many times. Because we are selling the best brands, they have the most to lose. They risk alienating their existing distribution channel or losing the lead position with our new emerging channel. So to have gone from over 1,000 noes to 1,000 yeses is pretty remarkable.

Q. Your focus on traditional advertising vehicles was unusual for a Web-based company. What was your reasoning?

A. E-commerce revenues had been driven through fixed-cost agreements with portals that provided a "click here" button. We believed that the same amount of dollars spent in traditional advertising would drive more revenue. It could create a whole new voice, a new image if the advertising was as information-rich and brand-centric as the store. That's impossible with a "click here" button.

Q. How will Value America evolve—and what are some possibilities for expansion?

A. We can create custom stores in almost any way that you can slice the people and products. For example, there are about 1,000 major charities in the U.S., and one of our strategies is to form alliances with them. Our biggest budget item is advertising. With these custom stores, we eliminate that cost.

Q. Are you troubled by the fact that PC penetration seems to be stalled at 40%?

A. No. We began Value America only when I became convinced that convergence was going to become a reality. TV and phone penetration are in the 99th percentile.

Q. What happens when somebody else says they think they can do this better?

A. I say, "Come on down!" Every day is a battle. And thank God the challenges are enormous. Otherwise, any idiot could do this. If I knew when I started this company what I know now, I never would have done it. I've spent 25 years preparing to do specifically what we're doing. I understand manufacturers and how to build relationships with them. I understand and love technology. I've been the middleman between manufacturer and retailer. And even with all of that— and hiring the brightest team of people and having backers with deep pockets— this is awesomely difficult.

Q. Have you found leading an Internet company to be different from leading a more traditional organization?

A. Yes. The biggest difference is the enormity of the dollars required to promote it. I have spent 90 percent of my time raising capital. Yes, there is a lot of capital available, but there are tens of thousands of people with wonderful ideas chasing it. Second, everything you do, you have to build yourself. Typically, when you start a business, the one thing you don't have to worry about is financial and accounting systems. But there is no accounting system you can buy for an e-commerce inventory-less model. You have to build it. And, this is the one space where patience is not rewarded. You have to be willing to go out to sea and fire your guns while you are still laying the keel. It's an environment where you must constantly be aggressive, where time moves in dog years.

Q. How did you manage to land Fred Smith?

A. Actually, Fred Smith—who I view as the Babe Ruth of business, a real world-class entrepreneur—called me out of the blue and left a voicemail saying, "I have been studying Value America and it is my opinion that it is the best business model I have ever seen." Now, in my opinion the best business model is Federal Express. So to have Fred Smith call and say that—that's some pretty powerful stuff."

In the end, after several days of intense investigation, the underwriter's attorneys couldn't find a single inaccurate nuance. The *Chief Executive* cover story remains the definitive published account of Value America.

To be helpful, Craig encouraged the lawyers to diminish their perceived liability by writing another risk factor. It seemed to work for everything else. He even offered to write it himself with a little help from Caise. In carefully worded legalese, they "asked" investors to ignore the February cover story. They warned that even though the article mentioned that Fred Smith and Paul Allen, founders of two of the world's largest and most innovative companies, had invested in Value America, this "should not be construed as an endorsement of our company." How these investments *should* be characterized, if not an endorsement, was left to the imagination of the reader.

What is perhaps most amazing, however, is that within a year's time so much would change at Value America, and within the dot-com world, that another business periodical would actually reuse the photographs of Craig found in the *Chief Executive* story without his permission to create an entirely different and false characterization. But more on that later.

A THOUSAND BRANDS and counting; we were not the same store we had been even six months before. We had more departments, and more depth within each department. The store layout that had served us well when we had fewer brands had begun to show the strain. So we hired a talented young Web designer as the new Creative Director for the store. I no longer had the time for such indulgences. My ad team and I were too busy composing ads for what had become one of the world's largest dot-com ad campaigns.

Interestingly, Paul Allen's only point of disagreement with our store in those heady days was the look of our homepage. He preferred what had become the standard approach, with links to everything under the sun arranged under tabs. We resisted this look, because it tended to look cluttered, confusing, and frankly, cheap. But there was far too much content in the store now for our old ultra-clean look. The compromise featured a gateway to each department, arranged in a checkerboard pattern of icons. It was handsome and scalable: as we added departments, we simply added more icons. Other key navigation and shopping features were handled neatly around the edges.

Glenda Dorchak, who considered herself to be in charge of everything, was proud as a peacock. Never mind that until the new designer started working with Craig her plan had been a catastrophe. She had tried to remake the store in her image: cold and clinical. Graphic suicide.

The compromise, however, failed in subtle ways, easy to miss. In some places, we lost ground. Craig noticed the shift, but few others did. Unfortunately, he was too busy closing the private equity rounds and reenergizing the IPO to steer the new creative team around all the inherent deficiencies in their new format.

So in the push to become more streamlined, the store ceased being polite: the page where we thanked customers for their last purchase and gave them the opportunity to comment was gone. We ceased being caring: the blue "genie," our visual metaphor for in-store help, was gone, as was my good-natured tutorial. The rich repository of information about the hows and whys of the store was jettisoned—it didn't fit the new, more clinical style. We ceased being fun: all the humor was sucked out of our presentations. We ceased being helpful: our thoughtful, well-reasoned explanations were gone, replaced with regurgitated ad patter. Craig was sick about it, but he couldn't put Humpty Dumpty back together again, not without shooting down all the queen's horses and all the queen's men.

One change was not so subtle, nor were its negative implications. From day one, our product presentations had been central to attracting brands, achieving factory authorization, and forming brand partnerships. When a shopper entered a product category, their shopping experience started with the presentation and then moved on to the purchasing panel (a page that was never more than one click away). Glenda, however, could see no value in the presentations, so she changed the order and made them an option. A tiny eyeglass icon led shoppers to them, but it was easy to miss, and easier still to ignore.

Even if Glenda didn't understand brand dynamics, the brands did. Almost immediately, the flow of capital from brand partners slowed to a trickle, magically transforming our corporate gold mine into an expensive white elephant. If Glenda had finished high school, she probably would have learned that every action has an equal and opposite reaction. Before the store was even open for business, Rex, Bill, and Craig had brought in many times more presentation revenue (at eighty percent gross margin) than General Dorchak's whole ill-managed army of merchants ever did.

ৎৡৡৣ৶

"I'VE GOT A bad feeling, Rex." Craig was slumped in a chair, rubbing his forehead and contemplating the impending IPO. "You know how we missed the summer window—the party was over before we showed up. Well, sure as shootin', we're heading directly into another round of dot-com jitters."

"You may be right. But, on the bright side, it looks like we did nineteen million in sales in Q4, a gain of four million over Q3, despite the fact we were too broke to advertise. The Series C round is finally closed, and we raised something like seventy-five million. The auditors are almost done screwing around, and we're about to re-file our S1 with the SEC. Unless something really bad happens, we'll be out there in four or five weeks. Think positive, Craig," Rex said brightly. "No more glitches."

Craig rose and smiled hopefully. "No more glitches."

ৎৡৡৣ৶

DEAN LOOKED PALE as a ghost. He grabbed Rex as he passed his office. Entering Craig's, Dean turned and closed the door. *Uh oh*, Craig thought.

"What?" he asked, not really wanting to know.

"How much was the ad budget for Q4?" Dean asked rhetorically.

Craig didn't have to look it up. "Three million. Six if the funding came through."

"Try *sixteen*. Glenda's overspent her budget by ten million dollars."

"Are you sure?" Rex asked. Stupid question. Dean had been over the numbers a dozen times. There was no mistake.

"I don't believe it," Craig lied. "She just ignored the constraints? We were sinking, and she spent money like a drunken sailor?"

"Well," Rex offered, "that explains how we were able to do nineteen million. She burned sixteen mil doing it! Hell, I thought this was the one thing she was supposed to be good at."

"Piss-poor ratio, that's for sure," Craig spat out. "Where was she advertising? Bus benches? *Magazines?* Get her in here!"

"It's not true," a watery-eyed Glenda cried when Dean appraised her of the problem. "It can't be," she protested. "Sixteen million? No way. Your numbers are wrong." She didn't like Dean very much. The feeling was mutual. "I'll straighten this out," she announced.

You do that.

It was a surreal episode. The problem, for once in our lives, wasn't the money. We had enough to propel all but the most gluttonous into the stratosphere. It was now a question of integrity and the merits of our business. Our analyst's models for the coming year had been based on a logical progression from the previous quarter. To have torched $16 million against a budget of $6 million could lead investors to one of only two conclusions. Either we were lying scumbags, as FedEx's CFO had assumed, or we were unaware of what was happening in our own company, incompetent buffoons. Investors never factored in treachery.

When Glenda returned, she tried to downplay the disaster. At first she announced triumphantly that she had found a $100,000 error. Dean called her on it. All the records were reexamined. With nowhere to hide, she eventually admitted that $16 million had indeed been torched. Then, true to form, she proposed misallocating some of her overindulgence into Q1 as a way to repudiate responsibility. Unethical, if not illegal.

"No thank you," was Craig's response.

Dorchak was never willing to accept blame. When the inquisition was over, she stormed out of his office vowing to find the responsible party. *A mirror*, Craig thought, *might be helpful.*

Cornered, Glenda did what any red-blooded American girl would do (she's Canadian, but who's counting). She lashed out at the most convenient target, in this case the soft-spoken Derick Roberts, whose job it had been to place our ads in accordance with Glenda's directives. Derick, a seasoned advertising professional, had been doing precisely that ever since Phil Ramsey had been dismissed from the job for questioning the appropriateness of overpaying *Business Week*.

Derick was in his office chatting with Doug Purvis, our photographer, when Glenda walked in. Ignoring Doug, she told Derick, "Sometimes a lieutenant has to fall on his sword for his general," or words to that effect, and fired him summarily, claiming it had all been his fault. She then turned to Doug and cooed, "I understand it's your birthday." Without warning, she grabbed him by the cheeks and kissed him full on the lips.

She hadn't fooled anybody except the bewildered Roberts and the nearly neutered Purvis. Craig reinstated Derick to his original job, but neither man was ever the same. Both had sacrificially invested their time and money when we had needed it most, and had been kicked in the balls for their efforts. As a company, it was not our finest hour.

As the extent of the damage became clear, Dean angrily observed, "Our first IPO failed, and against incredible odds we've earned a second chance.

But when the bankers find out about this, they're going to cancel the second one, sure as hell. We're dead men walking." He shook his head.

Craig looked up, wild eyed. "You're probably right, Dean. We're as good as dead—you can't cover up a ten million dollar mistake. But before they start throwing dirt on us, I've got one last idea. I don't know if it'll work, but we might as well go down fighting."

"Well, whatever you do, the funeral starts in two hours," Dean replied. "That's when the conference call with Dale Dandridge is scheduled. We're supposed to go over our IPO model—you know, the one that doesn't make sense any more. We need a miracle. Again."

Alone in his office, Craig reflected *it's not about history. It's about the future, about meeting and exceeding expectations.* It had always been his policy to under-promise and over-deliver. People liked pleasant surprises more than disappointments, of course, but the investment community seemed to like pleasant surprises even more than they did dead-on predictive accuracy. The answer to the present conundrum, then, was to tweak the model for 1999 to predict greater expenses and smaller revenues—in other words, lower expectations, especially in the first half. In so doing, Glenda's Q4 disaster wouldn't look so glaringly out of place.

In the two hours he had available, Winn lowered the coming year's revenue projection from $175 to $150 million. He increased expenses, especially advertising. This would serve to make the pitiful performance of Q4 blend into a logical, believable scenario. Craig pulled his calculator out, got a sharp pencil, and a clean pad of paper. He created a new model, a detailed assumption page, and a presentation strategy.

Without a second to spare, Dean came back to his office and sat at the antique table. He dialed Dandridge's number on the speakerphone as he instructed his assistant to fax Dale the new handwritten assessment. As the CFO sat, the CEO delivered his spiel. They held their breath.

"I'm glad you've done this," Dandridge exclaimed. "You guys were growing so fast, it was, frankly, unbelievable. This new scenario makes much more sense. It's more credible, an easier sell. As a matter of fact, it makes so much sense, instead of getting you three to four times forward revenues, I'll be able to get you five. Let's see. That's a gain of $150 million. We'll file the IPO at $625 million. How does that sound?"

Both men sat there looking like they'd been slapped silly with the good fairy's favorite wand. In curtailing expectations in a last ditch effort to save the company, they had actually increased our valuation by $150 million. Dean grinned and shook his head in admiration. "I think I have just witnessed the most incredible financial turn of fortune since some guy talked FedEx into changing their mind. Two hours ago we were dead.

Now we're worth more than ever. It's a pleasure to serve with you, sir!"

There were few people who could appreciate the magnitude of what had happened like Dean. But Craig simply smiled and said, "I've given the shareholders their money's worth today. I think I'm going to go home now."

⍦⋮⍦

THE VERY MOMENT we had raised the money we needed to survive, the founders turned their attention to ridding themselves of their incompetent, blackmailing President. They'd hired Russell Reynolds to find a COO so they could in due course torch the wicked witch.

"It isn't happening," Rex grumbled.

Craig, too, was perplexed. "We've engaged the biggest executive search firm around, and they've come up empty handed."

"Maybe it's the field—dot-coms are just too new. They can't find anybody who's experienced that can make the transition to our world."

"I dunno. We're really just a retailer in a new venue. I can't believe it— looks like we're on our own again."

It was an issue on which Craig and Rex were divided. With the specter of Dynasty's funeral pyre ever before him, Craig was convinced that as an entrepreneur/founder, he needed to turn over the reins of the company to a professional manager before it got too big—preferably as the company went public. Rex thought more of Craig's management abilities than Craig did; he wanted him to stay in the saddle a while longer. But they were on common ground when it came to Dorchak. She had managed to hang onto her job only because circumstances had prevented them from firing her. Ever since the unpleasant episode a few weeks after her arrival, the company had either been looking down the barrel of an IPO, as we were now, or had been desperately broke.

She still looked fine on paper, talked the talk, had all the right moves. Only a handful of people knew she was poison. But our founders knew, and that was enough. They felt there was no way they could ethically go public with an insecure, conniving President unless there was a solid plan in place to jettison her sorry butt.

"I know who I'd like to have, if we could get him," Craig said.

"Who?"

"A guy I've known for years, Byron Peters. He's the COO at Price Costco. He's an experienced retail pro, knows operations, and he's familiar with Sol Price's way of thinking. He's a known quantity."

"Okay. Anybody else? We ought to be looking at several candidates."

"You remember Tom Morgan, the COO at USOP?"

"He was there the day we played golf with John Ledecky, right?" Rex had a good memory for golf trivia.

"He's running an office supplies distributor. The category is important to us, so it's a pretty good fit. I got to know one of his execs pretty well, a do-nothing Harvard MBA named Tom Starnes. He loves Morgan. I asked Motley about him. He said he's got a decent reputation. 'Course, people tend to say nice things about guys who buy their products."

"Well, then. Let's try 'em both."

୨୬ଁ୫

PROFESSIONAL MANAGERS EXPECT employment contracts detailing their convoluted compensation packages, options, golden parachutes, and the rest. Value America, however, was a bit more democratic. We used a "one-size-fits-all" approach. Everybody from Craig and Rex on down signed the same exact agreement. It was supposed to be the company's first line of defense against the debilitating "every man for himself" philosophy so prevalent in corporate America. It is perhaps telling that one of Glenda's demands the previous September had been to get her own customized employment contract. After the fact, mind you.

For months now, Glenda's lawyers had been negotiating with our Justin Caise over contractual minutia, and still there was no signed agreement. At issue was her severance package—especially if we elected to dismiss her unceremoniously, or just demote her, pull her fangs, so to speak.

Glenda saw herself as the very picture of altruistic patience to have worked so long without a *special* contract granting her every whim. It was *so* unprofessional not to have one. So as the due diligence for the second IPO moved into its final week, she saw her chance to rectify matters.

As part of every IPO's due diligence, each officer is interviewed by counsel. They typically ask benign questions; it's boilerplate sort of stuff, but a necessary part of the process. One by one, they had checked off the boxes next to the names of the officers—all save one. Dorchak always seemed to be unavailable. The lawyers began to smell a rat, and called Craig. "You have a problem," they said. *No kidding*, Craig thought.

Now that she had garnered the desired attention, Glenda turned up conspicuously absent. She had confirmed her first blackmail by writing Craig a letter, and she did so again. Glenda informed the company that she would not be coming to work until she got a new contract, saying, "Before I move further, I want to come to an agreement on my personal matters, as outlined under separate cover. I cannot proceed..." unless I'm given everything I want, she implored.

Her showing up absent on the eve of an IPO caused jitters amongst those who are easily spooked. The practitioners of IPOs are universally allergic to the slightest sign of trouble. Was Dorchak aware our S1 couldn't be filed until she complied? Was she aware that she was putting employees and shareholders in peril for her own personal and selfish gain? *Of course. Why do you think I chose this particular time?*

A thoroughly disgusted Justin Caise and an utterly perturbed Rex Scatena spent hour after grueling hour with Glenda's lawyers, hammering out a contract she would sign. It was a watershed moment, the first self-centered legal document ever crafted on behalf of Value America. It would not be the last.

The only things Justin and Rex made sure not to give up were the right to hire someone over Glenda and to be able to fire her for cause without penalty. In the end, the contract was signed, the final interview was conducted, and the S1 was filed. Dorchak had magnanimously allowed the company she worked for to continue living.

ॐ

"PETERS SAYS HE'S interested," Craig told Rex, "but he's worried about losing his Price Costco stock options. His lawyer is overly fastidious, too."

Rex sighed. The process could take months. "What about Morgan?"

"I'm thinking we could bring him in as Chief Operating Officer, distance ourselves from Dorchak, and promote him to CEO after the IPO."

But Morgan wouldn't stoop to interview for *anybody's* COO position. "I'm the CEO of a Fortune 500 company," he proclaimed. "It'd be beneath me." He didn't mention that under his leadership, USOP was rushing headlong toward its new status as a Fortune *5000* company, splintered into impotent fragments of its former self and ultimately into bankruptcy. And he didn't mention that the only reason he was at USOP was that Ledecky had recruited him out of a lackluster twenty-year career in auto parts and office supplies, where all he'd had to do to "make it" was show up to work and accept responsibility for absolutely nothing.

So Craig suggested Tom could come in as CEO instead. This would be problematical at the IPO since he'd have none of the credibility only time and performance provide. The advantage for Tom would be that his stock option strike price would be set pre-IPO, a million-dollar advantage. Craig explained that an offer had been made to Byron Peters some time ago, but that negotiations were moving slowly. Tom, naturally, figured he had better move fast if he wanted to get his share of dot-com gold.

As part of the process, Craig called Fred Smith, seeking his advice about vacating the office of CEO. Fred complimented Craig as lavishly as he had ever been praised, saying, "This reminds me of me. I've always tried to hire the best COOs in the country. There's no limit to what a man can achieve if he is able to recognize his strengths and weaknesses. You're decision here is not unlike that made by some of history's great leaders."

"Fred, I'm told you've met one of the guys we're considering. His name is Tom Morgan, from USOP."

"Yeah, I think so," Smith replied. "We tried to buy one of their companies, Mail Boxes Etcetera. Morgan flew a leg with us on one of my planes. If he's the same guy I'm thinking about, he seems okay, kinda quiet, meat and potatoes. Could be a good fit for you."

Craig questioned, "Mind if I have him give you a call?"

"That'd be fine," Fred agreed.

Unbeknownst to Rex and Craig, Morgan was doing a little soul searching of his own. He called his spiritual advisor first, Mr. Goose Godfrey. Godfrey, who was paid handsomely for his counsel, put Morgan in touch with Dan Case and Gerry Roche. Dan, AOL's Steve Case's older brother, was CEO of H&Q, the technology investment banker. Roche was CEO of the giant headhunting firm Heidrick & Struggles. Both told Tom that the dot-com world was hot. If it didn't work out with Value America, they could always find him another job. So Morgan used the number Craig had provided and called Fred Smith. Fred was, as usual, passionate, articulate, and sincere in his praise of both Craig Winn and his company.

The final interview was conducted at Craig's home. Morgan was pleasant and polished. Craig was pleased with Tom's preoccupation with his faith and family. And he certainly looked professional, a picture of suave sartorial perfection. The founders liked what they saw (or thought they saw). Moreover, they desperately wanted to solve their Dorchak problem.

Craig explained that he had promised himself he would resign as CEO as soon as the company had grown large enough, and that time, he felt, had come. Tom took it all in, nodding knowingly.

Rex explained that Glenda Dorchak had to go. Tom, he said, must come up to speed on sales and advertising quickly. It was imperative that the firm's dependence on her be eliminated and that she become relegated to a minor role, or better yet, to the unemployment line. Morgan was told about Glenda's blackmail schemes and her willful disregard for budgetary restraint. Tom took it all in, nodding knowingly.

Rex spoke again. "The last thing we need from you is inspiration, Tom," he said. "In the person of Craig Winn, we have all we need of that. He's a charismatic, visionary leader. The best thing that can happen is for you to do your job, manage the company, keep the pieces tied together,

running smoothly. Free Craig up to do what he does, forming relationships, being out in front selling the merits of this thing to new partners
and brands. Frankly, there's no one who can do it better. If you can work
that way, the future's bright."

Tom took it all in, nodding knowingly.

Morgan said he was ready to leave USOP to join Value America. He
said he would need a special employment contract, of course, a huge
compensation package, stock options, and a partridge in a pear tree. He
also said that he wanted to give his old firm plenty of notice so as not to
leave them in a lurch. They, however, told him he could leave tomorrow.

For Byron Peters, it was better late than never. He joined our burgeoning executive team at a level equivalent to Glenda's, with his own shiny
new contract. His had to be better than Tom's, which had to be better than
Glenda's. Craig and Rex were so intent on removing Dorchak's stain, they
agreed to pay Peters $10 million out of their own pockets to cover poten-
tial losses on his Costco options should a particular set of adverse circumstances occur. The incident serves to demonstrate their resolve to
clean up their mess.

৵৽৽

CRAIG WAS NOT known for being a trend follower, but this one held
promise. It had become chic to exclude company executives from boards
of directors, the theory being that you could get input from your own
team any time you wanted it. This left more room for prestigious board
appointments from outside the company, appointments that bore the
potential for strategic partnerships of immense value.

Rex was by this time no longer President of the company. With the
advent of Tom Morgan as CEO, Craig too would be leaving his managerial role behind. They became merely Chairman and Vice Chairman of
the board, co-founders and the company's two largest shareholders, still
owning sixty-two percent of the stock between them after the dilution of
past investment rounds. But a Chairman is little more than a parliamen-
tarian, with no more influence than any other board member.

Dorchak's initial blackmail had landed her a seat on the board, and as
long as there were other insiders serving, she couldn't be forced off without sending up pre-IPO red flags. But if we went to an all-outside board,
she'd be history. Craig and Rex approached Johnson and Motley, explaining the situation. Both graciously sacrificed their positions in the interests
of removing Dorchak. She wasn't happy about it, but she was gone. One
down, one to go.

FORTUNATELY, INTERNET STOCKS had recovered, but *déjà vu* was starting to raise its ugly head. The market was showing signs of dot-com jitters. Amazon had stirred things up by doing the largest convertible debt deal in history—a $1.2 billion anchor. It had made a lot of folks nervous. Craig was convinced that if we didn't get our IPO on the road soon, we would find ourselves rowing up another waterfall.

This was where it had all started to unravel the last time we had tried to take our company public. The S1 was done, the SEC's comments had all been resolved, and the teach-ins for the sales force had been scheduled. They were to begin at Robertson Stephens, starting as before with a one-on-one preview for analyst Dale Dandridge.

At the conclusion of the new road show presentation, Dandridge rose, shook his head, and smiled. "I'd give that one a nine-point-five, gentlemen. It's probably a ten, but I've never given a ten. Don't change a thing."

The reaction they got from the Robertson Stephens sales force was roughly the same. Craig was happy and bewildered at the same time. We were the same company they had all but spit on six months before. Now all of a sudden we were God's gift to yuppies. Go figure.

As strained as our working relationship with Robbie Stephens had become, we were joined at the hip with them, for better or worse—like a marriage gone bad. Once a company selects its auditors and its lead underwriters, it's virtually impossible to change them—the Street automatically assumes there's a problem the firm is trying to conceal.

This was not necessarily true with the other support players. In our darkest days, Volpe Brown Whelan had stood by us—Mark McNay and Andrea Williams had been instrumental in helping to arrange capital, but Hambrecht & Quist had done nothing. As much as Craig and company loved H&Q's analyst, Suzzi Maupin, there was no way we were going to go into this IPO without rewarding Volpe for their tireless support.

"Suzzi," Craig explained to the H&Q analyst, "this is the right thing to do." Doing the right thing was important to Craig, even if it was out of step with the rest of the business world. "We're not going to shortchange Volpe Brown. They've been so supportive I can't in good conscience give them less than thirty-five percent of the deal. I have to give the lead house forty. That leaves a maximum of fifteen percent for H&Q, with Robinson-Humphrey getting only ten. Your work as an analyst is superb, Suzzi, but your investment bankers have been no help at all. They didn't show up. I don't even know their names. If you can't accept fifteen percent, it'll be a no go. I'm sorry."

The analyst sighed. "You're right. Everything you've said is true. But my firm won't accept fifteen. We're going to have to bow out, regrettably."

It was regrettable, Craig reflected, but in the end, good was rewarded. The final tally was Robertson Stephens forty-four percent, Volpe Brown thirty-nine, Robinson-Humphrey fifteen, and E*Trade two. It was the first time E*Trade was listed as part of an IPO syndicate. One detail down. A hundred to go.

✑✑✑

IT WAS BEGINNING to look like a classroom exercise in chaos theory. The Series C investment round had closed weeks previously. It was history. Who would have thought that in amongst that $75 million, a bad penny would come back and haunt us?

The Series C warrants indemnified investors if the company didn't increase in value, or if it failed to go public in a timely fashion. There was a "trigger price," below which there would be monetary consequences for us. But our value had passed that point some time back, making the warrants meaningless, like a man who had outlived the term of his life insurance.

The auditors couldn't come to terms with their possible non-cash consequence, so they hadn't released the Reds for printing. But in order to get out on the road, we had to have the Reds. Time was now our enemy.

Bentley Hollis, Robbie Stephens' syndicate manager, brought things to a head. He told Craig that he was unwilling to set the road show appointments without the Reds. For his part, Craig could envision the whole thing coming unglued again if he didn't force the issue. So he instigated a game of chicken.

"Bentley," he said, "the last time we tried this, your firm cost us big time. I don't like the way the market's acting. I'll get the Reds. You set the road show appointments."

"Alright. I'll set the appointments, but if the Reds aren't here by Tuesday, I'm going to cancel them."

Hollis would only flinch if Craig couldn't deliver. Like the bumper sticker said, "Get in. Sit down. Hold on. Shut up."

✑✑✑

"STAY AWAY FROM that man. He's dangerously unbalanced."

They were talking about Craig Winn, skiing down a Utah slope with a cell phone glued to his ear. Yelling.

Craig and Rex had come to the conclusion that it was silly to fly all the way back to Virginia from San Francisco, only to turn around three days later and fly back to the west coast to begin the road show. Since their kids were enjoying an early spring break, they met their families in Deer Valley to get a little skiing in before commencing the exhausting ordeal.

As usual, what had seemed like a simple solution to Craig had been a problem for the unimaginative auditors. If we took the company public now, our valuation would void the warrants, so he told the auditors to pick the worst possible number they could conjure up, and publish that in the Reds. Then, if the warrants, through some unforeseen twist of fate, did come into play, their impact would be less than they announced. Everyone would be happy. The auditors, being sticklers for detail, balked.

That explains why Craig was yelling into his cell phone. He was "negotiating" with PwC's Frank Noblock. "Listen to me, Frank," Craig threatened. "Dean Johnson is at the printer's. If you don't do this, my next call will be to him, and I'm going to tell him to print the Reds without your opinion. The fact that it's never been done before won't stop us."

"You can't do that!"

"Oh, yes we can. And we will. Either you act responsibly and choose the worst possible number for the non-cash consequences of the warrants—which aren't going to be exercised anyway because our valuation is already above their trigger price—or you'll go down as the first accounting firm in history that allowed Reds to be printed without an opinion. It's your call."

The Reds were printed. In the "Financial Pages" section, on page F-2 (following the seventy-seven-page body of prospectus material), the opinion of PricewaterhouseCoopers LLP appeared: "In our opinion, the accompanying balance sheets and related statements of operations...present fairly, in all material respects, the financial position of Value America...." Upon pages F-19 through F-21 appeared Point #12: "Subsequent Events," explaining in arcane accounting mumbo jumbo the ramifications of the Series C warrants. There is no extant evidence suggesting any investor ever read these pages, and far less to indicate that they might have been understood.

Craig had won his second game of chicken.

৩৯৵৲

"THOSE REDS AREN'T going anywhere."

Tuesday was approaching like a freight train. The Reds were edging their way toward the presses, but we had another battle on our hands. The Reds said, "Over a thousand brands have chosen to partner with us." We had actually printed the names of over five hundred of them. You couldn't buy that kind of credibility with all the tea in China. You had to earn it. There was just one problem. The underwriters' counsel found the number incredible. As in "not to be believed."

The problem was exacerbated by the fact that we couldn't just go to technology and ask the geeks to print us out a comprehensive list of our brands. There was no central repository where they were all listed together, nor should there have been. There were overlaps from department to department. There were esoteric issues concerning what constituted a brand, as opposed to a supplier or a manufacturer. The lawyers wanted proof, or the whole thing was toast.

Craig once again found himself yelling into a cellular telephone in a public place. This time it was in Robert Redford's Zoom Restaurant in Park City. They wanted proof. We would supply proof.

Dean enlisted his lieutenant, Tracey Wingfield, Richard Gerhardt, Andy Rod, and Isaac Saltzberg's Marketing group to do a physical inventory of brands. They worked for the better part of the night, reviewing the logo pages and putting the names on a master list. They checked the departments we'd created for firms that had brands in several categories, like HP, (with Colorado, DeskJet, LaserJet, OfficeJet, ScanJet, SureStore, Brio, LXPro Servers, Pavilion, Vectra, PhotoSmart, CopyJet, and DeskWriter). The ordeal came to be known as "The Night of a Thousand Brands."

The lawyers never did find out exactly how many brands we had in the store that night. When the documented list got well past a thousand, they backed down. But we continued counting. Gerhardt gave Craig the final tally. It was thirty-three pages long and contained the names of over 1,500 brands, all of which were in the store. Craig had won his third game of chicken. But this one came around for another go, squawking, with feathers flying. Some lawyers don't know when they're licked.

They took issue with the Red's overleaf, a page I had designed showing seventy major brand logos and a heading that read, "We're Known by the Company We Keep." Underwriters' counsel told Craig we couldn't show this brand logo page without the express written consent of each and every brand. "But that'll take weeks. Besides, we have other store pages with logos in the S-1," he protested.

"Yes," they said, "but those pages are actually in the store."

"Thank you," Craig said. Within the hour, we had Web-enabled the simulated page and put it up live in the store. Craig provided the lawyers with the URL, so they could see it for themselves. They were not amused.

Chicken, game number four: Winner, Mr. Winn.

❧

NATURALLY, IN ORDER to take a company public, you have to have the blessing of its board of directors. The step was supposed to be a *fait accompli.* Who would have thought the bad penny would show up again?

Rafe Durn had a problem with the way the auditors had described the Series C investments. He thought it might pose a tax problem for his investors. Dean reminded him that PricewaterhouseCoopers had come up with the formula. "And, as I recall, Coopers was the firm you relied upon when you questioned our policies back in '97. Besides, there's no time to change it now. The road show appointments are set."

Durn stood firm. "I don't care. I'm voting no until they're rewritten."

Dean called Craig in desperation. He had *had* it with Rafe Durn.

Craig calmed his trusted CFO and told him he would handle Rafe. Craig and Rex were sharing a beer in the Deer Valley Lodge after a day of cell-phone skiing. "Dean, have Tracey call each board member. Set up a conference call for nine o'clock eastern—that's seven o'clock mountain time. Get some rest. I'll get us through this."

They picked up separate phones in the condo that night. As predicted, everyone supported the IPO except Rafe Durn. For the fifth time in three days, Craig found himself playing chicken. "Rafe," he said, "I've done everything I can do to take our company public. Right now we're as ready as we'll ever be. The market is receptive, but it won't hold. Last time, your delays cost us. I'm not going to let that happen again."

Laying down ultimatums wasn't Craig's style. He knew that if you gave an adversary no room to maneuver, the situation could easily blow up in your face. He had learned that the hard way back in his days with The Winn Company. It hadn't been pretty. And yet, almost against his will, he found himself pushing Rafe Durn into a corner, giving him no way out.

"We've been down this road before, Rafe," he spat out the words. "I offered you the keys to the company. Well, I'm doing it again. You can either say 'yes' and give us a unanimous decision tonight so we can start the road show on Wednesday, or you can show up in Charlottesville and start running the company."

There was an unbearable silence. Somebody coughed. Durn finally spoke. "Alright, Craig," he said. "You've got my vote."

With a collective sigh, the final board meeting for Value America as a private company was concluded. As farewells were uttered, someone said, "Go out there and do us proud, guys!"

"That's the plan," Craig said as he jumped from the frying pan into a raging fire.

...And if I perish, I perish—Esther

BILLIONS AND BILLIONS

*E*xhilarating is the best word to describe the harrowing approach into San Diego, California. The chartered jet slipped in just above the buildings that pierce the sky east of Lindberg Field as the lights of the city twinkled brightly beneath them. The three-engine Falcon 50 would be Value America's magic carpet for the next two weeks as Craig, Rex, Dean, and the company's shiny new CEO, Tom Morgan, embarked on a nationwide tour of investors. Our *second* Initial Public Offering road show had officially begun.

The IPO was structured to sell five million shares of Value America stock at between $14 and $16 a share. We expected to raise about $75 million, roughly the same amount we had just raised in our Series C round. This $150 million nest egg, with careful stewardship, would be enough to fund the company's growth well into 2001.

As our guys had gathered, Craig had felt a little tickle in his throat, which he ignored, since there was little he could do about it. Now it was in flames. He was running a fever and was beginning to cough. Worse, when he opened his mouth to tell Rex, hardly anything came out.

Everybody had a role in the IPO presentation, but Craig's was by far the hardest. His remarks were carefully crafted to encourage questions and draw the audience into the fray. At fifteen minutes, his prepared speech was a miracle of brevity.

Our road show was a far cry from a succession of guys delivering canned speeches from behind a podium. Rex's and Craig's portions had to appear extemporaneous to properly convey the confidence and credibility necessary to prevail in this hostile environment. Dean's financial review was both memorized and brief. It, like the other parts, was supported with visual fireworks we had developed in-house. Every couple of sentences, a new graphic would appear on the screen, supporting the spoken words, bringing the complex concepts to life, making the whole add up to more than the sum of its parts.

When Craig finished, he would introduce Rex. With considerable flourish and maximum dramatic effect, Rex demonstrated how the store worked, especially our multimedia presentations. This was the fun part. Our store in the hands of someone who knew its unique features was totally captivating. Rex was at the top of his game. He exuded confidence as he courted the audience and played off the serendipity of their varied reactions. Then, following the store demonstration, Rex would introduce Tom Morgan.

In the preparation for the IPO, we had discovered that Morgan was considerably less capable than he appeared. The reason he was such a good listener was that he had little or nothing intelligent to say. The first hint was subtle. Tom was conspicuously absent from all of the high-level maneuverings that ultimately got our show on the road. But now, sadly, the founders recognized one of the reasons he said so little was that he couldn't speak, at least not very well. There was no conviction in his voice, none of the authoritative tone so essential for leadership, no sales ability of any kind. But while this was disturbing, especially considering Morgan's lofty salary, it wasn't debilitating; Craig and Rex possessed enough charisma and sales prowess to compensate for Tom's deficiencies.

Before our team arrived in San Diego, Craig had tried to help. He wrote Morgan's ninety-second part and coached him on its delivery. He relegated Tom's role to introducing our team, using the pictures we had taken for our first IPO. Craig titled the slides for Tom and composed a revealing thought he could add to his introductions. Morgan would conclude by introducing Dean, who after explaining our financial model turned the baton back over to Craig for a wrap up and Q&A.

That's how it was supposed to work. A Craig Winn with laryngitis and a hacking cough didn't exactly fit the game plan. In desperation, Rex took the script and retired with Dean to learn Craig's lines. The two worked 'til the wee hours. But the problem wasn't the speech; it was the questions it invited. Rex and Dean knew they were in trouble. As for Craig, he hit the nearest pharmacy, bought all the drugs he could carry, and went to bed.

The road show got under way at precisely six forty-five Wednesday morning at Wall Street Associates in La Jolla. Craig, Rex, and Dean vividly remembered having been slapped in the face the last time they were here. It had been the first clue we were in trouble.

Although Rex was ready, Craig's voice held. For the moment, at least, it seemed a good night's sleep had been just what the doctor ordered. This was a great relief to the silver-haired attorney. Rex knew from his initial road show experience that the prepared speech was seldom what investors heard. Rarely would the preamble have left Craig's lips before the questions started flying.

The vast majority of the investors knew nothing about retail, and little about Internet commerce except what they had read about Amazon. Craig's *modus operandi* was to use their questions to educate them on the realities of retail and how Value America had been invented to solve the problems others endured. Honest inquiries were met squarely with intelligent answers dredged from Craig's quarter century of experience. This, of course, was a problem for Rex. He had three years of observing his partner going for him, but that, he feared, was not nearly enough.

With Craig's voice, if not his normal temperature, temporarily restored, Rex was off the hook. The show went on as originally planned. Sort of. Tom Morgan had only ten short sentences to deliver, but to everyone's chagrin, he began with what amounted to an apology for not really knowing what he was doing, being new and all. Our new CEO either had a terminal case of stage fright, or he was not the business leader he had made himself out to be. Craig and Rex prayed that Tom's foibles weren't actually what they now appeared to be: an ominous sign that he wasn't very smart.

For their part, Wall Street Associates reacted enthusiastically. The market was receptive, having recovered from September's gloom. They agreed to buy as much Value America stock as Robbie Stephens would allot to them. One meeting down. Sixty-one to go.

The presentations were scheduled an hour and a quarter apart, which left no time for idle chatter and precious little for ground transportation. The group made two more meetings that morning in San Diego, and by noon they were in Los Angeles for three more. They received enthusiastic yeses from Duncan Hurst, Nicholas Applegate, Provident, Capital Research, and Trust Company of the West. We were on a roll.

༄༺✷༻

THE FOUR SPENT Wednesday night at the Mandarin Hotel in San Francisco. Thursday promised to be a big day: eight meetings in and around the city by the bay, packed into time slots like sardines in a can.

They started early at Van Wagoner Capital on California Street. Craig felt awful, but he answered the bell. He was running on drugs and adrenaline. Another yes. Then the group made the short trek to the Transamerica Tower, the skinny pyramid on Montgomery Street that had become the defining feature of the San Francisco skyline. At eight forty-five, they walked confidently into the offices of Transamerica Investments on the sixteenth floor, right into a brick wall. As Craig, refluent with Robitussin, began his corporate overview, he delivered the first of our dot-com heresies:

"We reach more people using off-line advertising to drive online sales. Last year we launched the first extensive print advertising campaign for any online store. It increases our credibility and brand share, and provides us with a throttle—we can ramp up rapidly to capitalize on opportunities. With off-line advertising, we benefit from vendor co-op, where brands pay us to sell their products. Brands understand the dynamics of traditional reach and frequency better than they do the more nebulous nature of virtual banners....

"Mature retailers invest as little as two percent in advertising, a ratio of fifty to one. Our model is more modest...yet advertising is a core competency. In cities where we advertise, we have achieved greater brand awareness in a shorter period of time, on less money, than most anyone...."

At that point, an investor, a self-proclaimed expert on all things dot-com, jumped all over Craig. With a big stake in Amazon, he had bought into the whole media metrics popularity myth. So he attacked our fanatical notion that e-tail was really another permutation of retail and that there were other ways to advertise than enriching portals. Craig held his ground, time and again letting the investor crawl out onto his limb, which Craig then proceeded to cut off using facts and insight honed by years of experience. The meeting went downhill rapidly and ended early. Transamerica declined to participate.

We didn't know it then, but this firm would be the only one to say no. As the days wore into weeks, sixty-one out of sixty-two meetings would cause cash to flow from those who had it to those who wanted it.

The ten o'clock spot was scheduled with J.H. Gambini, the firm whose namesake, Jake Gambini, Craig had bonded with so quickly the previous September. This promised to be interesting. During our darkest days following the failed IPO, Craig had tried to contact Jake, but had never heard back from him—strange for a man who had so strongly expressed his desire to be included in any future investments.

"Why didn't you return my phone calls, Jake?" Craig asked.

"What phone calls? I didn't know you called."

Craig was dumfounded. "You're kidding! I called you three times and left messages. Not only that, I called the father of your godson, Dale Dandridge, and asked him to call you on our behalf. Not once, but twice."

Jake shook his head. "That rascal. He never called me, Craig, I swear. You know I would have helped."

All the big words from Dale Dandridge and the other Robertson Stephens execs came rushing back: *Don't worry. We'll raise the capital to keep you going.* Jake Gambini had been the perfect candidate. All they had had to do was make a phone call, and he would have jumped in with both feet.

Before the presentation began, Jake said, "Look, Craig, it's obvious your IPO is going to be a big success. You'll be grossly oversold, and everybody's going to be begging for stock. I want ten percent of the deal, five hundred thousand shares. I'll be your most loyal holder. Do this for me. Call Bentley Hollis and Gordon Conover. You tell them I want half a million shares."

Craig passed Jake's request along, although he had serious concerns.

Gambini had never actually listened to a Value America presentation, and he was still loaded with Amazon stock. Our models were like oil and water. The relationship between Dale and Jake was becoming suspect, too. Yet Jake understood retail, and he said he was willing to hold his stock. Few investors seemed to fit that profile. Many are opportunists, clamoring for an anticipated first-day pop, planning to flip their shares for a profit. Craig and Rex were under no illusions. They knew they were just a piece of raw meat.

ভেঃৠ

IF ONE WERE to watch the faces of investors as they listened to the presentation, it wasn't hard to pick out the ones who liked us for the right reasons. But even the skeptics invariably came around when Johnson laid down the "boring" part of the pitch: the financials. To an investor on the lookout for a budding success story, his polished prose was pure poetry.

"Value America generates revenue from the sale of products," he began, innocuously enough. "This is pure e-commerce. We sell products on the Web and earn a margin. In addition, product presentations, site advertising, credit origination, and product renewals provide revenue diversity, all with gross margins over eighty percent.

"Our sales more than doubled from the first quarter of '98 to the second, and they tripled from the second to the third. Fourth quarter sales were impacted by our postponed IPO and the subsequent reduction in capital. However, when our future funding was assured, we resumed advertising and achieved sales in the last five weeks of the year that nearly exceeded the sales of the entire prior quarter! [There was no point in explaining how Dorchak had almost spent us into bankruptcy.] And speaking of funding, Value America has now raised one hundred and thirty million in private equity capital, more than any Internet company prior to their IPO, more than any of the previous leaders, @Home, AOL, Amazon, and Yahoo!

"Value America requires no working capital financing. We sell products out of the brands' warehouses. Credit card funding is swift, and payables average forty days. With no receivables and virtual inventory, trade financing generates cash. We're a self-basting bird!

"Value America's path to profitability begins with sales growth and leveraging our operations. Our inventory-less model is designed to run at four percent of revenue. Advertising is becoming more effective, and we expect brands to eventually fund over half our marketing budget. Once we've achieved scale, we will be profitable. As you can see, the Internet is the key enabler for very high levels of productivity.

"Over time we expect to achieve a fourteen percent overall blended gross margin. Overhead at four percent of sales and net advertising, after co-op, at five percent, yields a five percent operating profit. This is remarkable because, like a bank, we earn this margin on other people's assets."

September this wasn't. Although our team was doing the same thing they had done the previous fall, the reactions, and results, were radically different. Nobody was asking, "What price will you accept?" The only question on investors' minds was, "How many shares can we get?"

The team finished up in San Francisco, moved on to Janus, Invesco, and other big firms in Denver, and then flew back to Charlottesville for the weekend. Unlike the September attempt, the key cities of New York and Boston were not held in reserve for later in the road show. Bright and early on Monday morning, Craig and company began two grueling days—fifteen meetings—in the Big Apple, followed by a nine-meeting marathon day in Boston.

Craig was getting sicker. Whatever this bug was, it wasn't responding to medicine, and it wasn't overly impressed by a night's sleep. The fever grew, and Craig's voice faded, but the road show just kept going. The audiences, while showing none of the open hostility of the previous September, still asked a plethora of questions, most of which only Craig, of the four, could adequately answer. Our prospects were inevitably linked to his health.

These brief encounters aren't exactly cordial. Institutional investors have heard it all. They aren't easily persuaded. They're experts at disrupting presenters and probing for weaknesses. The game itself is rife with pitfalls. Investors can ask whatever they like, but thanks to the SEC, the company must be incredibly careful in how it responds. In the field of retail, Dean lacked experience and Rex lacked the financial understanding to stray far from their prepared scripts. Tom couldn't even introduce our team convincingly, much less provide extemporaneous elucidation on the finer points of e-commerce. Craig, fearful that the investors would be unimpressed with our new CEO, had to insulate Tom, but in order to do that, he had to be there, sick or not.

Fortunately, even as the quality of our presentations faded, we remained a scorchingly hot commodity. The sellers became the sellees. "Please lobby the bankers to allot us more shares," they were asked repeatedly. There were only five million shares to go around. By the time the road show was half over, the subscription had been oversold by a factor of ten: in other words, if we'd had *fifty* million shares to sell, we could have sold them all.

The ground rules for pricing a hot IPO go something like this: if interest in the stock is strong, then the middle of the range, in this case $15 a share, is where the price is set. However, if the offering is oversold several times over, the upper end of the range, $16, is a possibility. In rare cases of extreme demand, the price range might even be raised—instead of $14--$16, it might bump to as high as $15–$17 a share. Only the very best IPOs, with the investment community clamoring for stock, enjoy a lift in the range. It doesn't happen often, and seldom by very much.

As the road show wore on, it became obvious that there wasn't nearly enough Value America stock to go around. A lot of people were going to get less than they wanted. That worried Craig and Rex because they had promised to make stock available to the friends of the company, those who had kept us alive in darker days.

Problems like this, though, were the direct result of unmitigated success. The word had apparently gotten out. Unlike the previous September, when the typical luncheon had been attended by a dozen people, we were now filling the grand ballrooms of major hotels with hundreds of investors. We were drawing standing-room-only crowds, often with people stacked two to three deep along the back walls.

The media caught the buzz as well. Most everywhere the troupe went, the press corps were there to greet them. *Fortune* magazine wanted to give their readers an insider's look at what it was like to be caught up in the whirlwind of a dot-com road show. They asked a reporter to follow the team from city to city. Craig, of course, loved the idea. A major reason for going public was to gain free publicity. Media attention served as an accelerant for our advertising efforts. But the lawyers, ever in character, were horrified. A healthy Craig would have taken them on and prevailed, but in his present condition, he simply acquiesced.

By the end of the second day in New York, Craig looked like the walking dead. As they finished a meeting in the World Trade Center, his knees buckled. Rex caught him before he hit the floor and helped him into the elevator. "I'm not going to make it tomorrow, guys. We've done New York, but I'm finished." The last two days had included some of the biggest names in finance: Oxford, Oppenheimer, Fortis, Dean Witter Reynolds, Amerindo, Bankers Trust, Warburg Pincus, Ardsley, Scudder Kemper, and the venerable J.P. Morgan. They had been grilled, probed, and pounded by the hot-shot New York investment community and had emerged victorious: every one of them had said yes. But Craig's body was screaming *no!* He had run out of gas. "You're going to have to go on without me," he said, forcing the words out between hacking coughs.

Rex and Dean helped him to the limo. The team drove to the airport amid a pall of eerie silence. The moment was bittersweet—rife with irony, contradictory, glorious, and frightening.

The Falcon 50 was waiting to take them to Boston. It would be the longest and by far the hardest day on the schedule. The jubilation that accompanied earlier flights was now missing. They quickly ate on the plane and sent Craig to bed when they arrived. Rex and Dean went to the hotel bar.

"He'll make it," Rex said.

"Craig? No way," Dean responded. "I've never seen a person that sick still vertical. It's not going to happen. We're on our own, I'm afraid."

"He'll make it," Rex repeated. "It's Boston!"

જ઼઼૯ઃૡૢ

SIX THIRTY THE NEXT morning, Rex, Dean, and Tom were having breakfast in the hotel dining room. The conversation revolved around how they could expect to fare without Craig fielding the questions. "I'll be honest," Dean said. "I know my own world well enough, but not retail. You've been with him for three years, Rex. Besides, you're a lawyer— you're supposed to be a silver-tongued devil. The Q&A is yours."

Rex figured Dean was right, but it wasn't going to be pretty. "Well, I…" He stopped in mid-stammer and looked up. He then tossed his napkin on the table, grinned, and finished his thought, "…don't think that'll be necessary. Would you look at that? Lazarus walks!"

Craig, looking better than he felt, stumbled to the table. "Get him some hot tea," Dean said loudly, catching a waiter's ear, "with lemon and honey."

A road show waits for no one, so ready or not, the festivities began again with a seven-thirty meeting at Standish, followed by Fidelity, Massachusetts Financial, and State Street. At twelve thirty, there was a group luncheon at the Bay Club. Craig was fading fast, but he put on a bold face. The experience reminded Rex of a boxing match, where round after round, Craig would go out and do battle only to fall back into his corner a little more beat up than the round before. He and Dean would fan him with a towel, give him a drink of water, tell him he was doing great, and send him back out there again at the bell. Only problem was, every round Craig faced a new, fresh opponent.

Throughout the road show, the vast majority of their audience had been young, investors in their twenties and thirties, long on education and short on experience. But at Putnam, at least half of the seven or eight investors jammed into the small conference room had gray hair. Their senior managers had turned out *en masse* to check out the boys from Virginia and their scorching IPO.

Nobody had been a pushover, of course, but these guys were aggressive. They challenged everything, wanted to know why, how, when. It wasn't so much that they were belligerent; they were just merciless. These seasoned skeptics had seen it all, and they apparently wanted to impress their underlings. They were going to take some convincing.

By this time, our offering was hugely oversold, and we knew it. So Rex became protective, angered by Putnam's incessant probing. *If they can't see the value in this, screw 'em. Let's move on. We don't need these guys. We're better off letting Craig rest. His health is more important than this sale.*

Craig didn't see it that way. The harder they probed, the more aggressively he countered, providing answers they couldn't refute. Rex and Dean felt helpless and frustrated. These were the toughest questions yet. They couldn't answer them, and Craig didn't know when to quit.

Rex did the only thing he could do to protect his friend from the pounding. He got up and shut down the computer in the middle of Craig's response to a question about how co-op payments from brands are an offset to advertising costs, not revenue. Rex announced they were leaving. The investors were taken aback. *We are a big, respected outfit. You can't just get up and walk out.* Rex didn't care. He was in mother hen mode.

Everyone was surprised when Putnam asked for the maximum allotment. Treating us like garbage didn't mean they thought we were.

The day ended mercifully, surrealistically. By the time team Value America arrived at their last Boston meeting, they were a couple of hours late. It was well past seven o'clock. But to their surprise, these investors acted more like old friends than adversaries. "Can we get you a cold beer?" they asked, and then, "Why don't we just sit and chat for a while, get to know one another." This was followed by, "Forget about the presentation. You guys have this thing so oversold it's not going to matter anyway. We've already placed our order for as many shares as Robbie Stephens is willing to give us." Hard to believe, but true.

This was clearly turning into a phenomenon. As a result, the bankers decided to rethink their pricing strategy. With the stock oversold by fifteen times and demand rising rapidly, they acted. They told Craig that they were going to raise the price range, and not by just a smidgen. They would give it a huge shove, to $20 to $22 a share: one of the largest price range hikes for any IPO ever, dot-com or otherwise.

Putting this in perspective, there were over forty-three million shares of Value America stock outstanding. Bumping the price up by six dollars a share effectively raised the company's valuation by $260,609,170, and this was only the increase. Put another way, it put an extra $132 million in the net worth column of Craig Winn and Rex Scatena. Not bad for one phone call.

After Boston, it was on to Milwaukee, Kansas City, Philadelphia, Baltimore, Minneapolis, Detroit, and Chicago. The team had had it. They were exhausted, and Craig was still sick. They had visited, it seemed, every financial center that could boast an airport from California to New England. There didn't seem to be much point in going on, since the IPO was now oversold twenty times over. There was literally nothing left to sell. But two Texas towns, Dallas and Houston, loomed on the horizon.

"We're not going to Texas, Dale," a weary Craig told the analyst. "There's no point," he coughed into the phone. "Let's call it a day."

"Please, just two more cities. It isn't the shares. It's the relationships."

"Yeah, *your* relationships," Craig sighed. "We're just this week's hunk of meat." Coughing again, Craig surrendered. "Alright, we'll go, but not me. I *have* to be in Raleigh-Durham for an IBM meeting. I'll ask Rex and Dean to go to Texas. They'll do a fine job."

Craig couldn't bring himself to send Morgan. His performance had not improved with practice. As our new CEO had gotten more familiar with his part, his delivery had gotten sloppier, almost lackadaisical. In an environment where salesmanship and enthusiasm were base-line requirements, Tom's hesitant delivery had come to grate on everyone's nerves like a toothache. He was sent home.

✥

IT WAS AN easy taste to acquire, these perfect steaks at the restaurant owned by legendary baseball announcer Harry Caray, in the Windy City. Craig and Rex decided to indulge themselves, just the two of them—reflect on life's journey and the incredible place to which it had led.

So many dragons had been slain in the last three years. So many times, their backs had been against the wall. So many times, they had been mugged by fate and left for dead, only to recover, dust themselves off, and charge ahead. And now it had come to this—it was shaping up to be one of most incredible IPOs of the dot-com era. They speculated on where the deal would finally price. Craig sensed that it might actually end up above the newly elevated range.

The overwhelming demand for our stock had another ramification as well. IPOs have a feature known as "the green shoe," which gives the bankers the right to sell an over-allotment of shares, up to fifteen percent, should demand be sufficient. But unlike the five million shares created for the IPO, diluting everyone, this block consisted of shares that were already owned.

"Looks like they're going to exercise the green shoe," Rex said.

Craig smiled. "Good thing. Those shares belong to you and me."

"Paper wealth is all very nice, but with the lock-up, we won't be able to sell anything for six months. This'll put a little cash—hard-earned cash, I might add—in our pockets. Let's see. Five million shares times fifteen percent is seven hundred fifty thousand shares. If they price this at the upper end of the range, say at twenty-two bucks, it'll mean we'll split seventeen million."

Craig was starting to feel better.

Rex raised his glass. "Here's to birds in the hand, my friend."

It was a good news, bad news story. $22, the price they would receive from Robbie Stephens, would be less than a third of what the stock would be worth the following day.

The prospect of a deal well done wasn't the only reason to smile. Craig and Rex shared a secret that only a handful of people on earth knew at the time, and it was pure dynamite. The first quarter had ended a few days earlier, and they knew we had performed incredibly well. It's almost proverbial among companies going public that their first quarter out of the chute falls short of expectations. It's always the same story. It takes so much effort to achieve an initial public offering, businesses lose focus, execute poorly, and as a result miss their prognostications. But not Value America. We had beat our target by thirty percent.

In five weeks, our Q1 numbers would be announced. If there were any logic, any science, to this, the price of our shares would shoot into the stratosphere. Still, it was delicious indeed, sharing a secret that had the potential to make the dreams of everyone who had believed in us come true. Their New York strips were bland in comparison.

◈◈◈

CRAIG WAS PROUD of his old friend as Johnson described the masterful job Rex had done presenting the company in his stead. As the last meeting concluded, with AIM Capital Management in Houston, Rex reported that he had imbued the occasion with a heartfelt sense of destiny.

"History," he said, "is being made here today, and you're a part of it. This is the last presentation in the greatest road show of the dot-com era."

Moments later, in a quiet conference room at IBM's headquarters, Craig called Dale Dandridge, Gordon Conover, and Bentley Hollis. They were together in San Francisco, awaiting his call. Bentley began by reviewing the long list of people the team had encountered. As he read their names, he enumerated how much stock each had committed to buy and listed how much each was actually allocated.

"What we're witnessing here, Craig," Bentley said, "represents a success rate better than any IPO we've managed. Every investor but one of the hundred and forty firms you met with one-on-one or at one of your group luncheons has asked for the maximum number of shares. You're oversold more than twenty times."

The magnitude of the whole affair was only beginning to sink in. It was one thing to win an election. It was something else again to win with ninety-nine and a half percent of the vote.

"We have a problem, Craig," Conover said. "You told us that the people on your 'friends of the company' list would say yes, but we told you they wouldn't, because, frankly, they seldom do. They just talk a good game because they don't want to disappoint the company's founders."

"Uh huh."

"Well, we called everyone on your list," Gordon continued. "Every one of them committed to buy—every last one. Even your friend Jerry Falwell is in."

"So the problem," Dale explained unnecessarily, "is that the company's friends are only going to get a twentieth of the stock they want."

"C'mon, guys," Craig pleaded, "five percent of the shares they requested is meaningless. It's an insult. Without these people, we wouldn't be here. You've got to do better. "

"We can't. Not with five million shares."

"Well how about this?" Craig asked. "Increase the number of shares— say half a million, to five million five hundred thousand. Take care of our friends with the increase."

There was a long pause. Finally, Bentley spoke. "Umm, well, okay. I can't remember this ever happening before. If it has, it's rare. But it's legal, I suppose. Sure, why not! We'll do that."

"Thanks. Now, what's the price?"

"You know the drill. We want to give our clients a twenty percent bump. There appears to be plenty of support around thirty dollars. Twenty percent of thirty is six, netting twenty-four dollars a share. Right now, we have demand to spare. You can push it higher if you want, twenty-five dollars, maybe more. It's your call, Craig. What do you want to do?"

"They slaughter pigs. Let's be good guys, good corporate citizens. I think twenty-three dollars a share would be fine. The price will go up soon enough, I have a feeling."

Relieved chuckles were heard as Gordon Conover spoke for the group. "That's great, Craig. This is going to go over real well—it should endear you to all of your shareholders. Thanks a million." *Actually, thanks 4.5 million—Robbie Stephens' take on the deal*—Craig calculated in his head.

There was a pause. Now that the negotiations were done, Gordon cleared his throat. "Y'know, Craig, this IPO of yours was remarkable. I hope you know that."

Craig coughed again. His throat still hurt.

"You're going to raise..." Gordon paused as punched the numbers into his calculator, "a hundred twenty-seven million dollars. Plus we're going to exercise our over-allotment. That's another nineteen million, a hundred and forty-six million all together. That's twice what we expected." He paused again as he did another calculation. "It also means that your company is now worth one *billion* dollars. Congratulations!"

"But it goes beyond that," Bentley jumped in. "This was a class act. As a matter of fact, we are not aware of any IPO—whether at Robertson Stephens or elsewhere—where the deal was as greatly oversold as yours, where the price range was raised as much as yours, and then priced higher still. No IPO I've ever managed had as high a percentage of investor participation and demand per investor as yours. Add the unanimous participation of your friends of the company and...well, all I can say is that this was spectacular. I, *we*, want to thank you for letting us be a part of it. There may have been bigger ones, but Value America's IPO was among the very best."

Riches certainly make themselves wings; they fly away like an eagle toward heaven—Solomon

A FAILURE TO COMMUNICATE

eing "made up," is unnatural, yet that's what was happening to Craig the day after the IPO. Makeup artists were brushing, powdering, and generally fussing all over him. Nikki Norton, the company's new VP of Communications, had done her job. She had Craig booked on a series of newsmaker programs. Life had become a swirl, as unreal as the makeup itself.

The television appearances were produced remotely from studios in the nation's capitol. The moment Craig and Nikki arrived at FOX's, ABC's, or CNN's studio, they were immediately escorted into prep rooms. Studio executives briefed the pair on what to expect. All the while, Nikki grilled Craig with questions she thought the program's host might ask. She praised the answers she liked and coached Craig on the ones she didn't.

Without wasting a moment, Craig was led into a darkened studio. Someone switched on the lights, revealing a small stool strategically placed before a dramatic backdrop like a picture of Capitol Hill. A technician motioned for him to sit on the stool facing a robotic camera. An earpiece was placed in his right ear with its cable drawn down his back out of the camera's view. Then the lights were switched off, except the ones above the camera, which were so bright all else disappeared. Each studio had all the warmth of a hospital operating room.

Craig sat there for what seemed like an eternity, not knowing if the camera was on or off. The shows' hosts were already on the air, but he could neither see nor hear them. They were in another city, most often New York. As sounds began to enter his right ear, a voice would say, "Today, we have Mr. Craig Winn with us. His company, Value America, went public yesterday. It was one of the most successful IPOs ever. The price jumped to nearly five times the initial filing range. Mr. Winn, how does it feel to be a billionaire?"

"No different, really. My values haven't changed—only the value of my company has. But as a result, we are able to fulfill our mission of bringing people and products together."

"That's great," a faceless voice made itself heard through the earpiece. It was all so unnatural. "So what is Value America all about?"

Great, Craig thought, *I've got twenty seconds to explain what it took three hundred people three years to build.* "We use the power of the Internet to form an electronic conveyer-belt between factories and consumers, so we can sell the best for less. We produce informative multimedia product presentations so our customers can make better buying decisions. We're comprehensive, selling everything from toasters to televisions." Twenty seconds,

Craig thought, keeping track of time in the recesses of his mind. I wonder if my answer is going to pass muster with Nikki? No time for that now. Remember to smile, he thought, as his right ear buzzed again.

"Paul Allen, Microsoft's cofounder, is a backer, is he not?"

"Yes. Paul and I believe in using convergence to serve more people and to make technology less complicated. Convergence is the combination of the Internet with the telephone, television, and PCs. We use it to improve our customer service."

"So consumers can call you up as well as shop online? Isn't that a bit dated for an online store?"

"No. More people have phones than computers. Using the phone simply allows us to serve everybody. When people buy their Internet-enabled PCs from us, a whole new world awaits them."

"How many hits does your online store get a day?" the voice asked.

"We don't measure hits any more than Nordstrom counts how many people enter their stores. We believe e-tail is retail. We're just down the hall—not down the street."

"Well, that's nice, Mr. Winn, but tell me. Are you disappointed that the stock fell from its high yesterday and opened lower again today?"

"No. The IPO was filed at fifteen dollars a share. We were delighted when the range was raised to twenty-one dollars, and even more pleased when it was priced at twenty-three. The fact that it's well above that now is a good thing for our shareholders."

"That was Craig Winn, chairman of Value America. Now...."

With that, the lights were switched back on, the earpiece was removed, and Craig and Nikki raced off to do it all again. All the while, Nikki told Craig where he had performed well, and constructively criticized his weaker answers. All in all, she was pleased, and told Craig so. "I was Press Secretary for the House Judiciary Committee during the Clinton impeachment hearings," she said. "I served in the White House, too. But I've gotta tell you, you're better in front of a camera than any of 'em. Although," she added, "with practice, you can be *better*."

Nikki was smart, connected, and charming. But it was her faith that got Craig's attention. He was no stranger to religion. He'd been the youngest ordained ruling elder in the Presbyterian Church. He'd taught evangelism, led youth groups. But his faith had been all but crushed by the hypocrites who had ravaged Dynasty when she was down. Nikki's honest, open faith reminded him that Christianity was a *relationship*, not a religion. Like Craig's new friend Jerry Falwell, Nikki loved the world one person at a time.

REVEREND FALWELL INVITED Craig and Nikki to accompany him to Austin to meet with then-Governor George W. Bush. On the trip down, Norton coaxed Falwell into sharing some insights into his remarkable life. He told stories about his childhood as a bootlegger's son. Jerry had been a bad boy, wrecking his first car before he was old enough to drive. He, like Craig and the man they were going to visit, had been young and foolish when they were young enough to be foolish. They were all living examples of how God can transform lives, if only we are willing.

As they flew on, Falwell laughed about the Teletubby debacle. The media had broken a story claiming the conservative television evangelist was boycotting Teletubbies because he thought Tinky Winky was gay. There was little basis for the story; it was made up by some misguided jokester with the Associated Press. Falwell said, "When the story broke, the media had a field day with it. Reporters called me and asked, 'How could you be against a children's toy, against Teletubbies? Have you finally lost it?'" Jerry laughed, "I thought they were making fun of my weight. You know, I thought a Teletubby was an overweight television evangelist. I didn't even know what Teletubbies were when the media was accusing me of being against them."

"You mean the media *manufactured* the story?" Craig asked. "It was just one reporter parroting what another had said until they'd said it so often the whole country thought you were off your rocker?"

"Pretty much," Jerry answered, as if it shouldn't have been a surprise. The only thing actually connecting Falwell to this silliness was a story someone else wrote in the *Liberty Journal*. And even it only quoted other mainstream media accounts. "You can't believe much of what you hear or read these days."

"How do you handle bogus attacks like that?" Craig queried. "I mean, they made up the story just to embarrass you!"

Jerry smiled, "Much of what the Bible says is counter to the direction my critics are trying to take America. I'm a thorn in their side. Any time I stub my toe, make a mistake, and I make my share, they're on me like ugly on a monkey. I learned long ago that my friends know that most of these attacks are rubbish, and my enemies won't believe anything I say in my defense anyway. It's the price I pay for being willing to stand up for what I believe. Truth is seldom reported."

The Governor's mansion in Austin is grand, befitting a state replete with cattle and oil barons. As the four approached its iron gates, a guard recognized Falwell and, knowing he was on the list, motioned the driver through. Moments later, they were greeted by Karl Rove, George W.'s campaign strategist. Rove's hair was thin, long, and stringy at the time; he somehow looked unkempt even in a suit. Fortunately, he displayed none of the bark of Clinton's Carville. He seemed content to stand behind his man, support him, out of the media's glare. He was a servant in the most noble sense of the word.

But there was still something that made Craig uneasy. Perhaps it was just Rove's role in the game of perceptions, the political game of positioning. Like "professional" corporate types, political strategists usually pursue two agendas for their candidates. The first is public, rich with buzzwords, reasoned and compassionate, confident and competent. The private agenda, however, for both career politicians and corporate managers, is often about fame and fortune, *self promotion*. Winn, by contrast, is a builder, a pragmatic idealist, motivated by ideas, and excited by their execution. He has little regard for the gamesmanship far too many professionals display, whether corporate or political. Yet with the media more interested in good stories than in good journalism, with caricatures more important than character, the Carvilles and the Roves are necessary. Their mastery of positioning is the essence of the game.

The press, Craig reflected, has made the messenger more important than the message. As a result, enlightened debate gets swallowed up in self-serving agendas. "If you can't debate the message, malign the messenger" has become the standard, albeit lethal, operating procedure in far too many boardrooms, caucus rooms, and pressrooms.

With those thoughts in Craig's mind, the Virginians were escorted into a cozy, traditionally decorated reception room just off the main hall. George W. Bush's nomination was still more than a year away. It was a year in which Craig would be approached by three of W.'s rivals for the Republican nomination. First, the Forbes family invited him to cruise with them aboard their magnificent yacht, the Highlander. Next he met with Senator McCain, in John's Washington office, and later for dinner in Craig's Charlottesville home. He got to know Congressman John Kasich as well.

Few politicians possess Bush's charm, Craig would quickly learn. One-on-one, W. is warm, focused, and charming—a superb conversationalist. He's a tall, lean, strong man, yet unafraid to show his soft side. His family and his faith are his first loves. When Craig asked him, "Why run for President?" W. answered, "Because I'm good with people. Presidents are defined by the crises that arise during their time in office. This is where I'm best. Give me a problem, and America can count on me to work out a solution." The answer was reminiscent of his father's presidency. The senior Bush was also good with people and great in times of crisis. Falwell loved *him*, too.

Craig asked, "What issue stirs your passions, Governor."

"Underprivileged children," he said. "Craig, I want to see the kind of technology you're working with benefit every child."

"I believe it can, but it's a struggle. Why is it, Governor, that politicians fight things that will really serve underprivileged children: business-sponsored programs designed to make technology more available, vouchers for school choice, performance-based pay for teachers, and school accountability?"

"It's because they count on unions for votes and financial support," Bush said. "Maybe my compassionate conservatism will change that. But tell me, Craig, how's this e-commerce thing you're doing going to impact our ability to pay for schools?"

"It's a problem," Craig answered. "Right now, online sales aren't usually taxed. But sales tax helps fund our schools. Our Governor, Jim Gilmore, is heading the President's Commission on Internet Taxation. I've been asked to testify before it. I'm also serving on the Governor's Technology Taskforce. Paying for schools and getting PCs into the hands of disenfranchised children is essential if we hope to prosper and grow together as a nation."

They talked for the better part of two hours about a host of things, including W.'s fraternity brother at Yale, Fred Smith. On the way out, Nikki shared that her good friend, David Kuo, had just turned down the job of press liaison for Governor Bush. She proposed a meeting. Craig agreed, little suspecting how the connection would later impact his life.

On the return trip, the weary travelers coaxed Reverend Falwell into sharing how the Moral Majority had been formed, and why it had faded into the recesses of history. Jerry said, "A few of my preacher friends and I went to California to see Ronald Reagan. We wanted him to run for President. He was reluctant," Jerry added, "until we shared our plan to quietly mobilize the American faithful, good and decent people, hardworking family folks, through their churches and temples. We told him that the majority of Americans were moral and that they deserved a moral leader. He said yes. So we went back to our churches and started to mobilize other pastors. Before we knew it, we'd helped elect a President. Ronald Reagan and I were very close."

"Why did the Moral Majority die?"

"It was supposed to be low profile, kept under the radar screen. When the media discovered us, they mischaracterized everything we were doing. What started off as a good thing turned sour."

They had hardly returned home when the good reverend called again. This time he invited Craig to have dinner with former Secretary of State

Henry Kissinger. It would be an intimate affair, only four or five people, in a private dining room near Falwell's Listen America broadcasting studio. Kissinger had wanted to speak out against something President Clinton was doing, but as a former Secretary of State, he had to be careful. He told Craig that he chose Jerry's show because he trusted Falwell, calling him the nation's best interviewer.

To spend an evening with Henry Kissinger is to brush up against greatness. When Craig asked, "Who would you like to see in the White House?" Kissinger answered without hesitation.

"John McCain. He is a hero." He paused and said, "Let me tell you a story. As a good-will gesture, the North Vietnamese were willing to release John from prison. They knew his father was Pacific Fleet Commander. I told them, 'No. First in, first out. It's the military way.' When the fighting was over, both John and his father came to my office and thanked me.

"He is a good man," Kissinger continued in his slow, deep, resonant voice. "He knows everything he needs to know to be a great President. More than ever, America needs to elect a man of good character."

"What do you think," Craig posed, "of the Texas Governor?"

"He, like his father, is a fine man. I think he'd make a good President. I'm only afraid he may be a little too sure of himself. He's assumed he's already won the nomination. I believe he needs to study the issues more thoroughly to be effective in the debates," said the voice of legend.

"What was Richard Nixon really like?"

"A genius. Tireless. We would discuss things until he was sure he knew all there was to know. Then he would instinctively see his opponent's weakness. He'd go right for the jugular. We made a good team."

"Besides Reagan, who contributed the most to freeing Eastern Europeans from the shackles of communism?" Falwell asked.

"Pope John Paul," the Jewish Kissinger answered.

"Do you believe in God, Dr. Kissinger? Do you pray?" Craig felt compelled to ask.

"Yes, and often, ever since I was a little boy." Smart men know who's in charge.

Following the Kissinger dinner, Falwell invited Craig to join him for another meal, this time in the Senate Caucus Room on Capitol Hill. Their host was the *The Washington Times*, owned in part by the controversial Reverend Sun Myung Moon. The newspaper had decided to honor Reverend Falwell and other statesmen by bestowing on them their lifetime achievement award. Reverend Moon considers himself a special emissary of God, which makes fundamentalist preachers like Jerry Falwell a little nervous. "As divergent as some of our views are," Dr. Falwell told Craig, "it's important that we avoid the media picturing Reverend Moon and me together. It could be used to imply an endorsement of his religious views."

The photo op never occurred, but it wasn't thirty seconds after Falwell's admonition that Craig and the pastor headed to the men's room. Three stalls, three people. Guess where Craig first met the Reverend Sun Myung Moon. Quite a picture.

Of course, the most popular newspaper in the nation's capital is *The Washington Post*, not *The Times*. Craig had occasion to meet its CEO too, under no less unusual circumstances. We had become frustrated with Charlottesville's local paper. Their coverage at the time was consistently negative, despite the fact we had created hundreds of jobs, had donated hundreds of thousands of dollars to local charities, and were now the community's largest source of tax revenues. Craig considered encouraging *The Post* to buy and manage the paper. So he wrote to Don Graham, Chairman and CEO of *The Washington Post*. Graham promptly called and scheduled a meeting.

It was interesting for a host of reasons. The first was Graham's self-deprecating stories about his service in Vietnam, a conflict of which the *Post* vehemently disapproved. Then the warm and charming Graham candidly admitted that many of his writers might go out of their way to condemn something that was owned by *The Post* just to *appear* impartial. It sounded to Craig like he was implying they'd mislead their readers if it served their interests.

Then there was the paper's most treasured trophy. With all of their Pulitzer Prizes, only one trophy graces the *Post's* executive conference room. It's the press plate for the day Nixon resigned. They are inordinately proud of their role in bringing down a President. Journalists often tell us more about themselves than they do about whomever they're condemning.

Overall, *The Washington Post's* coverage of Value America was decidedly slanted. The only positive story was one in which there was *no* story. The senior editors of *The Post* invited Craig in for lunch and collectively conducted a recorded interview. Rather than write a story based upon their discussion, they simply decided to print the interview, Q&A style. It began with a review of Craig's recent George W. Bush meeting. It specifically addressed the importance sales tax plays in funding our public schools. Craig was opposed to letting our children's education suffer as a result of sales tax not being collected online. To him, it was a question of placing the collective good over his own self-interest. Not the kind of thing you'd expect from a dot-com founder.

TWO THINGS HAPPENED the following week that changed Craig's view of himself and his role in the world. First, Justin Caise called asking for two hours of Craig's time, without explanation. Around the old drop-leaf table, Justin talked about racism in America. He said, "Craig, I want you to run for Governor of Virginia, with the intention of ending racial inequality. I am politically connected. I can help make this happen. Only a conservative politician has a chance of ending racism. I believe you can do it."

Later that same week, he was asked by Virginia's Governor Gilmore to give the keynote address to his Technology Taskforce. Craig had given a thousand speeches and thought nothing of it. The venue was a giant tent. He began his talk by telling the crowd that the tent reminded him of old-time revival meetings. He said, "Because you all know how expensive building an Internet store can be, we'll be passing a collection plate. Please dig deep." Craig's talk was extemporaneous. It was scheduled to last thirty minutes; an hour later the audience was in a frenzy. They had laughed and cried. They had applauded so long, their hands hurt.

Nikki Norton jumped to her feet when it was over. "You were on fire! I've never seen anyone mesmerize a crowd the way you did today."

Word spread like wildfire. If there was a speech to be given, Winn was asked to give it. He soon found himself dining with Congressmen and Senators. He met the nation's top religious leaders, both black and white. The crowds grew larger, and the speeches became more frequent. But it wouldn't last. Nikki moved back to Washington to be closer to her fiancé. She introduced Craig to David Kuo, as promised, and David replaced her as VP of Communications for Value America.

It may not have been completely David's fault, but something got lost in the translation. David seemed bright enough. He had the contacts, too. He'd been around the horn, working over the past five years for the CIA, Ralph Reed of Christian Coalition fame, Bill Bennett's Empower America, Senator John Ashcroft, and even for his own charity, The American Compass. But both Craig's and Value America's public presence diminished precipitously immediately after David came on board.

David was connected to a group of religious power brokers in Washington called the United Brethren. Tom Morgan's spiritual advisor, Goose Godfrey, was also an active member. He was a former officer in the Reagan White House. Morgan told Craig on many occasions that Goose was his mentor, his "conscience." He said Goose was one of the most connected people in America, which wasn't suprising. They made a point of "ministering" to the rich and powerful.

In order to demonstrate his value to his next meal ticket, Goose invited Craig to Washington to meet with celebrities like news commentator Fred Barnes, and patriots like three-star General Mick Kicklighter and National Security Advisor Bud McFarlane. Goose told Craig that they had been invited to offer their input on the viability of him entering the public arena. But Godfrey had told his guests something entirely different, making Craig look like a fool when he talked of such things.

Setting a trap, purposely embarrassing folks, was something the Bretheren had mastered. The reasons they were interested in discrediting Winn would soon become as obvious as they were devious.

Godfrey was a glad-hander. He, like Kuo, loved to hug everyone in sight. He always had a series of syrupy platitudes ready to slather all over those with whom he was seeking favor. It was how he earned his living. "I love ya, bro, you know I'm praying for ya," he said with irritating repetition. Made Craig want to take a shower after each encounter.

None of this "positive reinforcement" came cheap. Morgan had "employed" Godfrey at US Office Products. And he did so again at Value America—to the tune of twenty grand a month. Morgan needed the constant reinforcement and praise that Godfrey was all too willing to lavish upon those who paid for his services. The Brethren—Godfrey, Morgan, and Kuo—soon began to cast a dark shadow across our company.

❦

THESE WERE HEADY days for Value America. The company was at the forefront of an economic revolution. Dot-com euphoria was permeating the national consciousness. The best and the brightest started making treks to Charlottesville. On one such occasion, *Chief Executive* magazine hosted a CEO Roundtable at Keswick Hall. Craig invited Fred Smith and Jerry Falwell. Morgan's Goose Godfrey invited his contacts, including General Kicklighter and Gerry Roche, CEO of one of the nation's leading executive recruitment firms. Whether Goose invited Newell/Rubbermaid's Vice Chairman, Wolf Schmitt, or just got to know him on this occasion, isn't certain, but it is certain that their relationship would later serve as a catalyst in a great corporate calamity.

As a result of the *Chief Executive* Conference, General Kicklighter resigned his leadership position in the Pentagon and started to work with Craig. The two bonded instantly, becoming a great team.

Favorable relationships were also formed between Fred Smith, the General, and Reverend Falwell this day. On Godfrey's recommendation,

Gerry Roche and Sam White, another Godfrey ally, were asked to join Value America's prestigious board. White, an African-American businessman, had triumphed over racial prejudice in the deep south. A fine and decent man, he always remained loyal to his pal Godfrey.

With one exception, the board was now set. It included our co-founders, Craig Winn as Chairman and Rex Scatena as Vice Chairman. Justin Caise had become a board member as a result of the pass-the-hat "Angel" financing round he had helped make possible. Rafe Durn and Don Tarpin had come aboard because of covenants carved out in the Series A investment round. Frank Flowers had joined by virtue of Series B, and Fred Smith by way of Series C. Gerry Roche and Sam White "earned" their places by virtue of their friendship with the company's new highly paid spiritual advisor, Goose Godfrey. Not to be outdone, David Kuo encouraged his former employer, Bill Bennett, to join the "most illustrious board in dot-com history."

৩৽৻৻

NOT LONG AFTER Value America's picture-perfect IPO, the leader of the dot-com pack stumbled. Amazon announced its quarterly earnings, or lack thereof. Their poor performance sent shivers though the tech world. Amazon delayed their expectations of profitability two years beyond their already distant aspirations. Worse, Amazon's retail metrics looked dismal. Operational costs as a percentage of revenue were climbing, not falling. They started calling their portal deals "unproductive."

Jeff Bezos unveiled his new game plan, saying that Amazon will triple its marketing spending, showering the customer with gift certificates. This sounded suspiciously like our ValueDollars. We didn't mind; imitation is the sincerest form of flattery. They had already adopted our comprehensive strategy and announced they were emulating our offline advertising formula too.

Trying to put a positive spin on bad news, Bezos said, "Our new marketing push is designed to stay one step ahead of other Internet-commerce companies that are launching ad campaigns—everything is now a dot-com commercial." Then stealing another move from the Value America playbook he said, "Much of Amazon's ad blitz is to be focused on print, radio, and television rather than other Internet sites. Amazon might not renew its marketing tie-ins with heavily trafficked portals. The rates they are charging now are so high," he said, "we don't think these deals are effective." Bezos made the words Craig had spoken at the Goldman Sachs meeting, nearly two years before, sound downright prophetic. But there was more.

Following Amazon's conference call, *The Wall Street Journal* reported, "The company and its analysts came under some pressure from investors who have repeatedly seen their forecasts stretched out for when the company will reach profitability." But the press, analysts, and media continued to tout Amazon, as evidenced by *The Journal's* commentary: "Ever since Amazon went public in May 1997, investors have been highly tolerant of the company's growth-before-profits strategy, and the company's latest results did little to shake that." The fallout from Amazon's failures only impacted their less-popular online brethren—like Value America.

Amazon's conference call was flattering because they had come full circle and were now preaching what Craig had predicted. Yet it was also debilitating, by virtue of its depressing effect on the price of *our* stock, not theirs. But all of this was child's play compared to what came next. Bezos was reported in *The Wall Street Journal* to have said, "The company's gross margins will shrink by two to three percentage points, because Amazon has been spending heavily to expand our warehouses and we don't have full efficiencies there. Fulfilling customer orders may cost fourteen to fifteen percent of total revenue."

The fact that gross margins are totally unrelated to warehouse costs or efficiencies apparently bothered no one. What really made the Amazon release problematic was that neither *The Journal*, the business media at large, nor any of Wall Street's illustrious analysts even noticed the absurdity of these statements. It was at this very moment that Craig came to realize he was in terrible, terrible trouble. We had a failure to communicate.

The way accountants calculate gross margins is simple. One subtracts the cost of the things that have been sold from the sales price. Thus, the cost of expanding warehouses has nothing to do with gross margins, only with operating profits.

Craig asked his new CEO, Tom Morgan, to read the article. He didn't get it either. If there was anything Morgan should have known, having managed distribution companies, it was that operating costs do not affect gross margins. Now Craig recognized that his life's work, his dream, was embroiled in a game in which neither the manager of his team nor the game's umpires—Wall Street's analysts—even understood the rules.

This was troubling because the centerpiece of our strategy to bring consumers and brands together was the replacing of distribution centers with technology, and inventory with systems. If Wall Street was clueless in this regard, our merits were beyond their comprehension.

The satisfaction of knowing he'd been right did little to make Craig feel better. Even when the media, Wall Street, and investors were told by

Amazon, the most sacred of their cows, "fulfilling customer orders may cost fourteen to fifteen percent of total revenue," they still didn't get it. Craig knew, and had said, that Amazon's commitment to warehouses and inventory would be their undoing, but those shaping the public discourse remained oblivious.

There was another problem brewing, and it was related to the first. Announcing good news in the face of a bad market is futile. Craig had known for five long weeks that our Q1 sales were off the chart. All our retail metrics were better than expected, and all were headed in the right direction. During the road show, Robertson Stephens had presented VUSA's financial model to each investor, predicting $21.4 million in revenue in Q1.

Beating a projection by five percent is considered good; ten percent is great. Value America beat its first quarter numbers by *thirty percent*. With news this spectacular, the stock should have soared. But instead, it fell.

The explanations the analysts gave were truly lame. They said Amazon's postponement of profitability had caused the sector to be viewed less favorably. The reasoning was that if they, Amazon, with their superlative model, gargantuan scale, and tremendous popularity, couldn't figure it out, no one could. It must have been mad cow disease.

One early message posted on VUSA's Yahoo Message Board said it all, "5/3/99 at 7:38 pm—Message Number 40: How come VUSA is plummeting with an upgrade?" He was referring to Dale Dandridge's report:

Revenues reflected an increase in customers, repeat buyers, and demand for increased product offerings. Value America ended Q1 with approximately 300,000 customers, up from just under 200,000 at the end of Q4:98. Based upon these results, we are raising our F1999 revenue estimate to $165 million. We are encouraged by the acceleration of revenue growth, which demonstrates the effectiveness of brand advertising and the attractiveness of the merchandising formula.

We believe Value America has built the right balance of price and fulfillment and is defining the value segment of the Web. Value America continues to ship over 90% of its orders within 24 hours. We believe the firm can scale to be one of the few big Web commerce destinations. We look to news of new branded products, affiliate partners, and growth to continue to move the stock higher.

But it didn't. The fact that the stock went down in the face of great news was inconceivable. *Charlottesville, we have a problem.*

Craig Winn and Value America were now on a collision course with destiny. Corporately, Craig had to choose between probable death and certain death. Personally, he had to choose between self-enrichment and the collective good of our team, company, and cause. If he did nothing, our company would fall victim to Wall Street's misguided illusions. Craig, however, would soon be free to sell his shares. At the time, they were worth over $650 million. If Craig spoke out, he would be the bearer of bad news. He knew all too well what those in power do when they're threatened, especially in the pocketbook. They nail the messenger.

Two thousand years ago, on a considerably more important issue—the fate of our tarnished souls—they crucified a Messenger when He was perceived to have threatened the wealth and power of the establishment. Today the powerful are more civil. They just ridicule them, demean their intentions, and malign their character. Craig knew Morgan wasn't up to the challenge—he didn't even understand the game. So Craig volunteered to face the critics alone. The choice was good but bad, right but wrong, all at the same time.

ৡঃৢ

AS EARLY AS their first interview sessions in February, Rex Scatena, Craig Winn, and Tom Morgan had discussed the obvious. Under the best circumstances, it takes a new CEO four to six months to come up to speed on a new company and become productive. That assumes the company is not inventing their industry as they go, building proprietary tools to sustain their business, and growing faster in one quarter than most companies do in five years. It also assumes the new CEO is bright and focused upon learning everything there is to know about the business.

Sadly, Morgan was not. But for better or worse, he was their guy, so Rex and Craig were committed to helping him. They tried to compensate for Tom's weaknesses by creating a scenario in which he could succeed. As a result, a division-of-labor strategy was formulated, recognizing Tom's need to focus his energies on the operations and management of the company. Craig would be the lightning rod, shouldering the burden of presenting the merits of our firm to investors and the media. Craig, it was agreed, would be Mr. Outside. He would form relationships with brands, and with Rex, build Demand Alliances with great institutions.

Tom would be Mr. Inside. The founders agreed to counsel him privately in their spare time about the nature of retail, explaining how Value America's model was designed to serve consumers by empowering brands. They would teach Tom the ins and outs of advertising, the Internet, technology, sales, and the implications of convergence. They would explain the business plan and share how it had been used to attract bright people, inspire them, and cause those who read it to manage their area of responsibility in harmony with the company's mission.

The founders recognized early on that the strength of their personalities would suffocate Tom's in any meeting they attended together. So they told him that they would not attend any of his management meetings, nor would they hold any of their own. Inside, Tom would sink or swim on his own merits.

The teach-ins never occurred. No matter how many times Craig and Rex offered to share their expertise, Tom, once empowered, rebuffed them. So much for the best-laid plans of mice and men. For reasons unknown to anyone, Tom chose not to avail himself of the opportunity to learn anything about retail, advertising, brand objectives, technology, or the value of Demand Alliances. On the contrary, during his very first weeks, Morgan began telling folks like John Motley, Byron Peters, Andy Rod, and Goose Godfrey that Winn and Scatena had to go. "It's my company now," he said behind their backs. The era of political maneuvering had begun.

Corporations, like nature, abhor a vacuum. The founders' departure from management left a black hole. To fill the void, the "come latelies" began to assemble their teams. While hiring Dorchak had obviously been wrong, hiring Morgan to replace her was a fatally flawed strategy. Individually, they would have been impotent. Corporate impotence is less than desirable, of course, but it's far better than paying people to be destructive. That, sadly, is precisely what happened.

In the eight months following the IPO, Morgan and Dorchak more than tripled the size of Value America, inflating our overhead *eight fold!* They hired 350 new employees, brought in 100 consultants, and employed 225 full-time contract workers—at a combined annualized cost of over $80 million. Too many of these individuals, especially the officers, mirrored the corporate morality of those who had hired them. After three years of extreme poverty and enforced frugality, the tide had turned. Those who hadn't struggled to raise capital evidently had no appreciation of its worth.

Glenda's Gang was in place first. She just needed to mobilize her vast army and make certain they were properly incentivized—linking their actions to her ambitions. This group was replete with former IBMers and assorted retreads from the PC world. They had their own language, culture, and way of doing things. They were experts at the game of positioning, politics, perceptions, and process. Pursuing the four "Ps" consumed their time. They were good at shirking responsibility and passing blame. And thanks in good measure to Dorchak's willingness to part with the company's money, their ineptitude was richly rewarded, making them dependent on her. Such favors, of course, came at a price. The devil would eventually collect her due.

Professional managers, like professional politicians, fall into one of five categories. Some are just plain evil. Adolf Hitler and Glenda Dorchak are examples in the political and corporate worlds. While the end results of their behavior were wholly dissimilar, some of their methods were comparable. Both, it turns out, were able to manipulate a small loyal following, deceive the establishment, and connive their way into power. They talked a good game and told people what they wanted to hear, but down deep they were bad apples, rotten to the core.

Some professional managers are hypocrites; they're sanctimonious, making them considerably harder to spot. Unlike the bad guys in classic westerns, they don't wear black hats. Hypocrites are masters at self-serving deceptions, prospering at the expense of others. They often prevail by projecting their weaknesses onto their opponents. They routinely mischaracterize their adversaries' achievements and personally take credit for whatever they cannot condemn. Bill Clinton, for example, demeaned the character of those who conceived the Contract with America. He fought against its implementation, yet when running for re-election he took full credit for all of the positive things the Contract had accomplished. Sanctimonious and self-righteous, our own Tom Morgan would prove to be the poster child for the hypocritical corporate manager.

The third type of corporate or political professional provides the power base necessary for their more evil and hypocritical comrades. They're mercenaries. Politically they're represented by the likes of Hitler's Joseph Goebbels. Corporately they are personified by our Goose Godfrey. They'll fight anybody's battle as long as the reward is high enough. Mercenaries lie, cheat, steal, and slander, without conscience, all in the name of the almighty dollar. Often failing at their jobs, they have the four "Ps" down pat. But, they, like killer bees, are impotent acting alone.

The fourth type of professional manager is the garden-variety incompetent buffoon. They're often likeable, but they provide little actual value for their wages. Unfortunately, they all too quickly align themselves with their more evil, hypocritical, and mercenary brethren. They go with the flow. Rather than stand up and fight evil, they become evil's unwitting accomplices. Sprinkle a little money and position their way, and those willing to misbehave can count on these folks to say and do pretty much anything they desire.

Fortunately, the base of the "professional" pyramid—politically and corporately—is composed of honest, hard-working, competent people. Were they not more numerous than the rest, America would have imploded long ago. They are builders, willing to do whatever it takes to make their company or country better. Builders routinely make personal sacrifices to promote the greater good. They don't much care who gets the credit; they just want to get the job done. They're motivated to do the right things for the right reasons. Most of the first fifty or so people who joined Value America's retail revolution were builders. Joe Page and Bill Hunt are names that come readily to mind.

When good people fail to unite and fight against the machinations of the evil, hypocritical, mercenary, and incompetent elements around them, all is lost. The good works and noble ambitions of the many are all too often recklessly destroyed and unjustly tarnished by the few. Progress is thwarted by process. Perceptions taint reality. Politics and positioning promote a cult of self-promotion and self-preservation. Simply stated, bad things happen when good people fail to stand up.

But enough preaching. Back to our story.

With Glenda's Gang formed, Tom was not about to be outdone. Thanks to the hard work of others, there was now plenty of money to spread around. So Morgan brought in his own group of loyalists. First was Tom Starnes, late of USOP, Morgan's old firm. He was asked to manage Business Development, the formation of outside relationships. This meant that Craig and Rex would now have to work through Tom's most loyal, dense, and unproductive minion as they endeavored to form productive alliances. It was like asking Dale Carnegie to work through Forrest Gump.

With Winn and Scatena handcuffed outside, Morgan focused inside, on operations. He recruited his friend Cliff Chambers, formerly a VP of Operations for NAPA. The fact that there were already two people doing the job Cliff had been hired to do didn't seem to bother Mr. Morgan. Maybe it was the reason Tom needed Cliff. After all, Byron Peters from Price Costco, Craig's friend, had been hired as Chief Operating Officer, and Ralph Murphy, Glenda's friend from IBM, was SVP of Operations. Their loyalties were at aligned elsewhere.

Morgan relished the thought that two of Value America's board members, thanks to his mentor, Goose Godfrey, were in his pocket. But that wasn't enough. Through Godfrey's United Brethren in Washington, he bonded with David Kuo, and then recruited Kuo's wife, Kim, to be his SVP of Investor Relations. He also hired Kim's sister as his personal assistant, and then hired *her* husband for Business Development.

We who had been around since the beginning merely kept our heads down and continued to work. That was how we had built the firm to the point that we could attract and pay the "professionals" in the first place. We didn't care about titles. Productivity, not popularity, meant everything to us. We didn't take sides; we thought we were all on the same side.

CRAIG WAS TOO FOCUSED on correcting Wall Street's misconceptions to get involved in these political games. He was, in fact, to our detriment, oblivious. Mr. See-the-best-in-everybody was blind to the dark corporate drama that was beginning to unfold. He had a plethora of outside issues to distract him. The problems we faced were now far worse than those he had encountered at Goldman Sachs. Companies were valued on ever more absurd criteria, like a cute name.

Wall Street's obsession with popularity prompted Winn to battle another illusion. Companies like Buy.com began selling goods below cost. While that might sound fine, especially if you're a consumer, it was the worst thing that could possibly happen. The media and investors alike touted the idea, suggesting that the e-tailer with the lowest price was the best managed, as if it took brains to give stuff away. Not only was Buy.com's practice unsustainable, which meant it was in no one's interest long term, it gave our whole industry a black eye. Although Buy.com's damage was inflicted only on brands they could buy through distributors, their bad example caused many great brands to back away from partnering with anyone online, for we were all tarred with the same brush.

Selling quarters for dimes made the registers ring, but it devalued our complex and synergistic strategy, our retail revolution, the power of Value America's brand-centric, presentation-rich model. The Street's willingness to reward ill-gotten revenue gains with an abundance of cheap capital was devastating; it made our metrics and value proposition seem less worthy. In a world enamored with illusions, it was one more dragon begging to be slain.

A lucid *Fortune* magazine editor reported the anomaly this way: "In a world where Wall Street seems to value revenues and growth more than profits, the ultimate business would be to create a website that sells dollars for 85 cents. As the argument went, you could always make up the difference through ad revenues. Today, Buy.com is doing just that, selling consumer products below cost with the hope of making up the deficit through advertising."

The story went on to say, "Of course, revenues may not be the proper metric for measuring the success of a company with negative gross margins. If all you were interested in was revenue growth, you could sell a commodity like oil below cost and probably hit $1 billion in your first year. It's easy to be skeptical of the seemingly crazy new model.... Capital is the natural limit to a business in which you lose money on every sale. However, the company has raised $60 million from Softbank, the

Japanese conglomerate that backed Yahoo!"

With all of this weighing heavily on Craig's mind, he was called to New York for a series of meetings. The first was with Tim Forbes, COO of *Fortune's* competitor, *Forbes Magazine*. Mick Kicklighter was now part of the team and traveled with Craig. The two discovered that the reason behind his invitation was curiosity. Tim Forbes had seen his world, the world of traditional business, turn green with envy over the upstarts, the dot-coms. Yet neither he nor his magazine were fans of those who were winning the popularity contest. In 1999 Forbes wrote, "Amazon fancies itself the future WalMart, the king of retailing. Don't bet on it. At the rate it burns through money, it will be out in less than three years. Amazon needs Wall Street as a source of cheap capital. If the company hiccups, the trance will be broken. Bezos needs to use his stock like currency to retain his hold on fickle Internet-generation managers and analysts...."

Tim Forbes told Craig and Mick, "You have the first online model that makes any sense. You're obviously playing by a different set of rules. I just wanted my team to meet you." Uncomfortable with the flattery, Craig diverted the conversation to forming partnerships like building a custom Forbes Business Marketplace appropriately called "Capitalist Tools."

With a couple of hours free between meetings, the retired General and our charismatic founder took a walk through New York's Central Park. As they strolled, Craig found a deserted bench at the edge of a large pond. It was a magnificent day. The azaleas and dogwoods were still in bloom. Inspired, Craig said, "We're faced with a difficult task. We need to teach the unteachable, and what we have to tell them is counter to the very illusions that are sustaining them."

Mick, after forty years of serving our nation in and out of uniform, knew little about business and nothing about retail. Yet he was great at sizing up the battlefield and formulating plans to correctly address reality. That made him the perfect sounding board. If Craig could explain to Mick, a retail novice, what was wrong with the way dot-coms were being managed and evaluated, he could explain it to Internet investors, analysts, and the media. They, as a group, knew just as little. Yet differences of experience and character would make teaching the latter more difficult than the former. Investment portfolio managers and tech analysts were mostly young hotshots in their twenties, lacking experience and the character experience brings.

"Mick, if you were trying to predict what a company, or any organization for that matter, might achieve, what tool would you use?"

"History," Mick responded. "As Solomon said, 'There's nothing new under the sun. That which is, has been.'"

"The best predictor of future performance is past performance. So since e-tail has no past, what should we use as our yardstick to measure the past and predict the future?"

"Retail." Mick stated the obvious: "It's the closest thing to e-tail."

"Right. We must convince analysts and the media that e-tail's retail."

"Sounds simple enough," Mick added casually as he watched a pair of ducks gracefully glide into the pond in front of them.

"But since retail *isn't* simple, how do we go about teaching it to the young know-it-alls and correlating it to e-tail?"

"You can't go wrong with a story. Do you have an example of something they're likely to know, relate to, that can bridge the gap?"

"I do." Craig nodded.

Mick, displaying the leadership skills that made him an outstanding General said, "Okay. Before you tell me your story, tell me specifically what you want your audience to understand."

"A couple of things," Craig answered. "First, that e-tail *is* retail. The best predictor of retail success is distribution efficiency. If they understand the importance of minimizing inventory cost, there's hope. But Mick," Craig said, "there's a lot more at stake here than Value America. The manufacture and sale of consumer products and services represents sixty-five percent of our GNP. It's the engine that fuels our economy. The engine's future is e-tail. If it crashes, we all lose."

"You're right. What's your second point?"

"I want them to appreciate the importance of forming partnerships— demand and supply alliances. It's the promised land of e-commerce. In a nutshell, Mick, I want analysts, investors, and the media to realize that most of their perceptions regarding our world are errant. Just because it's prevailing wisdom, that doesn't mean it's wise."

"And you think you can do all that in twenty minutes with some stories?" Mick asked, breaking into a good-natured chuckle.

"I'll share my stories, and you be the judge."

"Shoot," Mick said, enjoying the moment. Shoot was probably his favorite word. He was trained as an Army artillery specialist.

"Okay, Mick, pretend you're an analyst or investor in the audience at the upcoming Robertson Stephens Internet Conference. With that, Craig stood up, right there in Central Park, with his back to the pond. He began pulling words out of the fresh spring air…. "It is an honor to be here. If, as some have said, the collection of minds building technology companies is rivaled only by those in rural Virginia during the late eighteenth century, this conference is an amazing assemblage."

The words flowed with a natural rhythm. Craig's eyes twinkled; his smile was confident and disarming. "The last time I spoke here was just prior to our IPO. My talk was backed by a multimedia show and was perhaps more presentation than communication. Today's discussion will be different. In the teeth of this turbulent market, it's time to return to basics and focus upon what we know to be true—that e-tail is retail!" Craig stopped momentarily and asked, "Okay so far?"

"Sure," Mick said, "but cut out the part about your presentation not communicating. It did a fine job."

"Okay," Craig answered. "Today I shall endeavor to challenge your perceptions and perhaps inspire a new appreciation for the ultimate potential of the Internet and e-commerce. But before we begin, we must clear away some debris—the misperceptions that all too often accompany the formation of new opportunities." He paused. "Still with me, Mick?"

"Side by side."

In Craig's mind's eye, he visualized himself speaking in front of a skeptical audience. "I would like to share a couple of examples so I might earn the credibility needed to challenge today's misconceptions. Not too long ago, the perception was that WalMart would never successfully emerge from small-town America. In cities, it was thought, Sears and others would teach the Bentonville boys new lessons. But Walton's model was not about retail; it was about distribution. Unlike his larger competitors, it was about pull, not push. Sam improved upon Sol Price's FedMart, employing MacArthur's strategy of attacking where the enemy was weak. He was poorly understood, and his company remained under-valued. Then one day, America awoke, and WalMart was everywhere." Craig held up a finger indicating that that had been story number one.

"Not too long ago, the prevailing wisdom was that an upstart computer company named after its founder would falter in corporate America, especially when fighting Goliath. Big Blue was the darling of Wall Street, the undisputed technology leader. But Michael Dell recognized it wasn't about technology, it was about distribution. He eliminated the channel and constrained the supply chain. His model did not find favor with Wall Street until one morning, America awoke and Dell was everywhere, from Main Street to Wall Street. Prevailing wisdom was wrong." With a second finger held aloft, Craig asked Mick if he understood the comparisons.

"Your idea to start on common ground is solid. They should understand these examples."

A WEEK OR so passed, and Craig, along with other Value Americans, found themselves on the other side of the country. He was scheduled to speak at Robertson Stephens' Internet Conference in San Francisco. Unfortunately, this time the crowd was not particularly large. Amazon's first-quarter announcement had taken its toll on all things dot-com. To make matters worse, the prior speaker had run long, so Craig's prepared twenty-minute presentation would have to be shortened on the fly. Worse still, Dale Dandridge, Robertson's famed dot-com analyst, was too busy to either introduce Craig or listen to what he had to say.

A frustrated Winn began his speech with an abbreviated version of the words he had rehearsed with Mick in Central Park. Then he continued, saying, "Today, I believe much of the prevailing wisdom concerning the online retail world is errant. Some examples are: brick and mortar retailers with their buying clout, distribution, and brand names will dominate online. Second, inventory is an asset and is required to satisfy customers. And third, brands will simply go direct and bypass e-tailers like Value America.

"We salute WalMart. They are the undisputed masters of brick and mortar. But their three-year-old online store, designed by Microsoft, has been a self-proclaimed failure. Now they've hired different consultants to construct a new and improved version, so many consultants the list looks like the legal section of the New York Yellow Pages. And wouldn't you know it, once again the prevailing wisdom has it that they will dominate online. Yet every asset that drives their success in one realm is a liability in the other."

The media covered the reemergence of WalMart's Internet store like it was the second coming. Following Amazon's dismal Q1 announcement, they jumped to the conclusion that only traditional retailers, "bricks and clicks," would prevail online. For giggles, one even ranked the "Most Popular Web Retailers" by "Unique Audience" and "Average Duration of Visit."

Craig pressed on, trying to slay this dragon. "In their realm, WalMart's stores create a nexus requiring the collection of sales tax in every state, often an eight-percent disadvantage. Inventory is held at the retail price, devaluing their principal asset when goods are sold competitively online. Their product-mix and brand-image appeal to a customer demographic significantly below today's online shopper. Even WalMart's superior distribution is a liability online, which is why they don't use it. Meanwhile, Value America's inventory-less model does for the online world what WalMart's distribution once did for their world.

"WalMart recognizes that they must sell online, for it is the future. Yet, one world devalues the other. For one to grow, the other must be diminished." As predicted, this new incarnation of WalMart was disbanded, as was the next. But being right was now unimportant. Delusions were far more seductive.

Alternating glances between his notes and the audience, Craig attacked the inventory heresy. "Our largest online competitor recently postponed profitability another two years—seven years from inception—while they build warehouses and fill them with inventory. Yet our operational costs continue to decrease as a percentage of sales. Not only are we growing faster, we actually manage to satisfy customers without inventory. We have empowered ninety-five percent of our brand partners to ship our customers' orders within one day using our proprietary electronic fulfillment solutions." Incredibly, Amazon's admission that managing inventory actually cost fifteen percent, in a realm that averaged just twenty percent gross margin, didn't matter.

"Sure, brands envy Dell's direct model, especially as retailers become more abusive. But less than one percent will risk it all to compete against their existing customers.... And why should a brand build and promote its own costly e-tail solution when Value America is willing to give them one that's in complete harmony with its objectives. If this were not true, it begs the question: Why did the senior executives of over 2,000 brands decide to partner with us?" *Hello! Please wake up*, Craig thought as he mortally wounded another dragon. You'd think that in a world enamored with popularity, relationships would be meaningful, but the correlation escaped the judges.

The media was convinced that every brand ought to be able to sidestep retail and sell to consumers directly. The fact that only one in a thousand had the scale, resources, or will to do it escaped them.

"Last month, one of our board members, one of the most respected businessmen in America, Fred Smith, founder of Federal Express, said he was convinced Value America *would*, not just could, 'become the WalMart of e-commerce.'" The idea for Craig's attack on "prevailing wisdom" had actually come from Fred Smith. Some of the examples he stated, the comparisons he drew, as well as his conclusions, had been borrowed from the speech Fred had given at the *Chief Executive* Conference.

"Let's discuss brands, for they are the bright center of the retail universe. No one comes to a retail store to buy the store. They come to buy branded products. Value America has the most brands. That's one of our competitive advantages. We have forged strategic alliances with over two thousand of the world's top brands, enabling factory-direct, authorized, and supported sales. We have linked production and consumption, supply and demand. We use technology to eliminate inventory costs, and expedite delivery. It is that simple, and it is that profound.

"We have earned unparalleled brand support by giving brands what they want: broader distribution, customer intimacy, greater efficiency, and compelling product presentations. Wolf Schmitt, the vice chairman of Newell/Rubbermaid, said, 'Value America's brand-centric solution is exactly what every brand knows they need, but cannot achieve alone.'"

In any time other than one besieged by grand delusions, every point Craig made would have resonated with his audience. The value of our company would have risen, giving us—giving our whole industry—the time we needed to grow and prosper. We had the right solution at the wrong time. No one listened. No one thought. No one seemed to care.

"Value America's solution is friction-free commerce. We have built the first automated, electronic, paperless commerce link between consumer and supplier. Without inventory, stores, or warehouses, we operate with astounding efficiency. We believe our total overhead at scale will eventually be one-fifth that of the best regular retailer, and one-third the overhead needed to support a warehousing online model."

At this point, Craig explained the seven ways Value America served our customers, including setting the right example by donating one percent of every sale to charity. In the minutes he had remaining, he said, "We have created a means to efficiently mass-replicate ourselves in any image. That means we can build custom marketplaces for the way Americans congregate. Custom marketplaces are specially designed to raise money for, and communicate the mission of, charities, schools, religious groups, associations, and unions. These organizations encourage their supporters, patrons, customers, and members to support their custom marketplace through direct mail campaigns using their contact lists.

"Studies reveal we are eighty percent more likely to purchase from an organization that supports something we support. By direct marketing to these highly motivated shoppers, we can radically decrease advertising and increase sales. Value America's proprietary, customizable, convergence-based solution makes it possible. And our brand-centric inventoryless model makes it profitable. Good for you, good for brands, good for us, and good for America. The sponsoring organization earns a percentage of each sale, consumers get the satisfaction of knowing they're supporting a cause they care about, and we get to reduce our advertising costs as a percentage of revenue. It's a win-win-win value proposition. Our Demand Alliances enable us to do well by doing good."

Craig had just announced that we had found the Promised Land of e-business, and that it was flowing with milk and honey. We were the first to electronically link supply and demand. Nobody got it. The news went in one ear and out the other. *You say you found a cure for cancer? That's nice.*

"In this regard, Value America will unveil a revolutionary capability later this month," Craig continued, sensing the audience's apathy and feeling the energy drain out of him. "We will begin selling computers with Internet access to those who have neither credit nor credit cards. This initiative will empower our Demand Alliances and make their custom stores more effective. Those who have been disenfranchised will get the technology they need to close the widening gap that separates the haves from the have-nots—together we'll be closing the digital divide!"

Craig demonstrated the store and then took direct aim at the silliness of Wall Street's popularity-based metrics. He attempted to slay the myth that no e-tailer would ever profit, and reinforced his theme that e-tail was retail. "Today, we're encouraging a more enlightened debate. Let me share a couple of examples of why this is important. Take customer acquisition cost as a matrix. This is not a retail concept. In retail, which is what B-to-C is, the right metric is advertising-to-revenue. Acquisition cost is incomplete; it has little value unless you know how much customers buy. Is a ten dollar customer acquisition better than a hundred? Not if the ten dollars generated a twenty dollar sale and the hundred dollars produced a five hundred dollar purchase.

"We must also look at retail life cycles. New stores are introduced, they are built, they develop, and mature. Younger stores use price to change peoples' buying behavior and then use service to retain their patronage. Retailers, on and offline, launch with low margins to gain traction and gradually elevate their margins over time.... Thus most retail chains lose money in their first five years only to profit, as we will profit, when scale is achieved, when the shift is made from changing buying behavior to serving an established customer base." By connecting retail to e-tail, Winn was proclaiming reality to those intoxicated by the mass hallucination that had propelled the online world. But his words only angered this audience. Reality was uncomfortable. One investor compared Craig to "a TV evangelist" in a message he anonymously posted on VUSA's boards.

"Along these same lines, a recent and puzzling incomplete thought is gross margin without context." Although Craig didn't say it, the audience knew he was alluding to Goldman Sachs' recent attempt to justify Amazon's superiority. "Is a twenty percent margin better than ten percent? If gross margin without regard for the operational costs needed to consummate the sale were the principal matrix for valuation, catalogers, at sixty percent initial markup, should be the most highly valued of all retailers. If we follow this reckless logic, devoid of context, we would encourage Amazon not to stop at the expense of warehousing and inventory. Why not write and print the books as well? That would make their gross margins even greater. The added costs to write, publish, and promote would be unimportant, we are told.

"Well, they *are* important, and it is important to recognize that e-tailing is retailing, not rocket science. Results are predictable, especially if we use retail metrics like brand relationships, EDI implementation, turn, margins linked to operating costs, overhead as a declining percentage of revenue, and promotional costs net of coop, tied to sales.

"Folks, let's be serious. Do you think you're going to read in the next Nordstrom's annual report that they were 'popular?' Are they going to let us know how many people entered their stores (hits), how long they stayed (stickiness), how many shelves they looked at (page views)? No! Virtual or not, we live and work in the real world."

Finally, Craig drew from his past in trying to shape the future. "When you study the history of retail revolutions capable of changing the way America buys and sells, you come to recognize that superior distribution drives consumer value and corporate success. This is where Value America is most different, and we think, best. We have built the only brand-centric, automated, electronic link between people and products, linking production and consumption. It is a magnificent achievement."

The red lights flashed. Craig's allotted slot, one already shortened to fifteen minutes, ended with these words, "I like our model, believe in our people, and trust our brands. I believe that one day, America will awake and Value America will be everywhere. Until that day, we are dedicated to building a better company—to serving our customers by supporting our brand partners. By doing these things well, we shall grow, profit, and build shareholder value. This is a marathon, comprised of endless sprints. We believe we are building an extraordinary business and would be proud to have you share in our success." There was a smattering of polite applause as the under-whelmed investors scurried out of the room to resume their frantic lives. They hadn't gotten it. Craig had failed.

He gave the same speech to participants of Volpe Brown's Internet conference a couple of weeks later. It would be the last time he would talk to investors on Value America's behalf. The young portfolio managers in the audience were hostile, as was Volpe's new Internet analyst. They loved their popularity-based metrics. They thought Winn's view of the online world was heresy. Their view, even if it was a mirage, had made them a lot of money. And that, after all, was the whole idea.

They were incensed that someone had the gall to challenge the sanctity of their metrics. Their egos chaffed against his passion. They despised being taught. They were the top of the food chain. Nobody had the right to tell them anything. This rebel had to be dispatched, for if *he* were right, *they* were wrong—as phoney as the value of their over-inflated shares.

Some may assume that our decision to go public was a tacit endorsement of Wall Street's ill-fated metrics, implying that we, like all other dotcoms, deserved our fate. But was there really a choice? Building an enterprise requires capital. It's not optional. Investors don't fund businesses out of the goodness of their hearts. They need an exit strategy, either a public offering or the sale of the company. Accepting one necessitates the other.

Public offerings, as well as corporate mergers and acquisitions, require investment bankers. One may like gardeners or mechanics better, but that doesn't make them a viable option. Bankers work for a fee. Sending them flowers and slathering them with praise is all very nice, but it isn't enough. When you play on their field with their ball, you play by their rules.

Winn had simply wanted to fix retail for the sake of both buyers and sellers. He wanted to leave America a little better off for the experience. He never backed away from any of the core concepts that drove our desire to bring people and products together, to do well by doing good. Craig believed the power of his ideas combined with the soundness of our execution would ultimately awaken Wall Street. He was wrong.

By speaking out, Craig had made himself *persona non grata* with the left-coast investment community. It didn't take long for word to reach Fred Smith. Fred counseled him, once again sharing how he believed the two were cut from the same cloth. He explained his own reluctance to address investors, even on behalf of FDX. He observed, "You and I are too much for these people to handle. They're intimidated by us and misinterpret our passion and enthusiasm. They think we're trying to mislead them. Do what I do, Craig," Fred concluded. "Let someone else talk to the Street." *Someone less qualified* was the implication.

Craig followed Fred's advice. Rather than fight on, he capitulated. He recognized the cause was lost. The audience was too jaded, too set in their ways, too deceived by their own collective hallucination to trouble themselves with the truth. By speaking out, he had destroyed his reputation, and he knew it. He lost his confidence, lost his will to fight, and, uncharacteristically, gave up. Wall Street would henceforth be the domain of Tom Morgan, Dean Johnson, Glenda Dorchak, and Kim Kuo. But for reasons entirely their own, they would fare far worse.

The love of money is a root of all kinds of evil—Paul

WEAVING A WICKED WEB

*S*ummer's sultry grip had descended upon the small southern town of Charlottesville. The air grew hot and heavy. Despite the weather, these should have been the best of times, but they were far from it. Everything pointed in the direction of an approaching storm.

The tranquil eye was clearly in Morgan's office. It was immaculate, as spotless as its occupant. Craig's oak and green marble desk, the one upon which he had written Value America's business plan, was set against the inside wall. It had never looked so neat. If a cluttered desk is the sign of a sane mind, we were in trouble.

Tom's wardrobe matched his office. If anyone had ever earned the title, "dressed for success," it was him. Morgan bragged that he spent more than $50,000 a year on his wardrobe. In spite of his short stature, balding head, and perpetually red and running nose, he looked the part of the successful CEO. And that was true whether he was coming or going. His Mercedes was equally immaculate. It was so perfectly detailed that we used to joke that he spent more time at the car wash than most of us did doing our jobs. In a world rife with illusions, the image he projected was yet another mirage. Tom looked great, as long as you didn't look too closely.

Some, more mischievous than I, would sneak into Tom's office when he wasn't looking and rotate two or three of the things Morgan had carefully arranged on his desk. The game was to see how little they needed to be misaligned for him to notice, and how long he could handle the imperfection before dispatching the offending accoutrement back to its proper position. It seldom took more than a few degrees off kilter, or more than a few seconds, before his soul became too tormented by the intrusion to suffer the affront. The teasing was inspired by one of Tom's most annoying pastimes. While the rest of us toiled, he wiled away the hours bending paperclips into perfect right angles. Yes, he was an office products kind of guy.

Tom's preoccupation with order may have screamed, "I'm insecure!" but we weren't listening. Perhaps Morgan's tortured psyche was quietly trying to warn us, but we misdiagnosed the symptoms. We all wanted him to succeed, especially Craig and Rex.

Tom often pontificated about how his former boss, USOP's founder, had run afoul of his shareholders, board, and management shortly after his arrival. He explained that the charismatic founder had brought it all on himself by being *out there*, making things happen, speaking too boldly, and being unable to manage the firm he had built. Tom would say things like, "He just lost it, went too far. People lost faith in him; they couldn't trust him anymore. The board came to me. I told them I didn't want his job, but they were insistent. They wanted Ledeky out and me in," Tom said repeatedly. "So that's how I became the CEO of a Fortune 500 company. I know I'm not particularly bright; it's a mystery to me how I always end up being the senior executive." A mystery indeed, for later, the principal investors in the ill-fated USOP would tell Joe Page how thrilled they were that we had solved *their* leadership problem by hiring Morgan. *Swell.*

There were little things, as well as big ones, that painted a dark portrait. Tom told Craig multiple times how he was trying to stop berating his wife for doing things like misplacing one of a pair of socks. He was enraged that someone could be so careless. Why he would tell such a story once, much less several times, is also a mystery.

Tom's razor-thin wife spent an evening with Katharine Winn. What she said should have sent up all sorts of red flags, but Craig dismissed the warning. Morgan's wife thanked Katharine for Tom's job, and especially for the fact that her husband now lived in Charlottesville. She said, "The reason we never moved from Washington is that his being down here has given my daughter and me our first chance at a normal life." Could it be that the the the quiet, genteel, Bible-carrying executive had a dark side?

But no one worked harder at creating the illusion of integrity and competence than did Tom Morgan. The deception consumed his every waking moment. He carefully and purposefully crafted this image by manipulating his loyalists and deceiving everyone else. For the first seven months of Tom's tenure, Craig was one of those who were deceived. Tom's religiosity and soft-spoken demeanor, combined with Craig's overwhelming desire to see him succeed, caused him to buy into the illusion. After all, it was in his interest for Tom to be exactly what he was pretending to be.

Sure, Craig and Rex had recognized as early as the IPO that Morgan was a lousy leader, a poor presenter, and a marginal manager. Yet they believed their role in influencing outside relationships and shaping the company's public perception would compensate for their new CEO's deficiencies. They were wrong.

Glenda Dorchak, unlike Tom Morgan, was now a known quantity. Her prior actions had obliterated any doubt. While there is always a little good in bad people, her corporate behavior was about as evil as it ever gets. Multiple blackmail attempts, fun with numbers, personal enrichment at the expense of the team, and self-aggrandizement over all else painted a clear, horrid picture of a woman tormented by insecurity. She was a wreck, constantly coming into Craig's office in tears because something, or someone, had had the audacity to challenge her supremacy. In the letter that documented her second blackmail, she spoke of herself as the "single empowered leader at the helm of the operation," and said, "I can cannot proceed...unless I'm given the full responsibility."

Thin as a rail, hair shorter than most men's, Glenda wore expensive clothes and drove fast cars. She openly demeaned her opponents, routinely convoluting the truth for her own selfish gain. The consequences never seemed to matter. Her every move was predictable. In her view, she was the most qualified; others were simply in the way. It was *her* company, *her* opportunity, *her* money to spend however it served *her* ambitions.

Morgan, by comparison, was sanctimonious and self-righteous. He and his Washingtonian pals did so little, and were so inept, it was hard to see their more vile nature. Most missed it. Unlike Glenda, they carried Bibles, not cigars.

Corporately, they did more than their share of demeaning others, tearing down those they thought were in their way, but they did it insidiously, behind their backs, never to their faces. They were just self-serving hypocrites, nothing more, nothing less. I'm not sure which is worse.

Speaking of hypocrisy, remember Lad McCaile, the DBA who wanted to apply the Karl Marx approach to stock allocation? Even though he had participated in a blackmail scheme that nearly killed the company, his sense of fair play didn't prevent him from cashing in. He sold the stock that had vested prior to his "resignation" for $400,000—the biggest payday of his life.

❦

THE TECHNOLOGISTS all gathered in Morgan's office. Tom walked down the hall and, uncharacteristically, asked Craig to listen to what they had to say. It was the first time he had been invited to participate in a meeting following his resignation from management.

Listening was painful. Lacking any understanding of our company's unique mission, those assembled had decided they wanted to jettison our proprietary systems. The solution Joe Page and his team had built, overcoming tremendous obstacles, the solution designed specifically to serve our business, was now being viewed as a liability. The professionals wanted to buy an expensive generic solution. They wanted SAP, the biggest Enterprise Resource Planning application in the world.

It wasn't that our proprietary systems were inadequate. Collectively, our systems did more than any e-commerce suite on the planet. They suited *our* business perfectly. They enabled *our* brands to serve *our* customers. But the professional managers had a different agenda. They hadn't read our business plan, so they didn't understand our mission. But that didn't matter; they knew better. They wanted the same systems the elephants used—big, established, rustbelt dinosaur systems. That was the world they knew, and they were dying to recreate our world in their image.

The discussion started innocently enough. The technologists had grown weary of Glenda blaming them every time she failed. Made sense. They said they'd decided to replace NT with UNIX, SQL Server with Oracle. So far so good, Craig thought. That transition had been anticipated from the beginning. Then they said, "We want to upgrade our commerce engine with something more scalable, reliable, tested, and mission-critical." Any time Craig heard that many corporate buzzwords strung together, he knew it was time to run. But the words were spoken in such a reasoned tone, he just listened. They concluded, "We want to use SAP's ERP solution."

"Over my dead body!" Craig shot back. So much for listening.

"The business world is littered with the rotting carcasses of companies that botched their SAP conversions. Even those that succeeded nearly died in the process. A good SAP conversion is one that only takes twice as long as you think it will and only chews up three times the amount you budgeted." You could see Craig's blood boil. "It's built to run bulky battleships, not nimble cruisers. Are you crazy?" *Oh, what the heck, if you're going to be invited to a meeting, no sense in being shy. Might as well let the troops know where you stand,* Craig thought. *You might never get invited back. Could be a good thing.*

Craig thought his somewhat less than glowing endorsement of their plan would be sufficient to scuttle the idea. But no, it only galvanized their resolve. The execs interviewed a plethora of consultants to learn how, for a "reasonable" fee, they could shape our destiny. They met, they plotted, and finally they agreed. They needed SAP. It was the professional choice. The founder was wrong, and they would tell him so.

The second meeting took place in the enemy's camp, around Craig's hundred-year-old conference table. It was a mutiny of sorts, but there was no blood let, at least not on this day. The officers had voted. They had invested countless hours rationalizing and justifying. Now they had arrived at a unanimous conclusion—it had to be SAP.

They said they had a fixed price for the implementation—guaranteed by no less than the consultants at HP. They claimed to have a guaranteed completion date of September 1. It was all in writing, they promised. There would be no cost overruns, no time delays. So let it be said, so let it be done. But it was not done, not by a long and costly shot.

"How much for the upgraded RISC machines?" Craig asked.

"Just shy of two million in servers, plus another two million in ancillary equipment," Thor Anders answered without even looking at his notes. Thor was brilliant, a tireless and trusted leader. There were at least four technologists with titles bigger than his, but he had earned everyone's respect. Thor was the *de facto* leader of the team. "We're buying the best: HP N- and K-class servers, fully loaded. We're going to use the EMC storage arrays we spoke about in the last meeting. They'll replace our IBM RAID arrays. Our data backup capacity will increase to nearly two terabytes. We're also planning to install Cisco's ATM switches. They'll give us an all-glass network. Our plan is to have an hour of battery backup, and install a generator to power the servers and the new cooling systems."

"And how much will the software upgrades cost, including the gap work to get everything talking nicely together?" questioned Craig.

Thor answered again, "The switch to UNIX operating systems and the upgrade to Oracle databases will be reasonably cheap. We should be able to convert by late June."

Someone else in the group chimed in. "The really cool thing is we're going to run Oracle in Parallel Version. We'll be one of very few companies in the world with that kind of sophistication."

"We got a really good deal on the SAP software," Thor continued. "They don't have a large e-commerce conversion yet, and they're eager to partner with us. It'll cost less than a million dollars."

Trying to seem important, Tom Morgan looked down at the notes Thor had prepared for him and said, "Because you said you were worried about SAP, they've agreed to a penalty of half a million dollars if the conversion takes longer than promised. And better still, when it's done on time, they're going to give us the five hundred grand to run partnership ads." It wasn't. They didn't.

"How much does HP want?" Craig asked, looking at Thor.

Anders glanced at Tom, inferring that the answer was on the paper he had prepared. Tom looked down and answered, "One million seven hundred and fifty thousand dollars."

"And for the million seven, Tom, do we have a written plan that details every requirement, making sure the new SAP application integrates with our customer service tools, our Web store, the call centers, with EDI, the databases? Is all the gap work itemized and in writing?" Craig asked.

Tom, of course, hadn't a clue. He sheepishly looked down at the paper Thor had given him, but the answer wasn't there.

Sensing the new boss was in trouble, Thor coughed to gain Craig's attention. He shuffled through some papers and said, "Yes, we understand.

We're in the process of getting it done. It'll be comprehensive. SAP will work with every system and application. I guarantee it."

"Well folks, it appears you've already decided. Is there a dissenting vote?" They all shook their heads. Craig looked directly at Joe, praying he would voice an objection, but no. He just sat there, paralyzed. In reality, Joe hated SAP. He knew it was wrong for us, but the come-latelies had beaten down and maligned "JoeWare" until he'd finally capitulated. His surrender ultimately caused Craig to stifle that voice inside begging him to reject their costly and irrational plan. Limply, Craig struggled, "Am I correct in assuming, with all the offsite meetings you've held, every member of management has reviewed your proposal and is in accord?"

"It's unanimous," Thor answered.

"Tom, is this what you want to do?" Craig probed.

Tom coughed, rubbed his nose, looked around the room, down at his sheet, and then when no one came to his rescue, said faintly, "I support management's decision."

After a long and weighty pause, Craig succumbed. "Then gentlemen, I'll not stand in your way. I wouldn't go down this path, but you've obviously done your homework. And Thor, you're the most credible technology presenter I've ever encountered."

"Thank you," Thor swelled with pride.

"But gentlemen," Craig added in a tone that wiped the grins off their faces, "I want the following caveats met. Tom, are you listening?" Morgan nodded and picked up his pen. "First, there are to be no changes, no additions, no deletions. Is that clear?" Craig scanned the gathering to be certain he saw all nodding heads. "If you make a change, the guaranteed timetable and the fixed bid are out the window. You understand that, don't you?" All nodded again. "Second, the conversion must be completed by September 1, as promised, and be run in parallel the last month of Q3. If this thing slips into Q4, the company is as good as dead. Either we wait 'til next year, or we make certain the penalty for an HP or SAP failure is severe."

"I have met with them personally. We've got their commitment in writing for a Q3 conversion date," Morgan lied.

"Third, this is your responsibility, Tom. You must get everything in writing, negotiate the final price, confirm the timing—*everything*. If you screw this up, you'll destroy what it took us the better part of three years to build. Understand? Everything negotiated up front, fixed price, time certain, no additions, no changes."

"It's already done," Tom replied breezily. "I've personally invested a lot of time on this."

As the leaders of the technology team left, Craig sat alone. He buried his face in his hands. He could feel his body go limp. He wondered if his words, "Over my dead body," would come back to haunt him.

ᘒᘓ

WITHIN DAYS, GLENDA scheduled the first of a series of meetings with Tom. *She* was now managing *him*. "Our in-house CSR tool is holding me back. My sales team needs better. It's crippling our growth."

"So what are you saying, Glenda?" Tom asked apprehensively.

"I've been talking to Candy Clifford. She can't hit our Q4 numbers without better CSR and sales tools, Tom."

Morgan replied, almost stuttering, "We've got to hit our numbers! What do you need? What's it going to take?" Tom knew that he would be publicly ridiculed if we failed to meet the quarterly analyst estimates. He might even be dismissed as a result.

"Siebel. It's the best, and we need the best," she proclaimed.

"Well then, let's go with Siebel. We've gotta hit our numbers, Glenda!"

"Good," Glenda smiled, and then added, "Tom, you know I measure everything that moves, don't you?"

"Why, yes," Tom responded.

"Gus Birch has been looking into better reporting tools for me. We think ePiphany is best of class. Every manager can use it to make up their own reports. They can slice their data any way they see fit. We need ePiphany."

"Do we really *need* it, Glenda? It's another burden on technology."

"Only if we want to hit our numbers and be professional, Tom."

"Alright," Tom acquiesced. "Is that all?"

"No. We need to outsource sales to a professional outfit. We can't keep pace in this little burg. C'Ville's no place to run a professional call center."

"Are you suggesting we hire Convergys again? You know Winn hates the idea. He thinks we're better off keeping Customer Care and sales in-house as a core competency. It's all part of his convergence spiel."

"He's never run a call center. I have," she spat out. "He's wrong. We're in charge now. It's the right call, Tom. I've already negotiated the contract with Convergys. We can get a hundred fifty dedicated sales reps over night. We'll blow away Wall Street's expectations. We'll make you look great. Trust me on this one, Tom. It's the right move. Just don't tell him."

"You say you've already negotiated the deal, and they can give us over a hundred people right away?" Morgan asked, parroting Dorchak's words.

"Yes, Tom," she answered condescendingly. "Remember, I'm just here to make you look good. So it's all settled then. I'll tell Thurston and Gus."

As Glenda got up to leave, Tom asked, "What impact will all of this have on the systems conversion? Does Thor Anders know about this?"

"Not yet. He's on vacation. But Bill Poletti and Gus Birch are both IBM guys. They're up to speed on the changes. It won't be a problem," she insisted. "They'll inform Thor when he gets back." After congratulating themselves, Glenda left. Tom went back to bending paper clips.

Any one of these changes would be enough to mortally wound Value America. Collectively, death was now assured. Self-inflicted, suicide.

Suddenly, HP was no longer accountable to their timetable or fixed bid. As a result, the conversion would take twice as long as planned—concluding right in the middle of the Christmas selling season. Naturally, it would fail and cost several times the original bid. But the real cost was much higher. Ultimately, it would cost the entire company.

ᘉᕀᕹ

IRONICALLY, RUNNING on "JoeWare," Value America posted a spectacular second quarter. Revenues soared six hundred percent past the same quarter a year before. When we went public, the Street was told to expect sales of $26 million. But pulsing majestically through Joe Page's "hopelessly inadequate" proprietary code, the company's second quarter revenues reached $36 million. Fortunately, the mercenary managers' crippling decisions had yet to impact our performance.

Yet Tom and Glenda had been busy. Their Q2 press release pronounced that they had "filled many key management positions during the quarter." In the months following our IPO, Morgan and Dorchak did far more than doom the company's systems. They shaped a bureaucratic monolith of epic proportions. In twenty-nine weeks, they managed to accumulate 675 employees, consultants, and outsourced customer service and sales reps; that's twenty-four new people a week, every week. Yet ironically, the cast of characters that hired the cast of hundreds would soon cause them all to be extras in the most bizarre of corporate dramas.

The press release, incredibly, went on to compliment "JoeWare," the very system they were abandoning. It said, "The company's exclusive, automated, and electronic transactional solution was improved, making it more redundant, scalable, and effective. During the quarter, ninety-five percent of Value America's brand partners were able to ship our customers within one business day."

During the investor call that followed, Tom Morgan told the world that he was "in charge," and that under his "leadership" the company now reflected his professional demeanor. He said, "Perhaps what's most important about the quarter is that we largely completed building the framework of the company so that we are now prepared to scale as our business grows. To accomplish all this, we made necessary long-term investments in our future." If these words seem a little rich for Morgan's more simplistic vocabulary, it's because David Kuo wrote them.

The CEO sat up in his chair and pulled his notes closer. This was his proudest moment. He was telling the dot-com world what he had accomplished. "Our sales this quarter increased twenty-eight percent [Q1 to Q2 rather than Q2:98 over Q2:99, the more typical comparison.] This compares favorably to a seventeen percent increase in our media costs. Put another way," he continued to read, "our sales and marketing expenses represented sixty percent of our sales this quarter, compared to sixty-four percent last quarter. This means that our media purchasing is becoming more efficient." It's hard to believe, looking back, that a public company's CEO would brag that his cost of sales and marketing was *only* sixty percent!

But Tom didn't know any better. He was under Glenda's spell. Rather than replace her, he had become dependent, wholly owned and operated by Glenda M Dorchak. It wasn't that she was particularly bright. She, like Tom, had no intuitive feel for whether a number was good or bad, partly because she often just made them up. Jacob Mitchell, our tech-savvy call center manager, claimed that costs and revenues were routinely convoluted to create whatever illusion she was trying to achieve.

Joe Page would tease the Reporting Team, saying, "You guys should transfer to Marketing. They could use your creativity." Most responded to his chiding by blushing and rolling their eyes heavenward. But occasionally, Reporting Team members would get more of Dorchak's evil brew than they could swallow, angrily telling Joe, "At least we don't need your programmers anymore. We can just make the numbers up now."

While this was wrong, what made it intolerable was that Morgan didn't have a clue. Any reasonably intelligent person even vaguely familiar with the facts could have seen right through her. Tom, apparently, was not.

Unaware of the perils that lay before him, Morgan continued to proclaim his successes to investors. "We are changing our custom CSR, order pipeline, and financial tools to Siebel and SAP. In short, we are building the most scalable, redundant, fault-tolerant e-commerce engine. We are building the infrastructure it takes to efficiently run a multi-billion dollar Fortune 100 company."

These words were spoken on August 2nd. Morgan had been on the job five months. He had now publicly admitted that he had violated Craig's

caveats regarding changes to the SAP conversion. When Craig confronted him with this egregious breach, he whined, "Glenda claimed she
couldn't hit Q4 numbers without better tools. What was I to do? Besides,
I've got a commitment from HP to install Siebel in the same time and at
the same cost." The fact that he didn't never seemed to faze the sanctimonious Morgan. Tom would go on to blame this, and all other failures,
on, of all people, Craig.

An interesting insight into Morgan's public admissions was his claim
of building systems to serve a "multi-billion dollar Fortune 100 company." When Craig described Value America's aspirations in more humble terms to a reporter, Tom and his team of supporters quickly relayed
the "exaggeration" to the board, implying that he was out of control and
should be censured. Hypocrites just love a double standard.

Morgan continued his conference-call speech, turning his attention to
some of the people he had added to our payrolls. "We rounded out our
management team with some important new hires: Automotive President
Kirk Shepard, Communications SVP David Kuo, and retired Three-Star
Army General and current Habitat for Humanity Chairman Mick
Kicklighter, who is overseeing our Demand Alliances."

So what was Tom Starnes doing if someone else had to be hired to
manage Demand Alliances? Although Kicklighter was praised here,
Morgan would soon turn on him, too, referring to him as "General
Dunderhead." Value America's mercenary managers were now weaving
a wicked web.

Auto king Kirk Shepard would later share his portrayal of this cast of
characters: "Starnes is easily the dumbest manager I've ever encountered
in business, Kuo, the most naïve, and Glenda…well, Glenda would rather
tell a lie even if the truth sounded better." As for Morgan, he said, "It's
clear he doesn't care who he hurts so long as he gets what he wants."

Feeling his oats, a proud Morgan concluded his prepared speech by
telling investors, shareholders, and analysts, "It is hard to believe, but Q2
was the first quarter that the whole management team for Value America
was in place. As such, our accomplishments are even more amazing: We
announced our intention to buy InService America, a world-class call
center that will help improve both customer service as well as our
Demand Alliance partnerships."

The fact that "Demand Alliances" were built by Mr. Outside, without
the "whole management team's" help, makes you wonder why this was
listed as one of their two "amazing accomplishments." Their other great
feat, similarly, had been negotiated by Craig before Tom and his mercenaries ever graced our once-friendly confines. But taking credit for the

work of others is standard operating procedure for hypocrites.

Amazingly, even as Morgan was speaking these words, taking credit for Demand Alliances and the acquisition of InService, he and his pal Starnes were busy unraveling both of them. After Craig "sold" potential partners on forming a mutually beneficial relationship with us, the Toms called the organizations back, maliciously telling them, "Craig cannot be trusted," and "We're in charge now. He's not managing the company; we are. We have no intention of honoring his crazy commitments."

This is precisely what they told TBN, Trinity Broadcasting, one of the world's largest cable and satellite networks. They have a faithful audience in the tens of millions. Craig and others formed a mutually beneficial Demand Alliance with them. It included the creation of a custom TBN Marketplace, something that took maybe a day's time using the tools Joe and his team had crafted. He told TBN that if they used their mailing lists and airtime to promote their marketplace, we would donate five percent of the gross sales it generated.

Following their meetings with Craig, Morgan and Starnes undid everything that had been done. They informed TBN's representative, in the presence of InService, that there would be no such partnership. The deal was off. Value America didn't want their free advertising, endorsement, or access to their millions of loyal and faithful donors. "Five percent is *way* too much to pay," they said.

The Toms apparently had their reasons. The first may have been their dependence on Dorchak and her insistence on keeping the company reliant on her advertising. Second, neither Glenda nor the Toms understood the comparative math. They couldn't see the benefit of donating five percent promoting sales versus blowing sixty percent on advertising. No one ever accused them of being smart. Third, Craig was in their way. Anything he supported had to go if they were to rid themselves of his influence.

For Craig, "doing well by doing good" was part of a covenant he had made with the Almighty before any of us had engaged in building his dream. Yet he never presented these demand-generating relationships as anything other than "good business." The math was simple. Tom had just publicly announced, "Our sales and marketing expenses represented sixty percent of our sales this quarter." Craig thought five percent was better than sixty. So, if the allied organization, through their self-interest in raising money to do their good deeds, promoted their custom marketplace, why not donate five percent? If we had offered them *fifty percent*, we still would have been ahead of management's feeble performance.

Generating revenue cheaply, but outside of Tom's and Glenda's realm, was evidently threatening. Maybe it was only Mr. Outside they found threatening. Or perhaps it was simply beyond their scope, outside their comfort zone. Whatever the reasons, they dismantled relationships as fast as Craig and his Business Development team could build them.

The InService acquisition Tom had bragged about never materialized. The failure is a fascinating character study. Craig had negotiated the purchase during his tenure as CEO. Under the terms he'd worked out with Carl Townsend, InService America's founder, the call center and telemarketing firm would cost us $200,000 in cash and 115,000 shares of stock. Their '98 revenues were $7 million. The purchase included considerable assets, plus 275 trained sales and customer service employees tracking to earn an EBITDA of $650,000 this year alone.

While that was a pretty good buy on its own merits, there was a lot more to the deal. InService, as part of Value America, could staff and manage the company's burgeoning customer service requirements. They were good at it. They hired and trained great people, and paid them less, by virtue of being in Lynchburg, an hour's drive south of Charlottesville. Our most important relationship, the customer relationship, would remain in-house as a core competency. Moreover, InService had been a catalyst for providing high-quality introductions to many of America's premier charity and faith-based Demand Alliances. They had earned their trust by serving them well.

But even after taking credit for "acquiring the world-class call center," Morgan, with help from Starnes, Johnson, Clifford, and Dorchak, killed the deal. Then, for good measure, they misled Craig, claiming that, "Carl got spooked and backed out."

Carl Townsend tells a different story. "They told me," he informed Craig a year later, "that Value America wouldn't even be in business a year from now. So they said I'd be a fool to sign the agreement. They said I'd have to stop serving my existing clients, even though they were the same organizations for which Value America was building custom marketplaces. Then they told my board the breakup was *my* fault. To make matters worse," Carl continued, "they said something really bad would happen if I ever shared any of this with you, Craig. Tom Morgan claimed, 'Winn will fire all of us if he ever finds out what we're doing behind his back.'"

⚬⚬⚬

AS Q2 ROLLED INTO Q3, Value America's prestigious board met in person for the first time. For the most part, it was a group of strangers. And that in itself would soon be a problem.

But not on this day. The new board assembled at Keswick Hall, in Charlottesville: former Secretary of Education, Empower America's William Bennett; Global Crossing's Don Tarpin; Carson's Sam White; Caise Perkins's Justin Caise; Heidrick & Struggles' Gerry Roche; Paul Allen's William Flowers; the unions' Rafe Durn; and FedEx founder Frederick Smith. Wolfgang Schmitt, Vice Chairman of Newell/Rubbermaid, was an invited guest. And, of course, our cofounders, Craig and Rex, as well as the firm's senior corporate executives, Glenda Dorchak and Tom Morgan, were on hand.

In advance of the occasion, David Kuo issued one of his few press releases. He said, "Adding people of this magnitude, with such diverse and distinguished backgrounds, greatly increases the caliber and strength of our board. We have brought together a world-class team that will keep Value America at the forefront of the Internet economy." He concluded the release with a quote he wrote for Morgan, "'There is plenty of competition for great leadership—especially in the online world. We have assembled a team of the best business, political, and technological minds. Working with Chairman and founder Craig Winn and Vice Chairman and cofounder Rex Scatena, we have the business acumen, leadership experience, and vision to convert great ideas into great business.'"

Typically, a board meeting is led by the company's CEO and moderated by its chairman, if they are not one in the same. Unfortunately, Morgan was not very good at arranging things, so in his absence of action, Craig privately proposed a plan. "Tom, why don't you teach the board about the company so they'll be prepared to make good decisions? You could have each of your ten business units make a presentation. Board members can meet the people that make our company go and learn what we're all about. Without this knowledge, an outside board is a liability, you know."

Craig went on, suggesting, "It'll be great for our folks too, especially if you ask each department to write down what they do and how they do it. They could list their accomplishments and highlight their challenges. We can give each board member a binder that not only explains the company from inside out but also tells them who does what." *You might even learn something, Tom.*

Each department crafted their section of the textbook, *Value America 101*. The department heads prepared fifteen-minute overviews. Recognizing the sad reality that few, if any, of our board members had actually shopped in our store, Craig began the meeting by demonstrating the store's functionality, breadth, and content.

The Technology, Consumer, Office, and Automotive Products merchants were the first group to present. I was second, delivering the Advertising presentation, showing examples of our best work. It saddened me that the board seemed so bored by it all. My old department, Presentation Marketing, now led by Isaac Saltzberg, gave a dazzling demonstration of the powerful online multimedia tools Joe had built. The board remained comatose, already glancing at their watches.

If they didn't care to learn about the company, why were they here? How would they make informed decisions and protect shareholder interests without a basic understanding of our firm?

Communications was presented by its VP, David Kuo. He had invited his favorite PR firm to help him do his job, an outfit from Washington that had played a starring role for AOL. Then came Sales, with Candy Clifford. The only embarrassment of the day, Business Development, followed. Tom Starnes presented his one and only contribution to Value America. He proposed spending $9 million in cash plus 300,000 shares to buy a start-up technology company called eFed. Cute name, but little else. Although the price was forty times higher, eFed's sales were less than a quarter of InService's. They had no tangible assets to speak of, no technologists, and no plan for generating additional sales. The guys who had been running it since its inception were cashing out and leaving, so there was no management, either. The entire company consisted of twenty-four employees, and that was before the buyout.

eFed, the board was told, was designed to capitalize on the segment of government purchases that fell below the big boys (the bid process), the medium boys (the contract process), and the small boys (the GSA process). "Their crumbs," Tom shared, "were worth billions." He didn't know, of course, how to harvest them. He said, "Their toehold is in the procurement segment that could be converted to an off-contract, purchase-card purchasing e-commerce opportunity." I know. It doesn't make any sense to me either. It sure didn't sound like it was worth $15 million. But that was the best part of his presentation. The other seven things he spoke of on this warm summer morning, he actually dismantled. Under the Toms, Business Development had become Business Destruction.

Unbelievably, Tom Starnes would later whine to anyone that would listen, especially to the press, that he had been prohibited from doing his job because Craig had foolishly said no to eFed, even though Winn had simply asked Starnes a few questions. How was he going to complete eFed's technology without technologists? How was he going to generate sales without a compelling advantage over the companies that already focused on the government sector? How are you going to get factory authorization to sell the government, and what about GSA schedules? Tom, of course, had no answers.

Glenda had created a new department for one of her wayward sellers. It was called "Member Services." They presented next. I'm still not sure what service they provided, but as far as I could tell, our most outspoken lesbian employee managed the department professionally and with all possible political correctness. I'm told that no environments were plundered, no species were threatened (other than humans, who, as we know, have it coming), and that the only group discriminated against was wealthy, white, heterosexual males.

Leaving the world of fantasy and entering reality, the board reviewed Operations, replete with such scintillating topics as vendor compliance, EDI, freight, returns, facilities, and credit cards. And then, not a moment to soon, the Technologists, in *shoes*, some even wearing long pants, descended upon the board. They talked of hardware, software, custom code development, and networks. Then CFO Dean Johnson and Controller Karen Wiles introduced their staff and discussed human resources and cash management.

As the meeting concluded and the board members' departure times neared, they finally awoke, as if out of hibernation. Between stretches and yawns, they responded graciously and unanimously. Bill Bennett spoke first. He said, "I don't know much about business, but I know people. You can't fake what I saw here today. These are great people, and they care deeply about what they are doing. That kind of pathos is unstoppable."

Gerry Roche was the next to speak. He began by telling the others that it was his business to evaluate talent. After all, he was CEO of the world's most celebrated executive recruitment firm. He said, "I have never seen so much talent in one place. This team can do anything."

"I'm more convinced than ever," Fred Smith added, "that you've got the best model and the best people. One day America is going to wake up and Value America will be everywhere."

The visiting Wolf Schmitt said, "What you have built here is solid and compelling. You should be very proud." Remember those words.

ର୍ଚ୍ଚିକ୍ଚ

OUT OF THE BLUE, Craig's favorite accounting firm, Ernst & Young, came calling. They weren't looking for business; they were looking to praise a business: ours. On behalf of *USAToday*, CNN, and NASDAQ, they had singled out our company and its founder. They had nominated Craig as a finalist in their annual Entrepreneur of the Year Awards.

Unfortunately, he was so focused on consummating partnerships with Visa, Citibank, and FedEx, he was unable to meet with the panel of judges. In spite of this, they had nice things to say about him in a video production they played at their awards dinner. Set to music and against visual images of Value America's store, a professional voice boomed:

Craig Winn, founder and chairman of Value America, knows retailing from every perspective. Soon after graduating magna cum laude in business from the University of Southern Cal, he worked with the entrepreneurial team led by Sol Price, founder of FedMart and Price Club. Many of the core concepts that drove the success of the Price Club have been incorporated into Value America.

The Winn Company, one of the nation's leading rep firms, was formed and grew out of Winn's association with Price. His next venture, Dynasty, was a national company that went public in 1989. Winn was named Entrepreneur of the Year in California the same year he won Sears' Vendor of the Year Award, 1990. Winn's concept was derived from his work with Price Club, The Winn Company, and Dynasty—twenty years ago. Leveraging expertise in retailing, distribution, manufacturing, sales, and marketing with advanced e-commerce technology, Winn has created the Internet's premier one-stop retail destination.

Craig missed most of the black-tie event. He was tending to business, speaking at our IPO closing dinner at Keswick Hall. In a five-minute unprepared speech, Craig told the investment bankers from Robertson Stephens and Volpe Brown, along with members of our management team and their spouses, "It takes three things to change the world, especially the business world: a great idea, great people, and a great deal of money. Thanks to the culmination of events we are celebrating here tonight, we are long on all three."

During this time, however, it was getting a little harder to tell the "great people" apart. Morgan's first duty had been to replace Dorchak. But having become dependent upon her, he simply took her "President" title away instead. When her crying became unbearable, Tom solved the problem by taking everyone's title away. We became the titleless Americans. At considerable expense, everybody's business cards were reprinted without any reference to role, title, or responsibility. Mao would have loved it.

But all was not rosy in the workers' paradise. Craig, working with Bill Hunt, encouraged Whirlpool to partner with us in a most remarkable way. We agreed to manage the communications, logistics, and order fulfillment between Whirlpool and their nearly 5,000 authorized dealers. It was a tremendous business-to-business opportunity. So excited was the senior brass at Whirlpool, they loaded up their corporate jet with execs and made the trek to C'ville.

Rather than present Value America himself, Craig asked the managers of each department to do the honors. This time it didn't work. We now employed too many come-latelies, none of whom had read the business plan. They didn't know what Value America had been designed to accomplish, nor did they understand the merits of an eServices alliance. Craig found himself in the unfamiliar territory of having to clarify the company's position throughout the meeting. But that wasn't the worst of it.

Bill introduced Whirlpool to our titleless ex-president. Knowing that Glenda knew very little about anything other than the sale of computers through call centers, Bill explained the proposed alliance. He said, "Using our existing infrastructure, we can profit by reducing Whirlpool's cost of serving its dealers." Glenda responded flatly, "Well, if that's what you want to do, we're not interested." A shaken Whirlpool exec asked Bill as they beat an abrupt retreat, "Who the hell was that?" Good question.

❦

THE BIGGEST DOINGS during the long hot summer of '99 occurred outside Value America. Our *un*doings occurred inside. The company had arranged, approved, and all-but-funded an airplane for the Business Development team to use as it covered the country in search of less costly demand-generating partnerships. In addition to burning their share of jet fuel, they burned the midnight oil. Craig, Mick Kicklighter, Syd Kain, and Ken Erickson formed great relationships as fast as the plane could fly.

Their biggest achievement nearly crashed before it flew, however. Senior members of the Business Development team at the world's largest financial institution, Citibank, had taken notice of our early ads. They'd liked them, not just for what they sold, but also for what they said, and how they said it. Citibank wanted a way to reward their seventy million affluent cardholders. By rewarding their customers, they were more likely to remain customers. And when they used their credit cards, Citibank earned a fee. Value America's custom marketplace strategy was the perfect fit. Especially the fact that we were comprehensive—something that's essential if your goal is to serve the needs of a large and diverse audience.

Citibank wrote what's called an RFP, a request for proposal. It's what big organizations use to make certain their dealings with smaller firms like ours are fair and equitable. Value America's VP, Tom Starnes, had been the recipient of the Citibank's RFP. It wasn't because it was addressed to him or that he had done anything to prompt it. He held the position, so it came to his desk.

But Tom was apparently too busy undoing relationships and scheming against Craig to respond to a solicitation from the world's largest financial institution. Twenty-four hours before it expired, Ken Erickson got called into Starnes' office, being scolded, as usual, for some minor offense. Ken noticed the distinctive "Citi" logo sticking out from underneath a pile of papers and reached for it. As he did, Tom told him it was a waste of time, that he was about to throw it away. Ken replied, "Since my time is worth less than yours, let me handle it. If it needs to be trashed, I have a can in my office. You needn't be bothered with such rubbish."

Faster than you can say "imbecile," Ken and Syd got to work. The RFP was a dozen pages long. Although they had never seen it before, it bore an eerie resemblance to something Ken had seen before—Hewlett Packard's first online commerce partner proposal—the one they had written based upon the qualifications we had given them, the one Bill Hunt had answered by cutting and pasting sections of our business plan. This one was like that one, because Citibank had written it with us in mind.

Ken and Syd got hold of the right documents. They cut-and-pasted their fingers silly, made the FedEx pickup, and prayed they were not too late. They weren't. Citibank was so grateful to have finally received the response they were fishing for, they called the next day and said we were the lead candidate. The fact that we had been the *only* candidate did little to dampen their enthusiasm. That would come later. In time, we would all find out how great a chasm exists between being chosen and doing, between yes and go.

Our team would bleed "Citibank blue" before we were done, but it was worth it. Together, we built one of the most exciting alliances between supply and demand ever conceived. By Citi's own admission, the first phase of the relationship was worth over $325 million. It was the most mutually beneficial, symbiotic, and scalable partnership one could imagine. It was "win to the 100th power."

The Citibank initiative fit like a perfectly sized glove. It was the poster child for something Craig called the *Path to Profitability*. The *Path* was designed to diminish, and then eliminate, the firm's dependence on the four evils that were bleeding us dry: wasteful broad-based advertising, costly call center sales, the concentration of sales on low-margin, high-return computers, and the company's dependence upon Ms. Dorchak.

The plan was ingenious. Charities, associations, large corporations, and faith-based institutions had something Value America needed: patrons, members, customers, and believers. If our company could form mutually beneficial relationships with them, we could gain a privileged and endorsed introduction to the millions of people they served. The cost to reach these people directly where they lived, paid, prayed, and played was cheaper than any form of broad-based advertising.

These organizations used direct mailings to reach their donors, clients, and followers. All we needed to do was emulate them. Catalogs, on- and off-line, could be used to introduce ourselves, explain the nature of the alliance, and generate the initial sale. By sharing a percentage of the revenue with the sponsoring organization, everybody won.

The *Path to Profitability* was an economic and strategic plan to move from advertising dependence to direct-response partnerships. Craig gave a copy to management and repeatedly shared the concept with Morgan. He also sent copies to the board.

Interestingly, the *Path* actually cemented our relationship with its largest intended beneficiary, Citibank. They were concerned that even after they formed their far-reaching partnership with us, we would continue our wasteful ways. Forming partnerships with companies on a collision course with bankruptcy is generally considered poor form. So Craig sent the finance team at Citi a copy of his *Path to Profitability*, along with a list of the assumptions that underlay the numbers.

Citibank spent $1.5 billion a year in direct mail solicitations. They understood the *Path*. After a series of high-level conference calls, Citi's finance team had only one concern. They loved the plan, and they knew they would play the largest role in making it happen. But they also knew how the corporate world worked. "Mr. Winn, you're Chairman, not CEO. Has your management team adopted your *Path to Profitability?* Are we going to see the progress it predicts in your future financial releases?" Most insightful.

As good as it was, the CitiPrivileges Program wasn't the only stellar relationship on the table. There was one nearly as good afoot with FedEx and another with Visa. Together with Value America, these companies had the most to gain from the success of e-tail. They represented the world's largest express delivery service, the largest marketer of credit cards, and the largest issuer of electronic credit. Together these were the tools of e-commerce: the electronic money that made it go, the plastic that caused that money to flow, and the logistics that enabled delivery.

The Visa deal broke first. Richard Gerhardt learned that Visa was forming relationships with online stores in order to dispel old myths about credit card security and encourage credit card use online. Richard went so far as to arrange the first meeting with Visa in Northern California. Craig was out on the left coast with HP anyway, and was speaking at a business conference. David Kuo and Mick Kicklighter were with him. Rather than head back and return home at two in the morning, they pressed on and met with Visa. They talked of things that, given time, might revolutionize credit card solicitation, rewards programs, and online commerce.

David took the lead in building the relationship. He wanted out of communications. Many of the come-latelies were no longer content with the roles they'd been hired to play. David's reasons for wanting to enter the world of *doing*, and for departing the world of merely talking about what others had done, were as varied as his moods. Despite his reservations, Mick awarded the management of Visa to David Kuo.

After several months of discussions, the first phase of the Visa deal was launched. It wasn't particularly innovative. It was similar to most other online programs Visa was doing. We gave Visa customers a ValueDollar coupon when they came to our store from Visa's website. Our coupon was larger, though, because our typical checkout was larger. While the average Web-store register ring was around $20, ours was over $600 at the time. Our Visa ValueDollar coupon could only be used on the first purchase, it had to be used online, and it could only cover fifty percent of whatever the shopper was interested in buying.

It would have been impossible for the Visa promotion to perform any worse than the gluttonous Morgan-Dorchak Advertising/Call-Center Full Employment Act. As a worst-case scenario, if every Visa customer only shopped once, never returned, searched the store to find something that cost precisely $200, and only bought that one thing, Visa was still ten percent better than what management was already "proud" of accomplishing.

Since Craig was usually traveling, developing outside partnerships, it was no surprise that the Visa promotion debuted while he was on the road. The General had become the *de facto* manager of Business Development, so Mick was with Craig again. So was David Kuo. Struggling in his communications role, Craig wanted David to witness the development of demand alliances, hoping he would learn to communicate their benefits more frequently and effectively. The team was in Tennessee, meeting with Fred Smith, when David got the call.

Morgan, whipped into a frenzy by a hysterical Dorchak, had lost control. David, equal parts emotion and naiveté, turned white. The six-foot-three Kuo crumbled as Morgan screamed into the phone. He dropped it into Craig's lap like a hot potato.

The Visa deal, it seemed, was working. *Terrible thing.* It was generating $400,000 a day in sales. That made this one promotion as productive as the whole company was without it, even with all their expensive ads and call centers. Plus every Visa sale was online, so the transactions cost us nothing. Better yet, every sale was to a new customer, each with a computer and a credit card. Moreover, every sale helped cement a relationship between an upstart e-tailer and the largest credit card company on earth, with 600 million customers worldwide. You'd think that would be a good thing.

All Tom could see, though, were coupon-dollars flying out the window. He hadn't the capacity, nor desire, to reconcile the drastic savings in advertising that were now possible against Visa's more moderate and variable cost.

Craig was not pleased with Morgan's temper tantrum. "Tom," he said, "get a grip on yourself. You're acting like a child." These were the first cross words Craig ever spoke to his seven-month-old CEO. They would not be his last. Their relationship began to deteriorate rapidly. "Tom, I'm really disappointed by your reaction. I didn't broker this program, David did, but I've kept up with his progress. His Visa deal is superior in every way to your advertising and call center dependence. If you're concerned about some systems irregularities, call the tech team. When I return, we'll resolve those issues. Otherwise, stop criticizing Visa."

Perplexed, Craig looked at David, "Is Tom really that dense or has Dorchak got him bamboozled to the point he's no longer able to think for himself?"

"He's speaking for the evil one. Of that I'm sure." David hated Dorchak as much as he loved Morgan.

Like Craig, David's faith initially caused him to bond with Tom. Visa was Craig's wake-up call, shattering any illusion of Morgan being honorable. He would come to see Morgan as a charlatan, a hopeless hypocrite. Kuo, however, remained blind. David's complete lack of business acumen ultimately prevented him from seeing through Morgan. Ignorance was bliss.

That evening, Tom gathered the leaders of the tech team in his executive conference room. Craig was invited, but as a harbinger of things to come, Tom also invited one of Glenda's most trusted lieutenants, former Ms. Sales, then Ms. Member Services, and now Ms. Affiliate. She was the first to speak. "I'm here representing Sales," she barked. That was code for *Glenda sent me.* "I've already called Caise and put his office on notice." It would be the last thing she would ever say to Craig, for he was not pleased.

"This meeting was called to resolve technology issues, not to solve problems in sales. It is the *lack* of efficient sales that precipitates the kind of partnerships we formed with Visa. But before you go, I want you to understand something," Craig said, speaking in a controlled, ominous tone. "This is the last time I want any executive in this company calling a lawyer. We waste more money on lawyers than any ten companies. Good agreements are mutually beneficial partnerships, not legalistic constructs. Stop abusing our corporate wallet. The CEO, and *only* the CEO, has the authority to deploy a lawyer on the company's behalf. Now, as the representative of Sales, I would appreciate it if you would leave." Of the techs, only Joe had seen Craig angry. It was terrifying, but the group's open-mouthed, wide-eyed expressions hinted that they had rather enjoyed the encounter.

The technologists listed each of their problems. Most were challenges that had nothing to do with Visa, omissions that had occurred as a result of poor management. The distractions associated with the SAP conversion and outsourcing sales to Convergys had taken their toll as well.

As he had with Joe in days gone by, Craig provided the practical business guidance needed to resolve the system challenges, all save one. Somewhere along the way, the percentage of a purchase ValueDollars would buy had been hard-coded into our systems. It should have remained a variable. That was important now because David had an agreement with Visa to reduce the ratio of ValueDollars to twenty percent of the first purchase. When Craig asked Joe to change the variable, it was no longer that easy. He was able to make the necessary changes to JoeWare in less than an hour. Unfortunately, SAP was considerably less nimble.

If they'd had their priorities straight, they would have made it happen. After all, we had more than a hundred technologists, and the Visa promotion was responsible for nearly half our revenues. But they had abandoned the old JoeWare systems for their overburdened SAP-Oracle-UNIX-Siebel-GEIS-ePiphany-Convergys camel. They could no longer serve the real business, our online business, without pulling resources from the creation of their sacred camel, so the ratio of ValueDollars to purchase price never changed in SAP. The business partnership with the largest electronic credit company in the world would be scuttled instead. *Brilliant.*

When programs as good as Visa cause people to lose control, something is terribly wrong. And so it was. Riddled with insecurity, Glenda and Tom imagined Craig lurking around every corner. They were frightened, and their fear now caused them to say and do things, irrational and destructive things—behind his back, of course.

Glenda had only one agenda: Glenda. She lusted for power and money. They were like drugs to her. So long as the company continued its expensive advertising, the sale of computers, and sales through call centers, she was golden—she had a stranglehold on power. Her relative expertise made the less-capable Morgan helplessly subservient.

Yet Tom viewed his enemy's enemy as his ally. He wanted Craig disgraced and dismissed as much as, if not more than, Dorchak did—and for many of the same reasons. But he had no reason, he thought, to fear Dorchak. She was beneath him. Tom was convinced that he controlled the board too, thanks in no small part to the subtle maneuverings of his pal, Goose Godfrey.

But Dorchak was not without her supporters. Rafe Durn's man, esteemed "investment banker" Seth Rossi, had grown fond of her. And then there was Justin Caise. Dorchak had become his meal ticket. But Tom knew nothing of this. He was confident Glenda could be used to serve his purposes: disgrace, discredit, and ultimately distance the company from his nemesis, Craig Winn.

Morgan and Dorchak had come to an understanding. As much as Dorchak disliked and disrespected Tom, she despised Craig even more, for he had given Tom the job she thought she'd earned, the title she deserved, the position for which she was so much better qualified. So even as the animosity between Tom's Team and Glenda's Gang rose, they schemed together against our founder. The hypocrite and the evil one had formed an unholy alliance.

One who is slack in his work is brother to one who destroys—Solomon

THE PLOT THICKENS

We made our share of bad decisions. For example, we never should have moved the management team out of Hollymead and into smaller digs on Rio Road. The reasoning was sound enough: the growing horde of high-priced technology consultants needed to implement SAP-Siebel-ePiphany-GEIS-Convergys had consumed every available inch of space, and we were looking to put four or five people each in the offices occupied by Tom, Glenda, Craig, Rex, Mick, Dean, Byron, and others. Morgan and Peters suggested moving out.

The results, however, were devastating. Winn's open-door policy, ease of access, and proximity to most of the team had had a tendency to keep the mischief down to a survivable level. Even though Craig was on the road more than he was in the office, and even though he seldom did anything internally other than occasionally walk the buildings and inspire the troops, his presence was still large. The legacy of what he meant to the company, the stories we old-timers told, and the example he set made him a leader worth following.

The problem was that Glenda's loyalists and Tom's team were insanely jealous. In Craig's presence, they kissed his butt, which disgusted him. Behind his back, they demeaned everything he stood for, which disgusted the rest of us. They cowered under his shadow, scurrying about in the darkness like cockroaches, undoing what we had achieved. It was all part of their little game, a game as old as the ages, the game of elevating oneself by tearing others down. They were masters.

With the cat away, the rats did play. It got to the point that there were more closed doors than open ones. Whispers permeated the halls. Progress was stymied as the come-latelies scrambled to take sides, and we old-timers just kept our heads down, trying to dodge the crossfire.

❧⬥☙

VISA! TOM'S TEAM and Glenda's Gang had their opening at last. Their enemy was vulnerable, and they mobilized to take advantage. Management meetings were conducted in great haste. The theme: Visa is bad; Winn is responsible; thus Winn is bad and must be stopped.

Those who attended say the meetings were about as judicious as the Salem Witch Trials. They began with a proclamation of guilt and concluded with a litany of justifications. For the umpteenth time, the reporting team was told how to categorize, or should I say miscategorize, revenues and expenses. Once again they balked, refusing to perjure themselves.

Some time before the meeting, some members of the reporting team had bared their souls to Andy Rod, President of the Office Products Group. They told him of Glenda's propensity to alter numbers. Not knowing what to do, they asked the approachable Rod for help.

Andy took the problem to Morgan, saying, "I went bankrupt once on bad numbers. I don't want it to happen here." Tom, Andy recalls, went to Dean Johnson and asked him to oversee reporting, but he refused. The matter went unresolved. Glenda remained golden. Tom remained oblivious.

Not to be deterred, Ms. Dorchak simply prepared the reports herself. Inventing her own numbers, she told the department heads all about the horrid consequences of the Visa promotion. "This program Winn is sponsoring is going to cost each of your departments millions. It'll destroy our company."

Having "elicited" management's support, Dorchak prepared a "fun with numbers" response for Tom's review. It was perfect. It showed that her Advertising/Call Center business was wonderfully efficient and productive. It revealed that Winn's Demand Alliance revenues (at least those alliances they had not yet dismantled) were anemic and clearly unprofessional. The only problem was, her numbers were inaccurate; they didn't tie to the firm's public reports and were simplistic to the point of being childish. Tom, naturally, swallowed them hook, line, and sinker.

Dorchak, with Tom in tow, waltzed into Craig's office, numbers in hand. Glenda made what appeared to be a reasoned, professional pitch. Tom nodded knowingly. Craig listened. When Glenda was done, he asked for a copy of her report. As the unholy alliance slithered out of the room to reconnoiter, he grabbed a pencil and calculator. In less than five minutes, he had filled Glenda's conclusion page with a sea of notes. They all said pretty much the same thing: "This doesn't add up."

Craig headed to Tom's office. He was now alone. "May I close your door, Tom?" he asked. The plot was about to thicken.

"Yes. What's up?" Tom looked worried.

Craig reached behind him and shut the door. He laid the report on Tom's desk, his own old green marble-top desk, placing it right side up for Tom, upside down for himself. A salesman in a former life, Craig could read just as easily upside down as right side up.

Tom looked down at the sheet, now covered with handwritten numbers, then back up at Craig as he tried to assess his predicament. Craig knew his words were going to be devastating, so he began with a question and hoped for a miracle. "Do you see anything wrong with Glenda's report?"

"No. I asked her to do this evaluation. She got my management team together over the weekend and got it done." There would be no miracle.

"The numbers don't add up, Tom. The sales columns don't tie, nor do they correlate to our public reports. Either we've lied to the public, or we've lied to ourselves." He let that sink in. "The advertising, Value-Dollars, and promotional costs are all errant. Most everything is miscategorized to make the things Glenda likes look good and those things she fears look bad." Tom sat motionless.

"That is bad," Craig said, using small words to make sure Morgan would understand. "But it's not why I'm concerned." Tom looked up from the paper and met Winn's steely gaze. This wasn't going to be pretty. "The problem is you. How can you be CEO and not know you're being played for a fool?" Tom had been at the helm for over seven months. Craig had been patient far too long. Wishful thinking wasn't going to transform Tom into a real CEO. Nor was Craig's eternally optimistic nature.

Tom gulped but said nothing.

"There is nothing I've wanted more than for you to succeed. In deference to you, I haven't attended your management meetings. I don't get your reports. In fact, I'm hardly ever here. I no longer have any idea what is or isn't happening in most of the departments in this company. But thirty seconds into Glenda's presentation, I knew she was full of crap. Why didn't you? You're the CEO—the one guy who's got to know what's going on."

There was an interminable pause. "Why," Tom asked, trying to clear his throat, "do you think these numbers are wrong?"

Craig pointed out the four or five most glaring errors matter-of-factly and said, "Nothing she does surprises me. I told you she was evil, a liar, rotten to the core, a two-time blackmailer. You were hired to replace her, simple as that. Instead, you've become dependent upon her."

Morgan was speechless. Craig waited for what seemed like an eternity. Tom said nothing. "I've offered to teach you the business, Tom. I've tried to explain retail and advertising, yet you rebuff me. The simple truth is you're not qualified to manage this company."

☙∙❧

CRAIG AND I found ourselves in familiar territory. It hadn't been intentional, but it was a most welcome diversion. It was no fun creating the bastardized ads Glenda was forcing me and my team to design.

Our being together again was the result of someone else's failure. Dorchak had hired a high-priced, underproductive "professional" to preside over advertising, a tall, handsome zero named Nick Hofer. Like most of Glenda's clan, he had come our way via a PC company—Gateway, in his case. He had claimed to be an expert in direct response advertising and catalog production. It turned out he couldn't even *outsource* the job, much less *do* it.

Craig, even with Morgan and his pal Starnes working against him, had managed to pull off some pretty spectacular demand alliances. With the Christmas selling season fast approaching, we'd need catalogs to capitalize on these relationships. The catalogs would introduce the nature of our alliance, explain why it was of value, and sell some 200 products spread across our nearly thirty categories. The only problem was that after almost three months of throwing money at outside consultants, Nick had nothing to show for our money or time but some rough layouts.

Craig, watching the deadline approach like a freight train, went to Morgan and said, "The catalogs for Citibank, FedEx, Falwell Ministries, US Wired, and American Heart Association need to be in the mail in thirty days. Glenda's boy is nowhere." Politely, he asked, "Tom, I would like your permission to work directly with Ken Power. We can get it done in a week or ten days."

"Alright," Tom said reluctantly, "but are you sure Nick has nothing to show for his efforts? Glenda's telling me he's making it happen. The only holdup, they claim, is our brands and your demand partners."

"Tom, your management team are experts at passing blame. Problem is, that's *all* they're good at. Yes, I'm sure they've accomplished nothing, and I'm sure it's their fault. Dorchak can't manage anything, and her army of officers is just as useless."

Morgan nodded approval, but said, "I know how to manage Glenda. She's not a problem for me. My problem is with your guys." Morgan was getting feisty, still embittered by Craig's recent criticism. "To do my job, I need a better CFO than Johnson and a stronger CIO than Stark. I've already talked to them and told 'em I'm concerned."

"Tom, who you hire is up to you. I think you've made a mistake in technology, however." Craig paused to make certain what he was about to say would sink in. "I've encouraged you to manage tech in a committee forum until you understand it better. You've got one of the best developers on the planet in Joe Page, the smartest guy in the company, Dan Lucier in Networking, two world-class DBAs in Herrick and Intihar. You have a decent manager in Poletti and, perhaps best of all, an enterprise-caliber leader in Thor Anders. By listening to them collectively you'll learn technology and get first-rate input. I'm certain you'll find that Thor Anders is the CIO you're looking for."

"Well, Thurston Stark is not the right guy, of that *I'm* certain," Morgan said, obviously trying to get back at Craig for his earlier comments.

"Stark is a fine guy. Maybe he's not the right guy to be CIO, but that's not the point. You've got all the talent you need. You're just not managing them right."

"That's not my style, Craig. I have to have the very best people around me. The fewer direct reports the better. I've already asked Goose Godfrey and Gerry Roche to find a top-drawer CIO and CFO for me."

"Rex and I have a long history with Dean. Without him, you wouldn't be working here. He's the best there is when it comes to raising capital, which is something you need to do right now."

Craig wouldn't learn until later that Dean held Morgan in low regard. He was unimpressed with his managerial skill, leadership ability, and overall competence. The moment Craig left management and empowered Tom, Dean wanted out.

Craig was frustrated with Tom's lack of action in finance. Morgan had proposed convertible debt, which in this down market would have been suicidal. He even wanted Robbie Stevens to manage the offering, hilarious since we had heard almost nothing from them since their $4.5 million IPO payday. To be helpful, Craig had met with Dan Case, the head of H&Q, and arranged a $30 million equity deal with his favorite analyst, Suzzi Maupin, initiating coverage. Even with the deal teed up for him, Morgan couldn't seem to pull the trigger.

"I don't work that way," Tom continued. "Johnson just isn't the caliber I need. And another thing. Your friend Byron Peters isn't cutting it either. I've told you this before; neither Glenda nor I think he adds any value. He doesn't get anything done, and doesn't offer any new ideas."

"Peters' problem is that the deck is stacked against him. I asked you to fire Dorchak as soon as you came up to speed on sales and advertising, but you haven't. Then I asked you to at least take half her responsibility away; let her have either sales or advertising, but not both—with both she's lethal. She wastes ninety-five percent of our ad budget pushing cheap, low-margin computers. Byron is responsible for consumer products; that's where the ad dollars should be going, but they're not! It's little wonder you think he's unproductive. The situation is impossible."

Tom wasn't pleased. He hated criticism, even when it was constructive and done in private. His fragile psyche bristled. "I don't think Glenda is as bad as you think she is. At least she gets things done."

So did Genghis Khan, Craig thought. "Aware of her failings, I was able to keep her more sinister side in check, most of the time anyway. But someday you're going to have your back up against the wall—and that's when she'll strike. The best predictor of future behavior is past behavior."

"Like I said, I'm comfortable with my ability to manage her." Tom was blissfully unaware of what his overconfidence would cost him.

Craig knew he was about to sail into troubled waters, but he steamed ahead anyway. "While we're talking about under-performers, I have a problem with three of your people."

Tom squirmed. The little hair he had stood up, his face flushed. He knew who annoyed Craig, but he needed them—not to manage the business, but to promote his personal interests.

"Godfrey, Starnes, and Kuo—between them they cost the company what, fifty grand a month? They're doing nothing to earn it. I'm sure they're all nice guys, good fathers and all, but this isn't summer camp. It's a business, a business that's losing money, one that can't afford dead weight."

Morgan lamely defended their value. By now it was obvious: Craig and Tom were oil and vinegar. They may have been in the same vessel, but one was floating high above the other. They were adverse to one another—one still fueled what little flame flickered of the old dream, the retail revolution. The other had grown bitter.

Yet for one last fleeting moment, the flame flickered brightly, just like old times. Craig stepped into my small office, and we went to work. He had sketched out the catalog on paper, listing the products he wanted on each page. He stood behind me, facing my monitor, as we worked together each morning from seven to ten and each evening between four and seven. There were five catalogs altogether—similar, yet different. We placed pictures, wrote copy, tuned layouts, and chased details. As the days progressed, our direct response catalogs took shape.

They featured products from every area: Toys, Hardware, Jewelry, Home Improvement, Gifts, Apparel, Cameras, Electronics, Office, Computers, Peripherals, Software, Housewares, Specialty Foods, Books, Music, DVDs, Videos, Health and Beauty. In the end, Craig and I were on time, under budget, happy, exhausted, and maybe even a little proud.

࿐

"REX," ANDY ROD SAID, "I don't want to burden you, but there's some stuff happening here you need to know about." Andy was one of Rex's favorite people—and Craig's. He had been hired early on, while we were still in the Yellow House. Jewish, with the gift of gab, Andy got things done. His recent supply alliance with Esselte, the Office Products industry's largest conglomerate, had placed Andy fourth, after only Craig, Rex, and Bill Hunt, on the all-time Value America productivity list. The deal was a $15 million cooperative advertising partnership.

Andy was normally good natured, but today he was troubled. "Rex, do you and Craig have any idea what's going on here?"

"What now?" Rex asked innocently. Rex already knew more than he wanted to know. He had made a practice of staying close to his enemies.

"Can I close your door?" Andy asked. Rex nodded. "The 'Hitler Youth' are going to interrogate me for talking to you, but I owe it to you." The term had become standard corporate parlance describing Glenda's loyalists. "When I was in trouble," Andy went on, "you and Craig gave me a chance. Nobody else was willing to do that. You've been kind to me and my family," Andy said emotionally.

"Say what's on your mind, Andy," Rex insisted. Rex loved "A-Rod," as he was known, but could grow weary of his ability to talk endlessly, often without appearing to take a breath.

"I first noticed the problem a little while ago, when I went to my boss, Byron Peters, to ask for a raise. I'd been here for more than a year and thought that since I'd been so productive, I might be deserving. I began telling Byron how Craig had offered me the job, when he stopped me in mid-sentence. He put up his hand and said, 'Don't you ever talk to Winn again. Morgan, Starnes, Dorchak, and I are in charge now. Craig's got nothing to do with anything other than some outside partnerships. We'll decide when it's time for a raise.'" Andy shook his head.

"I'm sorry," Rex said, "but it's true. They're in charge."

"That's just the problem," Andy replied. "They're not!"

"What do you mean?"

"I mean they're not doing anything," Andy responded. "A couple of days ago, Starnes called me into his office. He said, 'Andy, it's come to my attention that you swear too much.' 'You're shittin' me,' I said. He didn't see the humor in it. 'Listen, sure I swear a little,' I told him, 'but at least I get stuff done. Unlike you and your friend Morgan, my life isn't a lie. I don't drink, do drugs, cheat on my wife, or screw the company I work for.'" The toxicity level had risen to the point that unsubstantiated personal accusations had become commonplace. "You won't believe what Starnes told me, Rex," Andy went on. "He said, 'Life is not about reality—it's all about perceptions.' What is it with these people? Who do they think they're fooling?"

"Their phony religious stuff, their Bible studies, and their prayer meetings give me the creeps," Rex added. "These clowns are total hypocrites."

"You know I don't think much of Starnes," Andy said. "The guy is useless. He asked me to do an OGSPM before my trip to visit the head of AOL Europe. I said I wouldn't. 'You and all your fancy reports and pretty charts,' I told him. 'I'll get to know the people, form a relationship, and beat you every damn time.'"

"You're right. They can't seem to get out of their own shadow. They spend all their time complaining about Craig."

"Morgan too. Tom's a real piece of work," A-Rod charged. "He had Byron and I jump into the corporate jet and fly with him to an office products deal in Chicago. Tom disappeared the moment we arrived. While Peters and I were working the brands for co-op money, he was out playing politics, feathering his nest. I swear, Rex, the guy spends most of his time promoting himself, making sure he's covered, just in case he needs a new job."

Rex was neither surprised nor amused.

"Let me give you an example," Andy moaned. "I found this office supply company. We've done all the due diligence, and everybody's agreed that we need to buy them if we want to be a serious player in the biz. The deal's cheap, they make money, and the founder's willing to stick around and run the joint. But Starnes and his buddy Morgan nixed the deal. I asked 'em why. Turns out Morgan's afraid he'll somehow violate his non-compete with USOP if we buy them! He's not thinking about us. He's only interested in himself. What are we paying him for, anyway?"

✦

KEN ERICKSON was another one of the good guys. He had come to talk to Craig while Andy was talking with Rex. As somebody who got things done, he was as universally despised by Tom's Team and Glenda's Gang as was Andy.

As Ken walked into his office, he looked over both shoulders to make sure nobody had caught him entering the forbidden zone—Craig's dark and lonely office on Rio Road. He asked if he could close the door.

Craig nodded, braced himself, and asked, "What was all that shouting I heard in the hall?"

"I was pissed at Kuo," Ken responded. "David's responsible for the Visa deal, but he doesn't have the balls to stand up and say so. I swear he's in cahoots with Morgan."

"Rumor has it Kuo's mad at me," Craig said. "I told him yesterday how disappointed I was at his lack of productivity—encouraged him to do more. He made a beeline to Morgan's office and spilled his guts. So, yeah, David's conflicted, but that's not why you're here, is it Ken?"

"No. I've got some really bad news. It's going to make you mad," Erickson sighed. "You've got to promise me you won't tell anybody where you heard this. The Toms already hate my guts. They hate everybody they think's close to you—threaten to fire us for even *talking* to you."

Craig put his elbow on his desk and cradled his head in his hand. It saddened him to see his baby, this company he'd nurtured from its inception, ripped apart. It killed him to know that the first twenty-five or so people, the ones he had hired and asked to change their lives, were now being abused—their only crime: devotion to the company they'd been instrumental in building. It made his stomach churn.

"It isn't why I'm here, Craig, but your mention of Morgan reminded me of something. He's got Kuo's relative, the one he planted in Business Development, trying to pull together copies of demand alliance agreements. The guy hasn't got a clue what he's looking for. Besides, Syd and I keep most of the agreements in our personal files. But I can assure you, he's up to no good. I think Tom wants to discredit what we're doing."

Craig sighed. "It's not like the job of managing the company is so easy he has the time to screw around with the relationships we've built."

Ken had been patient long enough. He took a deep breath and blurted it out. "Did you know Tom and Glenda are sending more than forty people to the Comdex show? They're planning to spend a million bucks. Glenda's on some panel, and she wants the attention. She's willing to spend *a million dollars* of our money just to make herself look important."

The words shot through Craig like an arrow to the heart. He was speechless, dumbfounded. "No. It isn't possible, not even for them. They *can't* be that...." Craig put his hand to his mouth and closed his eyes.

"Afraid so," Ken said softly. "Didn't think you knew. Eric Cherna tipped me off. Since he's our computer merchant, he knows better. He's sick about this, but he told me he didn't know you well enough—didn't know if you knew what they were planning. You don't talk to the troops much any more. Anyway, Cherna asked me to tell you. He was hoping you could do something before it's too late. "

Stunned, silent, Craig looked blankly at Ken.

"They've been planning it for months, Craig. The whole management team is in on it. I think Morgan and Dorchak are scared stiff you'll find out. I'll probably get fired when they learn who spilled the beans."

Craig knew, as did Ken and Eric (or for that matter, anyone who had ever spent five minutes in retail) that a broad-based retailer sending a large contingent to a computer show like Comdex was Dumb with a capital "D." Brands, companies with something to sell, send contingencies to trade shows. Retailers just send their buyers, and only the buyers for the category being presented. Our "brain trust" didn't have the sense God gave geese.

Dean Johnson had been right. Tom and team were clueless.

As Ken left, Craig allowed enough time to pass to give him plausible deniability. Then, unable to contain his disappointment, he marched into Morgan's office and slammed the door, this time without asking. "Tom, I pray that what I've heard is wrong. Please tell me you haven't committed to send forty people to Comdex and waste a million dollars."

"We've been working on this for months," a flustered Tom stammered, straining to get the words out. "The whole management team is in support of this initiative. It'll generate huge revenue and membership gains."

"No, it won't. No retailer in their right mind sends an army of people to a trade show, much less promotes themselves at one. This is the exact opposite of what we should be doing," Craig went on in desperation. "You'll be pissing away a million dollars plus wasting our people's time. For what? To promote Dorchak?"

"The plans have been made," Tom stated defiantly. "My management team doesn't agree with you. We're going to come back with a million new customers. We need this to hit our Q4 numbers."

"I've spent my adult life in and around retail, since I was seventeen years old. I have attended a hundred trade shows, in every imaginable capacity. I've been a manufacturers' rep, a brand, a retailer, an industry guest. I've served on the boards of the largest international shows. I've forgotten more about consumer products than you'll ever learn. You're *wrong*—it's not only a colossal waste of money; you won't sell a thing! Besides, we can't afford the distraction. We're entering Q4, your systems conversion is bogged down and late, and now you want to send everybody from advertising to sales, from operations to management, to a *trade show?*" Craig was seething. "This is insane!"

"I don't appreciate your criticism or lack of confidence," Tom mumbled. "This is our plan. We all support it. We're going."

"Like I said last week, Tom, I haven't overridden a single one of your decisions, no matter how harebrained. But my confidence is wearing thin. I disagree with your decision to outsource sales to Convergys, with keeping Glenda, Starnes, and Godfrey, with corrupting your systems conversion, with your antagonism toward Visa, and now, this Comdex fiasco."

It obviously wasn't going well. Tom didn't understand, and had no interest in learning. Craig was heartsick. His options were all bad. If he fired his CEO, which he obviously needed to do, and searched for a replacement, he would have to reverse most everything Tom and his team had done. He'd have to salvage the neglected JoeWare systems and scrap their botched $15 million conversion. He'd have to stop advertising, immediately, just to keep the company from bleeding to death. And the moment he did, he'd have to sell an already hostile Wall Street on his *Path to Profitability*, his demand alliance concept, and his eServices business model. He knew his chances of pulling that off were slim to none. They didn't understand retail, the engine of our national economy. How were they going to grasp these more complex strategies?

But that wasn't the biggest problem. Craig no longer knew ninety percent of the people on our team. He had no clue what we were doing. How would he go about culling the good from the bad? He'd been exposed to enough managers to know that the come-latelies were dangerously inept. Their loyalties were to themselves, not the company. If they were this destructive now, what would they do if he fired them? Craig Winn was clearly embroiled in a lose-lose game.

Then it got ugly. Most every officer was aligned in one camp or the other. Glenda's Gang, aka the Hitler Youth, were also called the FOGs, for "Friends of Glenda." They were paid exorbitant salaries—it reeked of bribery. Tom's Team, the Brethren, were all tied to the glad-handing, back-slapping Godfrey. They, like Goose, were even more unproductive and politically motivated, which shouldn't be surprising, considering most called Washington home. They, too, were grossly overpaid, under-worked, and self-absorbed. They did little but ridicule those who got things done.

Craig was in a pickle. This daring ship of commerce he had designed, built, launched, and sailed out to sea with guns blazing, was sinking. His choices were go back to the dock, make repairs, dismiss the officers, and train a new crew, or work with the existing crew and try to help them patch the hull and plot a new course. Out of touch, Craig chose the latter. It may have been the worst decision he ever made.

While still in Tom's office, Craig asked if he had a copy of the *Path to Profitability*. Tom didn't know, so Craig walked into his office, grabbed the file he had placed in the center of his desk, and returned. "Let's review this again," he said. "It's our only hope."

৵৽৽৻

"HEY MICK, could you do me a favor?"

"Sure, Craig" Mick replied as the two met in the hall.

"I've heard rumblings we're considering paying Dennis Conner serious money to endorse his America's Cup yacht, Stars and Stripes. If this is happening under the auspices of a custom store, and they're going to promote it for a share of revenue, okay. But if we're thinking about paying him money up front, make sure it doesn't happen in your area, Business Development."

"Okay. I'll check it out and get back to you."

It didn't take long. A deal was brewing with Conner. Morgan was responsible. Mr. Inside was trespassing outside. According to Mick, Tom was even territorial about it.

"Tom, not so politely, told me to butt out," the General said. "But you were right. He's committed to pay Conner seven hundred and fifty grand."

"Damn!" Craig moaned. "I knew it! Tom just doesn't understand demand alliances. There's no way we'll generate a dime's revenue from this. Sure as shootin', we've just thrown away three quarters of a million bucks. Where will it all end?"

"Say Craig," Mick said, wanting to change the subject, "what do you think about giving the Saks Alliance another try? You and their chairman, Brad Martin, came so close the last time we were in Memphis. The business plan you composed integrating the Saks opportunity into the Citibank program was the best I've ever seen."

"Mick, you know I respect your judgment, and if you want to do this, I'll support you. But I think it's a waste of time. The problem's not Brad, it's his bud Rob Hilton. It's not in Rob's interest to support an alliance, no matter how good it is for Saks. It could put him out of a job."

"You're right, but Brad's the boss, and ever since Kerr Tigrett and his mom, Pat, got you guys together, good things have happened.

"Yeah, but ever since your pal Goose Godfrey brought Hilton in, the deal's been a disaster. We work something out with Brad, confirm it in writing, and then, as quickly as we leave, Hilton scuttles it. It's worse than a waste of time, Mick. Somehow this relationship between Godfrey, Hilton, and Morgan is gonna cause us grief."

◈

EACH DAY WAS now interminable. Rex and Craig had become strangers in their own land. Every morning brought a new surprise, a new battle, a new bitter pill to swallow. Today's bout with Dorchak was no different. It was over Yahoo!

The Evil One slithered into Craig's office with her hypocritical ally shuffling behind. Not surprisingly, Glenda had a stack of reports an inch thick. She began, "I've negotiated a spectacular deal with Yahoo! As you probably know, last year's deal is about to go dark."

"Why are you coming to me with this?" Craig asked. "I thought you were in charge of spending money." Even the pretense of pleasantries had now been abandoned.

Tom cleared his throat. "This is a serious commitment, and we want your input."

Not likely, Craig thought. "Okay, how much do you want to spend?"

Glenda looked down at her paper. "Five and a half million."

"You want to do *what?*" Craig bellowed. He didn't know whether to laugh or cry.

"We need to build our Web traffic numbers," Glenda said, parroting the metrics Craig had trashed his reputation trying to debunk. "That's how websites are being evaluated, and we don't look as good as some of our competitors." As Glenda whined on, Craig wanted to throw up. "We need to do this if we're going to reach my goal of a million new members. Glenda fumbled through her computer printouts, found one she liked, and proclaimed, "After I worked with Yahoo!'s management to focus our last deal, I was able to achieve a five-to-one return on our investment."

"No, you didn't." Craig snapped back.

"I have the report right here," Glenda protested.

"You two are unbelievable. I'll bet your Yahoo! deal was less than *point*-five to one. You're wrong by a factor of ten, I guarantee it. Tom, how could you sit here and propose re-upping the most unproductive thing we've ever done?"

"Oops," Glenda said sheepishly, flipping through her sheets. "He's right, Tom. I read my numbers wrong. The number *is* point-five to one, not five to one. See it here?" she added, pointing. That little error was the difference between her $5.5 million generating $27.5 million in revenue or a paltry $2.75 million.

"We need a Web presence," Tom said, lamely defending the indefensible. It was rather amusing, Craig thought, that the CEO would defend a plan to waste $5 million when he'd just learned that the rationale for the plan had been misinterpreted by a factor of ten. "We can't afford to go dark, as Glenda has pointed out, if we are to achieve our numbers. The Street is looking for things like customer acquisition, hits, and site traffic. We're not as popular as some other sites." It was almost as if they were purposely trying to scuttle the company.

"If you're asking my opinion because it's over five million and you can't authorize spending that much without board approval, then I suggest you present the Yahoo! proposal at the next board meeting, along with your proposal to spend fifteen million on eFed. I'm just one vote. All you need is six of the other ten, and you're set."

✦

AS TEAM VALUE AMERICA winged their way to New York, a trap awaited. Craig was going principally to his attend his weekly Citibank alliance meeting. He had been asked to serve on their steering committee. Mick had arranged a meeting with the CEO of the Girl Scouts of America, a potential new demand alliance partner, and, to Craig's chagrin, another meeting with Saks Fifth Avenue.

The plane was full. Everyone had a reason to be in New York. Some, like Syd Kain and Ken Erickson, were coming to work with Craig at Citibank. Others, like Byron Peters and Richard Gerhardt, were there to meet with jewelry and giftware vendors. No one knows why Tom Morgan and David Kuo were there. Maybe they were looking for a good show.

The entire Value America contingent gathered in an upper-floor Saks conference room. The plan Craig and Brad had conceived for the Value America/Saks alliance was incredible, completely incremental for both firms. Saks and other Brad Martin department stores, including Chicago's Carson Pirie Scott, would have Value America sell their brands of appeal, soft goods, and giftware to Value America's customers online, as well as to the seventy million customers that were part of the CitiPrivileges program. Saks and Carson would then sell Value America's non-department store brands to their million or so customers. Each company reached the other company's customers and sold products they couldn't otherwise source themselves.

But it was not to be. Team Value America was treated to a show instead. While the meeting had been arranged because Mick had continued to work with Brad Martin, the fireworks had been arranged compliments of the incendiary insecurities of Morgan, Godfrey, and Hilton. They had been working behind the scenes.

Brad Martin introduced the Saks team and left the room. That was a bad omen. He left his pal Rob Hilton in charge. Craig thought it would be a good time to leave too, but he stayed for the entertainment value. He was curious to see just how Rob would defend his pre-orchestrated refusal not to engage. After the Saks team, especially technology, had embarrassed themselves, Rob introduced a young lady who epitomized everything Craig had grown to hate about retail, especially department stores. She personified arrogance, but it was clear Hilton loved her. As she finished explaining why Saks was going to build its own site without Value America, Craig responded.

"Why would you arrange this meeting for the purpose of enacting a partnership and then tell us you have no intention of forming one? They make telephones for that sort of thing." An angry Winn continued. "Just so we don't go through this charade again, I want to make certain you understand what I think will happen." Craig looked holes through Hilton. "The Saks technology team is not capable of building an e-commerce site.

They somehow think an IBM AS400 is a mainframe and that it will integrate with your future online store. As a result, you will have to hire consultants to build this. They will negatively impact your earnings and hurt your shareholders. You'll never justify the cost."

It would play out just that way. Saks put out a release telling investors that their failure to hit quarterly numbers was because their e-tail initiative was more costly and less productive than they had planned.

With that, Craig stood and walked out of the room. As our team left the building, he gathered them together and explained why he had responded so harshly. Craig had little tolerance for deceit. He didn't like having his time wasted or his chain yanked. That was clear. They had never seen him this angry. More importantly, our suits now knew, if they didn't before, that their largest shareholder had a bite. He wouldn't go down easily.

◈◈◈

IT WAS PAST TIME for a vacation. Rex and his wife, Jane, had arranged to whisk Craig and Katharine away on a week's tour of Florence and Venice. They stayed at a lovely inn nestled on the east bank of the Arno, just above the Ponte Vecchio. For seven glorious days, the sun shined brightly as our founders reveled in the magnificence of Michelangelo, the mastery of Cosimo, and the birthplace of the Renaissance.

Each evening, however, a little rain fell into their otherwise serene world—a fax from Morgan. Visa was still bubbling along. Online sales were averaging four hundred thousand dollars a day. Tom had neither the courage to kill it nor the backbone to stand up to those that wanted Visa scuttled.

Craig refused to bail him out. He answered each plea with, "Sorry, Tom, it's not my call. It's yours. You're the CEO. As much as I've disagreed with most everything you've done recently, you're running the company. I haven't overruled any of your decisions. You know where I stand on this. David's Visa deal is more productive than Glenda's advertising. Why are you bothering me?"

Tom never seemed to have an answer, only another fax, crying out for help. But the only help Craig provided was of no value to him. Craig simply said, "If I were in your shoes, I'd get my hands on some accurate sales and advertising numbers, and then I'd compare those results to what Visa is costing us in ValueDollars. Compare Visa's variable cost to the fixed upfront cost of placing ads in newspapers and magazines. Evaluate the real cost of taking an order through your new outsourced call center. Compare that to the Visa promotion, which is strictly online. I could answer these questions for you based on our public reports, but you need to discover the truth for yourself." Truth was, the first $6 million generated by the Visa promotion outperformed broad-based advertising by better than three to one. There *was* no comparison. Craig knew it. Tom didn't.

"Dean is getting pushback from Pricewaterhouse Coopers on this," Tom responded. "Their technology group says we can't treat ValueDollars as a promotional expense. It's going to hurt our margins."

"Whether it comes out of margins or advertising, Tom, it makes no difference on the bottom line, to earnings per share. That's how you should present it. On the other hand," Craig added, "why don't you get PwC to give us somebody who understands retail? Retailers have used promotional coupons for a hundred years. If that's beyond them, find a new accounting firm." Tom just squirmed.

With Craig and Rex out of the country, Value America grew darker still. In this dim light, I was actually able to see things more clearly. I finally came to the conclusion that it was no longer worth the grief. The company for which I had uprooted my family and trashed my business no longer existed. There was little left but broken dreams, busted systems, frayed nerves, and ferocious turf battles. I no longer recognized the company. I wanted out.

AS WE CREPT further into the stormy fall of our discontent, Tom Morgan was ground zero in what was looking more and more like a *coup*. The inbound executive phone logs told a sordid tale. Eighty percent of his unanswered inbound calls were from people he had little reason to talk to unless he was up to mischief. Cowering in Craig's shadow, he was finally consumed by his less-admirable qualities. His focus was now clearly on his own personal agenda.

Tom talked daily with Kuo, Starnes, Godfrey, and his pals on the board. They were scurrying in the darkness, maneuvering behind his back. They had set their trap, and Winn was now barreling toward it at 550 miles an hour, 35,000 feet above the Atlantic Ocean.

For Craig, it was one of the most inspiring moments of his life. His wife and his traveling companions Rex and Jane were asleep. Craig was awake, but growing weary trying to finish an opaque tome that Reverend Mathews, Bishop of the Methodist Church, had given him at a dinner hosted in Craig's honor at the headquarters of the United Brethren. The book, *The Unshakable Kingdom and the Unchanging Person,* had been written by Mathews' father-in-law, a great, aging missionary, E. Stanley Jones.

Craig's thoughts drifted back to his last visit with the United Brethren.

Their headquarters was an elegant converted old home called "The Pines," just outside Washington. The Brethren, still trying to recruit Craig, joined the chorus of those asking him to run for national office. Their leader's means, however, were a bit unconventional. After explaining why he didn't like being called a Christian, he encouraged Craig to follow the example of other great revolutionaries in his pursuit of a national revival. But the revolutionaries whose strategies he extolled were Adolf Hitler, Mao Tse-tung, and Jesus of Nazareth. Imagine, going forth to change the world with *Mein Kampf,* Mao's *Little Red Book,* and the *Bible* all tucked under your arm. Craig didn't didn't know whether to laugh or cry. So he simply rejected the Brethren. It was a move that would cost him dearly.

Craig caught himself shaking his head as he put the book down and rubbed his eyes. It was tough sledding. He had become convinced eighty-year-old men shouldn't be writing books. Yet as he did, he was moved to pick up his pen. In the inside back cover, he felt compelled to write these words, as if he were taking dictation from a higher source: "Service, Freedom, Education, Justice, Opportunity." Then, something told him to reopen the book. He read, "So He went to the little synagogue at Nazareth and announced His program for the reconstruction of the world. He delivered His manifesto...five important changes, regenerative changes. He said..."Good news to the poor" (service will abolish poverty), "freedom for the captives" (freedom), "recovery of sight for the blind" (enlightenment through education), "to release the oppressed" (justice), "to proclaim the year of the Lord's favor" (opportunity, for in that year debts were forgiven, slaves freed, and productive assets redistributed).

Craig sat for a moment in stunned silence. He looked out the window and saw the brilliant white light of the morning sun dancing upon the immensity of the Atlantic Ocean. He not only knew that he had been given his marching orders, but also that his orders were identical to those that had been proclaimed by the greatest Revolutionary of all time.

As he regained his composure, Craig picked up his pen again.

October 31, 1999—Italy to America (from the old world to the new world). Our future shall be of multiplication, not division. It is time to come together, and stop separating ourselves based upon skin color, preferences, and special interests. We must be one people, devoted to building a new and better world for all. We are called to serve—empowered by grace, motivated by love, encouraged by faith. It is time for a new American revolution where service abolishes poverty, where opportunity is created before responsibility is preached. A time in which the pursuit of truth inspires our youth and wisdom enlightens our souls. It's time for the chains of injustice and bonds of prejudice to be loosened. For I am a believer in the life and lessons of a carpenter, a builder, a Jew named Jesus. Humbled and imperfect,

I am but a servant and a messenger. Like the morning star, this is a new direction, a new promise, a fresh start to a bright new day.

As he lifted pen from paper and closed the book, Craig began a new chapter in his life—a chapter that would shake the very foundations of his faith. Summer was over; fall was in full swing. But the storms of winter were about to rock his world.

⤜⦂⤛

INSPIRED AND REFRESHED, Craig climbed the steps leading to the small but luxurious suite of offices housing Value America's management team. With each stride, he felt less comfortable. Unlike the spaces Craig had either found or designed for the company when he was managing us, the Rio Road offices were dark, moody, opulent, and "corporate." Craig disliked them nearly as much as he disliked the politics of those that occupied them. He desperately wanted out. Now, thanks to his inspired journey home, he had a reason to leave.

It was around eight when Tom Morgan stumbled into Craig's office, closed the door, and resigned. Just like that.

Morgan announced, "There can't be two cooks in the kitchen." Then he blurted out what was really bothering him. "I hate being second guessed."

Winn had only recently gone from examining nothing Tom had done to second-guessing everything. But Craig's criticisms had all been made in private, and he had always made a point of being constructive—sharing better alternatives.

Morgan had done just the opposite, and he knew it. He had been openly critical of everything Craig had done. Unable to sell himself, he resented Winn's ability. He had condemned Craig's efforts on behalf of the company, calling him an exaggerator, a liar, and worse. His attacks had invariably been made behind Craig's back, and always to audiences with whom Tom was seeking favor. Political, insecure, hypocritical psyches like Morgan's are terribly fragile. They rebel against any criticism, public or private, constructive or not. Thus Craig's recent focus on Tom's failings was intolerable. It haunted Morgan like a twisted piece of paper in his otherwise perfectly ordered world.

The two men pondered their fate. They had clashed over a variety of issues: overburdening the ill-advised system conversion, outsourcing sales and customer service, a multimillion dollar Yahoo! proposal, a yacht sponsorship, and a trade-show spending spree. Tom had failed to recognize Visa's superiority to broad-based advertising and had been unwilling to either endorse Craig's *Path to Profitability* or create a plan of his own. And then there was Morgan's continued dependence on Dorchak. Rather than demote and isolate her, his actions had actually empowered her, putting the company in harm's way, on a collision course with infamy— the most sensational corporate decline in American history.

The idea of "two cooks in the kitchen" was laughable. It's a wonder Tom said it and more amazing anybody bought it. The fact that Tom's plans, not Craig's, had been imposed at every point of disagreement should have tipped folks off. But no. Lies are more seductive than truth. And so it was that upon this false premise, Morgan launched his *coup,* justified his schemes, and ultimately attempted to dispel his culpability.

Craig had grown to distrust so many of those who had come, at considerable cost, to reshape his once noble firm in their image. He had wanted to part company with his company a long time ago. *As soon as the firm's new leadership understands our mission, I'm out of here,* he had so often promised himself. But if Tom left, Craig would have to return to management and actually *do* what Morgan had falsely accused him of doing. *Oh God,* he thought, *why now? Sure, I've done it before, but do I still have what it takes?*

To make matters worse, the CFO, Dean Johnson, and the CIO, Thurston Stark, had just resigned. Little wonder; Tom had made it clear that neither of them fit into his plans. In Dean's case, the transition from being at Winn's side to Tom's was unbearable. Dean often said that working with Craig was the highlight of his business career, while his time with Morgan was utterly frustrating.

Calamity was virtually assured. No matter the explanation, no matter the salesmanship, no matter the positioning, the CEO of a public firm resigning in the same quarter as the CIO and CFO is a recipe for disaster. It's fodder for class action suits, the impetus for an avalanche that unless checked, can consume everything. Under these circumstances, Morgan's resignation was impossible to accept. Craig knew it, and Tom was counting on it. So let the games begin.

"What is it going to take for you to stay, Tom?" Craig asked.

Morgan went through the same, "I-don't-really-want-anything-from-you," charade he had used so effectively at USOP. Then, "I miss my family. I'm just not happy here."

Craig laid it on the line: "When you took this job, you accepted a responsibility. You pledged to work for our shareholders, protect employees, and serve our customers and partners. Your happiness has nothing to do with anything. By announcing your resignation in the middle of the fourth quarter, right after the two guys you wanted out actually left, you're acting irresponsibly, breaching your fiduciary duty. If you want out, you need to give us ninety days to find a new CEO and CFO."

"No, I wouldn't be comfortable doing that." Tom said. He realized, of course, that what Craig had asked was both customary and reasonable. Yet he felt neither responsibility nor guilt. Morgan had already received Godfrey's blessing, and that was all he needed. Besides, this was all a ruse; he had no intention of leaving. He knew Craig couldn't accept his resignation. His agenda was to get a festering thorn, a thorn named Winn, removed from his side.

"Tom, we both know this isn't about having 'two cooks in the kitchen,'" Craig said. "You're just irritated that I've been critical of your decisions. You don't have the stomach for it." Tom squirmed in his seat and looked down at Craig's old table, unable to make eye contact. "So," Craig added, "I'll make this easy for you. If you'll stay, I'll leave."

"You'd do that?" Morgan perked up as the words he was hoping to hear were spoken. You could hear the childlike excitement in his voice.

"No one cares if a chairman leaves," Craig said solemnly. "Boards don't run companies, executives do. I was going to leave anyway. My plan was to work half-time next quarter and then half of that through June. I'll finish implementing the best of the demand alliances and teach you what you need to know to carry on. How's that for a plan?"

"Are you saying that you'll start phasing out as early as next quarter and be gone by the end of the second quarter?"

"Yes."

"Will you introduce Tom Starnes to the people at Citibank and FedEx, so he'll be up to speed on what you're doing? You've really misjudged him, you know. He's a great guy who can get things done."

"Yes, I'll introduce him, but I don't think I've misjudged him."

Tom ignored the affront. It wasn't important now. This was going as he'd dreamed it would, just as he, Godfrey, and Kuo had planned it. "These training sessions you mentioned, can they be done off-site?"

"Sure, wherever you'd like," Craig answered. *Good grief. The man's ego is so frail, he can't even handle being seen learning something.*

"Are you sure about this, leaving and all? This was your baby," Tom pressed, testing his luck.

"I'm sure. This stopped being my baby a long time ago."

With that, they shook hands and parted company. Craig marched into Rex's office. It was the second time this morning.

"You were right," he said.

"Yeah, that's why I warned you before he got in this morning. He's been bellyaching," Rex told his friend. "He thinks he can trust me, and I play along. So, how close was I?"

"It happened exactly as you thought it would. He resigned; I offered to leave; he agreed to stay."

"Good. He's not worth a damn, but that should buy us the time we need to find his replacement," Rex said calmly. "So just like we predicted —when you asked him to do the responsible thing, he refused."

"Yep. Funny thing, though. You and I want out worse than he wants us out," Craig said.

"Yeah, but there's no way we'll leave our company in *his* incompetent hands."

ও◦ৡ

AS WE CRUMBLED, Craig was invited to meet with Citibank's senior Business Development Officer. As promised, he now had Tom Starnes in tow. The General was also at his side.

Craig had arranged to see an old friend before the meeting began, the man who had first plucked my ads out of *The Wall Street Journal*. Over time, he had become more than a business acquaintance. He was now a compatriot, a kindred spirit. But he had moved out of the CitiPrivileges-Value America program. Having been promoted, he now headed up the solicitation of new customers with a direct-mail budget of $1.5 billion. As the Citi executive explained his new challenge to Craig, he said, "I'm counting on you to help me look good."

"How would you define looking good?" Craig asked.

"When you're working with a one-and-a-half *billion* dollar budget, it doesn't take much of an improvement to score big dividends. If you can find a way to improve acceptance, diminish churn, or cut the cost of our mailings, I'm a hero. A ten percent improvement in any area would be all I'd need."

"So if I can find a way for our best brands to partner in your direct mail solicitations and either diminish costs or improve results by ten percent, you're a hero?" The Citi exec nodded. "Piece of cake, my friend."

Craig explained specifically how the plan would work, how it was in the interests of each party, including the customers. He outlined the numbers. As he did, his Citibank friend was writing as fast as Craig could talk, which was saying something. They shook hands as Craig stood to leave.

"I'm looking forward to working with you again. We're gonna have some fun, Craig. You're not going to forget me now, are you?" he smiled.

With a question like that following an invitation to participate in a billion-dollar promotional campaign, Craig knew something was up. He gave his friend a sideways look. "What aren't you telling me?"

"You'll see. Just don't forget me."

The next meeting began with an incredible admission. An even more celebrated Citibank exec declared, "We are a hard company to partner with, and we know it. You, Mr. Winn, have impressed a lot of people around here. You've not only managed to succeed, no matter how many obstacles we've thrown your way, you've done it in record time. More importantly, you did everything you said you'd do and more. Your promises were great, but your follow-through was better."

"Thank you," Craig said humbly. "You've got a great team and a great company. It's been my pleasure."

"We do have a fine company, even in spite of ourselves," the executive said with conviction. "And that brings me to why I asked you here. You've earned our trust, so I'm offering you access to our most valued resource— our customers. We want you to help us serve and reward all seventy million Citibank cardholders—a totally integrated and comprehensive program."

Elation wasn't a big enough word for it. Craig and Mick could have flown home without an airplane. They had indeed done right by Citi, and they knew it, but it was altogether unexpected and most uncommon for a large organization to recognize something like this and be appreciative, even generous. For Starnes' benefit, Craig and Mick talked about the two kinds of trust needed to bring about such an awesome opportunity.

Mick began, "They're right to trust us, you know. We've earned it. They took a lot of risks, shared confidential information. A lesser man might have used what he'd learned to make a quick buck."

"Mick, the fact we did what we said we'd do is even more important. Lots of people are honest. But institutions like Citibank don't give you the keys to the kingdom just because they know you're not going to rob 'em. It's as much what we did as what we didn't do. We made them look good; we did what we said we'd do. We succeeded even when they made it difficult. You should be proud, Mick. I've been in business all of my adult life but have never experienced anything this good. You, your character, your way with people, is why this happened. Thank you."

The General tried to deflect the praise, but Craig was right. They made a wonderful team. Sometimes three's a crowd, though, and so it was on this day. Starnes had said nothing and done nothing all day. He'd been little more than a wet blanket. He didn't even comprehend that he had witnessed one of the most promising days e-commerce would ever see.

Sadly, it all started going downhill, and not because they were beginning their descent into Charlottesville. Craig began questioning Starnes about his accomplishments as they neared home. There were none. *None!* Even the deals that had been teed up by others before his arrival were now

comatose under his direction. It was one of the most depressing interviews he can remember. *Who hired this numskull, anyway? And why?*

⤜⦂⤛

PULSING MAJESTICALLY THROUGH our all-but-abandoned JoeWare,
we scorched Wall Street's expectations one final time. Value America, on
the evening of November 3, 1999, reported a 269 percent increase in third
quarter revenue. Sales had surged to an intoxicating $58 million for the
ninety days that ended September 30th. The press release said, "Gross
margins increased 110 percent while expenses as a percentage of revenue
fell significantly." As retail metrics go, this was as good as good gets.

According to the release, the company earned a gross profit of $3.5
million selling products from 3,000 brands in thirty categories. Total operating expenses declined from eighty-two percent of revenue to sixty-four
percent. While the trend was favorable, spending sixty-four cents to sell a
dollar was hardly something to brag about. Yet fully seventy-five percent
of the sixty-four cents was consumed by sales and marketing.

That meant that operating costs, apart from our wasteful advertising
extravagances, were now less than fifteen percent of revenue. Most retailers, at scale, in business for decades, would give their right arm for anything under twenty-five percent. We were so very close to achieving our
improbable dream! If we had only adopted the *Path to Profitability* and jettisoned broad-based advertising back when Craig had proposed it, we
would have been profitable, just as we'd predicted. But, alas, it wasn't to
be. As tantalizingly close as we had come, defeat was snatched from the
jaws of victory.

Tom's Team and Glenda's Gang had too much invested in their respective *coups* to let a little corporate success stand in their way. Morgan was
working feverishly with Godfrey and his sympathetic board members,
White, Schmitt, and especially Roche. Glenda maneuvered her schemes
by way of her secret admirer, the company's illustrious "investment
banker," Seth Rossi. He was clandestinely brokering her promotion.
Dorchak and her supporters were courting Caise, Durn, and Durn's new
boss, Don Tarpin. She even asked folks to sign an anti-Winn petition just
to make sure she was properly positioned. Then for good measure, she
managed to dig up some old stories on Dynasty's demise and passed them
around to promote her cause.

All this maneuvering left the seldom-available Flowers and Bennett,
good guys both, just dangling in the wind. While Smith denied being
worked by Dorchak, he certainly became her most public fan. But to be

sure, Smith was being set up by both Toms, Morgan and Starnes. Along with the Kuos, they were confident to the point of cockiness that they would prevail. Their only blunder was misjudging the resolve of Dorchak.

Glenda, thanks largely to her foe's incompetence, was in control, albeit lurking in the shadows. The company was reliant upon her sales volume. More importantly, she knew she controlled the hearts and minds, or at least the pocketbooks, of her mercenary managers. They had all adjusted their lifestyles to fit their inflated incomes. Dorchak owned them.

There is no evidence to suggest that either Dorchak or Morgan had considered the possibility that their actions could cause the company to fail. All they knew is that they wanted unquestioned control. Yet unable to manage anything, they quickly managed to lose control of the process they had set in motion.

Against this dreary backdrop, the company held its quarterly conference call for investors and shareholders. This was the Dorchak, Morgan, Kuo, and Kuo show. Winn opted out of the Q3 festivities. For some reason, they wanted to use Craig's speakerphone, so they all gathered around the antique table. Craig went to a downstairs office to listen in.

They claimed, "Customer relationship management software from Siebel systems was implemented to provide top-quality call center tools." In truth, it hadn't. The conversion, thanks to their burdens, wouldn't actually go live until the forth quarter. Even then, all the things they added to it would cause it to fail.

They said, "This quarter an enhanced EDI system was installed." Sorry, wrong again. It wasn't installed in Q3. The new GEIS Enterprise system wasn't in place until the seventh week of the fourth quarter, and even then, unlike the old system, it failed to transmit orders. In fact, the day the company jettisoned JoeWare, it began to implode.

Remarkably, in their comments to shareholders, management bragged about forming a business-to-business relationship with McGraw Hill, the parent of *Business Week*. That would come in handy a few months later.

It was an embarrassment. Dorchak misspoke, Morgan mumbled, and the Kuos were clueless. Their presentations were pitiful. But it was their prepared answers to the Q&A that sent a chill over the investment community. Morgan was worse than ever. Dorchak sounded better, but unfortunately the things she said were inaccurate or misleading.

When asked about "relationships with major Internet portals," they said, "We did not renew our contract with Yahoo! simply because it did not provide a good return on our investment." *Incredible, considering how strongly they had touted the deal to Craig, and even more incredible considering they actually signed a new agreement with Yahoo! just a few months later.* They claimed to be growing rapidly. *This was false, as we shall soon learn.* They declared their fondness for consumer products. *The world would soon discover how little consumer products meant to them.* They insisted their advertising was performing at a ratio of 3:1. *Glenda gave the board an entirely different number.*

The stock tumbled.

৩৽৽৻৶

NOT SO BRIGHT and early the morning of November 4th, Value America's esteemed board of directors assembled in Charlottesville for the second and final time. Once again, the event was held at Keswick Hall.

To his credit, Frank Flowers was actually there. So were Smith, Durn, Tarpin, White, Schmitt, and Caise. None of them bothered to visit the troops on their way into town, however, although Gerry Roche had. The previous night, he had asked Craig to show him around. After spending an hour going from building to building. Roche remarked, "This is as fine a team as I've ever seen."

Rex and Craig were in attendance. By invitation of the board, Tom Morgan and Mick Kicklighter were present. So was Biff Pusey, who listed himself on the official records as Senior Vice President & Corporate Counsel, Assistant Secretary. Nice title. Dean Johnson was there, even though he had officially resigned. The law firm Wilmer, Cutler & Pickering was also represented. But they, through no fault of their own, wouldn't last long.

Tom Morgan introduced the senior executives for each of the business divisions. First, Cliff Chambers, newly promoted to EVP, Operations and Information Technology. Then Byron Peters, recently demoted to Group EVP of Consumer and Office Products and Presentation Marketing. Quite a title, though. Third, Ms. Dorchak was introduced. Evidently as a reward for her complicity in the "oust Winn" campaign, she had earned her old title back, plus a new one to boot. She was introduced as "President and General Manager, Advertising, Sales, and Technology Products." Makes you wonder if she got new business cards printed. Probably not; her new title was too big to fit on a card. She'd need a poster: something large enough to be seen on the post office wall.

These grandiose titles told a story, one far bigger than the mere insecurity and incompetence of our management team. They spoke volumes about a business culture, and indeed an entire national climate, that had lost its bearings. Corporate America had come to emulate the worst in Political America. Our aspirations had once been about purpose and progress; now they were about positioning and perception, power and wealth. Noble ambitions were ridiculed as naïve. New agendas—personal, not collective or corporate—were set. The common good was forsaken. Value America had become a self-centered microcosm of misplaced American values.

Sure, we all go to work because we need money, but it's our *attitude* once we get there that makes all the difference. We learned that when making money became our principle aim, we miss the mark. Whatever the job, striving to create value, to be productive, ultimately enables both employee and enterprise to profit.

The board quickly tired as each suit droned on, recounting their stellar accomplishments. Funny thing though. A month later the same cast of characters would claim they were powerless to do anything. But I'm getting just slightly ahead of my story.

As this most obtuse of board meetings rolled along, Morgan introduced his favorite co-conspirator, Tom Starnes. He too had a new title, "Executive Vice President, Government and Business-to-Business Development and International." I *know* that won't fit on a business card. We had come a long way from being the "Titleless Americans." Starnes said nothing of value.

Morgan smiled as he proudly introduced his new Director of Investor Relations, Kim Kuo. "Kim," he said, "was formally in communications at America Online." He carefully avoided mentioning her previous role. She didn't say much, either.

Morgan then informed the board that CFO Dean Johnson, CIO Thurston Stark, and Controller Karen Wiles had all announced their resignations. Karen said she was leaving to rejoin her husband in the Carolinas. Thurston announced he was quitting so he could spend more time with his family. In truth, burned out and tired of the office politics, they were going to work for Dean's new e-tail firm.

But by forming an e-commerce business and hiring Value America employees, Johnson had violated the most salient conditions of his employment contract, prohibiting employees from going into a similar business in our immediate proximity and luring coworkers away. As CEO, Morgan was required to confront this breach of contract, but instead, he signed a document prepared by Dean releasing him from from these obligations. Tom didn't even read it. He was glad to have him gone.

While facilitating these departures, he managed to use their resignations to promote his own agenda. Tom and his minions hinted behind the scenes that the three had left because Winn was impossible to work with, claiming that Stark and Johnson blamed their departures on Craig.

In a way, it was true: Craig's hands-off approach in deference to

Morgan's management role had left Dean feeling orphaned, abandoned. A talented CEO makes his CFO his primary ally. For a year and a half, Craig and Dean had been joined at the hip. But now, having moved out of management following the IPO, Craig no longer worked with Johnson. So frustrated and uninspired, Dean left, hoping Craig would understand.

Morgan's contribution to the board meeting ended with these introductions and announcements. Makes you wonder what he did to earn his $600,000 compensation. With the allotted time nearly over, Tom asked Craig to discuss his progress in building demand alliances and their potential impact on our profitability.

Craig began by passing out copies of the holiday catalog he and I had created on behalf of the CitiPrivileges Program. "In the first phase," he said, "we earned the opportunity to market all of what we sell to the most active forty-two million Citibank credit card holders. Among these are Citi's two most successful affiliate card programs, American Airlines Advantage and their AT&T Universal Card."

Craig circulated a marketing letter Citi had prepared. "This letter from Citibank shows that they expect our program to generate three hundred thirty-six million dollars over the next twelve months. This revenue stream is greater than our entire company's expectation for next year. While the revenue is great, the credibility of partnering with the world's largest financial institution is better. The potential for profit is better yet in that advertising costs drop from fifty percent to less than five percent. And every contractual detail of this relationship has been approved."

The suits just sat in polite silence. "Our contract with Citi states that that our cost to generate sales is three percent on consumer goods and just one percent in technology. The catalog and direct mail inserts we used to promote this program cost us nothing! The portion of production and mailing costs our brands didn't cover through co-op, Citibank picked up. Yes, Citibank paid us to produce this catalog," Craig said, holding his copy up to underscore the point.

"It gets better. Twenty-one of the twenty-four pages in this catalog are devoted to consumer products, where our margins are three times greater than they are on PCs. And our returns are five times less. Citi has also given us a contract for a Value America Master Card. Its reward: one percent of whatever you buy anywhere in the world will be automatically, and electronically, applied to your ValueDollar account in our store. Citibank will cover the majority of this expense. Can you imagine the impact this will have on sales and profits?"

The board was conflicted. A half dozen disgruntled employees had deluged them with anti-Winn propaganda for weeks now, with intensifying doses over the past few days. Yet this was monumental. This partnership promised to deliver us from the bondage of gluttonous advertising, to rescue us from the ocean of red ink our company, like most dot-coms, was drowning in. It was the solution brands needed to pull free of retail abuse. It was the solution America needed to help fund her most productive charities and close the digital divide.

But the board was ambivalent. It's hard to crawl into the minds of others, but the only plausible explanation is a breach of trust. They had been told by six or eight misguided individuals that Winn was the problem, meddling, micromanaging, and exaggerating—your basic lying scumbag. So when the "scumbag" presented this partnership with the world's largest financial institution, they just yawned. When he told them that management's wasteful advertising spending could be slashed by *ninety percent*, they just closed the catalog and looked at their watches. *Sounds too good to be true. He must be lying. We're told he does that a lot.* But how could they dismiss Citibank's letter confirming the veracity of his statements. Was Citi lying too? This cast of strangers was clearly lost.

Bewildered by their lack of understanding, Craig shared, "Recently, two of Citibank's senior Business Development Officers sweetened the deal. One committed to include Value America in his one-point-five billion-dollar direct mail program. The other said we'd earned Citi's respect to such a degree that they were proposing a comprehensive marketing alliance based upon serving and rewarding every Citibank customer."

My, look at the time. Don't want to miss my flight. But Craig didn't let them off the hook that easily. They would soon have red ink, corporate blood, dripping from their hands.

Winn passed out our FedEx catalog. "Next week we'll announce a multi-phase agreement with Federal Express. Phase one is the FedEx Marketplace in which they provide a link from their home page to our FedEx/Value America Custom Store. One million people a day visit FedEx.com, and thanks to this alliance, we're prominent on their home page. We don't have to spend a dime promoting ourselves on- or offline. This catalog will introduce the alliance, but there's no cost associated with mailing it. The FedEx driver simply drops it off as they deliver packages. The value proposition is great too: 'The best products, from the best brands, delivered by the best...free!'"

Durn was livid. As Craig spoke, he remembered Rafe's threat: "*If you ever do a deal with that anti-union company, I'll bring you down.*" Yet he carried on. "Phase two of this alliance is an e-services business in which FedEx sells our e-commerce infrastructure under their name to their retail customers. We'll use our technology to empower many of the best catalog and specialty store operations in the country."

It's obvious in hindsight that this plan could have saved e-tail from dying a collective, suicidal death. Yet the board sat motionless, without question or comment. It was debilitating. *What's up with these people?*

Oh, what the hell, Craig thought, *I've come this far. Might as well finish the race.* "The third phase of this relationship is the best. It's called the FedEx Business Marketplace. Federal Express is one of very few companies in and out of most every business, every day. Who better to deliver your pens, paper, and packaging materials? FedEx is the perfect purveyor of office products, and Value America, with its commerce engine and brand relationships, is the perfect commerce enabler. It's win-win."

If the the multibillion dollar revenues of established office supply distributors like United Stationers, Boise Cascade, Office Depot, and Corporate Express were any indication, the FedEx Business Marketplace was a huge opportunity. Yet the board just rolled their eyes. You could build ten great companies out of the deals they had ignored. New on the job, lacking in understanding of the Internet and retail, they simply muffed it.

The official board records would read, "Mr. Winn led the board through a spreadsheet detailing the effects of a shift away from broad-based advertising in newspapers and television to direct response advertising. Promotions using catalogs are low or no cost to the company and have substantially higher response rates than broad-based advertising. They could result in the company becoming profitable in Q4 2000."

The actual discussion was considerably livelier than the historical records portray. Flowers said, "Your transition to an e-services business is probably your only viable alternative, but it's difficult. You're known as an e-tailer. Selling the new model to the Street won't be easy."

Smith was more animated. "Why haven't we spent more time on this? Why did we wait to the end of our second meeting?" Actually, the *Path to Profitability* had been discussed at board level. A copy of the plan had been sent to them months before it had been sent to Citibank. It was only management's disdain for the plan that had kept it from becoming a priority.

"This is the whole company," Fred said holding up his copy of the *Path*. "You can't spend fifty cents selling a dollar and ever make money." As he spoke these words, Craig's hopes soared. Fred added, "If you use this formula to get your brands and your Demand Alliance partners to underwrite your ad costs, you've got a hell of a business here."

If only the rest of the board, if only their management team, had seen what Fred Smith saw at this moment, dot-com might not have become dot-gone. But it was not to be. What followed instead revealed the depth of the abyss into which we had fallen—the new agenda.

Sadly, it wasn't about diminishing the cost of advertising or making it more productive. It wasn't about empowering brands, in harmony with our original business plan. It wasn't about bringing people and products together by enhancing our e-commerce engine. It wasn't even about achieving profitability. No, it was about Morgan and his frail ego; it was about Dorchak and her unquenchable ambition. The freshman board knew so little about our business they put politics ahead of profits.

For the first time, Craig and Rex were given an overt sign that revealed management's "plan." It exposed those who had hatched the scheme, and it proclaimed, ever so softly, that the founders' days were numbered, that there would be no retail revolution. It would instead fall victim to selfishness, greed, and an unrestrained lust for power. Gerry Roche, Godfrey's pal and Morgan's ally, asked, "What are your succession plans?"

Succession plans? Roche hadn't asked a single question about the business all day. But now, as the rest of the board was starting to deal with corporate survival and grand possibilities of alliance building, he wanted to discuss, as the record says, "transition plans in the event of executive departures." Craig had just laid opportunities worth billions of dollars at the feet of the board only to be asked how long it would take him to clean out his desk and leave the building.

Quietly, Craig wrestled with Gerry's about-face. The prior evening, he had been syrupy sweet in his praise. Why was he now so anxious to see Craig and Rex out of the company? There was only one possible answer: The Toms, the Kuos, and Goose Godfrey had all gotten to Roche and filled his susceptible head with their poison. It appeared that Justin Caise and Rafe Durn were up to their eyeballs in it as well.

Clearly, this was not the time or place for Craig and Rex to reveal that they were actively searching for a way to replace Morgan. Half the board was on Tom's side. The other half was rooting for Glenda. *It was Dumb and Dumber II.* So Craig's only comment was to reiterate the obvious. He tried to diffuse the situation. "Morgan is, and has been for some time, in charge of day-to-day operations while I focused on building outside partnerships and alliances. I am a builder, not a manager."

It was probably not the best thing he could have said. To the corporate establishment, there is no higher calling than to be a manager. They would harangue Craig unmercifully for not being part of their club, for demeaning their holy grail. For Craig though, the truth was clear: without the work of builders, there would be nothing to manage. The thought would prove prophetic.

Their tongue is a deadly arrow; it speaks with deceit—Jeremiah

THREE YEARS GONE IN THREE HOURS

espondent, Craig leaned up against the wall. "This place gives me the creeps. We've become strangers in our own land. It's a shame. We came so close to pulling this off."

"We left management too soon and hired the wrong people, that's all." Rex leaned back in his chair. "We should have stood up to 'em too, not rolled over, especially when we knew we were right. Of all the scoundrels, how did we end up with Morgan? Okay, I know; don't remind me."

Craig did anyway. "We were trying to ace the queen of scumbags."

"At least Morgan isn't evil," Rex sighed. "He's just dumb. You can fix a lot of things, but you can't fix stupid."

Not being bright isn't a crime, of course. But to accept the role of CEO in a public corporation, to accept a $600,000 salary, to make decisions that affect the lives and fortunes of thousands of employees and shareholders, one ought to be smarter, have greater skill, and display better character. Average people shouldn't take above-average jobs.

"Forget dumb," Craig reflected. "I smell trouble. Roche's 'succession' bit at the end of yesterday's meeting gave me the willies. I think we have a genuine sicko—a Judas—on our hands."

"Yeah. We're losing money hand over fist, especially in advertising. You gave 'em a way out on a silver platter, but they were more concerned about protecting their pal. What's up with these guys?"

"Maybe boards have just outlived their usefulness. A board stacked with company insiders is no different than having a managers' meeting. But an outside board, like ours, never seems to know enough to make the right call—especially when the chips are down. These guys don't know us, don't know our company. They don't even understand retail. It's no wonder they're lost."

"And without that knowledge," Rex mused, "they're so easy to manipulate. It's pretty obvious somebody's been yanking their chain."

"Well, whether it's Tom's gang or Glenda's, it's certain they haven't been running the business. The stock is down below ten bucks!"

"It's sad. But I say we stick to our original plan and get out of here as fast as we can," Rex proposed.

"Agreed. We don't know a tenth of these people—and I don't even *recognize* the company."

"We just own it, that's all."

"It's time to go to the Omni. You coming?"

Rex glanced at his clock. "Yeah, you're on in thirty."

"Can you believe it? Six hundred employees, and you and I are the only ones who can sell."

"The whole place is upside down. They're trying like crazy to drum us out, but who's going to present the company when we're gone?"

"When you get right down to it, without somebody convincing brands and others to partner with us, the company will just shrivel up."

With the exception of Dorchak and a few of the original merchants, none or our expensive suits had been able to get anyone to invest in our product presentations or advertising. Unlike the founders, the come-latelies had done little but worry about their positions and salaries.

"Hey, I've got some good news. I sold some stock yesterday. How 'bout you?"

"Naah. I know we're out of the six-month lock-up, but Robbie Stephens screwed up," Craig answered sadly.

"What happened?"

"The bankers were asleep at the switch. I sent 'em a letter two months ago approving their plan. They'd proposed selling two percent of what I owned each quarter. Then they forgot to process the paperwork! They say they're gonna sell some tomorrow."

৩৯ৎ৶

THE GRAND BALLROOM of the Omni Hotel was packed. There must have been over a hundred executives in attendance, many from the world's biggest brands. Over the past month, Craig had helped raise over a million dollars in co-op advertising with vendor days like this one. The audiences were getting progressively larger and more prestigious. The brands were here to partner with Value America and our allies: Citibank, Federal Express, Falwell Ministries, the AFL/CIO, and now the associations affiliated with KFS and MBNA. The promotional vehicle was direct response—the most productive tool in any promotional arsenal.

Craig arrived after lunch. His extemporaneous presentation was a brand-centric version of the *E-tail Is Retail* speech. This audience, unlike those with vested interests on Wall Street, understood and appreciated its themes. From retail metrics to partnering, promoting, and presenting, Craig's words were music to their ears. For an hour and a half, he held the audience in rapt attention. Well, *most* of the audience.

"There's another one, Rex," Tom Morgan groused as he scribbled a note on his pad. "That's ten now."

Rex wanted to hit him. Maybe it would shake some sense into his thick skull. But he remembered the promise he'd made to Craig. Rex would appear to be neutral, sometimes even sympathetic, to the pathetic behavior of Value America's management team. That way, at least, they had a shot at knowing who was doing what to whom. Rex believed in staying close to his friends—and closer to his enemies.

"Oh, there's another one. He's not telling the truth," Morgan mumbled as he kept scribbling. Having just lied to our shareholders in his written quarterly release about material things, the hypocritical Morgan was now nitpicking minutia in Craig's extemporaneous sales presentation.

Craig was now sharing with our brand partners how they could reach the patrons, members, customers, and cardholders of these great companies and institutions. The offer was concise and compelling. Everyone was feverishly taking notes. But unlike Morgan, they were making plans to *build* their businesses, not destroy them.

Craig finished to a standing ovation and thunderous applause. He was mobbed by brand executives on his way out of the room. Most wanted to express their appreciation for being included in what was clearly a win-win opportunity. Morgan scurried out the back. Rex cornered Craig.

"We've got a problem, pal," he said softly. "You were right. There's more to Morgan than dumb. He's on the warpath. Roche's succession bit is sounding more sinister every minute."

"Why can't the guy just do his job?" Craig moaned. "At least until we find a replacement. I'm sorry, but I can't stand this shit. The games have gotten downright perverse."

"Yeah. Watch your back, my friend."

❧

MORGAN RETURNED to Craig's office and closed the door. He started in, "I've decided to resign—again. I just can't live with myself. I'm tired of supporting you, sick of making excuses for you. I'm through explaining away all of your lies. You," he hissed, "are not a truth teller." Morgan shuffled and squirmed in his chair. His voice was weaker than usual. He was nervous, rubbing his perpetually red, runny nose, sniffling. He didn't even *look* like a CEO any more.

He gathered himself somewhat and continued to rant. "I sat in the back while you gave your speech. You are not a truth teller. I can't in good conscience continue to work here. I'm resigning."

"Well, that's twice in two weeks. Congratulations." Craig was too irritated to be polite. "Speaking of telling the truth, what happened to the commitment you made to continue—to not bail out in the middle of the fourth quarter? You made a commitment, Tom, for the good of the company, its employees and shareholders. How about honoring it? What about giving this company the time it needs to find your replacement?"

"I cannot continue to work here. I have to be able to live with myself. I am tired of defending you. I just can't do it any more. I *won't* do it any more. You're not a truth teller," he cried again.

"That's the third time you called me a liar. Mind telling me what I said that offended you?" Craig challenged. He was disgusted.

"I'd rather not," Tom sniffed. "I'd rather just walk out of here quietly. Don't want a thing from you or from the company. No severance. I just want to leave quietly. But I think you need help, professional help."

I thought that's why I hired you. "I'm unaware of a single comment I've made publicly or privately since I started this company that's inaccurate in any material way. So unless you have evidence to the contrary, I suggest you refrain from making such allegations."

"I didn't want to do this, but if you insist..." he squealed, "I brought my notes with me this time. But before we get to these lies," he said, shaking his notes, "I want you to know that you lied to me when you said you'd be gone by the end of the year."

"I said nothing of the sort. I said I'd go to half time in Q1 and quarter time in Q2. But based upon what I've heard around here, you've been telling folks otherwise."

Tom knew he had misrepresented what Craig had said, especially in his confessions to the Brethren. But admitting this to Craig's face took more courage than he could muster. Before and after each "resignation" meeting, Morgan, Godfrey, Starnes, and Kuo met in secret, compiling their demands. Then, buoyed by the Brethren, Tom would march off to Craig's office without his notes, recognizing that with them his "resignations" would have looked as contrived as they really were. But unable to think on his feet or remember what had been planned, Tom would end up listing a series of petty demands like lowering the strike price of his stock options. Then he'd retreat to the security of his entourage and profess that he'd stayed the course. Looking at his notes, he'd brag that he'd prevailed and reached an accord with Winn on all of the conditions they had conspired to achieve. When Craig acted in a manner consistent with what was *actually* discussed, they called him a liar.

Now with his rumpled notes in front of him, he coughed, rubbed his nose again, and began. "When you said our returns were one-half of one percent you weren't telling the truth. They're greater than that."

Craig snarled. "Who was I talking to, Tom?"

"What does it matter? It doesn't change the truth."

"Good God, you're lost," Craig snapped back. From a business perspective, he was conversing with a child. "It *does* matter. Those were all *consumer* brands, not computer brands.

"So what?" Morgan looked confused. This was beyond him.

"The thing that irritates consumer brands is non-defective returns, buyers' remorse," Craig explained. "Unlike PCs, their defectives are very low. They understand that our product presentations help customers make better buying decisions, so returns are diminished. Look more closely at your reports. What I said was accurate. These returns for consumer products are less than one half of one percent. The returns on PCs are probably six or seven percent. That's why we ought to stop selling them. Y'know, I offered to teach you this stuff, Tom."

Morgan was feeling even more squeamish, so he changed the subject rather than admit he'd been wrong. It's a common tactic of the vanquished. "Yeah, well, you didn't tell the truth when you said we'd signed an agreement with KFS."

Craig sighed. "Once again, you're wrong. But I'm glad you brought it up. In Boston last week, Kessler said that he was moving ahead with the first five KFS-MBNA associations. Howard's comments were based on the document we *signed* with his i-Belong organization. That contract defines the relationship between us, just as I explained during the brand seminar. This only shows that you, the CEO, don't know what's going on." Winn was about an inch from losing it. Being in the same room with Morgan was starting to make his skin crawl.

With every word, the animosity deepened. "Kessler called me yesterday," Craig continued. "He said he'd heard rumblings that there was dissension here at Value America. He reiterated that the deal he authorized was with *me*, because of *me*, because he trusted *me*. 'If you're not with that company, I'm not with 'em either,' is what Howard said. Just like Citibank, they trust me. Why don't you?"

Trying to change the subject a third time, Morgan grasped at Citibank, hoping Craig hadn't noticed that the score was now Winn-3, Morgan-0. "You're violating SEC regulations when you announce things like the CitiPrivilege and FedEx Marketplaces before they're publicly disclosed."

"Wrong again." Craig was wondering why he was having this conversation. "I've discussed this with our SEC counsel. Not only is it perfectly acceptable to discuss such things with our partners, we'd actually be violating our fiduciary duty if we *didn't* keep our brands informed like this. I know your buddy Kuo has you all up in arms over this, but in speeches to current or potential partners, you're *expected* to sell. Right from the beginning, I begged you to get involved in building partnerships with brands, to lead by example, but instead you've done nothing but complain, and that has no value. Selling is hard. You really ought to try it sometime. Now, what else do you have on your list?"

"Not so fast," Morgan said, hoping to salvage his assault. "We haven't signed an agreement with FedEx, yet you talked about their Marketplace."

Craig's exasperation was showing. "We've already printed—and *distributed*—half a million FedEx catalogs! The written documentation describing our current and future relationship is over twenty pages long. The founder and CEO of Federal Express shook my hand on it, confirming the relationship, in my cabin right after the last board meeting. And you're telling me we shouldn't talk to our brand partners about how they can participate?"

"I'm more conservative than you. I don't agree." Craig reflected that if "more conservative" meant Morgan was less likely to do *anything*, he had finally said something accurate.

Tom went through the remainder of his list. Each "lie" was just as silly, petty, and easily refuted as the one before it. But each clearly revealed Morgan's fundamental lack of understanding, ability, and more critically, his lack of character. "Board members agree with me," Tom revealed. The remark betrayed Morgan's complicity in his anti-Winn campaign, but it would take a day or two for that reality to really sink in. Today, as Tom claimed he had grown weary of "defending" Craig, the sad truth was that he and his useless friends had been the founder's most outspoken critics since the day they had arrived. But on this sad day, Craig only knew that Tom was incompetent. He knew nothing of the impending *coup* or the secret board maneuverings. His instincts had told him that Tom was up to no good, but he hadn't listened to his gut. He'd tried to think his way out of our predicament instead.

As Morgan reconfirmed his second resignation, he said he was taking Friday off to return home and watch his daughter's cheerleading squad (one he admitted to having financed with Value America's diminishing capital). He said he wanted to withhold his public announcement until the following week.

Unable to reason with Tom, Craig decided to *use* him. It wasn't a game he wanted to play, but he had to buy time to find his replacement. "Tom, you know as well as I do, this won't work. We've been over this ground before. You can't have the CEO of a public company leave in the same quarter as the CFO and CIO." Tom nodded knowingly. "We need time. We need you to hang in here for a few weeks. Call it a transition period for us to find your successor. I don't care if you spend the entire time on a paid vacation."

"No, I won't do that," Tom said. "I'm worn out. I can no longer defend you." Heavens! Tom was too worn out to take a paid vacation.

Must be brutal bending all those paper clips.

Craig repeated the vacation offer a couple more times, but to no avail. Morgan was so self-absorbed, he'd allow only two options. Either he and the Brethren would gain total control—immune from all criticism—or he'd aid and abet the destruction of our company, leave us dangling in the wind trying to explain his irrational behavior to the scandal-crazed media. There was no longer any pretense of honor.

So much for being rational, Craig thought. *All right, if he wants to act like a spoiled child, let's play.* "Tom, what would it take for you to stay?"

"I'm not interested in staying." *Yeah, right.*

"You were two weeks ago. You had a list of six concessions. I agreed to all of them, and you committed to stay." While Craig knew he had to quickly rid the company of Tom's debilitating presence, he was strangely comfortable with the concessions he'd made. He expected to abide by all of them. After all, he wanted out, and none of his concessions prevented Craig from searching for Tom's replacement. "Since I once again seem to be 'your problem,' tell me—how much more do you want from me?"

Tom didn't hesitate. His second "resignation" had been designed to elicit this very question. *Could this be the first sign of intelligence?*

Morgan tried frantically to remember the demands he had crafted with the Brethren, but sadly, he was unable, so he just blurted out a bunch of things, petty things. But it all boiled down to one thing—Morgan wanted Craig to leave in six weeks rather than six months as they had previously agreed. Craig said he would acquiesce to all of Tom's childish demands if he would agree to stay through the end of the quarter. Tom wouldn't. As he got up to leave, Craig, sensing that Tom was uncertain of his demands, asked him to write his requests down, so they could review them first thing Monday morning and resolve this matter professionally.

"I don't want there to be any misunderstandings. The last time we went through this, the conditions you proposed, and I affirmed, turned out to bear no resemblance to what I hear you saying now." Morgan said nothing. There was hollowness behind his eyes. Craig pressed one last time for a commitment, but Tom, as usual, was unable to speak for himself. He needed to consult his "advisors." Godfrey, Starnes, Kuo, and Kuo. Along with Morgan they were Dumb, Dumber, Dumbest, Naïve, and Naïver. If it weren't so sad, it would have been funny.

Craig was now in possession of materially adverse non-public information. He took the few steps to his desk, looked up a number and dialed.

"Robertson Stephens," said the voice at the other end.

"Hi, Tony. This is Craig Winn. Something's come up. Please refrain from selling any of my shares."

CRAIG WALKED DOWN to Rex's office and recounted the meeting. Without even the pretense of commitment from Tom, the founders were left with no alternatives. They knew that their first order of business was to immediately survey the troops, evaluate the condition of the company, and form a strategy to separate the firm from its floundering management.

Craig's first meeting was with Cliff Chambers. Chambers had been recruited by Morgan, so Craig entered his office like he was walking on eggs. "Cliff, I need some answers. First, have you attended any of the consumer brand seminars?"

Cliff nodded. "Good. You're responsible for operations and technology, right?" Cliff nodded again. "You know our numbers pretty well?"

"As well as anyone, I imagine."

"Did I misstate any fact?"

"No."

"Have you *ever* heard me misstate a fact?"

"No, never."

"What are our returns in consumer products?"

"You mean everything except PCs and technology?" Craig nodded. "I don't know for certain, but total returns for consumer products are less than one percent. You'd have to back out mis-shipments to get the net number but it's around one-half of one percent."

Cliff swallowed hard. "Does this have something to do with Morgan? I just got a call from Gerry Roche that sounded suspicious. Roche told me to hang in there. He said that he knew how difficult my job had to be with all of the crazy stuff *you're* doing. Gerry told me that he and some other board members would have the 'Winn problem,' as he called it, resolved soon enough. He implied that he was working with Tom to eliminate whatever problem they think exists with *you*."

I knew he was up to no good. Roche and his pals, Godfrey, Morgan, Kuo—they're up to their eyeballs in something that really reeks. Craig didn't know at the time that Caise, Durn, and Dorchak were in just as deep.

Cliff sat up a little straighter and added in his defense, "I told him he was wrong. There was no 'Winn problem.' In fact, I told him this place wouldn't survive without you. It's the truth. He didn't want to hear it. I don't think Gerry was very happy with me."

"Oh, my God. It's worse than I thought," Craig said under his breath, struggling to maintain his composure. "Listen, Cliff. I appreciate the support, and the company *is* going to need you. Morgan resigned again yesterday. But what you told me about Roche pretty much answers my next question. I recognize you're Morgan's friend and that he brought you here, but as you probably know, my phase-out plan is no longer acceptable to him. He wants me gone yesterday."

Chambers was normally so passive and soft spoken, Craig was taken aback by what came next. Cliff sat forward and looked him straight in the eye. "I don't know how you missed it. Tom Morgan is the most insecure man I've ever known. That's what this is all about, you know. He needs constant reinforcement and praise."

Craig sat in stunned silence. *No! It can't be. He seems so religious, so meek. This can't be happening again.* Craig's stomach tightened into knots. He became nauseated, dizzy. His whole business life flashed before him. Then he finally saw it, all of the symptoms: the fancy cars, the perfect wardrobe, the fanaticism with the orderliness of his desk, his wife's complaints, his rage over a misplaced sock, his sanctimonious attitude, his willingness to demean others for personal gain, his craving for attention. It had been Morgan all along. The slightest criticism, even constructive and in private, had been enough to set him off. His insecurities had finally gotten the best of him, and he was now lashing out, attacking. Winn was dazed. He wanted to scream, but nothing came out.

"Craig, *Craig!*" Cliff uncharacteristically shouted. "Are you okay?"

Craig shook his head violently. He wasn't okay. He had once again invited cancer into his company, not once or twice, but five times. Morgan, Dorchak, Godfrey, Starnes, and Kuo. Individually and collectively, they were doing what cancers do: infecting, multiplying, killing. He held his head in his hands. He thought he was going to vomit.

Cliff's quiet voice filled the void. "I've talked to Tom about this, pleaded with him. I'd like to see both of you here. That's why I came. But if I had to choose between you and Tom, that's easy. He's my friend, but this place wouldn't last six months without you."

It took every ounce of strength he could muster just to stand up. Wobbling, he nodded to Cliff, thanking him for his time. He floated down the hall in stunned disbelief.

He went back to Rex's office in hopes of regaining his composure. His friend's reassurance recharged his batteries just enough for him to continue his quest. He went from office to office, person to person. Craig avoided known Morgan loyalists, especially Starnes and the Kuos. They had accomplished nothing, so neither their opinion nor support mattered. He avoided Dorchak and her closest allies as well. They had their own agenda; he wasn't about to elicit the devil's support. But Craig talked to everyone else that mattered, in Technology, Operations, Customer Care,

Presentation Marketing, Sales, Business Development, Merchandising, and Finance (or at least what was left of it). He asked the same two questions twenty times. "Are you aware of any statement I've made that's inaccurate?—If I were to leave, could Morgan lead the firm?"

Twenty managers, forty questions, one answer: "No."

The path was now as clear as it was fraught with peril. Despite their reservations, despite the personal cost, Craig and Rex would have to return to management. There was no other choice. It was the only way to save the company.

෨෴෴

IT WAS A beautiful fall day. A cool breeze hinted that winter was nearing. Filtered sunlight danced off a nearby stream as it streaked through a stand of majestic hardwoods. The leaves had begun to fall, building a carpet of yellow, gold, and crimson. One leaf amongst the thousands caught Craig's eye as it released from a limb high above the forest floor. He watched it float gracefully down, glimmering in the soft light, translucent, almost iridescent. It finally settled silently near his feet.

Was God trying to tell him something, to let go and trust Him? Was he being told to prepare for a fall? Were the trees shedding their leaves in preparation for a long, cold, blustery winter? Should he do the same, prepare for stormy times? Perhaps it was all just part of the cycle of life— leaves fall and die, releasing their energy into the earth so the giants of the forest can sprout forth new life come spring.

A swirl of wind blew a whiff of smoke from the fireplace inside his cabin toward the deck upon which he was sitting. Craig took it in, and set his pen down. *The cabin.* It was here that he, Morgan and Starnes, Kuo, Shepard, and the General had met for Bible studies. Less than two weeks before, Craig had shared his willingness to accept the "marching orders" he felt he had received from the Almighty. He had also shared his premonition that something would soon happen to drive them apart. Sometimes there is no pleasure in seeing the future.

Craig picked up his pen and completed his hand-written press release.

Value America, in Charlottesville, Virginia, today announced that it is empowering its management team to strive toward profitability. Craig Winn, the company's founder, chairman, and leading shareholder, said he is returning to serve fellow shareholders, employees, brand partners, and customers as CEO.

Value America is entering the fifth phase of its strategic plan to revolutionize retail. In phase one, we conceived an innovative plan to serve all Americans, making the world of e-commerce more inclusive by converging the power of computers with the ease of telephones and the communication prowess of televisions to serve all, not just the privileged few with Internet access. We set out to conquer the digital divide that separates our nation by providing credit to those without it and linking customers directly to great values on Internet-enabled PCs. Our plan sought to revolutionize commerce by giving brands a turn-key solution to reach and serve consumers in a more efficient, direct, and inventory-free model. We sought to replace warehouses with technology and invest in systems rather than inventory, so we, working together with our brand partners, could sell the best for less.

In phase two, we brought together a bright and dedicated team. We are committed to enabling our shared passion to improve retail. Today, many members of our management team are being promoted.

Recognizing it takes three things to positively change our world, great ideas, great people, and a great deal of money, in phase three we sought to raise capital. Working together we raised $130 million in private equity and an additional $145 million in our IPO this April.

In phase four, we sought to execute our plan. In what may be record time, we have built one of the largest and fastest growing e-tail firms. Our Q3 results are proof of our scale and growth. They also reflect positively on our unique inventory-free model and innovative demand-generation strategy because operational, technological, promotional, and fulfillment costs are all continuing to decline as a percentage of revenue.

In phase five, we are committed to becoming profitable. We are aware that no business-to-consumer e-tailer has achieved this goal. We believe we can…so if you are a shareholder, investor, analyst, or journalist and would like to discover how Value America is changing retail you are invited to join us.…

Craig faxed a copy to Rex. He made some edits and added a note to the top of the release, "Craig—Here are my thoughts. Good letter. I'm glad! Let's get on with it."

Minutes after the exchange of faxes, the two men spoke on the phone. These were sobering times. The conversation was short and to the point. Rex began. "This is the last thing either of us wanted, but we've been given no alternative. Let's see if we can get this thing stabilized, find a leader we can trust, and then get out, like we planned."

"My sentiments exactly. The company is in rough shape. The systems conversion is our biggest problem—it was butchered. The outsourcing of sales was a huge mistake. Morale is low, but at least amongst the people that count, it appears to be salvageable. We're going to have to deal with Dorchak, stop wasting money in advertising, get a new CFO, and improve Customer Service. Immediately, if not sooner."

"First thing tomorrow morning we'll call each board member and let 'em know what's up. We should give them a heads up on your release." Rex paused for a moment. "You know, we may not win this one, pal. It's been a long time since we managed this thing. We don't even know most of these people anymore. We don't have a clue what they're up to."

"Yeah. We're out of touch. We're out of practice. And we may be out of miracles."

Craig called the General, the only other person who was aware of all that had occurred. Mick reconfirmed his unwavering support.

Then Craig called David Kuo, who was, unfortunately, responsible for issuing our press releases. "David," Craig spoke onto Kuo's local answering machine, "I've left a copy of a draft press release in my cabin. If you return this evening, pick it up. It's confidential. I want you to recommend changes and prepare it for release. As a public company, we have to keep investors informed. I'll call the board and get their support before it goes out."

David didn't do as Craig had requested. Instead, he and his bride did something that destroyed the founders' already-slim chance of saving Value America. They took the press release to Tom Morgan.

It was an incredibly foolish move but not out of character for Kuo. He had never built a business, never built *anything*, and thus lacked the ability to evaluate Craig's decision. Moreover, David was loyal to the Brethren above all else. He had to be. Based upon private confessions, David was the moral equivalent of a "made man" within the supposedly "Christian" United Brethren. He and Seth Rossi had more than one thing in common.

The press release hadn't even mentioned Morgan. Craig was willing to let Tom script his own departure in any manner he pleased. If he had really wanted out, as he'd claimed, if he'd been sincere when he said he wanted to leave quietly, David's treason wouldn't have mattered. But such was not the case. Morgan and his allies were more interested in positioning and enriching themselves than they were in the survival of the company they had been paid to serve. They threw a collective temper tantrum.

❧

FIRST THING MONDAY morning, Craig pulled out a copy of his Value America Directors phone list. He started at the top, placing a call to Bill Bennett, but he was out helping a struggling friend. Sam White was out of town, so he left a message. Next he called Caise. Justin listened to Craig's proposed release and said he supported it. Justin feared confrontation above all else.

Gerry Roche was next. In spite of his relationship with Morgan and Godfrey, Gerry seemed supportive as well. It was an Oscar-winning performance. But time would soon reveal the depth of his complicity.

Craig had Frank Flowers' direct line. Although it would be hours before Frank made it into Vulcan's Seattle offices, Craig thought it might be wise to leave a message. It usually took a week of exchanging voice-mails with Flowers before they actually got to talk. Scatena's name was next. Craig already knew where Rex stood—he had known precisely where Rex stood ever since the day they had stood together on the first tee of the Mauna Lani.

Craig called Wolfgang Schmitt. He was out at a Kimberly Clark board meeting. When Wolf returned the call, he seemed so understanding, Craig queried him about becoming more involved. Schmitt was retired (or more correctly, *had been* retired), following the sale of Rubbermaid to Newell. He volunteered to visit later in the week to discuss the possibilities.

The white knight was next, the Babe Ruth of business, Frederick W. Smith, Chairman and CEO of Federal Express. Craig brought Fred up to speed and then read his handwritten release.

Smith said, "That's beautifully written, Craig. I don't have an issue with anything you've said, but before you release it, you should schedule a board meeting."

"Time is not our friend, Fred. I'd prefer to keep calling board members individually. Tom has resigned, and his failed systems conversion is impacting customer service. We need to stabilize the company, tell the Street where we're going, and move forward."

"I don't think that's the right call. I'd rather you get Tom to go along with a transition period so that we can handle this thing professionally."

"My sentiments exactly, Fred. I told him to put our employees and shareholders' interests before his own. I asked him to do exactly what you just said many times. He refused. Then I asked him to take a paid vaca-tion. He even refused to do that."

"Listen, Craig, I'm no fan of Tom Morgan. I knew right off the bat that you were going to have a problem with him. He just sat there in board meetings like a damn bump on a log."

"Obviously, I hired the wrong guy. He never engaged. He didn't even understand the *Path to Profitability* you responded so favorably to."

Fred jumped back in. "Damn right, I liked it. It's the whole ball game, but why are we discussing it now? This board came together in June."

"Fred, I *wrote it* back then. I sent you a copy in response to a question you asked in July. The reason we haven't discussed it is Morgan. It's a budgetary plan. That's the CEO's job. Neither he nor anybody on his management team gave it the time of day."

"Well, that's just it, Craig. This is really awful timing. If you had come to the board months ago and told us what we already knew, that you were having a problem with Tom, we could have formed a committee, done a search, and announced his replacement." Fred was obviously unaware of the interworkings of the Brethren. "We shouldn't be in this pickle. Now, it's my opinion you've used this board poorly. You've wasted our time on stuff that's less important—like those department presentations."

"Fred, I appreciate your advice. You've been a good friend."

"Well, thanks, but I think you've got a bigger problem here than you realize. You may even lose some board members over this."

With that said, Craig dialed Rafe Durn's number, wondering if he was still with ULIC or if he'd already gone. Rafe, it transpired, had accepted a job with Pacific Capital Group, the venture company behind Global Crossing. Gary Winnick, the founder of both firms, was an Internet billionaire and a multimillion dollar investor in Value America's Series C round. Don Tarpin was also a Pacific Capital principal, serving on Global's board with Winnick as co-Chairman. Durn had awarded Tarpin one of the two Value America board seats ULIC had earned by virtue of its Series A investment. Durn's current, or former employer, depending on whether or not Craig had dialed the right number, had invested heavily in both Global Crossing and Value America. They had weaved a tangled web. Was Winn about to be ensnared?

"Hello, Craig, this is Rafe. What can I do for you?"

"Glad I caught you," Craig said. "I didn't know if you'd already left."

"Just cleaning some things up before I go."

"Rafe, I'll get right to the point. Morgan has resigned. The timing's terrible, fourth quarter and all, so I'm volunteering to return as CEO until we get the place back on track and find another candidate."

"Sounds fine to me," Rafe shot back quickly. Craig was relieved and worried, all at the same time. He was pleased that Durn wasn't going to make a meal of him, at least not yet, but he was worried. The board was universally supportive of his plan to return as interim CEO. That was both good and bad. They must have known no one internally was prepared to take the job, and they recognized it would be impossible to find a suitable CEO from outside quickly enough. Even then, a new CEO wouldn't be up to speed on the firm, and thus productive, for at least six months. The company was floundering, with busted systems, in the midst of the busiest quarter. It had *days*, not weeks, certainly not months, to get its house in order, or things would really get nasty.

Winn and Scatena were volunteering for a suicide mission. They had no better than one chance in ten of pulling it off. If they failed, they would earn all the blame and go broke doing it. Coming back to management would instantly make them both insiders, consequently barred by the SEC from selling any of their stock—twenty-one million shares between them. To save the company, they would be risking a personal fortune worth $300 million. They volunteered anyway; they felt it was the right thing to do. *Dumb?*

"Craig," Rafe went on, "you and Rex have done everything you said you'd do, and more. That's the reason I invested in Value America after the failed IPO. That's the reason I encouraged all of my friends to invest. You've earned our trust. I'll support whatever you guys want to do." Pretty strong sentiments for a guy who never visited the firm.

"Thanks, Rafe. That means a great deal right now."

Then Durn asked, "Have you called Tarpin?"

"He's my next call."

Don too was glowing in his praise. He said that the reason he was on the board, the reason everybody was here, was because of Craig. He counseled him to take charge and act decisively. It was the opposite of the advice Smith had given. As he said goodbye, Don told Craig how impressed he was with the way he was handling himself. Craig breathed a sigh of relief; every single board member was prepared to support the founder's plan to save the company.

But sadly it wouldn't last. His phone call with Tarpin was the last positive conversation Craig would ever have with a Value America board member. A lot can happen in twenty-four hours.

✺

MORGAN WAS IRATE. Apparently, it was perfectly fine for him to assail Craig's credibility, okay for him to renege on his commitments. But the shoe didn't feel so good on the other foot. When Craig's intentions to actually accept his resignation were revealed with the purloined press release, Morgan lost all semblance of decency. He stormed into Winn's office demanding to know why he had been misled. Morgan had thin skin, and his short fuse was ignited when his scheme was turned against him. He instantly moved from dumb to dangerous.

Tom had informants, but Craig thought he had circumnavigated them. He hadn't factored in David Kuo's treason. David lied so convincingly. He would waltz into Craig's office, tell him how much he "loved" him, feigning friendship, and pledging his undying support. He'd then pump him for information, only to spill his guts to Morgan, revealing whatever he thought he'd learned. There may be a psychological term for such behavior, but suffice it to say, David had a problem. David *was* a problem.

Tom knew his bluff had been called. Craig wanted to officially accept the idiot's resignation right then and there, but he delayed, in deference to

Smith's request. Listening to Fred's counsel, though, would carry a penalty. His hesitation would cost him—all of us, really—everything we had worked for.

No longer in an "asking mood," Craig told Tom to take a vacation—anything to get him out of his hair. There was work to be done.

In typical Winn fashion, Craig focused on the biggest and most lethal dragons first. He started with technology. It had become obvious that the company was operating in the dark. Overburdening the systems conversion had resulted in inoperative customer care, falling sales, and faulty reporting. There was hope: Joe Page and Thor Anders were making progress at a geometric rate. But they needed time, and time was in short supply.

Finance was next. Dean Johnson was long gone, as was his controller, Karen Wiles. So the remaining members of the team gathered around Craig's old maple table and painted a most unpleasant picture. Under the management of Morgan and Dorchak, the company had been burning through money as if there were no tomorrow.

Sales was next. Candy Clifford thought she would deliver a quarter with revenues of $75 million, about $8 million below their internal budget. She and her boss, Glenda, were armed with a mountain of reports, but they never seemed able to answer the same question the same way twice. As usual, they had more excuses than Craig had problems. Mostly, they blamed their performance on the company's failing systems. *Suits are certainly good at dodging responsibility.* He wanted to scream, but this was not a time for assessing blame.

Craig knew the company would need to chart a new course quickly if we were going to stay afloat. But he wanted to know whether we could handle the management transition separately from the course correction. That would depend upon the delta between our current expectations and Wall Street's. So Craig invited the senior managers into his office, along with Kim Kuo, VP of Investor Relations.

Craig began, "Folks, I have been trying to assess the damage we've sustained. The picture is neither encouraging nor debilitating. We have a chance to save our company, slim as it may be. But before we begin repairs, I want an accurate appraisal of the difference between our current reality and Wall Street's expectations. We have a fiduciary duty to bridge whatever gap exists before word trickles out via back channels. So Kim, let's begin with you. What do the analysts' models expect us to show in revenue and earnings in Q4?"

"I don't know," Mrs. Kuo said, fumbling through her things. "I didn't bring my notes with me, I think it's...."

"You don't know the numbers? What have you been doing?" Craig asked incredulously. Back in the days when he'd had a thousand times more on his plate, he had known the analysts' projections—by quarter, two years out—as well as he knew his children's birthdays. *This was Kim's only job.*

She sheepishly guessed, but made it clear that's all it was. Normally an attractive woman, she looked awful, an emotional wreck. It was certain there was something going on, but there wasn't time to deal with Kim's personal problems, so Craig carried on. He explained why he thought the Street's revenue expectation was $72 million. He shared a conversation he'd had with Tom back in August. He told the suits that he had privately encouraged Morgan to use his impending system conversion to increase expense estimates and diminish revenue projections in Q4. Craig explained the strategy and concluded, "I have no reason to suspect he would have done otherwise, so I believe the numbers we discussed are valid."

Kim Kuo somehow convoluted Craig's support of Tom in this regard into an attack on him. It was becoming obvious that she cared deeply for him. Hardly able to contain herself, Kim rushed out and called Morgan.

Moments later Tom called Craig, crying—literally. "I cannot believe you'd stoop so low as to assail my character."

Pretty good opening line, Craig thought, *from someone who's spent months doing that very thing to me.*

"I want you to know," Tom said between wheezes and sobs, "that I did exactly what we discussed. I called the analysts and lowered revenue expectations to seventy-two million."

"That's what I said," Craig responded flatly.

"You're *lying!*" Morgan had a very limited vocabulary.

"Tom! Get control of yourself. I did no such thing."

It doesn't pay to reason with the unreasonable. The relationship between Tom and Mrs. Kuo had apparently grown beyond business, throwing a whole new monkey wrench into the works. That was shock enough, but what came next was electrifying. "Up to this point, I have stayed away from the board," Tom lied, "but now that you've attacked my character, I'm going to take the gloves off! I'm going to go after you with all I've got! I'm going to tell them the truth about you."

"Tom, you're not thinking rationally. You're reacting—*overreacting*—to an unfounded allegation. Call any of the other people who attended the meeting. Find out for yourself what I said."

It did no good. *Good,* from that moment on, was in short supply, an endangered species.

"REX, IN LESS than twenty-four hours, we've gone from eight board members in our corner to eight against us," Craig said in disbelief. He felt punch-drunk, wobbling back on his heals, ready to fall. It wasn't so much the challenge of surviving the fight, of righting our ship. They had done that before, and against stiffer odds. But this time, the enemy was their own crew, the *officers*. They had mutinied; they were now serving their own private agendas.

"Today's board meeting was unreal," Rex responded. "How could they turn on us like that? Yesterday they were cheering us on as we volunteered to go to war on their behalf. Today they're asking for delays and dismissing our plans. Sure, they're new on the job and don't know us or the company very well, but...."

"Well, at least we've been discharged from our suicide mission. They clearly have no interest in us returning to management. They don't seem to have a clue what it took to build this company."

"You and I managed Value America for three years, '96, '97, and '98, as CEO and President. When we started, we were worth nothing; we had no money, no systems, no people, no sales. Three years later, the company we built was worth billions of dollars; we had hundreds of millions in the bank, hundreds of great people all doing their jobs, and we were growing faster than any e-tailer on the planet. Then we resigned from management. The 'professionals' we hired, who are now sliming our reputations, have managed to slash our value, cripple our systems, stifle our people's productivity, and blow through most of the money we raised." Rex had said a mouthful. "What do you say we send each of our board members a calendar? Just highlight the date and our value when we left management. They might figure it out."

"They may be smart people, but I doubt they'd get it. It sure didn't take much to mislead them."

"It's easier than you might think." Rex knew; he *was* a lawyer, after all. "They're all outsiders; they have their own businesses to run. I'd be surprised if any of them have invested any serious time in this thing. When you lack good information, bad information is seductive."

"Rex, I can't prove any of this, but I have a theory," Craig said. "It's just my opinion, mind you, but I think I might know who betrayed us."

"Who?"

"It all began with our failed IPO and the badly strained relationships between us and Robbie Stephens—especially Dale Dandridge."

"He's no friend of ours," Rex agreed.

"That's my point. Dale was more interested in defending Amazon and his damn media metrics than he ever was in promoting us. If we were right, he was wrong. Things went south when I delivered my first *E-tail Is Retail* speech at Robbie Stephens. Remember? You were there. Dandridge was so miffed he wouldn't even introduce me at his own conference. Then, partly as a result of him not supporting us, our stock tumbled, even though we were raising expectations and beating them. Do you remember our Q2 conference call? Dale's reaction?"

"Yeah," Rex answered. "You asked Dale to change his model to reflect the demand alliance strategy we'd touted on the Road Show—the *Path to Profitability*. He refused."

"That's right. And in so doing, two things happened. *Internally*, Morgan and Dorchak had a reason to discard our *Path*. Dale didn't like it. And *externally*, Dale, in my opinion, worked to shift blame for our stock's decline from himself to me."

"Well you've got to give him credit. If that's what he did, he did a darn good job," Rex offered. "But come to think of it, it's only natural. When things go south, people *always* need someone to blame. As our founder, you were the easiest target. You were our spokesperson. You did the most, said the most."

"That's probably why I have some enemies here, inside the company too," Craig said sadly.

It was true. "But anyway," he continued, "as it relates to the Street, what I think happened next is speculation, but it's the only rational answer I can think of for all the irrational behavior we've witnessed."

"Gambini," Rex said, sensing where this was going.

"Can't prove it, but yeah. Dale decides to leave Robbie Stephens. He's under attack because he's the lead analyst on our deal. He doesn't want to take the hit for not supporting us, so he blames it on me. He knows investors were put off by what I had to say. So," Craig asked, looking sideways at Rex, "how does our boy spread this load of crap quietly through the investment community?"

"Gambini," Rex answered again.

"Yep. Bet you dollars to donuts that's what happened. They were tight. Dale served on his board. Jake is even godfather to Dale's kid."

Rex surmised, "So her first week on the job, Kim Kuo flies off with our pal Morgan, and they run into a buzz saw. They visit with frustrated investors, and they hammer you. They need someone to blame, so you're it, the only target, because Tom hasn't done enough to be noticed. So they claim you're the reason our stock has fallen, even though you and I had nothing to do with it."

"By trying to save the company, I set myself up."

"So that's where they came up with the harebrained idea that the stock will double as soon as you're gone."

"The only problem with their theory is that the stock has climbed five bucks a share over the last week on rumors that Morgan's out."

"I don't normally look at the message boards, but this week A-Rod turned me on to 'em," Rex said.

"I don't either. What did you find?"

"First, we've got too many people around here with diarrhea of the mouth. If loose lips sink ships, we're in the Titanic. The Street knows Morgan is gone, and they're happy about it. They're comparing his eight-month tenure here to his USOP disaster."

"If that's the case, the board's postponement in dealing with Tom's resignation is a huge mistake," Craig added, stating the obvious. "Every day we go without a public announcement, we assume greater liability."

"A-Rod showed me a bunch of messages. They're not only speculating that you're returning to management, they're saying that's why the stock has jumped from ten to fifteen bucks a share."

"Great," Craig said, shaking his head. "That's just great. We volunteer, against our own self-interests, to act as interim managers, and the markets respond by increasing our value *fifty* percent. All the while, Morgan and his allies are shouting, 'Damn the facts, Winn is the problem, axe him and the stock will double.' Apparently, based upon our reversal of fortunes, the board's gulping *his* shit down."

"Well pal, I'm all out of options. What do we do?" Rex asked.

"What about Wolf Schmitt?" Craig questioned. "He's not doing anything. Maybe he'd consider being CEO while we find a replacement."

"You said he's coming in for the Citibank meeting later today. Why don't you ask him? You guys have known each other for years, right?"

"No, not really," Craig countered. "We served on an industry board back in my Dynasty days. He seemed pretty sharp. He talks a good game, anyway. Our board should like that. But I haven't really spent time with him in years."

Before the two could leave Craig's office, a disheveled David Kuo poked his head around the corner. Craig motioned him in.

David said, "I'd like to speak with you alone."

"Whatever you have to say to me, you can say in front of Rex. He and I have no secrets."

David sat down and read a letter of apology. He began by telling Craig how much he "loved" him, complaining that he felt like an "abandoned and unloved child of a divorce." He confessed to the inappropriateness of giving the draft press release to Morgan. It was anticlimactic; Mick had already informed the two founders that it had indeed been David's doing. As Kuo read his letter, both Craig and Rex became increasingly uncomfortable—Rex because it was entirely religious in nature and that gave him the creeps, Craig because it was entirely religious in nature and he had good reason to believe that the Brethren were the biggest hypocrites in God's creation, and that gave *him* the creeps.

The Brethren: Morgan, Godfrey, Kuo, and Starnes. Not an accomplishment between them. They had built nothing of value, here or anywhere they had ever been. Between them Morgan and Kuo had worked for thirteen different companies in half as many years. Godfrey and Starnes had simply remained dependent upon the charity of their temporary hosts. Pride, jealousy, covetousness, greed. Whatever the motivation, the results of their behavior are as undeniable as they are despicable.

Moments later, the prince of hypocrites slithered through Craig's still open door. Winn was ready for him. A secret source had tipped him off.

"Can we talk about my position in the company?" Starnes asked.

"Sure, Tom," Craig replied coldly. "Just as soon as you tell me why, all of a sudden, you're calling Fred Smith at home. What, or should I ask, whom, have you been discussing, Tom?"

That one caught the Harvard MBA by surprise. *Craig couldn't have found out so soon. He must be bluffing.* He had no idea Craig would uncover his complicity in the save-Morgan-oust-Winn *coup*. Starnes didn't have the courage to challenge Craig, not to his face, anyway. Nor did he answer his question. Morgan's lap dog mumbled something about calling an attorney, put his tail between his legs, and scampered out of the room.

What made this so hard for Craig and Rex was knowing how incredibly close they'd come to pulling off their improbable dream. The Citibank relationship alone would have diminished the cost of demand generation to pennies on the dollar. Then there was Visa, KFS, and MBNA, not to mention the potential of the Federal Express Marketplaces for consumer and business products and their e-services alliance. Any one of these relationships was sufficient in itself to break the chains of advertising dependence and launch the company toward profitability. But now, rather than capitalize, the company was rendered rudderless by its mutinous crew and its clueless board. Treachery is expensive.

Later that same afternoon, Wolf had the privilege of attending another mind-numbing Citibank meeting. Their business development team had made their way to Charlottesville to work out the details and the timing for implementing the grand relationship they had proposed in New York. In the unbalanced "praise-one-minute, attack-the-next" style of Gerry

Roche, Wolf Schmitt oozed admiration for Craig's propensity for conceiving innovative and value-laden strategic partnerships. He said, "Others just see the dots, but you manage to connect them in a way that's almost magical. It's a gift."

Following the meeting, Schmitt agreed to accept the role of interim CEO while the board searched for a permanent replacement. A third telephonic board meeting was arranged to discuss the matter.

On November 19th at 5:00 PM EST, ten of Value America's eleven board members met telephonically to discuss Tom's departure and the Wolf solution. Rex began, "I move that we accept Morgan's resignation."

There was no second, so Craig said, "I second the motion. Any discussion, gentlemen?"

"Yeah," Durn barked, "I want to talk to Tom. Why isn't he on the call?"

"Because he resigned, and he's not a board member," Craig said calmly.

"I don't give a damn! I said I want to talk to Morgan. Get him on the phone," a hostile voice screamed back. The seeds of deceit had taken root. Dorchak's relationship with Seth Rossi was paying off.

Craig asked Biff to find Morgan and connect him to the call. Seconds later, as if prearranged, a voice he had come to loathe said, "Morgan here."

"Hello, Tom. This is Rafe. I asked you to join us so we could hear it directly from you. Why are you leaving?"

"There can't be two cooks in the kitchen, two generals on the field," Morgan answered. "Craig hasn't allowed me to do my job. I'm tired of being second-guessed. Since I don't feel comfortable working with him, one of us has to go. Since I'm the newcomer, I thought it should be me."

"Then you're not saying you don't *want* to be CEO. You're just saying you don't want to be CEO so long as Winn is here."

"That's right," Tom answered.

"How about you, Craig," asked Durn. The former lawyer was enjoying his cross-examination. "Are you willing to step aside and let him do his job?"

"I *did* step aside—before the IPO. Contrary to what Tom told you, I haven't overridden any of his decisions. I focused on outside relationships because the company needed them, and it freed Tom to manage the business without interference." *Heck, he's so paranoid he threatens to fire anybody who even tries to talk to me. I don't even know the people I'm being accused of managing. The very allegation is moronic.*

"You're not acting like a traditional Chairman," Fred Smith charged. "Cultivating relationships outside of the company is the CEO's job, as is strategic planning. I don't want to beat a dead horse, but when you said at our last board meeting that you were not a manager, you put this board in tremendous peril." Sadly, the intelligent are not always wise.

"Fred, I have a great deal of respect for you, but we differ on both accounts," Craig answered, futilely trying to defend himself from the lynch mob. "I have consistently referred to myself as a builder rather than a manager. But builders have to be managers—good ones—or nothing gets built. They must conceive and design what they intend to build, raise the capital, hire the talent, buy the materials, and coordinate construction. That takes management. It takes leadership. Builders are leaders. I am proud to be a builder. But once something is built, I don't much enjoy the day-to-day managing, the meetings, the personnel squabbles." *Like this one.*

"Sorry to say it," Smith said, "but that's what managing is all about."

It was like the Salem Witch Trials. No matter what the accused said, it was quickly convoluted and used to fan the fire in which Craig was standing.

"We've been over this turf before, Fred, but I'll try again. New-technology companies are different than asset-based firms like yours. Your assets are warehouses, planes, and trucks. Ours are ideas, people, and partnerships; While both need managers and builders, new-economy firms need to be led longer than traditional asset-based industries. Consider the world's two most successful tech firms: Microsoft and AOL. Both are led and managed the way I believed Value America should be. Gates and Case are visionaries; they're builders, leaders. Ballmer and Pitman are tough, effective managers. What makes their companies successful is their ability to work in harmony with their visionary founders."

Craig realized what he had just shared was of no interest to the assembled. Although it was pointless, he continued. "In the Internet Age, alliances are uncommonly valuable. There is no better use of a chairman's time than to increase the quantity and quality of these partnerships."

"Fred Smith here," he said. "Listen, I disagree. I could spend the next week giving you chapter and verse on proper organizational protocol, but I think it boils down to a founder trying to do too much and a CEO who's neither prepared nor able to work within that kind of environment."

"Durn here." Rafe wanted back in. He evidently enjoyed executions. "Craig, it sounds like Tom is willing to come back. If he were to stay, would you be willing to move aside?"

"No. Not now. Not after what I've learned this past week."

"Why not?"

"He's not the right person for the job," Craig replied. *You want Tom Morgan to form strategic partnerships and lead this company? Are you crazy?*

Morgan couldn't sell water to a rich man dying of thirst.

Durn thanked Morgan profusely for his glorious eight-month service. Others passed along their goodbyes, hoping, as Tom was, that it wasn't over yet. Everybody knew now that Morgan had had no intention of actually resigning.

As they settled down, Craig told the board that Wolf Schmitt had expressed a willingness to act as interim CEO while the board formed a committee to search for a permanent replacement. Smith, Roche, and Caise were assigned the responsibility of confirming the appropriateness of naming him acting CEO. The meeting was adjourned at 6:35 PM.

By all accounts, the Saturday morning conference call between Smith, Roche, Caise, and Schmitt went well. They were all in agreement. At the next board meeting, Wolf would be crowned acting CEO. Craig was relieved.

WHEN A ROCK starts to roll down a hill, it usually just goes a few feet and stops. But sometimes it gains momentum, kicks up debris, and starts an avalanche. That's what happened here. Craig and Rex had picked the wrong stone—again. In scrambling to save the company, they doomed her.

Wolf told Craig to send the company jet to pick him up—the second time he'd asked for this special treatment. The plane wasn't supposed to be used to pamper board members. Even so, Wolf didn't seem to enjoy the flight. He arrived a changed man. At dinner with Rex, Craig, and the General, he suddenly and boldly proclaimed the firm was too fragile for him to lead it. Someone had obviously gotten to him prior to his arrival.

At dawn the next day, Wolf asked Craig to arrange meetings with the managers of each department. He waltzed in announcing that the board had placed him in charge, waxing poetic about his glorious career at Rubbermaid. (Some believe Wolf had been instrumental in destroying his former firm, forcing the merger with Newell. But we had long ago entered the land of make-believe.) By the time the meetings concluded, Wolf had developed a nasty repetitive-motion disorder patting himself on the back.

Throughout the day, the solid citizens who remained at Value America, of which there were many, marched into Craig's office to ask what was going on. They had thought *he* was returning to management to lead us back to the Promised Land. "Who was this Wolf? Why was he here? What was happening to the company we'd worked so hard to build?" They saw right through him.

I was one of them. But I had not come to burden him with these questions. I had come to resign. The company he had conceived, the one we had so lovingly nurtured and raised, had become an unruly, rebellious adolescent. I no longer knew these people, so childish, rude, and greedy. Our firm had been without adult supervision ever since Craig and Rex had left management. So I told Craig I was leaving. Even though he was no longer my boss, he was the only person to whom I felt I owed an explanation.

I had never seen Craig so despondent. It wasn't the news I had brought him, although he was clearly saddened by it. It was as if something, or someone, had sucked the life out of him. He was a hollow shell of his former self. He told me that he was not at liberty to explain, but I could clearly see that whatever it was, it was bad, very bad. Craig thanked me. Then, as I was leaving, he reminded me one last time of the curious thing he'd said countless times before: "You were our patron saint. I always knew God would never let anything bad happen to our company so long as you were here." *Why does he keep saying that?*

After I left, Wolf made his way into Craig's office. He was joined by Rex and Mick around the old table. The telephonic board meeting was scheduled to start in ten minutes, promptly at four o'clock.

Wolf repeated the "fragile and unfocused" diatribe he had delivered at dinner the night before. He said the participants in each meeting had echoed his sentiments, and claimed that our technologists viewed our dilemma to be of crisis proportions, with no end in sight. As he told his tale, Wolf was confident, even pompous. He had ulterior motives to be sure, a separate agenda. And whatever it was, it was clear he had the blessing of at least enough board members to carry the day. Wolf was about to give wolves a bad name.

The good guys were screwed, and they knew it. Still, they fought on, though goodness knows why. It was in their interests to leave, dump their shares, and retire in style. Who could have blamed them if they had? They were *persona non grata* in a world they themselves had built. It was still their world; they owned it (at least their stock certificates said they did). But they were being treated like a pack of hyenas treats dinner.

Craig, rather than backing down, challenged Wolf's statements. Yes, he knew the company was fragile and unfocused. That was Morgan's doing, and thankfully, within the hour, he'd be gone. But Craig knew from the steady stream of visitors that the meetings had not been as Wolf had described them. "So who in technology said our systems are as far from remedy as you just described?

"I had every technology manager in the meeting. They all said it," Wolf bristled arrogantly.

"So you're telling me Joe Page and Thor Anders were in the meeting and they told you that our systems were desperately faulty?"

"Yes, I've already told you that," Wolf bellowed in a tone calculated to show his superior status. "You and Rex are both so out of touch. This company is in worse shape than you realize."

"This past week, I've seen how bad a shape we're in, and I've learned how we got into this mess. I'm also aware that you're lying. Neither Joe nor Thor attended the technology meeting I arranged for you. And those who did said they never gave you their opinions. They said you were too busy talking about yourself."

"We'll just see about that," Wolf growled as he jumped up and stormed out of Craig's office. The founders were watching their own funeral. As they struggled to regain their composure, they saw Wolf dart into Morgan's old office. There was no question what he intended to do. Whomever he had cajoled on the board to support whatever plan he had concocted was being called with an update. It had taken three years to build Value America. Within three hours it would be gone—poof.

The founders scrambled to form an alternate plan. The board meeting was now less than five minutes away. Plan A had been trashed when Tom resigned a second time. Plan B had crashed when the board turned south and rejected their return to stabilize the firm. Plan C, Wolf as interim CEO, was now in flames. Plan D?

They gathered the four most senior managers together: Dorchak, Peters, Chambers, and Ewert. Craig and Rex explained the Wolf conundrum and asked the assembled if they had any ideas. Ewert considered it promotion enough making him responsible for all merchandising categories. Peters seemed pleased with his move into the management of demand and supply alliances. He, like Chambers, said he didn't want the job. Dorchak remained mostly silent. She had already sowed her seeds of discontent, and she knew they were about to take root.

"Alright folks," Craig said, "since none of you has a plan, I'll propose one. I'll volunteer to be interim CEO for ninety days. During that time, you'll manage the company as an Executive Committee. I'll teach each of you some aspect of what you'll collectively need to know to lead a public company. I'll ask the board to choose one of you to be CEO, another to be President, another COO. Are you all willing to work together in support of this plan?"

Three said yes. Dorchak squirmed. Craig asked them to stay, and then returned to his office for the start of the board meeting. Wolf was already there with a smirk on his face. Craig, Mick, and Rex sat in the other chairs surrounding the antique table. The octopus-looking conference phone sat between them. It was 4:00 PM EST November 23, 1999. As each board member called in, they announced their names. "Justin Caise is on."

"Hi, Justin. This is Don Tarpin."

"Rafe Durn is on."

"Hello, Rafe," Craig said, "I've been trying to reach you." Rafe didn't respond.

"This is Fred Smith calling in from Memphis."

"Hello, Fred. This is Rex. I'm joined here by Craig, Wolf, and Mick. We've also got Biff Pusey as Corporate Counsel."

"Hello," Gerry said, "Roche here."

"White here."

"This is Frank Flowers. I'm on."

"That's everybody except Bill Bennett," Biff Pusey said, acting official. "He's out of town and will be unable to join us. Mr. Chairman, you have a quorum and may call the meeting to order."

The meeting started with a discussion of CFO candidates followed by a quarterly update, performance *versus* expectation. It moved to personnel.

"We still need to resolve the Morgan issue," Craig said. "There has been a motion and a second to accept his resignation. Any discussion?"

"What about severance?" Roche questioned. Gerry was good at spending money on people. That was his job.

Don Tarpin said, "I was assigned the responsibility of working out a separation package for Tom, but I wasn't successful. Tom is now saying that he hasn't resigned, and he doesn't want to resign."

Justin Caise and Rex Scatena, attorneys both, jumped into the fray. They reviewed the facts and rendered their opinions. Morgan had constructively resigned, regardless of what he was saying now.

Then Craig stepped up. "Tom has told me repeatedly that he doesn't want anything from us—no severance, nothing. As you've confirmed, he's resigned and thus is not entitled to any severance. He only worked here eight months, so we shouldn't pay him anything."

But Tom, either directly or through his lawyer, had called Justin Caise, threatening an SEC investigation if he wasn't given a year's severance— salary *and* bonus. The fact that Tom had once again lied didn't surprise Craig. An SEC investigation didn't worry him either. He was concerned only about our dwindling cash reserves. Treachery, he discovered, didn't come cheap. Tom's compensation was $600,000, plus a six-figure loan he never bothered to repay. Caise said, "I've talked with his attorney, and I can assure you he wants a year's severance. But he's also saying Tom has not resigned."

"If we pay, let's limit our exposure to six months," someone said.

For the first time all evening, Flowers chimed in. "If the bid and the ask are six months and a year, let's split the difference and pay him nine."

Caise then responded, "I'll negotiate the settlement." What he failed to do was to negotiate a non-disparagement clause, the only conceivable reason to offer a resigning eight-month disgruntled employee *any* severance. Pretty poor lawyering, Craig thought. It would get worse.

"Gentlemen, do I have a motion to accept Mr. Morgan's resignation?"

"So moved," someone said. It was quickly seconded.

"Is there any more discussion?" Craig asked. There was silence. *Good.* "All those in favor." There were some audible "Ayes." "All those opposed." There were no audible noes. "The motion is carried," he said with some semblance of relief. *At least one nightmare is over.*

Craig wanted the minutes to reference some comment memorializing Morgan's eight-month tenure. It seemed like the right thing to do, so he made what he thought was an innocuous statement: "Tom Morgan tried to do what he thought was right, but he just wasn't the right guy to be running an Internet retail business."

"Stop right there!" Rafe shouted at the top of his voice. His tone was so angry, the assembled backed away from Craig's old table. "I don't know about the rest of you, but I'm not going to tolerate *you* demeaning Tom Morgan."

After a moment of stunned silence, our peacemaker, Justin Caise, tried to keep the meeting from deteriorating further. He said, in a significantly less hostile voice, "Caise here. I was of the opinion we were going to get a report from Wolf today." There had been no prior board discussion about Schmitt providing a "report." Justin's admission was proof positive the board was now scheming behind the founders' backs.

"Yes," Wolf said, sitting up and clearing his throat. "I have spent the day in meetings I've arranged with the managers of every department. What I found is that the company is unfocused and fragile, especially its systems. They're in very bad condition. The technologists have been distracted trying to accommodate Winn's whims rather than focusing on their jobs. The company is too weak for me to consider acting as CEO."

Right again, Craig thought. *Damn. I knew it!*

"Wait a minute!" Fred shot back, clearly annoyed. "Saturday, you accepted the role, and we confirmed the terms of your engagement. And now your telling us you're not going to do it?"

"Frankly, I think the company has been so badly mismanaged that it's more than I feel comfortable doing. But," Wolf added with a rise in his voice, "you haven't asked me what I think you should do."

Here it comes, Craig thought. *The ulterior motive. Wolf's real agenda.*

"If it were my company, I'd bring Morgan back."

Apparently, neither sanity nor rational thought was any longer a prerequisite for a board position. How does one reconcile, "The company has been so poorly managed I'm not willing to work here," with "bring back the manager who managed so poorly?" At least Craig now knew that it had been the Brethren who had betrayed us. Morgan, Godfrey, Starnes, and Kuo had seduced Wolf and persuaded him to join their *coup*, not that it mattered any longer. Hope was getting pummeled. One more blow and it would be all over.

"Well, we've got ourselves a pickle here," Craig said. "Morgan's gone, Wolf's out. Does anyone have a plan?" An indeterminable silence followed. With more heart than head, Craig filled the void. "I'm willing to return for ninety days as acting CEO while this board forms a search committee to replace me. I neither want the job, nor is it in my interest to take the job, but somebody's got to do it. I've just talked to the four most senior managers and there's support for this plan. They'll manage the company as an Executive Committee. I will teach them what they need to know to run a public company."

"Smith here. I'm told more people will resign if you return."

"We have too many people, not too few, so with cash the way it is, that would be a good thing. However, I have talked to everyone who's crucial. No one who is essential will resign if I return. In fact, they're pleased."

"What about Tom Starnes?" Smith asked incredulously.

"He's not essential. He's not even *useful*," Craig answered.

About a dozen come-latelies like Starnes had rallied in support of Morgan, claiming they would leave the company if Craig remained. Their motivations were transparently simple: as CEO, Tom controlled their compensation; he held the power of the pen—hiring, firing, contracts, titles, bonuses, and even severance packages. Craig had no real power, and they knew it. In fact, most most didn't even know him.

"Gentlemen, I don't check the VUSA message boards, but I'm told they claim the reason the stock climbed from ten bucks a share to a high today of *seventeen* is because the Street is anticipating my return to management."

"And *I'm* told the stock will double the day after we announce you're gone!" an angry Durn shot back.

That was it. With that single sentence, hope's faint light blew out. Three years gone.

"I've been quiet too long," a clearly angered Rex Scatena stood up and spoke confidently into the phone. "I know this man you're abusing here today better than anyone. I'm proud to call him my friend. He's the reason this company exists. None of you built it; he did. None of you would even be here if it weren't for him. Frankly, it disgusts me to sit here and watch you all tear him apart. I'd follow Craig Winn into hell."

"I don't appreciate your tone or your implications," an angry Fred Smith responded. "I'm his friend too, and I'm here because of our friendship. You're comments are inappropriate and out of line."

"Roche here. I don't want an acting anything. We need to have a real CEO, not an acting one. Tell us about your four top managers. Is any one of them qualified to be CEO?"

"No!" Craig answered. "Not now." He was more dazed than ever. "I think they may have the potential, but none of them is ready."

"We need to announce a CEO tomorrow morning." It sounded like Fred's voice. "This has gone on too long." Wasn't this the same man who had asked Craig to "hesitate" back when this problem could have been solved without calamity?

"This is Roche. Tell us about your four candidates." Gerry's question was as eerily predictive of turmoil as was his question about succession.

Craig went through the motions anyway. Sometimes he didn't know when to shut up. "I know the least about Paul Ewert, but he was the Senior Merchant and SVP at CompUSA, a multibillion dollar company. He appears to be polished and well regarded. He knows the PC business. Cliff Chambers doesn't want the job. He's responsible for Operations. I'd like to see him promoted to COO. He's a fine man. He was responsible for Operations at Genuine Parts, NAPA, a billion-dollar distribution company. Cliff understands most everything we do operationally."

Craig caught his breath and scratched his head. He wanted to make sure it was still attached. "Byron Peters is the most qualified of the four. Byron was EVP and COO of Price-Costco's eastern operation. He knows retail and distribution. He knows what brands want. He grew up in the Price organization and thus understands our core philosophy and mission. Byron has had the most people reporting to him, and managed the largest budgets—several thousand people and several billion dollars." As Craig listed Peter's qualifications, it was obvious the crowd was oblivious. You could hear coughing and other distracted sounds. *To hell with qualifications. We're not interested in Byron.*

With the last once of strength he could muster, he turned his words to Glenda. It pained him. But in contrast, with each word Craig uttered, he could sense the board's rising enthusiasm. He said things like, she's been here the longest and works hard. She's in charge of sales and advertising, and that's where the money is. He was careful to point out that there were character issues that caused him concern. It didn't matter.

"Durn here. I'm impressed with her. She's experienced."

I guess Rafe's man Rossi has done his job. Wonder what he got paid this time?

"Roche here. I've already taken the liberty to talk to my people about Glenda." His comment clearly revealed that the board had already decided. "You all know," Roche went on gleefully, "that my firm was retained by Compaq to find Pfeiffer's successor. The leading candidate for that job had good things to say about her. She checks out great throughout my organization. So Craig, if you had to pick one of them, who would you pick?" Roche asked, begging the question.

Let's see. I've just told you that none of them were prepared to be CEO. I've stated as clearly as I can that Peters is the best qualified. I've told you that Dorchak's rotten. But she's obviously who this board wants, and nothing I could possibly say will make one bit of difference. If I told you guys that the earth was round and revolved around the sun, you'd burn me alive as a heretic. "Dorchak?" *You deserve each other.*

"Great, good choice," enthused the assembled. "Winn, go and see if she'll accept the job." As if they didn't already know. While Craig was out, Caise promoted a scheme that had also been hatched behind the scenes in smoke-filled rooms. "Wolf, would you consider being Chairman and guiding Glenda through this process?"

"Why yes, I suppose I would. Anything I can do to help."

"Then let's see if we can get Winn to resign," another said.

The board gushed all over Glenda as she walked triumphantly into the room. Craig doesn't recall who made the motion or who seconded it, but it was done; that much is certain. Glenda became CEO, and Wolf became Chairman. The founders joined generation ex.

Craig stumbled over to an old leather chair in the corner that had come from his oceanfront office in California, the very office he had used to craft Value America's business plan. He sat down and buried his head in his hands. His revolution was over. Our dream was dead.

WALKING THE PLANK

*Q*uoting the great Yogi Berra, "It was *déjà vu*, all over again." The employees of Value America were celebrating Thanksgiving within the friendly confines of Rococo's Restaurant. A year before, we were announcing the arrival of Glenda Dorchak. Today we were proclaiming her coronation.

The troops were restless. Craig tried to calm them, saying he wasn't going anywhere. "The only titles I ever wanted were founder and owner anyway. *Founder,* because I take pride in having been part of all that made our company special. *Owner,* because I'm proud to be one of you."

Bill Hunt, sitting in the audience, knew better. The pain was etched in his friend's eyes; he could hear it in his voice. Their dream was over. The bright flame that had been Value America had been snuffed out. The body was still there, but the soul had departed.

Joe Page got up and walked over to the bar. He asked for a beer. He would drink many more before the day was through. He knew that with Craig leaving, we were finished. *Of all the "Dilbert" executives from which to choose,* he thought, *why did they pick the most conniving and manipulative?*

Rex was stunned. I was gone.

Dorchak gave the same speech she'd given before. "It's time to pass the baton from the entrepreneurs to the professionals." Her press release read:

"Glenda Dorchak named CEO, Wolf Schmitt named Chairman. On November 24 Value America (VUSA) announced a change in its management designed to focus on quality growth and a drive to prosperity. Dorchak, *who joined the company as President in October 1998* after 23 years at IBM, will become Value America's new CEO. "Our innovative business model is becoming a viable and exciting business," Dorchak said. "As we advance toward profitability, we are determined to focus on...increasing the depth of products in our store. A top-quality management team is being empowered to generate explosive growth and focus its efforts on achieving profitability."

The fact it was a lie didn't seem to matter. What mattered was that Value America's board had been wrong. Apart from Glenda's Gang, no one was celebrating. The stock didn't double as they had predicted. Following the announcement that Winn was gone, it tanked.

But all was not lost. Dorchak and Morgan discovered you can use the press to rewrite history in any form that serves your interests.

The phone rang off the hook. Countless callers, one question: *Why?* And the big surprise? It seems that Wolf Schmitt was as universally disliked as Dorchak! They were two peas in a pod. Craig was devastated.

The first call came through David Kuo's cell phone. He and his comrades were in mourning. They openly despised Dorchak. The phone call was from *The Wall Street Journal*. David handed it to Craig as he stepped outside, behind the restaurant, so he could hear above the chatter. Glenda followed, afraid she'd miss an opportunity. The reporter asked Craig three questions a dozen ways, fishing for dirt. He didn't bite; he bit his lip instead. Trying to support the company that had just humiliated him, Craig said, "Morgan resigned. He was not fired. Tom returned home to be with his family." He said, "I am pleased for Glenda. As the largest shareholder, I am counting on her performing well." And, "No, I was not forced out of the company. I've had no managerial role, nor title, for over eight months. I was the one who invited Wolf to join our board. I'm responsible for encouraging him to accept a more significant role."

The whole time, Glenda paced like a caged leopard. When Craig gave her the phone, she scurried away and stood talking next to the restaurant's dumpster. Alas, once again Craig blew a perfect opportunity.

The Reverend Jerry Falwell called on Mick's cell phone to comfort Craig. He said, "I believe your best days are ahead of you. You are a man called out by God to lead his times."

A senior *Fortune* editor called David Kuo and asked how the company could have promoted "arguably the worst CEO in America?" According to David, she had written a feature about Wolf's destruction of Rubbermaid. Ray Kennedy of Masco called too. He asked Craig the same question a different way, "What in the world were you thinking? No one in the home improvement industry has a worse reputation than Schmitt." Plan D, their desperate move to save the firm, had failed.

Value America's message boards would prove to be eerily accurate:

Wolf is at the Helm   12/1/1999 8:32 am EST
Watch for the following developments now that Wolf is in charge. 1) If there are any good people left, they will leave due to Wolf's arrogant leadership style. 2) He will surround himself with people who agree with him no matter how wacko the idea. 3) He will reorganize and announce huge savings and efficiency gains, which will fail to materialize. 4) He will bring in hordes of consultants, thereby wasting any available cash for absolutely no benefit except to the consultants. Sell this stock and put your money under your mattress—you'll be way ahead.

Everything happened exactly as they foretold. A week later this appeared on Rubbermaid's board:

Hoser Wolf   12/6/1999 7:30 pm EST
My Gawd! I feel like weeping! I read the messages on VUSA's Yahoo! board. They haven't a clue! No one even asked a question about Wolf's past. The poor

unlucky investors don't know what's in store for them now that Wolfman is at the helm of the U-Boat. Can you believe that guy actually got a job?... This is really pathetic! On 11/23 VUSA traded as high as seventeen, which is the highest it's traded in months. On 11/24 the press release came out on Woofie's appointment. The stock price traded down that day and every day since. Closed at twelve today, down another half. Nobody on that company's board has made the connection."

On Tuesday, November 30, Craig met Fred Smith in New York City. The two were co-hosting an Internet Conference for CEOs at the request of *Chief Executive* magazine. Fred gave the morning's keynote address, complimenting Craig and Value America throughout his talk. Craig delivered the afternoon's address, returning the favor. Between the two speeches, the two men huddled in a back corner of an upper room of the World Trade Center overlooking the financial district.

"Fred, you and every other board member have been misled, purposely misled. A small group of Morgan's loyalists mounted a pro-Tom, anti-Craig campaign to discredit me and entrench him. As you no doubt deduced, Tom had no intention of resigning."

"I'm really disappointed in him," Fred responded.

"Their *coup* blew up in their faces, and they got Dorchak instead, whom they despise even more than me. Fred, you asked what I meant when I said there were issues with her character during the last meeting. I answered but there was too much pro-Glenda sentiment bubbling up for me to be heard. She's conniving, insecure, and a blackma...."

"Now, Bub, Glenda was not one of those that lobbied me against you," Fred interrupted, trying to squelch the news he didn't want to hear.

"Yes, I know. She got to Caise, Durn, and Tarpin and later, when all was lost, to Roche." Tom's spiritual advisor and paid company consultant, Goose Godfrey, was wooing his contacts on the board, Roche and White, on Morgan's behalf, while the Toms and the Kuos were working on Fred.

Godfrey, Craig later learned, did more than boost Morgan's ego. He played a pivotal role in unraveling the company. Jerry Falwell shared that opinion. He had seen Goose Godfrey and the religious power brokers that made up the United Brethren in action. Falwell, in fact, had narrowly saved a prominent faith-based organization from slipping into their greedy hands. He said their attempt to gain control had all been perpetrated at board level through sympathetic board appointees and a coordinated attack on their rival's character. Sure sounds familiar.

"The board has made some terrible decisions based on incomplete and inaccurate information," Craig told his friend. It was the understatement of the millennium.

"What's done is done," Smith shrugged, stating the sad but legitimate truth. "You assembled an all-outside board. All of us are busy. Truth be known, none of us have time for this. We had a problem; we tried to resolve it as best we could."

Craig had made a tragic mistake. He had brought together the most prestigious board of any dot-com firm. They were all good men, successful men, powerful men. But that was the problem. A handful of people with ulterior motives had been able to use half-truths, stereotypes, exaggeration, and slander to cloud their thinking. And it had all happened so quickly, Craig hadn't seen it coming.

"Many of the company's senior merchants and I," Craig said, "have been overrun with calls regarding Wolf. I brought him in, so I'm at fault," Craig admitted. "But he's bad news, Fred. You're the most respected man on our board. If you don't check into Wolf's past, as I have now done—too late, mind you—and dismiss him, we're in trouble. I'll give you the names and numbers of people who can confirm what I'm telling you."

Fred answered condescendingly. "I understand, you'd like to have your chairmanship back. I agree. Give it some time. It'll happen."

"Fred, this is not about me; it's about the company! It may not survive without your intervention."

"We've just made a change," Fred said, trying to be both compassionate and wise. "Give it time; settle down." Craig was now being viewed as Chicken Little. Unfortunately, the sky really *was* falling.

꒰◦⦂◦꒱

IT DIDN'T TAKE LONG for Glenda to impale herself on her own words. On Wednesday, December 1, 1999, at 1:48 PM, she sent an email to everyone@valueamerica.com. In it she said, "With only one month left in this quarter, we are in the unfortunate position that we are *well below* our revenue objective for the quarter due to our need to slow advertising during system changes, product shipment issues, and challenges with customer service. In order to succeed in Q4, we need to have the biggest month in Value America history!" Glenda M Dorchak, CEO, Value America.

Like Craig had said, *no one* was prepared to be CEO. Rex, recognizing the peril associated with this email, faxed a copy to our SEC counsel, Wilmer, Cutler, Pickering. They correctly advised the company to issue a public revenue warning before the email found its way to the VUSA message boards. Rex and Craig drew straws for which of them would gain the dubious honor of informing their new CEO that she had started poorly. Craig lost.

He invited Glenda into his office and explained the fiduciary duty and disclosure rules of a public company CEO. Dorchak was incensed. She seethed, "Now that I'm the CEO, you have no right to talk to me like I'm a child." She stormed out, scurried down the hall, ducked into her office, and slammed the door behind her. She picked up the phone and told one of her minions to fire Wilmer, Cutler, Pickering—arguably the finest law firm in the mid-Atlantic states and among the best SEC lawyers in the nation. Glenda couldn't handle the humiliation of being rebuked; her insecurity couldn't countenance a challenge to her supreme authority.

What Dorchak did next was even more amazing. She hired the very same firm that had been so badly outmatched during the IPO process. From all accounts, the law firm of Caise, Perkins is a fine regional firm, well suited to small entrepreneurial, pre-public companies. But it had about as much business being Value America's SEC counsel as Dorchak had being the CEO of a public company. At least now Craig knew why Caise may have been so supportive of Ms. Dorchak's coronation. *Quid pro quo* and all. His firm would be paid over $2 million defending ours, and that's a lot of reasons.

An earlier Dorchak email, sent at 8:24 AM that same day, was less dangerous to the firm's public standing. But it clearly revealed the private turmoil brewing inside Value America's new CEO. Ironically, it was written to Linda Harmon, the administrative assistant who had recognized Tom Morgan's character flaws as far back as IPO day, long before anyone else had seen them. Now she would be among the first to read Glenda's— in glorious, unmistakable, black and white.

The email to Linda was sent to every manager, although it specifically listed Starnes, Peters, Ewert, Chambers, and Pusey. It began, "To all Value America Managers: As an executive team we are undertaking a detailed planning effort to ensure we have a sound business plan for 2000." Read: It's December already, and yet none of us "professional managers" have come up with a plan for the coming year. What, pray tell, are we doing to earn our lofty salaries?

The email continued, "No agreements should be signed or verbal commitments made until approved.... Delay any prospective partner or alliance visits to C'Ville.... The following approval process is in place effective immediately. Any external document which commits us to financial or other conditions can only be approved by an EVP and myself.... Ensure that everyone understands that any deviation from this process could be grounds for dismissal."

Translated, this meant, "I don't trust anybody. All progress will cease immediately. Nothing will happen without my approval. If you don't please me, I will fire you." It was pure, unadulterated insecurity screaming, *I need to be in control, total and absolute control, the center of attention, even if it brings everybody else down, even the company.* As you might imagine, it was great for morale. From this moment on, no forward progress was made. The company's decline was even more rapid than its rise.

What followed was particularly fun. *The Industry Standard*, a magazine that calls itself, "Intelligence for the Internet Economy," as if there were such a thing, published a feature story on Value America. Arranged by David Kuo, it was entitled, "Value America's Palace Coup." It said:

"First the CEO quit. Then the board deposed its chairman. Now the general merchandise e-retailer thinks it can turn a profit. Nothing says 'Christmas' like a good old-fashioned corporate bloodletting. In keeping with the spirit, Value America, the general-merchandise e-retailer headquartered in Charlottesville, recently announced its founder, Craig Winn, would move away from oversight of day-to-day operations. Then, a couple of days before Thanksgiving, the company's board voted to oust Winn as chairman, replacing him with another board member, Wolf Schmitt.... The recent behind-the-scenes maneuvering left Winn with a 'nothing burger' in the words of one Value America exec." *Thanks, David.*

The announcement of Winn's move away from day-to-day operations had taken place in early March, not late November. But this was not a casual mistake or a careless error. The Brethren were anxious to write themselves out of our history. Though fallen, their hero needed an alibi, and so did they. A little lie can do wonders for one's reputation.

It was unthinkable that they might be held responsible for the company during the time they were paid to manage it. The possibility of having their failed *coup* linked to the company's demise was beyond comprehension. So Morgan and his fan club concocted a story, and the press lapped it up. "Winn was a meddling entrepreneur who just couldn't let go," they said. "It wasn't our fault," they whined, "Winn micromanaged everything. He cut us off at the knees, reversed our every decision." It fit the stereotype nicely and provided a great alibi for them, not to mention the regime that followed. It also made for a juicy story. To hell with the truth. Seduction and betrayal.

"According to company insiders [read: Starnes and Kuo], Morgan, who joined the company as CEO in March, was frustrated over Winn's refusal to hand over the corporate reins. *[And I thought it was because he wasn't a 'truth teller.']* To contrast Winn's style with Morgan's, insiders point to a recent deal that Winn brokered with Visa, which gave Visa cardholders 100 'value dollars' for their first $200 in purchases on Value America's site.... Value America was forced to cancel the arrangement, which company executives claim Morgan never would have made without first carefully studying the ramifications."

Bravo. Fine job, David and Tom. You really nailed Winn with those clever insights. Never mind that Kuo, not Winn, brokered the Visa deal. Never mind that it brought millions of dollars of revenue into the store while costing less than newspaper ads. You could even be forgiven for falsely stating that the company was forced to cancel the deal because you finally said something right: "Morgan would never have done the deal." He never did *any* deal.

Staying out of management, not being an insider, was in Craig's financial interest. It freed him to sell fifteen million shares at $10 to $17 a share. Yet he was portrayed as wanting to commit economic suicide. Let's see, a smart man willing to throw away hundreds of millions of dollars to gain operational control of a company that he had voluntarily given up control of just nine months earlier. Not on this planet. Any business journalist worth his laptop should have been able to connect the dots, put two and two together. Or in Craig's case, multiply fifteen million shares by $10 to $17. But why be rational? Logic doesn't sell magazines. Besides, logic requires thought, and that's too much to ask.

"What started as a contest between the two men for operational control ended with neither man victorious," the fantasy continued. "Winn is banished to a position of no real responsibility, and Morgan is looking for a job. Glenda Dorchak, Value America's president since October 1998, has been installed as the company's new CEO...."

"Right again," Craig mumbled to no one in particular. "The biggest problem isn't that the ship's on fire. It isn't even the crew. It's the mutinous officers." Craig picked up the phone and called Caise's direct line.

"I didn't call to chastise you for your lack of support the other night, Justin, although I'm disappointed. Personally, I think you're a fine man, but corporately, your behavior is reprehensible. You of all people should know better. *You* wrote the blackmailer's employment contract, for cryin' out loud." Justin was silent. His words could only incriminate him.

"You know as well as I do, in my absence an unrestrained Dorchak will destroy Value America. Everyone will lose." *Except the lawyers.* "And *you* could have stopped this." Craig was hard on Caise. He struggled with the dichotomy between the upstanding nature of Justin's personal life and the depravity of his current corporate behavior. Craig did all he could to instill some courage into Justin's feeble heart. It did no good. Caise had gone from ally to adversary. "This board has plotted its own course. I can no longer help. You are on your own," Craig stated defiantly.

Justin responded with a syrupy diatribe about how they were eager to get Craig's valuable insights, but he stopped him in mid-sentence. "It's far too late for that, and you know it. I called to tell you that Value America will be lost if you don't find out who's misinforming the press and fire them. Those willing to put their personal agendas above the shareholders have no business in this, or any, company. We're paying them, or should I say, *you're* paying them, to serve the interests of the shareholders, yet their actions show they're simply serving themselves!"

Sadly, Justin said and did nothing. Going along, keeping the peace, was more important to him than anything (except money, perhaps). Before they parted, Craig arranged to meet Caise in his office the following evening to discuss his role in the failed *coup*.

In the presence of General Kicklighter, Justin vehemently denied his complicity. Caise insisted that he, more than anyone, trusted and respected Craig Winn. He recounted the many promises, the bold claims Craig had made. Then he shared in painstaking detail how every promise had been fulfilled, how every claim had been verified. Caise once again urged Winn to run for Governor. He not only said he would be supportive, he actually catered a gala affair in Craig's honor for several hundred notables at his magnificent home. Justin's introduction was one for the ages. Personal good and corporate evil were now inextricably intertwined.

Over the next few days, Craig's phone bristled with activity. The press smelled blood and they wanted stories. *The Wall Street Journal*, *The Washington Post*, and *The New York Times* all called. Craig did his utmost to walk the party line, trying to say something good or nothing at all. It worked—to a point. In each interview, the reporter would inevitably ask, "Why were you so foolish as to kill the eFed deal? Why did you throw away money supporting Visa? Why couldn't you let go, and let Morgan manage?" After hours of, "have-you-stopped-beating-your-wife," questions, a reporter with the *Journal* asked, "If you could do it all over again, what would you do differently?"

Craig finally bit. "I should have stayed on as CEO after the IPO. New economy companies need to be led longer."

Then the journalist asked, "Anything else?"

"Sure," Craig said. "Having an all-outside board was a mistake. They're busy men. They have neither the time nor the background to make well-informed decisions."

"And...."

"And after all this rubbish you just told me about what Morgan and his boys have said, I wish I hadn't hired him."

❧

DURING THE FINAL moments of the last board meeting, Fred had made it clear that Wolf was to work with Rex and Craig on all strategic issues and alliances. But Wolf made a mockery of the request. He canceled every meeting. He was too important to be expected to spend time with mere entrepreneurs. When he finally did grace the two founders with his presence, he was so belligerent, arrogant, and obnoxious, Rex reacted. "Get the f--- out of this office, before I throw you out." Craig just looked at his friend in wide-eyed admiration.

Not wasting a moment, they went back to work. They formed "Plan E"—sell the company before it implodes. As much as he hated to make the call, Craig dialed Gordon Conover, Managing Director of Robertson Stephens. They reasoned that even with a mile of bad road between them, no investment banker knew the company better or could respond as quickly. *Quickly* was everything now. We had become a lemming convention, racing hell-bent toward death. The Wolf and the Witch were leading the charge.

"Hello, Craig. Hi, Rex," Gordon said over the speakerphone. "What can I do for you, gentlemen?"

"Collectively, the five founders of Value America own fifty-one percent of the company. We'd like to sell it," Craig stated calmly.

"Do you wish to sell just your controlling interest, or the whole company?" Gordon asked with admirable equanimity. Fifty-one percent was twenty-two million shares, still worth over $300 million. This was a whole lot of business to fall into his hands.

"We would prefer to sell the whole company for the benefit of all shareholders," Rex answered.

"But we only control our shares, Gordon," Craig interjected. "We propose marketing our shares to a prospective company and then offering whatever deal we're able to negotiate to all shareholders."

Gordon responded, "We can do the deal either way, but we'd prefer to act with management and board support, not without it."

"Gordon, this is Rex. We're not in a position to offer you board support. We have no influence over management either. We just want to know if you can sell our shares to another firm—someone who can use what we've built."

"Yes, of course."

"How much and how fast?" Rex queried.

"Sixty days to get a binding letter of agreement. You've already got most of the book done. We just need to update portions of your prospectus. We've done the due diligence. So I'd say the last week in January."

"Good. The price?"

"That's a little harder to say. You're trading at $12, down from a high of...*whoa,* $17 just two weeks ago! The market for dot-coms is strong, but you guys are falling like a rock—down thirty percent in ten trading days. Wow! Guess the market didn't react very favorably to...."

"Yeah, we know," Rex said, cutting him off. "Too bad our board hasn't made the same connection. But go on..."

"Sure," Gordon said, regaining his composure. "You'd be in good hands. We're by far the biggest and most aggressive firm in dot-com mergers and acquisitions. And it's for damn sure you guys can sell. Yours is still the best IPO we've managed. Plus there are a lot of companies that need what you've built. But nothing's for certain; there are risks and all."

"You sound more like a lawyer than an investment banker," Rex interrupted. "What are the shareholders going to realize, Gordon?"

Gordon answered with a question. "Have you thought about which companies we should present Value America to, and how your commerce engine might be attractive to them?"

"Yes," Craig said. He rattled off twenty names in staccato fashion. As he started to explain the synergies, Gordon cut back in.

"If one of these firms shows interest, we should be able to get a fifteen to twenty percent premium above your average trading price—around $15 a share. If we can make it a horse race, with two or more firms interested, you'd be looking at $20 or more a share." That was nearly a billion dollars.

"Put it in writing," Craig said. "Send us a proposal."

"Sure, I'll even include an engagement letter," a happy Conover shot back. "We've still got most of the day here. You'll get it tomorrow, FedEx. You know, guys, time is critical here. Your value is falling fast. I suggest we schedule our first working session for tomorrow morning, say ten-thirty your time. I'll get a team together. We'll get this done."

"Good." Craig added, "I'll pull the materials together for the book and write a *Strategic Partnering Plan* so you'll know how to present us to the big guys like Microsoft and AOL. I'll even explain how e-commerce can be profitable with the right blend of demand and supply alliances."

"Sounds great. Talk to you guys tomorrow."

As Gordon hung up, Craig asked Rex, "Why don't you tell Biff Pusey what we're doing, so we don't run afoul of the Hitler Youth again."

With that, hell's fury was unleashed. You'd think from the way the Wolf and the Witch responded, Rex and Craig were stealing their favorite toy.

The founders' plan was to save shareholder value by selling a controlling interest in the company to a larger Internet firm. It was undeniably their last shot. If Plan E failed, there would be no tomorrow. Probable death would become certain. If you listened closely, you could hear "Taps" being played softly in the background.

Schmitt and Dorchak were incensed. Leading Value America was their big chance to prove themselves and redeem their tattered reputations. The very thought of having it snatched from their tightly clenched fists was unthinkable! Forget shareholders' interest; they only *owned* the company.

Remarkable, really, to think we had built a company so exciting organized labor tried to buy us, as did Paul Allen, the world's second wealthiest man. Even "America's Entrepreneur," Fred Smith, invested, along with his company. All but one of 140 institutional investors we had met on our road show had clamored to buy our stock. We had raised hundreds of millions of dollars. We had built one of the world's largest etailers. Yet today all that meant nothing to those who were in control. What were they thinking?

The board, thoroughly weary and totally disgusted, was called back into session telephonically. They were told Chicken Little was on the rampage—again. It was after dinner on December 6th, around eight o'clock. The purpose: stop Winn and Scatena from selling Value America.

Craig, Rex, and Mick participated from a speakerphone in Winn's home. The new chairman called the meeting to order. He, Tarpin, White, Caise, Roche, Flowers, Smith, and Durn were on the line. So was Biff Pusey, along with the new CEO and her new legal counsel, Caise, Perkins. Craig and Rex asked the deposed company counsel, Wilmer, Cutler & Pickering to attend as well, to represent shareholder interests. You could almost hear someone cry, "Let's get ready to rumble!"

Mr. Schmitt, in his most condescending voice, said, "We have called this special meeting to hear proposals by Mr. Winn and Mr. Scatena regarding their engagement of an investment banker to sell their shares of the company." He introduced Caise's henchman, who went on for a goodly time explaining the fiduciary duties of directors in acting in the best interest of the company (which he took to mean them) and the company's shareholders (which he took to mean everybody except the two guys who owned most of them).

The fact that no board member bothered to ask why we had changed SEC counsel, a fact now plainly obvious, did not bode well. That meant they were either oblivious and didn't care about a major legal development in the midst of a clearly litigious situation—not likely—or they had all been briefed via back channels. If so, the outcome was predetermined, just as Craig and Rex suspected had occurred at the coronation.

In a tone more taunting than professional, Wolf invited the founders to present their views. Rex and Craig now knew the jury had been tampered with, the outcome rigged. But they pressed on as hope's light dimmed. They took turns presenting their strategy. They outlined the reasons that the company, its employees, brand partners, and shareholders would fare better if a controlling interest were sold to a firm that already had customers, one that could halt the advertising burn. They shared how an acquiring company could capitalize on Value America's commerce engine, supply partnerships, and demand-alliance relationships.

Craig and Rex expressed their concerns about the company's prospects under its current management structure. Craig said, "A part-time chairman, overseeing an inexperienced CEO in light of the company's cash burn and current capitalization, is a recipe for disaster." Together they explained how the company's biggest problem, its gargantuan sales and advertising expense, could be eliminated following an acquisition by the right company.

They told the assembled that they had not yet signed an engagement letter and that they had only offered their own shares, not anyone else's—although, they said, "If any of you, or any other shareholder, would like to join us at any time, you're welcome. We'll bear the burden of the process. You can enjoy the benefit."

Some bickering followed as Craig told the board that the airing of dirty laundry in the press was intolerable, especially mischaracterizations. Then he added, "The demand alliances we've cultivated are of great value to an acquiring company. If Rex and I are disparaged, these relationships will all dissolve, as will shareholder value."

Wolf demeaned these concerns. "He's on a witch hunt. Glenda and I have met with Rex and Craig often," he lied. "We have sought and received their input. The *Industry Standard* article does not reflect management's position on Mr. Winn's role in the company." *Yeah, right.*

Don Tarpin quickly voiced his support for Wolf's assessment. It was as if it had been scripted.

Fred Smith was next, "I'm concerned about the pattern we're developing here. Just two weeks ago we resolved the matter of management structure, and we're already debating it again. We must give the new management team time to produce a business plan. Craig, you're my friend, but you need to settle down."

Now Glenda, as she had done a year ago, stepped in and gave the board an earful. It sounded so reasoned, so professional. She used all the right words: planning, process, objectives, examination, profitability, focus, and stabilization. They ate it up. No surprise: boards almost always support management, and the founders had been out of management for a very long time.

Craig, realizing he was fighting a losing battle, thought full disclosure would be good for the soul. He told the board that Wolf was a fraud, a charlatan. Although he did not use these specific words, the board was put on notice: the company's two largest shareholders had no confidence whatsoever in the competence or character of their new chairman.

Sensing the reprieve she was getting at Schmitt's expense, Dorchak threw Craig a bone. She said, "It is my understanding that the board has directed me to keep Mr. Winn engaged in the demand alliance process throughout 2000." *Swell,* Craig thought. *What could be more fun? Negotiating good deals for evil people.*

With the positioning games over, it was now time for the main event. Wolf, angered by Winn's assessment of his character and ability, or lack thereof, naturally tried to steer the discussion away from himself and the evaluation of his fitness for duty. The more the board knew, the worse shape he would find himself in. "This board must resolve whether or not the company should put itself up for sale, as Mr. Winn and Mr. Scatena have proposed." This was a battle Wolf was prepared to win.

Craig began, "Rex and I have Gordon Conover, Managing Director of Robertson Stephens, standing by. He is prepared to make a presentation to this board tonight regarding the feasibility and appropriateness of a sale or merger."

"I don't wish to hear from them," someone said.

Another chimed in, "It's premature. We don't even know if we have any interest in a sale yet."

"Well, *we* do," Rex responded, "and we own fifty percent of the outstanding shares." The board couldn't be bothered with such trivia.

It was time for Justin's hired gun. "Companies typically appoint a Special Committee to examine strategic options. This committee should be comprised of independent directors who are not officers of the company." That tidbit wasn't worth what we'd paid for it, considering there were none. He went on to say, "Mr. Winn, I advise you to get counsel from your own legal advisors about your role on such a committee, as a director, the most significant shareholder, and leader of the initiative."

When a lawyer tells you to "get your own legal advice," two things are happening. The attorney making the recommendation is indicating that he is against, not for, the person to whom he is offering this advice. And second, he is in the process of evaluating the legal strategies he might deploy to thwart the plans of his new opponent. Such was the case here. The King was dead. Long live the Queen.

Craig and Rex had already done as much. They had sought the legal advice of the most highly respected SEC law firm in the mid-Atlantic states, Wilmer, Cutler & Pickering (having just been fired, they were available). It is not wise for clients to discuss matters they have reviewed with their lawyers; some courts had ruled that in so doing they have waived their privilege of confidentiality. Suffice it to say, however, that no one could come up with a scenario in which the interests of Craig and Rex were divergent from other shareholders.

Craig jumped back into the fray. "I believe this process should be led by the board member with the most comprehensive understanding of the company, the person who knows the most about how our firm would benefit an acquiring entity, the person whose interests are most closely aligned with fellow shareholders." *Gee, I wonder who that might be?*

For a moment, hope's faint light flickered brightly. The founders' spirits rose. The board started discussing the composition of the Special Committee. They discussed how the bankers should work with the committee, the company, and the board. They discussed issues regarding access to management and confidentiality. It was decided that the committee should be composed of two or three directors in addition to Winn and Scatena. Board members suggested listening to presentations from several investment banking firms in addition to Robertson Stephens.

Victory was within their grasp. This was familiar territory. Selling the company, especially presenting the benefits of Value America's solution to other companies, was what Craig and Rex did best. In this arena, they had always been victorious. Everyone was going to win after all—their fellow shareholders, their dedicated employees, their brand partners, the alliance organizations too—*everyone*. They were going to sell Value America for twenty dollars a share.

Craig spoke, "I move that Tarpin, Winn, Smith, and Scatena serve on the Special Committee, with Mr. Tarpin acting as chair."

Scatena seconded the motion.

Mr. Schmitt killed it. Selling the company was not in his interest. He was not a shareholder. Neither was his co-conspirator, Dorchak. She had already sold her few vested shares. It was in *their* interest to maintain control. The Golden Goose was *theirs*, not the shareholders, certainly not Winn's and Scatena's.

A voice asked, "Wolf, would you consider serving on the Committee?"

"No," Schmitt responded. "I wouldn't feel comfortable serving. The company is too fragile and unfocused. It's a house of cards! In my opinion, it wouldn't survive due diligence."

A house of cards that wouldn't survive due diligence. Stunning. Perhaps he was just confused, disoriented. Might he have been hallucinating? Was he harkening back to his final days at Rubbermaid, when he had been accused of turning that once proud company into a pile of rubble?

Value America had successfully endured two consecutive *years* of due diligence. From March through September of '97, it was the Venture Capitalists. In October, November, and December, the company had been examined so closely by the unions, on behalf of their pension funds, we had had to hire Mr. Due Diligence himself, Dean Johnson. Then it was the first IPO. Starting in January '98, Volpe Brown, Robertson Stephens, underwriter's counsel, company counsel, Price Waterhouse, and then PricewaterhouseCoopers had overturned every stone, examined every haystack, and probed every orifice. During March, April, and May, the IPO due diligence was augmented by the studious investigation of the world's foremost technologist, Paul Allen, and his team of techno-wizards. The due diligence for the first IPO carried on right through September, at which time the company was investigated by the "loan-shark" lenders, the techno-legions from Federal Express, Compaq, Paul Allen a second time, and ULIC a third time. Then, for good measure, it was time for a second round of DD from the IPO team of Robertson Stephens, Volpe Brown, underwriters counsel, company counsel, and PricewaterhouseCoopers, all leading up to the second IPO in April of '99. "A house of cards that wouldn't survive due diligence!" What were these people thinking? What were these people *drinking*?

Craig and Rex were horrified. Sure, the management team of Morgan, Dorchak, Peters, Chambers, and Starnes had been destructive. But even *they* couldn't have destroyed this once-strong, vital company *this* quickly.

What's even more amazing is that no one, not a single solitary soul on this "board to end all boards," questioned the absurdity of Wolf's incendiary allegation. Yet these were the same folks that got caught up in their underwear over Craig's innocuous statement that he was a builder, not a manager. *A house of cards.*

Sensing victory, Wolf deployed the same strategy that had nearly worked for Morgan. "I am considering resigning as chairman and as a director." *Okay. Let me open the door for you. Have a nice life. Goodbye.*

"Smith here. I would be extraordinarily disappointed if you resigned, Wolf. If you were to resign, I would consider resigning myself."

"So would I," a different voice chimed in.

"As would I," said another.

Smith carried on. "The rapidity of management restructuring issues coming before this board is a real problem. It's essential that a business plan for 2000 be completed and presented before we entertain any more changes. Wolf, will you continue to serve at least until that date?"

"Yes, Fred, so long as Winn's and Scatena's plans to sell the company are tabled," he said, amid favorable murmurings.

It was over. Plan E was sneakers up, just like A through D before it. Self-interest had once again prevailed over the greater good. Hope's candle no longer flickered. It had been blown out by the sultry winds of deceit. Worse, if Craig and Rex sold their shares now, they'd be faced with a full-on board meltdown. The shareholders were screwed.

"Our next scheduled meeting isn't until February," Wolf said. "I propose something earlier. How about December 20th, in Washington."

"Will you be prepared to present a year-2000 plan?" Durn inquired.

"Yes," Dorchak and Schmidt answered in unison.

"Then there's no need for a Special Committee," Caise concluded.

"There's no need to review proposals from Robertson Stephens or any other investment bankers either," said another.

"Mr. Winn, Mr. Scatena," another hammered. "That's only two weeks from now. We want you to refrain from authorizing an investment banker to sell your shares as a block between now and then."

Craig chose each word carefully, as if he were under oath, "Neither I nor Mr. Scatena will sign a letter of engagement with an investment banker to sell our shares as a controlling block between now and December 20. We believe, however, that this delay is counter to the interests of *all* shareholders. There is no plan this management team can prepare that will extricate this company from its wasteful advertising before it runs out of money. Asking them to form a new plan is therefore unwise. Their energies must be focused on systems and customer care, or the company will suffer irreparable harm."

"It sounds to me like you're accusing this board of acting counter to shareholder interests, breaching our fiduciary duty," Rafe Durn responded angrily. "If that is your intent, it is a very serious allegation."

"I don't believe you have *knowingly* acted counter to shareholder interests. But that's precisely whose interests have been injured as a result of your decisions here tonight."

At 10:05 PM the meeting was adjourned.

Slumped in their chairs, the founders simply stared at each other. After what seemed like an eternity, Rex spoke. "We need to hire the best damn lawyers in the country. These guys are going to take the company down, and us with 'em."

Stunned, Craig haltingly choked out the words, "It's—it's hard to imagine anything deteriorating so rapidly. You'd think our words were poison. We need to resign. We've done all we can do."

"Yes," Rex replied. "But before we do, let's get a great lawyer."

With that, they said good night, turned out the lights, and were enveloped in darkness.

∽•∾

BRIGHT AND EARLY, Craig and Rex made their way to Building E. If there were a house of cards, the deck was being shuffled in Technology. The founders invested six hours among the techs, taking twelve pages of detailed notes. They questioned everybody they could, from leaders like Joe, Thor, Dan, and Phil, to the doers, guys like my son CL in Testing.

"The problem's simple," the techs said. "The conversion was overburdened. We'd have been fine if they'd stayed with the original plan. We pulled off the UNIX and Oracle conversions on time and on budget. But then, while Thor Anders was away on vacation," they charged, "management gummed up the works: Seibel was added without his knowledge or support. Then Ms. D decided she didn't like her reports and threw ePiphany into the mix." It wasn't her money. Besides, a little chaos does wonders for a well-orchestrated *coup*.

The camel, though, continued to limp, so Cliff Chambers, not to be outdone, added an all new EDI solution. *The camel's still quivering,* they must have thought. *What else can we load on? Yes, I know. Why don't we rewrite all the sales and customer care applications, so we can fire our people and outsource the task to Convergys. At triple the cost, it's the epitome of professional management. And the fact that Winn hates the idea makes it even better.*

That was the last straw. The camel crumbled under the load, half dead.

"Okay, forget how it happened," Craig said. "How can we extricate ourselves from this predicament? How long is it going to take?"

"We're good with SAP," Thor answered.

"It came up without a major hitch. It's big and bulky, and hard to work with, like you warned us, but at least it's running," Joe interrupted. "Seibel is getting better, but we've got quite a way to go, especially because nobody knows how to use it yet. That's a problem in the middle of the Christmas selling season, you know."

Then Thor. "ePiphany is a black hole too. It's optimized on NT and SQL Server, so we'll have to undo a lot of what we've accomplished just to get it to work with our new RISC systems and Oracle applications."

"Dumb move," Joe shook his head.

"We're not real sure about the new EDI ap either," Phil added. "It's getting good transactional data, but we don't know what's happening from there. With Glenda's lame decision to use ePiphany instead of SAP reports, it's hard to tell what's what."

Craig sighed. "Best guess, fellas. When is it all gonna work?"

"We're functional now," Thor answered. "We're solving problems quickly, at least the ones we're told about. If we could get better feedback, I'd say we'd be in okay shape by the end of the week, and in fine shape a couple of weeks from now."

"What do you mean, 'Get better feedback?'" Rex asked. "Testing?"

"No. I mean we haven't seen anybody in senior management in weeks. You guys, but you're not really part of management," Thor answered.

Craig spoke slowly as he asked, "You mean we are the only non-tech types you've seen over here? Glenda and Wolf are blaming technology for all their woes, and they haven't even *been* here?"

"That's right," Thor, Phil, and Joe answered in unison. Then they asked, "Who's Wolf?"

An interesting email came out of the founders' walk through tech. My son, CL, wrote to Craig, "What happened to the company I joined back in the Attic? We had fun then—we got things done. Ever since the IBMers descended on us, everything's changed. Those in power are giving me a hard time just for talking to you. Imagine that. I remember a time any of us could talk to you anytime we wanted. Your door was always open. Now it's a criminal offense. What's become of us?"

❧❧❧

CRUISING IN THE fast lane, Craig and Rex were on Interstate 66 heading eastbound toward Washington and meetings with their new lawyers. They evaluated every possible scenario—agonizing over their beleaguered list of dwindling options. Their stomachs were in knots. Their heads were spinning. Then suddenly, as if in sympathy with their plight, their car sputtered, choked, and rolled to an ignominious stop. They were out of gas. Literally.

Immobilized, they watched the world speed by. No one was willing to give up a moment's time to assist a pair of stranded strangers. Finally, a Hispanic lady stopped to help our founders fetch a gallon of gas. Ironically, she too was out of work. As they parted, Craig tried repeatedly to give her a hundred dollars for her trouble, but she refused. A true saint, she knew something the rest of us would do well to learn.

Now late and frustrated with themselves, Craig and Rex continued on. They met with their lawyers and finally headed for home. The trip back was symbolic of just how far they'd fallen. Dazed, they ran out of gas again as they left the District. They had forgotten to refuel.

It hit them both at that moment. They cared so much about their company, its employees, and the relationships they'd built, trying to save it had nearly done them in. They were no longer able to function, no longer able to deal with life's simplest challenges. The firm's despicable managers—both past and present—their confrontational, hallucinating board, the wanton destruction of their business coupled with their inability to do anything about it, had finally brought them to their knees. The dragons had won. Craig and Rex coasted into a service station, exhausted, agitated, and once again completely out of gas.

"Rex, my friend," a weary Winn told his buddy, "It's time we admit defeat. I'm done. I'm going to resign."

"They won. We lost," Rex agreed. "Truth be known, we all lost. We'll resign at the next board meeting. It's only a week away."

"Okay, but let's finish the *Strategic Partnering Paper* and the explanation for the *Path to Profitability* we promised to give Robbie Stephens. That way, they'll understand our business and know what needs to be done."

"Can't hurt. The board can't scream at a letter. I reckon they have a duty to read what we send them. They might find it sobering. After all, when we left management and formed this board, we were growing. We had nearly two hundred million in the bank, and were worth three billion. You'd think they'd want to know how that happened."

"At least we'll know we gave it our best shot."

With that, they finished their "sell-it-now" *Strategic Partnering Paper*. They detailed the possibilities of e-commerce in their *Path to Profitability*. They sent copies of both to every board member, in advance of the Washington showdown. Considering they were written by a couple of guys that no longer realized cars needed fuel, the two documents seem pretty lucid.

To: Value America's Board of Directors
Re: Strategic Partnering Paper   Date: December 16, 1999

While our *Path to Profitability* demonstrates that it is possible to prevail as an independent advertising-centric e-tailer, we think the potential benefit to our shareholders is outweighed by the risk. In light of the company's current stock price, its current and projected financial performance, and its current cash position, we firmly believe that it is in the interests of our shareholders to find a strategic partner for the company.

Gentlemen, by crafting this position paper we are not prejudging management's year 2000 plan. We simply recognize our current and historic reality. Last quarter we lost 55 cents on every dollar we sold.... Sales and marketing represents 75% of our operating expenses. No plan, however well conceived or presented, changes this reality....

We strongly favor selling the firm because many, if not most, of our challenges are mitigated with a partner. In fact, some of our challenges become assets with the right partner. If the acquiring corporation is already a significant advertiser, if they have an established customer list, or a large Web presence, our advertising expense can be quickly and substantially diminished. With advertising diminished there is no need for additional capital…. Management's 2000 plan…will have little bearing on our value to an acquiring company that would replace our advertising with theirs, and our customer acquisition with their customers.

The debate between us focusing on our advertising-centric e-tailing model and our proposed infrastructure-enabling solution becomes unimportant. The fact that we can do both with our existing systems just makes us more valuable. The right partner, like AOL, Microsoft, or AT&T, could use our existing infrastructure to create a specialty retail marketplace, a brand direct marketplace, and still feature our store in its present form but without the burden of our inefficient advertising…. Without the distractions of public life, our entire team could focus on completing our system conversion, delivering on our corporate promise of serving brands, and delivering value to the consumer.

E-tailing is not as favored by the investment community as it once was. The rules for valuation have changed since our IPO. While we have performed better than we promised, valuations based solely upon revenue gains are no longer a reality… Additionally, too few analysts and portfolio managers understand retail, distribution, inventory management, or advertising productivity. This makes the task of prevailing as an independent e-tailer far more difficult….

E-tail success requires management to adopt a plan that implements sweeping changes in demand generation…. Yet no stand-alone plan that diminishes losses by improving advertising efficiency meaningfully influences our value to a strategic partner with existing advertising, web traffic, or customer base….

Any new plan, no matter how well executed, will still require recapitalization in the range of $50 to $100 million. The dilution will be extreme. The closer we get to needing money, the more costly it is likely to be. If the market turns south, it could be impossible to obtain. Recognizing it could be a year or more before our valuation reflects a changed operating strategy, who is going to give us $50 to $100 million to continue on as an advertising-dependent e-tailer with our high losses, high advertising cost, and low margins?

Today e-services firms are highly valued, and we are in a position to capitalize. We have created a remarkable set of e-commerce infrastructure tools: the most flexible, scalable, reliable, and efficient business-to-consumer solution. We have created and built a proprietary front end and enterprise caliber back end with a pragmatic understanding of retail, distribution, and brand strategy….

Our unique ability to create custom marketplaces has tremendous value. Our ability to tie the telephone, television, mailbox and online experience together to be a more inclusive solution places us at the cutting edge. Our credit card capabilities, instant credit ability, and fraud detection solutions are best of class.

We have been able to successfully ramp revenues through our proprietary e-commerce engine at *quarterly* growth rates of $2 million, $5 million, $15 million, $19 million, $36 million, and most recently $57 million in Q3. This clearly demonstrates the system's scalability and functionality.

Value America's unique ability to present brands, specialty retailers, or credit card issuers in unique custom marketplaces makes our infrastructure very valuable. As an infrastructure company our demand generation becomes the burden of the strategic partner. There is no advertising expense. The company simply earns a fee on gross revenue. As a result, we become a Business-to-Consumer and Business-to-Business version of Ebay.

While the company has many of the attributes of an infrastructure company today, the ability to reposition the firm as such, independent of a strategic partner, is difficult.... Value America's existing systems, however, in their present form, enable this incredibly valuable and desirable capability.... In the hands of AOL or Microsoft this capability is far more valuable than our current valuation... making the company easier to sell.

Understanding, selling, building, and enabling the kind of strategic partnerships needed to capitalize on this strategy requires vision, leadership, salesmanship, retail and brand experience, and entrepreneurial skill. Doing this while simultaneously managing our core e-tail business away from its huge advertising-induced losses to profitability is unlikely....

We realize that our infrastructure capability is imperfect. But our solution is ten-fold superior to that which existed during the two years of due diligence we underwent preceding our private equity rounds and our IPO. We passed intense legal, audit, and operational scrutiny with substantially inferior systems...

We are aware that customer service is currently our most formidable challenge. The addition of Siebel to our SAP conversion was challenging in the midst of Q4. Siebel came up far less than optimized. We struggled to process returns and credits. The new system initially performed more slowly, and our customer care staff was less familiar with its operation. Technology, Operations, and Customer Care believe we have made progress in resolving these issues over the past five weeks. While we are not yet optimized on these tools they are superior in their present form to the solution we deployed preceding our IPO. Sixty days following our mid-November conversion, we will be a magnitude better again.

Strategic partnering, becoming part of a large company, is the best path to enhancing shareholder value. This course ensures the longevity of the company and supports the interests of our employees... Most importantly, it generates increased shareholder value with greater certainty, and it does so more swiftly.

The board has asked us not to sign an agreement with an investment banking firm to sell our shares prior to the December 20th presentation of management's

2000 plan. We have honored that commitment. We are, however, concerned that the majority of senior management's time has been devoted to forming a plan rather than to enhancing customer care during this critical time....

It is our hope that the board, after reviewing our position paper, will render the same conclusion as us, the company's largest shareholders. We believe that the company must be sold and we encourage the board to approve the formation of a Special Committee to capitalize on this opportunity.

Like I said, not bad for a couple of guys so dazed they ran out of gas twice in the same evening. Their arguments in favor of selling the company were compelling. The fact that they were ignored is downright amazing.

Their *Path to Profitability* was equally thoughtful. It was a treatise on e-commerce, circa late 1999, Value America style. It served several functions. First, it showed that Winn and Scatena had a firm grasp on reality, something the board had come to doubt. Second, it revealed that the original business model was sound. Third, it demonstrated that there was little chance current management could save the company. Fourth, it would leave the board with no excuses; they would never be able to claim they didn't understand the business or know that what they were doing was inconsistent with our mission. Today these documents show what could have been, what *should* have been:

To: Value America's Board of Directors
Re: Path to Profitability   Date: December 16, 1999

The principal question facing Value America, and indeed all e-tailers, is can we operate profitably? I believe with great management and great leadership the answer is yes. But achieving profitability is dependent upon meeting three requirements and establishing the right strategic alliances.

The first requirement for achieving profitability in e-tail is diminishing the cost of inventory and distribution. Value America's model is the natural extension of what Sam Walton initiated with WalMart three decades ago. Walton turned the retail world upside down by making his customers buyers and by making his buyers merchandisers. He created the technology to place orders directly to manufacturers by week, by store, based upon customer purchases.

WalMart's merchandisers were merely responsible for building a relationship with the right brands, putting a small representation of their products, properly priced, on the shelves, and working to assure each manufacturer could ship each store's order reliably and swiftly. Value America has taken this strategy to its natural conclusion. Our *customers* are our buyers, but rather than gathering orders by store by week, we order goods by customer, by moment. Our merchandisers perform in identical fashion to WalMart's. They form relationships with brands, select products, price them, and work with brands to promote their products cooperatively and assure rapid and reliable shipment.... Ironically, the very requirements placed upon leading consumer products brands by WalMart helped enable Value America's business model....

For us or any e-tailer to achieve profitability, we must replace inventory with systems, and distribution with technology. The continued enhancement of our inventory-free distribution model is central to our path to profitability, and gives leading brands a direct and efficient relationship with the consumer....

The best managers of inventory typically buy, manage, and store goods at 10% to 12% of revenue. To perform at this level, they must have superior systems, sell a narrow or focused range of products to a broad customer base, have excellent forecasting tools, and long operating histories. E-tailing margins are likely to evolve to less than 20%. This means there is not enough gross margin to cover sales, advertising, operations, and inventory—profitably.

The second requirement for Value America, or any e-tailer, to profit is that demand must be generated more efficiently. Sam Walton recognized this challenge when he started WalMart. He deployed the MacArthur strategy of attacking where the enemy was weak. He put his stores, his "demand generation centers," in small town America, away from his largest competitors. He was able to promote and drive revenue where his competitors were weak. WalMart prospered, developed scale, and ultimately became an irresistible force.

Value America recognized the need to generate revenue away from the standard operating procedures of its online rivals. At the time of our advertised launch, e-tailers were focused on buying anchor and tenant positions and banner ads with the large portals. Our concept for generating demand where our competitors were not was radical for its time. The e-tailers in existence at the time of inception were ISN (Internet Shopping Network, which later became Outpost), Amazon, OnSale, and CUC (which later became Cendant, and then NetMarket). The portals were, and continue to be, AOL, Yahoo, Excite, and Lycos. The former paid the latter many tens of millions of dollars.

At the time of our launch in February, 1998, advertising for an online store in newspapers was quite uncommon.... It was our belief that we could drive revenue and build our brand name more efficiently in this manner. The events of the last two years have proven our strategy to be wise, particularly when compared to the online alternative. We have developed a brand name, sold product more efficiently, and have grown more swiftly than our competitors. We created an advertising style that is innovative and memorable.

However, the ongoing prospects of this strategy are dismal. Stunning amounts of venture capital have been given to e-tailers with the express direction to create excitement and brand awareness, which in a world devoid of profit has been linked to market capitalization.... Today, dot-coms represent the "advertising agency full employment act." As a result, the cost of breaking through and selling product using broad-based offline advertising is crippling.

Today, we believe we have gone at least two quarters too long relying on broad-based advertising to generate revenue. As a result, we no longer have the time to test, or the luxury of a gradual transition.

Mature retailers typically spend from 1% to 5% of their revenue in advertising.... Therefore, the retailers Value America competes against are driving revenue at between 20 and 100 times their promotional investment compared to our 2 times. This is particularly painful when one recognizes that over 60% of e-tail sales are from traditional retailers—bricks and clicks.

Traditional retailers use catalogs to generate revenue. Best Buy, for example, distributes more than 35 million product catalogs each week by inserting them in leading newspapers. WalMart, K-Mart, Target, Home Depot and Office Depot do the same. Nordstrom's, The Gap, and REI also create catalogs but mail them to current or prospective customers.... No retailer has ever successfully sold consumer goods, especially non-computer goods, efficiently using broad-based advertising. It is no surprise our sales are generated so inefficiently and that we are so PC-centric.

Catalogs are the principal revenue generation tool in all three of our business segments. Dell, Gateway, CDW, and others in the PC business are catalog dependent. So are office supply leaders, Corporate Express, Boise Cascade, and United Stationers. Catalogers, the retail forum most similar to Value America, are obviously dependent upon their catalogs to generate demand....

The worst possible performance of a catalog is superior to what we are currently achieving. Unfortunately, the people most responsible for creating our only catalog...have been isolated by management and by this board.

The third requirement for Value America, or any e-tailer, to achieve profitability is aligned with the first two. Brands must choose to participate in our demand generation and order fulfillment. Most mature retailers cover most, or all, of their advertising costs by partnering with brands....

To achieve this...we must rely upon catalogs, where brands are accustomed to investing their cooperative advertising funds. They understand the cost per contact in the direct response world. They understand them because catalogs are the most prevalent and productive medium of their largest customers.

Without these cooperative advertising dollars there is no way for Value America, or any e-tailer, to profit. The cost of generating demand will exceed operating margins.... This is why I created the *Path to Profitability*. Its initial version was drafted back in Q2. At the time I encouraged management to move a significant portion of its demand generation to direct-response catalogs in Q3 and move a substantial portion in Q4. The initial version of the *Path to Profitability* was distributed to senior managers seven months ago.... I asked our former CEO and our President to use it as the basis for developing a year-2000 plan back in July. During that time it was mailed to every Board member. It was later used as a means to demonstrate to Citibank's senior financial team that an e-commerce company could become profitable in a method they understood, direct response.... While this plan is achievable, the leadership necessary to accomplish it, in time, is extraordinary. This is why we have drafted this analysis....

The ultimate challenge in moving to direct response demand generation is getting the names and addresses of interested people with money. This is why we worked so hard to form Demand Alliances.... We created partnerships with companies like Citibank, FedEx, Visa, American Heart Association, U.S. Wired, Falwell Ministries, KFS (iBelong, the AFL/CIO) and others. In so doing, we were given access to extremely high-quality customer lists. Citibank estimates our CitiPrivileges program will produce over $330 million in revenue in 2000. I have included their estimate. To be a patron of a charity or the holder of a platinum credit card, one must have money. Better yet, we know what they are interested in buying. Financial institutions, particularly credit card companies, are expert at direct response marketing and know how to generate acceptance via targeted mailings. They have credibility and are trusted by their customers, so we benefit from a quality introduction. Therefore, Value America, through associations, charities, financial institutions, and logistics companies, has acquired the second element in shifting demand generation: a quality list of prospective customers. Yet maintaining and capitalizing upon these partnerships is going to be very challenging, for we are relatively small and they are large....

The motivations, flexibility, and normalized operating procedures of brands with regard to their market development and cooperative advertising budgets are complex. So are the methods that should be employed to motivate brand partners. However, in our initial attempt with the Q4 catalogs, we generated 90% co-op against the cost of production and mailing. We can prevail at this requirement only if we are properly focused, managed, and led, if our brand partners are motivated, and if our demand alliance partners are fully engaged....

The *Path to Profitability* and the *Strategic Partnering Paper* were signed, sealed, and delivered. They were not, however, *read*. Most board members ignored them, as unbelievable as that might seem. In fact, few things are as unbelievable as Value America's final board meeting of the millennium.

The time was 7:30 AM, December 20, 1999. The place was the mezzanine conference room of the Westfield's Marriott. The stock that day would open at $9.43. It would close at $8.13. The meeting wouldn't go any better.

In fact, in the twenty-seven days following the coronation of the Wolf and the Witch, our stock lost half its value. The board failed to see the correlation. Maybe they didn't read newspapers either.

Craig and Rex drove up from Charlottesville (this time with a full tank of gas). Most board members had flown in the night before. The day's events began with a Compensation Committee meeting. Justin Caise was the chairman of the committee, but he wasn't there. A family matter had arisen, and he'd rightly decided to perform his duties from home, by phone. The long walk to the committee room provided the first hint of trouble. Wolf Schmitt and Gerry Roche were seen kibitzing as if they were old friends, close confidants. It sent a shudder down Winn's spine.

Was there a connection? Roche's board position had been a derivative of his relationship with Godfrey, as had White's. Wolf had reentered Winn's life at the CEO Roundtable in May, where a high percentage of the guests had been Godfrey's invitees. If Schmitt fit into that group, if he'd joined the Brethren, his complicity in the bungled *coup* and his childish we'll-make-you-pay-for-what-you've-done behavior made sense. Roche and Schmitt laughed and tugged at each other like a pair of silly schoolboys as Craig watched in horror, sensing that the fate of his company had been predetermined. It was apparent they had it backwards again—the jury deliberations had preceded the trial. The verdict had already been rendered.

✂••✂

CRAIG AND REX had fought the right battle for the right reasons, but in the wrong place. Their strategy in times of crisis had always been to put out the fire, determine what had happened, rally the crew, chart a new course based on what they'd learned, and then report to the authorities. This *modus operandi* had served them well. But Tom's Team and Glenda's Gang deployed a different scheme. They *set* the ship afire, abandoned the sailors, and falsely blamed the fire on the people who built the ship. Then they threw the cargo overboard and called in the architects to design a fancy new vessel while the old one burned.

Sadly, the founders found themselves battling the board, not the problems "fueling the fire." It was during this time that the firm's best and brightest made repeated pilgrimages to Craig's home, asking the obvious, "Why was the Wicked Witch empowered? Don't they know she's evil? Can't they tell Wolf is a fraud? Why have they done this to us? What can we do to save our company?" Good questions all, and all too late.

"Call the board," was Craig's only response. "Those who undermined what we've built did so there. Bad things happen when good people don't stand up," he admonished.

As a result, about a dozen Valuable Americans called an *ad hoc* meeting, congregating at Cliff Chambers' home. Cliff's neighbors, coincidentally, included both Glenda Dorchak and Byron Peters. Glenda was hosting a party that night; when Peters arrived for the affair, he recognized the cars at Cliff's house and joined them—providing the wet blanket. "I would advise all of you against calling board members."

Most were afraid; their families depended on the wages they brought home. As a result, they heeded Peters' admonition. Joe Page did not; he just wasn't built that way. He called Fred Smith at home. Page, unlike Morgan's cronies earlier, had earned the right to call. Joe had been there from the beginning. He not only knew the truth, he was also responsible for building the technology that ran the store. The Brethren had done nothing except abet the ensuing calamity. They left their fingerprints on the murder weapon but little other evidence that they'd ever been here.

Uncharacteristically, Fred responded harshly. Maybe Joe interrupted him at the wrong time. Perhaps he had just grown weary of the whole sorry mess. Whatever the reason, "Fred wasn't pleased that I called him," Joe would report.

❧

THE THREE MADE their way down the last corridor, entering the suite that had been configured for Compensation Committee. But Justin Caise wasn't on the line. Schmitt wasn't a member of the committee, so he couldn't vote. With only Roche and Winn present, his plans would be thwarted, victims of deadlocked votes. He was panicky. But his fears were eased as Justin's voice finally announced his presence.

Craig already knew what he was up against. As a member of the committee, a package had been delivered to his home the night before. It said that his and Rex's salaries had been diminished to $0. That had annoyed Rex, but it didn't bother Craig—he had come to resign. It merely confirmed management's lack of character. What bothered him was the huge compensation package being proposed for Dorchak's new Human Relations Director—a cool $290,000. He was troubled by Dorchak's proposed package too. It weighed in at a hefty $525,000. Mr. Schmitt's comp of $200,000 and his equally gargantuan grant of 300,000 options also seemed a bit much for somebody donating only a day or two a month to the cause. Every vote that morning was two to one. Big surprise. The meeting ended forty minutes late. It seems not all Germans can make the trains run on time.

As they made their way up the stairs, Craig, now with Rex, bumped into Rafe Durn and his new partner, Don Tarpin. One last time, Craig pleaded with Durn to help him save the company for the sake of his own investments and his investors. His pleas fell on deaf ears. Durn just threw *Time* magazine in Craig's face. Amazon's Jeff Bezos had just been named "Person of the Year." He growled, "This should have been us."

Besides Winn and Scatena, the board attendees were Fred Smith, Gerry Roche, Rafe Durn, Don Tarpin, and Wolf Schmitt. Frank Flowers, Justin Caise, Sam White, and Bill Bennett "attended" telephonically. Glenda Dorchak and her new corporate counselor were invited guests.

The meeting did not begin well. The most routine of all board activities is the approval of minutes from prior meetings. But they were full of errors, glaringly slanted. Craig was the first to say they were a disgrace. Caise concurred, telephonically, asking for them to be rewritten. Craig would later learn, from the woman asked to type them, that their errors were not the result of carelessness, but purposefulness: they were designed to deceive.

Wolf should have been ashamed of himself, but he wasn't. He simply changed the subject. For the sheer pleasure of it all, he announced that Winn and Scatena had been removed as bank signatories. Then, pleased with himself, he grilled Winn on the ninety-day interest-bearing corporate loan that had been made to Liberty University. While all of the documentation for the loan had been handled by the company's CFO at the time, Dean Johnson, and while all of the paperwork was in order, payment was a little late.

Wolf chastised him about the appropriateness of supporting an institution that had been at the core of the company's demand alliances. That played particularly well amongst the board's Democrats. Liberty had been founded by Jerry Falwell. Durn was once Vice Chairman of the Democratic National Committee. But Falwell, as always, was as good as his word; the loan was repaid promptly, with interest—but not before Wolf and his cronies had their fun.

While on the subject of loan repayments, monies due Winn and Scatena for the corporate aircraft came up next. Dorchak squelched the discussion, promising, "I'll make certain they're reimbursed in full. They won't be left a dollar out of pocket." She was lying, of course. She stiffed them. *What the hell—It's only $650,000. They won't miss it.*

Wolf invited the auditors to make a presentation. Telephonically they reviewed the system conversion and another looming problem—cash: there wasn't enough of it left to be what's called "a going concern." Craig had warned the board about the lack of capital in his *Strategic Partnering Paper*. It was why the company needed to stop advertising and find a buyer. Incredibly, they snarled at Craig as the indictments were read against the systems. It was as if they'd been told the conversion had been *his* idea.

Craig told the board that he'd invited the company's most senior technologists to discuss the condition of the firm's systems. "You've heard our chairman say they won't stand up to due diligence. You've heard the auditor's appraisal. This is important. Wouldn't you like to get the story straight from those who actually know what's happening—the technologists themselves? They're here, waiting downstairs to speak with you."

"No," was their collective, adamant answer. So much for fiduciary duty.

Schmitt smiled at his apparent mastery of the board, delivering the most arcane, obscure, self-aggrandizing diatribe ever uttered by one in a position of influence. It was utterly incomprehensible. He spoke of organizational stabilization, strengthening controls, increasing processes, focus, and yes, the implementation of restructuring actions, just as the message boards had so accurately predicted. The board listened politely, giving him his fifteen minutes of glory. Then, in as demeaning a tone as he could muster, the chairman asked the founders to present their plan.

"We," Craig responded, "sent you all a written copy of our proposal." He left unsaid, *We wrote it because we've become accustomed to you attacking our spoken words.* As Craig scanned the room, he could see board members fumbling through the documents, hastily distilling what little they could on the fly. From all appearances, most had never opened the cover. "There is little we can add to what we've written."

"I'd like the floor," Roche said. He began a ten-minute dissertation on his view of the business world, "It's all about the people," he proclaimed. "I don't see anything about the people in your proposal. That's why I'm unable to support it." Obviously, he hadn't read it.

With that, Dorchak took the floor and unfurled her PowerPoint presentation. Her plan: save the company by firing half the people. How ironic.

Her presentation was perfectly suited to what the company itself had become. The new management team of Schmitt, Dorchak, Chambers, Ewert, and Starnes had "studied the facts" and come to the conclusion that *people were the problem.* "Fire half of 'em and we'll be fine. And while we're at it, why not discard eighty percent of our brand partnerships too, constraining sales to the categories with the lowest margins and highest returns. Let's dismantle those awful demand alliances as well. If we get rid of all this dead wood, we'll have enough money to advertise our way into prosperity, and even more to reward ourselves for the effort."

As incredible as it may seem, that was their plan: lay off half the employees, about 300 people, rather than cut advertising. And then say goodbye to most of the brands and alliance partners. Of course, there was no actual basis in fact for any of what Glenda presented. She'd just made it up. She had produced a plan. It looked good on the screen. It was plenty detailed. The board just smiled. They had already decided.

Before Dorchak was through, Fred interrupted. "You know, I can read seven times faster than you can speak. I've read through your proposal, and I must say I'm very impressed with what you have been able to do in such a short time." Then he turned toward Craig (whose plan had evidently proved too much for the speed-reading Smith) and said, "I'm going to support this plan over yours. I, better than perhaps anyone on this board, know how hard it is to develop a mailing list to make a catalog operation go. It takes years. And that's all your plan is—a catalog operation."

Develop a list? Dismayed, Craig replied, "Our plan was to *sell* the company, not *manage* it. We've made that abundantly clear. But while we're on the subject of lists, Fred, you should know we've already earned access to the best mailing lists in the country. They don't *need* to be developed."

The board was utterly unable to grasp the obvious. Craig agonized over the catastrophe their failures would precipitate. They were smug in their belief that Craig and Rex were the problem, but now their own hands were dripping with blood. The company had stumbled, but rather than nurse her back to health, they stabbed her in the back while she was down. Having been seduced, they were now ready to betray the shareholders' trust.

Craig's report said there was no viable plan to save the company. It had to be sold—now. How could such smart men be played for fools? He was awash with emotions: pain, frustration, desperation, disgust. Yet somehow he mustered the composure to say, "Gentlemen, if you'd read our plan, you'd know we aren't recommending the continuation of Value America as it exists, or even as it was once conceived. No. It must be sold before all is lost."

Craig studied the room. No one could look him in the eye. They were impatient, checking their watches with annoying frequency. It was like witnessing the James Gang rob a bank; all they could think about was getting out of Dodge. But Craig wasn't about to let them off that easily. "I'd like to point out the most glaring flaws in management's plan. First, it's based upon a false premise. Every reference to productivity per person is contrived. For example, we *don't* have fifteen people in the jewelry department, as they claimed; there's only *one!*" After similar disclosures for other departments, Craig paused to see if Glenda had the courage to defend her numbers. She didn't. She just sat there silently, as did the board. She knew, as did they, that the outcome had already been decided—privately, behind closed doors, in the smoke-filled rooms. Craig had just called the chairman and CEO liars, and no one cared.

"Second, seventy-five percent of the company's operating losses are devoured by Sales and Advertising. There's been no mention, none whatsoever, of how this plan will change this debilitating reality."

With that, Glenda interrupted. She had an answer. After all, she was an *expert*. "Our plan calls for an increase in advertising productivity to ten-to-one." She never bothered to explain how, of course. She didn't have to. This board meeting was a charade. Why, if she could do it now, hadn't she done it before?

With so much at stake, you'd think they would have overwhelmed her with questions. But no. You could almost hear them thinking, *the less we know, the better.*

"Third, the plan says that five days before Christmas, half the people who built Value America will be laid off. That's just plain wrong! Cut *advertising,* not people!" Craig thought that might get a rise from "it's-all-about-the-people" Roche, but he dipped his head in cowardly silence.

The experience was surreal. *They don't care about the truth. Neither our brands nor alliance partners mean anything to them. They're willing to ignore the opinions of shareholders who own fifty percent of the stock, and they're willing to trash the lives of 300 families without a second thought.*

"I wish to leave you with these thoughts. We live in a small southern town. Harming good people in this way in a place like this will soil the company's reputation beyond repair. Cutting back in an industry that's expanding will make the company a laughingstock. Discarding the brand relationships we've worked so hard to build will destroy much of the company's remaining value. Disbanding our demand alliances is inexcusable. Your failure to curtail management's wasteful advertising spending will be your downfall. But ignoring the largest shareholders' plea to sell the company before it's too late is—is...." Craig searched for the right word, but it didn't come.

The irate chairman asked Winn and Scatena to leave, so the remainder of the board could go into Executive Session.

Craig was still chairman of the Executive Committee. If there was to be an "Executive Session" *he* would have to call it. He and Rex were being told to leave the room by a bunch of ill-informed suits who were under the spell of the self-absorbed, the come-latelies. He snarled at Wolf.

Craig wanted to fight to the last breath to save the company, the jobs, the brand relationships, the alliance partnerships. They deserved no less. But it was a losing battle, and he knew it. The odds were impossible. Still, it's better to die fighting for something you believe in than just *die*.

Rex was more realistic. He knew there were *no* odds. The war had been lost more than a month ago. The continued anguish was as futile as it was valiant. He took Craig's arm and said, "Come, my friend. There's nothing more we can do here."

Dazed, Craig followed his pal downstairs. They found Joe Page, Thor Anders, and Mick Kicklighter and thanked them for coming. Craig apologized for the disruption to their lives and told them they were free to leave. With that, he and Rex walked back upstairs and entered an unused ballroom across the hall from where the remaining board members were conferring. The cavernous room was heavy with silence. There was nothing left to say.

Only a few minutes passed before Fred Smith walked in. He was polite. "The board in Executive Session has decided to support management's plan. Management would like you and Rex to move to a separate office. They will provide a secretary and pay your rent."

Craig spoke. "Fred, that won't be necessary. We came here to resign. We have no interest in staying."

"Alright, but that's your choice."

"We've made our choice, and the board has made theirs," Rex said.

Smith took a deep breath. "Craig, I'm only doing this because I'm your friend. Because of our friendship, I've agreed to head a Special Committee to sell the company. The committee will be comprised of Tarpin, Flowers, I think Durn, and myself. We're going to meet shortly after Christmas, interview investment bankers, and then review our strategic and financial options. I don't know if we'll be able to raise money, or if we'll be able to get this thing sold, but I'll give it my best shot. You know I need this like I need a hole in my head."

"Fred, there is no one we'd rather have sell this company than you. Thank you," Craig offered his hand in support.

The three rose, left the grand room, and walked across the hall.

Motions were made and seconded. Then came the votes. Chairman Wolf said, "All those in favor of accepting management's plan say aye."

"Aye," most of those gathered said in unison.

"All those opposed...."

"Nay," Craig and Rex said defiantly.

"*Naaay?*" queried Smith, as if the word were eight syllables long. "I thought we just worked all this out."

Craig spoke slowly as he looked directly at Smith. "No. We are pleased that a Special Committee has been formed to sell the company. We are pleased you'll be chairing it. We don't, however, support this plan to 'save' the company by cutting it into pieces and throwing them away."

They meet with darkness in the daytime, and grope at noontime as in the night—Eliphaz

CRASH AND BURN

"Well, that was fun," Craig said sarcastically to his traveling companion. He and Rex were in Craig's truck again, headed home to Charlottesville.

"Our friends are going to get nailed," Rex moaned. "You know they'll be the first ones fired. It's going to be a bloodbath. *Damn!* After all the times we brought the company back from the dead."

"That's no comfort to those being laid off."

"We gave it the good fight. We lost the last round."

"How do you lose a company to a pack of strangers?"

"They're so damn arrogant about it." Rex slumped in his seat.

"Oh, yeah. They actually think *we're* the problem. They think the stock's going to go up. They're in denial. Just use the right words and Wall Street will buy this harebrained scheme. Can you believe how many times they told the Witch to use the word 'focus' in her release?"

"Hocus Focus, is more like it," Rex cringed. "What we've got here is a mass hallucination. They finally drank the koolaid, but not until it was laced with cyanide. Thing is, it's going to kill *us* as well as them."

"Well, that's convenient, 'cause we just left our own funeral."

"They ignored the package we sent 'em, sure as hell. None of the issues we raised were even discussed. With so much at stake, they never even bothered to read our plan. *Or hers,* for that matter!"

"Like you said, pal, we were sneakers up a month ago. Our goose was cooked the moment the board elected Dorchak. Right or wrong, boards support management—that's what boards do. From that point on, we were just background noise, an irritant."

"And I thought they existed to protect the shareholders."

Craig sighed. "Is it us, or them?"

"What do you mean?"

"I mean, are *we* wrong? Our corporate types, the board, Wall Street analysts are all saying we're nuts."

"Yeah, maybe, but the people who count know we're right. Thousands of brand and alliance partners have invested in us. Our original team knows better too, as do our customers. We've got a lot of support."

"But, our management and board, wrong as they may be, are in charge now. So let's face it. We've empowered our own executioners.

A few moments of quiet slipped by as the two unemployed dot-com founders turned off US 28 and merged onto the westbound lanes of I-66. Rex broke the silence. "There may be a bright side to all of this."

"Oh, a funeral with a happy ending. This I want to hear."

"I'm serious. You know how all the analysts hammered us because our business model didn't fit theirs?"

"Yeah. Ours made sense."

"Well, this new plan doesn't. So they're gonna love it."

"The plan is so ridiculous, the Street'll actually buy it?"

"Stranger things have happened," Rex mused.

"While I'm not buying your 'It's-stupid-enough-to-be-smart' argument, you're right about one thing. The day wasn't a complete loss. We resigned," Craig said thankfully. "We'll never have to walk into purgatory again." *Purgatory* was what everybody had come to call the executive offices on Rio Road, also known as the "den of thieves."

"We got more out of the meeting than that," Rex noted, still endeavoring to make the rape and plunder of their dream look like a little misunderstanding. "We're free to sell." He shook his head. "Can you believe that little prick actually told us not to sell our shares while 'the Special Committee evaluates its options?'"

"What an a-hole," said Craig, using an uncharacteristic vulgarity. Alas, the founders' vocabulary had deteriorated to match their mood.

Rex replayed the encounter, "Let's see. They abuse us, ignore us, slander us, and dismember the company we built. Then they expect us to love and cherish our..." Rex left the expletive deleted, "shares."

"Makes perfect sense. Most people I know would be *thrilled* to own a company stupid enough to piss off their largest shareholders. Hold on to our shares? What color is the sky on their planet?"

"I must say, you did a nice job clarifying our position when Caise's donkey tried to get us to bend over and capitulate. 'We have no intention whatsoever of restricting our property rights.' Well put."

"Thank you. You hammered him too, right there on the stairs on the way out. You gave that pompous buffoon both barrels: 'I wish to confirm that you understand it is our intention to sell our shares. We waived none of our rights. Make certain the record correctly reflects our position.' Based on the creativity they showed drafting the last set of minutes, who knows what this set will say."

"I don't trust that boy as far as I could throw him. It's guys like that who give lawyers a bad name. We haven't heard the last of him."

"You know, Rex, apart from us, the board is united. They've chosen a plan. It's their plan. There's no way on God's green earth they can blame us if their plan tanks."

"You're right. It's our company, but it's their plan. We're gone. *Hasta la vista*. They're on their own. They've got to make this thing work. It's a big damn deal challenging a firm's largest shareholders, especially when they're the founders. They've drawn a line in the sand. If the company craters now, they're in deep shit." Rex paused, "They're not only risking their reputations, they're *begging* for a humongous class action suit."

"All the stuff we wrote them, pleading with them. Our letters are going to come back to haunt them," Craig said as he glided down the exit ramp and turned south on US 29. They were headed home. "I really hate this," he groused as they waited for the light to turn green. "We're pledged to secrecy. For seven long days we've got to carry this burden. This is going to be a miserable Christmas. Three hundred families are going to get torched by the Witch's broom, and there's not a damn thing we can do to stop it. We can't even warn them."

"Don't get yourself depressed any more than you already are. We don't even know the names of ninety percent of the folks they're gonna lay off. Like I've been telling you, this stopped being our company a long time ago."

"I still feel responsible," Craig moaned, "like there's something more I could have done, should have done differently."

"Yeah. We should have fired that lying blond bitch when we had the chance. But who knew? We should never have hired Morgan, and even after we did, we should have canned him the day we came back from the road show. He was worthless: couldn't talk, couldn't think, couldn't even manage his own damn *coup!* No wonder nobody blames him for anything. How do you blame a guy who never does a damn thing?"

"He's living proof of the adage, 'It's better to remain quiet and seem dumb, than to open your mouth and remove all doubt.'"

"Speaking of dumb, forming an all-outside board wasn't real bright, either, pal."

❧❀❧

WHEN CRAIG REACHED home, he went to his office and opened Dorchak's plan to see if it was really as bad as he'd thought.

VALUE AMERICA PLAN OF RESTRUCTURE

Management's review of the business revealed that the number of product categories served significantly affected the Company's efficiency, headcount [as if they were cattle] and capital requirements. The number of distributors and brands has negatively a67ffected [*sic*—just carelessness] our service.

Management plans to eliminate the following product categories and non-core revenue streams: Suppliers from 450 to 25; Business Alliance Development; Custom Stores; Direct Mail; Marketing Services; Presentation Revenue; Account Sales; Radio, Broadcast, Magazine, and Online Ads."

That pretty much eliminated everything of value. Jettisoning magazine and online ads would have been a good thing, of course, but it didn't occur. The company's brilliant new CEO, unconstrained, promptly signed the $5.5 million Yahoo! deal Craig had thwarted. She even blamed Winn for approving it! Funny thing, though. Reference to the elimination of online ads mysteriously disappeared from the December 28th version of her plan. Perhaps she thought no one would notice.

"Management intends to reduce office space from 14 locations with a total of 77,668 square feet to 8 locations with a total of 32,568 feet." And waste $165,000 canceling the leases. But that was chickenfeed compared to what came next. Thinning the herd was going to cost…

WARN Act—60 days (required)	$1,750,000
One week for each year of completed service	$25,000
Reemployment package	$175,000
Employment Contract breakage penalty	$100,000
Non-compete agreements	$500,000
Total Severance Costs	$2,550,000

$2,550,000 to pay people not to work. *Amazing.* But not nearly as amazing as the revelation that came from Joe Page. His father was no longer Counsel for the UAW; President Clinton had appointed him General Counsel for the National Labor Relations Board. He had co-authored the WARN Act and had lobbied Congress for its passage. He said Value America didn't qualify, for a number of reasons. So much for great legal advice. But heck, Caise, Perkins only charged $375,000.

Funerals were getting expensive. As Craig waded through the plan, he lived a succession of emotions: disappointment, sadness, anger.…

There was a new organizational chart, just in case someone missed an earlier memo and wondered who was in charge. Kari Meyer, the new $290,000 SVP of Human Resources, was already on board. I guess there was no reason to wait for Compensation Committee approval. Imagine *her* first day on the job—*Welcome. You're in charge of human resources; now fire half the humans.*

Tom Starnes was also listed prominently on the new org chart: "T. Starnes, EVP & CMO." That's Chief Marketing Officer, for those without their secret decoder rings. Sounds important, doesn't it?

It must have been amusing watching Starnes, the Kuos, and the other Morgan co-conspirators trying to suck up to Dorchak, whom they openly loathed. Their *coup* hadn't gone exactly as they'd planned.

There were a plethora of new committees. Cliff Chambers headed the "SWAT Team" to monitor order fulfillment and improve reporting. Then there was the "Customer Delight Taskforce." No, I'm not making this stuff up, I swear. They even assigned someone the responsibility of "Process Management." They must have fought over that one.

Team Value America claimed they had *already* shipped $65 million in the fourth quarter, and expected to ship $72 million by the time it was over, twelve days off. Remember those numbers, because before they were through, something mysterious would happen to them. As Craig sat there alone in his office, he could still hear General Glenda M Dorchak's stirring words, "We are focused. We are not admitting defeat. Our team is still trying to achieve our goal of $83 million for the quarter." They were having such fun with numbers. Think they could spell "fraud?"

Flipping the page, Craig read, "Value America has a membership database of 562,113 and customer base of 143,040." These factoids were followed by an asterisk that indicated that the customer data was provided courtesy of an outside consulting group, apparently because they recognized their own reporting was no longer credible. The report went on to say that there were 613 FTEs. That's people. It means "Full-Time Equivalents."

Craig had scribbled some notes in the margin during the meeting. He listed the number of people Glenda had concluded were working in each product category and the amount of revenue they were generating. The numbers were entirely contrived, but they were presented as the very foundation of her reorganization plan. There were sixty-plus pages recounting every last minuscule detail of this elaborate scheme, yet she managed to omit any written record of the very premise upon which her charade was based. Do you think it was a careless oversight?

So as not to throw up on his desk, Craig turned the page. It made him laugh. Good. It said the firm's most glaring weakness was, "Business Processes and Process Management." That was them. They were that. Why were they condemning themselves? That was all they were good at.

He laughed again. Citibank was listed as a "marketing opportunity." *Yeah, right. They won't generate a dime's more revenue from this relationship. They didn't build it, and they're too unethical to deal with such a fine firm.* Besides, it was based on the premise of having a comprehensive store, something they had now destroyed. *Oops.*

Some pretty graphs followed. They were real audience pleasers. They depicted "eKiosks, eCall Centers, eStores within a Store." Then, a couple of pages later, it all came together:

Our new and improved ads are going to generate a 20:1 ROI. We will replace ValueDollar offers with Free Freight, a tested value proposition... A site redesign will increase customers seven fold. We will deliver the new VA value proposition and limited product specials in newspapers with less frequency and with a new style. It will transform our 2.5:1 performance in 1999 to 8:1 in 2000.

So how were they planning to magically enhance their dismal track record four to eight fold? Details, details.

Then Craig saw his dream of a direct-response solution. "Catalogs performing at a ROI of 4:1 by using a small, high-density catalog approach developed thematically around the Consumer Electronics and Business Segments." *What?* Didn't they just say they were incurring huge savings by eliminating direct mail catalogs? Who writes this stuff anyway?

This utter waste of ink and paper ended with a recitation of "Strategy Proof Points" and their "Benefits," (translations provided):

STRATEGY PROOF POINTS:	BENEFITS:
Clear Message	[We're going to bankrupt this company.]
Effective Communication	[Fooled the board, didn't we?]
Focus on Priorities	[Watch us line our pockets.]
Operational Efficiencies	[Let's scrap everything we don't understand.]
Headcount Reductions	[Merry Christmas, cows.]
Demand Generation	[We demand hefty retention packages.]

And famous last words… "The effective communication of this plan can create a short squeeze that will drive significant gains in the stock price."

The stock ended the year at five dollars a share. Even with dot-com math, it's hard to make five look like twice seventeen. Maybe the board goofed.

ฬฬฬ

IT WAS EASILY the worst Christmas Craig can remember. His friends were going to get fired in three days, and he was powerless to stop it.

No longer in the Christmas spirit, Katharine asked her extended family to stay away. The Winn household was no place to be. The news articles were flying with reckless abandon. The story line was always the same: Winn got fired because he managed the company so poorly after the IPO. But now Glenda was riding in to save the day.

Craig wrote one last letter. It was a bazillion-to-one shot, but the board needed to be awakened from their collective trance-like state of denial before they officially ratified their suicide pact.

To: Value America Board Members
Re: Maximizing Shareholder Value   Date: December 27, 1999

Rex Scatena and I voted against the adoption of management's restructuring plan and we elected to resign our employment with the company because we believe the plan will make the sale of the company more difficult, and believe it will diminish the company's value in a merger. We are convinced that the company, its employees, and its shareholders are at greater risk if the firm is not merged into a larger corporation. Therefore, we believe Value America must be managed to sell with the greatest certainty, the greatest speed, and at the highest valuation. Cutting the company in half is inconsistent with these objectives.

We are pleased that a committee has been formed to select investment bankers and manage this sale. We are pleased that the committee is moving toward this goal. However, the manner in which the company conducts its affairs in the next three months will have a great impact on the value, speed, and certainty of a sale. It is our opinion that if the board gives its final approval to the restructuring plan, the company we built, its core competencies and many of its best people will be lost. Additionally, we believe a restructuring of this magnitude will inevitably slow the sale process. As the company's largest shareholders we view any delay of a sale to be against our interests and counter to those of fellow shareholders.

Board members seemed surprised by our rejection of the restructuring plan during the conclusion of our last meeting. To minimize any misunderstanding we have written the remainder of this letter to constructively communicate our rationale. We believe that any restructuring aimed at diminishing Value America's losses and prolonging cash reserves in preparation for a merger or acquisition should focus on the company's most expensive and least productive area: advertising. Promotional expenditures can be reduced quickly and substantially without diminishing the value of the company.

Management's plan actually burns more cash in the short term and eliminates the company's business development team, demand alliances, presentation marketing and most consumer products merchants and brands. Incredibly, 75% of the company's expenditures, as evidenced by our Q3 statements ($28M of $37M) are in Sales and Advertising. The answer is simple: cut advertising, not people.

The *Path to Profitability* focused on Value America's requirement to reduce advertising, to make it more productive, and to diminish the its net cost by increasing brand co-op. Our strategy to diminish the company's largest expense area, and thus diminish the company's cash burn, was rejected. Similarly, our efforts to obtain access to affluent Americans through Demand Alliances must not have been valued, because the approved plan eliminates all of the Business Development team that built and managed these relationships.

We earned access to the names and addresses of over 100 million of the wealthiest Americans. We were given the opportunity to use targeted data and promote to those that shopped the most, bought the most, even those that favored direct response sellers. For the first time, we proved we could get our brand partners to pay for our advertising. We proved that we could use direct response to successfully sell a wide range of consumer products.

Success was within our grasp. Yet the board approved a plan that will negatively impact people's lives, rather than cut advertising. It will eliminate consumer products, and cast aside much of the business model and people that attracted you all to this company. It will also eliminate all the Demand Alliances that would be viewed so favorably by an acquiring firm.

Tomorrow, as a result of this decision, half of Value America's employees will be laid off. Many have been with the company for more than two years and have been devoted to its success. The impact of a restructuring of this magnitude in a small town will be devastating to the company's credibility and thus its ability to attract talented people. A 50% reduction in employment in an Internet business where growth often exceeds 50% quarterly will be equally devastating to the company's ability to retain the talent it now has, most of whom joined the firm because of its powerful model, inventiveness, and growth.

A reading of the VUSA message board on Yahoo! shows that we have fostered an environment that fails to discourage employees from communicating misleading or confidential information. Posted there you will find that the firm intends to lay off hundreds of people and will miss revenue estimates this quarter. This is not conducive to the sale or management of the company.

Bright, passionate, and dedicated people make a company valuable. Their excitement and vitality are the first things a prospective buyer notices. It is the very thing every member of our board noticed during our first meeting. Empty buildings and the cumulative depression that will most assuredly follow the dismissal of over 300 people in a company of 600 will have an equally negative impact on how a prospective buyer will value the firm. This is a tremendously painful and unnecessary risk.

Sadly, we will waste money on severance and facility closures. Not only will we receive no benefit from these employees over the next several months, they will actually cost the company more than if they were working to serve our customers, brand partners, and shareholders. And Value America will become less valuable and salable as a result. This deplorable situation is unnecessary because the alternative is to do the right and obvious thing: reduce sales and advertising spending. Under one strategy we spend a lot less cash and have a whole company to sell. Under the other plan we spend a lot more cash in the short term and have half a company to sell. What are we missing?

As a result of management's reorganization plan, all of the expense and enormous effort to form relationships with thousands of consumer brands will be wasted, negating the value of these relationships to a prospective buyer. In the wake of this decision the company must rely on the sale of low margin and high return goods. Value America will become a more expensive version of Buy.com, OnSale, and Outpost—a more expensive version because the same executives that managed our poor advertising performance are now elevated without addressing their failures, or without proposing a more productive alternative. An acquiring company can quickly resume advertising, but they will not be able to quickly hire 300 skilled people, or be able to resume relationships with our demand alliances or with thousands of quality brands.

It is possible to diminish costs outside of advertising without delaying a sale of the company or diminishing its value. We can eliminate Convergys, the outsource call center management brought on line in Q3. Those managing this relationship claim we pay them twice as much per hour than we do our own people, and receive less than half the performance. They claim we contract for between 125 and 150 people at Convergys. If this were in-house, we could lay off 50% fewer people, we would be more valuable as a result of the increased in-house capability, and we would spend much less money, short and long term.... We could eliminate the hiring freeze in technology and replace the fifty $200 to $300 an hour consultants with $20 to $30 an hour employees. If we are managing the company to maximize the value, swiftness, and certainty of a sale, these actions should be taken rather than the alternative of enduring the great risk and cost of management's plan.

Please review the three documents we sent to you two weeks ago. We believe it is clear that we must sell Value America to a strategic partner, now, not later. The board, in our view, has been misled into believing our technology would not endure due diligence. We were told a sale should be postponed until our systems are fixed. Those responsible for our integrated e-commerce solution were never given the opportunity to refute this charge. They resolutely believe, and can substantiate, that Value America's infrastructure is superior to the systems and capabilities that endured years of intense inspection preceding our funding rounds.

Even our challenges, in particular our excessive advertising, are eliminated with the right buyer because a more established company can replace our advertising with theirs and our customer acquisition cost with their customers. The crown jewel of Value America is its superior e-tailing engine. A strategic partner will be able to capitalize on this capability with minimal cost while simultaneously building our custom marketplaces. We are more valuable to our shareholders and more responsive to our employees following a successful merger.

The company must be managed in a manner that maximizes value while it minimizes risk. This course of action ensures longevity and supports the interests of our shareholders, employees, customers, and brand partners. As a result, Rex and I voted yes on focusing on the swift sale of the company and voted no on terminating half of its employees and brand relationships. During today's teleconference meeting of the board you will have the opportunity to concur with the position of the company's two largest shareholders...."

It's hard to imagine rational men ignoring such words, but they did. Reading takes time, and thinking is...well, who thinks anymore? So Wolf made a mockery of it. Caise said he would support it only if it were the unified will of the entire board. Smith bristled, asking Craig why he bothered to write it. Based upon their actions, there is no evidence the others even read it. Most board members, in fact, didn't even bother attending the December 27th teleconference. The new chairman struggled to obtain a quorum. If Craig had hung up, the board would not have been able to conduct its business.

Perhaps it's understandable. After all, this board had served less than six months. They were openly defying the firm's founders, rebuking their largest shareholders, firing half their people, disposing of their most valuable assets without gaining any benefit, inviting—*begging for*—a class action suit, and dispatching shareholder value—all because of incomplete and inaccurate information. *Important? Why should I attend? It's Christmas.*

CEO Dorchak began the meeting by revealing that with three days left in the quarter her sales outlook had fallen from $75 million to $70 million. The Street already knew it. The previous day, someone using the code name "gotnomomoney" had posted this message on Yahoo!'s VUSA board: "VUSA will miss earnings estimates. Whispers are $70 million, maybe less. Rumors are they are going to lay off hundreds of people. This is going belly up." Another said, "Major announcements are coming. Layoffs are coming. News on Wednesday."

Dorchak's other numbers "migrated" a tad as well. The $2.5 million she proposed paying 300 people not to work jumped to $4.1 million. Even that wasn't close; in the end, the direct cost of cutting the company in half would exceed *$8 million*. While wasting $8 million is foolish, destroying people's lives and a company in the process is downright criminal.

They got nothing for their eight mil except a class action suit. But to their credit, they'd anticipated that. In their plan, they wrote, "The costs detailed above are limited to those liabilities management believes currently exist and those that can be reasonably estimated. Costs associated with possible litigation resulting from implementation of this plan of restructure have not been included above and could range up to, or be in excess of, $7,000,000." It took only a few weeks for the shareholders to turn management's fears into reality.

The highlight of the December 27th tele-board was the "Key Personnel Retention Packages." It was approved by majority vote. The board must have thought it was in their shareholders' interests to guarantee the top brass a "one-year salary for termination on Change of Control with immediate stock option vesting." The new CEO explained that it was important to make the company "difficult to sell." She said, "We think it's important that we put a prospective acquirer on notice that if they wish to buy this company, it will cost them an additional $3.4 million."

Later she conveyed her high treason in writing: "An acquirer of Value America would be liable for $3,410,000 if all executives covered were dismissed due to change of control. It is imperative that we move quickly to reduce anxiety and contain turnover." Why would one be concerned about reducing turnover if they planned to "turn over" half the employees the very next day? Perhaps there was an ulterior motive for their "Key Personnel Retention Packages."

The one-year bonus babies included Ewert, Starnes, Anders, Chambers, and stunningly, the two-day-a-month Chairman, Wolf Schmitt, along with Dorchak herself. It was *their* plan, so why were they "anxious?" Some of the six-month bonus babies were Kim and David Kuo, Biff Pusey, HR's Kari Meyer, Nick Hofer in Advertising, and Candy Clifford in Sales.

The twenty-three page fax Ms. Dorchak sent the board this day was hilarious. Glenda had screwed up and was desparately trying to cover herself. She had sent a letter to Byron Peters, firing him. Only then did she discover that he had an employment contract. Her move wasn't particularly professional. So she did what came naturally: she lied. She told the board she "was considering" firing him, because there was no longer anything for him to do. Since her restructuing plan was already three times over budget, she needed to elicit their complicity.

Glenda had gotten herself into this pickle because she didn't like the fact that Peters had worked with Craig. At the same time, she wanted to reward Starnes for the role he'd unwittingly played in her ascension.

One of them had retail experience; the other had none. One had ability; the other had, well, let's not go there. One had an employment contract she now revealed would cost $1,368,856 to sever; the other had *nada*. So Glenda besieged the board, hoping they would bail her out and indulge her childish whim. Besides, how could she maintain her "professional image" if she admitted she'd already blown the money.

Craig knew she was lying, but he elected not to say anything. In each of the last two board meetings, he had gone out of his way to show that the new CEO and Chairman were not "truth-tellers," but he had been trained, like Pavlov's dog, that such revelations would not be well received.

He argued the merits of doing the intelligent thing but the board was, well, the same board who had approved the restructuring plan. Value America's "brilliant" new CEO, now with board approval, promptly re-fired the guy with ability, experience, and a contract and promoted the guy who had none of the above. Kiss another million bucks goodbye.

Rex was out of the country this day, so Craig cast the lone dissenting vote. "Hell no," he said defiantly. It would be the last vote either of them would ever cast—the last board meeting either of them would ever attend.

As the festivities drew to a merciful close, a deeply saddened Winn pressed what he thought was the disconnect button on his new speaker-phone. *Oops, wrong button.* Before he could figure out what was wrong, his sadness turned to revulsion. As others signed off, Fred Smith and Glenda Dorchak remained on the line. Fred was positively gushy, praising Glenda and her new plan with unbridled admiration. Craig's heart fell a mile before he was finally able to get the technology to release him.

"They completely ignored your letter." Craig's coworker, friend, and neighbor, Sean Flynn had listened in on the conference call. Winn had wanted a credible source to attest to the fact that his letter had been faxed to every board member—no excuses, no denials. With Rex out of the country, he thought that another set of ears might be helpful. The board's behavior had become so bizarre, an independent witness might help to corroborate the absurdity.

"Based on the last set of board minutes, it's not beyond these folks to doctor what was said today. I'm glad you were here, Sean."

"Isn't that illegal?"

"Probably. I'm not a lawyer, but it's never good when you have to change the facts to keep from looking bad."

"I don't have much experience with this sort of thing. But how do you explain the fact that they never so much as discussed any issue you raised in your fax? I read it. It told them the truth—that by approving this plan they would kill the company. With so much at stake—so many lives, so much money—they ignored it. Sounds crazy to me."

"And to me. Listen, I had thought they'd study the material Rex and I sent them prior to the *last* board meeting. It would have taken them an hour or so, but they were evidently too busy with their own issues—family, business, politics, who knows? These guys were all chosen because they were successful doing something else, and *that* something took pre-cidence over *this* something."

"So they destroy a company rather than alter their priorities long enough to make an informed a decision?"

"They didn't mean to kill it. They probably think they saved it."

"Not a chance," Sean exclaimed. "Ask anybody who counts. I have. We all know this company is doomed without you."

"Well, they haven't, so they believe the opposite, that the stock will double with me gone."

"Don't they read the message boards, see what the shareholders think? Check the newspapers for the stock price?"

"No. All they knew was that the stock was below the IPO price. They needed a scapegoat. I wasn't only the easiest target, I was the *only* target, because neither Dorchak nor Morgan did enough to get noticed. They got a half dozen idiots to say I was the problem, and these fools fell for it."

"No way!" Sean couldn't believe what he was hearing.

"Do you really want to know what happened?"

"Yeah."

"It's the board. Start with Bill Bennett. He's a nice guy. Damn smart, but claims to know nothing about business. He's a friend of Kuo's, so guess how he votes. Second, Rex, Dean, and I replaced Justin Caise's firm with a more qualified outfit after the IPO. He loses his biggest client. Then Justin picks up two million bucks in billings when Dorchak fires the big firm and rehires him. How do you think he votes?"

"You're oh for two."

"It gets worse. Rafe Durn, Mr. Union, threatens to 'bring me down' if I do a deal with the 'anti-union FedEx.' I do, and he does. He even gets his new partner, Don Tarpin, to go along. So now it's four to nothing."

Sean's eyes were big as saucers.

"We're just getting warmed up. Take Gerry Roche and Sam White. They were introduced by that overpaid idiot of a spiritual advisior— Goose Godfrey. They remain loyal, for whatever reason, to the Bretheren. So it doesn't take a PhD to figure out how they voted. Do you think it was hard to convince them that Morgan was grand or that I was scum?"

"But Godfrey doesn't know anything about the inner workings, the operations of Value America."

"He doesn't have to. He knows the board members, and therefore is in a position to 'influence' them."

"This is really sickening."

"It's six-zip. So now in a knee-jerk reaction to save the company in the midst of all this foolishness, I stupidly empower Wolf Schmitt. The very second he's promoted, his true colors come out."

"Nobody in the company even knows who he is. How could he have any credibility? The few people who've met him think he's arrogant."

"But not the board. He speaks their language. And they don't know enough about the company to realize he's just blowing smoke."

"So he votes against you. That leaves only Fred Smith and Frank Flowers. What's their story?"

"I'm not sure Flowers even knows what business we're in. He's super smart, plenty talented, but he's become a cable guy. He's managing umpteen billion bucks for Paul Allen, so even though I think he wants to do right, he doesn't know how."

Sean slumped back in his chair.

"As for Smith, he was worked over by the Brethren. They pounded him relentlessly, somehow convincing him that everyone would bail if I returned to management."

"That's absurd. You're the only reason we're all here. In fact, the opposite is true. Guys like Dean Johnson and Ken Power left *because* you got out of management."

"You know that. Smith doesn't. I have irrefutable confirmation that the Brethren got to him big time. All they needed him to do was waver on one vote. After that, it was all over. From that time on, they knew that his military experience combined with the corporate culture he'd created at FedEx would cause him to support management blindly. So long as I wasn't brought back into management at the November 23rd meeting, it was curtains. I became nothing more than a friendly irritant. Smith is as predictable as the sunrise. Chain of command, 'proper organizational protocol,' in his corporate parlance, is supremely important. He has always and will always vote in favor of management. During his six months on the board, I was never a manager. So guess how he voted?"

"That's it. Nine against you and Rex. Bye-bye company."

"And come to find out, we can't fire them, even though we own the company. It's sick. Sad. But not all that mysterious."

The press release was issued the following morning. It used the word "focus" a lot, but that didn't help. The stock continued its free fall. Buried at the end of the release:

'The board of directors has been very involved in this process. We are supportive of the management team and the potential of this new business focus,' said Wolf Schmitt.... The company also announced that the board has appointed a special committee to explore strategic opportunities for Value America. In addition, they announced that its two founders, Craig Winn and Rex Scatena, had resigned.

Unable to think on their feet, the management team prepared talking points. They said, "We are moving from an entrepreneurial start-up to a more professionally managed public company. Even without focus, Value America has become e-commerce's leading computer reseller. With focus, we will become e-commerce's leading technology superstore." Anticipating the obvious, they wrote, "Q: Aren't you just the first dot-com failure? A: We'll focus on our winners and more tightly manage costs for acceleration toward profitability. Backed by a world-class board of directors, we think we can be one of dot-com's great success stories." It was incomprehensible drivel like this that caused the stock to plunge seventy percent in the first month of the Wolf & Witch era. *Yep. Craig and Rex are the problem. Get rid of them, and the stock will double.*

༄

THE LAYOFFS WERE as cold and calculated as the schemes that had precipitated them. Everyone was asked to attend a company-wide meeting at the Doubletree, the same hotel in which Joe had met Craig their first day together in Charlottesville.

Some thought little of it; Glenda loved meetings as much as Hitler loved a good pep rally. She had just held one a few days before Christmas. In addition to spending and lying lavishly, she had arranged for everyone to have a token of her esteemed adoration—a five-cent badge that said, "BEST." It was evidently an acronym for some corporate agenda.

Other invitees were considerably more concerned. They had read the VUSA message boards and knew something was brewing, something ominous. As they gathered in the hallways and prepared to leave, someone opened an email to everyone@valueamerica.com. It was a copy of the press release announcing the D-Day festivities. Dismantling Value America was to be Dorchak's crowning achievement. She was so proud of herself she couldn't suppress the temptation to spread the news. She wanted everyone to know who had done this magnificent thing.

The troops did what they had become accustomed to doing: they sent a copy of the announcement to the press, who quickly dispatched reporters to the scene. The news reports said Dorchak, filled with pride and passion, announced her plan to axe 300 employees: "Half of you are being laid off today."

The whole room gasped, then exhaled in unison. Joe Page recounted, "It was the most painfully emotional experience I've ever witnessed."

The CEO then turned the meeting over to her new CMO, Tom Starnes. Few even knew who he was. He gave this room full of strangers their marching orders: they were to go back to their workstations, sit with their hands folded, and wait. Their immediate supervisor would tell them if they were friend or foe, victor or vanquished, *en route* to the Promised Land or Poland.

As Starnes concluded his address, he laced his final words with threatening overtones. "If any of you talk to the press about the company or its management, you'll jeopardize our generous severance package." All the while, Starnes and his cronies were spewing venom to the press like famished rattlesnakes. Perceptions were more important than reality. The lapdog had a new mistress.

The vanquished were banished, unceremoniously told to gather their personal effects, without touching their phones or computers, and were escorted out of the buildings. Each was given an envelope inviting them to a "counseling session" the following day.

The officers were nervous. They must have seen it coming, must have known the crew would be miffed. Those who were laid off were coerced into signing a document that released the company and its management from all claims the dearly departed might have, along with a promise not to disclose their feelings to the media, forever and ever, or there would be no severance. So Caise, who had lawyered a gargantuan severance for Morgan *without* a non-disparagement clause, wrote a suffocatingly restrictive non-disparagement agreement tied to a piddly little severance for these who were being fired without cause, these who had served in the trenches, some as long as three years. I don't get it.

All the while, *der* Dorchak hunkered down in her bunker on Rio Road. Elaborate electronic locks were installed on the doors to keep the critics at bay. An armed guard was stationed at the entrance. She didn't make another appearance. She didn't go out to comfort those whose lives had been ravaged by her actions. She didn't try to inspire those who were spared. Instead, she left. Dorchak had the company charter a corporate jet to whisk her off to a vacation in sunny Arizona. Why not burn twenty-five grand of company money?

The board stood idly by as Value America was torn asunder. They were busy and couldn't be bothered. Not a single member of the company's illustrious board said a word. To this day, none of them have had the courage or the character to accept responsibility for the travesty they unleashed, a travesty precipitated by a convoluted notion that wonderful people serving a company with noble aspirations were somehow less productive than advertising.

One board member, who shall remain nameless, was still willing to talk to Craig this day, to his credit. As Craig pleaded one last time for sanity, the response he got sent a cold shiver down his spine: "Your concern over the hardship this is causing your people isn't healthy. I learned a long time ago to separate business from people. You should do the same."

Craig couldn't. His first call was to his lifelong friend, Bill Hunt. His wife, Judy, answered the phone. She was crying. Bill, Value America's fifth employee, had been discarded like yesterday's newspaper. There was pain in Judy's voice, melded with a sense of bewilderment as she tried to comprehend how a group of strangers could wreak such havoc on the firm her husband had worked so hard to build. There were no good answers, only sorrow. Judy, through her tears, asked but one question: "Why?"

"REX," CRAIG SAID, "I'm at a loss. I don't know what to do."

"I pride myself in being able to size things up," Rex said, "understand what makes people tick, good or bad. But nothing I've experienced has prepared me for this. It's like we're breathing different air than they are."

"They're so callous. Will they ever wake up?"

"No. Never," Rex cautioned his friend. "When prideful people make bad decisions, they work overtime justifying them, rationalizing what they've done. That's what this board will do."

"And so will the come-latelies. They'll shirk responsibility for the pain they've inflicted. I'm sure they'll blame us. I'm so damn sick of reading my name in the paper. It's nothing but one revolting lie after another."

"Get used to it, my friend. It's going to get worse before it gets better."

ళ×త

THE FOLLOWING DAY, there were two meetings at the Doubletree. One was for the saved, the other for the damned. The two groups passed in the hall. The new professional management team had not been astute enough to schedule them at different times. It was a sad affair—friends holding one another, comforting and supporting each other. Those who still had their jobs seemed embarrassed by it. It was hard to know whom to be happy for and who was to be pitied.

Curiously, about ten percent of the people management took credit for laying off were not actually dismissed. They were simply transferred to InService's payroll to create the illusion of savings. InService was told to pay them even though they had no idea who they were or what they did.

Meanwhile, the professional managers did what they do best; they held meetings—meetings with consultants, meetings at hotels, meetings at expensive corporate retreats. They held meetings just so they could blame each other for what wasn't happening—business. No plan ever materialized. No direction was ever forthcoming. Under the Witch's watch, the business just melted away, dissipated in the vacuum of leadership.

Against this backdrop, Winn and Scatena resigned their board positions. On February 3, 2000 they both wrote, "Please be advised that I hereby resign from the Board of Directors of Value America, Inc. effective immediately. Please be further advised that until such time as I otherwise advise the company in writing, I do not want to receive any non-public information about Value America."

The only thing now that tied them to the company they'd founded was twenty-one million unwanted shares. But parting with them would not be easy. The company, at the direction of Schmitt, Dorchak, and Caise, conspired to deny Winn and Scatena their right to sell their stock. In a desperate attempt to thwart the founders, they wrote a convoluted letter falsely claiming Craig and Rex had agreed not to sell their shares. Caise's henchman, the very guy Rex had predicted would come back to haunt them, did. He lied on behalf of his employer—and his pocketbook— denying that the founders had proclaimed their intent to sell. And the practice of law used to be *such* an honorable profession.

In time, the founders circumvented the bogus challenge by pointing out that: a) no such commitments were made; thus there was no supporting evidence, b) the opposite was indeed true, and c) even if everyone in the room had heard one thing though another was actually said, there was no consideration paid; thus no contract was possible.

Not to be outdone, the conspirators then lamely implied that Craig and Rex were still insiders, with access to material, adverse, non-public information, and should therefore be prevented from selling their shares. In actuality, they had been so isolated by the company's management, they were little more than disgruntled mushrooms left in the dark to rot. In the end, Craig went to Smith and relied on his sense of fair play. Fred promised to correct the record, and did. Though easily misled and sometimes wrong, Fred Smith proved himself to be an honest and decent man.

Others were not. The new management team and their hired gun, the law firm of Caise, Perkins, seemed to enjoy torturing shareholders. They simply refused to provide a clean opinion on the founders' shares. According to Robertson Stephens, this was easily the most underhanded and unethical move their firm had ever witnessed. For Craig and Rex, it was just one more insult, par for the course.

The crowning blow came when Smith told Craig that their lawyers had discovered a Virginia law that prevented them from conveying their voting rights to a company that might buy their shares as a block. This, of course, killed any incentive for a firm to buy Value America.

An equally bitter pill was one that had been swallowed years before. At Caise's suggestion, the board had been set up with a staggered structure. This meant that only one third of its members came up for reelection in any given year. So even if Craig and Rex had called a shareholders' meeting (which would have taken ninety days), they could have ousted only three of the nine members of this board that was now unanimously aligned against them.

A letter Craig wrote captured the moment:

At no time since the inception of Value America have Rex and I known less about the firm than we do now. The company we founded and helped build has completely distanced itself from us and charted a new course in which we were neither involved nor supportive....

Rex and I have consistently expressed our willingness to assist the Special Committee with matters related to selling the firm. We have expressed our willingness to manage Value America in a manner that maximizes the value, certainty, and swiftness of a sale. These offers have been rejected; thus we are sellers."

Value America's stock continued to fall. About the time NASDAQ hit a high of 5,000, VUSA hit a low of $3.50. The investment community was as impressed with the company's management and their prospects as Winn and Scatena were. By the time the board and their management team were through with their shenanigans, Rex and Craig were worth less than five percent of what they'd been worth when they left management on IPO day. Their first miniscule stock sale as *persona non grata* from the company they'd founded brought them just three dollars a share.

༄

IT WAS A bright, wintry afternoon, the 24th of February 2000. Craig and his farm hands had cleared several acres for a new orchard. Early that evening, they began burning the large pile of debris their labor had created. As the fire began to rage, Rex arrived unexpectedly, pulling his blue pickup truck over to where Craig was standing. Dressed in overalls, he was still dirty from having toiled all day in his vineyard.

Both had talked to Robertson Stephens over the course of the afternoon. They hadn't sold anything. The volume had dropped to an insignificant 200,000 shares a day—far too little volume to sell a block of any quantity. By contrast, on November 23rd—the day the Street anticipated their return to management, the day the board rejected them—2,300,000 shares had been traded at a high of $17 a share. That reflected a trading volume of $39 million *versus* this day's sobering $700 thousand—a ninety-eight percent reduction.

Robbie Stephens said that institutional interest in VUSA was nil, as was analyst support. Even the day-traders were sitting on their hands. The only hope, they felt, was a sale or merger, and none was in sight.

To make matters worse, both Craig and Rex had been named in a class action suit filed against Value America the previous day. Even though they had voted "hell no" to the plan that prompted the suit, it didn't matter. VUSA was damaged goods.

The harassment didn't end there. Management couldn't accept the fact that the collapse of Value America's stock might actually be their fault. They routinely blamed it on Craig and Rex, crying, "Winn and Scatena are dumping their shares. They're purposely flooding the market, trying

to undermine the company, just to lash back at us for rejecting them."
Sure, it sounds far fetched, but as many an evil regime has shown, the bigger the lie, the better it sells. The truth: between them they had sold 15,000 shares since November, an insignificant fraction of one percent of what they owned.

Rex, like Craig, had been stymied by the board and by the company's hostile management. Yet that didn't matter as much to him as it might have to a lesser man. To Rex, it had never been about the money. It was about working together to build something of value. They had accomplished what they'd set out to do. The beginning had been glorious, but the end, ignominious. In the dwindling light, near the warmth of the raging fire, they embraced. It had been a long journey from the first tee of the Mauni Lani.

It was over for them. They knew they weren't going to be able to sell their shares after all. Yet there were no complaints, no bitter feelings, no harsh words. They just stood there, side by side, watching the fire rage and then die, just like a certain company they had once known.

❧

FOR REASONS ONLY God knows, our story didn't end there in front of the smoldering fire. The very next day, out of a clear blue sky, lightning struck: Craig and Rex were each able to sell their first meaningful block, 50,000 shares of Value America stock. It wasn't over after all. Sure, it was just two-tenths of a percent of what they owned, but to them it was like manna from heaven.

That evening, Value America did something no company in their right mind ever does after the close of the market. They announced good news. Good news is supposed to be proclaimed at the opening of the market, and early in the week. Bad news is released at the close, and preferably late in the week. While Craig and Rex knew nothing of the sales alliance with IBM before it was announced, it is likely other investors knew of it earlier in the day. The company had earned its reputation for loose lips.

Under heavy trading, the stock shot up to $4 a share. Acquisition rumors suddenly filled VUSA's message boards. Over several weeks the stock rose from $3 to $6, fueled by talk of a buyout. Predictably, it settled back down to $3.50 when it became clear the rumors were unfounded. But during this aberration, the daily trading volumes were in the millions. On one day alone, over six million shares of VUSA were traded—600,000 each belonged to Rex and Craig. Around eighty percent of the value the founders derived from their "post-part-Tom" sales occurred during this remarkable time—about $35 million each. It was delicious. In the end, the company's mutinous crew and rebellious board had put daggers to their backs and forced them to walk the plank—right into an ocean of gold.

Thankfully, the traders wanted their shares more than Craig and Rex did. That, of course, wasn't saying much. According to the message boards, the reason so many suddenly considered VUSA's shares worth owning wasn't the company's "experienced management team." It most certainly wasn't the merits of their "focused restructuring plan." Nor was it the prospects of the advertising-centric e-tailer "growing profitability." It was their fascination with Fred Smith at the helm of the Special Committee. *Institutional Review* said, "An increase in VUSA takeover rumors has persuaded us to select VUSA for our stock buy for this coming week. Our short-term traders should play this stock up to $7." Everybody, it seemed, other than the company's misled board and its mercenary managers, knew what to do.

As successful as Value America had been at raising money and forming strategic alliances, investors believed that the "Babe Ruth of American business" would "get a deal done in excess of $10 a share." Then they thought $7, then maybe $5, or perhaps $2. Sadly the illusion didn't last. Even Babe Ruth struck out sometimes. As quickly as the bubble had formed, it burst.

The stock quickly fell below two bucks. It never recovered. The average volume shriveled. Craig was left with nearly five million worthless shares. Rex, happily, had been able to sell all of his.

They couldn't help but laugh at the irony. Had the board accepted any of their offers to stabilize and sell the company, they wouldn't have sold a share. They would have been insiders, prohibited by SEC rules from trading. But as a direct result of the abuse the board and management had heaped upon them, they had become free and motivated sellers.

For Winn and Scatena, it was a glorious moment in time. If living well was really the best revenge, they had bested their tormentors. They had had the last laugh.

Or so they thought.

The plans of the diligent lead to profit...as surely as haste leads to poverty—Solomon

UNDER THE SHADOW

There were good days, and there were bad days, but there were no worse days than April 20, 2000. The May issue of *Business Week* was posted online. Craig's smiling face was on the cover. It had all started a month earlier. The first quarter had not yet been publicly announced, but Dorchak and her management team knew the score. It was a shutout. No amount of spin or propaganda was going to deflect the criticism they would soon have to endure as a result of their humiliating failure. Using "focus" six times in the same release wasn't going to help this time. Worse, there was no one left to blame. Even after using their restructuring plan to stack the deck, pushing every possible liability back into Q4 and pulling every possible sale into Q1, the numbers told a sorry tale: the once proud company was now in the hands of an incompetent and gluttonous crew.

The problem had begun to manifest itself several months before. The fourth quarter goal of $83 million General Dorchak had rallied the troops to achieve failed to materialize. Her promise to the board of $75 million vanished. The $70 million she confirmed she'd sold as late as December 27 evaporated. Even the $65 million she claimed had already shipped two weeks before the quarter's end went poof. Mysteriously, they managed to post only $61 million. Even that included $6 million from the dreaded Visa program. Without it, Q4 would have been smaller than Q3.

According to the holocaust survivors, Glenda had it all figured out: make Q4 look as bad as possible. She could blame the quarter on Winn and make herself look great in Q1 by comparison. Just slide revenue out of "his" quarter and into "hers." That was the plan, but it hadn't worked out quite that way. Sure, she'd managed to convince a scandal-hungry press that Winn was an irresponsible scoundrel, but she failed Part Two. General Dorchak couldn't pull off a quarter that looked good by any standard. Even after she'd magically transferred some $10 million in sales out of "his" Q4 into "her" Q1, she still looked pathetic.

No matter how you looked at it, for the first time in Value America's history—for the first time in *dot-com* history—quarter-to-quarter sales fell. They fell precipitously. Q1 eventually settled in at $47 million, which meant they had actually sold only $37 million—against a Street expectation of $65 million. That should have been enough to convince the board that their glorious management team was full of shit (pardon the language—that's the standard business terminology for this particular scenario). But they held their noses, closed their eyes, covered their ears, closed ranks, and somehow ignored dismal performance.

In spite of management's arrogant self-appraisal, announcing their Q1 performance would cost them their jobs. It *had* to. Revenues had dropped nearly forty percent below the previous quarter's, and a similar percentage below Wall Street's expectations. Miscues this severe are invariably irrecoverable for a public company and fatal for its officers.

But it got worse. While the revenue picture was appalling, management's "stewardship" of cash was reprehensible. After consuming $8 million cutting the company in half, the mercenaries really got down to business. Over the first ten weeks of the quarter, they devoured nearly a million dollars—*every business day!* During this period, available cash reserves fell from $74 million to less than $24 million. They burned through $50 million in support of rapidly declining sales! There was no way to keep this a secret. With nowhere to hide, the Wolf and the Witch needed a diversion. They needed an alibi. They needed to call in an old IOU.

There may be no way to prove the connection, but the fact remains, they started cooperating on a story with *Business Week* at the very moment they needed to cover up their dismal failures. And that fact begs the following questions: Why had Glenda clandestinely struck such an odd, secretive, and overpriced deal with *Business Week*? Why had she done it outside the confines of the contract the company had signed with our media buying service? Why had she paid twice the rate our agency would have paid for the same space? Why did she buy prohibitively expensive two-page full-color ads at a time when the company was so desperately poor that meeting payroll would have been impossible if our employees hadn't contributed? And why did Dorchak announce an alliance with McGraw Hill, the parent of *BW*, during the previous quarter?

On April 4, a day or so after Dorchak would have known how dismal her Q1 performance had actually been, John Byrne, a senior writer for *Business Week*, called Craig at home. He said he wanted to interview him for a story he was writing on Value America. Fact is, his story line had already been determined. He, for some odd reason, had been given Morgan's number, and true to form, Tom had already done a number on Craig.

Winn refused the interview and naively encouraged Byrne to contact management. Frustrated, he sent Craig a letter. Wrongly addressed, it wasn't delivered until long after the damage was done.

Dear Mr. Winn: April 5, 2000

We spoke yesterday on the telephone about a story I am doing on you and Value America. I understand your reluctance to speak, but I'm hoping you'll reconsider. For one thing, despite what has occurred at Value America, nearly everyone agrees that your original business model and underlying premise for the company was solid. I'd like to get your early thinking on this "straight from the horse's mouth" instead of picking it up from secondary sources and clippings from *Chief Executive* magazine.

For another, current and former executives at the company say that Tom Morgan found it impossible to succeed at the job of CEO while you were there as chairman. They claim that you were "micro-managing every decision Tom made." I know you don't want to get into a tit-for-tat spat with the current management. But it would be unfair to publish these charges without giving you an opportunity to respond.

I'm going to be in Charlottesville Monday, April 10th, through Wednesday to do reporting on this story. I would greatly appreciate the opportunity to meet and speak with you. Either way, I intend to do a fairly significant story for *Business Week* on what has happened at Value America and what other Net-entrepreneurs can learn from the experience.

Sincerely, John Byrne, Senior Writer

On April 11, John called again and pleaded for an interview. Craig said, "No." Had Byrne's letter not been carelessly mis-addressed, he would have said, "Hell no!" The last thing Craig wanted was his name in the press, especially associated with the company he had come to loathe. The fact that the letter revealed that Byrne had already spoken to Morgan and his pals, and listened to them, was all Craig would have needed to know to stay a million miles away. He had no interest in jumping into their cesspool.

So why was Morgan's number one of the first given to Byrne? Perhaps someone needed an alibi. Why did Morgan continue to stay in character, falsely accusing Craig of "micro-managing everything?" Craig hadn't even second-guessed Tom until his final month, and even then, Morgan's will, not Winn's, had been implemented. Did Tom, like Dorchak, need a way to hide his complicity in the destruction of Value America? Was he willing to lie to achieve his ends?

Pleading, Byrne said, "This is my last day here, and I'm going to write this story on the rise and fall of Value America anyway. Can't we talk about the rise? There's no one left that knows anything about it."

"I've learned not to trust the media," Craig observed. "But I'm damned if I talk to you and damned if I don't." Sad but true. "So I'll talk about what propelled our rise, but I've got some game rules."

"What are they?" a hopeful Byrne inquired.

"First, short and sweet. You've got thirty minutes, starting at seven-thirty tomorrow morning. Second, I'll have three witnesses present to corroborate anything we discuss. Third, we'll only talk about Value America from its inception through the IPO, nothing after. Fourth, you will share any derogatory statements made against me by those seeking to use your story as an alibi for their failures. While I will not answer their charges, I will give you the names of people who can. And, fifth, you must arrive with a letter confirming your commitment not to discuss or quote me on events following the IPO."

"Agreed. I'll see you at seven-thirty."

On lined, three-hole notebook paper, like we all used in grade school, Byrne handwrote and signed the following letter:

Mr. Craig Winn
Charlottesville, VA   *12 April 2000*

I understand that you have agreed to meet with me today to discuss events leading up to Value America's initial public offering in April of last year. I understand that at today's interview session you will not be expected to comment on the company's existing plans. I also understand that you have only agreed to meet me today for an interview if the above conditions are in effect. As a result, I agree to these ground rules for our meeting.

Mr. Winn will not be quoted regarding any issues after the IPO.
Sincerely,
John Byrne, Senior Writer, Business Week

It wasn't worth the paper it was written on. Nor was his story.

Almost a year to the day after Craig led Value America's IPO, he found himself with a reporter talking about the great people and noble ambitions that had propelled the firm from a mere idea into one of the world's largest e-tailers. Retired General Mick Kicklighter was present, as was Andy Rod, former President of the Office Products Group, even Byron Peters, the highest-ranking officer to receive the axe at the Great Restructuring.

During the interview, Craig remained circumspect, choosing his words carefully. Mick observed when it was over, "No matter how many times you were prodded, you never took the bait, never said anything critical about anybody or anything. You were humble to a fault. There's no way," he concluded, "this fellow will be able to use this against you."

A day or so later, Craig received another call from Byrne. This time he wanted pictures. Craig vehemently refused. "No! Do not send a photographer here. I do not want my picture in your magazine. No pictures. Is that clear?"

Byrne complained but said he understood. Then as promised he delineated the gripes Craig's former employees had against him. There was nothing new, only the same lies he had heard before. Following each Craig gave Byrne the name, position, and phone number of someone he could call to verify the absurdity of the charge. "If you're still in doubt over who to believe after talking to these folks, call me back. I'll send copies of whatever documentation you may need to set the record straight."

Byrne responded, "It's amazing, in light of their deteriorating condition, that they find it useful to make all of these charges against you, especially, if as you say, they're not true."

"I don't get it either. You'd think they'd focus on implementing their plan, whatever it is. Why do they need to recreate history? By doing so, they alienate their largest shareholders. It just doesn't make any sense. Based upon their comments, it appears that *their* problem isn't that they're nearly financially bankrupt, it's that they're morally bankrupt." Winn's concluding comment was prophetically perceptive, not only of what was threatening Value America, not only the dot-com world, but much of corporate America.

❧❦❧

CRAIG'S RESPONSE TO the *Business Week* cover story, "Fall of a Dot-Com" would begin with these words: "I am surprised the *Business Week* cover story failed to say, 'Winn was abducted by aliens while dining with Elvis.' It would have been equally sensational and equally fictitious. It is mystifying that so many false, malicious, and reckless charges could reside in any story. The documentary evidence to disprove these charges is so strong, plentiful, and available. It begs the question… why?"

Loosely translated, the ten-page article said that Dorchak and Morgan weren't responsible for anything because Winn micromanaged everything. They claimed that Winn was a charismatic super-salesman who managed to part the best and brightest businessmen in America from their money by selling them a "house of cards." Further, Winn was portrayed as someone who knew nothing about planning, managing, technology, brands, or logistics. And for good measure, they alleged, he was a crook.

Everybody got what they wanted. Morgan and his cronies got the alibi they so desperately needed. By virtue of this revisionist history, they were exonerated from their complicity in the company's demise. That's a pretty neat trick. Their lack of management was presented as inescapable. Their botched *coup* was now merely a justifiable resignation. Of course, if true, it meant Tom and his accomplices had been paid a couple million dollars for doing nothing. Doesn't sound like high moral ground to me.

The Wolf and the Witch couldn't believe their good fortune either. Just when they needed it most, they got the distraction they were so desperate for. Their catastrophic Q1 failures would fade under Winn's looming shadow once again. The purveyors of painful propaganda got their cover-up. Their inadequacies would be swept under the rug. And *Business Week?* The hideous exposé sold magazines. Everyone won except Value America's shareholders and employees. But they weren't important to this crew.

୬:୯

PRESIDENTIAL ADVISOR, television commentator, and Democratic Party operative Lanny Davis was *real* unhappy. Mr. Davis and his law firm had been hired by *der* Dorchak and the Hitler Youth to represent the company and its co-defendants in the class action suit their actions had both inspired and predicted. Glenda had, of course, offered the very lucrative job to Justin Caise, but the company's insurance carrier, AIG, wisely applied the brakes. They had come to the undeniable conclusion that Caise was conflicted. It was hard to square voting in favor of the plan that had led to the suit with making money defending it. The view was obviously clearer outside Value America than it was inside. Less fog, perhaps.

It's hard to overlook a resigned CEO, after fleecing a company for a million dollars, lying publicly to cover some personal inadequacy. But that wasn't why Davis was so angry. The problem was the idiocy of a chairman and CEO, in the midst of a class action suit, telling the press that their company was a sham. Even to a lawyer, this was vile, an indefensible breach of fiduciary duty. It spoke volumes about the depravity and desperation of Morgan and his Brethren, Schmitt, Dorchak, and the FOGs.

Lanny Davis and his firm, working with others, conducted a month-long investigation into the charges made by current and former managers. They reviewed ten thousand pages of documentation. They conducted extensive interviews. They filtered the facts through the sieve of their collective experiences. Then they put their findings in a letter they asked management to release. Management, of course, refused. The truth was counter to their interests. Davis naturally asked them to justify their refusal with some corroborating evidence, a little documentation to support their "the-company-and-its-founders-are-slime" theory. Knowing they couldn't, they initially stalled, saying they were too busy. Pressed, they finally refused, admitting that there was no such evidence. So Lanny Davis took his letter to the company's illustrious board. *They* refused to release it as well.

So what did the Davis letter say that those in control didn't want said? Only that, "A team of professionals conducted a thorough investigation

IN THE COMPANY OF GOOD AND EVIL

of the serious allegations made in the *Business Week* cover story and found them to be without substance." That should have been great news for the shareholders and employees of a company whose value was evaporating, a firm embroiled in a nasty class action suit. So why were management and the board afraid to set the record straight and save their sorry assets from the angry plaintiffs?

With Wolf, Dorchak, and the FOGs, the answer was painful and predictable. Their collective need for an excuse, a cover-up, a distraction, was all-consuming. Chairmen and CEOs of public companies with rapidly declining sales, those that miss their earnings projections by forty percent, get fired, especially when they torch seventy-five percent of their company's cash reserves doing it.

But what was the board's excuse? Were they so lazy, so poorly informed, so gullible, that they actually believed management's drivel? Or were they simply displaying group dynamics? Having told themselves they'd made the right choice so many times, they actually believed it, even in the face of overwhelming evidence to the contrary. Or was fear starting to creep in, fear that they had made the wrong call, fear that they might be held accountable for their actions? *If we just stay united, if we keep on blaming Winn, we'll get out of this with our reputations intact.*

What few real insights we have into this perplexing drama occurred as a result of a series of conversations between Davis, Smith, and Winn. After a month of delays and scrutiny, Craig posted his response to the *BW* story at www.VADefense.com. He wrote an *Open Letter to Shareholders* and included his December board communications. This, naturally, made management's assertions and the resulting story look ridiculous.

Apparently, Craig's letters were causing board members considerable heartburn. Who knows? Maybe they finally read them. According to Davis, Smith complained and asked Lanny to use his influence to get them off the Web. But then Fred called Craig and said he hadn't read what he'd posted. Smith said it was Davis who wanted *him* to use his influence to get them removed. Somebody wasn't telling the truth.

Craig told both men that he would remove his board letters, but he wanted something in return. First, he wanted the company to reimburse the $650 thousand it owed him and Rex for the company airplane. Confiscating his money and then falsely accusing him of stealing theirs wasn't very nice, Craig thought. Fred was angry that the firm had failed to honor this debt and said he'd make certain it was paid. (It never was.) Second, Winn asked Smith to do the right thing and release Davis's "*Business Week* got it wrong" letter. Smith said he would so long as it was okay with Davis and Caise. Davis was the one promoting the release, so either Fred failed to do as he promised or Caise was motivated by something other than shareholder interests. The letter went nowhere.

Craig's *Open Letter* shines a revealing light on the character and motivations of the players in our drama. Consider his motivation for responding to the attacks in the first place:

I wanted to leave Value America quietly. As the company's largest shareholder, I had the most to gain if the new strategy prevailed. Today, however, as a result of the continuing slander and the media's willingness to disregard fact and suspend reason to tell a good story, I can no longer remain silent. I must defend myself for the sake of my family and for the sake of those who invested their money and their lives in Value America. It is now abundantly clear the false and malicious attacks will continue until they are repudiated.

Craig had more than enough reasons to defend his character. *Business Week* not only altered the facts, the graphic imagery they used boldly proclaimed their intent to deceive. The *Business Week* cover story was filled with pictures, some so large they spilled over onto subsequent pages. Craig's smiling face was scattered throughout the story, although he had expressly withheld his permission to use his likeness. And where had the photos come from? They had been mysteriously lifted from the glowing *Chief Executive* article printed over a year earlier.

That painted an ominous picture, and not just for Craig. He's just one guy. He may or may not rise above the scurrilous attacks on his character. But what about the rest of us, our treasured institutions, our productive economy, and our once-noble nation? Should we—can we—trust the media? It's one thing to question what we *read*; journalists are fallible, just like the rest of us, despite the burden of responsibility the job carries. But if deception is the *purpose* of their stories, rather than the byproduct of carelessness, what does that say about our national character, about our prospects for a future as great as our past?

Honest criticism goes with the territory. Anytime you enter the arena and dare to be different, you invite controversy. You're guaranteed to make enemies. It's par for the course. But you'd hope the critics, especially in the media, would make an honest effort, and barring that, you'd hope they'd at least refrain from purposely distorting the truth.

Craig was disappointed by the attacks on his character and the assault on what had once been his company. He was angered by *Business Week's* willingness to lie in an effort to craft their distorted caricature. But he was revolted by their willingness to use pictures that were intended for one purpose and alter them to impart another, entirely false, impression. When their ethics stooped so low as to invade his home and family,

Craig's disgust turned to rage. He felt violated, raped. Fact is, he was.

Pictures are more powerful than words. Craig and I had relied on the communication prowess of the "picture-caption-copy" formula to present the merits of our company and its products. *BW* used the same tools, but to deceive their readers. Not only were the pictures taken from another magazine, used without permission, they were even altered. The captions were crafted to purposely mislead the reader into believing that Craig was gloating, thumbing his nose at all the suckers he'd swindled.

The captions were textbook examples of tabloid journalism. The cover screamed: "Winn has been ousted...the inside story of what went wrong." Above the table of contents was a picture of Craig and Katharine in their living room: "How hype and hubris destroyed Value America." The third picture was huge, so large it covered a page and a half of the magazine. Beside it they began, "Blinded by Net fever...Craig Winn's chaotic Value America." Inferring Craig was an arrogant fat cat, they wrote, "SET FOR LIFE. Value America may be short on cash, but Winn gained $53.7 million."

Each picture was designed to misrepresent Craig's character and malign the truth. On one page, they got *everything* wrong: "November 23, 1999—The board fires Winn. He begins dumping his shares into the market," and "Winn had little of his own money at risk. His business experience consisted mainly of leading another public company into bankruptcy. His technology experience: nil."

BW had the audacity to use a picture *Chief Executive* had shot of Craig's wife, Katharine, and dog, Crystal, sitting next to him in their home, smiling during better times. The caption read, "HOME AND HEARTH, The Winns relax in their mansion, set on a 150-acre estate in Virginia." Byrne added, "Sitting in his very sturdy mansion, which he calls Windom Hall, with majestic views of the Blue Ridge Mountains, Winn wants his millions and the last word." Gee, it certainly *sounds* like Craig invited the reporter and his photographers into his home to gloat, doesn't it?

Having set up his deception, Byrne concluded: "The Value America saga goes beyond the excesses of the Internet era. Serious questions are also being raised about alleged gross mismanagement, abuse of corporate funds, and the sometimes erratic and bizarre behavior of Winn."

Of course, if John Byrne had made up all this stuff himself, he'd be the next John Grisham. But Byrne isn't nearly that good. He required a lot of help crafting his grim fairy tale. Enter the seven dwarfs. "'Everyone figured he was more genius than crazy,' says a former senior executive. 'As time went on everybody got more concerned.'" *Thanks, David.*

There isn't much doubt that the attacks were designed to help Dorchak, Morgan, and the board by mischaracterizing all that Winn, and we, had done. But there was more to this than merely wanting a good story that would sell magazines by titillating that part of us that somehow relishes character assassination. Something more sinister was going on. Their own words tell the tale.

"'There have been a fair amount of decisions and expenditures of funds that were questionable,' says director Schmitt." Byrne intoned, "In retrospect, the story's most surprising aspect is how long the public—and the board—continued to believe in Winn." He went on to claim, "Winn quickly embraced the worst excesses of the New Economy.... He spent money lavishly, running through the company's cash as if it were unlimited."

Wow. And the Craig I knew had Tyranosaurus hands, you know, too short to reach our corporate wallet. As our CEO, he was so tight he squeaked. He was the best negotiator I ever met. But what do I know? I've only been joined at the hip with him for the better part of seven years.

The crusade against truth marched on. Six of the next seven statements are false. Based on conversations with Schmitt, Dorchak, and Morgan, Byrne wrote, "Other expenditures were even harder to understand. Winn agreed to purchase a 34.4-acre expanse of land for $5 million.... The property was later appraised at less than $2 million.... After a newly recruited CEO discouraged Winn's purchase of a corporate plane, Winn and co-founder Rex Scatena spent $650,000 for a down-payment anyway. They began expensing their trips to the company...and claim the company still owes them the down payment [bingo: that one's true]. Scatena couldn't be reached for comment."

Actually, Byrne was given Rex's home number, but he never bothered to call. He was, in fact, given the home numbers of all five founders as well as many of the most tenured current and former executives. He never called us, not even one of us. Was he reckless, or just too busy polishing his illusion?

Imagine that—writing a cover story for a supposedly serious business journal, owned by an even larger publishing company, McGraw Hill, and not bothering to call any of the people who actually know the most about the story you're writing. Imagine being willing to trash a man's reputation and invade the sanctity of his home without even making the effort to get the facts right. Imagine being given access to the documents you need but ignoring them and filing a story as fanciful as it is irrational. But he wasn't alone. Prominent newspapers and leading networks parroted many of the same false allegations—and nobody checked!

The absurdity of the more inflammatory charges revealed the underlying motivations of the participants. They demonstrated that the delusion was purposeful, not careless, that it was malicious, not just entertaining. And if reckless, purposeful, and malicious, a lot more is at stake than one man's reputation.

In his defense, Craig countered the charge that he'd misappropriated funds for land:

"I did not negotiate, nor even participate in the negotiations, to purchase the land in question. But before I present the facts, let's first examine the absurdity of the charge. The story infers that I was either stupid and paid twice what the land was worth or that I was a crook and was willing to risk jail to pick up my share of an overpayment. The "dumb" alternative is counter to the claim that I defrauded the smartest and richest men in America. The "criminal" inference is even more irrational. During the time this deal could have been concocted, my stock was worth over $300 million. My home was completed, I had no debt, and had millions in the bank. To think that I would risk losing everything, including my freedom, to illegally share in an overpayment defies reason.

While I was CEO, I negotiated land and office contracts. I worked with the area's leading commercial realtor, Lane Bonner, and with our Facility Manager, Sean Flynn. Neither Lane, Sean, nor I was a participant in this deal. Following my resignation as CEO in March '99, Byron Peters was assigned responsibility for facilities, property, and leases. Byron found this property, negotiated its purchase, and managed the process....

Mr. Bonner believes the land is more valuable than that offered at $200,000 an acre by the University of Virginia in their adjoining parcel. (34.4 times $200,000+/acre is $6.9 million, not less than $2.0 million.) I am neither a developer nor an expert in commercial land. Yet to prove my point, I'll reimburse the company the four hundred thousand they spent canceling this contract if the owner will sell me the land for the price Value America says it's worth. More importantly, if the land is worth anything close to what the area's leading expert claims, what does it say about those that are willing to soil my name by claiming it is worth less?

Good question, one that deserves an answer. And what about the airplane? Was this story concocted as well? Here's what Craig had to say:

"The charge that I misappropriated corporate funds related to the airplane is equally absurd. Funds were misappropriated, but I was a victim, not the perpetrator. Use your common sense to answer these questions. First, how could the "newly recruited" CEO be against the airplane if there was no airplane until the fifth month of his eight-month career at Value America? Second, why, if he was against the plane, did he fly on it so many times, including nine times in

September and October alone? Third, why, if the airplane was just my personal extravagance, did the company write an aircraft policy, obtain Board approval, conduct lease negotiations, hire pilots, schedule business trips, and pay the fuel bills? Fourth, why, if there was no truth to our claim that the company owes us money, did the firm's auditors book a "reasonable reserve" to pay us back in Q4?

Value America's aircraft policy was written by Dean Johnson. It was presented to the board without any dissent, and was approved unanimously, with Fred Smith saying we had made the right choice on a necessary tool. Johnson wrote, "Were Value America located in a metropolitan area its payroll costs would be 50% higher ($12 million annually) and its office leases would be 170% higher ($1.4 million annually). Unfortunately, Charlottesville is not well served by air transportation so [the aircraft is a relatively inexpensive tradeoff]. The primary use of the corporate aircraft is for high-level strategic Company-related business with a clearly stated business purpose."

The airplane was the principal tool used to consummate the company's best and most productive relationships. If the entire cost of the airplane were attributed to just two relationships, CitiPrivileges and the FedEx Marketplace, the plane was a sound investment [at one third of one percent of the revenues it generated, it was 150 times more productive than any advertising money Ms. Dorchak ever spent]. Value America's aircraft logs show that it was used productively by most every member of management including the current CEO (9-8, 9-9, 10-18), former CEO (7-7, 7-8, 9-2, 9-7, 9-14, 9-15, 9-28, 9-30, 10-13, 10-14), current Chairman (11-19, 11-22, 11-23, 11-29), and board Members (7-13, 7-14, 11-4). Rex and I made the initial deposits on the airplane while the company's finance department worked out acceptable lease terms. The lease was approved by the board but never executed. The company still owes us our initial deposits. It is unconscionable that the loss of our own personal money has been convoluted to infer we misappropriated the company's money.

Under the headline: "BAILING OUT" Byrne wrote, "Most Value America investors have lost big. But both Winn and Scatena have been feverishly dumping their stock since being forced out of the company in November." He included a pretty chart showing Craig selling shares worth nearly $3 million in December. In actuality, he sold *no* shares in December or even in January for that matter. But why be accurate?

To his credit, John Byrne actually asked one intelligent question, "So where were the directors during this debacle?" He illuminates his question with an observation, "When an executive-suite *coup* erupted in November, they had barely settled into their roles. Directors contacted by *BW* say they acted appropriately and still express confidence in the company."

But then, just when you think the lights are on, they dim again. "Winn shows little regret about the fate of Value America or of the well-heeled backers who believed in him." Actually, Byrne never asked, and Craig never said. The charge was neither true, nor a careless error.

As Value America's current and former managers scrambled to contrive their cover-up, and concoct their elaborate diversion to save their sorry souls, *BW* entertained readers with a plethora of witty attacks. Dorchak said, "It's like icing a cake that hasn't been baked. We had someone here who was just icing an unbaked cake." "'We played vendor bingo,' says one former executive." Nick Hofer, Glenda's inept VP of Advertising, toed the company line, calling Craig's passion for direct response catalogs, "his whim of the week." Technology merchandiser Paul Ewert supported the woman who had promoted him as well, claiming, "Now we have adult supervision." Frank Flowers, as if talking about a different company, said, "Attempting to deal directly with consumers probably wasn't the smartest idea on their part." *And I thought we were a retailer.*

One of my personal favorites came courtesy of an infamous, nameless former manager: "Value America began to operate less like a business and more like a cult. 'When you're around him, you get caught in the swirl,' says one former manager. 'It's like drinking the Kool-Aid.' Winn would gather his employees and speak for a full hour at a time, promising that everyone standing before him would someday be a millionaire. At one session, recalls employees, he stood on top of railroad ties on a chilly May morning in the parking lot and spoke for an hour about his life and career. 'As he talked, the sun rose higher in the sky and the air became warm and comfortable.... I wonder if Craig planned it that way?'"

At this point, Mr. Byrne's hatchet job was done. He had crafted an elaborate ruse designed to sell magazines by appealing to the worst in his readers. But he owed his collaborators their due. There was a reason the morally challenged had trashed the company's largest shareholders publicly, condemned the company in the teeth of a class action suit, and breached their fiduciary duties. Remember, they needed an alibi in the worst possible way. In the face of clear and unmistakable warnings, they had implemented their plan, and it had failed—more miserably perhaps than any in the history of American business. Lucky for them, John Byrne was all too pleased to comply:

"Winn, say insiders, had trouble giving up control to his new CEO. Although Winn denies it, several present and former executives [Read: Morgan, Kuo, and Starnes] say he frequently undermined Morgan and continued to micromanage nearly everything. 'There was never a major decision he was not involved with,' says Morgan. 'Craig would just do what he wanted to do and informed me after the fact.'"

Later, next to a picture of Dorchak (one *Business Week* actually took for the occasion), Byrne portrayed Glenda as a victim, saying, "Dorchak now finds herself trying to pick up the pieces." Makes you want to vomit. But at least with Morgan, one doesn't have to wonder if he were just misunderstood. His lies were clearly premeditated, unprovoked, reckless, material, malicious, and purposely designed to demean Craig just to save his tattered reputation. According to *Business Week's* lawyers, the allegations made against Craig were defensible because Tom Morgan said they were true.

Craig's *Open Letter* begs to differ. So do the facts.

According to the *Business Week* cover story, neither Morgan, the former CEO, nor Dorchak, the current CEO, are willing to accept responsibility for their time as managers. To shirk responsibility, the former CEO now alleges that 'Winn micromanaged everything.' If this is not true, feasible, rational, or in keeping with factual evidence, the remainder of the story, and their alibi, disintegrates. Since I was not the CEO, President, COO, CIO, CTO, CFO, EVP, or SVP of anything following the IPO, unless I micromanaged everything I could not have been responsible for under-funding technology and over-funding advertising as they claim. The charge of "micromanaging" is neither factual, feasible, nor rational.

We raised $275 million dollars from June '98 to April '99 through four private and two public rounds. As any entrepreneur knows, managing a private investment round is incredibly time consuming. The entrepreneur has to find potential investors, present the company's merits, justify the valuation, survive due diligence, keep tedious and contentious legal negotiations moving forward, and close the transaction. IPOs are even more time consuming and challenging. It is not remotely possible that anyone, not Fred Smith, not Lee Iacocca, not Andy Grove, and especially not Craig Winn, could micromanage a lemonade stand, much less a fast-growing technology business with 300 people, while managing six investment rounds in nine months.

Following the IPO, the micromanagement charge is equally fictitious. In fact, following the IPO and my resignation as CEO, I neither managed nor *micromanaged* anything. I built relationships on the firm's behalf with other great companies and institutions. It is hard to be in two places at the same time. The micromanaging charge is neither feasible nor in keeping with the evidence. Most importantly, it is not even rational. If I wanted to micromanage, why did I voluntarily give up the role of CEO and recruit a CEO, President, and EVP of Operations, all with compensation packages greater than my own?... The charge defies reason and logic. Its only support is that it fits the typical entrepreneurial stereotype and, if true, mitigates other people's responsibility.

Byrne's story linked Craig to lavish ad spending. In reality he was its biggest opponent. All of his letters to the board confirm this indisputable reality. Yet those in need of an excuse seized upon the opportunity to thrust their wanton extravagances upon the firm's founder. The *BW* article said, "Meanwhile in [his] zeal to meet the unrealistic expectations of Wall Street, the company was making ever more desperate and wasteful marketing deals. The company paid Yahoo! $4.5 million for a year's worth of website ads that several insiders say brought in less than $100,000 of revenue. The company spent $1 million for a booth at Comdex, the computer show...and wasted another $750,000 sponsoring Dennis Conner's America's Cup yacht. 'We kept spending money like it was going out of style,' said one former top executive."

But the Open Letter described reality:

I was not an advocate for big advertising spending to inflate the stock price, as is charged. In fact, I thought it would have exactly the opposite effect. It is astonishing that as the most outspoken critic of the Comdex show, America's Cup yacht endorsement, and spending more with Yahoo!, I am portrayed as the fool that proposed them. Fortunately, the *Path to Profitability* I prepared on behalf of shareholders proves the foolishness of this charge. The decisions of the board, the merits of the restructuring plan, and the rejection of our *Path* are now public, and thus our letters represent nothing more than the losing side of a debate. Today, they may actually help shareholders by demonstrating that the charges alleged in the story are unfounded.

Craig's May 2000 *Open Letter* answered the most serious allegations. The other seventy false and misleading statements he refuted in a document he cleverly entitled "False and Misleading Statements." He posted it all online at VADefense.com, a website which has its own revealing history.

Joe Page had sent CMO Tom Starnes an email asking if he wanted to pay the renewal fees on twenty or so unused URLs, or just let them go. These included two web addresses the company had bought on behalf of its founder: craigwinn.com and cwinn.com. Tom returned Joe's email confirming the appropriateness of relinquishing the useless domains. So when Craig needed an appropriate Web address in which to post his defense against the company's libelous attacks, he naturally choose craigwinn.com. It was his name, after all. He had the URL transferred to a local ISP, and posted his rebuttal there. Dorchak had a hissy fit. She instructed her loyalists to misuse the company's autonomous system status to misdirect traffic away from Craig's site. But she wasn't done. She ordered the Hitler Youth to commit another offense, acquiring craigwinn.net and -.org. Amused but undaunted by the chicanery, Craig simply bought the URL VADefense.com and posted everything there.

Craig's *Open Letter* was five thousand words, half the length of *Business*

Week's attack. I can hardly imagine what it must have been like to write it. The company we had worked so hard to build was now publicly humiliating my friend. And it wasn't only in *Business Week*. Management spewed the same venom to *The New York Times*, *The Washington Post*, and *The Wall Street Journal*. NBC even sent a helicopter to hover above Craig's home. They foolishly implied that he had built it by ripping off the shareholders.

In that his words were written concurrently with these events, they provide us with an insight into his personal anguish and a perspective into the builders and destroyers of our once proud firm:

It is not surprising that I attract attention and sometimes inspire animosity. Those who are willing to accept the challenges of building and innovating almost always attract unwanted attention and criticism. I have, as a matter of practice, avoided responding to my critics, most of whom have never built anything. I have always asked people to remember what the critics say, for critics impale themselves on their own words. This is no exception.

Fortunately, builders like me also have a redeeming quality. We can inspire good people to accomplish great things. There are no quotes in *Business Week* from Rex Scatena, Joe Page, Ken Power, or Bill Hunt. Together we were Value America's first five employees. Each name and number was given to the author of this story, but he never bothered to call or listen to what they had to say.

In direct conflict with the story, Rex and I were not fired, or forced out, by the Board in November, or ever. We were both still employees through December 20th. We resigned following the Board's decision to implement management's restructuring plan. At the time, no one had a greater incentive for the company and its future plans to work than did Rex and I. We were the company's largest shareholders with combined ownership of nearly 50%.

We believed, however, that the company needed to cut its advertising, not its employees. We believed, as evidenced by my letters, that there were better alternatives. I thought the case for those alternatives, and against the restructuring plan, was so compelling, its rejection was unequivocal evidence we no longer had any ability to influence the board or the company in any positive way. As a result, Rex and I resigned from the board on February 3rd after first complying with all of the requests made by the chairman of the Special Committee. Three weeks later, in the final days of February 2000, the [Rule] 144 specialists at Robertson Stephens began to sell significant amounts of our stock in compliance with all SEC regulations.

It is completely false and purposely misleading to report, "They have been feverishly dumping their stock since being forced out of the company in November." We did not sell until the second half of February, after both Rex and I had resigned from the board, three months after we had been isolated by management, and demeaned in the press by those whom we empowered. And for the record, I volunteered, verbally and in writing, before and after my resignations from the company and from the board, on ten occasions, to manage the sale of the company on behalf of the shareholders. The board knew, as I knew, if they had accepted my offer I would have been prohibited from selling any meaningful quantity of shares, because managing this process would put me in regular contact with material non-public information. But they rejected my offers, and thus I was able to sell my shares in a company I no longer understood, I no longer influenced, and in one that no longer valued me or my contribution.

In defiance of reason, no one associated with the company ever did anything positive to encourage their largest shareholders to retain their shares. In fact, they did just the opposite. They chose to slander us in public forums. Why management thought it was in their interest to harass the company's largest shareholders is as perplexing as *Business Week's* callous disregard of evidence and reason.

The charge that "the story's most surprising aspect is how long the public, and the board members, continued to believe in Winn" is as inconsistent with the facts as "almost anyone can find buyers for a house of cards if he has a good enough pitch." The notion that America's best and brightest, who collectively put the company and its entire team through two years of constant due diligence and audits, invested, not once, but multiple times, in a house of cards requires a complete suspension of reason. During the years I was CEO of Value America, we consistently under-promised and over-delivered. The only suspension of belief required here is that it is remotely possible to pass through two years of intense scrutiny and professional audits with just a good sales pitch. The premise of the story is not only untrue...it's *impossible*.

I find it interesting that *BW* describes November as the "eruption of an executive-suite *coup*." While their coverage is inaccurate, a *coup* may have been what was intended. With regard to the board, I am certain they believed they made the best decisions they could, with the information they had available to them, and that they believe they acted on behalf of the shareholders. However, an all outside board is easier to influence with a coordinated blend of misinformation and character assassination. Sadly, it takes very few misguided individuals to destroy the good work of many. It's happened before. For example, the former CEO's company, USOP, was sliced into pieces, and like ours, USOP's stock plummeted during his tenure. It is also interesting that USOP's founder and Chairman was was gone less than a year after Morgan joined the firm through what some say was a character-assassination campaign conducted at board level.

During the years Rex and I managed the company, its value increased from $30 million in September '97 to $1 billion in April '99. The fact that the stock price increased from $10 to $17 in late November amongst rumors we were returning to management, and has since dropped to $2 following the announcement of our resignation and the restructuring plan, may not be coincidental. We will never know if our proposed alternatives would have prevailed, but in the aftermath of the company's decline and the *Business Week* story, our proposals make interesting reading. So why did the board reject our *Path to Profitability* last December and choose to support management's restructuring plan that cut the company into the pieces they "now find themselves trying to pick up"? I do not know, but it is not hard to imagine, considering the way misinformation and character assassination were used to weave this grossly fictitious tale.

I am sure that there will be some, following the release of this letter, that will think that all I accomplished was to get into the mud with my attackers. Others will come to believe that truth lies somewhere in-between the charges and my defense. The truth is, my open letter is just a defense, a long defense indeed, but just a defense. I believe it is right to defend that which one knows to be true. Yet, a good offense is more stimulating and sells magazines. I hope, however, that many find my defense helps them justify the soundness of their decision to invest their money and lives in a company we called Value America.

This all brings us back to the initial question.... Why did some say, and why did others write, something that is not, and could not, be true? For some the proliferation of these stories, no matter how false or ridiculous, provides an excuse for what actually occurred preceding and following our departure. They know that the truth will never get as much public attention as their attacks. For *Business Week* it is a good story that sells magazines, even if there is no correlation between what actually occurred and what they wrote. For the great men and women who devoted themselves to building Value America only to be discarded and demeaned, this story just adds insult to injury. As for my family and me, we dedicated ourselves to building a company based upon the noble idea of doing well by doing good. While I know we did everything in our power to make Value America a success, I am troubled by the disappointment that must be shared by all who invested their lives and their money in this company.

❧❧

MANY OF THOSE who had helped build Value America made their way to Craig's farm. We had come to support our fallen friend, who was as low as a worm on a hot day. For a man who had fought and won so many battles, who had sacrificed so much on our behalf, to be depicted as trash in that pretentious rag just wasn't right. We were angry, not so much at the media, but at the weasels who had used them. The *Business Week* story and others like it in *The Post, The Times,* and *The Journal* had said far more about the collaborators, Value America's desperate and mercenary managers, than they had about Craig.

One of the most revealing attacks came courtesy of David Kuo. He supplied Byrne with detailed "information" about Craig's brush with advertising and politics. He claimed Winn wanted to create a series of TV ads featuring himself as a spokesperson in order to promote his budding political career. In actuality, it had been David's two public relations firms who had concluded that featuring Craig would be the only way our firm could successfully convey our unique message. David conveniently elected to omit this "detail" from his conversations with Byrne. He also somehow managed to forget that he himself had invited Ralph Reed, his former employer, to meet with Craig to discuss the political landscape.

What drives people to set up others in this manner, wrongfully embarrassing them in the media? Perhaps, having failed to seduce Craig into aligning himself with the Brethren, they thought a little public humiliation might be appropriate. Without facts to support their condemnation, they just made 'em up. It was all designed to make Craig look foolish, of course. But I would soon learn that he was in good company. David's whoppers about Jerry Falwell, another foe of the Brethren, were as entertaining as they were absurd. Mess with the Brethren, they'll slander you.

Byron Peters, strangely enough, was bitter. He seemed to almost relish Craig's condition. Sure, he acknowledged that nothing in the articles had been true, but he saw *himself* as the principal victim of this calamity. He said, "You made money on Value America, so no one cares that you were trashed." The implication was, "I'm the one who got hurt; you should feel sorry for me."

Craig challenged him. "This isn't about feeling sorry. Why would anybody in their right mind want people to feel sorry for them?" That concept was beyond Craig's comprehension. "It's about right and wrong, good and evil," Craig told Peters, encouraging him to stand up and rebuff the lies. "Bad things happen when good people don't stand up." Sadly, the six-foot-four Byron Peters, professional manager *extraordinaire*, once again ducked for cover.

Joe Page, Jacob Mitchell, and Phil Intahar rose to the occasion. Early one morning, they found Craig working on a tractor in his barn. They had come to demonstrate their support and to share some of what they had learned. Jacob said he had gone to the new CIO, Niles Edwards. Edwards, like Tip Lawson, Glenda's new CFO, had made his way into Value America's employ through the continuing machinations of Goose Godfrey. Amazingly, Godfrey was still being paid his "consulting fee." He had found a kindred spirit, I suppose.

Anyway, Jacob said that Edwards had been troubled by the *Business Week* story and had challenged Glenda, asking her why she had been willing to inflict such terrible damage upon the company. What Edwards told

Jacob is hard to believe. "She told me that it had been Frank Flowers' idea. He wanted Craig punished for having sold his stock. She said she was only doing what she'd been asked to do."

"Liars lie; that's what liars do," Craig responded with a shrug. "Frank Flowers is a smart man. He has a wealthy boss to protect. It doesn't make sense. It's just Glenda doing the only thing she's really good at—blaming others for her failures."

As some reached out to Craig in person, others did so by letter. Value America's friend, John Motley wrote, "I realize there has been a great deal written about both you and Value America. Although plans did not develop as we hoped they might, I want you to know that from my perspective, you have been a great friend and have done more for me than I ever imagined. I cannot begin to tell you what a tremendous thrill it was watching Value America develop and grow. I will never be able to adequately express how much I appreciate what you have done for my family. While some will argue that mistakes were made, and certainly there were some, I have always thought of you as one of the most talented and brilliant people I have ever met. You never backed away from any commitments you made to me, and for that I am very grateful. I have always been proud to say you are my friend."

Sean Flynn wrote, "I first met Craig Winn in the summer of 1996. He described his plans to clear his overgrown fields and his desire to build his home. It was the first of a thousand times that he told me what he was going to do and he did exactly what he said. The Craig that I know is a man of integrity and moral strength who earned the respect and admiration of all who know him." Another said, "In all my dealings with you, I found you to be honest. A handshake with you is the way it ended up in the paperwork."

India Hamner was one of the many great people who had helped build the dream that had once been Value America. She and Craig seldom spoke, but today her words speak for all of us. On May 29th she wrote:

Craig, I have waited for the storm to blow over and for the air to clear but I just can't wait any longer. I'm the Helpdesk supervisor at Value America. I have been in the position for some time and I've watched what has happened to your dream. I am so sorry. I can't speak for "the company" but I can certainly speak for myself. I believe we are now bleeding from the inside.

I remember my first day at work. Your dream was being lived each day. Each of us came to work with such excitement and enthusiasm. I could stand in the hall and hear the developers pouring into the office talking about what they could do. I remember the day we went public. That was one of the most exciting days I have ever experienced! We were running up and down the halls hugging each other. We were all a part of the "Great American Dream" being fulfilled. That team spirit is what drew me to Value America.

I remember the day I received my first Value America shirt. I was so proud to wear it everywhere. I remember the day we were setting up the call center at Hollymead. Your wife, children, and dog dropped by. Your wife was so kind to me and she didn't even know me. I told her how proud I was to be part of it all.

I have gone over and over it in my mind trying to figure out what I could have done differently to make things better. Those of us in the trenches doing the day-to-day work have had so little say and so little control. Until the last few weeks I still believed the dream of Value America could be a reality. I wish I could have made things better. I'll always be proud of being a part of a great company. Thank you for making that possible. I pray that you and your family will continue to love and support each other. Thank you for the beautiful example you have set.

I too wrote a letter. Though mine was addressed to *Business Week* rather than to Craig, my words echoed India's sentiments.

John Byrne's article, "The Fall of a Dot-Com" (May 1, 2000), tries valiantly to place the blame for the imminent demise of Internet retailer Value America squarely on the shoulders of its founder, Craig Winn, portraying him alternately as a silver-tongued super salesman, a meddling and avaricious flim-flam man, and a financial loose cannon. This characterization may make the story line tidy; too bad it's so very far from the truth.

I am in a position to know. I was there four years ago when Craig Winn dusted off a business plan he had written almost twenty years earlier describing the future of retailing, a world where better information, not merely lower price, drove sales; a world where the inherent inefficiencies of brick and mortar stores could be reduced or eliminated, making it possible to sell better products for less money; a world where a percentage of every sale could be donated to a worthy charity. It was a stunning concept, and I felt privileged to be a part of it.

I knew Craig Winn. I had worked shoulder to shoulder with him for months on end. I felt that if there were any man on earth capable of pulling off this palpably difficult endeavor, it was him. He knew sales. He knew manufacturing. And for a non-technologist, he had a remarkably good handle on how the emerging technology worked. So I signed on as Value America's Creative Director.

Over the next three years, I watched us grow from three people to over six hundred. As long as we kept Mr. Winn's vision clearly before us, our presence grew at a phenomenal rate. But by the time there were 150 or 200 of us, something had changed. More and more employees neither shared nor cared about Craig Winn's vision. Executives and managers were hired who had their own agendas and methods. Our newspaper ads, which had started out so information-rich and brand-centric, became increasingly focused on little more than price, until we finally earned our unwanted reputation as a "cheap-computer store." It seemed that every time we strayed from Mr. Winn's original business plan, we became more like every other struggling retailer. And with every three-hour manager's meeting, we strayed ever farther off track.

But was it Craig Winn's fault? Without his vision, enthusiasm, and good old-fashioned hard work, there would have been no Value America to discuss. So let's discuss some of Mr. Winn's "faults":

Greed: Byrne seems miffed with the opulence of the Winn estate near Charlottesville. But Mr. Winn built it with money earned long before Value America went public...and he did a surprising amount of the actual site preparation with his own two hands, a tractor, and a chainsaw. Not your typical yuppie scum. And stock sales? Mr. Winn began to systematically sell off his Value America shares only after it became clear the board had discarded his business plan. No one ever said he was stupid.

Lavish ad spending: Before Glenda Dorchak was hired to head up our advertising program, Craig had us running ads with a modest and manageable schedule. It was under Dorchak's management, not Winn's, that our ad program grew to over twenty newspapers a week, plus magazines, radio, and television.

Micromanagement: Ah, if only he could have spread himself even thinner. Craig has better instincts in more diverse disciplines than anyone I've ever met.

Ego: Presidential aspirations? Yes, for a brief moment he considered it. Why? Because several of Virginia's most influential citizens asked him to, recognizing his abilities, his high moral standards, and his heart for the practical realization of racial equality through his plan for increased educational and economic opportunity. But to my mind, he's too idealistic to make it in Washington.

I still think Value America was a wonderful concept. It should have worked. But don't blame Craig for its failure. It's not his fault. It's mine—along with six hundred or so of my Value America coworkers. He did not fail us. No, we failed him, in failing to execute his grand and worthy vision.

It's been said a thousand times, "Those who can, do; those who can't, write." John Byrne, many of Wall Street's dot-com analysts, and most of our professional parasites, shared something in common: they *couldn't*. They couldn't build a business if their lives depended on it. So they wrote, or at least contributed to the writing of the *Business Week* article and other published illusions. If Craig is right, and I fear he is, they shared something else as well: insecurity. It's the reason those who *can't* try to bring others down in order to elevate themselves. The behavior is rampant, contagious, and cancerous. Unstopped, it can do immeasurable harm.

Where you have envy and selfish ambition, there you find disorder and every evil practice—James

THE WICKED WITCH

As time slipped out of Value America's hourglass, General Kicklighter introduced Craig to a group of Australian businessmen. They wanted to build the kind of infrastructure tools our board had rejected. Fortunately for the Australians, many of Value America's best and brightest were now either unemployed or desperately looking to be reemployed in a more ethical environment.

This all led to what came to be called "The Craig Dinner." Those interested in a new challenge joined him one evening at the Downtown Grill to discuss the possibilities. Spotted by the FOGs, word quickly spread that Winn was up to no good. The FOGs, at Dorchak's direction, grilled the participants like SS troopers.

Joe Page, whom it was impossible to intimidate, sent the Hitler Youth an email: "I don't see any reason for being asked to sign another non-disclosure letter, other than that it's the company's reaction to the 'Craig Dinner.' I have already signed multiple non-disclosures. On a professional level, I would never leak out information. Personally, I am offended by the inference. Specifically regarding Mr. Winn, he is, and always will be, my friend. In addition, he is very insistent upon keeping Value America out of ANY conversations in his presence. Therefore, I consider this whole exercise to be nothing other than harassment."

Just for fun, Craig had his lawyers call the company and ask for his employment records. He knew that the one-size-fits-all employment contract he had signed had never been countersigned by the company. But lo and behold, when he received a copy, it bore Dorchak's signature, even though she had not even been with the firm at the time it was executed.

Craig somehow talked the Australians into buying a controlling interest in the now buck-fifty-a-share firm rather than building their own e-services business from scratch. So the Australians studied the juicy parts of the recently released annual report and came to the inescapable conclusion that Value America was running out of time and money. It was a win-win scenario, so the Australians went out and collected commitments for over $50 million in venture capital.

Within days, they contacted the Special Committee's investment bankers. Fred Smith had hired Alex Brown to "explore strategic opportunities," but they couldn't be bothered. Rather than facilitate a legitimate offer to bail the company out of its cash-deprived predicament, they rebuffed the advance. The company's nervous management had told them to stonewall the Australians and challenge their motives. So afraid were Glenda and Wolf of losing their personal enrichment machine, they ordered Caise to craft a convoluted confidentiality agreement to thwart them, keep them at bay. Frustrated, the Australians faxed a letter to Smith, explaining the affront. He didn't respond.

᭡᭡᭡

VALUE AMERICA'S mercenary managers put out press releases with reckless abandon. They all said pretty much the same thing: *The company is announcing a nothing relationship with nobody. This is proof that the focused restructuring is taking hold. It is further evidence that the company's superior management team is worthy of their lofty salaries.* The market yawned. The stock dropped. This time it fell below a dollar a share.

To be fair, they did do something. As soon as Glenda and her beloved FOGs were empowered, they eliminated the store's charity contribution feature. It was inconsistent with their corporate character. So in effect, they changed the beneficiary from great organizations like Habitat for Humanity and American Heart Organization to the pocketbooks of Glenda Dorchak and her devoted fan club.

But she wasn't without a heart. On one occasion the benevolent CEO roamed the halls with her HR Director in tow. In a move that would make Marie Antoinette blush, the Charitable One graciously handed each and every remaining employee a donut. The beneficiaries were speechless.

Unimpressed, Linda Harmon left. As a single mom, she needed the job desperately, but she couldn't take it any more. A woman of strong faith and good character, she had been stationed in Purgatory, the heart of darkness. She realized that all hope was lost. The dream of "doing well by doing good" had been turned into "get what you can while the getting's good." She watched in disgust as Glenda courted her girlfriend at *Business Week*. She overheard the heated conversations, witnessed the finger pointing among the loyalists as they blamed each other and jockeyed for position. She agonized over the repeated pleas from shareholders wanting to know what was going on. She passed the messages on to Mrs. Kuo, SVP of Investor Relations, but Kim just let them pile up on her desk, too busy painting her nails to be bothered.

Not surprisingly, Kim was the only employee Tom recruited from Value America for his next stint. She had done such a fine job, he whisked her off to Atlanta to work with his new company. But like most Morgan endeavors, it didn't last long. His next victim, though, was a larger, more established firm, so he was able to reward Goose Godfrey, Tom Starnes, and Cliff Chambers, bringing them all aboard. True to form, Starnes told the press that Morgan was the most wonderful professional he had ever served. You can't pay a man too much for that kind of support.

David Kuo, of course, followed his bride to Atlanta, where he wrote a book about his life and times on the periphery of Value America—his seventh job in less than seven years. Without any business background or understanding, it's amazing he'd even attempt it. Equally amazing was his next job. His new address? 1600 Pennsylvania Avenue, the West Wing: assisting the President to enact his faith-based initiative.

Meanwhile, back in Purgatory, *der* Dorchak and the Hitler Youth squabbled over who were going to get the best chairs. They pondered which overpriced consultant they would get to craft a business plan. They must have reached a consensus, for they hired—and paid—a small army of them. On the way down, they enriched every lawyer and consultant east of the Blue Ridge.

Katharine Winn was not immune from the fallout. She received a call at home one morning from the CEO of Wachovia Bank, complaining about the company's bizarre behavior. He wanted Craig to explain why the bank should continue the company's merchant account—its ability to accept credit card payments. Katharine patiently explained that Craig was no longer with the firm and that he should call Ms. Dorchak. When Katharine offered to provide the banker with her direct line, the bank's senior executive said, "Thanks anyway. I've called her. She won't return my calls. She's left me with no alternative." Wachovia put the company on notice that within sixty days it would stop all credit card payments. Sadly, it wouldn't matter.

Another episode indicative of the company's collective moral bankruptcy involved Apple Computer. Against the advice of Eric Cherna, her sole remaining productive merchant, *der* Dorchak commanded her entourage to blow $200,000 filming an infomercial for the colorful new line of Apple PCs. Then, after it was done, she instructed them to solicit Apple's support. The FOGs lied about it, telling Apple they would consider filming an infomercial if *they* would pay for it. Not only didn't Apple bite, they said they hated infomercials. *Don't sell our radically new machines like some sort of kitchen gadget!* Another two hundred grand squandered.

Unfortunately, that was now the norm. One day, for no apparent reason, Dorchak decided to change infomercial agencies. Her choice was fifty percent more expensive than the one it replaced. The agency not only cost more, the time they bought was less productive, so the new infomercials failed miserably.

Undaunted, the professionals filmed another infomercial. This time, the brain trust tried to sell *business* technology between Veg-o-Matics and Miracle Hair products. I don't have to tell you how it performed. Cherna cried foul, but his complaints fell on deaf ears. Eric, who was now responsible for eighty percent of the firm's revenues, resigned in protest.

As April rolled into May, something came up that compelled Fred Smith to call Craig. The discussion led to Value America. Craig once again volunteered to give up the right to sell his remaining shares to help the Special Committee. "Rex and I will work for a buck a day just to keep this thing from disintegrating any further."

Smith replied, "The company is finally focused and making progress. A change at this time would be destabilizing. Thanks, but no."

Destabilizing! "Fred, do you have any idea how screwed up this company is? Every day somebody important leaves. All the best merchants are gone. Nothing's happening in technology, or anyplace else. If it wasn't for *Dungeons and Dragons* and *Age of Empires*, they'd have nothing to do. From what I hear around town, everything's ground to a halt. There's no plan. There's no leadership. There's no sales. There's no money." *And check the stock price: there's no value, either.*

Craig waited for a reaction, but got none. "I have no relationship with any of the folks supposedly running this company of yours. God knows what little I get is hearsay, stuff from the trenches, mostly from people long since discarded. It's the kind of stuff you'll find plastered all over the VUSA message boards. But Fred," Craig paused to make sure he would choose the right words, "everybody is saying the same thing. The company's sales have evaporated. Revenues may have fallen to as little as a million dollars a week. If the scuttlebutt is true, Value America will miss this quarter's revenue expectations by *seventy percent!*"

"It's not true!" Fred shot back angrily. "Management is telling us no such thing. They're doing a fine job! You just need to let go."

"I did, Fred. That's the problem."

৩৶:৶৶

MANAGEMENT CONTINUED to delay reporting their earnings for their devastatingly inept first quarter. Normally, a company closes its books ten days after the end of a quarter. They invest another ten days reconciling, adjusting, and fine tuning prior to giving the auditors about the same amount of time to review their work. This is why public companies typically report their quarterly numbers four weeks after the quarter's end. Our brain surgeons were caught off guard when the May issue of *Business Week* debuted in April, weeks before they were ready to hide under Craig's shadow. Sure, they now had a great alibi, but unfortunately they would need a new diversion.

As these events unfolded, Wolf elected to trot off into the sunset. Glenda was crowned Chairwoman. Failure has its rewards. But the rewards were not shared equally. Remember Seth Rossi, the man who had worked so hard to broker Dorchak's promotion to CEO? So enamored was he with her seductive story, he continued investing in Value America stock. All the way down. He ultimately lost everything he had "earned."

But he was not alone. A supportive Smith, as poorly informed as ever, was again quoted praising Dorchak's superior management, her ability to stabilize and focus the company, and her tireless devotion to duty. The board danced to every note she played. Then they decided to pay—handsomely—for the privilege. For reasons even they may not fully comprehend, the members of the Special Committee—Durn and Tarpin on behalf of Pacific Capital, Smith on behalf of himself and Federal Express, and Flowers on behalf of Paul Allen—reinvested. They did what every entrepreneur knows should never be done: They threw good money after bad, torching another $30 million.

Dorchak touted the news, claiming she'd raised *$90 million*. She bragged to the press, "Today is the biggest day in Value America's history!" I'd beg to differ, but she had the podium. "The company has more than enough cash to make it all the way to profitability." The May 10, 2000 press release gushed:

Value America to receive up to $90 million in equity…. The first set of agreements provides $30 million from a new issue of convertible preferred stock to existing investors including Vulcan Ventures, Pacific Capital, Fred Smith, and Federal Express. The company also has entered into an agreement with Acqua Wellington for up to $60 million. "These financing commitments represent a significant vote of confidence in the steps Glenda Dorchak and her management team have taken to stabilize and refocus Value America," said Fred Smith, Chairman of Federal Express, who serves as Chairman of the Special Committee.

"We have streamlined our model and achieved significant improvements in key operating indices including revenue per head and advertising efficiency," Dorchak observed…."We believe we can *continue to grow revenues* and increase satisfaction while rationalizing costs and improving advertising efficiencies."

Buried deep in the rubbish was the dirty little secret that made all her exuberant claims a lie. Normally, e-tail firms begin their quarterly releases by proudly proclaiming that their astonishing growth is proof positive they are worthy of their lofty valuations. But for the first time, Value America could make no such claim. It was dying. At the last possible moment, they announced Q1's dismal results: "Revenues were $47 million." The company wasn't "continuing to grow" as Dorchak and her propaganda machine had claimed. $47 million was less, not more, than the $61 million the company eventually reported in the previous quarter.

But that wasn't the worst of it. The mercenary managers were failing at an ever-accelerating pace. While pathetic, their $47 million Q1 revenues were nearly three times better than the $17 million they would ultimately sell in the current quarter, Q2, a quarter already sixty percent over at the time Dorchak claimed to be "growing." She knew the truth, yet, as in the past, elected to lie. Value America wasn't doing any of the wonderful things she claimed.

So the groundswell Craig had heard regarding the second quarter was true. Revenues had fallen to less than a third of what they had been during his final quarter as chairman. Glenda missed her revenue expectations by $50 million, a scant seventy-five percent below the numbers she had given Wall Street. I'm sure it must have been Craig's fault.

〜✿〜

BELEAGUERED SHAREHOLDERS RECEIVED an expensive, elegantly bound copy of the electronic annual report that had been posted online some time before. It pictured the Wicked Witch garbed in her favorite color, black. With black covers, black text, and black news, it had all the effulgence of asphalt at midnight. Although she had been with the company since '98, Ms. D. began her three-page letter to shareholders by reassuring investors that the company was now being, in her words, "led by a completely new but very experienced management team headed by CEO Glenda Dorchak, formerly with IBM." Evidently pleased with herself, she carried on, and I quote, "Our talented, experienced management team plays a critically important role in our future success. In addition to the board having named *me* Chairman & CEO, Value America has appointed a new CFO and CIO." She didn't mention the company's founders in the 1999 annual report. She didn't mention Tom Morgan, either, although he'd been CEO most of the year. Courtesy of the gullible press, Morgan had now been written out of Value America's history, like an unpopular Pharaoh whose cartouche has been chiseled off all his monuments by a gloating successor.

The end of Glenda's letter was particularly delusional. "Our future opportunities are many. We received a significant vote of confidence as represented by a cash infusion that gives the company access of up to $90 million in available cash." This was purposely misleading, of course, but she wasn't finished. "We believe that Value America is well positioned to flourish in the coming years." This, the perfect epitaph for her corporate tombstone, was followed by her parting salvo: "We believe we have quickly proved that the stewardship of Value America is in good hands, thanks to our employees who have demonstrated an unending commitment to shareholder value and in whose capable hands the future of Value America lies." Well, at least she got the last word right.

❧❧❧

THE FOLLOWING MEMO pegged the evil-meter. On Monday, May 22, 2000, at 11:56 AM, Kari Meyer sent Biff Pusey the following email. She cc'd its beneficiary. The subject: "Loan Forgiveness."

I have spoken with Gerry Roche, Compensation Committee Chair, and he has agreed that the loan of $250,000 between Value America and Glenda Dorchak is to be forgiven in full including interest. The Compensation Committee has agreed that the minutes will need to be amended to reflect this forgiveness....

A smoking gun if ever there was one. "The minutes need to be amended" means this action never occurred in the context of a duly authorized Compensation Committee meeting. That's bad. Post-dating the "forgiveness" was worse, especially because if a company were to file Chapter 11, there would be a statutory ninety-day moratorium on the repayment of moneys. But because Value America was "flourishing" in her "capable hands," there was no danger of that. Was there?

❧❧❧

BY LATE JUNE, Value America's "experienced management team" was prepared to reveal their latest hoax. They called it ESB—it stood for Electronic Services Business. It was essentially the same idea Craig and Rex had proposed to the board six months before. *That* plan had been ignominiously rejected, as I recall, in favor of the touted but fatally flawed Restructuring Plan. But that was then, and this was now. Now, they heralded ESB as if it were the firm's salvation, the professional choice.

Their report to the board began with a description of the "five main processes." Value America's managers were in their element. The only problem was, they forgot to enable any of the five processes. They produced revenue projections, by week, out fifty-two weeks; they just forgot to generate any revenue. They missed all fifty-two projections by one hundred percent. They never sold *anything*. After all, the Hitler Youth and the Brethren had worked overtime to make a scandal-hungry press believe that "selling" was despicable, the domain of delusional and over-zealous entrepreneurs. Selling was beneath them.

But ESB looked great, and they were paid handsomely for having conceived it. At fifty pages, it was filled with a sea of numbers so small they could hardly be read. But it didn't matter. The FOGs had long since learned that nobody reads this stuff anyway. To fool professionals, all you have to do is look professional. It's all a matter of perceptions.

Their PowerPoint presentation, replete with fancy flowcharts, colorful pie charts, and a plethora of bar graphs, was magnificent by all accounts. They even had a slide entitled, "Infrastructure Point of Pain." But the FOGs' love affair with "focus" was evidently on the rocks. "Focusing" hadn't worked quite as well as they'd planned. The board, of course, gave ESB rave reviews. Anything to avoid admitting they'd been wrong.

In the final analysis, ESB had nothing to do with the Electronic Services Business. It was simply another scheme to confiscate what rightly belonged to the shareholders.

The money Dorchak and company had just swindled from Durn, Flowers, and Smith wasn't going to last long in a two or three hundred person advertising-centric e-tailing business. There would have to be another round of layoffs, and soon, if the FOGs were to retain enough capital to pay their elevated salaries, retention bonuses, and multi-million dollar severance packages. But a new layoff of any magnitude could not happen without an excuse, a new *plan*. ESB was it. So let the layoffs begin. You could almost hear the Hitler Youth screaming, "Firings will continue until morale improves!"

The rank and file knew the company was imploding. Yet when they expressed their legitimate concerns over the firm's falling fortunes, management misled them. They encouraged those who remained to go on about their lives, buy homes and such. The mercenary managers inferred that in the unlikely event they stumbled, Federal Express would save Value America in the end.

And stumble they did. July 26, 2000 dawned fraught with portent. At the request of Fred Smith, the FedEx team gathered in Value America's executive conference room. At eight-thirty sharp, Dorchak called the meeting to order. This was to be the second and final début of the e-Fulfillment Services Business, eFSB (a more professional version of ESB, I suppose). Outside the arena, the troops, who had been led to believe FedEx had simply come to kick the tires before consummating the purchase, waited for a glimmer of hope.

The grand plan was unveiled by the consulting firm of Blair, Crawford, McKinsey. Evidently the mercenaries realized they had lost what little credibility they had once posessed, so they simply bought some. After demos, tours, and process reviews, the meeting ended at three o'clock.

No go. This time the presentation failed. Federal Express neither engaged the company's e-services tools nor consummated a purchase of the now drowning firm. Smith, in the end, was rumored to have wanted to do the deal, but was voted down by his Executive Committee.

So that was it. The music stopped. The dancers ceased their fancy foot-work. The clock struck midnight, and Value America turned into a pumpkin. What had once been valued at three billion dollars, the second largest e-tailer on the planet, was *kaput*.

You don't just wake up one morning and say, "I think I'll bankrupt my company today." It takes preparation, expensive lawyers, and time. Dorchak must have started planning her get-even-richer-quicker scheme within days of the $30 million heist from Durn, Flowers, and Smith. She had to. She had a colossal problem. Her Q2 revenues were seventy percent below Wall Street's expectations and about a third of the prior quarter's. If that were announced, she would instantly become the laughing stock of the dot-com world, the poster girl for failure. She'd do anything to avoid that.

The last possible date for making her failed Q2 performance public was fast approaching. As soon as she released her quarterly results, the entire business world would know she was a fraud. She had burned both Winn and her fellow board members to cover her butt *last* quarter. She was fresh out of diversions.

This time the answer to her little credibility problem lay in the arcane language of bankruptcy law. A bankrupt company doesn't have to publish a quarterly report card. And make no mistake, Glenda Dorchak was willing to do *anything,* no matter the cost, to keep from revealing that her tenure as CEO had been a con, an elaborate snatch-and-run.

By filing bankruptcy this soon, she could still claim she had done her best, but that the disaster Winn had left behind was beyond redemption. That was good, but it got better. The $30 million they just received could be legally diverted from the shareholders and creditors to—you guessed it—the "capable hands of the experienced and professional" management team.

It looked like Christmas in August. But *surely* she wouldn't bankrupt a company that had tens of millions in cash for her own personal gain! *Surely* she wouldn't do it within months of her glowing "we're growing; we're flourishing; we've just had the best day in Value America's history" diatribe. *Sure* she would, and did. Dorchak was as easy to predict as a bad girl on prom night. She and Value America were going down.

JUST FOR FUN, on Chapter eve, the characters played one last charade. CMO Tom Starnes hosted the first annual "Value America-InService Partners for Life" party. The hosts even bought celebratory t-shirts for the entire Value America team at InService to commemorate the occasion.

Starnes had been a leading contributor to the e-services plan. He knew the score, yet he purposely deceived the good folks at InService, asking Carl Townsend, their CEO, to do things that would have been disastrous for his people if Value America were to file for bankruptcy. Then, to add insult to injury, the sanctimonious Starnes called Carl moments after the big announcement and told him "to accept the news like a Christian." Hypocrite is too soft a word.

As this drama was unfolding, the investor community was also being purposely duped. Yes, Dorchak knew how to keep a secret. Against SEC regulations, she was withholding material, adverse information: both of the company's payment sources, the company's credit card and its merchant account with Wachovia Bank, had been revoked. That was plenty "material," and certainly "adverse," but there was no announcement. The quarterly performance was well south of pathetic as well, requiring an earnings warning. But releasing such news, in compliance with SEC regulations, would have been more humiliation than she could bear. So without notice and without explanation, Dorchak ordered the company to cancel its scheduled earnings release and investor conference call. Her Investor Relations team told shareholders not to worry, implying the delay was in preparation for a positive announcement, a merger, perhaps.

The Great Dismantler had no intention of ever letting the public know how badly she had abused their trust. Dorchak bankrupted the company rather than accept blame. Two out of every three remaining employees lost their jobs as a result. Over 180 more people were now sacrificed on the altar of greed.

On August 11, she filed Chapter 11. For the founding fathers, it is a date that will live in infamy.

The company announced that it was leaving the retailing business forever. They turned off the store that day. The company's servers never registered another sale of any kind. Glenda and the FOGs landed on their feet, of course. They kept their jobs, a remarkable achievement in light of their failure, which was arguably among the most magnificent in corporate history.

Funny thing about the timing, though. August 11th worked out to be exactly ninety-one days from May 10, the date to which Glenda had arranged for her quarter-million dollar loan forgiveness to be back-dated. How fortuitous.

Every Glenda loyalist was retained, even though there was little or nothing for him or her to do. Dorchak kept Nick Hofer, her VP of Advertising, even though there would be no more ads. She kept Candy Clifford, her VP of Sales, although there was nothing left to sell. Dorchak retained her VP of Investor Relations—sick, considering the shareholders were now toast. She even managed to save her VP of Human Resources, though most of the humans were now long gone.

The list of overpaid, under-employed professionals went on and on. Who they kept and who they discarded spoke volumes. It was obvious to everyone except Value America's esteemed board that they had no intention of making e-services work. Dorchak was simply paying her dues.

But the hoax didn't end there, not by a long shot. They tried the same trick on the bankruptcy judge they had deployed so successfully on the board. The FOGs told the court that they were the company's greatest assets—that they must be retained at any cost. And the cost was astronomical. For starters, Glenda asked the judge for $50,000 a month. Annualized, that's $600,000. She recommended $42,000 a month for Tip Lawson, her CFO. Newcomer Robert Lamb, EVP of Operations, was slated for a handsome $37,000 a month, $444,000 annualized. Not bad for a guy three weeks on the job. Niles Edwards, the other Goose Godfrey find (along with CFO Lawson) was to be paid a cool $40,000 a month. And lest I forget, the SVP of HR for the company now in the midst of its second fifty-percent reduction in force scraped the bottom of the barrel, pulling in a measly $32,000. An HR director for a bankrupt company with maybe seventy employees left earning $394,000? Why not? I'm sure the Comp Committee would have approved it.

The FOGs justified their ransom demands with the following words: "In order to implement its e-fulfillment services business, the Debtor needs to induce its remaining top five key executive employees to remain as a team during this reorganization.... These five are charged with leading the Debtor's capital restructuring and operational transformation. Their mission is daunting.... It is imperative," they told the judge, "that this retention program must be approved in order to give this Debtor the best chances of success." It was all contained in a twenty-page tear-smeared document, artfully crafted by a team of high-priced lawyers.

For added measure, the co-conspirators had the nerve to beg the court for severance packages. CEO Dorchak: another $375,000. The CFO: $270,000 more. The CIO: $300,000. The EVP: $265,000. And the SVP: $102,000. Then there were "emergence bonuses." But enough already. It's perfectly clear this was not about the e-services business; it was about corporate necrophilia.

Oh, and guess who profited again, to the detriment of the shareholders? Listed proudly as bankruptcy counsel for the company was Caise, Perkins. The mismanagement of Value America had indeed become a profitable affair—Justin's firm had over two million reasons to celebrate.

Glenda, according to public documents, made dismantling Value America a wonderfully enriching experience. She earned $266,000 in salary, a bonus of $443,000, another $250,000 courtesy of a forgiven loan, plus the sale of options worth $242,000. Of course, that $1,200,000 didn't include her raise to $525,000 for the smash-up job she'd done managing the company in 2000. Nor did it include her recent bonus, severance, and emergence rewards.

Investors and employees posted messages on VUSA's message boards with reckless abandon. Dorchak was so enraged by these public postings, she personally led a Witch-hunt trying to expose the authors. In light of the pain so many have endured at her hand, it's only fair to give the employees and shareholders of Value America the last word....

"I heard it on the radio this morning. I must have been asleep and didn't hear things right. According to the filing chairwoman Glenda Dorchak wants $603,000 a year. It's no wonder that they filed for bankruptcy! This company is ridiculous...these managers are trying to suck it dry."

"Let Them Walk, Your Honor!... As the first to blow up and the first to file Chapter 11, the VUSA team already has a leg up on the rest of the world. I see no reason why the people who ran VUSA into the ground and lied repeatedly shouldn't continue to get paid through the nose for performing this service. Without a guaranteed severance that exceeds the money she wasted at Yahoo, how could our Ms. Dorchak survive?"

"The Real Scoop: They are hiding behind Chapter 11 just to set themselves up for a big chunk of the change while hurting the lives of 185 former employees and their families. ANY judge HAS GOT TO SEE THROUGH WHAT THEY'RE DOING. They're used to working with crooks, aren't they?"

"The court should reject everything these jerks are proposing. First they file bankruptcy, then they enrich themselves.... Sad."

"Wow, and you guys want more money. Can you at least tell us for what? You don't have any clients. You're not bringing any money in. What's the deal? I really do hope VA survives just for the shareholders and the remaining great employees, but geez, you all have to understand how shitty you all look. Shame on you, Glenda, Craig was right about you. Choke on your bonus."

"Oh please Glenda, you and your cronies are f------ unbelievable!!!! Bonuses again? Your gall is amazing, you worthless b----. Here's a thought—pay the employees and the creditors what you owe them. Oh, sorry. That would mean you were honest. Gee, what was I thinking?"

"They tell the judge 'the company will be hindered if any of us clowns leave.' Stop it, you're killing me! Why would anybody hire people that lose money as fast as they lie? The inmates have taken over the asylum."

"Working there taught me about walking the line between legal and illegal. No one cared that we were on the wrong side of the line."

"Our integrity sunk to the levels of our leaders. Glenda took us for a ride. Now she's sitting with the FOGs and paying them to make her, a high school dropout, feel smart, powerful and well liked. Value America is down to 65 employees. That just makes more bonus money available to the FOGs."

"Anyone know if Glenda will be in court tomorrow? Hopefully I'll get my fondest wish and see the nasty woman squirm. Her lies are so entertaining, as anyone who ever attended one of her stat chats can tell you. She raped the shareholders. It's a shame so many bright people were wasted."

"I asked someone still at VA how Glenda was doing. He said, 'Remember Typhoid Mary? She was more popular.'"

"The first duty of a politician is to perpetuate themselves in office. Apparently these people want to model themselves after politicians. They even lie like them."

"How can VUSA have a chance when its CEO is an idiot. All she knows is how to rip off people, profiting herself by getting away with crime. Glenda is not a leader. Employee morale is unbelievably low. They fire their best people and retain the worst. VUSA no longer has anything to offer. The only ones benefiting from all of this are the big shots (they are still milking the company). I cannot understand how employees and investors are letting this take place."

"All Glenda has to do is ride this e-services monkey business through the end of the year and she won't be leaving potato chips on the table. Current employees who have leveraged big pay increases can thank the board. The only reason she's paying others for doing nothing (no, it's not the Dorchak Apprentice Program) is because she doesn't want to tell the judge that she...has no prospects of success."

"The Dorchak method is so much more direct.... Take the money and stiff everyone else. Their new e-biz plan is a scam. Close the doors, judge."

"Dorchak and Larson are cheap at half the price. It's not easy to find a pair that have both run two companies into the ground in less than five years. I'll bet the headhunters are buzzing around the place like killer bees! Between them they wrote the book on B-to-B: Business to Bankruptcy. And on B-to-C: Business to Cayman Islands bank accounts."

"Reasons Why Glenda Needs the High Salary, Bonus, and Severance: 1) This job will be her last. After the fiasco of turning a $20 stock into a penny stock, she needs to pad her retirement account. 2) She's ugly, and ugly people have been treated unfairly. 3) She needs to confirm her supreme authority so she can say, 'Hey, I'm...better than you are.'"

"Good morning, Glenda. Are you embarrassed or ashamed of yourself yet? Didn't think so. It's not your style, huh? Remember, your number one responsibility was to the shareholders. Boy you f----- them, didn't you? Take any chartered planes recently? That was the first clue."

"Glenda must be the most deceptive human being I've ever known. I bought into this company based upon her restructuring plan. But rather than saving it she runs it right into the ground. Glenda, all you are is a con-artist, a thief who stole our money... 'a wolf in sheep's clothing.'"

"Glenda is nothing but a high school dropout with a failed resume. While she worked at Ambra, she abused more people than she did at Value America. No doubt, based upon her ability to deceive, whoever brought Dorchak into VUSA looked at the Ambra massacre as the crown jewel on her resume."

"Check out Craig Winn's website at VADefense.com. I've been led to believe that Winn was one of the big problems with VUSA. I have rethought that and now believe that his contributions to the demise of the company pale compared to Tom, Glenda, and the FOGs. Then again, he did hire them. Like everyone else, I thought he was dumping his stock to drive the price down and make it harder for us to raise new funding. According to his site, he didn't. Only reason I accept this is that his statements are so easily verifiable."

"You stood up there at the Doubletree and told the entire company when we were 185 people stronger that the problem was that Craig and Rex won't stop dumping their shares. You said that once they were finished, we could look for the sun to shine again and we would start to make money. You're a liar. We knew you were insulting our intelligence. Now you have proved it through your actions. I can't understand why the board continues to keep you. Craig was right about you, and we all knew it."

"Many were naïve and bought the VUSA propaganda. Some are still buying it. If you believe these people will salvage something from this corpse, you're living the embodiment of P.T. Barnum's belief."

"Look at the bright side. After months of doubt, you can now be sure they weren't too dumb to steal. All they needed was a new vehicle, a new stage so that their previous failures would be hidden—and their new schemes enhanced—by the fact there would be no surviving corporate entity left to reveal their thievery."

"Thank the whole team: Glenda, the FOGs, and the whole Severance Club. Nobody can accomplish something like this on their own!"

"I cannot even comprehend what this management team has done. The lies and false promises they have spewed in their press releases. Loser leadership at the helm of the biggest hoax in history."

"Glenda knew we were going to file bankruptcy prior to her early June vacation in Italy. She told her team to put the plan together before she left."

"I found it hard to believe that Glenda would lie to my face, but you know what? She did it without batting an eyelash!"

"The problem is that Glenda and the FOGs are working for their own benefit, not for the good of the company. That has always been the problem. Why would they be asking for large bonuses and severance packages if they didn't see this thing continuing to head downhill? One would think that if they really wanted to succeed, they would be focusing on the business rather than their own pockets."

"Obviously they are closing the doors, but not before they set themselves up for early retirement with hefty severance packages. The anger is immobilizing! All I keep hearing is 'don't worry, Glenda will get what's coming to her?' WHEN? Somebody PLEASE tell me how this will happen and help us all put this bad nightmare to rest!!!"

You shall not covet.... You shall not steal—God

THE SUN ALSO RISES

*O*n August 11, 2000, the whole world learned what I had known for some time: Glenda and her plan were *wrong*—as wrong as Wall Street. The same hype and hubris that was smothering e-tail's once-bright promise had strangled Value America.

It was inevitable, I suppose, that the five founders would find themselves together again on this day. One by one we made our pilgrimage to Craig's Carriage House, a brick barn nestled in the trees a short walk from his home. Upstairs from where his big tractor sat in majestic green repose, a large cedar-paneled room served as his office and retreat.

A great craggy stone fireplace occupied one corner. On the other side of the room, Craig's desk, littered with computers and books, stood guard beneath a large Palladian window. Nearby was the old maple drop-leaf table, rescued from Purgatory, providing its quiet service once again. The floor was strewn with box upon box of documentation—thousands of pages of notes, correspondence, and articles gathered over the last five years, the lifespan of his ill-fated dream. The guy apparently never met a piece of paper he didn't like.

Crystal woofed a greeting as I climbed the stairs. Rex and Bill were already there. Let the *post mortem* begin.

❧❧

IT WAS NOT as cathartic as it should have been to merely say, "I told you so." The conversation devolved into a search through our collective soul. What could we have done to change the outcome? Craig was in agony, blaming himself for letting his improbable dream implode.

"It's my fault," he said. "There are a dozen things I could have done that might have made a difference. I'm sorry, guys. I let you down."

We weren't buying it, and we told him so. "Yeah? Like what?" Rex asked. "Your decisions were sound. Your motivations were never suspect. If anything, you were too damn devoted. If you hadn't tried so hard to save the company, we'd be a couple of hundred million dollars richer. I'm not complaining, mind you." Eyes rolled heavenward.

A dozen thoughts vied for Craig's attention. "I should have pushed harder to close the Paul Allen deal. My gut told me a delay would take the IPO into troubled waters, and I was right. Two weeks earlier, just *two weeks*, and we would've made the summer window. We would've had a great IPO in July, instead of a failed one in September. We would've fired Dorchak, never hired Morgan, and April would have been our secondary.

We would have had all the time and money we needed...."

Bill cut him off. "You know a lot of stuff, but you're not a prophet."

"But I *knew*," Craig protested. "It was my job to be a visionary. I saw it coming. I just didn't get it done."

Better late than never, Joe climbed the stairs. "You got any beer in the fridge?" He headed for the little kitchen without waiting for an answer. "Y'know, this was all Glenda's fault," he said as he emerged, "The Wicked Witch. If you hadn't hired Glenda...."

Craig nodded. "You're right, but she appeared to be exactly what we needed—she sure talked a good game. I'll give you this. I should have fired her at the first sign of her shenanigans. She wasn't here a week before she kicked Ken out of his office and clawed Kim DeJong's eyes out."

"Right," I said. "A lot of CEOs would have fired an SVP her first week on the job for wanting a workspace bigger than a broom closet."

"Okay, Ken, I'll grant you that, but there's no excuse for not dumping her when she blackmailed us two weeks later. If only I'd thrown her sorry butt out of the car when I had the chance. No jury on earth would have convicted me."

"I beg to differ," Rex said. "We have littering laws in this state."

Amid the morbid chuckles, Craig continued to beat himself up. "Things would have been different if only I'd had the courage..."

"The heart," I added.

"The brains," Joe said, as if on cue.

"...to throw a bucket of water on the Witch when we had the chance," Craig picked up on the theme. "We may not have made it to Oz, but at least she wouldn't have made monkeys out of us."

"You're forgetting something," Rex reminded him. "We couldn't fire her without fatally delaying the IPO. Then, after it failed anyway for lack of a market, we had to raise big-time capital fast or die. We couldn't fool around trying to fill her job." Then he laughed as it finally dawned on him. "'Course, in retrospect, canning Glenda would've turned out great. If the IPO had been delayed, we would've avoided the embarrassment of failing, and would have gone public when the market recovered in early November. But who knew? Twenty-twenty hindsight."

"What about the next time?" Craig asked. "We should have fired her when she blackmailed us again, before the second IPO."

"Okay, say we had," Rex countered. "We would've delayed the process a week or so to write her out of the S1. But don't you remember? Everything came to a screeching halt for dot-com IPOs the very week we ended our road show. We would have missed the window again."

Craig sighed. Rex was right. "My wife figured it out years ago. Katie calls me a scum-magnet. Glenda was scum, so I hired Morgan to replace her. All we got was a different kind of scum. Must have moved too fast."

Rex bristled. It had been his job to keep the scum at bay. But his friend had overlooked something important. They had *tried* to do it the orthodox way. "Remember the headhunters? We interviewed the biggest: Russell Reynolds, Korn/Ferry, and Roche's firm, Heidrick & Struggles. We engaged Reynolds to find somebody so we could dump her. They searched for months, but failed."

"Right. So when they came up empty handed, we hired Morgan and Peters, hoping one of 'em would work out."

"Best laid plans," Joe said. "Neither did. Realistically though, the problem wasn't just the executive wing. The whole company grew too quickly, not that we had much of a choice."

"The average business grows at what—ten percent a year? At that pace, it takes five, six years to double, ten years to triple. How's my math, Joe?"

"Not bad for a lawyer."

"Lawyer turned wine maker," Rex smiled. "We didn't have the luxury of growing at a leisurely pace. At the time, we were tripling in size every quarter. It was all we could do to assimilate people, bring them up to speed. We didn't have time to examine their life histories."

"Morgan never did come up to speed. He never accomplished anything. Hell, he couldn't even engineer his own *coup*. Look at all those boxes over there," Craig said, glancing in the direction of the dozen or so large file boxes he had stuffed to the brim with papers. "I must have twenty or thirty thousand pages here documenting the rise and fall of Value America. But would you believe, not one sheet came from the hand of Tom Morgan. We got nothing of value for the million dollars he was paid. Oh, a couple of faxes bellyaching about Visa, but that's all. Should tell you all you need to know about Tom Morgan and his pals. But that's not what really bugs me. It's that guys like Morgan have burned me before, yet I didn't see it coming. He had insecurity written all over him, but I missed the signs for seven long months. It wasn't until his own man, Cliff Chambers, pointed it out that I finally saw him for what he really was."

Joe, who didn't have an insecure bone in his body, had no idea what he was talking about. "What signs?"

"It's always the same sort of thing. I'll give you a description, and you tell me who it sounds like. Perfectly attired; spends lavishly on clothes. Drives fancy cars, always perfectly detailed. Thin, without an ounce of fat. A perfectionist; perfectly organized desk, not a piece of paper out of place, everything aligned. Totally self-absorbed. Who does that sound like?"

"That could be either Morgan or Dorchak."

"Right, Joe, but I was describing a guy Bill and I knew way back in our Price Club days...."

"Yale Conrad," Bill nodded.

"Precisely, but it could have been any of a score of people I've met along life's way, all destructive and delusional."

In all fairness, Craig had attracted, led, and inspired more than twenty good and decent people for every shallow, self-serving scumbag who weaseled their way in. Far more good was done than bad. But it doesn't take much bad, if unchecked by good, to destroy everything.

Besides, in reality Craig wasn't and probably never had been a "scum magnet." Even with the Toms, the Kuos, Dorchak, and Godfrey, we had about the same percentage of "scum" you'd find anywhere. Our problem was simply exacerbated by Craig's tendency to empower everyone, give us the reins, encourage us, and let us go. Ninety-five percent of the time, it worked great, creating a productive work environment. Unfortunately, the insecure five percent abused the privilege and wreaked havoc.

None of that seemed to matter to Craig today. He sighed deeply. "It started with my own father. I paid him a bundle for his little business, and he repaid me with a mountain of hateful letters. He ended each attack just like Kuo did: 'love, Dad,' or 'love, David,' as the case may be. Too weird for words. Rex has seen them; so has Bill. I know all about insecurity, guys. I have no excuses."

The room grew quiet. "There's no winning with these people," Craig continued at last. "They'll stop at nothing to get their way. No matter what you do, no matter how much you give them, they always need more. To satisfy their cravings, they start to spread lies. They lie so often, they even start to believe their own rubbish. Pretty soon, others start buying into it. I've seen it time and again. Insecurity is a cancer. It kills things."

Rex moved forward in his chair. "Y'know, you're right. The press releases from the Witch's era, as well as Morgan's, were all about how wonderful they were, how experienced, how professional. It was all about *them*, wallowing in the moment, self-absorbed."

Bill summed it up. "So we hire Morgan to smoke Dorchak, but he becomes dependent upon her, 'cause she's smarter than he is, which, by the way, isn't saying much. Then they join forces and turn on you."

Now I was confused. "I thought they couldn't stand each other."

"They couldn't." Bill explained by quoting the ancient Chinese book, *The Art of War*. "The enemy of my enemy is my friend."

"The ancient wisdom that comes to *my* mind," I said, "hits a bit closer to home. 'What profit has a man from all his labor in which he toils under the sun?'"

"Solomon," Craig said softly. "Vanity of vanities. Futility of futilities."

"Cheer up," I said. "That wasn't Solomon's final conclusion."

"Maybe, but it seems like everything we tried in the end was futile."

"In the end," Joe responded, "is the operative phrase. In the *beginning*, we put Wile E. Coyote to shame. We died a dozen deaths, got up, dusted ourselves off, and got the job done."

"So long as the levers were in our hands, we managed to save the day," Rex observed. "Sometimes I think we willed our way back from the dead."

It was my turn to get something off my chest. "The moment you left management, we went straight to hell. Why'd you leave?"

"Dynasty."

"Care to elaborate? I think I'm entitled."

"In the end, I didn't have what it took to save Dynasty. I failed. I've never stopped blaming myself or, more importantly, doubting myself."

"I *knew* it," Rex exclaimed. "I tried my level best to talk you out of it. You're the best damn leader I ever served under, and a great manager, too. If you'd only had more confidence, we'd have pulled this off."

"Thanks, but you know how I felt. I thought management should be left to managers. I got out as soon as we were on our feet, had enough money, and plenty of momentum. Okay; it was the wrong call."

Rex nodded. "So *now* you agree with me. Leaving management too soon was our biggest mistake." No decision had cost us more.

"Sure, in hindsight. It's pretty obvious. New economy companies need to be led, not just managed. I was wrong."

"What really irks me," Bill said, "is that we build the business from nothing and hire the parasites. Then they fail and blame it on us. Talk about 'weird beyond words.'"

Softly, Rex said, "You know what set them up, don't you, Craig? Your fight with Wall Street. If I remember, there's some sage advice in *The Art of War* about that as well...."

"Never fight a battle you can't win," Bill quoted.

"So what were my choices? It was certain death *versus* mere probable death. If we'd gone along with Wall Street's mantra—that the value of an e-tailer was its popularity, not its business—we would've collapsed with the rest of the dot-coms. Oh, it may have taken longer, and we might have cashed out with hundreds of millions like Rex said, but death was certain."

Four heads nodded in recognition of the grim truth. Our model was perfect for rational times, but perfectly *wrong* for the insanity of the dot-com era. "I told them that '.com' stood for commerce, that e-tail was retail, and should be allowed to mature, as such. If they'd been willing to listen, we'd have succeeded. Truth is, we came darn close."

Joe knew the numbers. "Our costs, apart from ads, were less than fifteen percent of revenue. At the pace they were dropping, overhead would've fallen to under five percent pretty quickly."

"Net of brand co-op, our alliance catalogs cost us less than five percent of revenue, just like we promised."

"And sales of high-margin consumer products were growing, so we were home free. We'd have netted more than five percent on other people's assets—we'd have been a money machine," Bill concluded.

"When we left management, we had what, two hundred million dollars in cash, Craig?" Rex asked. "Plenty of money to get it done."

"It's sickening," Bill agreed, "to think the board allowed the Brethren and the Hitler Youth to destroy the company instead."

"The maddening thing is that even now, nobody gets it." Craig slumped in one of his overstuffed leather chairs. "We were merely the first rock in the avalanche. It'll be months before anybody figures it out, if ever. Sure, it's too late for us, but by the time Wall Street wakes up, I'm afraid it'll be too late for most every dot-com."

I jumped in again. "At least you have a clear conscience. You did what you could. You threw Wall Street a lifeline."

"Yeah, and they used it to hang me."

Rex looked up and smiled. "How appropriate. Seems we spent half our corporate life looking death in the face."

"Yep. While we were all drinking the koolaid, somebody laced it with cyanide. We were in the company of good *and* evil."

Craig disappeared into the kitchen, emerging with another round. "You know where I really blew it? I was blind as a bat—all those closed-door meetings, all that sneaking around undoing everything we'd done."

"They buried themselves," Rex said. "By not listening to us, they made it possible—hell, they motivated us—to sell our stock. In a way, they made us rich." He took a sip of his beer and smiled at the irony.

"Rich or not, I'll tell you what we should've done, Rex. We should've told our board to go to hell!" Craig said with the benefit of hindsight. "Outside boards have no business managing a business the way they mismanaged ours. Like they say, a little knowledge is a dangerous thing."

"We were told the worst possible scenario was a board meltdown. Then of course there was Caise's staggered board—*that* made it impossible for us to fire the fools, even though we owned the company."

"Ironically, Rex, the very board that harassed us would've been better off if we *had* thrown 'em out. They bought into Morgan's lies—and Dorchak's. Then they plunked down another thirty million bucks, only to see the company go toes up weeks later. Lost it all. If we'd sold the company when we wanted to, most everyone would've made money."

Rex agreed. "Robbie Stephens figured that with our track record for getting deals done, we could've sold the company for nearly a billion bucks."

"Hard to pull off that kind of deal when your own team is working against you, my friend."

"We've sold less, lots of times!"

Joe jumped in. "*Forget* the business; our infrastructure alone was worth a fortune. If only the board hadn't bought into the idiocy of the restructuring plan, somebody would've scooped us up. I guarantee it."

"Oh, come on. I think their plan was great," Bill said. "Save the company by getting rid of half the people, most of the brands, and all the money!"

We laughed at the absurdity of it all. What else could we do? Our dream had died long ago. As the late afternoon sun poured through the western window of the Carriage House, it cast deep shadows on the rough-hewn cedar walls, not unlike the shadows that had descended upon Value America. The sun had set on our dream, never to rise again. Time had dulled the pain. Well, maybe a little.

Rex leaned forward and spoke wistfully. "We were so close."

Craig nodded. "We were a lousy six months away from pulling it off. Brands were clamoring to capitalize on our demand alliances. That was the last hurdle. We would've been profitable."

Profitable. The word hung in the air like sweet perfume, but she whose scent it was had departed, never to return. There was no point in hanging on, but still, it was hard to let go.

"Somebody ought to tell the world what happened here," Bill announced. Instinctively, we all looked at Craig. It had been his dream; he had led us all to this place, and he bore its scars, not unlike those of Melville's Captain Ahab; beyond the flesh, they tore into his very soul. We couldn't ask him to reopen those wounds. He had nothing to gain, and so very much to lose.

"The story is much bigger than Value America," he said prophetically. "The lessons...." His voice trailed off as he pondered the implications.

"Sure," Bill interjected. "Value America is a parable. Think about it. Dot-com was touted as the greatest economic opportunity since the industrial revolution. It exploded onto the world scene, destined to enhance people's lives. Then, mysteriously, it died a collective death. Why?"

"That's not what I meant, Bill," Craig said gently. "It's bigger than dot-com. Oh, sure, by telling our story, we'd reveal what really happened, why dot-coms rose, why they fell, and how and why e-tail will rise again. But dot-com was just an accelerant, a catalyst that helped make our characters seem larger than life. And it caused everything to happen so much faster. What occurred to me, Bill, is this. The real story is that *corporate* America is dying from the same thing that ultimately killed Value America."

"Glenda?" Joe asked.

"No," Craig laughed. "People like Glenda, the Toms, and the Kuos aren't worth the ink we'd give them. It's only what they represent that's important. There's no shortage of insecurity. It's a cancer that eats away at every human endeavor. Business? Sure. It's easy to see why insecure and greedy people with personal agendas show up there. Same with politics. But it's also infecting our churches, universities, charities, the press...."

"Oh, don't get me started on the press," Rex hissed. "They were Wall Street's most willing accomplices. Without their complicity, it would have been impossible to fool so many so long. They had a responsibility to ferret out the truth. Instead, they perpetuated the myth and misled everybody. What's worse, when we challenged their illusions, they attacked us rather than debate our message. Nobody wants to think anymore. As a nation, our reasoning muscles have grown fat and flabby."

"You know what Winston Churchill said about the press?" I asked. "'The essence of American journalism is vulgarity divested of truth.'"

Not to be outdone, Craig got up and thumbed through a familiar work on Thomas Jefferson. He found the passage he was looking for and read it aloud: "'Our newspapers present caricatures of disaffected minds,' said Jefferson. 'The abuse of freedom of the press has been carried to a length never before known or borne by any civilized nation.' He went on to say, 'Nothing can now be believed which is seen in a newspaper. Truth itself becomes suspicious by being put into that polluted vehicle.'"

"Ouch," I said. "Don't hold back, T.J. Tell us what you really think."

"There is nothing new under the sun" was Craig's smiling refrain. "The point is, what killed Value America has the power to kill *corporate* America. When lies outsell truth, when evil is unchecked by good, and when self reigns supreme, it's all over. Those are the big three; any one of them is capable of strangling the life out of a company—or a nation.

"You see," he continued, "the corporate behavior that built Value America emerged from a spirit of sacrifice. In the beginning, the collective good was more important than any individual gain."

"Right," I said. "It was all about building something worthwhile."

"But then the Brethren—Tom and his clique—came. They were focused on their own mission, and we failed to stop them."

"What do you mean, *their* mission?"

"I thought you guys knew. The United Brethren's stated agenda is to 'minister' to the rich and powerful."

"Not much point in robbing poor people, is there?" Bill quipped.

"No," Craig laughed. "In order to gain control of an organization and siphon off its its resources, they 'minister' to its leadership, get them in their pocket. Their *modus operandi* is always the same. First they try to recruit the leader, seduce him if you will, dangle a carrot or two. For me, it was access to power. I didn't bite.

"If recruitment fails, they try to compromise their target. Remember Grisham's novel, *The Firm?* The girl on the beach? With pictures to commemorate the occasion, the hero became a 'made man.' They owned him. Just like in that story, the Brethren probe for a weakness—power, sex, or money. Again, I didn't take the bait, thank God.

"Failing that, the Brethren simply assassinate them. Oh, not with a gun to the head, like in the movies. No, they just kill their character, malign them by spreading false rumors, right Rex?"

"'Fraid so," Scatena nodded. "Gestapo tactics. How do you fight something like that?"

"There's only one remedy." Craig looked at each of us. We had all heard him say it: "Bad things happen when good people don't stand up." There had been good people in our management, good people on our board, but they had cowered, unwilling to be counted when it mattered most. I had been one of them, I had to admit, hunkering down, trying to wait out the storm, just doing my job. *I was only following orders.* Not much of an excuse. Never is.

"Seventy-five years ago," Craig explained, "only three percent of Germans were Nazis. They were empowered by misinformed business leaders who were terrified of Communism. Hitler figured out that it doesn't take much. Tell people what they want to hear. Prey on their fears. Demean your opponents, falsely accusing them of doing the same awful things you're planning on doing yourself. Sprinkle your lies with just enough truth to make them seem plausible, and hope no one figures it out until it's too late. If good people don't stand up, if they're not willing to accept the risk, you're free to rape and plunder at will. They didn't in Germany, and the world paid a horrible price. Less than twenty years later, nearly a hundred million people lay dead."

"Oh, thanks, Craig. I feel so much better."

"I'm not implying that the pain the come-latelies inflicted is in the same league as the devastation wrought by World War II. But their motives and their methods were all too similar."

"You're right."

"If what we endured is as prevalent as I think it is, the consequences, unchecked, could be worse. See, the thing that sets America apart, that pays all the bills, that provides the kind of life that's the envy of the world, is *business*. If corporate America falters, so does America, and with it the world as we know it."

Craig stood, walked toward the western window, then turned and faced us. "Dislodged, a single stone can gain momentum, pick up loose debris along the way, and bury everything. One stone was all it took to nudge NASDAQ from its pinnacle of 5000. Our government in their infinite wisdom decided that it was in our interest to attack Microsoft. That started the avalanche. They didn't mean to bury our economy. They were just naïve, more interested in positioning themselves than in the productivity of our nation. Politicians love to attack business. It's all part of the same mentality that killed Value America. Elevate oneself by tearing others down—especially builders."

The room grew silent for a short eternity. Finally Rex inquired, "How many employees did we have at the time of Morgan's botched *coup*?"

"Over six hundred."

"And the active collaborators, between the FOGs and Morgan's incompetent gang—how many were there? A dozen, in both camps? What's twelve as a percentage of six hundred?"

"Two percent," Joe said sadly.

"And yet," Rex concluded, "because good people didn't stand up, bad things happened. Morgan, Dorchak, and their cronies sucked the company dry. They killed the vision, maligned our mission, and hurt a whole lot of people in the process. Why? So they could satisfy their cravings for power and wealth. Corporately, character counts, my friends."

"Indulge me for a minute." Craig turned and looked toward the setting sun. "You all know the Dynasty story. What happened when we were staring bankruptcy in the face?"

"You made payroll out of your own pocket," Bill said.

"And what did Rex and I do when our first IPO failed—when we were broke?"

"You dug into your own pockets, led by example," Joe said. "The rest of us followed your lead."

"Uh huh. And what happened when Glenda found herself failing?"

"She contributed nothing, and paid herself a couple million bucks," Rex said bitterly. "She and the FOGs stole the company blind."

"Right. And what did Morgan do after his failed *coup*? Walk away quietly? Wish us well?"

"Not hardly. He threatened suit and got the board to pay him another four hundred grand. That's fifty thousand bucks in severance for every month he worked, if my math is right."

Joe grimaced. "Your math is fine, Rex. Your definition of *work* is all wrong. You know, neither Tom nor Glenda repaid their loans. They raked in millions between 'em hacking our company to death."

"Gee," Bill joked. "Crime *does* pay!"

"Seriously though," I said, "Rex is right. Character counts. During our first three years, we worked together. We grew from nothing, no money, no people, no brands, no sales, no value, to three hundred people, the second or third largest e-tailer on the planet. We raised nearly three hundred million bucks, and we were worth three *billion*. As long as we served something bigger than ourselves, we grew. Then came the parasites. In half the time it took us to build the firm, they took it all the way back to where we started—no people, no brands, no sales, no money, and no value. Zero. Zip. Zilch."

"So you're saying the measure of one's corporate character is whom or what you serve—yourself or the cause—whatever that may be, country or company," Joe observed as he set his beer down.

"Well, nothing so profound as all that. But it's been my experience that ninety percent of the bad stuff that happens it the result of somebody wanting something that doesn't belong to them. It all started back in the Garden of Eden. Eve found herself wanting something that wasn't hers— the knowledge of good and evil. She bit into the apple, got Adam to go along, and since then nothing's changed. Power, wealth, land, sex, food, self-esteem, you name it. If someone's got it, others want it, and don't care what they have to do to take it."

Craig shook his head. "Some of us work for it, Ken. If we want something, we build it. We *create* good things, we don't steal them."

"That's just my point," I said. "If you build something, it *belongs* to you. If you build something good, you'd hope others would follow your lead. But all too often, they simply try to steal it, or failing that, ruin it so you won't have anything they don't. That's what happened to us.

"Without sacrifice nothing gets built." Craig shared. If nothing gets built there's nothing to steal, exploit, or even destroy."

"It's like there were two different Value Americas," I agreed, "the one we built and the one they killed. It's hard to imagine how we got from one to the other."

We were still proud of what we, hundreds of us, had built. But the buzz, the excitement, the optimism disappeared when the baton was passed. The Brethren and the FOGs hadn't *tried* to kill the company. There was no conspiracy. They couldn't help themselves. Ever in character, they just did what came naturally.

Still, the good times were not forgotten. Rex commented, "Hardly a week goes by when I don't run into somebody who says, 'Let's do it again.'"

"You too, huh?" Joe shared. "We *ought* to build it again. We had the right solution; our timing was off, that's all. And our choice of managers sucked."

"Just yesterday, I got calls from three of our guys," Craig said. "Somebody calls me most every day, and they all say pretty much the same thing. They came to be part of something worthwhile. Working here was somethin' special. Call me crazy, but we could revive JoeWare for a song and put the custom marketplaces back together. Like before, we could help great organizations raise money. But this time, we should empower specialty retailers along with the best brands. What do you think?"

"*Somebody* needs to link supply and demand," Joe said. "Now that we're gone, nobody's even close."

"There's only one problem, Joe," Bill retorted. "The market has to recover. No one's gonna fund anything in its present condition."

"But don't you see?" Craig pondered. "Our plan was good; only our timing was bad. In a normal market, all the things we set out to do actually *work*—they make sense. We don't need the market to revert back to what it was—hot air. Bubbles burst, but values never go out of style."

Values. That's why we all came and, in the end, why we all left.

Craig summed it all up. "Ask not what you can do for your company. Ask what your company can do for you," he paraphrased. "*That* was the rallying cry of the parasites."

"They never understood our mission or appreciated what made our company strong," Bill acknowledged. "It's kind of like America. We've distorted our history to the point we no longer understand why our forefathers risked so much to come here, what they fought for, or even what they believed."

"Yes, indeed. Just as our gang recreated history in their own self-serving image, we as Americans have too. I'll give you an example," Craig said, flopping back down in a leather chair. "Politicians and their like-minded friends in the media have tried their level best to convince us that there's a clause in our Constitution that requires the separation of church and state. They've said it so many times, most Americans now believe it's actually there. But all the Constitution says is, 'Congress shall make no law respecting an *establishment* of religion, or prohibiting the *free exercise* thereof.' It's not the same thing, not even remotely."

"Right," I said. "A lot of what's troubling our nation can be attributed to this delusion. When we distance ourselves from God, self-interest becomes the only thing that matters. You can't take morality out of corporate behavior and still prosper. The end *doesn't* justify the means. Like Joe said, it all comes down to whom or what you choose to serve."

"Exactly. Ask yourself, Ken, whose interests are served by this 'separation of church and state' delusion? Who benefits from creating a dependence on government?"

Craig chose not to answer his question, letting the implications sink in. Instead, he admonished us: "History has proved that the separation of God from our public life is even worse than a politicized clergy. Stalin, in a society that spurned God, killed twice as many Russians as Hitler did. But the opposite extreme, the church in the Dark Ages with their Crusades, or the Islamic states today with their *Jihad,* is nearly as bad."

The whole church-state conundrum sounded a lot like us. Craig hadn't made a big deal about his Christianity when he'd written the business plan. Yet service, faith, and charity were woven into the fabric of the company from its inception. Doing well by doing good. But then, in a very real sense, we unwittingly empowered a politicized "clergy" when we brought in the Brethren. These misguided hypocrites came to work with Bibles under their arms, conducting prayer meetings in their offices while they convoluted faith to advance their own selfish ambitions.

When they failed, the pendulum swung back, and we witnessed the disastrous results that total a separation from God invariably brings to any organization. The FOGs made no pretense of service or faith, while the Brethren *only* pretended.

"Corporate character really matters. It's the dividing line between positioning and progressing, between truth and deception, between good and evil. It was the dividing line between the rise and fall of Value America."

Sure, we were getting a little preachy, but this was a eulogy, after all. I stepped up on my soap box. "I guess that means the next time we find the media demeaning something important, we ought to question the presenter's motives and veracity. Not be judgmental, you understand, just discerning. If we don't, we're just puppets, no better than those on our board who let our company die rather than invest the time to learn the truth."

"You know something?" Craig said. "Bill's right! We need to tell the world what happened."

"Are you suggesting we collaborate on a story, say, an article in *Forbes* or *Fortune?*" Joe asked.

"An article?" Rex laughed. "It'd be more like *War and Peace.*"

"More like *War and Getting a Piece,*" Bill countered.

Everybody laughed but Craig. He was thinking. "Value America," he said at last, "is a parable, like Bill said. It's a window into a larger world in which the forces of good and evil ultimately shape our destiny. Value America became a microcosm of misplaced American values. We either learn from our mistakes, or we're destined to repeat them. If we tell our story, maybe we can prevent our problems from becoming America's problems. Stop the avalanche before it's too late. It's a cautionary tale."

"If we tell our story," Joe said, "the mercenary two percent who got rich plundering the company are going to scream bloody murder. It's going to get nasty. They'll continue to act in character. They won't refute anything we say with fact. They'll make stuff up and use it to smear us, personally. And you know, the press'll eat it up. Like you said, the best predictor of future behavior is past behavior."

"If we tell our story," Bill interjected," we're gonna get our butts sued. The truth is going to tick a lot of people off. The first thing they'll do is band together like hyenas—form a unified front to make us look crazy. It's worked for them up til now."

"Just because a dozen people see the same mirage, that doesn't mean it'll hold water," I said. "Just once, I'd like to see a journalist act like one, rather than just repeat the slander, scratch one layer below the surface—they'd see that the lies are irrational, impossible, really.

"Bill, if the truth is upsetting, whose fault is that anyway?" Craig asked. "We built the thing. They destroyed it. All we'd be doing is holding them accountable for their actions. When did that go out of style?"

Rex still had his wits about him. "The successes we achieved when we were in charge are as obvious as their failures. In hindsight, only a fool could see the Morgan era as productive, the board decisions as wise, or Dorchak's behavior as anything other than, well, *evil*."

It was all true, we had to agree. There was no other rational explanation.

"Actually, it's even better than that," Rex assured us. "They destroyed our company, so by the time a book's published, there won't be any confidentiality issues. The limitations that might otherwise be imposed are all gone. We can tell the whole truth, warts and all. And as a result, Craig, those three letters you wrote are going to *haunt* them. You predicted exactly what was going to happen, and why."

"I'll tell you what'll haunt them," Craig said with visible emotion. "I got a letter from our helpdesk supervisor, India Hamner. It describes the real spirit of Value America, the sacrifice and the joy. If there's any humanity at all in these people, they won't run to their lawyers; they'll fall on their knees."

"Still," Bill came back, "guys like Fred Smith aren't going to like us revealing what they said—and we'll have to. But I guess that's why our forefathers wrote the First Amendment, isn't it? They knew that holding our leaders accountable was in our interest. The men who sat on our board still influence the lives of hundreds of thousands of people. They need to understand the consequences of their actions."

"So does every board member of every company in America—every leader for that matter." Joe knew from experience. "And I suppose writing them another letter won't get the job done."

Rex thought about it for a minute. "Smith is a good guy; he was misled, but he always meant to do the right thing. Some, though, set themselves up—they chose to publicly disparage us and our company in the press, and that makes them public figures, at least as it relates to Value America. So in trying to cover up their own misdeeds, they gave us great liberty to tell the whole sordid tale. The irony is delicious, don't you think? When we tell the truth about them, expose their ill-gotten gains, they'll have no remedy, no matter how much it stings."

"You know what this story is?" I reflected. "It's *Moby Dick* for the twenty-first century. Did you guys ever read that?" Joe admitted to having seen the movie. "It's based on the true story of a ship that got rammed by a whale, and get this: their last day in port was August 11th, and it sank on November 23rd. Those dates sound familiar to anybody?"

My four friends had no idea I was such an afficionado. "*Moby Dick*. Half of the book was a treatise on the whaling business in the nineteenth century. You couldn't really understand what the crew of the Pequod were up against if Melville hadn't explained it all. Anyway, it's the same with us and the new economy. The pursuit of dot-com gold was the western world's white whale, the one that got away."

Rex spoke up. "Problem is, the Value America story would read like a tall tale, just like *Moby Dick*. Who'd believe it? It's stranger than fiction."

"Who cares if they believe it," Craig asked, "so long as they learn from it? Look. I've got thousands of pages of documentation. We all know what went on—we lived through it. Let's tell our story. Maybe it'll do our country some good. We can't just roll over and play dead." *Bad things happen when good people don't stand up.*

I knew what that meant. For the next year, I would be joined at the hip with Craig Winn. Again. For some reason, I didn't run away, screaming.

Call me Ishmael.

శ్రీజ్

FIRST BILL, THEN Rex and Joe, said their goodbyes. Craig and I were left to reflect on the course we had just set. "Are you really sure you want to do this?" I asked him. "It's going to open up all kinds of old wounds. You need this like you need another hole in the head."

"It's worse than that, Ken," Craig said solemnly. "I'll be burning my last bridge to the only world I know. To tell this story, we'll have to expose investment bankers, boards of directors, retailers, auditors, lawyers, politicians, even the media. We'll be exposing the dirty little secrets they've swept under the rug. I'll become a pariah, never able to return."

Craig quietly agonized for a long moment and then said, "You don't believe in fate, do you, Ken?"

"No. I believe in providence."

"Remember what I always called you?"

"Yeah. It was embarrassing. You called me the company's patron saint."

"What else did I say?"

Like a schoolboy reciting his lesson, I repeated the words Craig had said so often. "You said that as long as I was with the company, God would never let anything bad happen to us."

"Remember the date you resigned? And the time?"

"No, not exactly. Sometime in November."

"I do. It was November 23rd, 1999, 3:45 PM. Fifteen minutes later, the board met. They presided over the company's execution."

"I...I had no idea." My head was swimming.

"Still think we shouldn't do this?"

"No. You're right. The world needs to hear it. But think about it. The heat's off you for the first time in ages. Dot-coms are starting to drop like flies: you're not only vindicated, you're anonymous. You've got enough money to live ten lifetimes, a beautiful family, real friends. You don't have to relive the pain—and it will be painful, you know. You could just let the whole thing drop, enjoy your life. Living well is the best revenge, right?"

Craig smiled, walked over to his desk, and picked up his Bible. "Think so?" It fell open to the book of Ecclesiastes, the wisdom of Solomon again. Craig didn't even flip the page. This is what he read:

"What does pleasure accomplish? I planted vineyards. I made great gardens, and planted all kinds of fruit trees. I amassed silver and gold. I denied myself nothing my eyes desired. I refused my heart no pleasure. Yet when I surveyed all that my hands had done and what I had toiled to achieve, everything was meaningless, chasing after the wind.... There is a time for everything, and a season for every activity under heaven. A time to tear down and a time to build, a time to weep and a time to laugh, a time to mourn and a time to dance, a time to search and a time to give up, a time to tear and a time to mend, a time to be silent and a time to speak...."

The sun rises and the sun sets, and hastening to its place it rises again—Solomon